# Macroeconomic Causes of Unemployment: Diagnosis and Policy Recommendations

Veröffentlichungen des
Instituts für Empirische Wirtschaftsforschung

Band 36

# Macroeconomic Causes of Unemployment: Diagnosis and Policy Recommendations

Makroökonomische Ursachen der Arbeitslosigkeit: Diagnose und Therapievorschläge

Edited by

Wolfgang Filc and Claus Köhler

Duncker & Humblot · Berlin

Die Deutsche Bibliothek – CIP-Einheitsaufnahme

**Macroeconomic causes of unemployment: diagnosis and policy recommendations** = Makroökonomische Ursachen der Arbeitslosigkeit: Diagnose und Therapievorschläge / ed. Wolfgang Filc and Claus Köhler. – Berlin : Duncker und Humblot, 1999
(Veröffentlichungen des Instituts für Empirische Wirtschaftsforschung ; Bd. 36)
ISBN 3-428-09758-0


Fremddatenübernahme und Druck:
Berliner Buchdruckerei Union GmbH, Berlin
Printed in Germany

ISSN 0720-7239
ISBN 3-428-09758-0

Gedruckt auf alterungsbeständigem (säurefreiem) Papier
entsprechend ISO 9706 ♾

# Contents

## IV. Country Studies and Country Comparisons



## V. Macroeconomic Policy Designs to Regain High Employment

# Editorial Introduction

The *Institut für Empirische Wirtschaftsforschung* (Institute for Empirical Economic Research) held its seventh symposium on March 19/20, 1998. The subjects discussed referred to the most pressing economic, social and political problem which has affected many industrial countries since the beginning of the 1990s – the permanently high rate of unemployment. There is advice galore of how to overcome the debacle: getting fit for international economic competition, changing location to meet economic needs, reducing the labor and payroll fringe costs, making the wage structure, the working hours and the working conditions more flexible, relieving the corporations from the tax burdens and so on. Unemployment has been diagnosed mainly as a structural problem of the labor market that can only be solved by making corrections to this very market, namely by giving an incentive to companies to employ more people and to the unemployed to also take up a job even if the wage earned does not come up to the previous level. A striking feature is that the macro-economic dimension of how to overcome unemployment is not being considered in the discussions in Germany. This is why economists from universities, economic research institutions and banks, who – in recent years – had voiced their opinions on the issue of stabilizing the employment situation under macro-economic aspects, have been asked to explain the macro-economic aspects of how to tackle the dilemma on the labor market. This book is now introducing the papers discussed at the symposium.

The institute also intended to afford a better understanding of the teachings of foreign scholars and to discuss their points of view. Therefore, as compared with previous symposiums, the number of foreign participants was much higher. In order to improve the response to the conference proceedings, they have been published under an English title and most of the papers have been written in English. Furthermore, an English abstract has been added to the German papers.

A symposium attended by 32 scholars and 20 papers read will be very expensive. The conference could not have been organized without the generous financial support of the *Südwestdeutsche Landesbank* and the *DG Bank,* for which the editors would like to extend their thanks to both institutions.

The papers in the first section of this book put the subject of the symposium in the general context of theoretical paradigms that explain the permanently high rate of unemployment. In his introductory paper *Wolfgang Franz* uses a micro-economic reference model, which takes into account macro-economic causes for unemployment exclusively with demand shocks that he does not detail any further. In his view, which would probably be supported by a majority of economists, the high unemployment rate in Germany is almost exclusively a problem of the labor market and must be solved in this context. Rather than taking into account the overall requirements of the labor market, the wage determining process is more concerned with the interests of the employees (the insiders) and the corporations (efficiency wages). This results in a quasi-balanced state of unemployment as a consequence of which the overall economic demand further decreases. However, structural unemployment can only be rectified by reforming the labor market. Attempts to explain the high unemployment under macro-economic aspects are only of comparatively marginal importance.

In his refreshingly written paper, *Rudolf Richter* describes the tendencies how the reasons for unemployment have been interpreted by different economic theories over the recent decades. He reviews the contribution of the economic approach of both industry and institutions. Five possible main reasons for unemployment are being emphasized: excessive real wages, a lack in the demand for goods, insufficient capital, the mutual blockage of the economic and political decision-making bodies and wage cartels. For the author, it is a matter of course that a permanently high unemployment rate can only prevail if it is useful to at least one social group of people who share this interest. This may be the unions, that represent mainly the interests of the insiders and not of the people unemployed, the employers associations, that try to maximize the corporate profits in the short run by efficiency wages that are not market-clearing and the political class, that follows the wishes of the broad majority of the insiders on the labor market, i.e. those who have a job already. The political class wishes to be re-elected and wants to avoid putting any further burdens on the insiders, which would be the consequence if the outsiders, i.e. the jobless, were to be returned to permanent employment. Hence, unemployment may be permanently high if it benefits those forces that intend to abolish the present form of the social market economy by fundamentally changing the economic and social structure one way or the other. In order to prevent such a development, there is one thing which is required before anything else: Those who have the final say as regards the level of unemployment have to be informed and economically enlightened, i.e. the collective bargaining parties, the political class, the legal profession. This interpretation corresponds to the economic analysis of both industry and institutions which the author has been carrying out over a long period.

*Jan Priewe* takes a totally different approach. For him, unemployment is – above all – a result of an unsatisfactory demand for commodities. The differentiation between keynesian and classic unemployment is considered unconvincing and not plausible, analytically blurred and thus unusable for formulating recipes aimed at stabilizing the employment situation by economic and political measures directly out of the labor market. Unemployment is not a purely micro-economic problem that solves itself once the individuals act economically and in conformity with the market. From the author's point of view, a decrease in real wages is only a suitable means of creating employment when capacities are fully utilized and the investment rate increases. This, however, is wishful thinking. Normally it must be assumed that unemployment is a consequence of the commodity market rationing the labor market, i.e. a missing overall demand and weak investment activities. Any expansion of the demand for labor therefore requires a higher demand on the commodity market. In this case, the classic reason for unemployment – namely the low returns of the corporations in comparison with the wage rates – will also vanish.

In view of the globalized markets, the question which is being asked more and more is whether the employment problem can still be solved at national level on the basis of a macro-economic approach, or whether international competition for economic locations is entirely unavoidable by dismantling the social network, cutting the labor and payroll fringe costs and competing in tax decreases. However: All countries together will not be able to make any progress in the employment situation in this way. The three papers in the second section consider these issues under different aspects. *Hans-Joachim Heinemann* summarizes the globalization debate, above all from a German point of view, that favors an analysis approach based on the supply side. The paper describes that individual national efforts aimed at improving the employment situation can hardly be successful in globalized markets. Instead, international cooperation is required, that should limit instabilities resulting from inefficient financial markets and ensure the international coordination in the field of employment policies, such as at the level of the European Union, but rather under demand aspects, i.e. taxes and working conditions. This descriptive contribution refers to some of the approaches to stabilizing employment under globalized economic conditions, that have been dealt with more in-depth in other papers of the book.

*Paul Davidson* looks beyond national employment policies and turns to the international implications of the problem. Any national attempt to raise the employment level alone can only create jobs at the expense of other countries. If all countries followed the recommendations of those that are expecting advantages in international economic competition as regards their own location, deflation and a world-wide depression would be the result. The time between 1950 and the beginning of the 1970s was characterized by high economic growth, low unemployment and vigorously increasing international trade. This "golden age" ended in 1973 when the fixed exchange rates were abandoned. Since then, the world economy has been staggering from one crisis into the next. Flexible exchange rates, if detached from fundamental factors, slow down economic activities at international level. The proposal was made to introduce an international payment system with fixed exchange rates, a reserve medium to be retained by all central banks and a clearing agency for the short-term compensation of deficits on external accounts by surplus balances of other countries. Moreover, pressure should be exerted on the surplus countries to reduce excessive internal savings by more imports or transfers to deficit countries. From these far-reaching proposals the author expects a global expansion of the overall demand as a prerequisite for a global increase in employment.

*Henning Klodt* reviews whether the level of Germany's direct investments abroad results in the loss of employment at home. First of all, the paper refers to the considerable problems of establishing direct investments in a reasonable way, since different statistics reflect the most diverse data for Germany as far as direct investments are concerned. Theoretical approaches suggest that direct investments abroad may lead to both a loss and an increase in employment at home. The crucial factor are the motives for the direct investments. Empirical investigations into both the regional and industrial structure confirm that direct German investments abroad rather accompany exports than substitute them. At the moment, the primary cause for direct investments of German companies abroad must be seen to a lesser extent in the production cost differentials between Germany and other countries rather than in securing specific returns to scale from headquarter services that are generated by the company at home and that secure jobs. Hence, the high level of direct investments abroad is neither an indicator for a weak economic position at home nor for the export of jobs.

The third section of the book deals with the effects the developments in financial markets have on the economic growth and the employment situation. *Alexander Juchems* and *Willi Leibfritz* describe the connection between monetary conditions and an indicator for the course of the fiscal policy on the one hand and cyclical growth in the Federal Republic of Germany on the other, the latter being reflected by the ifo-business climate index. The monetary indicator has a closer connection with the cyclical indicator than the indicator for the course of fiscal policy. The overall indicator as a summary of the individual indicators is superior to the fiscal and monetary indicators as mere reflections of the cyclical development. In order to assess the future cyclical development and its effects on the employment situation, it is therefore important to pay attention to monetary conditions foremost. Nevertheless, the monetary and fiscal policies must not be overrated as regards the economic and employment situation. Only one third of the economic growth can be attributed to monetary and fiscal measures as well as changes in the external value of the deutschmark. Although the financial and monetary political strategies must necessarily be adapted to the economic requirements, they alone cannot create full employment.

*Peter Winker* demonstrates that financial restrictions for companies hamper their economic activities, block investments and lead to cuts in the research and development funds, thus affecting the rate of employment negatively. Empirical research carried out at a micro-economic level has shown that loan rationing for companies is relevant in Germany as it is tantamount to limiting the budgets for economic activities. On the other hand, loan rationing could not be empirically proven at macro-economic level as sufficient data and a suitable theoretical model is not available at the moment. However, simulation studies show that loan limits to finance the acquisition of capital assets may well become a decisive obstacle for raising the employment level. Permanent imbalances in the loan markets resulting in rationing the demand for commodities may possibly be put down to the insufficient equity of the financial institutions. In that case it would not suffice to call for low interest rates in order to raise the employment level, as this cannot overcome the rationing of funds of commercial banks.

*Michael Frömmel* and *Lukas Menkhoff* discuss methods and results of the latest empirical studies concerning efficient information processing in financial markets. The mainly unanimous result is that information about financial market prices happens to be correctly processed and expressed only very seldom. One reason may be that the participants in the financial markets expect more from the methods of technical analyses that they apply than from new information, and that information is used for more intuitive decisions rather than at the basis of analytic processes. This has been suggested by the results of a survey among participants in the foreign exchange market. The authors therefore make the assumption that financial market prices, such as the exchange rates, may have a destabilizing effect. Discretionary attempts of official institutions to intervene in the price formation in financial markets or a better cooperation between the proponents of macro-politics aimed at avoiding the destabilizing deformations of financial market prices are viewed with scepticism. In contrast to this, a transaction tax and similar regulations are recommended in order to make destabilizing speculations more difficult and to increase the contribution of the financial markets to establishing the macro-economic balance.

The fourth section of the book includes papers devoted to the experience gained with strategies in other countries that are aimed at raising the employment level. *Lothar Funk* summarizes in a very comprehensive manner the results of combinations of different economic and political measures in various countries to stabilize the employment situation. The paper concentrates on those measures that were directly connected with the labor market, while macro-economic approaches are only dealt with in a lax fashion. The paper opposes the view that the high and permanent level of unemployment is an expression of hysteresis effects and could thus be reduced with the help of an expansive course in macro-policies, above all in monetary policies. The alternative is, as an assessment of the experience gained in Britain and The Netherlands shows, that a solution to the employment problems in Germany would first of all require a more flexible labor market and a sensible wage restraint over several years. But, apart from a structural reform of the labor market, it would also require a reasonable macro-policy, such as a monetary policy aimed at securing employment. However, the paper does not make any suggestions as to the contents of a reasonable macro-policy and how to bring macro-policy and structural policy in line with each other.

*Michael Heise* and *Mathias Moersch* compare the development of the employment situation in the USA and Germany against the background of structural differences in the labor markets of both countries. They also probe into the question whether different strategies for macro-economic policies of stabilizing the employment situation in both countries can help to answer the question why the trends in the employment situation have developed along opposing lines since 1992. The sectional economic development certifies that the more rapid expansion of employment in the service industry in the USA as compared to Germany does not sufficiently explain the generally opposing trend in the employment situation of both countries. Considering similar growth rates in real income, the high employment gains in the USA is attributed to a lower increase in labor productivity, a higher wage differentiation than in Germany as well as the lower regional mobility of the German labor force. In other words, it is above all the encrusted German labor market that hampers any increase in the employment level as well as weak dynamic entrepreneurial activities as a result of supply obstacles. It is also noted that the capital intensive production in Germany is a result of excessive wage agreements in this country. It must be added, that the substitution of labor through capital should be reflected in an investment boom in Germany which, however, cannot be found. The chance to raise the employment level permanently by introducing monetary measures without endangering the price stability is considered to be low. The employment policy in Germany requires first of all reforms of the labor market. Only then the prerequisites will have been created to orientate the monetary policy – like in the USA – along such lines as economic growth and employment.

*Arne Heise* emphasizes different aspects. He searches for an explanation of the different trends in the employment situation in Britain and Germany and addresses both micro-economic and macro-economic aspects. In Britain, the structural changes have made more progress than in Germany while the employment level in lower-skilled areas has risen less than in Germany, despite a more distinct wage differentiation. Consequently, the micro-economic interpretation of the different developments of the employment situation in both countries does not seem to be conclusive. A macro-economic approach can explain the differences better: The real devaluation of the Pound Sterling and higher structural deficits of the government budgets in Britain as compared to Germany are much more decisive for the increased employment level in Britain. Apart from that, micro-economic prerequisites for a higher employment level in Germany must not be underestimated, either. As the comparison shows, the wages in Britain, which are based on the distinct standards in skills, show a much higher degree of differentiation than in Germany.

*Derek Hum, Wayne Simpson* and *Norman Cameron* use Canadian data and probe into the question whether any progress in slowing down even moderate inflation rates will lead to higher employment or whether – quite the opposite – too ambitious attempts to curb inflation will also harm the employment situation. These connections are discussed in Canada under the catchphrase of "grease versus sand in the economy". It is striking in this context that the Canadian economic upswing, which has not let off since 1993 and had an inflation rate from under 3%, has virtually not made any contribution to a higher employment level. All other previous economic upswings since the end of the 1970s went along with a higher inflation rate but also with an increased employment level. Inflation rates leveling at about 4% offer the opportunity for a better differentiation of the wage structure, which goes along with a decrease in real income in some segments of the labor market without effectively reducing the nominal wages. The Canadian data confirm this interpretation: In times of higher inflation rates from the end of the 1970s onwards right up to the mid-1980s, changes in the real wage structure were implemented nearly exclusively by a differentiated increase in the nominal wages. With its increasing proportion of constant or even lower nominal wages, such as in the mid-1980s and from 1993 to 1995, the high economic growth did not have any employment effects. The reason given is that the workforce resisted cuts in the nominal wages heavily and accepted more willingly decreases in real income as a result of price rises. The empirical research supports the assumption that the unemployment rate in Canada since 1993 has been one percentage point above values that could have been attained had the real incomes been adapted by differentiated changes in nominal wages without cutting nominal wages. Therefore, record values achieved as regards price stability will become a problem for the employment situation under high economic growth conditions.

The contributions to the fifth section of the book do not look back but into the future. Is there a macro-economic approach to a higher employment rate? The discussion, which is mainly based on the theory of supply in Germany and supported by some of the papers in this book, denies that. *Attiat F. Ott*'s paper confirms this viewpoint. It is investigated on the basis of the Solow model and the strategies of endogenous economic growth, whether economic growth can be stimulated by macro-economic measures and whether economic growth brings about positive employment effects. Although economic growth is largely endogenous, a macro-economic policy of stabilization has surely an effect on it but only to a lesser extent on the rate of employment. The interpretation of other studies and of the results of her own empirical findings are summed up in a rather sceptical conclusion. The development of the nominal national products in Britain and Germany demonstrates that fiscal impulses have a considerable and long-lasting effect, while the real economic effects of an expansive financial policy, including the rate of employment, remain undetermined.

*Loek Groot* and *Ronald Schettkat* probe into the effects of unified wage increment rates on production, prices and employment under different conditions of the productivity increase in various economic sectors. Nearly identical wage increases on the basis of the average productivity increase are beneficial to industries with a high productivity so that the employment level rises at the cost of other industries with a low growth in productivity. Productivity differentials are largely a consequence of a different degree of the technological progress and sector-specific demand developments. In order to take these differences into account, wages must develop in a differentiated way. If not, labor may become permanently redundant, which has been demonstrated with the help of two simulation models for two economic sectors with a different productivity development. If the wage policy is based on the average productivity development, redundancies shall be created permanently in the less productive sectors. In the case of low economic growth and hence restrictions to the technologically leading sectors, an expansion of the demand for products of the less productive sectors is an alternative to permanently increasing unemployment.

*Ewald Nowotny* analyzes the connection between economic growth and employment as well as the role of monetary and financial policies for the overall economic activity. The chief reason for the high unemployment in Western Europe is the weak economic growth that remains below the employment threshold in most countries. Insufficient economic growth is above all the result of the restrictive European monetary policy which is aimed exclusively at price stability and measured by the gap between the interest rate and the growth rate of the national product. However, only income growth rates above the interest rate will provide companies and government budgets with an opportunity to stabilize the quota from indebtedness and revenue without restricting expenditures for the purchase of goods and services. After the transition into the European Monetary Union the conditions for a monetary policy aimed at employment will improve, as this policy will no longer be exclusively aligned with the inflation rate but also with the differences between the interest rates and the values for economic growth. Wage restraint is – from the author's point of view – no suitable means of creating employment. Both Germany and Austria have shown parallels with regard to a sinking labor's share in the national income and rising unemployment for some years. The unemployment rate in Austria – comparatively low in the European context – has been attributed to the "Social partnership" system practiced there. This cooperative strategy, that contains both macro-economic and micro-economic elements – facilitates a better flexibility of the real wages and a financial policy aimed at stability. The Austrian experience proves that a coordination of all institutions and representatives of a stability-oriented policy, including the central banks, may contribute to a policy mix that furthers employment and improves price stability.

*Carl-Ludwig Holtfrerich* supports the central hypotheses put forward in the above paper. It will not be possible to tackle the employment problem without brisk economic growth. Supply-oriented measures alone, such as the announced tax reform in Germany, will not suffice to achieve this objective. It is necessary to closely coordinate monetary and fiscal policies with the aim of achieving low interest rates as a prerequisite for high economic growth.

*Heinz-Peter Spahn* subjects some of the central and widely accepted tenets of a macro-economically oriented stabilization policy, above all on the monetary policy, to a critical assessment. The thesis, central banks or governments had an incentive to create short-term employment effects by a surprise inflation, is assessed as extremely unrealistic. Hence, inconsistency over time in monetary matters is a sham problem, but may lead central banks to pursue a permanently too restrictive course. Moreover, the paper discards the assumption that central banks could use the inflation rate both as a political aim and as a variable in their monetary instrumentarium. Central banks may set interest rates but do not directly influence inflation rates. Inflation is therefore not the result of a game of central banks versus the market, but the result of the market itself that, in turn, will cause central banks to respond. As a matter of fact, increasing interest rates will cut income and employment. Since monetary measures – due to interest-induced changes in the demand and through their influence on the expected inflation – will have an overall economic effect, monetary policy can only have a positive effect on economic growth and thus on the employment situation, if monetary measures are introduced through market channels, i.e. if they do not raise expectations for a higher inflation. This necessitates the co-operation of all those contributing to the policy of stabilization. If successfully implemented, a low-interest policy may increase the employment level even in the case of structural unemployment, when wage policy and financial policy follow suit. Hence, monetary policy is not a match against the market and may even further employment, even it is not a match against wage and financial policies, either.

*Hans-Jürgen Krupp* and *Karen Cabos* provide a summary of the literature concerning the issue whether monetary policy creates an employment effect or not. If at all, the employment effects of monetary measures can only be found in economic growth. What then is the influence, the monetary policy has on economic growth? It does not suffice to just name alternative theoretical hypotheses. Many empirical studies on the information quality of the monetary indicators for future economic growth prove with regard to several countries that short-term interest rates, which can be well controlled by the central banks, are superior to long-term interest rates or monetary aggregates. Monetary measures have been found to have a real effect over a period of three to four years, thus for longer periods than had been previously assumed. The theoretical explanations of real effects of monetary policy clearly have not got past the rudiments, with loan rationing, the influence on expectations, effects of changes in the interest rates on a company's net asset policy and hence its creditworthiness, the effects of interest-political measures on exchange rates being suggested. In any case, the results of empirical research indicate that considerable real economic effects of the monetary policy can be shown, which are in contrast with the traditional concepts of monetary transmission mechanisms. It may therefore be concluded, that monetary policy – although primarily responsible for price stability – will have to take into account the employment effects which have been generated by interest impulses all the time. Measures of the monetary policy will first of all have an effect on the real economic sector and only later, if at all, on the general price development.

The paper by *Gustav-Adolf Horn* concludes this section and the conference proceedings as a whole with clear instructions as to how to lower the high employment rate in many West European countries by implementing measures of the macro-economic stabilization policy. The empirical analysis centers around the interaction between monetary and wage policies in the USA and in Germany, with the response of the monetary policy to wage developments and the wage policy to monetary policy decisions being examined. The paper lays open different response pattern of those two proponents of the stability policy in both countries. The wage development in the USA is shown to have a higher information content for monetary decisions than in Germany. In the USA monetary measures are implemented at an early stage, if wage developments create inflationary impulses so that an expectation of higher inflation rates could build up. Quite the contrary in Germany, where the current inflation rate, followed by the unemployment rate and – ending a poor last – the exchange rate development, are of decisive significance for any monetary steps to be taken. On the other hand, there is no indication that the Bundesbank would consider wage impulses as a harbinger of a forthcoming inflation and take preventive monetary measures to suppress an expected increase of the inflation rate. A reversal of this interaction – from the monetary policy to the wage policy – also highlights considerable differences between the countries compared. While the wage policy in the USA does not respond at all to changes in monetary policy, it has been found in Germany that the wage policy has clearly taken monetary signals into consideration since the beginning of the 1990s: The wage rises have slowed down after the Bundesbank has increased interest rates. On the whole, the results show that there is no mutual interaction between the monetary and wage policies in either country by taking into account the expected responses of the one policy area to measures implemented by the other. The available information to avoid unemployment and inflation before it is created in the first place is insufficiently used. The decisive lack of cooperation in the USA has its origin in the fact that the wage policy does not take into consideration monetary measures, while the monetary policy in Germany orientates itself mainly towards the current inflation rate rather than taking those measures of the wage policy into account that could bring about inflationary pressure. The cooperation deficits in the USA have a higher inflation danger potential that in Germany, while insufficient cooperation in Germany has an inherent tendency to lower employment. From this, the European Central Bank should draw its conclusions for its own monetary policy that is based on price stability and high employment.

The papers contributing to the symposium and the subsequent discussions make it clear that a strategy for rising employment is insufficient, if it is solely restricted to a supply-oriented and hence micro-economic point of view. Macro-economic strategies for stabilizing employment must not be excluded. This does not mean to disqualify the manifold and necessary reforms of the labor market and the conditions for a job-creating economic growth as minor considerations. Surely, the companies need incentives to expand the supply of commodities and the labor demand. This is as sure as it is necessary to take measures for improving the readiness to take up work at the existing wage level. However, since mass unemployment has become the outstanding economic, social and political problem, one should refrain from the luxury of not probing into all possibilities and of using every possible way and means to overcome this problem (cf. also the initial quote in *Lothar Funk*'s paper). This can also be achieved by macro-economic approaches, although micro-economic aspects are given priority in some papers. The message of these contributions may be summarized as follows:

1. All contributions with one exception (*Attiat F. Ott*) see a high economic growth as the primary prerequisite for higher employment.
2. The globalization of the economic relations must not be equated with a loss of jobs at home (*Heinemann*). Direct investments of German companies abroad may also create jobs at home, i.e. they do not mean job export (*Klodt*).
3. The employment level is determined to a large extent by the labor costs and other micro-economic determinants (*Franz, Heise/Moersch*), but also by the interaction between the fiscal and monetary policies (*Juchems/Leibfritz*) as well as by adapting the monetary and wage policies to each other (*Horn*).
4. Most authors emphasize that an insufficient overall demand is a major reason for the permanent and high unemployment (*Priewe, Holtfrerich, Heise, Nowotny*), especially in industries with a low productivity growth (*Groot/Schettkat*).
5. Any central bank, that sees itself under the obligation to maintain absolute price stability as it is considered to be a precondition for rising employment, will in fact decrease the employment rate (*Spahn, Krupp/Cabos*). A moderate inflation up to a rate of 4% helps to make the real wage structure more flexible without decreasing nominal wages, which would be difficult to implement (*Hum/Simpson/Cameron*).
6. Developments in financial markets have always an effect on the real economy, such as income and employment. Incorrect price signals coming from the financial markets disturb the allocation and lower the overall economic activity level (*Frömmel/Menkhoff*). The same applies to loan rationing (*Winker*). Monetary and exchange rate policies as well as regulations to supervise commercial banks are necessary to restrict the financial markets to their service role within the economy.
7. A competition for specific economic locations in the wake of globalization cannot create additional jobs at an international level. Quite the opposite, national initiatives with the aim of gaining advantages over foreign competitors would result in international deflation and depression. An international payment system with fixed exchange rates is a prerequisite for a macro-policy that has an expansive effect on income and employment, so that countries with a surplus are enticed to reduce accumulated funds. (*Davidson*).
8. Most papers consider concerted economic and political measures on the basis of an overall strategy that secures employment to be an important prerequisite

for a considerable improvement of the employment situation. This applies to the representatives of the macro-economic policy of stabilization (*Spahn*) and the connection of the necessary micro-economic incentive structures of different decision-makers (Richter) with a labor-market orientated macro-policy (*Funk*). Consequently, it applies also to the social partners including the central bank (*Nowotny*), if possible at international level.

It goes without saying that all this will be difficult to implement. However, it will hardly be possible to solve the European labor market problem without any progress in these fields. The prerequisites in this respect will, however, improve with the transition to the European Monetary Union. Not only will there be a single European monetary policy, a single European currency will also highlight integration deficits in other fields more clearly, such as in the financial policy, in the wage policy or in the reconciliation between the various political areas, and thus enforce the process of further integration.

Wolfgang Filc and Claus Köhler

# I. Macroeconomics and Employment

# Macroeconomics and Joblessness: An Introductory Statement

By Wolfgang Franz[1], Mannheim

It goes without saying that high and persistent unemployment is the prominent topic among all things which go wrong in these years. In order to understand the sources of unemployment and to look for measures to fight against it, a reference model is required which is capable to incorporate major causes of joblessness. To outline briefly such a framework is my duty at this conference and, hence, the theme of this introductory statement. Given severe time restrictions only an extremely brief sketch can be offered here. Moreover, to facilitate the following discussions at this conference I shall concentrate on a model commonly agreed upon in the academic profession.

## I. Basic Analytical Framework

A model explaining the rise and persistence of unemployment needs three ingredients: labor demand, labor supply, and wage determination as depicted in *figure 1*[2].

1. The labor demand curve LD reflects profit-maximizing labor demand dependent on the real product wage.[3] Shifts of the LD-curve to the left cause lower employment and, if labor supply and wage setting remain unchanged, higher unemployment. Reasons for such a shift include determinants of pricing behavior of firms, higher taxes levied on firms, technological change, loss of international competition, reductions of productive capacities, and the like.
2. For the sake of simplicity labor supply LS is treated exogenously although it is influenced by individual preferences and income taxes, for example.

---

[1] Center for European Economic Research (ZEW, Zentrum für Europäische Wirtschaftsforschung), Mannheim, University of Mannheim and Council of Economic Experts (Sachverständigenrat zur Begutachtung der gesamtwirtschaftlichen Entwicklung). The usual disclaimer applies. This note is based on a previous paper titled "The German Unemployment Problem: What We Know and Do Not Know".

[2] See Layard et al. (1991), Lindbeck (1993), Wyplosz (1994) and Franz (1996).

[3] An alternative interpretation of this curve is based on the hypothesis of mark-up pricing in a world of imperfect competition.

3. The wage setting curve WS reflects the importance of institutional rules and social arrangements on the labor market which influence wage determination. An incomplete list of factors which in principle and for theoretical reasons may affect the WS-curve adversely (in terms of high unemployment) includes an increasing power of insider forces, a higher tax wedge, greater generosity of unemployment benefits, higher minimum wages. Put differently, this approach avoids walking right into the pitfall of treating wages as exogenous variables. The WS-curve is positively sloped due to higher wage demands by unions if employment increases or because employers pay wage premiums for efficiency reasons (such as to avoid unwarranted turnover of qualified workers or to reduce incentives for shirking).

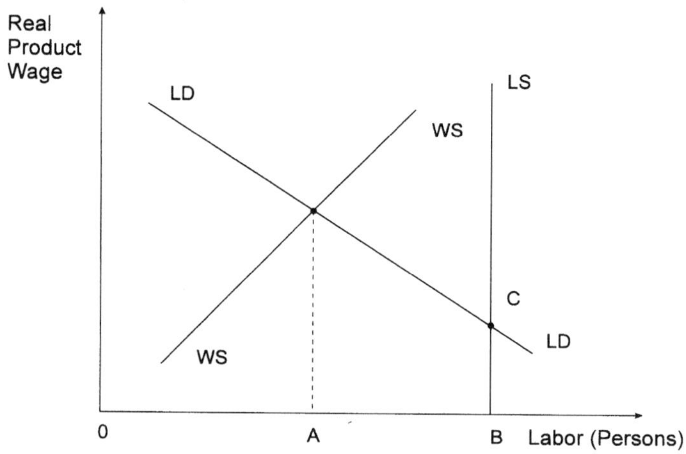


Figure 1: Theoretical Reference Model

The intersection of the LD-curve with the WS-curve gives the amount of employment $\overline{OA}$. Given LS, unemployment amounts to $\overline{AB}$ and the resulting unemployment rate (i.e. $\overline{AB} / \overline{OB}$) has been coined "quasi-equilibrium rate of unemployment" (QERU). "Equilibrium" means that this unemployment rate balances labor demand (or pricing behaviour) and wage setting so that the real product wage has reached an "equilibrium" value. However, this "equilibrium" is quasi in the sense that there is an excess supply of labor at the same time. Full employment is at point C but not consistent with wage setting behavior (the WS-curve has to shift to the right and intersect the LS- and LD-curves in C). Taken together, this basic theoretical framework forms a suitable work-horse to explain the stylized facts:

1. Actual unemployment can be decomposed into two parts, the QERU, or "structural unemployment" for short, and deviations from this value caused by adverse demand shocks, for example.

2. The QERU may increase in the course of time because the LD-curve and / or the WS-curve shifted to the left. Hence, observed trends in unemployment may be due to greater structural factors and / or greater deviations from the QERU.
3. Unemployment rates exceeding the QERU may affect the QERU itself when, for example, temporary unemployment due to, say, a lack of aggregate demand creates long-term unemployment. If long-term unemployed persons are not viewed as suitable to fill vacancies (in contrast to short-term unemployed persons) the resulting pressure of wage growth declines, i.e., the WS-curve shifts to the left thus producing a higher QERU.

This theoretical approach is now used to evaluate possible sources of unemployment in Germany.

## II. Possible Sources of German Unemployment

In the following major candidates for an explanation of German unemployment are reviewed along the lines suggested by the analytical framework outlined in the previous section.

Unemployment due to economic fluctuations constitutes a non-negligible part of unemployment. As is evidenced by the estimation of a macroeconometric disequilibrium model, a considerable share of firms are rationed by aggregate demand during various time periods such as the past recession 1993 / 95.[4] Moreover, the German Council of Economic Experts estimates for West Germany that in the year 1994 around one quarter to one fifth of total unemployment stems from the then recession.[5] It is unlikely that this figure has decreased dramatically.

As has been shown in the previous section both wage setting (WS-curve) and labor demand (LD-curve) affect the QERU both its level and its likely increase as it is evidenced by the shifts of the NAIRU (although the QERU and the NAIRU differ).[6]

### *1. Sources Resulting from Wage Setting*

– Insider and union power: Reviewing recent wage negotiations especially at the firm level there is reason to argue that in West Germany insider forces are at work. Wages are set trying to keep the insiders' workplaces rather than to mod-

4 The type of such a disequilibrium model and estimates for various countries are described at some length in Drèze and Bean (1990). A short introduction into the German model is given in Franz and König (1990).

5 See Sachverständigenrat (1994).

6 The QERU requires a constant price level, the NAIRU an unchanging inflation rate.

erate wage demands so that the unemployed as the outsiders get a chance to become employed.

- Outsider ineffectiveness: The high share of long-term unemployment increases wage demands ceteris paribus (see below).
- Unemployment benefits: Despite a huge body of literature trying to econometrically evaluate the effect of unemployment benefits on the duration of unemployment, there is still a considerable uncertainty surrounding the resulting estimates.[7] At the risk of an oversimplification but based on more recent studies there is evidence that, firstly, the length of the period a person is entitled to unemployment benefits matters but not the replacement ratio, and, secondly, that even significant effects tend to be rather small and concern only certain groups of unemployed persons. Moreover, there is hardly any evidence that these effects contribute to an explanation as to why the QERU has possibly increased.
- Mismatch: It is safe to say that a considerable amount of mismatch between labor supplied and demanded exists both with respect to regions and qualifications. It is less clear to what extent mismatch increased causing a higher QERU.[8]
- Tax wedge: Higher taxes on labor income and increasing contributions to social security (levied on both the employer and the employee) put a substantial and broadening wedge between product wages and consumption wages.[9]
- Minimum wages: In the absence of effective legal minimum wages the most important issue here is that the wage structure with respect to qualifications remained fairly stable in contrast to other studies such as the UK and the US.[10] A wider dispersion of wages especially for less qualified labor might help, however, to create more jobs in that segment. It should be noted that in the industrial sector low wage groups do exist but are not filled for reasons whatsoever. Moreover, lowering real wages at the bottom of the wage structure must be accompanied by other measures in order to circumvent the US problem of the "working poor".

---

7 A short but valuable survey of this literature for Germany is given by Steiner (1997). Most if not all of these studies are based on an estimation of hazard rates using large sets of individual data.

8 Greater mismatch shifts the wage setting curve to the left because unemployed applicants not suitable for filling the vacancy in question exert less pressure on wages.

9 This increases wage demands ceteris paribus, shifts the WS-curve to the left and causes a higher QERU.

10 See OECD (1996), chapter 3.

*2. Sources Stemming from Labor Demand*

- Firing Restrictions: In the presence of severe firing restrictions (legal and / or in form of severance payments) employers may reduce employment as theoretical models of labor demand in an intertemporal setting show. For obvious reasons those effects cannot be detected by inspection of unemployment series (especially if reduced hires balance less firing exactly). In the German case such firing restrictions are prevailing especially for special groups for social reasons (such as elder employees, pregnant women, handicapped persons) and for members of the workers' councils. Moreover, more important than legal firing restrictions are casual decisions of labor courts which are uncomprehensible on economic grounds. While firing restrictions may indeed protect those employees (but, of course, do not the unemployed belonging to the same group), general firing rules do not seem to have such an impact. Firms may be interested in a long attachment of those workers in whose education they have invested.
- Supply Shocks: These have been extensively named as candidates for explaining higher structural unemployment. In terms of the QERU framework supply shocks such as the spurt in raw material prices in the seventies cause the LD-curve to shift to the left (for example, if the mark-up is also on prices on imported goods). Higher unemployment can be avoided, however, if wage setting takes into account these shocks by lowering wage demands (the WS-curve shifts to the right). This was not the case in West Germany in the midst of the seventies, hence, the QERU may have risen indeed. Given that the oil price has returned to its pre-shock level in the eighties, this line of argument clearly cannot explain why the QERU might have increased in the eighties.
- Skill Biased Technical Progress: The argument is that technical progress (such as arising from the computer revolution) has accelerated and is increasingly in favor of skilled labor to the disadvantage of unskilled labor. Indeed, during the time period from 1976 to 1985 employment of unskilled workers declined by 36 percent but that of skilled labor increased by 30 percent in West Germany.[11] Again, the resulting unemployment can be mitigated by, for example, a greater wage dispersion as has been mentioned above (including other measures). However, this point should not be overemphasized. As has been pointed out by Nickell (1996), low skilled workers in West Germany are paid more than twice as much as equivalent workers in the US and yet their unemployment rates are much the same.
- International Capital Mobility: A major problem for the German economy is that firms located in Germany invest abroad but that foreign firms hesitate to invest in Germany. For example, the share of investment by foreign firms among total domestic investment during the period 1991 to 1995 was 0.8 percent in Germany but 3.5 percent in the US and 10.7 percent in the UK. The correspond-

11 See Sachverständigenrat (1994), p. 257 for details.

ing figures for the share of outgoing investments are 4.9 percent for Germany, 5.6 percent for the US and 16.1 percent for the UK.[12] Hence, for Germany the former figures constitute the problem but not the latter ones. Among other reasons international differences in taxes and unit labor costs contribute to an explanation of the low inflow of foreign investment into Germany.

### *3. Transmission from Non-Structural Unemployment to Structural Unemployment*

The most important issue here are hysteresis effects. This is the notion that past unemployment affects current unemployment, i.e., unemployment is path-dependent. Channels through which hysteresis in unemployment may work are the depreciation of skills during long-term unemployment or a discouragement of long-term unemployed so that their search intensity declines. If so, long-term unemployed exert little influence on wage bargaining, hence, the QERU increases. Put differently, deviations of actual unemployment from its quasi-equilibrium value due to, say, demand deficiency influence the QERU. While supply factors are certainly more important in explaining the behaviour of the QERU, in the presence of hysteresis the dichotomy between supply and demand determinants breaks down.[13]

There are numerous econometric studies which try to identify to what extent hysteresis effects can contribute to an explanation of the evolvement of German unemployment. While they are based on various econometric methods most if not all wind up with the conclusion that the hypothesis of hysteresis in unemployment cannot be rejected; but they differ in their judgement to what extent hysteresis is present. Taken together, there is plenty of empirical evidence that German unemployment is plagued by hysteresis effects but it is still not known whether they are strong enough to generate the time pattern of German unemployment since the eighties.

## III. Conclusions

Some determinants of unemployment are likely to play a major role in explaining unemployment in Germany. Among these are economic fluctuations and hysteresis effects as well as factors which induce wage setting to be hostile against (a recovery of) full employment such as a tax wedge, mismatch, and insider power. Moreover, we know that the higher degree of international competition and capital mobility implies that Germany has to pay a rising price, in terms of joblessness,

---

12 Source: Sachverständigenrat (1996), p. 67. It should be kept in mind that these figures are plagued by considerable data deficiencies.

13 See Stiglitz (1997).

for domestic failures in reforming the tax system, in removing barriers for investment, and in making the wage bargaining process more flexible. However, we do not know the quantitative importance of those partial explanations. In the absence of this knowledge each of the aforementioned issues has to be taken seriously.

## References

*Drèze,* J. H., C. R. *Bean* (1990): Europe's Unemployment Problem. Cambridge. – *Franz,* W. (1996): Theoretische Ansätze zur Erklärung der Arbeitslosigkeit: Wo stehen wir 1995? in: B. Gahlen, H. Hesse, H. J. Ramser (eds.), Arbeitslosigkeit und Möglichkeiten ihrer Überwindung, Tübingen, 3 - 45. – *Franz,* W., H. *König* (1990): A Disequilibrium Approach to Unemployment in the Federal Republic of Germany, European Economic Review 34, 413 - 422. – *Layard,* R., S. J. *Nickell,* R. *Jackman* (1991): Unemployment. Oxford. – *Licht,* G., E. *Nerlinger* (1997): New Technology-Based Firms in Germany: A Very Rapid Survey, Manuscript, Zentrum für Europäische Wirtschaftsforschung (ZEW), Mannheim. – *Lindbeck,* A. (1993): Unemployment and Macroeonomics, Cambridge. – *Nickell,* S. (1996): Unemployment and Wages in Europe and North America, Centre for Economic Performance, Discussion Paper No. 6, Oxford. – *OECD* (1996): Employment Outlook, Paris. – *Sachverständigenrat zur Begutachtung der gesamtwirtschaftlichen Entwicklung* (1994): Jahresgutachten 1994 / 95 "Den Aufschwung sichern – Arbeitsplätze schaffen", Stuttgart. – *Sachverständigenrat zur Begutachtung der gesamtwirtschaftlichen Entwicklung* (1996): Jahresgutachten 1996 / 97 "Reformen voranbringen", Stuttgart. – *Steiner,* V. (1997): Extended Benefit Entitlement Periods and the Duration of Unemployment in West Germany, Zentrum für Europäische Wirtschaftsforschung (ZEW), Discussion Paper No. 97 - 14 E, Mannheim. – *Stiglitz,* J. (1997): Reflections on the Natural Rate Hypothesis, Journal of Economic Perspectives 11 (1), 3 - 10. – *Winker,* P. (1996): Rationierung auf dem Markt für Unternehmenskredite in der BRD, Tübingen. – *Wyplosz,* C. (1994): Demand and Structural Views of Europe's High Unemployment Trap, Swedish Economic Policy Review 1, 75 - 107.

# Warum Arbeitslosigkeit?

## Antworten von Wirtschaftstheoretikern seit Keynes (1936)

Von Rudolf Richter, Saarbrücken

Die Frage „Warum Arbeitslosigkeit?“ gehört seit der Weltwirtschaftskrise zu den zentralen Themen der Wirtschaftstheorie. Über einige wichtige Antworten soll hier berichtet werden. Die moderne, bis heute anhaltende wissenschaftliche Diskussion beginnt mit dem Erscheinen der *Allgemeinen Theorie der Beschäftigung, des Zinses und Geldes* von John Maynard Keynes (1936). Sein Buch richtet sich gegen die von ihm so bezeichneten „klassischen Ökonomen“, zu denen er außer David Ricardo, James Mill und James Stuart Mill auch Marshall, Edgeworth und den von ihm immer wieder zitierten „Professor Pigou“ (Oxford) rechnet. Jedoch: Trotz seiner vernichtenden Kritik haben die Vertreter der klassischen Schule bis heute nicht aufgegeben und – etwa im Gewande der Monetaristen – den Lehren von Keynes kräftig entgegengehalten. Beide Richtungen, Keynesianer wie Klassiker, sehen sich als „Sieger“ im nicht endenden Streite. Und beide Richtungen beeinflussen bis heute im Gewande unterschiedlicher Parteien und politischer Gruppierungen die Beschäftigungspolitik der Industrienationen.

Bei der Beantwortung der Frage „Warum Arbeitslosigkeit?“ gehe ich wie folgt vor:

Ich beginne mit der klassischen Lehre in Reinform, gehe auf Keynes' „Allgemeine Theorie der Beschäftigung“ ein, berichte über den zeitweiligen Burgfrieden zwischen Keynesianern und Klassikern – die „neoklassische Synthese“ –, komme auf die Attacken von Friedman und Lucas gegen eben diesen Burgfrieden zu sprechen und gehe auf das Problem fehlender Arbeitsplätze ein. Nach diesen typisch makroökonomischen Argumenten behandle ich „strukturelle“ oder (besser) institutionenökonomische Argumente: Arbeitslosigkeit aus politökonomischer Sicht, aus industrieökonomischer Sicht, und aus Sicht der Neuen Institutionenökonomik. Ein Rückblick schließt den Artikel ab.

### I. Die klassische Antwort

Die klassische Antwort auf die Frage „Warum Arbeitslosigkeit?“ lautet: Weil der Reallohn höher als sein Gleichgewichtswert ist. Man spricht von Mindestlohn-

oder genauer Mindestreallohn-Arbeitslosigkeit. Vollbeschäftigung besteht, wenn der Reallohn seinem Gleichgewichtswert entspricht – also dem Wert, bei dem Angebot von und Nachfrage nach Arbeit einander gleich sind. In dem Falle ist die Grenzproduktivität der Arbeit gleich dem Grenzleid der Arbeit (gleich den Alternativkosten der Arbeit). Man vergleiche dazu Hicks (1932/1966).

Das sind Sätze der neoklassischen Mikroökonomik. Die Nachfragefunktion nach Arbeit wird vermöge der Theorie der Unternehmung hergeleitet unter der Annahme, daß die Unternehmung ihren Gewinn maximiert, gegeben ihr technisches Wissen und die von ihr zu zahlenden Produkt- und Faktorpreise. Die Angebotsfunktion von Arbeit folgt aus der Haushaltstheorie: der Haushalt (das Individuum) maximiert seinen Nutzen, gegeben sein Vermögen (Finanz-, Sach- und Humanvermögen), die Güterpreise und Löhne.

Mindestlohnarbeitslosigkeit ist nach klassischer Lehre eine vorübergehende Angelegenheit – besteht nicht lange –, weil der zu hohe Reallohn nach dieser Theorie „automatisch“ so lange sinken wird, bis er seinen Gleichgewichtswert erreicht hat. Allenfalls politische Aktivitäten (die Anwendung von Gewalt, darunter Streiks mit anschließend überhöhten Tarifabschlüssen) verhindern sein Absinken und sorgen für den Fortbestand „klassischer“ Arbeitslosigkeit.

Keynes hatte keine Mühe, die klassische Theorie des Arbeitsmarktes – und damit der Arbeitslosigkeit – zu kritisieren. Ihre Annahmen sind von geradezu bizarrer Wirklichkeitsferne. Unter den Bedingungen der klassischen Theorie funktionieren alle Märkte – auch der Arbeitsmarkt – ähnlich einer Börse oder Versteigerung – und dies kostenlos. Man stellt sich vor, ein Makler ruft versuchsweise einen Lohnsatz aus. Ist das Arbeitsangebot größer als die Arbeitsnachfrage, versucht er es nochmals und ruft einen niedrigeren Lohnsatz aus usw. solange, bis Angebot und Nachfrage einander gleich sind. Erst dann kommt der Zuschlag, die Verträge werden rechtsgültig, es wird getauscht: Geld gegen Arbeitsleistung zu dem vereinbarten Stundenlohnsatz. Getauscht wird also erst im Gleichgewicht. Streng genommen kennt dieses Modell keine Arbeitslosigkeit. Es ist eine Gleichgewichtstheorie der Beschäftigung, behandelt insofern nur einen Spezialfall. Genau das kritisiert Keynes (1936, 16), der sich bemüht eine „Allgemeine Theorie“ zu liefern, die auch auf Situationen mit Arbeitslosigkeit („Unterbeschäftigung“) anwendbar ist. Das muß eine Theorie sein, die zugleich erklärt, wie die Akteure ihre Pläne koordinieren, wenn Preise und Löhne als Koordinationsinstrumente „versagen“, weil sie zum Beispiel temporär starr sind.

Tatsächlich sind auch die Geldlöhne häufig nach unten starr und dies nicht nur infolge Tarifvertrag oder Mindestlohngesetzgebung (Entsendegesetz etwa). Desgleichen bewegen sich die Güterpreise zum Teil nur zögerlich, wie eine frühe Studie von Mills (1927) zeigt, die Keynes bereits gekannt haben könnte. Es gibt Güter, deren Preise sich häufig ändern, (Salat) und andere Güter, deren Preise sich nur selten ändern (Stahl, Automobile). Nach einer neueren Studie von Blinder (1991) ändern weniger als 15% der Unternehmen ihre Preise häufiger als einmal im Vierteljahr und 55% ändern ihre Preise allenfalls einmal jährlich.

Für Vertreter der Neuen Institutionenökonomik sind starre Löhne und Preise leicht begründbar. Sie werden auf die von der Klassik ausgeklammerten Transaktionskosten zurückgeführt – auf die Kosten der Marktbenutzung wie Such- und Informationskosten, Verhandlungskosten oder Kosten der Überwachung und Durchsetzung von Leistungspflichten.

## II. Die Argumentation von Keynes

Charakteristisch für den Ansatz von Keynes ist, daß er die Frage warum Arbeitslosigkeit besteht, nicht vom Arbeitsmarkt, sondern vom Gütermarkt her erklärt. Er bezieht sich dabei auf das „Paradox der Armut mitten im Überfluß"(1936, 30), zu dem es infolge mangelnder Güternachfrage komme. Mit dem Arbeitsmarkt beschäftigt sich Keynes dabei nur am Rande. Dementsprechend kommt bis heute der Arbeitsmarkt in den Lehrbüchern zur keynesianischen Beschäftigungstheorie entweder überhaupt nicht vor (McKenna, 1955; Dornbusch und Fischer, 1978; Branson, 1979), oder er wird nur sehr kurz behandelt (Mankiw, 1992, Chap. 5, 20 Seiten von 483! – Blanchard, 1997, Chap. 15, 21 Seiten von 609!).

Keynes argumentiert, daß bei einem exogenen Schock – z. B. einem Rückgang der (autonomen) Investitionsnachfrage oder der Exporte – die Güterpreise und Geldlöhne nicht reagieren. Die herrschenden Preise und Löhne sind bei der Sachlage „falsch", die Unternehmen können auf der Grundlage dieser falschen Preise nicht mehr ihre Produktion und damit ihre Arbeitsnachfrage planen. Sie richten sich jetzt nach der am Gütermarkt herrschenden „effektiven" Nachfrage $Y^*$ und fragen nur so viel Arbeit nach, wie sie zur Herstellung von $Y^*$ benötigen. Die Arbeitsnachfragekurve bricht als Folge an dieser Stelle ab. Es herrscht „keynesianische Arbeitslosigkeit", d. h. Arbeitslosigkeit trotz unverändertem Gleichgewichtsreallohn. Eine Senkung des Reallohnes hilft in dem Falle nicht. Das Mittel der Wahl ist vielmehr die Ausdehnung der gesamtwirtschaftlichen Nachfrage – etwa durch zusätzliche, defizitfinanzierte Staatsausgaben oder durch Steuersenkungen. Nur durch „Nachfrage-Management" läßt sich keynesianische Arbeitslosigkeit überwinden und Vollbeschäftigung wieder herstellen.

*Zwischenbemerkung:* Diese Kur funktioniert nur, wenn der Reallohn in der Zwischenzeit entweder nicht gestiegen ist oder im Zuge der keynesianischen Vollbeschäftigungspolitik wieder auf sein altes Gleichgewichtsniveau zurückgeht. Keynes und die „alten" Keynesianer diskutieren dieses Thema nicht, obgleich Preisrückgänge zum Bild des „Paradox der Armut mitten im Überfluß" gehören. Bei nach unten starren Löhnen bewirken sinkende Güterpreise eine Erhöhung der Reallöhne. Lautet das gewerkschaftliche Verhandlungsziel „Reallohnsicherung," dann kann es sein, daß am überhöhten Reallohnniveau festgehalten wird – zumal wenn zwischen dem ursprünglichen Beschäftigungseinbruch und dem Beginn beschäftigungspolitischer Gegenmaßnahmen so viel Zeit vergangen ist, daß die Öffentlichkeit die Ursachen der Arbeitslosigkeit aus den Augen verloren hat. Die Unternehmen werden bereit sein, zu höheren Reallöhnen abzuschließen – wenn sie nur ihre Anlagen „voll auslasten" können und zu Grenzproduktivität der Arbeit = Reallohn (also zum gegebenen Reallohn gewinnmaximierend) produzieren können. Sie könnten natürlich ihren Gewinn durch Zahlung niedrigerer Löhne erhöhen, werden aber aller Erfahrung nach wegen der hohen Verhandlungskosten (Streiks etc.) davon Abstand nehmen. Eventuell sind sie selbst an höheren Löhnen interessiert, um die Kosten ihrer (potentiellen) Konkurrenten heraufzuschrauben (Haucap et al. 1998). Resultat: Weder die Gewerkschaften als Vertreter der Arbeitsplatzbesitzer, noch die Unternehmen werden für eine Beseitigung der „Reallohnschranke" kämpfen. Die Reallohnschranke verhindert den vollen Erfolg des keynesianischen Nachfrage-Managements. Ein Rest von Arbeitslosen bleibt dann nach dem exogenen Schock übrig, wird nicht wieder ins Arbeitsleben zurückgeführt. Dies ist eine Variante der Erklärung für das Zurückbleiben (der „Hysteresis") von Arbeitslosigkeit nach größeren Schocks und der damit einhergehenden „Stagflation".[1] In der Neu-Keynes'schen Literatur wird in dem Zusammenhang (Arbeitslosigkeit als Konsequenz gleicher Lohn- und Preissteigerungsraten) der Begriff „quasi-gleichgewichtige Unterbeschäftigung" verwendet (*quasi equilibrium rate of unemployment,* QERU; Franz 1996, 8). Wir kommen weiter unten erneut darauf zurück.

*Zurück zu Keynes:* Statt den Arbeitsmarkt im Auge zu behalten, konzentrierten sich also Keynes und die „alten" Keynesianer auf den Gütermarkt und dort auf die Frage, was die effektive Güternachfrage $Y^*$ bestimmt. Die Antwort von Keynes ist genial einfach: Die Güternachfrage $Y$ selbst dient als Steuerungsinstrument und bestimmt $Y^*$.

Das geht bekanntlich so: Die Konsumgüternachfrage $C$ der Haushalte hängt nicht vom Reallohn, sondern vom Realeinkommen $Y$ ab – ausgedrückt durch die Konsumfunktion $C(Y)$. Die Unternehmen fragen für Investitionszwecke die Gütermenge $I$ nach. Lassen wir Staat und Ausland unberücksichtigt, dann muß im güterwirtschaftlichen Gleichgewicht die Gleichung

$$C(Y) + I = Y \qquad \text{mit} \quad Y \leq Y_v$$

erfüllt sein ($Y_v$ = Vollbeschäftigungs-Einkommen). Wir haben eine Gleichung mit einer Unbekannten $Y$. Die effektive Nachfrage $Y^*$ ist der Wert von $Y$, der die Gütermarktgleichung erfüllt – ist also die „Lösung" dieser Gleichung.

Eine zentrale Rolle spielt die Konsumfunktion mit der Annahme, daß die marginale Konsumquote $dC/dY < 1$ ist. Darauf geht Keynes im 8. und 9. Kapitel seines

---

[1] Vgl. unten „insider-outsider approach" von Lindbeck und Snower (1988) und das Argument der Hysteresis von Blanchard und Summers (1986).

Buches ausführlich ein, desgleichen behandelt er im 10. Kapitel den sich aus obiger Gütermarktgleichung ergebenden Investitionsmultiplikator

$$dY/dI = 1/(1 - dC/dY) > 1 \ .$$

Der Investitionsmultiplikator ist größer als 1 wegen $dC/dY < 1$. Das ist ein zentrales Stück der Beschäftigungstheorie von Keynes. Durch den Investitionsmultiplikator wirken, so Keynes, die Schwankungen in der Investition verstärkt auf Volkseinkommensnachfrage und Beschäftigung. Die Stabilisierung der Investitionstätigkeit auf einem ausreichend hohen Niveau ist deshalb, so Keynes, von zentraler Bedeutung für die Beschäftigung. Durch die Geldpolitik – über den Zins – würde sich das nicht unbedingt erreichen lassen (1936, 207).

Ansonsten sei monetäre Beschäftigungspolitik einer in nicht-totalitären Staaten schwer zu verwirklichenden Politik flexibler Geldlöhne vorzuziehen. Eine flexible Geldpolitik bei starren Geldlöhnen und flexiblen Wechselkursen sei politisch klüger als eine Politik flexibler Geldlöhne – auch wenn beide theoretisch auf dasselbe hinauslaufen (Kapitel 19, 267 f., 270).[2] Aber selbst dann kann seine Theorie, wie er 1936 im Vorwort zur deutschen Ausgabe schreibt,

> „viel leichter den Verhältnissen eines totalen Staates angepaßt werden als ... unter Bedingungen des freien Wettbewerbes und eines großen Maßes von *Laisser-faire* ...“, (Keynes, 1936*).

## III. Die neoklassische Synthese

Bei der neoklassischen Synthese handelt es sich um eine Eingliederung der Allgemeinen Theorie von Keynes in die temporäre Gleichgewichtstheorie von Hicks (1939, 1946), einer klassischen Theorie, in der wegen flexibler Preise (und den üblichen Existenzbedingungen) stets Vollbeschäftigung herrscht. Der Kapitalmarkt, auf dem finanzielle Titel („Bonds“) gehandelt werden, und der Geldmarkt, mit der Nachfrage nach Kasse und dem nominellen Geldangebot $M$, kommen vor – beides wichtige Bestandteile der Allgemeinen Theorie von Keynes. Die Güterangebotsseite, die in der älteren Makroökonomik unberücksichtigt blieb, (Ackley 1961) findet zögernd Beachtung (Dornbusch und Fischer 1987, 477 - 482, 5 Seiten von 770!).

Das Modell wird nicht nur für den Fall flexibler Löhne und Preise, sondern auch fester Löhne und/oder Preise verwendet. Sind Löhne und Preise fest, dann wird im Stile der aus Güter- und Geldmarkt bestehenden keynesianischen Theorie diskutiert, graphisch dargestellt durch das bekannte IS-LM Diagramm. Keynesiani-

2 „... it can only be a foolish person who would prefer a flexible wage policy to a flexible money policy, ...“, (1936, 268).

sche Arbeitslosigkeit besteht. Sind Löhne und Preise flexibel, herrscht stets Vollbeschäftigung. Vollbeschäftigung ist in der neoklassischen Synthese also ganz im Sinne von Keynes ein Spezialfall der Allgemeinen Theorie der Beschäftigung.

Die neoklassische Synthese beherrschte die Beschäftigungstheorie der 60er und frühen 70er Jahre. Unser Lehrbuch Richter, Schlieper, Friedmann (1973, 1981) folgt dieser Konzeption, allerdings berücksichtigten wir ausführlich sowohl den Arbeitsmarkt als auch das gesamtwirtschaftliche Güterangebot.

Zu erwähnen ist hier die Phillipskurve (Phillips 1958), der empirisch ermittelte negative Zusammenhang zwischen Geldlohnänderungsrate und Arbeitslosenquote. Von der Stabilität dieser Beziehung war damals alle Welt überzeugt. Allerdings bezieht sich die Phillips-Kurve allenfalls auf klassische Arbeitslosigkeit, denn wie dargelegt, reagiert keynesianische Arbeitslosigkeit nicht auf Lohn- oder Preisänderungen. Aber Keynes ist in dem Punkt auch nicht eindeutig. Jedenfalls erfreut sich die Phillips-Kurve großer Beliebtheit bei Keynesianern. Samuelson und Solow (1960) transferieren die Phillips-Kurve zu einer Beziehung zwischen der Änderungsrate des Preisniveaus (der Inflationsrate) und der Arbeitslosenquote und entwickeln das Konzept des „Phillips-Kurven Trade-Off." Danach kann sich ein Land eine dauerhaft niedrige Arbeitslosenquote um den Preis einer dauerhaft hohen (aber festen) Inflationsrate „eintauschen". Helmut Schmidt, damaliger Bundesminister für Wirtschaft und Finanzen, drückt das in einem Interview für die Süddeutsche Zeitung von 27. Juli 1972 wie folgt aus:

> „Mir scheint, daß das Deutsche Volk – zugespitzt – 5% Preisanstieg eher vertragen kann, als 5% Arbeitslosigkeit".

Dahinter steht die Idee, daß Unterbeschäftigungsgleichgewichte vermeidbar sind, da ihr Niveau durch Inkaufnahme einer Dauerinflation verringert werden kann.

Helmut Schmidt war, wie viele Ökonomen seiner Zeit, von der Stabilität der Phillips-Kurve überzeugt. Dieser Vorstellung widersprach Milton Friedman in seiner berühmten Rede als Präsident der *American Economic Association* im Dezember 1967.

## IV. Die Attacken von Friedman und Lucas

Friedman argumentiert in dieser Rede, daß die Arbeitslosenquote unmöglich durch eine permanente (konstante) Inflationsrate auf einem festen (niedrigen) Niveau gehalten werden kann. Die Beschäftigung werde letzten Endes nicht vom Nominal- sondern vom Reallohn bestimmt. Allenfalls könne es eine der Phillipskurve ähnliche Beziehung zwischen der erwarteten Reallohnänderungsrate und der Arbeitslosenquote geben (Richter und Diener 1987). Friedmans Angriff auf die Phillips-Kurve und den Phillipskurven Trade-Off fand jedoch damals bei den Keynesianern kein Gehör. Paul Samuelson veröffentlichte noch 1970, also zwei Jahre später, die 8. Auflage seines Lehrbuches „Economics" mit unverändertem „Phillips Trade-Off" Bild (ebenda 810). Erst als aus der fortschreitenden amerikanischen Inflation bei Arbeitslosigkeit die Stagflation eine unleugbare Tatsache geworden war und die Phillipskurve gänzlich aus den Fugen geriet, begann die Profession die Einwände Friedmans gegen den Phillipskurven Trade-Off zu akzeptieren. Die Idee der natürlichen Arbeitslosigkeit und langfristig starren Phillipskurve setzte sich durch.

Einen weiteren Schlag gegen das Gedankengebäude der Keynesianer führte Robert Lucas (1972) durch seine Anwendung der Rationalen Erwartungshypothese (REH) auf das Konzept der (monetären) Stabilitätspolitik.[3] Seine Überlegung knüpft am Phillipskurven-Konzept an, also an der Reparatur klassischer Arbeitslosigkeit, nicht keynesianischer. Lucas verwendet eine um die Preiserwartungen ergänzte Phillipskurven-Version der güterwirtschaftlichen Angebotsfunktion. Seine „Lucas-Angebotsfunktion" ist dementsprechend vom Typ

$$Y = Y_v + a(p - p^*) + \varepsilon \; ;$$

$p^*$ ist der erwartete Preis, $a > 0$, $\varepsilon$ eine normalverteilte Störgröße mit Mittelwert Null. Im Unterschied zu der in der neoklassischen Synthese angewendeten gesamtwirtschaftlichen Produktionsfunktion fehlen die Argumente: Arbeitseinsatz (und damit der Bezug zum Arbeitsmarkt) und Kapitaleinsatz. Das Modell ist allein darauf abgestellt, die „Politik-Ineffektivitätshypothese" von Lucas (1973) zu illustrieren – nämlich die Behauptung, daß eine systematische und damit von den privaten Wirtschaftssubjekten genau vorhersehbare Geldmengenpolitik (Beispiel: erhöhe morgen $M$, wenn heute $Y < Y_v$) wirkungslos ist (Sargent und Wallace, 1975, Barro, 1976). In diesem Modell haben nur noch zufällige (also nicht einer Regel folgende) Geldmengenänderungen eine Beschäftigungswirkung[4].

*Zwischenbemerkung:* Das Modell unterstellt (implizit) flexible Preise und Löhne sowie Freiheit von Geldillusion. Gewerkschaften und Arbeitgeberverbände kommen nicht vor. Wir können natürlich die REH auch auf den oben andiskutierten Fall Keynesscher Arbeitslosigkeit anwenden bei Annahme mächtiger Gewerkschaften und Arbeitgeberverbände. Die Gewerkschaften maximieren ihre Einnahmen aus Mitgliederbeiträgen, die vom Bruttolohn der Beschäftigten abhängen, die Arbeitgeber sind daran interessiert, sich Konkurrenten durch hohe Produktionskosten vom Leibe zu halten. Arbeitnehmer und -geber bilden ein Tarifvertragskartell zu Lasten Dritter (der Arbeitslosen und der Steuerzahler). Als Konsequenz werden die Tarifparteien sich darauf vorbereiten, sofort in die zu erwartenden „tiefen Taschen" der monetären Beschäftigungspolitik zu greifen und die Geldlöhne um die

---

3 Bei der Rationalen Erwartungshypothese handelt es sich um die Annahme, daß die Individuen bei ihrer Erwartungsbildung das ökonomische Prinzip anwenden, d. h. die „beste" Erwartung aus der Gesamtheit aller ihnen zur Verfügung stehenden Informationen bilden.

4 Leicht lesbare Übersicht bei Maddock und Carter (1982).

zu erwartende Inflationsrate zu erhöhen. Als Ergebnis steigen nur die Preise. Die Beschäftigungslage bleibt (im Schnitt) unverändert (Stagflation). Durch Nachfrage-Management läßt sich bei rationaler Erwartungsbildung der Gewerkschaften die von mir so bezeichnete „Reallohnschwelle" nicht überwinden. Aber nicht nur die Gewerkschaften, auch die Unternehmungen bereiten sich auf die nächste, von der Keynesschen Beschäftigungspolitik angefeuerten Lohnrunde vor und beginnen damit, ihre Arbeitsproduktivität um den Betrag zu erhöhen, um den nach ihrer Einschätzung (oder Ankündigung der Gewerkschaften) die Lohnforderungen die Inflationsrate übersteigen werden. Der Abbau von Arbeitsplätzen wird vorbereitet. Rationale Erwartungsbildung der Unternehmungen bewirkt eine weitere Zunahme der Arbeitslosigkeit oder verfestigt die Hysteresis.

Im Ergebnis halten sich die Lohnerhöhungen an die Grenzen, die ihnen die Arbeitsproduktivitätsentwicklung setzt. Die Tarifparteien stehen dem Rest der Gesellschaft gegebenüber, wie es aussieht, „gut da". Tatsächlich jedoch drehen sie sich in einem Teufelskreis. Die Unternehmen akzeptieren die hohen oder sogar erhöhten Reallöhne, wenn sie nur ihre Produktionsmenge an der Stelle „Grenzproduktivität der Arbeit gleich Reallohn" absetzen können. Die Gewerkschaften akzeptieren die zunehmende Arbeitslosenzahl (selbst bei 20%iger Arbeitslosigkeit ist mit 80% immer noch die überwiegende Mehrheit der Arbeitnehmer beschäftigt!), wenn sie nur ihre Mitgliederzahl und ihr Beitragsaufkommen halten können. Die Tarifparteien, Gewerkschaften und die Arbeitgeberverbände, beschuldigen die Regierung, die Arbeitslosigkeit nicht wirksam zu bekämpfen. Diese kann den Teufelskreis wegen der Tarifautonomie nicht unterbrechen. Sie kann ihn allenfalls durch Keynessche Beschäftigungspolitik ein Stück weiter drehen. Gegebenenfalls stabilisiert sich der Teufelskreis auf einem quasi-gleichgewichtigen Unterbeschäftigungsnivau QERU (einem „limit cycle" bei hoher Arbeitslosigkeit). Das ist eine denkbare Interpretation unserer gegenwärtigen deutschen Beschäftigungslage.

## V. Verteidigungsstrategien der Neuen Keynesianer

An „Revolutionen" und „Gegenrevolutionen" fehlt es in der Ökonomik nicht, und die Keynesianer hatten in dieser Beziehung von den Monetaristen alsbald ihre Lektion gelernt. Nach einer Zeit der „Makrokonfusion" (Nordhaus 1982) übernimmt Gregory Mankiw die Führungsrolle unter den Vertretern der sich herauskristallisierenden New Keynesian Economics (NKE). Mankiw ist nicht nur ein ideenreicher Forscher sondern auch ein erstklassiger Lehrer, der 1992 mit einem inzwischen vielbenutzten Lehrbuch zur Makroökonomik hervortrat. Dazu kommen von ihm gut plazierte, die Position der Neuen Keynesianer darstellende Publikationen, darunter ein mit David Romer 1991 herausgegebener zweibändiger Sammelband mit 34 Zeitschriftenaufsätzen führender Vertreter der NKE, ferner ein süffig geschriebener „Quick Refresher Course in Macroeconomics", erschienen 1990 im Journal of Economic Literature und (1993) ein von Mankiw eingeleitetes *Sympo-*

*sium: Keynes and Economics Today,* im Journal of Economic Perspectives (mit Beiträgen von Romer, Greenwald und Stiglitz, Tobin, Robert King). David Romer (1996) zielt in die gleiche Richtung mit seinem 1996 erschienenen Lehrbuch „*Advanced Macroeconomics.*“

Die Hypothese rationaler Erwartungsbildung wird von den NKE Vertretern voll integriert. Unverändert abgelehnt wird hingegen die klassische Hypothese der automatischen Markträumung, an der die Neuen Klassiker wie Lucas weiter festhalten (Greenwald und Stiglitz, 1993).

Generell geht es den Vertretern der NKE darum zu zeigen, daß antizipierte Schwankungen im Geldangebot auch unter den Bedingungen der REH Einfluß auf reale Größen, darunter die Beschäftigung, haben (Mankiw und Romer, 1991, 2). Dafür sprechen ökonometrische Tests, z. B. von Mishkin (1982). Erklärt werden diese Effekte durch nominelle Preis- und Lohnrigiditäten, aber auch – zwei neue Gedanken – durch reale Rigiditäten oder als eine Konsequenz unvollständiger Konkurrenz. Die Arbeiten beziehen sich allerdings auf die amerikanischen Erfahrungen, also ein Land mit schwachen Gewerkschaften, auf das meine obige Argumentation nicht anwendbar ist.

Es gibt eine wachsende Zahl mikroökonomischer Begründungen für starre Löhne und Preise. Ihnen gemeinsam ist, daß sie irgendwelche „Unvollkommenheiten“ (im Vergleich zur klassischen Theorie) unterstellen, darunter mangelnden Zugang der Arbeiter zum Kapitalmarkt, asymmetrische Information der Arbeitgeber gegenüber den Arbeitnehmern (oder umgekehrt), die Kosten der Preisanpassung oder Gewerkschaftsaktivitäten. Als Mikrotheorien der Arbeitslosigkeit treten hervor die *Theorie impliziter Verträge* (Azariadis, Bailey, Gordon), die *Theorie der Kundenmärkte* (Okun), die *Theorie der Menü-Kosten* (Akerlof und Yellen, Mankiw), die *Theorie der Arbeitslosigkeit als Folge gewerkschaftlicher Aktivitäten* (McDonald und Solow, Oswald, Gylfason und Lindbeck, Calmfors und Horn), die *Effizienzlohntheorie* (Schlicht, Solow, Akerlof, Stiglitz) und der *Insider-Outsider Ansatz* (Lindbeck und Snower, Shaked und Sutton). Während diese Theorien unfreiwillige Arbeitslosigkeit modellieren, benutzen andere Vertreter der Neuen Keynesschen Makroökonomik die Markträumungshypothese – allerdings unter Berücksichtigung von Marktstörungen, die sie auf „Marktmacht“ und andere „Unvollständigkeiten“ (wie Suchkosten) zurückführen. Es sind die Vertreter der Theorie des *Kooperationsversagens* (Hart) einerseits sowie andererseits der *Theorie des Koordinationsversagens* (Cooper und John, Ball und Romer; Überblick über die beiden Varianten: Silvestre 1993).

Hier sei kurz über die letzten vier Theorien berichtet:

(1) Die *Effizienzlohntheorie* wurde Ende der 70er, Anfang der 80er von Schlicht (1978), Solow (1979), Akerlof (1982) u. a. entwickelt (Überblick: Akerlof und Yellen 1986). Sie zeigt, daß unfreiwillige Arbeitslosigkeit nicht nur eine Folge gewerkschaftlicher Aktivitäten sein muß, sondern auch durch das Verhalten von Unternehmungen zustandekommen kann. Es wird angenommen, daß das Anstren-

gungsniveau $e$ der Arbeiter von den Unternehmen nicht beobachtet werden kann. Es wird ferner angenommen, daß das Anstrengungsniveau der Arbeiter mit wachsendem Reallohn steigt. Durch Angebot eines hohen Reallohns können die Unternehmen ihre Informationsasymmetrie also ausgleichen. Modelliert wird wie folgt: Der Arbeitseinsatz $N$ in der Produktionsfunktion $\Phi$ ist ein Produkt aus Arbeitszeit $n$ und dem vom Reallohn $\omega$ abhängigen Anstrengungsniveau $e$ der Arbeiter. Die Optimierungsaufgabe der Unternehmung lautet dann:

$$\max_{\omega,n}, n\ Y = \Phi\big(K, ne(\omega)\big) - \omega n\ .$$

Bei dem Wert $\omega^*$ maximieren die Arbeiter ihre Anstrengung $e$ pro Arbeitsstunde (arbeiten sie „am effizientesten"). Aus der Arbeitsnachfragefunktion $N = ne(\omega)$ ergibt sich die Beschäftigungsmenge $n$, die das Unternehmen zum Effizienzlohn $\omega^*$ einstellt. Solange $n < A$ ist, herrscht Arbeitslosigkeit. Dennoch senkt die (annahmegemäß reallohnfixierende) Unternehmung nicht ihr Reallohngebot, weil eine Lohnsenkung das Anstrengungsniveau der Beschäftigten verringern würde. Damit erklärt die Effizienzlohnhypothese das evtl. Bestehen unfreiwilliger Arbeitslosigkeit. Das monopolistische Verhalten der Unternehmung auf dem Arbeitsmarkt ist allerdings für gewerkschaftsgewohnte Deutsche schwer einzusehen. Auch ist zu beachten, daß die Effizienzlohnhypothese starke Lohnunterschiede innerhalb einer Industrie vorhersagt, was mit den in Deutschland bislang üblichen Flächentarifen nicht vereinbar ist.

(2) Eher auf deutsche Verhältnisse zugeschnitten ist der *Insider-Outsider-Ansatz* von Lindbeck und Snower (1988 a, b). Die Autoren nehmen an, daß nicht nur die Unternehmer, sondern auch die Arbeitnehmer eine gewisse Machtstellung haben. Zentral ist die Annahme, daß ein kompletter Austausch der Beschäftigten einer Unternehmung (der Insider) gegen Arbeitslose (Outsider) eine kostspielige Affäre ist. In der Sprache der Neuen Institutionenökonomik: die Unternehmung ist in den Vertrag mit ihrer Arbeiterschaft „eingeschlossen". Die Insider können daraus für sich einen gewissen Vorteil (eine „Rente") bei den Lohnverhandlungen herausschlagen mit dem Ergebnis, daß ihre Löhne über dem Gleichgewichtslohnsatz zu liegen kommen. Unfreiwillige Arbeitslosigkeit ist das Resultat. Die Outsider können ihre Position durch Unterbieten der Insider nicht verbessern, da diese ihre Vormachtstellung ausnützen würden, wodurch ein Beschäftigungswechsel die Unternehmung teuer zu stehen käme. Vier Typen von (Transaktions-)Kosten spielen eine Rolle: die Kosten des Heuerns und Feuerns (*turnover costs*), die (arbeitsvertrags-) spezifischen Investitionen,[5] die Produktivitätsverluste, die sich aus nichtkooperativem Verhalten der Insider gegenüber Outsidern ergeben und die Produktivitätsverluste infolge sinkenden Anstrengungsniveaus der Insider bei abnehmender Arbeitsplatzsicherheit (zunehmendem Feuern und Heuern).

---

5 Zur Berücksichtigung der *turnover costs* und *specific investments* in der Theorie der Arbeitsverträge vgl. die Übersicht von Malcomson (1997).

(3) Zum *Kooperationsversagen* hat Oliver Hart (1982) eine viel zitierte Arbeit geschrieben. Arbeitslosigkeit wird als Konsequenz gewerkschaftlicher Aktivität erklärt, verstärkt durch monopolistische Praktiken auf den Gütermärkten seitens der Produzenten.[6] (Die Gewerkschaften setzen den Lohnsatz und die zugehörige Arbeitsmenge fest, bei der die Lohnsumme maximiert wird. Die Arbeitsmenge wird nach einer Quotenregelung auf die Arbeiter verteilt, die allerdings zu dem Monopol-Lohnsatz gerne länger arbeiten würden, vgl. Hart 1982, 114). Unter bestimmten Bedingungen bietet hier Keynessches Nachfrage-Management eine (wohlfahrtstheoretisch) zweitbeste Lösung des Kooperationsproblems. Silvestre (1993, 136 f.) bemerkt dazu jedoch treffend, daß die Ausgabenpolitik des Staates zumindest eine gewisse Preissteigerung bewirken dürfte und damit eine Lohn-Preis-Spirale mit keinem oder sogar einem negativen Beschäftigungseffekt in Gang setzen könnte. Geldpolitik ist in diesem Modell eo ipso unwirksam, da hier Geld, wie bei vollständiger Konkurrenz, neutral ist.

(4) *Koordinationsprobleme* treten in spieltheoretischen Marktmodellen mit multiplen Gleichgewichten auf, darunter effiziente und ineffiziente. Eine allgemeine Darstellung liefern Cooper und John (1988). Wenn alle Akteure z. B. glauben, das schlechte Gleichgewicht (Unterbeschäftigungsgleichgewicht)[7] tritt ein, dann wird es nach dieser Theorie auch eintreten. Das Problem besteht dann in der Koordination der (in diesem Beispiel) individuellen Erwartungen, wofür es keinen „Marktmechanismus" gibt.[8] Staatliche Interventionen, so D. Romer, seien dann angezeigt. Durch temporäre Stimulanzien könnte die Wirtschaft eventuell auf ein besseres Gleichgewicht gebracht werden (D. Romer 1996, 297). Das ist die alte Investitionsmultiplikator-Idee im neuen Gewande.[9] Allerdings weist Greif (1997a) darauf hin, daß in spieltheoretischen Ansätzen, wie sie in der Informationsökonomik zur Anwendung kommen, die Ergebnisse stark von den Annahmen abhängen.

The result is „a proliferation in the numbers and types of micro- and macroeconomic models, each aimed at highlighting particular, potentially important aspects of economic systems", (1997a, 401).

Im übrigen sind die Neuen Keynesianer bescheidene Leute. Sie freuen sich, die Attacken von Lucas abgeschlagen zu haben und zu einem Stand „ähnlich dem der 60er Jahre" zurückgekehrt zu sein (so Mankiw und Romer 1991, 15). Ein eigener Schritt nach vorn, ein großer theoretischer Wurf, vergleichbar mit dem der Friedman-Lucas-Linie, wird nicht gewagt. Es bleibt bei der Restauration der Keynes-

---

6 In der Fortentwicklung wird gezeigt, daß Arbeitslosigkeit allein eine Folge monopolistischer Praktiken der Produzenten auf den Gütermärkten sein kann. Vgl. D'Aspremont, Dos Santos Ferreira und Gérard-Varet (1991).

7 Gemeint ist ein Gleichgewicht bei niedrigem Beschäftigungsniveau *aller,* kein Gleichgewicht mit unfreiwilliger Arbeitslosigkeit: „underemployment" und nicht „unemployment".

8 Das Problem wird beim Studium der temporären Gleichgewichtstheorie von Hicks deutlich.

9 Zur Illustration vgl. Matsuyama (1995).

schen Position – keine Aufbruchsstimmung, keine Übernahme der intellektuellen Führung, keine neue Beschäftigungspolitik. Die Neue Keynessche Theorie bleibt eine Theorie der Nachfrageschocks und des Nachfrage-Managements.

## VI. Fehlende Arbeitsplätze

Keynes' „Allgemeine Theorie der Beschäftigung" verallgemeinert die klassische Lehre in Richtung *Arbeitslosigkeit wegen Absatzschwierigkeiten* der Güterproduzenten. Das Problem der *Arbeitslosigkeit wegen fehlender Arbeitsplätze,* wie wir sie in den Neuen Bundesländern, in Westdeutschland 1948 ff. oder in Entwicklungsländern beobachten, behandelte er nicht. Es ist auch bis heute nicht Gegenstand der (amerikanisch geprägten) Standard-Makroökonomik. Die gängige Wachstumstheorie – obgleich von Keynesianern erfunden (Solow, Romer) – ist neoklassisch. Es gibt in ihr keine Arbeitslosigkeit. Nur die alte Harrod-Domar-Wachstumstheorie geht von Unterbeschäftigung mangels Arbeitsplätzen aus und illustriert, wie in dem Falle Arbeitslosigkeit zu beseitigen ist, nämlich durch Sparen (wie im Westen Deutschlands nach der Währungsreform), nicht durch Konsumieren (wie heute im Osten). Die entscheidende, von Solow (1956) über Bord geworfene Annahme der Arbeitslosigkeit wegen fehlender Arbeitsplätze ist die Annahme der Komplementarität von Kapital und Arbeit: Zu einem Kapitalgut bestimmter Technik gehört eine bestimmte Arbeiterzahl: Zur Dampflok Lokomotivführer und Heizer, zur E-Lok nur ein Lokführer usw. (Harrod 1939). Nehmen wir dazu im relevanten Bereich abnehmende Skalenerträge an, dann erhalten wir bei gegebenem Kapitalstock $K_0$ eine an der zugehörigen Stelle $N_0$ abbrechende Arbeitsnachfragekurve. Sie ist äußerlich ähnlich der Keynes'schen Arbeitsnachfragekurve, auch gilt wie dort, daß Reallohnsenkungen keine Beschäftigungszunahme bewirken. Es ist aber nicht mehr Nachfrage-Management das Mittel der Wahl sondern im Gegenteil Sparen! Je größer die Sparquote $S/Y$, desto schneller das Wachstum des Kapitalstocks und damit die Zunahme der Arbeitsplätze (gegeben der Kapitalkoeffizient $k = K/Y$).

Die Diagnose „fehlende Arbeitsplätze vom Harrod Typ" ist, wie die Erfahrung lehrt, in unserer ideologiebeladenen Welt nicht einfach zu stellen. Selbst im Falle Deutschlands der Nachkriegszeit, als Bombenlöcher „fehlende Arbeitsplätze" drastisch demonstrierten, hielten britische Keynesianer wie Dr. T. Balogh (später Lord Balogh) im Jahr 1950 der britischen Besatzungsmacht in Deutschland vor, Professor Erhard und seinen „satellite economists" und „Experten" zu gestatten, eine „aufgeklärte Keynesianische Wirtschaftspolitik" zu diskreditieren. Nach Dr. Balogh basierte die Politik der deutschen Regierung auf „completely outmoded and erroneous economic theories," die nicht zum Erfolg führen würden (zitiert nach Hutchison 1979, 438). Ähnlich argumentierten andere englische Ökonomen.[10]

---

[10] Richter (1979, 449 - 453).

"Fehlende Arbeitsplätze" können aber auch das Resultat von Mindestlohnarbeitslosigkeit bei im übrigen Substitutionalität von Kapital und Arbeit sein. Vollbeschäftigung kann auch in dem Fall nicht durch Nachfrage-Management hergestellt werden. Halten die Tarifparteien am Reallohnniveau fest, dann kann nach einiger Zeit Vollbeschäftigung durch eine Rechtsverschiebung der Arbeitsnachfragekurve – also durch ein Harrod-Domar-Wachstum des Kapitalstocks – hergestellt werden. Das geht um so schneller, je größer die Sparquote $S/Y$ ist. Man versteht so den starren Blick der Politiker auf die Wachstumsraten des BSP. Aber: nicht zusätzlicher Verbrauch – etwa mehr defizitfinanzierte Staatsausgaben –, sondern zusätzliches Sparen – etwa Haushaltsüberschüsse wie in den 50er Jahren – ist dann angezeigt. Das klingt eher „sozial verträglich" als eine Reallohnsenkung. Das Problem dabei ist, daß mit der Rechtsverschiebung der Arbeitsnachfragekurve die Arbeitsproduktivität der Insider steigt. Die Gewerkschaften müßten bereit sein, an dem Ausgangs-Reallohnniveau festzuhalten, *obgleich* die Arbeitsproduktivität der Insider (also ihrer Mitglieder) steigt! Verlangen sie höhere Reallöhne wegen gestiegener Arbeitsproduktivität, wird die Reallohnschwelle wieder nach oben verschoben und das Langfrist-Ziel der Vollbeschäftigung nicht erreicht. Für die Unternehmen ist es, wie erwähnt, entweder zu teuer oder nicht erwünscht, Lohnsenkungen herbeizuführen. Vollbeschäftigung werden die Tarifparteien im allgemeinen nicht herstellen. Es bleibt bei einem „schlechten Gleichgewicht" – bei quasi-gleichgewichtiger Unterbeschäftigung (QERU).

## VII. Arbeitslosigkeit aus polit-ökonomischer Sicht

Keynes war, wie Harrod schreibt, ein Elitist. Für ihn galten die Voraussetzungen der Harvey-Road, die Vorstellung, daß die Politik der Regierung, insbesondere ihre Wirtschaftspolitik von einer kleinen Gruppe kluger und aufgeklärter Leute gemacht wird.[11] Keynes hat sich seine wirtschaftspolitischen Vorschläge nicht unter dem Aspekt der modernen Demokratie überlegt, in der die Regierung dazu neigt, dem Druck von Gruppeninteressen nachzugeben, um an der Macht zu bleiben. Inzwischen gibt es polit-ökonomische Modelle mit ersten Ansätzen sowohl im Lager der Keynesianer (angefangen mit Nordhaus, 1975) als auch bei eher klassisch orientierten Ökonomen (Beispiel: Olson, 1984).

Nordhaus beschreibt einen polit-ökonomische Konjunkturzyklus. Die Regierung erhöht direkt nach der Wahl die Arbeitslosigkeit, um sie dann bis zur nächsten Wahl kontinuierlich wieder sinken zu lassen, mit dem Ziel der Wiederwahl bzw. der Maximierung ihres Stimmenanteils bei der nächsten Wahl.

Olson (1984) schreibt, statt zu fragen „Warum Arbeitslosigkeit?" müsse man fragen „Wem nützt die Arbeitslosigkeit?". Sie nützt bestimmten Interessengruppen (darunter Gewerkschaften als Vertreter der Arbeitsplatzbesitzer und Arbeitgeber-

11 Harrod zitiert nach Buchanan, Burtan und Wagner (1978, 16).

verbände als Vertreter von Angebotsmonopolisten) bei der Förderung ihrer Spezialinteressen.

Saint-Paul (1995) beschreibt Fälle *polit-ökonomischer Komplementaritäten,* die einen Teufelskreis von hoher Arbeitslosigkeit und pervertierten politischen Entscheidungen zur Folge haben. Beispiele sind (1) die hohen Kündigungskosten, (2) die Finanzierung der hohen Suchkosten von Langzeitarbeitslosen, (3) das Problem, arbeitslose Bergleute u. a. Arbeiter absterbender Industrien neu zu beschäftigen. Die drei Teufelskreise laufen so: Zu (1) Hohe Kündigungskosten verringern den Arbeitsumsatz und damit die Einstellungschancen Arbeitsloser, die Dauerarbeitslosigkeit wird erhöht, was zur politischen Unterstützung von Vertretern führt, die den Kündigungsschutz weiter hoch halten oder verstärken usw. Zu (2) Die hohen Suchkosten bewirken bei, infolge wachsender Arbeitslosigkeit, schrumpfenden Steuereinnahmen einen zunehmenden Fiskalkonservatismus des Medianwählers, was zu einer Reduktion von Fortbildungs- und Suchprogrammen führt usw. Zu (3) Die Schwierigkeiten, arbeitslose Bergleute usw. einzustellen, verstärkt die Aktivitäten der Bergbaulobby usw., mit der Konsequenz weiterer oder erhöhter Subventionszahlungen an den Bergbau oder andere sterbende Industrien.

Mit der Politökonomik der Arbeitslosigkeit eng verwandt ist die *Ökonomische Analyse des Arbeitsrechts.* Hier treibt die Juristerei Blüten (vgl. Rüthers 1996). Man betrachte etwa den Kündigungsschutz und in dem Zusammenhang die Lehre vom Arbeitsverhältnis als Lebensbund (Herschels 1958, 1981 zit. nach Rüthers 1996, 70 ff.). Vergleiche mit dem Wesen der Ehe werden gezogen – was nicht völlig falsch ist, denn Ehe und Arbeitsvertrag haben einen stark relationalen Charakter (s.u.). Volkswirtschaftlich (und auch allgemein gesellschaftlich) unangebracht jedoch ist die Tendenz zur Verabsolutierung des Bestandsschutzes von Arbeitsverhältnissen nach den Wesensargumenten der Ehe, wie sie sich in der Rechtsprechung des BAG entwickelt hat (Rüthers, 90).

## VIII. Arbeitslosigkeit infolge der Kartellstruktur von Arbeitsmärkten: Industrie-Ökonomik der Arbeitslosigkeit

Hier geht es um die Erklärung der Arbeitslosigkeit als Folge einer Koalition von Gewerkschaft und Unternehmerverband gegen den Rest der Gesellschaft.

Vorab einige elementare mikroökonomische Überlegungen zum *„Grundrecht der Koalitionsfreiheit“* (Grundgesetz Art. 9 III). Dahinter steht das Vertrauen des Grundgesetzgebers in das „Gleichgewicht der Kräfte“ (Dreschers 1994, 509).

Die regelungsmäßige Zurückhaltung des Grundgesetzgebers basiert auf der prinzipiellen ordnungspolitischen Distanz, die der Grundgesetzgeber mit seinem Bekenntnis zur „neutralen“ oder – besser ausgedrückt – offenen Wirtschafts-, Arbeits- und Sozialverfassung verfolgt oder verfolge (Maunz und Dürig, 1996, 109).

Die freiheitliche Bildung von Koalitionen werde

> im öffentlichen Interesse die Aufgabe übertragen, „im Verein mit dem sozialen Gegenspieler das Arbeitsleben zu ordnen und zu befrieden.“ (BVerfGE 18, (27).

Von Verfassung wegen ist den Koalitionen die Aufgabe zugewiesen, im *Prozeß freiheitlicher Interessenauseinandersetzung und autonomer Interessenausgleichung* das Arbeitsleben bzw. den dieses maßgebend mitprägenden Gegensatz der Produktionsfaktoren von Kapital und Arbeit zu ordnen und zu gestalten. *Antagonistischer Koalitionsgegensatz* und *privatautonome Koalitionseinigung* heißen danach die ... Funktionsprinzipien der Koalitionsfreiheit (Maunz und Dürig 1996, 110 f.).

Der Wirtschaftstheoretiker wird an die Theorie des bilateralen Monopols erinnert, die ja auch unter den Lohnverhandlungstheorien zu finden ist. Bilaterale Monopole stören nicht die Paretoeffizienz des Allgemeinen Konkurrenzgleichgewichts. Sie haben nach verbreiteter Auffassung nur eine Verteilungswirkung – bestimmt von der Verhandlungsmacht der Parteien. Voraussetzung sind jedoch „gläserne Menschen“: jeder kennt des anderen Nutzen- bzw. Gewinnfunktion, jeder kennt des anderen Verhandlungsmacht (sein Potential privater Gewaltausübung). Anders ausgedrückt: es gibt keine Transaktionskosten.

So verstanden ist die Koalitionsfreiheit ein „soziales Schutzrecht“ (Maunz und Dürig 1996, 109), das zur Verteilungsgerechtigkeit beiträgt, ohne die Effizienz der Wirtschaft zu beeinträchtigen.

Man wird an John R. Commons (1934) erinnert, einen bedeutenden „Alten Institutionalisten“, und seine energische Unterstützung der Pressure Groups, die die tatsächliche gesetzgebende Körperschaft des Landes bilden sollten.[12] Commons' Denken lag die Ansicht zugrunde, daß der Markt wegen der Ungleichheit der Verhandlungspositionen der verschiedenen Gruppen der Volkswirtschaft nicht für gerechte Ergebnisse sorgt. Die Interessengruppen erschienen ihm deshalb als unentbehrliches Mittel zur Herstellung gerechter Ergebnisse. „... Kooperation der Individuen ergibt sich nicht aus einer *im Voraus angenommenen* Interessenharmonie, wie die älteren Ökonomen glaubten. Sie ergibt sich aus der Notwendigkeit, *eine neue Interessenharmonie zu schaffen* – oder zumindest eine Ordnung, wenn Harmonie unmöglich ist – aus dem Interessenkonflikt der potentiell miteinander Kooperierenden.“ (1934, 6) Kooperation ist das Ergebnis der bei der Verhandlung angewandten Überzeugungspsychologie, Zwang oder Nötigung (coersion or duress). Harmonie ist mithin nicht eine Voraussetzung der Volkswirtschaftslehre – es ist vielmehr eine Folge von Gemeinschaftshandeln „designed to maintain rules that shall govern the conflicts.“ (Commons 1934, 7)

Diese Argumentation trifft allerdings nur dann zu, wenn für die bilateralen Monopolisten „nach außen“ – also am unteren und oberen Ende des bilateralen Mono-

---

[12] Zitiert aus Olson 1992, 112.

pols – vollständige Konkurrenz herrscht und wenn sie nicht nur den Lohn, sondern auch die zu tauschende Arbeitsmenge vertraglich bestimmen. Inhalt der Tarifverträge muß also für den naiven Mikroökonomen sowohl Geldlohnsatz als auch Arbeitsmenge (Zahl der Arbeitsstunden mal Arbeitsplätze) sein („Effiziente Arbeitsverträge“, Franz 1991, 283 f.). Die Bestrebungen der Gewerkschaften, die Tarifverträge in Richtung „Arbeitsplatzsicherung“ auszuweiten, erstaunen den naiven Mikroökonomen deshalb nicht. Was ihn allerdings erstaunt, ist die völlige Außerachtlassung der „äußeren“ Konkurrenzverhältnisse. Sie mögen für die Konsumseite der Arbeitnehmer in etwa „vollständig“ sein, auf der Verkaufsseite der Arbeitgeber sind sie es in vielen Fällen jedoch nicht. Die umfangreiche Literatur zur Oligopoltheorie und unvollständigen Konkurrenz, das große Gebiet der IO (Industrial Organization) bleibt unberücksichtigt. In einer Entscheidung des BAG vom 27. 6. 1989 heißt es z. B.,

> daß die von Art. 9 III GG garantierte Befugnis zur autonomen Regelung der Mindestarbeitsbedingungen auch die Befugnis beinhalte, die Schutzinteressen der Arbeitnehmer und die wettbewerblichen Interessen der Arbeitgeber auf dem Gütermarkt selbst unkontrolliert zu bewerten (Dreschers 509).

Dreschers fährt fort:

> Die hierin liegende Betonung einer „Richtigkeitsgewähr des Tarifvertrags“ und das Vertrauen auf das Gleichgewicht der Kräfte wird wohl auch in Zukunft für die höchstrichterliche Rechtsprechung bestimmend sein und in der Praxis eine Prüfung der Tarifverträge am Maßstab des § 1 GWB ausgeschlossen erscheinen lassen (ebd.).

Die Frage der Effizienz wird von deutschen Gerichten nicht geprüft, den Ausschlag gibt die „Rechtsnatur“.

Die Monopolkommission dagegen argumentiert ökonomisch. Sie arbeitet das uns in diesem Zusammenhang interessierende Konzept der *Tarifvertragskartelle* heraus, sie unterscheiden sich von reinen Unternehmenskartellen dadurch, daß in den Abschlußmechanismus ein vertikales Gegenmachtelement eingebaut ist: Dem Arbeitgeberverband steht eine Gewerkschaft gegenüber. Dies berührt freilich nicht die typische Kartellwirkung, nämlich soweit sie als Vertrag zu Lasten Außenstehender wirkt. Dies sind hier nämlich die im Zeitpunkt der Vereinbarung tatsächlich Arbeitslosen oder die zukünftigen Arbeitslosen.

Zu den belasteten Außenstehenden gehören nicht nur die Arbeitslosen, sondern auch (in der Arbeitsmarktliteratur bislang unbeachtet) die potentiellen Konkurrenten der Unternehmer (darunter die von den Politkern immer wieder animierten Neu- und Jungunternehmer) – und die Steuerzahler, die zur Abdeckung von Defiziten der Arbeitslosenversicherung oder zu Wohlfahrtsleistungen herangezogen werden oder zu Subventionszahlung absterbender Industrien.

Das Problem des Tarifvertragskartells, daß durch hohe Lohnkosten pontentielle Konkurrenten ferngehalten werden, hat früh Williamson anhand des *Pennington Case* beschrieben (Williamson 1968). Er kommt zu dem Schluß, daß

> ... wage premiums *can* be used to erect a barrier to entry, and thus the uniform wage agreement may indeed be a device by which monopoly advantage is secured.[13]

Zum deutschen Tarifvertragskartell vgl. im übrigen die im Anhang zusammenfassend geschilderte Arbeit von Haucap, Pauly und Wey (1998).

## IX. Arbeitsmarkt und Arbeitslosigkeit aus Sicht der Neuen Institutionenökonomik

Was den naiven Mikroökonomen weiter erstaunt, ist (1.) warum rationale Individuen unter den geschilderten Bedingungen („gläserne Menschen") überhaupt streiken („Hicks-Paradox", Kennan 1986, Antworten vgl. Franz 1991, 281) und (2.) die völlige Vernachlässigung der Theorie des Kerns.

Was letztere angeht, ist zu berücksichtigen, daß das Grundrecht der Koalitionsfreiheit eng mit der neoklassischen Idee der Effizienz bilateraler Monopole zusammenhängt, und zwar bilaterale Monopole als Ausschnitt einer großen Wirtschaft mit Null-Transaktionskosten. Informationsbeschaffung und Koalitionsbildung kosten hier nichts. Der Staat hat das Gewaltmonopol, das er allein zum Schutz von Eigentumsrechten und zur Durchsetzung frei vereinbarter Leistungspflichten aus Verträgen einsetzt. Den Individuen steht es frei, sich beliebigen Koalitionen anzuschließen oder sie zu verlassen. Wie wir nun von der Theorie des Kerns her wissen, ist das gesamtwirtschaftliche Gleichgewicht unter diesen Bedingungen identisch mit dem Walrasianische Konkurrenzgleichgewicht (Varian 1992, 389). Auf den Arbeitsmärkten bilden sich mithin so oder so Konkurrenzlöhne. Der Grund ist: die neoklassische Welt ohne Transaktionskosten ist institutionenneutral (Richter und Furubotn 1996, Kap. 1). In ihr spielt es keine Rolle, ob die Löhne zwischen Gewerkschaften und Arbeitgeberverbänden ausgehandelt werden oder sich frei am Markt bilden, ob das Kapital die Arbeit anheuert oder die Arbeit das Kapital mietet, ob wir eine Privateigentumswirtschaft oder eine sozialistische Wirtschaft mit zentraler Planung (oder auch mit Quasimärkten) haben usw. – solange nur dem neoklassischen Optimierungsschema Folge geleistet wird. Das Modell ist ungeeignet, zwischen verschiedenen Institutionen zu diskriminieren und damit nicht in der Lage, eine wie immer verstandene Effizienz des Grundrechts der Koalitionsfreiheit zu begründen. Die neoklassische Begründung des Grundrechts der Koalitionsfreiheit (und der sich daraus ergebenden Tarifautonomie) ist mithin inhaltsleer.

Um das Konzept der Koalitionsfreiheit wirtschaftlich begründen zu können, brauchen wir einen Denkansatz, der die Kosten „der Betreibung des Wirtschaftssy-

---

13 Das ist Williamsons Antwort auf die Frage: „... in what circumstances (if any) agreements between one group of employers and a union to impose uniform wage rates throughout an industry could be used to establish a barrier to entry or (as alleged in the present case) force small rivals to abandon the industry". (Williamson 1968, 86).

stems“ (die Transaktionskosten, Arrow) berücksichtigt. Dazu gehören die Kosten der Marktbenutzung und die Kosten, die sich aus der Tatsache ergeben, daß wir nicht wissen, was uns die Zukunft alles bringt. Das sind die Kosten der Begründung und Erhaltung von Institutionen – also von Normensystemen wie Märkte und Austauschverträge. Mit dem Einfluß der Transaktionskosten auf die Institutionenwahl und Vertragsgestaltung befaßt sich die Neue Institutionenökonomik, ein Mix aus Property Rights Analyse, Transaktionskostenansatz, Vertragstheorie, ökonomischer Analyse des Rechts, Politökonomik, Public Choice Theorie, u. a. m. (Richter 1998). Wir knüpfen hier am Transaktionskostenansatz von Williamson (1985) an und behandeln den Arbeitsmarkt in freier Interpretation des von Williamson, Wachter und Harris (1975) beschriebenen „Beschäftigungsverhältnisses“.

„Beschäftigungsverhältnisse“ sind Langfristbeziehungen zwischen Arbeitgeber und Arbeitnehmer, „relationale Verträge“ im Sinne von Macneil (1974). Der dem Beschäftigungsverhältnis zugrundeliegende Arbeitsvertrag ist ein Paradebeispiel dafür, wie erfolgreich den Ungewißheiten der Zukunft begegnet wird: Da nicht im Voraus bekannt ist, was die Zukunft alles bringt, sind minutiös ausgearbeitete kontingente Dienstverträge unmöglich. Der Arbeitgeber behält sich ein Weisungsrecht vor. Vereinbart wird nur ein „Vertragsrahmen“, an den sich die Parteien zu halten haben. Aber auch der Rahmen kann veralten, weshalb Änderungs- oder Kündigungsvorbehalte vereinbart werden. Die Ungewißheit der Zukunft betrifft natürlich auch und gerade die Entlohnung und die Regelung der Arbeitsbedingungen. Deswegen einigen sich die Parteien darauf, sich immer wieder von neuem zu einigen. Das ist das „relationale“ Element des Arbeitsvertrags (Richter und Furubotn 1996, 149 f.).

Zum ökonomische Problem wird der relationale Vertrag durch die Notwendigkeit transaktionsspezifischer Investitionen der Parteien bei oder nach Vertragsschluß. Das bedeutet, nach ihren spezifischen Investitionen sind die Parteien in das Vertragsverhältnis „eingeschlossen“, sie sind nicht mehr so frei wie sie es vor Vertragsschluß waren (Williamson (1985/90, 70): „fundamentale Transformation“). Damit wird, wie es im Jargon heißt, „ex post Opportunismus“ (ein „hold-up“) für die Seite mit den geringeren spezifischen Investitionen interessant.

Das ist von Einfluß auf die Gestaltung des Arbeitsvertrags und spielt, wie zu erwarten, in der ökonomischen Theorie des Beschäftigungsverhältnisses eine Rolle (Überblick: Malcomson 1997). Das ist auch ein wesentliches Argument für Gewerkschaften, „... und wenn das ihre einzige Funktion wäre, so würden Unternehmen nichts gegen sie einzuwenden haben ... [aber] Unternehmen fürchten das umgekehrte Risiko, daß Arbeitnehmer die Quasirenten der Arbeitgeber enteignen“ (Alchian und Woodward, 1987, 131). Sicherung gegen ex post Opportunimus bei Tarifneuverhandlungen ist auch ein Argument für das Kampfmittel der Arbeitgeber (Aussperrung).

Es gibt auch Rechtsschutz, aber nur während der Laufzeit des Tarifvertrags (andererseits besteht dann Friedenspflicht, Arbeitskampf ist rechtswidrig). Arbeitskampf kommt allenfalls bei Neuverhandlungen zum Tragen. Sie sind grob gesprochen in der Abfolge „Verhandlung, Schlichtung, Streik“ strukturiert. Entscheidend ist, daß der Staat (die Rechtsprechung) sich aus der Lohnfindung heraushält. Die institutionenökonomische (also rationale) Begründung dafür ist, daß der Staat (Gerichte, Verwaltungen, Parlamente) mangels Insiderwissen – im Jargon: aus Gründen asymmetrischer Information in Verbindung mit hohen Kosten der Information – nicht in der Lage ist, die Angemessenheit der Lohnhöhe zu beurteilen. Allenfalls „trilateral governance“ (Williamson 1985/90, 84 f.) kann helfen, d. h. die Einschaltung eines sachkundigen Schlichters. Ultima ratio, nach Ausschöpfung aller Verständigungsmittel, sind Streik und Aussperrung. Sie passen in die Welt mit Transaktionskosten als ein Instrument, die „wahre“ Höhe des Gleichgewichtslohnes (und damit zugleich das „wahre“ Machtverhältnis der Verhandlungspartner) festzustellen.

Man beachte jedoch: „Arbeitskämpfe“, die Androhung oder Ausübung von Gewalt, ist eine dem neoklassischen Modell fremde Schattierung der Übertragung von Verfügungsrechten. Die Neoklassik lebt von der Idee der Konvention, des Übereinkommens aus freien Stücken. Gewalt, wenn sie überhaupt eine Rolle spielt, wird allein vom Staat verwaltet.

Im neoklassischen Modell gibt es keinen Streik, keine Aussperrung, keinen Boykott, keinen sozialen Druck, keine Erpressung oder andere Zwangsformen privater Gruppen. Die Macht, Zwang auszuüben, liegt beim Staat, der sie frei vom Lobbyismus und von Rentensuchern allein für das öffentliche Wohl anwendet, insbesondere den Schutz der Rechte einzelner (Gesetzgebung, Rechtswesen, Polizei, Militär).

Im Ansatz der NIÖ hat dagegen private Gewalt (private ordering) durchaus Platz. Sie dient dazu, Rechtspositionen einzelner zu sichern, für die der Rechtszwang zu kostspielig oder mangels Beweisbarkeit vor Gericht unmöglich ist. Private Durchsetzungsinstrumente spielen deshalb eine wichtige Rolle unter den Instrumenten der „ex ante Sicherung gegen ex post Opportunismus“.

Aber es ist eine Sache, ob die Androhung oder Anwendung privater Gewalt die Parteien allein betrifft oder Außenstehende in Mitleidenschaft zieht – wie im Falle des Arbeitskampfes. Streik und Aussperrung bekommen ja nicht nur die streitenden Tarifparteien zu spüren, sondern auch der Rest der Gesellschaft – und dies nicht nur im Sinne des oben geschilderten Tarifvertragskartells. Die nicht direkt betroffenen Mitglieder der Gesellschaft sind ebenfalls durch spezifische Investitionen in das relationale Vertragsnetz „Marktwirtschaft“ eingeschlossen. Ein Weggang („exit“) wäre für sie außerordentlich teuer. Von der Alternative „voice“ können Sie nach deutscher Rechtslage praktisch nicht Gebrauch machen. Zwar besteht die vage Forderung der „Sozialadäquanz von Arbeitskämpfen“, aber wie ist sie zur Abwehr von – beispielsweise – der Beschäftigungswirkung eines Tarifvertragskartells anzuwenden? Davon abgesehen: Es bleibt dem „Rest der Gesellschaft“ nur das Mittel der „voice“, sie können sich über Auswüchse der Tarifautonomie nur über Regierung, Gesetzgebung, Verwaltung zur Wehr setzen, etwa durch Einschaltung einer Regulierungsbehörde. Wir haben, institutionenökonomisch gesprochen, eine dem „Argument gegen das Argument gegen Regulierung" (Goldberg 1976) ähnliche Situation – die Abwehr des Rests der Gesellschaft gegen ex post Opportunismus der Tarifpartner nach Übertragung der Tarifautonomie. Das ist ein klassisches neoinstitutionalistisches Problem.

Die Regulierungsbehörde müßte u. a. stark genug sein um zu verhindern, daß die Notbremse des Nachfrage-Management zu nichts anderem als zu höheren Einkommen der Arbeitsplatzbesitzer und steigender Arbeitslosigkeit führt – wie oben geschildert.

Eine sehr unerfreuliche Antwort auf die Frage: „Wem nützt die Arbeitslosigkeit?" ist: Sie nützt den politischen Kräften, die die Marktwirtschaft abschaffen wollen – generell oder in der heutigen „kapitalistischen" Form. Trifft das zu, dann haben wir es nicht nur mit einem politökonomischen Teufelskreis, sondern einem politökonomischen Teufelsplan zu tun. Die Arbeitslosen dienen dann – institutionenökonomisch gesprochen – den Gegnern der Marktwirtschaft als Geisel, mit der sie Andersdenkende erpressen können. Sie können etwa argumentieren, daß sie nur dann bereit sind, auf den Griff in die sich öffnenden tiefen Taschen des Deficit Spending zu verzichten, wenn die Marktwirtschaft, wie wir sie kennen, in Richtung ihrer politischen Vorstellungen geändert wird. Das mag harmlos und „verständlich" klingen, ist aber nicht von der Art, wie wir uns eine Demokratie vorstellen, in der private Gewaltanwendung systemfremd ist. Wird sie dennoch in einem Teilbereich unseres politischen Lebens zugelassen, genügt nicht die gesetzliche Beschränkung sondern ist – wie die Erfahrung lehrt – eine Regulierung der Ergebnisse unabdingbar. Die Erpreßbarkeit der Wähler – das ex post opportunistische Verhalten, der Einsatz privater Gewalt eines Teils der Partner unseres *contrat social* – muß durch geeignete Institutionen nach Möglichkeit ausgeschlossen werden.

## X. Zusammenfassung

Fassen wir zusammen. Wir haben fünf Typen von Arbeitslosigkeit kennengelernt:

- klassische Arbeitslosigkeit – Ursache: zu hohe Reallöhne,
- Keynessche Arbeitslosigkeit – Ursache: zu geringe Güternachfrage,
- Arbeitslosigkeit wegen fehlender Arbeitsplätze – Ursache: zu geringer Kapitalstock,
- Arbeitslosigkeit als Resultat politökonomischer Teufelskreise,
- Arbeitslosigkeit als Resultat von Tarifvertragskartellen.

Die Liste ist nicht vollständig. Arbeitslosigkeit hat unterschiedliche Ursachen und verlangt unterschiedliche Kuren. Es gibt nicht nur ein Mittel der Wahl. Soviel zur Ätiologie. Die Schwierigkeiten beginnen mit der Diagnose. Wie die Erfahrung lehrt, sind die Meinungen der Fachwelt in dieser Beziehung geteilt, selbst in scheinbar so klaren Fällen wie dem Westdeutschlands nach dem II. Weltkrieg. Und dann erst die Kur: Sie darf nicht aus „billigem Gerede“ *(cheap talk)* bestehen, sondern verlangt den umsichtigen Einsatz anreizkompatibler Regeln.[14] Die moderne Institutionenökonomik bietet hierzu Orientierungen.

- Das Mittel der Wahl zum Abbau *klassischer Arbeitslosigkeit* ist Reallohnsenkung, die, wie Keynes richtig betonte, am einfachsten über einen inflatorischen Schock zu haben ist. Aber das setzt Stillhalten der Gewerkschaften voraus. Werden die (deutschen) Gewerkschaften das tun? Die Anreizlage spricht nicht dafür. Sie haben den Anreiz, ihre Mitgliederzahl möglichst auszudehnen und ihr Beitragsaufkommen, das vom Bruttoeinkommen der Mitglieder abhängt, zu erhöhen. Zehn oder zwanzig Prozent Arbeitslose, zumal am unteren Ende der Einkommensskala, lassen sich durch mitgliederwerbendes Heraufdrücken der Bruttolöhne verschmerzen. Die Gewerkschaften hätten einen Anreiz, die Arbeitslosigkeit klein zu halten, wenn sie z. B. verpflichtet würden, das Geschäft der Arbeitslosenversicherung ganz oder zum Teil zu übernehmen. Was die Unternehmen angeht, so sind sie zufrieden, wenn sie ihre bei „Grenzproduktivität der Arbeit gleich Reallohn“ anfallende Produktion verkaufen können. Ein Anreiz, die Arbeitslosigkeit möglichst gering zu halten, besteht auch für sie nicht. Für die Lohnführer unter ihnen besteht eher der Anreiz, sich durch hohe Löhne Konkurrenten vom Leibe zu halten. Der Staat als dritte Partei darf das Grundrecht der Koalitionsfreiheit nicht antasten und deshalb nicht in die Lohnfindung eingreifen. Er kann allenfalls versuchen, die Lohnnebenkosten zu senken. Das bedeutet, Senkung der von den Unternehmern getragenen Versicherungsbeiträge etc. pro Arbeiter, und zwar zu Lasten der Steuerzahler – nicht (direkt) der Beschäftigten, deren Einkommen einschließlich *fringe benefits* nicht sinken soll. Im Effekt handelt es sich bei diesem Vorgehen um eine Senkung der Lohnkosten für die Unternehmer in Verbindung mit gleich hoher Lohnsubventionierung zugunsten der Arbeitnehmer. Die Anreizlage für Gewerkschaften und Unternehmen ist die gleiche wie zuvor. Die Gewerkschaften haben den Anreiz, die Entlastung der Arbeitgeber durch entsprechend höhere Lohnforderungen abzuschöpfen, die Lohnführer unter den Unternehmern haben den Anreiz, sich durch Lohnzugeständnisse die Konkurrenz vom Leibe zu halten. Die Senkung der Lohnnebenkosten bleibt beschäftigungspolitisch erfolglos. Der Steuerzahler zahlt doppelt.
- Das Mittel der Wahl zum Abbau *Keynesscher Arbeitslosigkeit* ist *deficit spending,* eine Expansion der Güternachfrage ohne Steuererhöhung oder Steuersenkung. Der Preis besteht in dem Fall in der Hinnahme einer Erhöhung der Staats-

[14] Zur Bedeutung der Begriffe *cheap talk* und *incentive compatibility* vgl. etwa Binmore (1992, 309).

schulden. Das ist kein großes Problem, wenn die Extra-Schulden konjunkturell magerer Jahre in den folgenden fetten Jahren wieder abgebaut werden. Aber die Erfahrung lehrt anderes und Ökonomen wie Buchanan und Wagner (1977, 1978) zeigen, warum die Politiker – die keine Götter, sondern ganz normale eigennützige Menschen sind – Schwierigkeiten haben, sich wie ein wohlwollender Diktator (oder Patriarch) zu verhalten. Die Anreizlage für die Tarifparteien ist ähnlich wie im vorhergehenden Fall. Für die Gewerkschaften besteht der Anreiz, in die sich öffnenden tiefen Taschen des Finanzministers zu greifen, für die Unternehmungen besteht der Anreiz mitzumachen. Dem Staat (dem Steuerzahler) werden die Extralasten aufgebürdet. Er darf in die Lohnfindung und Tarifgestaltung nicht eingreifen. Rational handelnde Tarifparteien werden den Steuerzahler über ihre Tarifvereinbarungen bis an die Grenze seiner Mitmachbedingung „melken" – d. h. bis zu dem Punkt, bei dem der Medianwähler gerade noch mit der derzeitigen Regelung der Tarifhoheit einverstanden ist. Die Regierenden (die Agenten der Steuerzahler) denken im übrigen an ihre Wiederwahl. Für sie besteht der Anreiz, je nach Wahltermin und Popularität die öffentlichen Ausgaben und Einnahmen zu gestalten. Politische Konjunkturzyklen sind die Folge (Blankart 1998, 7. Kap.).

– Die Mittel der Wahl zum Abbau von *Arbeitslosigkeit wegen fehlender Arbeitsplätze* bestehen in privatem und öffentlichem Konsumverzicht und in der Förderung der heimischen Investitionstätigkeit. Von Interesse ist außer der Anreizlage auf dem Arbeitsmarkt insbesondere die auf dem Kapitalmarkt. Kapitalanleger sind vorsichtige Leute. Mit importiertem Kapital (Fremdkapital) allein läßt sich eine Marktwirtschaft so wenig finanzieren wie eine Unternehmung. Das ist plausibel, wird aber gerne übersehen. Anreize zu heimischem (oder lokalem) Konsumverzicht und zur Anlage im Inland (oder in der Region) sind von Nöten. Der westdeutsche Wiederaufbau der frühen 50er Jahre illustriert den Punkt (vgl. Stolper und Roskamp 1979). Wegen der Komplementarität von Kapital und Arbeit sind die Reallöhne von Bedeutung. Desgleichen sind die sehr erheblichen Einrichtungs-, Anlern- und Anlaufkosten (set-up cost) sowie die Investitionen in Sozialkapital zu beachten.[15]

  – Arbeitslosigkeit als Resultat *politökonomischer Teufelskreise.* – Sie sind die Folge pervertierter Anreizstrukturen (Selbstdurchsetzungsmechanismen) und deshalb nur durch deren Restrukturierung zu durchbrechen. Der Politökonom denkt im Stile des methodologischen Indidvidualismus (Richter und Furubotn 1996, 3). Er sieht auf die materiellen und immateriellen Anreize (Präferenzen) der Beamten, öffentlich Bediensteten, Parteimitglieder, Gewerkschaftsfunktionäre, Verbandsmitglieder usw., den Agenten der Empfänger und Zahler öffentlicher Leistungen. Die These lautet: Wo straflos betrogen werden

[15] Schlicht (1984); Coleman (1990, 300). Sozialkapital ist für soziales Handeln (darunter für die Arbeitsplatzsuche) von Bedeutung. Es besteht aus Verpflichtungen, Erwartungen, wechselseitigen Normen und Sanktionen, die sich aus vorausgehenden sozialen Interaktionen entwickelt haben (Starr und MacMillan, 1990, 80).

kann, wird betrogen. Opportunismus ist allgegenwärtig. Wegen der Asymmetrie der Informationen und der Unmöglichkeit, alles vor Gericht zu beweisen, gibt es keinen perfekten (Pareto-optimalen) Selbstdurchsetzungsmechanismus (Richter und Furubotn 1996, 5. Kap.). Eine einfache Herstellung funktionstüchtiger Selbstdurchsetzung besteht darin, die Empfänger und Zahler öffentlicher Leistungen direkt abstimmen zu lassen – nach Schweizer Vorbild. Das ist nicht immer möglich und führt auch nicht immer zu guten Resultaten (Blankart 1998, 7. Kap.). Die ökonomische Theorie der Politik (Social Choice Theory) beschäftigt sich mit diesem Komplex (Bernholz und Breyer, 1994).

- Arbeitslosigkeit als Resultat von *Tarifvertragskartellen:* Hier helfen wieder nur anreizkompatible institutionelle Arrangements wie die Anwendungen des GWB – von der Monopolkommission gefordert und in den USA längst praktiziert –, Einführung einer Regulierungsbehörde, die die monopolistischen Praktiken auf dem Arbeitsmarkt unterbindet und die Tarifgestaltung überwacht, Verbot von Flächentarifen und Übergang zu Firmentarifen u.ä.

So viel zur Skizzierung denkbarer Kuren der fünf Typen von Arbeitslosigkeit. Man beachte dabei zweierlei:

(1) Die Anwendung privater Gewalt (Streik, Aussperrung) wirkt sich nicht allein auf die streitenden Parteien aus, wie es der Grundsatz des „antagonistischen Koalitionsgegensatzes" unterstellt. Nennenswerte externe Effekte sind unvermeidbar und werden von den Tarifparteien zu ihren Gunsten genutzt. Die neoklassische Theorie des effizienten bilateralen Monopols, die dem Prinzip der Tarifautonomie zugrundeliegt, unterstellt eine Null-Transaktionskosten-Welt, fernab jeder Realität. In dieser Welt sind ironischerweise Koalitionen irrelevant. Sie führen zum gleichen wirtschaftlichen Ergebnis wie Konkurrenz aller gegen alle.

(2) Unsere Betonung der Anreizkompatibilität beschäftigungspolitischer Maßnahmen, also der Mikroökonomik, schließt makroökonomische Eingriffe nicht aus, wie etwa im Falle der Weltwirtschaftskrise. Was das deutsche Beispiel dazu angeht, behalte man jedoch im Auge, daß im Jahr 1936, als Keynes sein Vorwort zur deutschen Ausgabe der Allgemeinen Theorie niederschrieb, das deutsche Nachfrage-Management bereits einen kritischen Punkt erreicht hatte. Ein allgemeiner Preisstop wurde 1936 für notwendig angesehen und eingeführt. Anreizkompatibilität wird im übrigen in einer Diktatur auf sehr einfache Weise hergestellt: durch Androhung drakonischer Strafen bis hin zur Todesstrafe (für Devisenvergehen). An frei verhandelnde Gewerkschaften und Arbeitgeberverbände war damals in Deutschland nicht zu denken. Keynes hatte insofern recht, daß seine Theorie „viel leichter den Verhältnissen eines totalen Staates angepaßt werden" kann als denjenigen einer freien Wirtschaft (Keynes 1936*, IX). Ob „leichter" oder „schwerer", Makrokuren ohne Rücksicht auf die Anreizkompatibiltät beschäftigungspolitischer Maßnahmen funktionieren nicht – gleich ob Diktatur oder freie Wirt-

schaft. Sie funktionieren nur in unseren Standard-Makrotexten – einschließlich Richter, Schlieper, Friedmann (1973 / 1981).

Unsere Ergebnisse sind trotz allem nicht entmutigend. Im Gegenteil, anhaltend große Arbeitslosigkeit ist von vornherein vermeidbar bei entsprechend anreizkompatibler Gestaltung der Marktordnung. In dem Sinne können wir Keynes zustimmen, der in seinem Aufsatz über „Wirtschaftliche Möglichkeiten unserer Enkelkinder" (1930) schreibt: Die Menschheit sei dabei ihre wirtschaftlichen Aufgaben zu lösen und sehe „für nicht so ferne Tage den größten Veränderungen entgegen, ... in denen die Fragen der wirtschaftlichen Notwendigkeit praktisch aufgehoben sind." (Keynes 1956, 272) Sein Optimismus verlangt allerdings, daß wir in unseren Köpfen aufräumen und damit beginnen, unseren quasi-physikalischen Denkstil aufzugeben und zu einer eher institutionenökonomischen Orientierung überzugehen. Tatsächlich spielt institutionenökonomisches und politökonomisches Denken zunehmend eine Rolle sowohl in der Standard-Mikroökonomik als auch in der Neuen Keynesschen und der Neuen Klassischen Makroökonomik. Wir haben keine andere Wahl als diesen Weg fortzusetzen, denn wie die Erfahrung lehrt, wird kaum etwas Gutes (oder Schlechtes) in Politik umgesetzt, was nicht zuvor – Jahre zuvor – irgendwelche Volkswirte oder Philosophen geschrieben oder gesagt haben. In den Worten von Keynes (1936*, 323): Es sind „... die Gedanken der Ökonomen und Staatsphilosophen, sowohl wenn sie im Recht, als wenn sie im Unrecht sind, einflußreicher, als gemeinhin angenommen wird. Die Welt wird in der Tat von nicht viel anderem beherrscht." – Die Fortsetzung des berühmten Zitats bleibt hier besser unausgesprochen.

## Summary


### Why Unemployment?
### Answers by Economists since Keynes (1936)

Five types of unemployment are surveyed: classical unemployment resulting from too high real wages, various kinds of Keynesian unemployment – largely resulting from a too low demand for goods, unemployment for lack of jobs because of a too small or outdated capital stock, unemployment caused by political economic vicious circles and by wage cartels. The first two types of unemployment result largely from business fluctuations, the third has to do with economic growth, the last two with „structural" problems. In all five cases microeconomic issues play a vital role. Central pieces are *methodological individualism* (not collective entities but utility maximizing individuals are the main focus of research) and *rational formation of expectations.* Because of *transaction costs* opportunism is prevalent. Under these conditions empty promises (*cheap talk*) lead nowhere. *Incentive compatibility* of institutional arrangements matters. Examples are self enforcing agreements, credible commitments, credible threats, material incentive schemes.

There exist different cures for unemployment depending on its cause. Thus, unemployment has to be first well diagnosed to be then effectively attacked. Whatever its cure – a decrease in real wages; a stimulation of demand; an investment in machinery, human or social capital; a reformation of labor law, the application of antitrust legislation to the results of collective bargaining etc. – to be effective, it has to be incentive compatible for the participating individuals. Neither Keynes nor mainstream macro textbooks deal with this issue. Instead, economists are fascinated by the reasoning style of physicists. Nevertheless, a more institutional or political economic way of thinking begins to penetrate standard microeconomics as well as New Keynesian and New Classical Macroeconomics. Still, a long road remains to go, and we have no choice but to march on in this direction – knowing full well that not much good (or bad) is transfered into practical economic policy which has not been written before or touched upon somewhere sometimes by economists. As Keynes (1936, 383) put it: „. . .the ideas of economists and political philosophers, both when they are right and when they are wrong, are more powerful than is commonly understood.“ The rest of the famous quote is better left aside here.

So much for the general idea of this paper. One of its special considerations goes as follows: The German constitutional right of free coalition is based on the neoclassical theory of bilateral monopoly understood as a segment of a large economy with zero transaction costs. Information and coalition formation are, *inter alia,* costless. Force and compulsion are safely locked away by the state and only applied by its police and courts to protect property rights and to enforce liabilities from freely concluded contracts. People are free to form and leave coalitions at will. As we know from the theory of the core, the resulting equilibrium is the same as under perfect competition. Thus, the formation of unions and employers' associations is here allocational neutral in the sense that it does not matter whether they are formed or not. This is not true, of course, for a real world economy with transaction costs, and in which the state transferred the right to apply certain kinds of force (strikes, lockouts) to particular coalitions of private individuals. Under these circumstances, though, the hypothesis of the „equilibrium of powers“, assumed by the legislators of the German constitutional right of free coalition, does not apply anymore. External costs of strikes and lockouts (and their potential for blackmailing) aside, there exists an incentive for the wage bargainers to collude at the expense of the rest of the economy. They may tacitly agree to increase real wages, and thus leave or increase unemployment, at the cost of institutions like unemployment insurance or unemployment assistance. In any case, neither union leaders nor firm managers have an incentive to reestablish full employment. Union leaders wish to increase (or maximize) their unions' income from membership fees. Unemployment ratios in the range of 10 to 20 percent do not matter much in this context; there still remains 80 to 90 percent of the work force as potential union members. Managers are content with the rule of „marginal cost equals real wage“ as long as they hope to be able to sell what they had produced. Because of high bargaining and strike costs, and managerial inconveniences, they will shy away from profit increases achieved by wage cuts. Some of them, the wage leaders, may even prefer higher wages to steer clear of potential competitors. The German rule of nationwide pay scales combined with the practice of wage increases through pilot collective bargaining with highly productive firms (e.g. in south-west Germany) fits well with the plans of tacit wage cartels. In addition, firms expecting wage increases may gear up their labor productivity in advance by reorganizing their production and by investing in labor saving machinery before the fact. Thus, because of the rational formation of expectations, expected inflationary shocks, demand pulls, wage pushes etc. will be neutralized by the activities of unions and firms. Monetary or fiscal employment policy becomes ineffective. Of course, both sides will stress later that they were good citizens who faithfully observed their „wage increase equals labor productivity increase“ restriction and will heavily criticize the government for having done nothing (or not enough) to overcome unemployment. They know, of course, that the German government cannot encroach on their constitutional right of free collective bargaining. A bizarre situation – and seemingly nowhere there is the political will to change it.

## Literatur

*Ackley,* G. (1961): Macroeconomic Theory, New York. – *Akerlof,* G. A. (1982): „Labor Contracts as Partial Gift Exchange", Quarterly Journal of Economics, 97, 543 - 569. – *Alchian,* A. A. und *Woodward,* S. (1987): „Reflections on the Theory of the Firm", Journal of Institutional and Theoretical Economics, 143, 110 - 137. – *Arrow,* K. J. (1974): The Limits of Organization, New York. – *Ashenfelter,* O. und *Johnsen,* G. E. (1996): „Bargaining Theory, Trade Unions, and Industrial Strike Activity", The American Economic Review, . . . , 35 - 49. – *Barro,* R. J. (1976): „Rational Expectations and the Role of Monetary Policy", Journal of Monetary Economics, 2, 1 - 32. – *Bernholz,* P. und *Breyer,* F. (1994): Grundlagen der Politischen Ökonomie. Band 2: Ökonomische Theorie der Politik, Tübingen. – *Binmore,* K. (1992): Fun and Games. A Text on Game Theory, Lexington, MA. – *Blanchard,* O. J. und Summers, L. H. (1986): „Hysteresis and the European Unemployment Problem", NBER Macroeconomic Annual, 1, 15 - 78. – *Blankart,* Ch. B. (1998): Öffentliche Finanzen in der Demokratie. Eine Einführung in die Finanzwissenschaft, 3., völlig überarbeitete Auflage, München. – *Blinder,* A. S. (1991): „Why are Prices Sticky? Preliminary Results from an Interview Study", American Economic Review, Papers and Proceedings, 81, 89 - 96. – *Branson,* W. H. (1979): Macroeconomic Theory and Policy, 2nd ed. New York. – *Buchanan,* J. M. / *Burton,* J. H. und *Wagner,* R. E. (1978): The Consequences of Mr. Keynes, Hobart Paper 78, The Institute of Economic Affairs. – *Coleman,* J. S. (1990): Foundations of Social Theory, Cambridge, MA. – *Commons,* J. R. (1934): Institutional Economics, Madison, WI. – *Cooper,* R. und *John,* A. (1988): „Coordinating Failures in Keynesian Models", Quarterly Journal of Economics, 103, 441 - 463. – *D'Aspremont,* C. / *Dos Santos Ferreira,* Rodolphe und *Gérard-Varet,* L.-A., (1991): „Imperfect Competition, Rational Expectations, and Unemploymernt", in: W. A. Barnett et al. (eds.), Equilibrium Theory and Applications: Proceedings of the Sixth International Symposium in Economic Theory and Econometrics, 353 - 381, Cambridge. – *Dornbusch,* R. und *Fischer,* St., (1978): Macroeconomics, 6th ed. 1994, New York. – *Dreschers,* M. (1994): Die Entwicklung des Rechts des Tarifvertrags in Deutschland. Eine rechsthistorische Untersuchung über den Verlauf der Durchsetzung des Kollektivvertragsgedankens, Frankfurt am Main. – *Franz,* W. (1991): Arbeitsmarktökonomik, Berlin et al. – *Friedman,* M. (1968): „The Role of Monetary Policy", American Economic Review, 58, 1 - 17. – *Furubotn,* E. und *Richter,* R. (1996): Institutionen und ökonomische Theorie: Eine Einführung und kritische Würdigung der Neuen Institutionenökonomik, Tübingen. – *Goldberg,* V. (1976): „Regulation and Administered Contracts", Bell Journal of Economics, 7, 426 - 452. – *Greenwald,* B. und *Stiglitz,* J. (1993): „New and Old Keynesians", Journal of Economic Perspectives, 7, 23 - 44. – *Greif,* A. (1997a): „Cliometrics After 40 Years", American Economic Review, Papers and Proceedings, 87, 400 - 403. – *Harrod,* R. F. (1939): „An Essay in Dynamic Theory", Economic Journal, 49, 14 - 33. – *Hart,* O. (1982): „A Model of Imperfect Competition with Keynesian Features", Quarterly Journal of Economics, 97, 109 - 138. – *Haucap,* J. / *Pauly,* U. und *Wey,* C. (1997): „Employers' Associations Raise Rivals' Costs and Induce Involuntary Unemployment", Manuskript: Arbeitsstelle für Neue Institutionenökonomik, Universität des

Saarlandes. – *Herschel,* W. (1958): „Beschränkung der Befugnis zur außerordentlichen Kündigung", in: Festschrift für Arthur Nikisch, Tübingen. – *Herschel,* W. (1981): „Gedanken zur Theorie des arbeitsrechtlichen Kündigungsschutzes", in: Mayer-Mali / Richardi / Schambeck / Zöllner (Hrsg.), Arbeitsleben und Rechtspflege – Festschrift für Gerhard Müller, Berlin. – *Hicks,* J. R. (1932 / 1966): The Theory of Wages, London. – *Hicks,* J. R. (1946): Value and Capital. An Inquiery into Some Fundamental Principles of Economic Theory, 2nd ed., Oxford (1. Aufl. 1939). – *Hutchison,* T. W. (1979): „Notes on the Effects of Economic Ideas on Policy: The Example of the German Social Market Economy", Zeitschrift für die gesamte Staatswissenschaft, 135, 426 -441. – *Kennan,* J. (1986): „The Economics of Strikes", in: O. Ashenfelter und R. Layard (Hrsg.) Handbook of Labour Economics Vol. II, 1091 - 1137. – *Keynes,* J. M. (1936): VII The General Theory of Employment, Interest and Money, London: Macmillan. – *Keynes,* J. M. (1936*): Allgemeine Theorie der Beschäftigung, des Zinses und des Geldes, Ins Deutsche übersetzt von Fritz Waeger, München und Leipzig: Duncker & Humblot. – *Keynes,* J. M. (1956): „Wirtschaftliche Möglichkeiten für unsere Enkelkinder", (1930) in: E. Rosenbaum (Hrsg.) Politik und Wirtschaft. Männer und Probleme, Ausgewählte Abhandlungen von J. M. Keynes, S. 263 - 272, Tübingen. – *Lindbeck,* A. und *Snower,* D. J. (1987): „Efficiency Wages versus Insiders and Outsiders", European Economic Review, 31, 407 - 416. – *Lindbeck,* A. und *Snower,* D. J. (1988a): „Cooperation, Harassment, and Involuntary Unemployment: An Insider-Outsider Approach", American Economic Review, 78, 167 - 188. – *Lindbeck,* A. und *Snower,* D. J. (1988b): The Insider-Outsider Theory of Employment and Unemployment, Cambridge. – *Lucas,* R. E., Jr. (1972): „Expectations and the Neutrality of Money", Journal of Economic Theory, 4, 103 - 124. – *Lucas,* R. E., Jr. (1973): „Some International Evidence on Output-Inflation Tradeoffs", American Economic Review, 63, 326 - 334. – *Macneil,* J. R. (1974): „The Many Futures of Contracts", Southern California Review, 47, 691 - 816. – *Maddock,* R. und *Carter,* M. (1982): „A Child's Guide to Rational Expectations", Journal of Economic Literature, 20, 39 - 51. – *Malcomson,* J. M. (1997): „Contracts, Hold-up, and Labor Markets", Journal of Economic Literature, 35, 1916 - 1957. – *Mankiw,* N. G. (1990): „A Quick Refresher Course in Macroeconomics", Journal of Economic Literature, 28, 1646 - 1660. – *Mankiw,* N. G. (1992): Macroeconomics, New York, (2nd ed. 1994). – *Mankiw,* N. G. (1993): „Symposium on Keynesian Economics Today", Journal of Economic Perspectives, 7, 3 - 4. – *Mankiw,* N. G. und *Romer,* David (1991): New Keynesian Economics, Cambridge, Mass. – London. – *Matsuyama,* K. (1995): „Complementarities and Cumulative Processes in Models of Monopolistic Competition", Journal of Economic Literature, 33, 701 - 729. – *Maunz,* T. und *Dürig,* G. (1996): Grundgesetz Kommentar, München. – *McKenna,* J. P. (1955): Aggregate Economic Analysis, New York. – *Mills,* F. C. (1927): The Behavior of Prices, New York. – *Mishkin,* F. (1982a): „Does Anticipated Monetary Policy Matter? An Econometric Investigation", Journal of Political Economy, 90, 22 - 50. – *Mishkin,* F. (1982b): „Does Anticipated Aggregate Demand Matter?", American Economic Review, 72, 788 - 802. – *Nordhaus,* W. D. (1975): „The Political Business Cycle", Review of Economic Studies, 42, 169 - 190. – *Olson,* M. (1984): „Microeconomic Incentives and Macroeconomic Decline", Weltwirtschaftliches Archiv, 120, 631 - 645. – *Phillips,* A. W. (1958): „The Relation Between Unemployment and the Rate of Change in Money Wage Rates in the U. K. 1862 - 1957", Economica, 25, 283 - 299. – *Popper,* K. R. (1957): The Poverty of Historicism (deutsch: Das Elend des Historizismus, Tübingen 1965, 6. Aufl. 1987). – *Richter,* R. (1979): „Currency and Economic Reform. West Germany after World War II: A Symposium. Editorial Preface", Zeitschrift für die gesamte Staatswissenschaft / Journal of Institutional and Theoretical Economics, 135, 297 - 300. – *Richter,* R. (1998): „Neue Institutionenökonomik. Ideen und Möglichkeiten", Johann-Heinrich-von-Thünen-Vorlesung, Jahrestagung des Vereins für

Socialpolitik in Kassel 1996, G. Krause-Junk (Hrsg.), Steuersysteme der Zukunft, Berlin. – *Richter,* R. / *Schlieper* U. und *Friedmann,* W. (1973 / 1981): Makroökonomik. Eine Einführung, 1. Auflage, Berlin; 4. korrigierte und ergänzte Auflage, Berlin, 1981. – *Richter,* R. und *Diener,* F. (1987): „Phillips Curves in West-Germany 1975 - 1985: On the Role of the German Bundesbank as an Expectation Determining Institution", Weltwirtschaftliches Archiv, 123, 346 - 353. – *Romer,* D. (1996): Advanced Macroeconomics, New York. – *Rüthers,* B. (1996) Beschäftigungskrise und Arbeitsrecht. Zur Arbeitsmarktpolitik der Arbeitsgerichtsbarkeit, Bad Homburg: Frankfurter Institut – Stiftung Marktwirtschaft und Politk. – *Saint-Paul,* G. (1995): „Some Political Aspects of Unemployment", European Economic Review, 39, 575 - 582. – *Samuelson,* P. A. und *Solow,* R. M. (1960): „The Problem of Achieving and Maintaining a Stable Price Level – Analytical Aspects of Anti-Inflation Policy", American Economic Review, Papers and Proceedings, 50, 177 - 194. – *Sargent,* T. J. und *Wallace,* N. (1975): „Rational Expectations, the Optimal Monetary Instrument, and the Optimal Money Supply Rule", Journal of Political Economy, 83, 241 - 254. – *Schlicht,* E. (1978): „Labor Turnover, Wage Structure, and Natural Unemployment", Journal of Institutional and Theoretical Economics, 134, 337 - 346. – *Schlicht,* E. (1984): „Cognitive Dissonance in Economics", Normengeleitetes Verhalten in den Sozialwissenschaften, Berlin, 61 - 82. – *Schmoller,* G. v. (1900): Grundriß der Allgemeinen Volkswirtschaftslehre, München. – *Silvestre,* J. (1993): „The Market-Power Foundations of Macroeconomic Policy", Journal of Economic Literature, 31, 105 - 141. – *Solow,* R. M. (1956): „A Contribution to the Theory of Growth", Quarterly Journal of Economics, 70, 65 - 94. – *Solow,* R. M. (1979): „Another Possible Source of Wage Stickiness", Journal of Macroeconomics, 1, 79 - 82. – *Starr,* J. A. und *Macmillan,* I. C. (1990): „Resource Cooptation via Social Contracting: Resource Acquisition Strategies for New Ventures", Strategic Management Journal, 11, 79 - 92. – *Stolper,* W. F. und *Roskamp,* K. W. (1979): „Planning a Free Economy: Germany 1945 - 1960", Zeitschrift für die gesamte Staatswissenschaft, 135, 374 - 404. – *Williamson,* O. E. (1968): „Wage Rates as a Barrier to Entry: The Pennington Case in Perspective", Quarterly Journal of Economics, 82, 85 - 116. – *Williamson,* O. E. (1985 / 90): The Economic Institutions of Capitalism, New York (deutsch: Die ökonomischen Institutionen des Kapitalismus, Tübingen 1990). – *Williamson,* O. E. / *Wachter,* M. L. und *Harris,* J. E. (1975): „Understanding the Employment Relation: The Analysis of Idiosyncratic Exchange", Bell Journal of Economics, 6, 250 - 280.

# Klassische und keynesianische Arbeitslosigkeit – eine Kritik hybrider Typologien

Von Jan Priewe, Berlin

## I. Die hybriden Typologien

Heute dominiert die Auffassung, daß die hohe und seit Mitte der 70er Jahre ansteigende westeuropäische Arbeitslosigkeit vorrangig „struktureller“ Natur sei. Die konjunkturelle Komponente sei eher gering und ohnehin nur vorübergehend relevant; ein beträchtlicher Teil sei „mismatch“- Arbeitslosigkeit – der Sachverständigenrat zur Begutachtung der gesamtwirtschaftlichen Entwicklung (SVR) hatte ihn für Westdeutschland vor einigen Jahren auf etwa ein Viertel geschätzt –, und der Rest, d. h. der überwiegende Teil, sei im Grunde klassische Arbeitslosigkeit im weiteren Sinne. Und gerade dieser Teil macht den großen Anstieg der Arbeitslosigkeit in den vergangenen beiden Jahrzehnten aus. Neben zu hohen Reallöhnen ist diese „strukturelle“ bzw. klassische Arbeitslosigkeit aus diesem Blickwinkel durch wachstums- und beschäftigungsmindernde Regulierungen bedingt, wodurch indirekt die Arbeitskosten steigen bzw. rentable Produktionsmöglichkeiten behindert werden. Auch eine steigende inflationsstabile Arbeitslosigkeit (NAIRU – „non-accelerating-inflation-rate of unemployment“) wird zur Begründung dieses expandierenden Teils der Arbeitslosigkeit angeführt. Demnach wäre trotz Unterbeschäftigung der lohnmindernde Wettbewerbsdruck auf den Arbeitsmärkten fortwährend gesunken, so daß eine immer größere Arbeitslosigkeit erforderlich sei, um Inflationsbeschleunigung bei steigender Beschäftigung zu vermeiden.

So unterschiedlich die Begründungen für die Dominanz der „strukturellen“ Arbeitslosigkeit auch sein mögen, es handelt sich aus dieser Perspektive nicht um keynesianische, also unfreiwillige Arbeitslosigkeit, die mit makroökonomischer Politik abgebaut werden könnte.

Für Keynes machte freiwillige, allein durch zu hohe Löhne bedingte Arbeitslosigkeit, wie sie jene Theorien, die er klassisch nannte, als alleinige Form der Arbeitslosigkeit (neben friktioneller) behaupteten, nicht den Kern von Massenarbeitslosigkeit aus. Heute findet man in der zeitgenössischen Wirtschaftstheorie eine Vielzahl von Varianten, die die Möglichkeit klassischer wie keynesianischer Arbeitslosigkeit und auch ihre empirische Gleichzeitigkeit konzedieren. Dies gilt vor allem seit dem Beginn der „neoklassischen Synthesen“ mit Hicks’ IS-LM-Interpretation und anderen Hybriden, in jüngerer Zeit vor allem seit der Entfaltung neukeynesianischer Ungleichgewichtstheorien. Auch wenn die theoretische Möglichkeit keynesianischer Arbeitslosigkeit von der neoklassischen Seite akzeptiert wird, so dominiert doch die erwähnte Sichtweise, daß es sich allenfalls um kurzfristige, temporäre Arbeitslosigkeit handele, die nicht unbedingt wirtschaftspolitischer Intervention bedürfe; persistente Arbeitslosigkeit dagegen sei im Kern klassische Arbeitslosigkeit im weiteren Sinne.

Bei klassischer Arbeitslosigkeit gelten drei Charakteristika: (a) Die Reallöhne sind zu hoch, da sie über der Grenzproduktivität der Arbeit liegen; (b) durch autonome Nominallohnsenkung bzw. mehr Nominallohnflexibilität nach unten kann klassische Arbeitslosigkeit abgebaut werden (insofern handelt es sich um freiwillige Arbeitslosigkeit, auch wenn es kollektiver Lohnzurückhaltung der Beschäftigten und Arbeitslosen bzw. der Gewerkschaften bedarf); (c) es existiert entweder kein Mangel an Güternachfrage oder aber mit Reallohnsenkung entsteht automatisch – unmittelbar oder zeitverzögert – zusätzliche Güternachfrage. Klassische Arbeitslosigkeit ist damit weitaus enger gefaßt als in vielen theoretischen und empirischen Untersuchungen üblich. Das erste Kriterium beschreibt einen Zustand mangelnder Kapitalrentabilität infolge einer zu hohen Lohnquote. Dabei wird meist eine negativ geneigte Arbeitsnachfragefunktion unterstellt. Das zweite Kriterium stellt die klassische Auffassung dar, wie niedrigere Reallöhne erreicht werden können: diese führen aus dieser Sicht unmittelbar zu niedrigeren Reallöhnen, weil das Preisniveau quantitätstheoretisch durch die gegebene Geldmenge fixiert ist. Mithin sind die Reallöhne ein direkt beeinflußbarer Handlungsparameter der Arbeitsanbieter. Das dritte Kriterium gibt an, daß niedrigere Nominallöhne notwendige und zugleich hinreichende Voraussetzung für mehr Beschäftigung sind, da entweder die Güternachfrage automatisch steigt oder aber der vorhandene Kapitalstock einfach mit mehr Arbeit kombiniert wird, ohne daß es größerer Güternachfrage bedarf. Wie noch zu zeigen ist, ging auch Keynes bei seinem Begriff unfreiwilliger Arbeitslosigkeit von zu hohen Reallöhnen aus (jedenfalls in der „General Theory"), die bei ausreichender effektiver Nachfrage automatisch sinken würden. Aus Keynes' Sicht waren niedrigere Reallöhne eine *Folge* hinreichender effektiver Nachfrage. Die Kriterien (b) und (c) bestritt er bekanntlich vehement.

Klassische Arbeitslosigkeit im Sinne der drei Kriterien entsteht allein auf dem Arbeitsmarkt und wird dort auch wieder beseitigt, unabhängig von der Interaktion mit dem Güter- und Kapitalmarkt. Sie ist ausschließlich ein reales Phänomen, dem durch monetäre Veränderungen nicht beizukommen ist. Und sie ist ein mikroökonomisches Problem, das durch marktkonformes einzelwirtschaftliches Handeln wieder verschwindet. Bei Dominanz klassischer Arbeitslosigkeit ist folglich makroökonomische Politik fehl am Platze, sie würde die Probleme eher verschlimmern. Dies ist das Credo des *mainstream* unter den Ökonomen wie auch die Meinung der großen Mehrheit der Wirtschaftspolitiker. Neben Maßnahmen zur Deregulierung ist demnach entscheidend, daß die Arbeitskosten über längere Phasen langsamer als die durchschnittliche Arbeitsproduktivität ansteigen und somit die Lohnstückkosten fortwährend sinken[1].

Auf den ersten Blick sind die Unterscheidungsmerkmale für die beiden Typen von Arbeitslosigkeit in den verschiedenen Varianten dieser Grundposition recht ähnlich, während sich auf den zweiten Blick eine ganze Reihe von Unterschieden offenbaren:

(1) Weit verbreitet ist die These, *konjunkturelle* Arbeitslosigkeit, die auf unausgelasteten Produktionskapazitäten beruhe, sei keynesianisch, während die darüber hinausgehende Arbeitslosigkeit *strukturell* sei, wobei häufig auf Sachkapitalmangel verwiesen wird.

(2) In der *neukeynesianischen Ungleichgewichtstheorie* entsteht keynesianische Arbeitslosigkeit durch einen Mangel an Güternachfrage bei fixen Preisen und Löhnen, wobei das Reallohnniveau vollbeschäftigungskonform ist. Klassische Arbeitslosigkeit ist durch zu hohe Reallöhne und eine Überschußnachfrage auf dem Gütermarkt gekennzeichnet (z. B. Malinvaud).

(3) Aus der Sicht der Theorie *natürlicher* Arbeitslosigkeit ist vorübergehende Arbeitslosigkeit entweder keynesianischer Natur im Sinne nachfrage- und konjunkturbedingter Ursachen oder durch vorübergehende Anpassungsträgheiten bei Löhnen und Preisen verursacht, während der persistente Bodensatz der Unterbeschäftigung eben natürliche Arbeitslosigkeit sei, die vor allem durch mehr Flexibilität am Arbeitsmarkt gesenkt werden kann. Natürliche Arbeitslosigkeit wird als Teil klassischer Arbeitslosigkeit verstanden.

(4) Gemaß Theorien einer *inflationsstabilen Arbeitslosigkeit* existiert nachfragebedingte keynesianische Arbeitslosigkeit insoweit, als sie ohne Inflationsbeschleunigung durch Wirtschaftswachstum bzw. nachfragesteigernde Wirtschaftspolitik abgebaut werden kann. Die NAIRU wäre dann strukturelle oder im weiteren Sinne klassische Arbeitslosigkeit, die über die natürliche hinausgehen kann.

(5) Zu hohe Reallöhne als Ausdruck einer *Lohnlücke,* wodurch auch immer bedingt, führten zu „profit squeeze" und einem Regime klassischer Arbeitslosigkeit, die nur mit Reallohnveränderungen, die hinter dem Produktivitätszuwachs zurückbleiben, abgebaut werden könne. Die bei vollbeschäftigungskonformen Reallöhnen verbleibende vorübergehende Rest-Arbeitslosigkeit wäre demnach keynesianisch.

Im folgenden werden die fünf Varianten der Unterscheidung keynesianischer von klassischer Arbeitslosigkeit kritisch untersucht. Im Ergebnis zeigt sich, daß sie nicht schlüssig sind, was ihre hybride theoretische Fundierung ausdrückt, und daß sie ganz überwiegend in krassem Gegensatz zu Keynes' eigenen Vorstellungen stehen. Danach ist „keynesianische Arbeitslosigkeit" nicht eine unter anderen Varian-

---

1 Anstelle vieler anderer vgl. Krelle, Wilhelm: Notwendige Änderungen des Arbeitsmarktes: Die Lohnhöhe hat einen Einfluß auf die Beschäftigung. In: Sadowski, D., Schneider, M. (Hrsg.), Vorschläge zu einer neuen Lohnpolitik. Optionen für mehr Beschäftigung I. Frankfurt/M.-New York 1997, S. 17 ff. Krelle schlägt vor, die Tarifverträge solange automatisch zu verlängern, bis die Arbeitslosigkeit unter 4% gesunken ist.

ten – es ist die entscheidende! Allerdings wird abschließend vorgeschlagen, den immer wieder mißverstandenen Begriff keynesianischer bzw. unfreiwilliger Arbeitslosigkeit zu präzisieren und dabei zwei Varianten zu unterscheiden.

## II. Konjunkturelle und „capital shortage unemployment“

Unter konjunktureller Arbeitslosigkeit wird meist der während einer Rezession entstehende Zuwachs an Arbeitslosen verstanden, der bis zur vollen Auslastung der Produktionskapazitäten im nachfolgenden Aufschwung anhält. Demnach wäre der jenseits des Punktes der Vollauslastung des Produktionspotentials verbleibende Sockel an Arbeitslosen „strukturelle“ oder klassische Arbeitslosigkeit im Sinne eines für Vollbeschäftigung zu kleinen Sachkapitalstocks – *„capital shortage unemployment“*. Dabei muß eine bestimmte „normale“ oder trendmäßige Kapitalintensität unterstellt werden; bei einer streng substitutionalen Produktionsfunktion (mit ex-post-Substitutionalität) kann es ja keine Kapitalmangel-Arbeitslosigkeit geben, da jedweder Kapitalstock mit jedweder Menge an Arbeitskräften kombinierbar ist. Sieht man davon ab, dann gilt: Bis zur Potentialauslastung existieren physische Arbeitsplätze, die mangels Nachfrage zunächst noch nicht besetzt werden können (also auch noch keine „offenen Stellen“ darstellen); jenseits dieses Punktes mangelt es an physischen Arbeitsplätzen. Beispielsweise schätzt das Ifo-Institut die „nachfragebedingte“ Arbeitslosigkeit in Deutschland aufgrund des Auslastungsgrades des Produktionspotentials für das Jahr 1997 auf 40%[2]. Bis zur Normalauslastung existieren aus dieser Sicht Nachfrageprobleme, danach Angebotsprobleme. *Mismatch*-Arbeitslosigkeit bleibt zunächst ausgeklammert. Bis zur Vollauslastung der Kapazitäten wäre „Nachfragepolitik“ angeraten, zur Bekämpfung der darüber hinausgehenden Arbeitslosigkeit „Angebotspolitik“. Nachfragepolitik bei Vollauslastung wirke inflationär.

Obwohl diese Sichtweise allerorten anzutreffen ist, ist sie keineswegs plausibel:

(1) Ein zu kleiner Sachkapitalstock ist Ausdruck zu schwacher Investitionstätigkeit in den Vorperioden bzw. in der Gegenwart. Es ist also ein Nachfrage- und zugleich ein Angebotsproblem, und zwar sowohl in der Phase der Unterauslastung als auch danach. Jenseits des Punktes der Vollauslastung spielt die Investitionsgüternachfrage die entscheidende Rolle für die Schaffung von weiteren Arbeitsplätzen. Um Kapazitätseffekte zu bewirken, muß die Investitionsgüternachfrage steigen. Diese wird nur steigen, wenn die Nachfrageerwartungen hinsichtlich der zukünftigen Kapazitätsauslastung positiv sind. Entscheidend wäre die Klärung der Frage, warum die Investitionstätigkeit zu schwach ist.

---

2 Schalk, H.-J., u. a.: Wachstum- und Arbeitslosigkeit – gibt es noch einen Zusammenhang? In: Ifo-Schnelldienst 17 - 18 / 1997, S. 3 ff.

(2) Ein in einem konjunkturellen Aufschwung steigender Auslastungsgrad beruht normalerweise in besonderem Maße auf steigender Investitionsgüternachfrage, da diese eine größere konjunkturelle Amplitude aufweist als andere Nachfrageaggregate. Ein Aufschwung signalisiert also steigende Güternachfrage und zugleich – zeitverzögert entsprechend den Ausreifungsszeiten der Investitionen – steigende Produktionskapazitäten. Mit steigendem Auslastungsgrad, soweit er durch vermehrte Investitionen bedingt ist, steigt also auch zeitverzögert das Produktionspotential. Die Angebotskapazitäten nehmen nicht erst jenseits der Vollauslastung zu. Ein langanhaltender Aufschwung ist also ein mehr oder minder gleichgewichtiges Wachstum von Produktionspotential und Güternachfrage. Idealerweise wird die volle Kapazitätsauslastung nie ganz erreicht, um im Wettbewerb erwünschte Reservekapazitäten vorzuhalten. Ein gewisses Maß an chronischen, gewissermaßen „gleichgewichtigen Überkapazitäten" könnte auch wettbewerbspolitisch erwünscht sein, so daß Käufermärkte dominieren. So könnte idealtypisch die vermeintliche Kapitalmangelarbeitslosigkeit vollständig abgebaut werden, ohne daß die vollständige Kapazitätsauslastung je erreicht wird. Bleibt aber im Aufschwung bzw. in der Hochkonjunktur ein Sockel an Arbeitslosen bei annähernd voller Kapazitätsauslastung, so drückt dieser Sachverhalt nur aus, daß die Konjunktur ins Stocken geraten ist bzw. das Wachstum, vor allem das der Investitionen, zu schwach ist. Es ist ebenso sehr ein Angebots- wie ein Nachfrageproblem. Man könnte durchaus auch für diese Phase von konjunktureller Arbeitslosigkeit im Sinne einer zu schwachen Konjunktur oder aber – synonym – von *wachstumsdefizitärer* Arbeitslosigkeit[3] sprechen.

(3) Es macht wenig Sinn, Konjunktur und Wachstum zu trennen. Eine starke Konjunktur, ein kräftiger langanhaltender Aufschwung erzeugt einen wachsenden Kapitalstock und zusätzliche Beschäftigung, so daß der Wachstumstrend, das Potentialwachstum, nach oben verlagert wird – und umgekehrt. Das Problem der steigenden Arbeitslosigkeit in Deutschland seit Mitte der 70er Jahre ist ja gerade die explosiv ansteigende Unterbeschäftigung in den Rezessionen und der für Vollbeschäftigung des steigenden Erwerbspersonenpotentials viel zu schwache Anstieg der Zahl der Arbeitsplätze in den aufsteigenden Konjunkturphasen, die über lange Strecken eher *„semi-slumps"* als Hochkonjunkturen waren.

(4) Ist der Kapitalstock bei Vollauslastung für Vollbeschäftigung zu klein, ohne daß die Marktkräfte hinreichend expansiv wirken, wäre staatliche „Investitionsförderung" bedenkenswert, sofern Inflationsbeschleunigung vermieden werden kann. Wie auch immer eine derartige Politik aussehen mag, sie unterscheidet sich nicht von investitionsfördernder „Nachfragepolitik" bei unterausgelasteten Kapazitäten. Die Unterscheidung von Angebots- und Nachfragepolitik ergibt hier einfach keinen Sinn. Eine direkt konsumfördernde „Nachfragepolitik" wäre sicher nicht in einer Vollauslastungsphase angezeigt (in einer Unterauslastungssituation wird sie

---

3 Damit ist nicht gesagt, daß Strukturwandel keine Bedeutung für den Abbau von Arbeitslosigkeit hätte. Wachstum ist immer mit Strukturwandel verbunden.

aber ebenfalls, vielleicht nicht ganz so einhellig, für fragwürdig gehalten), wenngleich Investitionsförderung in aller Regel zugleich auch indirekte Konsumförderung ist (durch den Kauf von Investitionsgütern entstehen in der Regel zusätzliche Lohn- und Gewinneinkommen). Wenn bei investitionssteigernder sog. „Nachfragepolitik" bei Vollauslastung Inflationsbeschleunigung befürchtet wird, so müßte dies in gleicher Weise für investitionsfördernde „Angebotspolitik" bzw. endogene kräftige Wachstumsprozesse gelten. Um stärkere Inflation zu vermeiden, kommt es im Kern auf die Minderung der Nominallohndynamik an, nicht auf geringere Reallöhne.

Die entscheidende Frage ist, ob die für hohe Beschäftigung zu schwache Investitionstätigkeit ihre Ursache in zu hohen Reallöhnen hat, wie es die These klassischer Arbeitslosigkeit unterstellt. Im folgenden sollen sechs Argumente geprüft werden, die Reallohnsenkungen (relativ zur Produktivitätsentwicklung) ab dem Punkt der vollen Kapazitätsauslastung postulieren, um die Beschäftigung weiter zu erhöhen.

(1) *Physischer Mangel an Kapitalgütern?* Unterstellt man starre Kapazitätsgrenzen und vollständige Auslastung des Sachkapitalstocks, dann kann dieser nur ausgeweitet werden, wenn produktive Ressourcen aus anderen, nämlich konsumtiven Verwendungen abgezogen werden, also weniger konsumiert und mehr investiert wird. Nehmen wir an, es gebe keinen Mangel an geeigneten Arbeitskräften unter den Arbeitslosen, so daß sich der Ressourcenmangel allein auf Kapitalgüter bezieht. In einer Ein-Gut-Volkswirtschaft ist die Reallokation der Güter problemlos möglich. Güter, die bislang dem Konsum dienten, werden nun als Kapitalgüter verwendet, so daß der Kapitalstock steigen kann. Nimmt man der klassischen Einfachheit halber an, daß aus Löhnen nur konsumiert, aus Gewinnen nur investiert wird, dann ist natürlich eine Reallohnsenkung und spiegelbildlich eine Gewinnsteigerung unumgänglich. Schon in einer Zwei-Gut-Ökonomie (mit Konsum- und Investitionsgütern) ist die Umschichtung der Güter kaum noch möglich, und erst recht nicht bei heterogenen Kapitalgütern, die nur in einer einzigen Verwendungsart produktiv genutzt werden können. In dieser Situation würden Reallohnsenkungen zu Unterauslastung der Konsumgüterindustrien führen, aber nicht zur Erhöhung des Kapitalstocks. In der Realität entsteht die prekäre Situation des physischen Mangels an Kapitalgütern meist deshalb nicht (oder es handelt sich nur um einen kurzfristigen Übergangszustand), weil die Märkte – in dieser Hinsicht – gut funktionieren: Marktsignale führen über die Erwartungsbildung zu rechtzeitigem Kapazitätsaufbau; ferner werden begrenzt variable Kapazitätsauslastungsgrenzen eingeplant und zudem existieren in einer stark internationalisierten Produktion Importmöglichkeiten für fehlende Kapitalgüter. Schließlich spricht vieles dafür, daß in einer technologisch hochentwickelten Dienstleistungsgesellschaft die Ausreifungszeiten von Investitionen gegenüber der Hochzeit der Schwerindustrie gesunken sind. Insgesamt kann man mit einer beachtlichen und historisch vermutlich steigenden Produktionsflexibilität rechnen.

(2) *Vermeidung von Nachfrageinflation bei voller Kapazitätsauslastung?* An der Kapazitätsgrenze könnten sich Produktionsengpässe bilden, insbesondere auch selektive „bottlenecks", die bei starker Nachfrageexpansion inflationär wirken. Wenn diese Inflationsimpulse durch Lohnkostensenkungen, also niedrigere Reallöhne, aufgefangen werden können, bliebe die Inflationsrate unverändert. Allerdings wäre dies nur eine vorübergehend notwendige Reallohnsenkung, bis die Angebotsengpässe dank der Kapazitätseffekte der Investitionen wieder verschwinden. Dann entstehen erst die neuen Arbeitsplätze, und zu diesem Zeitpunkt sind die Lohnsenkungen nicht mehr erforderlich. Die unter (1) erwähnten Gründe sprechen dafür, daß das Problem vorübergehender Kapazitätsdefizite eher von abnehmender Bedeutung ist. Vorübergehende konjunkturelle Preisimpulse wären unter stabilitätspolitischen Erwägungen weniger problematisch, solange eine Preis-Lohn-Spirale vermieden werden kann. Es käme also in dieser Phase auf *Nominallohn*zurückhaltung an.

(3) *Reallohnsenkung zwecks Finanzierung höherer Investitionen?* Bei konstanter Geldmenge und unveränderter Umlaufgeschwindigkeit des Geldes erfordere vermehrtes Investieren erhöhtes Sparen, das nur durch Reallohnsenkung bzw. durch eine steigende Gewinnquote erreichbar sei, sofern man unterstellt, daß die Sparquote der Lohnempfänger konstant und geringer als die der Gewinnbezieher ist. Alternativ könnte der Ausgleich von Sparen und Investieren durch steigende Zinsen zustande kommen, die den Konsum senken und das Sparen erhöhen, wenn man (unrealistischerweise) zinselastisches Sparen unterstellt. Zudem würden steigende Zinsen die Investitionsbereitschaft dämpfen. Beiden Argumentationen ist entgegenzuhalten, daß der für höhere Investitionen notwendige Anstieg des Sparens auch durch Kreditschöpfung des Bankensystem – gewissermaßen aus dem Nichts – zustande kommen kann. Dadurch steigt die Geldmenge (oder die Umlaufgeschwindigkeit des Geldes steigt), und es entsteht bei voll ausgelasteten Produktionskapazitäten eine vorübergehende „Kreditinflation", bis die neuen Produktionskapazitäten das Güterangebot erhöhen. Mit Schumpeter ist diese Art Inflation, die bei hoher und rascher Produktionselastizität nur während einer kurzen Zeitspanne auftritt, für eine dynamische Wirtschaft unumgänglich und ganz anders als „normale" Inflation zu bewerten[4]. Diese temporären Inflationsimpulse mindern in der Tat die Reallöhne. Problematisch wäre, wie erwähnt, eine nachfolgende Preis-Lohn-Spirale. Kann diese vermieden werden, dann erhöhen steigende reale Investitionen das reale Volkseinkommen, und es entsteht auch bei unveränderter Einkommensverteilung und konstanten Sparquoten der Lohn- und Gewinnempfänger das erforderliche höhere Sparen[5]. Reallohnsenkungen erfolgen also nur vorübergehend. Wenn aus Gründen der Furcht vor Inflation im Aufschwung stärkere Lohn-

---

4 Schumpeter, J.: Theorie der wirtschaftlichen Entwicklung, 8. Auflage, Berlin 1993, S. 158 ff.

5 Vgl. auch Hagemann, H.: Lohnhöhe und Beschäftigung in Keynesscher Sicht. In: Hagemann, H., Steiger, O. (Hrsg.): Keynes' General Theory nach fünfzig Jahren, Berlin 1988, S. 203

zurückhaltung praktiziert wird, die zu Reallohneinbußen und schwächerer Konsumnachfrage führen, kann nicht ausgeschlossen werden, daß die Investitionsneigung beeinträchtigt wird.

(4) *Reallohnsenkung bei steigender Investitionsquote?* Unter Punkt 3 war von steigenden Investitionen die Rede, die die Investitionsquote unverändert lassen. Sollen die Investitionen jenseits des Punktes der Vollauslastung jedoch schneller steigen als das Volkseinkommen, muß auch die Sparquote steigen, was bei konstanten Sparquoten der Lohn- und Gewinnempfänger nur durch Verschiebung der Einkommensverteilung zugunsten einer steigenden Gewinnquote erfolgen kann. Bei konstanter Arbeitsproduktivität muß der Reallohn in der Tat sinken bzw. bei steigender Arbeitsproduktivität muß der Reallohnanstieg geringer ausfallen. Dies kann entweder durch Inflation oder durch Nominallohnzurückhaltung geschehen. Die Reallohnsenkung ist in der Regel *die Folge* der gestiegenen Investitionsquote. Sinkende Reallöhne sind eine notwendige, aber keine hinreichende Voraussetzung für eine steigende Investitionsquote. Zur Erhöhung des Sachkapitalstocks zwecks Verminderung der Arbeitslosigkeit ist eine steigende Investitionsquote zwar nicht unbedingt notwendig, aber sie könnte natürlich den Beschäftigungsanstieg beschleunigen. Normalerweise geschieht dies auch in einem kräftigen Aufschwung mit Multiplikator- und Akzeleratorprozessen. Während des Anstiegs der Investitionsquote bleibt die Lohn- hinter der Gewinnentwicklung zurück, und wenn sich die Investitionsquote auf erhöhtem Niveau stabilisiert, muß auch die Einkommensverteilung stabilisiert werden. So erfordert gerade ein kräftiger *konjunktureller* Aufschwung (und dieser ist durch eine steigende Investitionsquote gekennzeichnet) sinkende Reallöhne, ein gleichgewichtiges *Wachstum* dagegen konstante Reallöhne (bzw. produktivitätsorientierte Reallohnzuwächse).

Nun könnten sinkende Reallöhne bzw. eine sinkende Lohnquote im Aufschwung die Konsumgüternachfrage absolut schrumpfen lassen, so daß hier die Kapazitätsauslastung abnimmt und von dieser Seite die Investitionstätigkeit gebremst wird. Jedoch tritt dies nur ein, wenn (bei konstanter Konsumquote der Arbeitnehmer) die reale Lohnsumme fällt. Ist der Beschäftigungszuwachs infolge der Investitionen stärker als die Rate der Lohnsenkung oder sind die Gewinnerwartungen stärker als die investitionshemmenden negativen Kaufkrafteffekte des privaten Konsums, dann kann dieses Problem vermieden werden. Freilich wächst die Konsumgüterproduktion langsamer als die der Investitionsgüter – was nicht Unterkonsumtion, sondern starkes Wirtschaftswachstum ausdrückt.

(5) *Reallohnsenkung aufgrund einer negativ geneigten Arbeitskräftenachfragefunktion?* Gilt die übliche negativ geneigte gesamtwirtschaftliche Arbeitskräftenachfragefunktion entsprechend der Grenzproduktivitätstheorie, die Keynes als „erstes Postulat" der klassischen Beschäftigungstheorie in der „General Theory" akzeptierte[6], dann besteht natürlich nicht der geringste Zweifel an der Notwendig-

[6] Keynes, J.M.: The General Theory of Employment, Interest and Money. The Collected Writings of John Maynard Keynes, Vol. VII, London 1973, S. 4 ff.

keit sinkender Reallöhne für mehr Beschäftigung. Bei starren Nominallöhnen und konstanter Produktivität bedarf also jede Zunahme der Beschäftigung steigender Preise, was Keynes ja auch in „General Theory“ annahm, ohne daß ihn Inflationsangst plagte. Aber Keynes selbst stellte das „erste Postulat“ bekanntlich 1939, drei Jahre nach Erscheinen der „General Theory“, unter Verweis auf Unterauslastung und ansatzweise auch unvollständigen Wettbewerb wieder in Frage[7]. Die Grenzproduktivitätstheorie unterstellt partielle Faktorvariation bei gegebenem Kapitalbestand und voller Kapazitätsauslastung. Zumindest annähernd bis zur vollen Kapazitätsauslastung könnte von mehr oder minder konstanter Grenzproduktivität ausgegangen werden, denn es wird zusätzliches Sachkapital eingesetzt, das zuvor wegen Nachfragemangel nicht genutzt werden konnte[8]. Für jeden Auslastungsgrad müßte eine andere Grenzproduktivitätskurve gelten[9]. Die Arbeitsproduktivität bleibt also bei steigendem Auslastungsgrad mehr oder minder konstant. Dabei wird von Skalenerträgen und technischen Fortschritt abgesehen[10]. Nach Erreichen der Vollauslastung sinkt jedoch die Grenzproduktivität der Arbeit, so daß nun, so scheint es, tatsächlich „klassische Arbeitslosigkeit“ vorliegt. Sobald jedoch die Kapazitätserweiterung realisiert ist (unterstellt, daß technischer Fortschritt dabei nicht stattfindet), ist wiederum die bisherige konstante Grenzproduktivität bis zum neuen Punkt der vollen Kapazitätsauslastung gegeben. Wenn also fortwährend knapp unterhalb dieses Punktes bei stetiger Kapazitätserweiterung produziert wird, gilt die kurzfristige waagerechte Arbeitskräftenachfragefunktion auch längerfristig. Wird der kritische Punkt etwa in einer Hochkonjunktur überschritten, wovon Keynes zumindest in der „General Theory“ überzeugt war[11], sind natürlich Inflation und Reallohnsenkung unvermeidbar. Klammert man diesen Fall aus, dann ist die Unterscheidung von kurz- und langfristiger Perspektive in dieser Hinsicht überflüssig. Steigende Beschäftigung hängt dann allein von der steigenden Güternachfrage ab, solange der Reallohn konstant bleibt.

---

7 Keynes, J.M.: Relative Movement of Real Wages and Output. Abgedruckt in: Keynes, J.M.: The General Theory, S. 394 ff.

8 Vgl. u. a. Spahn, H.-P.: Makroökonomie. Theoretische Grundlagen und stabilitätspolitische Strategien, Stuttgart 1996, S. 89 f.

9 McCombie, J.S.L.: Why cutting real wages will not necessarily reduce unemployment – Keynes and the „postulates of the classical economics“. In: Journal of Post Keynesian Economics, Vol. 8, 1985 - 86, S. 233 ff.

10 Hier wird der Einfachheit halber homogene Arbeit unterstellt. Bei heterogener Arbeit mit Einsatz zunehmend weniger qualifizierter Arbeitskräfte bei steigender Kapazitätsauslastung muß natürlich mit abnehmender Grenzproduktivität der Arbeit gerechnet werden. Werden Skaleneffekte und unvollständiger Wettbewerb systematisch berücksichtigt, wie insbesondere J.Robinson immer wieder forderte, bleibt von dem „gesetzmäßigen“ inversen Zusammenhang von Lohn und Beschäftigung nicht viel übrig. Dies gilt erst recht, wenn man die neoricardianische Kritik einbezieht. Eine allgemeingültige Aussage läßt sich kaum treffen.

11 Vgl. Keynes, J.M.: The General Theory, S. 405

Sicher kann man Zweifel hegen, ob die hier angenommene kurz- und längerfristige waagerechte Arbeitskräftenachfragefunktion empirisch jederzeit zutreffend ist. Entscheidend ist vielmehr, daß von einem allgemeingültigen inversen Zusammenhang von Reallohn und Beschäftigung, wie ihn die neoklassische Produktionstheorie postuliert, nicht gesprochen werden kann. Wie erwähnt waren ja Keynes' selbst Zweifel nach Hinweisen von Viner, Dunlop, Tarshis und Kalecki gekommen. Empirisch läßt sich jedenfalls für die Bundesrepublik Deutschland feststellen, daß es mehr Evidenz für prozyklische Lohn- und Beschäftigungsdynamik gibt als für eine inverse Beziehung. Die Lohnquote weist in vielen Ländern über lange Phasen eine erstaunliche Stabilität auf, unabhängig von Veränderungen im Beschäftigungsgrad.

(6) *Steigende Renditen – Voraussetzung für mehr Investitionen?* Welche Investitionsfunktion man auch immer unterstellt, daß die Investitionen auch von den erwarteten Renditen abhängig sind, wird kaum jemand bestreiten. Dies gilt aus keynesianischer Sicht zumindest bei konstantem Kapitalmarktzins, so daß steigende Renditen – bei ansonsten unveränderten Zukunftserwartungen der Investoren – eine größere Grenzleistungsfähigkeit des Kapitals signalisieren. Höhere Renditen führen bei konstantem Kapitalkoeffizient zu einer steigenden Gewinnquote und einer spiegelbildlich sinkenden Lohnquote, so daß die Reallöhne relativ zur Produktivität sinken. Mit dem Hinweis auf die Investitionsfunktion könnten sinkende Reallöhne (immer relativ zur Produktivität) sowohl bei konjunkturell-keynesianischer Arbeitslosigkeit in einer Rezession, in der Gewinne und Investitionen schrumpfen, wie in einem für Vollbeschäftigung zu schwachem Aufschwung sowie auch nach erreichter voller Kapazitätsauslastung bei wachstumsdefizitärer Arbeitslosigkeit postuliert werden. Konjunkturelle und kapitalmangelbedigte Arbeitslosigkeit würden sich in dieser Hinsicht nicht unterscheiden.

Daß eine derartige wachstumsfördernde Konstellation *möglich* ist, ist nicht zu bestreiten. Fraglich ist, ob sie zwingend notwendig ist und ob sie, angenommen sie ist notwendig oder wenigstens wünschenswert, durch Nominallohnzurückhaltung erreicht werden kann. Notwendig sind steigende Renditen bzw. eine steigende Gewinnquote dann nicht, wenn der gleiche investitionsstimulierende Effekt durch eine Zinssenkung oder eine autonome Nachfragesteigerung bei konstanten Renditen erreicht werden kann. Häufig ist dies beispielsweise in der Rezession der Fall, wenn die Zinsen sinken oder automatische Stabilisatoren bzw. die Fiskalpolitik oder andere Faktoren (Auslandsnachfrage, autonome Investitionen etc.) die Nachfrage stimulieren. Ebenso kann die Reduktion von Unsicherheit die Investitionsneigung bei unveränderten Renditen erhöhen. Bei persistenter hoher Arbeitslosigkeit kann man sich fragen, ob all dies hinreichend ist. Die entscheidende Frage ist, ob höhere Renditen bzw. eine steigende Gewinnquote durch eine zurückhaltende Nominallohnpolitik erreichbar sind. Die Gefahr ist groß, daß diese erstens im Falle unflexibler Güterpreise kaufkraftschwächend und damit investitionshemmend wirkt, was nur durch sehr starke Investitionsanreize überkompensiert werden könnte, oder daß bei flexiblen Güterpreisen und Wechselkursen disinflationäre oder deflationäre Folgen entstehen; Deflation würde Wachstum und Investitionen schwächen. Um *im Ergebnis* niedrigere Reallöhne bzw. eine höhere Gewinnquote bei mehr Beschäftigung zu erhalten, erscheint es sicherer, auf die akkumulationsstimulierende Funktion der Geld- und / oder Fiskalpolitik als auf Lohnsenkung zu setzen.

Die Diskussion der sechs angeführten Argumente ergibt, daß lediglich in einem Fall Reallohnsenkung für mehr Beschäftigung ab dem Punkt voller Kapazitätsauslastung zwingend notwendig ist, nämlich bei steigender Investitionsquote – etwa in einem kräftigen Aufschwung (oder bei steigendem Kapitalkoeffizienten). Indes ist eine steigende Investitionsquote für einen Beschäftigungsanstieg mit parallelem Wachstum des Produktionspotentials nicht unbedingt erforderlich, allerdings sicher wünschenswert. Daß automatisch aus im Verhältnis zur Produktivität sinkenden Reallöhnen eine steigende Investitionsquote oder überhaupt steigende Investitionen folgen, ist unsicher. Im Zuge eines konjunkturellen Aufschwungs wie auch bei starkem investitionsgetriebenen Wirtschaftswachstum wird die Gewinnquote steigen; dies ist das *Resultat* starker Investitionsdynamik, die in der Regel nicht durch entsprechende Nominallohnpolitik initiiert werden kann. Das Argument der Nachfrageüberschüsse bzw. evtl. steigender Grenzkosten bei hoher Kapazitätsauslastung legt *vorübergehende* Reallohnsenkung an der Kapazitätsgrenze nahe, um Inflationsimpulse zu dämpfen. Bei hoher Produktionsflexibilität kann „vorübergehend" sehr kurz und damit vernachlässigbar sein. Obwohl die Gefahr einer Preis-Lohn-Spirale besteht, insbesondere wenn über den Punkt optimaler Kapazitätsauslastung hinaus mit steigenden Grenzkosten produziert wird und die Kapazitätserweiterung unzulänglich vorankommt, kann von einer generellen und anhaltenden Notwendigkeit zur Reallohnsenkung zwecks Abbau der Arbeitslosigkeit bei voller Kapazitätsauslastung jedenfalls nicht die Rede sein. Mithin ist die Unterscheidung von konjunktureller und kapitalmangelbedingter (in diesem Sinne „struktureller" oder klassischer) Arbeitslosigkeit analytisch wenig ergiebig. Konjunkturelle und wachstumsdefizitäre Arbeitslosigkeit liegen nahe beieinander.

## III. Neukeynesianische Ungleichgewichtstheorie: Malinvauds klassische und keynesianische Arbeitslosigkeit

In der ungleichgewichtstheoretischen „Neuen Keynesianischen Makroökonomie" werden im Anschluß an Patinkin, Clower und Leijonhufvud bekanntlich kurzfristig starre Preise und Löhne und damit vorrangige Mengenreaktionen bei Ungleichgewichten unterstellt. Unter den inzwischen weitverzweigten neukeynesianischen Ansätzen sei hier lediglich einer diskutiert. Vor allem Malinvaud[12] ar-

---

12 Vgl. Malinvaud, E.: The Theory of Unemployment Reconsidered, Oxford 1977. Vgl. auch Benassy, J.P.: An introduction to the Non-Walrasian approach, London 1986, Kap. 3. Malinvaud bezieht in anderen Arbeiten stärker die längerfristige Perspektive ein. Hier wird

beitet unterschiedliche makroökonomische „Regimes" als Kombinationen von Arbeits- und Gütermärkten heraus, insbesondere keynesianische und klassische Arbeitslosigkeit. *Keynesianische* Arbeitslosigkeit herrscht demnach, wenn Arbeits- wie Gütermarkt Käufermärkte sind, auf denen das jeweilige Überangebot durch die zu geringe Nachfrage rationiert wird. Obwohl die Reallöhne vollbeschäftigungs- bzw. grenzproduktivitätskonforme Gleichgewichtslöhne sind, mangelt es infolge exogener Schocks an Güternachfrage. Bei *klassischer* Arbeitslosigkeit ist der Arbeitsmarkt ein Käufermarkt, der Gütermarkt ein Verkäufermarkt, auf dem eine Überschußnachfrage existiert, die seitens der Anbieter wegen der zu hohen Reallöhne auf dem Arbeitsmarkt nicht voll bedient werden kann[13]. Die anderen möglichen Marktkonstellationen (vor allem zurückgestaute Inflation) werden hier ausgeklammert. Die eigentliche „Keynessche" Arbeitslosigkeit ist nach Malinvaud ein Grenzfall zwischen seinen Typen keynesianischer und klassischer Arbeitslosigkeit (geräumter Gütermarkt bei Unterbeschäftigung). Malinvauds Modell, das hier nicht dargestellt werden soll, impliziert u. a. geräumte Investitionsgütermärkte mit konstanter Investitionsgüternachfrage. Die Konsumgüternachfrage ist eine steigende Funktion des Reallohnsatzes, des Realwerts des Geldbestandes (Realkasseneffekt) sowie des Beschäftigungsstandes. Die Arbeitskräftenachfrage ist neoklassisch invers mit dem Reallohn gekoppelt, sofern sie nicht durch die Güternachfrage rationiert wird.

Bei beiden Typen von Arbeitslosigkeit entstehen temporäre nicht-walrasianische Gleichgewichte durch Mengenanpassung. Malinvaud beschreibt drei mögliche Wege zur Beseitigung keynesianischer Arbeitslosigkeit: Erhöhung der autonomen Güternachfrage durch Fiskalpolitik; bei verzögert wirksam werdender Preis- und Lohnflexibilität Geldlohn-Preis-Deflation, die über Realkasseneffekte zu größerer Güternachfrage führen soll; und in beschränktem Maße durch sinkende Güterpreise bei konstanten Geldlöhnen, wodurch ebenfalls Realkasseneffekte eintreten, sofern das Arbeitsangebot nicht infolge höherer Reallöhne steigt oder klassische Arbeitslosigkeit entsteht. Klassische Arbeitslosigkeit kann einfach durch steigende

---

nur Malinvauds Analyse der kurzen Frist behandelt. Vgl. Malinvaud, E.: Profitability and Unemployment, Cambridge 1980, und derselbe: Wages and Unemployment, in: The Economic Journal, Vol. 92 (1982), S. 1 ff.

13 Bhaduri kritisiert die in der Ungleichgewichtstheorie übliche Zuordnung von keynesianischer Arbeitslosigkeit zu niedrigen Reallöhnen bei Angebotsüberschuß auf dem Gütermarkt (bzw. hohe Reallöhne und überschüssiger Güternachfrage bei klassischer Arbeitslosigkeit). Es läßt sich nämlich nachweisen, daß unter bestimmten Annahmen hinsichtlich des Verhältnisses von Reallohnniveau zur aggregierten Güternachfrage auch die Kombinationen von niedrigen Reallöhnen und Nachfrageüberschuß auf dem Gütermarkt sowie hohen Reallöhnen und defizitärer Güternachfrage möglich ist. So können etwa niedrige Löhne, die unter dem Gleichgewichtslohn liegen, in einer Art Unterkonsumtions-Regime zu niedrigem Wachstum der Güternachfrage führen, sie können aber auch u.U. die Investitionen und die Exportnachfrage sehr stark stimulieren (umgekehrt für hohe Reallöhne). Daher macht nach Bhaduri die übliche Unterscheidung von klassischer und keynesianischer Arbeitslosigkeit keinen Sinn. Vgl. Bhaduri, A.: Keynesian and classical unemployment: a false distinction. In: Economie Appliquée, Vol. XLIV, No. 1, S. 43 ff.

Güterpreise abgebaut werden. Da auf dem Gütermarkt ja in Malinvauds Modell eine Überschußnachfrage existiert, ist hier bei einsetzender Preisflexibilität nicht mit Deflation, dafür aber mit Inflation zu rechnen, und trotz sinkender Reallöhne kommt es nicht zu einer für Vollbeschäftigung unzureichenden effektiven Nachfrage.

Bei beiden Marktkonstellationen führt Preis- und Lohnflexibilität, sobald das Modell sie verzögert zuläßt, zu walrasianischen Gleichgewichten auf allen Märkten. Im Unterschied zur herkömmlichen neoklassischen Analyse wird nachfragebedingte Arbeitslosigkeit als Möglichkeit konzediert, und ihre Beseitigung erfordert keine Reallohnsenkung. Wenn Vertrauen in den Realkasseneffekt besteht, ist eigentlich eine nachfragesteigernde Politik überflüssig; allenfalls ist sie zur Beschleunigung der Wiederherstellung von Vollbeschäftigung hilfreich. Die Analyse des Abbaus klassischer Arbeitslosigkeit durch Preis- und Lohnflexibilität weicht in gewisser Weise von dem bekannten neoklassischen Muster ab: Sobald das Modell Preisflexibilität zuläßt, sorgt der per Ungleichgewicht unterstellte Nachfrageüberschuß auf dem Gütermarkt für steigende Preise und sinkende Reallöhne, ohne daß es einer Nominallohnsenkung bedarf. Implizit wird damit eine restriktive Geldpolitik ausgeschlossen, die die Preiserhöhung „verbietet". Paradoxerweise ist dies eine Art der Beschäftigungssteigerung, die Keynes, allerdings via Nachfrageankurbelung, zum Abbau *unfreiwilliger* Arbeitslosigkeit im Auge hatte. So hat Malinvauds klassische Arbeitslosigkeit durchaus Ähnlichkeit mit Keynes' unfreiwilliger Arbeitslosigkeit!

Persistente Arbeitslosigkeit erklärt Malinvaud nicht[14]. Zwar hält er keynesianische Arbeitslosigkeit für in der Realität häufiger anzutreffen, weil es nicht gerade selten reale Nachfrageschocks gäbe und die Preisreagibilität nach unten – die ja für die Initiierung der Realkasseneffekte entscheidend ist – geringer als die nach oben sei. Aber ein anhaltendes nicht-walrasianisches Gleichgewicht bei Unterbeschäftigung ist dies nicht. Währenddessen kann klassische Arbeitslosigkeit, die nach Malinvaud vor allem bei starken sozialen Spannungen, die zu hohen Löhnen führen, oder bei plötzlichem Produktivitätsrückgang entsteht, relativ leicht durch die höhere Preisreagibilität nach oben geheilt werden.

Fragwürdig ist Malinvauds Basisprämisse der sofortigen Mengenanpassung bei verzögerter Preisflexibilität. Eine schlüssige mikroökonomische Begründung liefert er nicht, während andere Ungleichgewichtstheoretiker so viele verschiedene mögliche Begründungen liefern (man denke an die vielfältigen neukeynesianisch-mikroökonomischen Begründungen für Nominallohnrigiditäten in den Effizienzlohn-, Kontrakt-, Insider-Outsider-Theorien etc.), daß die Auswahl schwer fällt. Zumindest sollte die *generelle* Gültigkeit der Basisprämisse in Zweifel gezogen werden, denn: Preisanpassungen nach oben erfolgen häufig viel rascher als entsprechende Mengensteigerungen; das Verhältnis von Preis- und Mengenflexibilität

---

14 Vgl. auch Priewe, J.: Zur Kritik konkurrierender Arbeitsmarkt- und Beschäftigungstheorien und ihrer politischen Implikationen, Frankfurt / M. usw. 1984, S. 201 ff.

ist nicht unabhängig von Kapazitätsauslastung, Investitionsentscheidungen, Marktformen und Homogenitätsgrad der Güter; Existenz von Informationskosten; Arbeits-, Güter- und Geld- bzw. Kapitalmärkte unterscheiden sich erheblich. Freilich löst diese Kritik nicht die Frage des Verhältnisses von Preis- und Mengenflexibilität in dynamischen Marktwirtschaften, der man, zumindest in der Tradition von Keynes, vermutlich nur durch die Analyse von Erwartungen und Unsicherheit beikommt[15]. Die berechtigte Kritik am Walrasschen Auktionator kommt nicht weiter, wenn sie in einer 180-Grad-Wendung zu vollständiger Preisinflexibilität Zuflucht nimmt.

Malinvauds keynesianische Arbeitslosigkeit trifft in wichtigen Punkten nicht Keynes' unfreiwillige, gleichgewichtige Unterbeschäftigung, aber in einem anderen Punkt stellt sie eine wichtige Erweiterung dar. Bei Keynes ist der Gütermarkt auf niedrigem Niveau geräumt, die Nachfragefunktion hat sich nach links verschoben, es herrscht am Ende eines kontraktiven Prozesses ein Gütermarktgleichgewicht, das keine Preisveränderungen induziert[16]. Es hat also infolge eines Nachfragerückgangs eine kontraktive Preis- und Mengenreaktion stattgefunden (unterstellt, die Güterangebotsfunktion ist positiv geneigt). Da der Keynessche „Beschäftigungsmarkt" vom Gütermarkt abhängig ist, kann die Beschäftigung nicht größer sein als die Güternachfrage zuläßt. Allerdings kann der Reallohn in dieser Unterbeschäftigungssituation durchaus höher sein als für Vollbeschäftigung erforderlich, wenn dem oben erwähnten „ersten Postulat" der Klassik gefolgt wird. Wenn es zu Lohnunterbietung und Deflation kommt, kann gerade nicht auf Realkasseneffekte vertraut werden, wie Keynes im 19. Kapitel der „General Theory" argumentierte. Malinvauds keynesianische Arbeitslosigkeit hat jedenfalls in dieser Hinsicht mit *Keynes'* unfreiwilliger Arbeitslosigkeit wenig zu tun. Andererseits wird Keynes' Begriff unfreiwilliger Arbeitslosigkeit an einer wichtigen Stelle erweitert: Selbst dann, wenn der Reallohn unterhalb oder auf dem Niveau des grenzproduktivitätskonformen Lohnes liegt, existiert nachfragebedingte Arbeitslosigkeit, weil der Gütermarkt – aus welchen Gründen auch immer – rationiert ist. Es mangelt allein an Güternachfrage; die Preise müssen nicht steigen oder die Nominallöhne sinken, um zu mehr Beschäftigung zu gelangen.

Analog tauchen bei Malinvauds Analyse klassischer Arbeitslosigkeit Probleme auf, wenn man annimmt, daß die Rationierung der Überschußnachfrage auf dem Gütermarkt durch das Angebot zu negativen Multiplikatorprozessen (starre Güterpreise seien unterstellt) führt, die eine Linksverschiebung der Güternachfragefunktion auslöst, so daß sich nun ein Gütermarkt*gleichgewicht* auf niedrigem Outputniveau einstellt. Wenn jetzt die klassische Arbeitslosigkeit beseitigt werden soll,

---

15 Vgl. Leijonhufvud, A.: Über Keynes und den Keynesianismus, Köln 1973, S. 71 ff.

16 Dieses Gleichgewicht bei Unterbeschäftigung widerspricht nicht dem Walrasschen Gesetz (vgl. Leijonhufvud, A., S. 80 ff.). Die Arbeitslosen fallen aus den Tauschprozessen und Geldkreisläufen heraus. Dem Überangebot am Arbeitsmarkt korrespondiert – in Clowers Worten – eine „spekulative Güternachfrage", die die Arbeitslosen entfalten würden, wären sie beschäftigt.

muß nicht nur der Reallohn sinken, sondern zugleich die Güternachfrage wieder auf ihr ursprüngliches Niveau steigen (die Nachfragefunktion muß sich wieder nach rechts verschieben). Malinvaud umgeht dieses Problem, indem er einfach die Fortexistenz des ursprünglichen Güternachfrageüberschusses unterstellt, obwohl es eine rein „spekulative" und keine „effektive" Überschußnachfrage in Clowers Terminologie ist[17]. Läßt man die Prämisse der verzögerten Preisreagibilität *nach oben* fallen, dann wird klassische Arbeitslosigkeit gar nicht erst entstehen, weil weder die Reallöhne zu hoch geraten noch eine Überschußgüternachfrage entsteht.

So ergeht es Malinvaud wie einst Hicks' mit seinem IS-LM-Schema. Die Analyse läßt sich leicht neoklassisch vereinnahmen. Malinvaud unterstützt dies, wenn er Ungleichgewichte aufgrund des Fixpreissystems für die kurze Frist und gleichgewichtsträchtige Preisflexibilität für die lange Frist reklamiert. Mit der Begründung von Arbeitslosigkeit durch Hinweis auf temporäre Preis- und Lohnrigiditäten argumentiert man ebenso neoklassisch wie mit zinsunelastischen Investitionen und Zinsstarrheiten als keynesianischen Ausnahmetatbeständen. So vermag auch Malinvauds Unterscheidung keynesianischer und klassischer Arbeitslosigkeit letztlich nicht zu überzeugen, weil sie den Kern von Keynes' Kritik an der Klassik nicht übernimmt.

## IV. Natürliche und inflationsstabile Arbeitslosigkeit – klassische Arbeitslosigkeit?

Eine andere Typologie von klassischer (oder struktureller) Arbeitslosigkeit und vorübergehender keynesianischer (oder mehr oder minder konjunktureller) Arbeitslosigkeit stellt das Begriffspaar *„natural rate of unemployment"* (NRU) auf der einen und die sonstige, meist nicht genauer titulierte Arbeitslosigkeit (also faktische Arbeitslosigkeit minus NRU) dar. In einer zweiten Varianten wird die NRU durch die eingangs erwähnte NAIRU[18] ersetzt.

Für Friedman ist bekanntlich die NRU jene bei jedweder Inflationsrate dauerhaft bestehende freiwillige und damit gleichgewichtige Arbeitslosigkeit, die mit Vollbeschäftigung vereinbar ist. Sie beruht auf Friktionen und Marktunvollkommenheiten auf den Märkten, insbesondere dem Arbeitsmarkt, die institutionell oder soziologisch bedingt sind und normalerweise nur langsam verändert werden können[19]. Sie ist ausschließlich durch reale Faktoren bedingt und höchstens vorüber-

---

17 Vgl. Clower, R.: Keynes and the Classics: A Dynamical Perspective. In: Quarterly Journal of Economics, May 1960

18 Genau genommen handelt es um eine nicht-*steigende* Inflationsrate.

19 „Das natürliche ‚Unterbeschäftigungsniveau' ist ... jenes, das sich aus dem Walrasianischen Gleichgewichtssystem ergeben würde, vorausgesetzt die aktuellen Strukturcharakteristika der Arbeits- und Gütermärkte sind eingebaut, und zwar einschließlich Marktunvollkommenheiten, Zufallsvariabilität von Angebot und Nachfrage, Kosten der Informationsbeschaf-

gehend durch Inflation zu vermindern, so daß sich die langfristige Phillips-Kurve in die Vertikale verdreht. Häufig wird die NRU mit friktioneller sowie Such- und Mismatch-Arbeitslosigkeit beschrieben. In manchen Standard-Lehrbüchern[20] ist die NRU einfach die langfristig verbleibende Arbeitslosigkeit in annnähernd konstanter Höhe (etwa 4 - 6% in den USA), die unabhängig von vorübergehender konjunktureller Arbeitslosigkeit persistent ist. Aus neoklassischer Sicht wäre sie durchaus zu reduzieren, wenn die durch die Arbeitslosenunterstützung bestimmten Reservationslöhne sowie die Minimumlöhne gesenkt und andere deregulierende Maßnahmen ergriffen würden. Tatsächlich handelt es sich um ein Konglomerat verschiedener Komponenten, die unterschiedliche Ausmaße annehmen können. Die meisten empirischen Untersuchungen haben erhebliche Mühe, die NRU einzugrenzen und von der tatsächlichen bzw. der konjunkurellen Arbeitslosigkeit abzugrenzen. Daß es einen harten Kern mikroökonomisch bedingter friktioneller sowie Mismatch-Arbeitslosigkeit gibt, wird wohl niemand in Abrede stellen, allerdings scheint Friedman weit darüber hinaus zu gehen und einen erheblichen Teil „normaler“ freiwilliger bzw. klassischer Arbeitslosigkeit in die NRU einzubeziehen, für die die übliche keynesianische Kritik gilt.

In Westeuropa hat die NAIRU größere Bedeutung erlangt, da der starke Anstieg der persistenten Arbeitslosigkeit seit Mitte der 70er Jahre nur schwer mit dem NRU-Konzept vereinbar erscheint, zumal dieses von einer Konstanz bzw. nur langsamen und graduellen Veränderungen ausgeht. Die NAIRU umfaßt die NRU, übersteigt diese aber normalerweise. Es ist ebenfalls eine gleichgewichtige Arbeitslosenquote, die allerdings kein walrasianisches Gleichgewicht allseits geräumter Märkte impliziert. Um eine bestimmte Inflationsrate stabil zu halten, also eine steigende Inflationsrate bzw. Dis- oder Deflation zu vermeiden, bedürfe es einer bestimmten Arbeitslosigkeit. Bei der NAIRU-konformen Inflationsrate kann es sich um die politische gerade noch tolerierte Inflationsrate handeln, was häufig implizit unterstellt wird, aber auch um eine höhere Inflationsrate.

Sind nun Güter- und Arbeitsnachfrage so stark, daß die Arbeitslosigkeit unter die NAIRU sinkt, werden die Arbeitnehmer bzw. Gewerkschaften inflationsverstärkende Nominallohnforderungen stellen. Dieser Fall wird als *lohninduzierte Arbeitslosigkeit*[21] verstanden, die bei restriktivem staatlichen Nachfragemanagement, das Inflationssteigerung vermeiden muß, zu zu hohen Reallöhnen und zu zu niedrigen Gewinnen führt[22]. Arbeitslosigkeit oberhalb der NAIRU, die zu Disinflationie-

---

fung über freie Stellen und Arbeitsreserven, Mobilitätskosten usw.“ (Friedman, M.: Die Rolle der Geldpolitik. In: Brunner, K., Neumann, M.J.M. (Hrsg.): Geldtheorie, Köln 1974, S. 322) Zur kritischen Diskussion der außerordentlich problematischen Definition vgl. Kromphardt, J.: Zur Erklärung der Persistenz nichtnatürlicher Arbeitslosigkeit. In: Franz, W. (Hrsg.): Mikro- und makroökonomische Aspekte der Arbeitslosigkeit, Beiträge zur Arbeitsmarkt- und Berufsforschung 165, S. 212 ff.

20 Z.B. Dornbusch, R., Fischer, St.: Makroökonomik, 5. Auflage, München-Wien 1992, S. 571 ff.

21 Franz, W.: Arbeitsmarktökonomik, 3. Auflage, Heidelberg 1996, S. 366

rung (oder Deflation) führt, wird auf eine zu niedrige Güternachfrage zurückgeführt – *nachfragemangelinduzierte Arbeitslosigkeit.* In anderen Darstellungen führt Arbeitslosigkeit oberhalb der NAIRU zu geringeren Nominallohnzuwächsen und – bei konstant bleibender Inflationsrate – zu geringeren Reallöhnen. Damit wird die NAIRU nicht nur nach ihrem Wortlaut gedeutet, nämlich als jene Arbeitslosigkeit, die die Inflationsrate stabil hält, sondern auch als *verteilungsstabilisierende* Arbeitslosigkeit: „Die NAIRU stellt also die Höhe der Arbeitslosigkeit dar, bei der ein Gleichgewicht zwischen den Verteilungsansprüchen erreicht ist."[23] Damit wird die NAIRU in einer Weise interpretiert, daß sie zur Wegscheide zwischen klassischer und keynesianischer Arbeitslosigkeit wird, auch wenn die meisten NAIRU-Theoretiker nicht direkt diese Begriffe verwenden.

Die NAIRU teilt ihr Schicksal mit der NRU. Beide passen sich im Zeitablauf zunehmend der persistenten, faktischen Arbeitslosigkeit an, wie viele empirischen Untersuchungen ergaben[24]. Auf jeden Fall scheint es eine langfristig stabile NAIRU nicht zu geben, die relevanten Parameter, die eigentlich das Lohn-Verhalten der Arbeitsanbieter (vor allem der Gewerkschaften) sowie das Preissetzungsverhalten der Unternehmen widerspiegeln sollen, sind keineswegs stabil[25]. Die Veränderung der Parameter scheint von der makroökonomischen Situation mitbestimmt zu sein. Der Verdacht ist nicht von der Hand zu weisen, daß die NAIRU mehr noch als die NRU ein ökonometrisches Artefakt ist. Häufig wird der Anstieg der NAIRU mit *Hysteresis* begründet, vor allem über die mit steigender Dauer der Arbeitslosigkeit zunehmende Entwertung des Humankapitals, wodurch die Mismatch-Arbeitslosigkeit und damit faktisch die NRU zunimmt. Ein wachsender Teil der Arbeitslosen verliert seine Wettbewerbsfähigkeit, wodurch die lohntreibende Knapp-

22 Vgl. Franz, W.: Theoretische Ansätze zur Erklärung der Arbeitslosigkeit: Wo stehen wir 1995? In: Gahlen, B., u. a. (Hrsg.): Arbeitslosigkeit und die Möglichkeiten ihrer Überwindung, Tübingen 1996, S. 3 ff.

23 Sesselmeier, W., Blauermel, G., Arbeitsmarkttheorien. Ein Überblick, Heidelberg 1997, S. 24. Damit kommt der NAIRU jene profitratenstabilisierende Funktion zu, die Arbeitslosigkeit bei den Klassikern hatte, insbesondere bei Ricardo und Marx, dessen „industrielle Reservearmee" die NAIRU-Funktion übernimmt, allerdings mit dem Unterschied, daß zugleich das Reallohnniveau auf dem Reproduktionsniveau stabilisiert wird. Diese Parallele tritt ein, weil nicht hinreichend unterschieden wird, ob die NAIRU die *Nominal*löhne oder die *Real*löhne stabilisiert. Erklärt man wie die Klassik und Neoklassik das Preisniveau quantitätstheoretisch durch die exogene Geldmenge, dann erübrigt sich freilich diese Differenzierung, denn jede Nominallohnänderung ändert in gleicher Höhe den Reallohn.- Die NAIRU-Konzeption wird nicht klarer, wenn man sie zur QUERU modifiziert: „quasi-equilibrium-rate-of-unempoyment", bei der die Lohn- und Preissteigerungsraten gleich, aber nicht – wie bei der NAIRU – auch konstant sind (vgl. Franz, W.: Theoretische Ansätze, mit Literaturhinweisen). Während die QUERU nur die Verteilung stabilisiert, stabilisiert die NAIRU demnach die Verteilung und die Inflationsrate zugleich.

24 Vgl. z. B. Tobin, J.: Stabilization policy ten years after. In: Brookings Papers on Economic Activity, No. 1 / 1980, S. 60; Horn, G.A., Scheremet, W.: Ursachen struktureller Arbeitslosigkeit. Zur Theorie und Empirie neuerer makroökonomischer Ansätze. In: Konjunkturpolitik, Heft 5 / 1990, S. 298 ff.

25 Vgl. Heise, A.: Arbeit für Alle – Vision oder Illusion? Marburg / Lahn 1996, 144 ff.

heit der „Insider" verstärkt wird. Demnach würde bereits eine geringe Reduktion der Arbeitslosenquote aggressives Lohn-Bargaining der Gewerkschaften induzieren. Bei Kapitalmangel-Arbeitslosigkeit könnte auch infolge einer Nachfrageinflation an der Kapazitätsgrenze die Inflation über die bisherige gleichgewichtige Inflationsrate hinaus beschleunigt werden, wodurch die NAIRU weiter anstiege. Eine steigende NAIRU, was auch immer die Ursachen sind, scheint die alte neoklassische Auffassung zu bestätigen: Nachfragebedingte keynesianische Arbeitslosigkeit ist temporär, klassische ist persistent, sofern Lohnrigiditäten dauerhaft bestehen.

Zunächst ist zu fragen, ob die NAIRU wirklich klassische Arbeitslosigkeit im Sinne der eingangs genannten Kriterien ist. Entscheidend ist, daß eine unter die NAIRU sinkende tatsächliche Arbeitslosigkeit inflationserhöhend wirkt, dies aber von den geldpolitischen Instanzen nicht toleriert wird, so daß eine Einkommensumverteilung zugunsten der Löhne entsteht, was wiederum die tatsächliche Arbeitslosigkeit auf NAIRU-Niveau erhöht. Man könnte auch sagen, die NAIRU ist durch restriktive Geldpolitik (steigende Zinsen) verursacht, die notwendig ist, wenn nicht eine akzelerierende Inflation akzeptiert werden soll.

Kann nun aber Nominallohnzurückhaltung mehr Beschäftigung ermöglichen? Folgt man Keynes' zentraler Überzeugung der Abhängigkeit von Preisniveauveränderungen von Veränderungen der Nominallöhne, dann würde die Nominallohnmoderation – von Zeitverzögerungen abgesehen – nicht zu sinkenden Reallöhnen führen, sondern zu einer niedrigeren Inflationsrate, die unter der bisherigen NAIRU-konformen Inflationsrate liegt; damit würde die NAIRU gesenkt, so daß der Anteil der nachfragebedingten keynesianischen Arbeitslosigkeit an der Gesamtarbeitslosigkeit steigt. Der Abbau der Arbeitslosigkeit hängt jetzt in stärkerem Maße von der effektiven Nachfrage ab. Die Geldlohnmoderation hat nur die Voraussetzung für die Stabilität der Inflationsrate geschaffen. Zumindest einige der NAIRU- (und QUERU-) Deutungen bestreiten diese Lohnabhängigkeit des Preisniveaus, da sie das Reallohnniveau bzw. dessen Veränderungsrate als abhängig vom Bargaining um Löhne und Preise betrachten.

Die Nominallohndynamik wirkt *asymmetrisch* auf die Reallöhne bzw. die Einkommensverteilung: Sind die Nominallohnsteigerungen so hoch, daß die tolerierte Inflationsrate überschritten wird und die Geldpolitik restriktiv reagiert, dann wirken sie lohnquotensteigernd. Gehen umgekehrt die Geldlohnsteigerungen zurück, so daß in der Folge die Inflationsrate sinkt, bleibt die Lohnquote konstant.

Eine keynesianische Interpretation legt es nahe, jegliche Arbeitslosigkeit, soweit sie nicht „friktionell" oder durch „mismatch" verursacht und in diesem Sinne „strukturell" zu nennen ist (sie wäre also der NRU zuzurechnen, sofern man diesen Begriff verwenden will), als keynesianisch anzusehen, gleichgültig ob sie Teil der NAIRU ist oder darüber hinausgeht. Die NAIRU beschreibt nur eine mit einer stabilen Inflationsrate nicht vereinbare Nominallohndynamik, deren Eindämmung eine *notwendige* Voraussetzung für den Abbau nicht-natürlicher Arbeitslosigkeit ist, aber keine *hinreichende,* solange es an effektiver Nachfrage mangelt.

Auf zwei weitere Probleme der Interpretation der NAIRU soll hingewiesen werden: Welchen Einfluß haben *konjunkturbedingte Preisfluktuationen* sowie *Disinflation* auf die NAIRU? Das NAIRU-Konzept orientiert sich an einer bestimmten Inflationsrate, die zu stabilisieren ist. Mithin dürfen auch konjunkturbedingte vorübergehende Preisschwankungen nicht zugelassen werden. Sobald ein konjunktureller Preisauftrieb über die NAIRU-konforme Inflationsrate hinaus entsteht, der nicht durch Lohnmoderation aufgefangen wird, führt die dann für notwendige gehaltene geldpolitische Restriktion zu steigender Arbeitslosigkeit. In der Hochkonjunktur steigt demnach die NAIRU, in der Rezession sinkt sie. Je weniger die Geldpolitik konjunkturelle Preissteigerungen zuläßt, desto früher werden aufsteigende Konjunkturphasen abgebrochen. Bei steigendem Erwerbspersonenpotential – wie in der Bundesrepublik – ergibt sich das Bild treppenförmig steigender „Sockelarbeitslosigkeit", weil der Beschäftigungsanstieg in Zeiten guter Konjunktur abgebremst wird. Dabei kommt es auch auf das Ausmaß der geldpolitischen Restriktion an. Reagiert die Geldpolitik sehr hart auf relativ geringe konjunkturelle Preissteigerungen, wie etwa nach Ansicht zahlreicher Beobachter 1992 in Deutschland, dann erscheint dies als Anstieg der NAIRU. Mithin indiziert der ökonometrisch ermittelte Anstieg der NAIRU *auch* die Art und Weise der Geldpolitik.

Häufig wird die NAIRU-konforme Inflationsrate als politisch tolerierte und zugleich gewünschte Inflationsrate (z. B. zwischen 0 und 2%) interpretiert. Beim eigentlichen NAIRU-Konzept geht es jedoch um jedwede Inflationsrate, wenn sie nur stabil gehalten wird. Wenn der Übergang von einer stabilen hohen NAIRU-konformen Inflationsrate $p_h$ zu einer niedrigen, politisch gewünschten Ziel-Inflationsrate $p_Z$ angestrebt wird (Disinflation), ist in der Regel eine restriktivere Geldpolitik erforderlich, sofern eine inflationsmoderierende Einkommenspolitik nicht betrieben wird oder nicht gelingt. Wenn dabei die Arbeitslosigkeit ansteigt, dann nicht, weil mehr Arbeitslosigkeit nötig ist, um die ursprüngliche Inflationsrate $p_h$ zu stabilisieren, sondern weil die Restriktionspolitik – zumindest vorübergehend – im Übergang zu $p_Z$ die Güter- und Arbeitsnachfrage dämpft. Der Anstieg der Arbeitslosigkeit ist also disinflationsbedingt, nicht aber Ausdruck einer gestiegenen NAIRU. Wieviel Arbeitslosigkeit erforderlich ist, um $p_Z$ zu stabilisieren, läßt sich erst feststellen, wenn $p_Z$ erreicht ist. Die neue NAIRU liegt an dem Punkt, an dem Nachfrage- und Lohnexpansion die Inflation über $p_Z$ hinaus beschleunigt. Bei einer Zielinflationsrate von $p_Z$ erfordert dies eine konventionelle Lohnpolitik produktivitätsorientierter bzw. kostenniveauneutraler Art in der Grundform einer Geldlohnsteigerung von „Produktivitätszuwachs plus Kaufkraftausgleich $p_Z$". Entspricht die tatsächliche Inflationsrate der Zielrate, und würde diese auch bei fortschreitendem Abbau der Arbeitslosigkeit gewahrt, muß die dabei verbleibende Arbeitslosigkeit allein durch Nachfragemangel bedingt sein.

*Fazit:* Auch die Konstruktion einer inflationsstabilen Arbeitslosenquote bringt keine analytisch scharfe Scheidung klassischer von keynesianischer Arbeitslosigkeit. Ein Teil der NAIRU ist „strukturelle" Arbeitslosigkeit, die hier als friktionelle plus Mismatch-Arbeitslosigkeit verstanden wird; sie ist nicht im üblichen Sinne keynesianisch, aber auch nicht klassisch, weil sie nicht ohne weiteres durch niedrigere Nominallöhne verschwindet. Der restliche Teil der NAIRU sollte – ebenso wie die die NAIRU übersteigende Arbeitslosigkeit – als keynesianisch verstanden werden, da er nur durch Nachfragesteigerung vermindert werden kann, wobei die Reallöhne konstant bleiben, jedoch die Nominallohnsteigerungen zurückgehen müssen.

## V. Zu hohe Reallöhne und „Lohnlücke" – klassische Arbeitslosigkeit?

Versuche, die tatsächliche Arbeitslosigkeit in klassische und keynesianische Komponenten zu zerlegen, beruhen meist auf der Schätzung eines vollbeschäftigungskonformen Reallohnes mittels einer Produktionsfunktion[26]. Hintergrund ist in der Regel die Annahme einer negativ geneigten neoklassischen Arbeitsnachfragefunktion. Prämisse ist, daß es nur eine Kombination von Reallohn und Beschäftigung gibt, also keine beschäftigungsneutralen Verteilungsspielräume, wie sie in verschiedenen Theorien behauptet werden (z. B. in Monopolgradtheorien der verschiedensten Art oder auch in monetären Theorien, die den Zins als eine zentrale Determinante der Profitrate ansehen). Sieht man davon ab, dann besteht die Aufgabe darin, von einem Vollbeschäftigungsjahr ausgehend eine beschäftigungsneutrale Reallohnentwicklung zu schätzen. Dabei wird die tatsächliche Lohnquote bzw. eine produktivitätsorientierte Lohnpolitik als Maßstab verworfen, weil die zugrunde liegende Produktivitätsentwicklung möglicherweise aufgrund zu hoher Lohnsteigerungen realiter höher ausfällt als eine beschäftigungsneutrale Produktivitätsrate. Es müßte also eine lohninduzierte Komponente des Produktivitätsfortschritts eliminiert werden. Bei einem hypothetischen niedrigeren Produktivitätspfad ergäbe sich dann bei Vollbeschäftigung erneut eine konstante Lohnquote.

Hier ist nicht der Ort, die verschiedenen empirischen Studien zu resümieren[27]. Statt dessen sollen die theoretischen Grundlagen des Vorgehens infrage gestellt werden. Die Schätzung des beschäftigungsneutralen Reallohnes bzw. des vollbeschäftigungskonformen Reallohnes setzt *erstens* voraus, daß nicht nur die lohninduzierte Produktivitätskompenente ermittelt werden kann, sondern auch, daß von einem schwächeren Produktivitätstrend keine beschäftigungsmindernden negativen Wachstumsimpulse ausgehen. Dies ist jedoch wahrscheinlich, denn eine langsamer wachsende Kapitalintensität führt ceteris paribus zu geringerem Wachstum der Investitionsgüternachfrage, so daß möglicherweise gar kein Beschäftigungsimpuls entsteht[28]. Außerdem müßte unterstellt werden, daß das Faktoreinsatzverhältnis

---

26 Vgl. stellvertretend für viele andere Klodt, H.: Lohnquote und Beschäftigung – Die Lohnlücke. In: Jahrbücher für Nationalökonomie und Statistik, Band 201 / 5, S. 480 ff.

27 Vgl. u. a. Heise, A., S. 162 ff.

28 Vgl. auch Sievert, O.: Die Steuerbarkeit der Konjunktur durch den Staat. In: von Weizsäcker, C.C. (Hrsg.), Staat und Wirtschaft,. Schriften des Vereins für Socialpolitik, Band 102, Berlin 1979, S. 823 ff.

von Arbeit und Kapital tatsächlich von dem Verhältnis der Faktorpreise (Lohn bzw. Zins) gesteuert wird[29]. *Zweitens:* Will man vollbeschäftigungskonforme Reallöhne schätzen, dann müßte zudem die „Produktivitätsfähigkeit" der Arbeitslosen geschätzt werden können, bei wachsendem Erwerbspersonenpotential auch die der zusätzlichen Erwerbspersonen. *Drittens* - und dies ist entscheidend – kann nicht kausal von einer bestimmten Reallohnentwicklung auf die daraus vermeintlich resultierende Beschäftigung geschlossen werden. Eine empirisch beobachtbare negative Reallohnelastizität der Beschäftigung gestattet keine Aussage über einen Kausalnexus. Der neoklassischen Deutung könnte die keynesianische entgegengehalten werden, daß steigende Investitionen kreislauftheoretisch zu – relativ zu den Löhnen – steigenden Gewinnen führen und damit steigende Güternachfrage und steigende Beschäftigung induzieren. Die Reallohnentwicklung wäre die *Folge* einer Ursachenkette, die von den Investitionserwartungen ausgeht – nicht umgekehrt. Aus dieser Kritik folgt, daß selbst eine – wie auch immer – empirisch ermittelte Lohnlücke keineswegs ein Indiz für klassische Arbeitslosigkeit ist. Abgesehen davon gibt es, wie bereits erwähnt, nicht nur in Deutschland längere Phasen steigender Beschäftigung, die mit konstanter oder gar steigender Lohnquote einhergingen.

Verbreitet ist die neoklassische Interpretation der Lohnquoten- und Beschäftigungsentwicklung im Rahmen des Konjunkturzyklus. Normalerweise eilen Gewinne und Gewinnquote den Löhnen bzw. der Lohnquote voraus, aber häufig schon vor dem oberen Wendepunkt zieht die Lohnquote nach. In der Rezession geht die steigende Arbeitslosigkeit mit steigender Lohnquote und Gewinnverfall einher. Argumentiert man mit Keynes („General Theory"), als er noch der Grenzproduktivitätstheorie folgte, dann führen die positiven Erwartungen der Investoren, gestützt durch niedrige Realzinsen, zum Aufschwung, infolge von tolerierten Preissteigerungen sinken die Reallöhne, ohne daß die Nominallöhne nachgeben; die Gewinnquote steigt. Wenn die Preise infolge getrübter Zukunftserwartungen bzw. bei restriktiv umgeschalteter Geldpolitik langsamer expandieren, sinkt die Grenzleistungsfähigkeit und die Investitionen gehen zurück.

Ein weiterer zentraler Kritikpunkt an dem Lohnlückenkonzept ist die implizite Annahme, daß die Reallohnentwicklung nicht endogen erklärt, sondern durch die Arbeitsanbieter durch Nominallohnforderungen gesteuert werden wird. Dies ist ja eines der konstitutiven Merkmale der Konzeption klassischer Arbeitslosigkeit. Es müßte also nicht nur nachgewiesen werden, daß die Reallöhne gegenüber einer vollbeschäftigungskonformen Lohnentwicklung zu hoch sind, sondern daß dies auch durch entsprechende Nominallöhne veränderbar ist – nur dann wäre es klassische Arbeitslosigkeit. Entscheidend sind aus keynesianischer Sicht die Auswirkungen der Nominallohnsenkung auf die drei wichtigsten Bestimmungsfaktoren der effektiven Nachfrage, nämlich auf die Zinsen, die Grenzleistungsfähigkeit des Kapitals (und damit auf die Investitionen) und den Konsum.

---

29 Vgl. neuerdings kritisch dazu Sachverständigenrat zur Begutachtung der gesamtwirtschaftlichen Entwicklung, Jahresgutachten 1997/98, Wiesbaden 1997, Ziffer 371.

Man könnte einwenden, daß unter den Bedingungen einer *offenen Volkswirtschaft* der inverse Zusammenhang von Reallöhnen und Beschäftigung sowie die Parallelität von Nominal- und Reallohnsenkungen in stärkerem Maße gegeben ist. Keynes selbst wandte sich in Großbritannien nach der Rückkehr zum Goldstandard 1925, wodurch eine Überbewertung des Pfundes eintrat, gleichwohl gegen Lohndeflation (vgl. die Argumentation in der „Treatise“[30]). Unter modernen Bedingungen ist die Art des Wechselkursregimes entscheidend, ferner die Entwicklung der Löhne im Ausland sowie das Verhältnis von exportsteigernden und die Binnennachfrage schwächenden Nachfrageimpulsen. Auch in einer offenen Volkswirtschaft, vor allem bei flexiblen Wechselkursen, bleibt Geldlohnsenkung ein extrem unsicheres, wahrscheinlich kontraproduktives Vehikel zur Beschäftigungssteigerung.

Anders gewendet: Arbeitslosigkeit, die mit zu hohen Reallöhnen und komprimierten Renditen („profit squeeze“) einhergeht, kann durchaus, wie bereits eingangs dargestellt, mit keynesianischer, unfreiwilliger Arbeitslosigkeit vereinbar sein[31]. Gerade dies ist bei der eben erwähnten konjunkturellen Arbeitslosigkeit der Fall – in der Rezession ist die Lohnquote meist höher als bei hohem Beschäftigungsstand. Dies ist eine *Folge* des Zusammenbruchs der Investitionen und der mangelnden Kapazitätsauslastung. Für Keynes selbst – solange er dem „ersten klassischen Postulat“ noch folgte – war unfreiwillige Arbeitslosigkeit (anders als bei Malinvaud) durchaus mit zu hohen Reallöhnen und zu niedrigen Gewinnen verbunden[32] – der Reallohn ist aber die abhängige Variable. Damit sei nicht behauptet, die Nominallohnentwicklung sei irrelevant. Unter politischen Rahmenbedingungen, die der Geldwertstabilität sehr hohe Bedeutung zumißt, können die Reallöhne infolge aggressiver Tariflohnpolitik in der Tat so stark steigen, daß bei harter geldpolitischer Disziplin „profit squeeze“ eintritt, der Arbeitslosigkeit bewirkt. Dies war sicherlich in den 70er Jahren nach der ersten Ölpreisexplosion in der Bundesrepublik der Fall, als die Lohnpolitik die Kostensteigerungen weiterwälzen wollte, die Zentralbank jedoch auf geringere Inflationstoleranz umschaltete. Ob eine Tariflohnpolitik, die die Verschlechterung der terms of trade berücksichtigt hätte, über die Preisniveaustabilisierung hinaus auch zur Beibehaltung der Vollbeschäftigung geführt hätte, ist jedoch ungewiß.

Aus der Kritik an den „wage gap“-Berechnungen, insbesondere aus dem Hinweis, daß die Reallöhne nicht Gegenstand von Tarifverhandlungen seien, resultierte das Konzept der *„Nominallohnzurückhaltung“*[33]. Demnach steigt die Be-

---

30 Keynes, J.M.: A Treatise on Money. Vol. II. Collected Writings of John Maynard Keynes, Vol. VI, London 1971, S. 162 ff.

31 Vgl. beispielsweise Marglin, St., Bhaduri, A.: Profit squeeze and Keynesian theory. In: Marglin, St., Schor, J. (eds.): The Golden Age of Capitalism: Reinterpreting the Postwar Experience, Oxford, S. 153 ff.

32 Vgl. Hagemann, H., S. 192 f.

33 Lehment, H.: Lohnzurückhaltung, Arbeitszeitverkürzung und Beschäftigung. Eine empirische Untersuchung für die Bundesrepublik Deutschland 1973 - 90. In: Die Weltwirtschaft,

schäftigung, wenn die Nominallohnsteigerungen hinter dem erwarteten Zuwachs des nominalen Volkseinkommens zurückbleiben. Sieht man einmal von dem Problem der Erwartungsbildung ab[34], dann tauchen ähnliche Probleme wie bei den Lohnlückenkonzepten auf. Aufgrund definitorischer Beziehungen gilt, daß die Beschäftigungsmenge (definiert als Arbeitsvolumen in Stunden) nur steigt, wenn der Stundenlohn langsamer wächst als das Volkseinkommen (der Einfachheit halber seien konstante Preise angenommen). Bei konstanter Lohnquote mit Beschäftigungsanstieg sind die Wachstumsraten von Lohnsatz und Produktivität gleich, aber kleiner als die des Volkseinkommens. Demnach kann die Beschäftigung bei konstanter Einkommensverteilung durchaus steigen, Lohnzurückhaltung im Sinne einer hinter der Produktivitätssteigerung zurückbleibenden Lohnsteigerung ist nicht zwingend erforderlich[35]. Natürlich gelten die Zusammenhänge nur ex post, d. h. auch die produktivitätsgerechte Lohnsteigerung folgt eben jener Produktivität, die sich ergäbe, wenn mehr Personen – unter Umständen mit schwächerer „Produktivitätsfähigkeit" – eingestellt würden. Freilich sagen die definitorischen Zusammenhänge nichts über die Kausalbeziehungen. Die aufgrund von Schätzgleichungen ermittelte Nominallohnelastizität gestattet mithin nicht die gewünschte neoklassische Aussage: *„Eine Lohnzurückhaltung von einem Prozentpunkt erhöht die Erwerbstätigenzahl um rund 1 vH ...* "[36] bzw. 300.000 Personen pro anno[37].

## VI. Keynesianische Arbeitslosigkeit – zwei Varianten

Arbeitslosigkeit ist *freiwillig* im Sinne der klassischen und neoklassischen Typologien, wenn eine individuell oder kollektiv konzedierte Nominallohnsenkung zu einer mehr oder minder gleich großen Reallohnsenkung führt, die unmittelbar die Beschäftigung zusätzlicher Arbeitskräfte rentierlich macht. Die erforderliche zusätzliche Güternachfrage kommt von selbst, allenfalls ein wenig zeitverzögert. Bei

---

Heft 2/1991, S. 72 ff.; Siebert, H.: Geht den Deutschen die Arbeit aus? München 1994, S. 98 ff.

34 Heise zeigt, daß es 1973 - 91 stets ex ante Lohnzurückhaltung gab, gemessen an den Prognosen des Volkseinkommens durch den Sachverständigenrat (Heise, A., S. 168).

35 Ist A das Arbeitsvolumen, L der Stundenlohnsatz, Y das Volkseinkommen und P die Arbeitsproduktivität je Stunde (alles bei konstanten Preisen), dann gilt für die Lohnquote Q: $Q = (A \times L) / Y$. Bezeichnen Kleinbuchstaben die Wachstumsraten, dann gilt: $q = a + 1 - y$. Bei konstanter Lohnquote, also $q = 0$, gilt: $y-a = p = 1$. Wenn $a > 0$, dann gilt: $1 = p < y$. Ein Abbau der Arbeitslosigkeit – konstante Arbeitszeiten je Erwerbstätigen unterstellt – erfordert also eine Wachstumsrate des Sozialprodukts, die über der der Stundenlöhne liegt, sofern diese produktivitätsorientiert wachsen. Die Kernfrage ist natürlich, ob dieses hohe Wachstum, das hohe Investitionen erfordert, bei konstanter Lohnquote gelingen wird. Für eine steigende Lohnquote bei steigender Beschäftigung gilt $p < 1 < y$, und für eine sinkende Lohnquote bei steigender Beschäftigung : $1 < p < y$.

36 Lehment, H., S. 77

37 Siebert, H., S. 99

konstantem Kapitaleinsatz und variabler Kapitalintensität wäre dies in einer Marktwirtschaft mit *Naturaltausch* auch zutreffend: Mit den zusätzlich beschäftigten Arbeitskräften entstünde uno actu die erforderliche „Güternachfrage“. Die Nutzung von Arbeitskraft würde ja gegen Lohngüter getauscht. In einer *Geldwirtschaft* wollen die Arbeitskräfte jedoch Geld als Gegenleistung. Als Gruppe der Unterbeschäftigten sind sie nicht in der Lage, der Summe der Unternehmen zu signalisieren, daß sie potentielle Nachfrager nach Gütern sind, wenn diese sie beschäftigen würden. Die „Transaktionsstruktur“[38] ist eben in einer Geldwirtschaft anders als in einer Naturalwirtschaft. Um so mehr gilt dies für eine dynamische Wirtschaft, in der die Kapitalintensität nur begrenzt variabel ist und die zusätzliche Beschäftigung mehr Sachkapital und zusätzliche Investitionen erfordert, wobei die Investitionsentscheidungen unabhängig von den Sparentscheidungen erfolgen.

Manches, was empirisch als reallohnbedingte Arbeitslosigkeit beschrieben wurde, ist in Wirklichkeit Teil dessen, was Keynes mit unfreiwilliger Arbeitslosigkeit meinte. Freilich blieb seine Definition durchaus dunkel und klärungsbedürftig: *„Men are involuntarily employed if, in the event of a small rise in the price of wage-goods relatively to the money-wage, both the aggregate supply of labour willing to work for the current money-wage and the aggregate demand for it at that wage would be greater than the existing volume of employment.“*[39] Die entscheidende Ursache, so meine Interpretation, ist ein Mangel an effektiver Güternachfrage, dessen Ursache wiederum nicht in zu hohen Reallöhnen liegt und nicht automatisch durch niedrigere Nominallöhne beseitigt werden kann. Der entscheidende Grund hierfür liegt nicht darin, daß einfach Nominallohnstarrheit, bedingt durch soziologische Faktoren oder Geldillusion der Arbeitsanbieter, unterstellt wird, sondern daß die Wahrscheinlichkeit groß ist, daß in der Folge von Nominallohnsenkungen auch die Güterpreise sinken, so daß die Reallöhne starr bleiben und zugleich Deflation mit investitionshemmenden Folgen droht. Daß Geldlohnsenkung zu niedrigeren Reallöhnen, mehr Güternachfrage und mehr Beschäftigung führt, ist zwar nicht ausgeschlossen, aber unsicher. Entscheidend sind letztlich die Erwartungen der Investoren.

Keynesianische Arbeitslosigkeit in dieser Fassung ist mit Reallöhnen verbunden, die für die Zunahme der Beschäftigung zu hoch sind; Keynes’ entscheidender Grund für diese Annahme liegt in der Akzeptanz der Grenzproduktivitätstheorie in der „General Theory“: *„... in general, an increase in employment can only occur to the accompaniment of a decline in the rate of real wages.“*[40] Reallohnsenkende Preissteigerungen sind demnach hinzunehmen. Diese entstehen tendenziell bei steigender Güternachfrage. Daß zuvor die Reallöhne zu hoch waren, kann verschiedene Ursachen haben, u. a. auch sinkende Güterpreise in der Folge mangelnder effektiver Nachfrage. Auch wenn man sich von der Grenzproduktivitätstheorie löst und die Annahme einer negativ geneigten Arbeitskräftenachfrage aufgibt, kön-

---

38 Leijonhufvud, A., S. 86

39 Keynes, J.M., General Theory, S. 15

40 Keynes, J.M.: The General Theory, S. 17

nen zu hohe Reallöhne und damit ein „profit squeeze“ einer Zunahme der Beschäftigung entgegenstehen. Diese Erweiterung des Begriffs unfreiwilliger Arbeitslosigkeit ist mit Keynes zentralem Anliegen vereinbar, nämlich den beiden Einsichten, daß die Reallöhne nicht auf dem Arbeitsmarkt gebildet und verändert werden können und daß die Beseitigung unfreiwilliger Arbeitslosigkeit zusätzliche effektive Nachfrage erfordert. In dieser ersten Version unfreiwilliger Arbeitslosigkeit wäre also die Senkung der Reallöhne (relativ zur Produktivität) eine notwendige, aber nicht hinreichende Bedingung für mehr Beschäftigung, die nur auf dem Umweg über die Gütermärkte realisierbar ist.

Was aber passiert, wenn jene leichten Preissteigerungen, die Keynes für notwendig hielt, geldpolitisch nicht toleriert werden? Oder wenn die Arbeitnehmer im Falle derartiger Preissteigerungen rasch mit Nominallohnsteigerungen reagieren? Unter diesen Bedingungen ist die Wahrscheinlichkeit groß, daß sich unfreiwillige Arbeitslosigkeit verfestigt. Nun kommt es auf ein kluges, abgestimmtes Verhalten von Geld-, Tariflohn- und Fiskalpolitik an. Diese Variante keynesianischer unfreiwilliger Arbeitslosigkeit, bei der ein mehr oder minder kräftiger „profit squeeze“ eingetreten ist, ähnelt zwar der klassischen Arbeitslosigkeit, weil in beiden Fällen die Lohnquote sowie die Lohnstückkosten zu hoch sind, jedoch sind die Unterschiede aufgrund der eingangs erwähnten Kriterien (b) und (c) in Wirklichkeit sehr groß. Die Herausbildung „richtiger“ Reallöhne bzw. einer „angemessenen“ Gewinnquote ist keine Sache des Arbeitsmarktes, sondern marktendogenes Resultat der gesamtwirtschaftlichen Dynamik. Eine „Keynessche“ Sicht des Verhältnisses von Nominal- bzw. Reallohn und Beschäftigung postuliert einen je nach makroökonomischen Konstellationen variablen Zusammenhang, im Gegensatz zur starren neoklassischen „Gesetzmäßigkeit“[41].

Die zweite Variante keynesianischer Arbeitslosigkeit trägt sowohl Keynes' Distanzierung von der Grenzproduktivitätstheorie im Jahre 1939 als auch Malinvaud Rechnung. Diese Form unfreiwilliger Arbeitslosigkeit liegt dann vor, wenn die Reallöhne der Grenzproduktivität entsprechen oder darunter liegen, so daß die Kapitalrentabilität nicht beeinträchtigt ist (abgesehen vom Einfluß schwacher Kapazitätsauslastung). Die Arbeitsnachfrage ist allein wegen mangelnder Güternachfrage zu gering. Das Güterangebot ist zunächst durch die Nachfrage rationiert; im Zuge der nachfolgenden Anpassungsprozesse verschieben sich jedoch die Nachfrage- und / oder Angebotsfunktion dergestalt, daß ein neues markträumendes Gleichgewicht auf niedrigerem Output-Niveau erreicht wird (Gleichgewicht bei Unterbeschäftigung). Klammert man Realkasseneffekte infolge von Lohn-Preis-Deflation aus, dann führt nur eine exogene bzw. politisch induzierte Steigerung der Güternachfrage zu mehr Beschäftigung. Die Reallöhne brauchen dabei nicht zu sinken (sie dürfen es auch nicht), aber es darf auch keine inflationäre Geldlohndynamik entstehen.

---

41 Vgl. Bhaduri, A., Marglin, St.: Unemployment and real wage: the economic basis for contesting political ideologies. In: Cambridge Journal of Economics, Vol. 14 / 1990, S. 375 ff.

**Typologien zur Unterscheidung klassischer und keynesianischer Arbeitslosigkeit**

| Theorieansatz | klassische Arbeitslosigkeit | keynesianische Arbeitslosigkeit |
|---|---|---|
| Neoklassischer „mainstream" | Reallohn > Grenzproduktivität der Arbeit, Nominallöhne bestimmen Reallöhne, kein Mangel an Güternachfrage | temporärer Nachfragemangel, konjunkjunkturell oder durch Nachfrageschocks bedingt |
| Konzeptionen konjunktureller / struktureller Arbeitslosigkeit | strukturelle Arbeitslosigkeit, Sachkapitalmangel bei ausgelasteten Kapazitäten, Reallöhne zu hoch | konjunkturelle Arbeitslosigkeit bei unterausgelasteten Kapazitäten, Nachfrageschwächen |
| neukeynesianische Ungleichgewichtstheorie (Malinvaud) | zu hohe Reallöhne, Überschußnachfrage am Gütermarkt | Mangel an Güternachfrage bei fixen Preisen / Löhnen, vollbeschäftigungskonforme Reallöhne |
| Theorie der natürlichen Arbeitslosigkeit | persistenter Bodensatz an Arbeitslosen aufgrund mangelnder Arbeitsmarktflexibilität | temporäre konjunkturelle / nachfragebedingte Arbeitslosigkeit |
| Theorie der inflationsstabilen Arbeitslosigkeit (NAIRU) | NAIRU = „strukturelle" Arbeitslosigkeit, zu hohe Nominal- bzw. Reallöhne | temporäre Arbeitslosigkeit, durch Nachfrageexpansion inflationsneutral abbaubar |
| Konzept der Lohnlücke | Reallohn > geschätzter vollbeschäftigungskonformer Reallohn, durch Nominallohnsenkung abbaubar | bei vollbeschäftigungskonformen Reallöhnen bestehende Arbeitslosigkeit, meist temporär |
| Keynes / keynesianische Theorie | friktionelle und freiwillige Arbeitslosigkeit | Mangel an effektiver Nachfrage, vor allem schwache Investitionstätigkeit, konjunkturelle und wachstumsdefizitäre Arbeits losigkeit, Reallöhne entweder zu hoch oder vollbeschäftigungskonform, Reallöhne nicht am Arbeitsmarkt bestimmbar, unfreiwillige Arbeitslosigkeit |

Keynes bestritt nicht die Möglichkeit jener Formen von Arbeitslosigkeit, die die „Klassiker" für die alleinigen Formen von Arbeitslosigkeit hielten: friktionelle und freiwillige Arbeitslosigkeit[42]. Im weiteren Sinne wäre auch Mismatch-Arbeitslosigkeit hinzuzufügen. Aber Keynes war überzeugt, daß diese Formen der Arbeits-

[42] Keynes, J.M., General Theory, S. 6

losigkeit, die simultan neben der unfreiwilligen existieren, nicht den Kern moderner Massenarbeitslosigkeit ausmachen.

Die meisten Versuche zu Typologien von keynesianischer und klassischer Arbeitslosigkeit, wie sie im Schema zusammenfassend dargestellt sind, sind aus keynesianischer Sicht Hybride, theoretisch brüchig und fragil – Keynes' Analyse wird nur in verstümmelter Form integriert. Keynesianische Arbeitslosigkeit wird viel zu eng gefaßt, insbesondere weil zu hohe Reallöhne und ein zu geringer Sachkapitalstock als mit ihr nicht vereinbar angesehen werden. So wundert es nicht, daß der überwiegende Teil der heutigen Arbeitslosigkeit als klassisch (fehl-)diagnostiziert wird und folglich die makroökonomischen Ursachen der tatsächlich existierenden Arbeitslosigkeit bei weitem unterschätzt werden. Daß damit die Bedeutung makroökonomischer Politik zum Abbau der Massenarbeitslosigkeit ebenfalls unterschätzt wird, ergibt sich daraus.

## Summary


### Classical and Keynesian Unemployment – A Critique of Hybrid Typologies

There are numerous variants of hybrid typologies distinguishing classical and Keynesian unempoyment. Their common feature is perceiving classical unemployment as characterized by three criterions: too high real wages with respect to marginal productivity of labour; classical unemployment can be reduced by autonomous money wage decreases including more downward nominal wage flexibility (voluntary unemployment); no lack of effective demand on commodity markets (or automatic demand increases due to lowering money wages). The broad consensus among mainstream economics is the proposition that the high and persistent European unemployment is mainly „structural" and „classical" (in differing meanings) but with the exception of a small temporary part not Keynesian; thus macroeconomic policy is rejected as inappropriate and futile or even counterproductive.

The paper reviews four alternative typologies: (1) cyclical and capital-shortage (in this sense structural) unemployment; (2) Malinvauds disequilibrium approach of classical and keynesian regimes according to different combinations of buyers' and sellers' markets on labour and commodity markets; (3) the conceptions of natural unemployment (NRU) and „non-accelerating-inflation-rate of unemployment" (NAIRU), both of which might be interpreted as classical unemployment whereas the remaining temporary unemployment is Keynesian; (4) measurement of wage gaps which are supposed to indicate the extent of classical unemployment. None of these alternatives can furnish a consistent theoretical base for distinguishing classical and Keynesian unemployment. Keynes' critique of the classical concept of voluntary unemployment is applicable to all four variants of classical unemployment; almost all typologies rest on rather traditional classical or neoclassical assumptions which deny the possibility of a persistent underemployment equilibrium due to involuntary unemployment.

This perception of Keynesian or involuntary unemployment is far away from being reduced to temporary cyclical unemployment; Keynesian unemployment can be persistent; it can include deficient growth unemployment due to capital shortage and low investment; it is at least similar to both types of Malinvaud's unemployment; it can be part of the NAIRU. There are two types of Keynesian unemployment – the first with a profit squeeze, the second without: Reducing the first requires as a necessary but not sufficient condition lower real wages (relative to productivity) and a change in the income distribution, the second does not. The common crucial points for both types are the lack of efficient demand and the conclusion that adequate real wages cannot be achieved on the labour market via lower money wages but only as a result of the macroeconomic process. Those hybrid typologies reviewed in this paper integrate only a truncated and narrow version of Keynesian unemployment. When the understanding of Keynesian unemployment is broadened, the major part of current mass unemployment must be identified as Keynesian due to macroeconomic causes (except frictional and mismatch-unemployment). This diagnosis underlines the impact of macroeconomic policy.

# II. Globalization and Employment

# Nationale Beschäftigungspolitik bei globalisierten Märkten?

Von Hans-Joachim Heinemann, Hannover

I. Der Überlegung, ob es auf globalisierten Märkten noch eine nationale Beschäftigungspolitik geben kann, sollte die Frage vorangestellt werden, ob überhaupt, also auch gegebenenfalls in einer geschlossenen Volkswirtschaft, noch eine (staatliche) Beschäftigungspolitik möglich ist. Die heute dominierende angebotsorientierte Sichtweise, die inzwischen auch weitgehend die Position des Sachverständigenrats zur Begutachtung der gesamtwirtschaftlichen Entwicklung beherrscht, läßt den Schluß zu, daß beschäftigungssteigernde Effekte nur durch Flexibilisierung und Lohnzurückhaltung auf den Arbeitsmärkten möglich erscheinen. Obgleich wir in der Bundesrepublik Deutschland seit längerem zumindest in Teilbereichen steigende Gewinne der Unternehmen bei zugleich stagnierenden bzw. sogar sinkenden Realeinkommen der Arbeitnehmer verzeichnen, sind der Sachverständigenrat und wohl die Mehrzahl der Ökonomen der Meinung, daß die Unternehmens- und Kapitaleinkommen immer noch nicht ausreichend sind, um einen Umschwung auf dem Arbeitsmarkt herbeizuführen. Nun läßt sich nicht leugnen, daß in den USA, Großbritannien und anderen Ländern deutliche Beschäftigungserfolge zu verzeichnen sind, die u.a. auf einem Ausbau des Dienstleistungssektors beruhen, allerdings auch zunächst in manchen Bereichen mit Lohneinbußen und vor allem mit der Verteilung der Gesamtarbeitszeit auf mehrere Jobs verbunden sind. In Kontinentaleuropa sieht die Situation oftmals wesentlich schlechter aus, wobei die Länder unterschiedliche Vorstellungen von der Lösung des Problems haben: Während Deutschland auf Veränderungen auf dem Arbeitsmarkt setzt, neigt die französische Regierung traditionellen beschäftigungspolitischen Wegen zu, möglicherweise ungeachtet früherer Mißerfolge während der ersten Präsidentschaft Mitterand.

Offizielle Meinung hierzulande ist, daß trotz möglicher Gefahren für die Binnennachfrage unter dem Produktivitätsanstieg bleibende Lohnsteigerungen zu fordern sind, um die Wettbewerbsfähigkeit der deutschen Volkswirtschaft zu sichern. Hier kommt nun erstmals das Globalisierungsargument zum Zuge. Was die Wettbewerbsfähigkeit anbelangt, ist auf Paul Krugman (1996 a, b) zu verweisen, der Wettbewerbsfähigkeit zwar für Unternehmen, nicht aber für Staaten als sinnvolles Argument sieht, da im zweiten Fall immer der Gedanke eines Nullsummenspiels herumgeistert. Im wesentlichen liegt der angebotsorientierten Sichtweise die Vorstellung zugrunde, daß die Effizienz der Märkte durch die richtigen Preissignale erreicht würde, was für den Arbeitsmarkt eben entsprechende Löhne ohne Beachtung möglicher Interdependenzen zu anderen Märkten bedeuten würde. Für die Finanzmärkte hat Wolfgang Filc kürzlich (1997) nachgewiesen, daß diese keineswegs immer hinreichend effizient sind, so daß von ihnen auch falsche Signale auf Geld- und Gütermärkte ausgehen können. Vergessen sind bei der angebotsorientierten Sichtweise oftmals makroökonomische Ungleichgewichtstheorien wie von Clower, Barro oder Malinvaud, ein Handel zu falschen Preisen scheint nicht mehr zeitgemäß.

Die triste Situation auf dem europäischen Arbeitsmarkt veranlaßt Viviane Forrester (1997) dazu, vom Terror der Ökonomie zu sprechen. Sieht man die Unruhen vor einigen Wochen, v. a. in französischen Vorstädten, merkt man, wovon sie spricht. Weniger spektakulär, aber für den Wirtschaftswissenschaftler vielleicht wichtiger, ist die Kritik von Richard Hauser (1997) an der oftmals zu einseitigen Sichtweise des Sachverständigenrats, die entgegen früherer Zurückhaltung Überlegungen zur Wirtschaftsordnung und zu Gerechtigkeitszielen meist der angebotsorientierten Betrachtung unterordnet, ohne mögliche Alternativen genügend zu berücksichtigen. Nimmt man die offene Volkswirtschaft, kommt man auf das Buch von Peter Martin und Harald Schumann „Die Globalisierungsfalle“ (1996). Beide sehen in der Globalisierung der Märkte die Gefahr, daß nur noch 20 % der Arbeitswilligen Beschäftigung finden und daß z. B. in Asien und Afrika entstehende Reservearmeen die Arbeitsmöglichkeiten in der „ersten Welt“ drastisch verändern.

II. Globalisierte Märkte sind keineswegs neueren Datums, auch wenn die Bedeutung internationaler Produktion in den vergangenen zwanzig Jahren deutlich gewachsen ist. Die rasche Zunahme internationaler Handelsbeziehungen – aber auch der Arbeits- und vor allem der Kapitalmobilität – hat die Möglichkeiten nationaler Wirtschaftspolitik einerseits erheblich beeinträchtigt; andererseits hat die gestiegene Interdependenz der Finanz- und Geldpolitik auch neue Möglichkeiten eröffnet; vor allem aber hat die Liberalisierung der Weltwirtschaft wohlfahrts- und beschäftigungswirksame Entwicklungen gefördert, nicht zuletzt durch einen hohen internationalen Technologietransfer.

Das einfache nachfrageorientierte Multiplikatormodell zeigt, daß durch die dem Inlandskreislauf entzogenen Importe der Einkommens- und Beschäftigungsmultiplikator umso kleiner wird, je stärker die Importabhängigkeit einer Volkswirtschaft ist. Berücksichtigt man Wechselkurs- und Preiseffekte, so kann eine Investitionszunahme über Zinssteigerungen wechselkursmindernde Kapitalimporte bzw. über die Gütermärkte Preissteigerungen auslösen, die beide zu einer realen Aufwertung führen, welche den ursprünglichen expansiven Effekt nicht nur dämpft, sondern möglicherweise beseitigt. Aus dem Mundell-Fleming-Modell wissen wir, daß je nach dem Wechselkursregime und entsprechend zinsreagiblen Kapitalbewegungen Fiskal- oder Geldpolitik wirkungslos bleiben. Auf der anderen Seite profitiert – wenn man vom Laursen-Metzler-Effekt absieht – ein Land von der Beschäftigungspolitik anderer Länder, solange diese nicht mit einer Nachfrageverschiebung, sondern mit einer Nachfrageexpansion verbunden ist.

Die klassische güterwirtschaftliche Außenhandelstheorie kennt üblicherweise keine globalen Beschäftigungseffekte. Das vorhandene Potential an Arbeit und Kapital wird stets voll beschäftigt; internationale Handelsbeziehungen beeinflussen also nicht die Einsatzmenge, sondern die Verteilung der Ressourcen. Dies wird anders, wenn aufgrund irgendwelcher Marktunvollkommenheiten (z. B. Mindestpreise oder sektorspezifische Faktoren) Import- oder Exportänderungen den Faktoreinsatz insgesamt verändern (z. B. Vent for Surplus-Gedanke bei Adam Smith).

Grundsätzlich braucht sich dieses Bild nicht zu ändern, wenn man neben Handelsbeziehungen auch zwischenstaatliche Kapitalbewegungen berücksichtigt, die sowohl in Verbindung mit Außenhandelsströmen als auch als reine Finanztransaktionen heute eine noch vor zwanzig Jahren kaum erwartete Höhe erreicht haben und bei manchen die Besorgnis ausgelöst haben, ob nicht die weltwirtschaftliche Stabilität gefährdet sei, so daß z. B. Tobin an Steuern auf spekulative Kapitalströme denkt. Übrigens hat schon Keynes in internationalen Kapitalbewegungen nicht nur eine Chance, sondern auch ein Risiko für die Weltwirtschaft gesehen und nicht von ungefähr sieht das Bretton Woods-Abkommen zwar die Konvertibilität für Leistungstransaktionen, nicht aber unbedingt für Finanztransaktionen vor.

Expansive beschäftigungspolitische Maßnahmen z. B. können sowohl Kapitalzuflüsse wie -abflüsse anregen. Ist eine entsprechende Fiskal- und Geldpolitik mit Zinssenkungen verbunden, so sind – v. a., wenn sie auch Abwertungserwartungen auslösen – Kapitalabflüsse zu erwarten. Eine mit Zinserhöhungen verbundene expansive Finanzpolitik braucht keineswegs Kapitalzuströme auszulösen, wenn nämlich an ihrem Erfolg gezweifelt wird, so daß hier Abwertungserwartungen wahrscheinlicher als Aufwertungserwartungen werden.

Globalisierung wird meist im Zusammenhang mit der wachsenden internationalen Produktion gesehen. Zwar reagieren Direktinvestitionen sicher nicht so kurzfristig wie Portfolioinvestitionen auf Zins- und Wechselkursänderungen. Neben der Erschließung von Absatz- und Beschaffungsmärkten spielen aber auch geld- und finanzpolitische Veränderungen im Gefolge beschäftigungspolitischer Maßnahmen eine große Rolle. Hohe Unternehmenssteuern können dann kontraproduktiv sein, selbst wenn sie zur Finanzierung zusätzlicher Staatsausgaben dienen.

III. Daß die traditionelle makroökonomische Beschäftigungspolitik in einer Welt es umso schwerer hat, je stärker die Güter- und Faktormärkte und Produktionsvorgänge international miteinander verbunden sind, könnte ein Argument für eine internationale Koordinierung der Beschäftigungspolitik sein. Auf Gipfeltreffen der Europäischen Union wurde auch genau dies verschiedentlich angeregt, von der Bundesregierung allerdings abgelehnt. Deutschland möchte die Beschäftigungspolitik in nationaler Verantwortung belassen, wobei freilich nicht an die Konjunkturpolitik alten Stils gedacht wird. Während in der Europäischen Union und teils auch darüber hinaus die Stabilitätspolitik zumindest bei der Geldwertstabilität Erfolge aufweist, gilt dies für die Beschäftigungspolitik nicht. Trotz hoher Arbeitslosigkeit wird hier ein Handlungsbedarf nicht gesehen, da die angebotsorientierte Sichtweise Maßnahmen zur Nachfragesteuerung nicht als erfolgreich ansieht und da die Angebotsseite sich eben nicht für eine koordinierte Konjunkturpolitik zu eignen scheint. Trotz der Begrenzung öffentlicher Beschäftigungsprogramme über Budgetdefizite z. B. aufgrund der Maastrichter Verträge sind aber Verschiebungen zwischen verschiedenen Staatsausgabenbereichen möglich, die Beschäftigungserfolge haben können.

Die angebotsorientierte Sichtweise geht zwar davon aus, daß die Märkte und vor allem der Arbeitsmarkt für den Abbau von Ungleichgewichten verantwortlich sind, was aber die Wirtschaftspolitik nicht aus der Verantwortung entläßt, geeignete Rahmenbedingungen zu schaffen. Das heißt einmal, die Steuersätze so festzulegen, daß unternehmerische Investitionen angeregt werden. Hierbei mag es wünschenswert sein, bei einer allgemeinen Investitionsschwäche vor allem auf Inlandsinvestitionen zu setzen und ausländische Unternehmer zu veranlassen, hierzulande zu investieren. Aber auch deutsche Investitionen im Ausland können die inländische Produktion und Beschäftigung anregen. Das zu geringe Investitionsvolumen in Deutschland – das im übrigen nicht für alle Bereiche gilt – ist freilich nicht allein auf zu hohe Steuern zurückzuführen. Investitionen und Produktion leiden auch unter staatlichen Regulierungsmaßnahmen und oftmals sicher auch unter zu hohen Lohnkosten.

Regulierungsfehler sind mit verantwortlich für Inflexibilitäten auf den Arbeitsmärkten; zu geringe Abstände zwischen niedrigen Löhnen und Sozialhilfesätzen schaffen zu wenig Anreize, auch schlecht bezahlte Arbeitsplätze anzunehmen. Strittig ist, ob nicht Lohnkostenzuschüsse zum Abbau von Arbeitslosigkeit beitragen könnten. Weniger umstritten ist, daß erhöhte Beschäftigung in (keineswegs nur schlecht bezahlten) Dienstleistungen wünschenswert wäre, auch wenn dies für den einzelnen bedeuten kann, daß er gleichzeitig oder in kürzeren zeitlichen Abständen mehrere Tätigkeiten ausübt.

Ohne Zweifel gehört zu einer sinnvollen Angebotspolitik die Verbesserung des Bildungswesens. Zwar hat die Bundesrepublik durch ihr duales Ausbildungssystem Vorteile gegenüber manch anderen Ländern. Die Schwierigkeiten, genügend Ausbildungsplätze bereitzustellen, ist sicher auch den Arbeitgebern anzulasten; die Wirtschaftspolitik hat hier jedoch ebenso Aufgaben wie in der Verbesserung der Studienbedingungen!

Nachhaltige Produktivitätsverbesserungen sind entscheidend für die Zunahme der Wettbewerbsfähigkeit von Unternehmen, für das Einkommen von Arbeitnehmern, Kapitaleignern und Unternehmern und damit auch für die Standortbedingungen eines Landes in der Weltwirtschaft. Und es ist sicher irrig zu glauben, dauerhafte Wachstumserfolge ließen sich allein auf Inputzuwächse gründen (Krugman 1996c diskutiert dies z. B. im Zusammenhang mit der Entwicklung in den sozialistischen Ländern und dem „Wachstumswunder“ in Südostasien).

Auf manchen der genannten Gebiete hat die Bundesrepublik Nachholbedarf. Nicht nur die USA oder das UK sind hier weiter; auch die Niederlande, Dänemark oder Neuseeland stehen besser da. Eine so verstandene Angebotspolitik gehört zwar zunächst zur nationalen Beschäftigungspolitik, eine internationale Koordinierung könnte jedoch sehr vorteilhaft sein. Allerdings ist zu erwarten, daß Erfolge hier mit Einschnitten in der Vermögens- und Einkommensverteilung verbunden sein können. Zwangsläufig erscheint das aber nicht: Eine stärkere Hinwendung von der direkten zur indirekten Besteuerung und eine Belastung nicht produktiv genutzter Vermögen, könnten sich als sinnvoll erweisen.

Auf jeden Fall scheint die Abstimmung solcher Strategien auf der Angebotsseite erfolgversprechender als der Versuch, nachfragewirksame Programme international zu koordinieren.

IV. Internationale Wirtschaftsbeziehungen haben als Kernstück seit längerem nicht mehr allein den Handel mit Gütern und Dienstleistungen; die Globalisierung reicht in die Finanz- und sonstigen Faktormärkte und in den weltweiten Wettbewerb unternehmerischer Entscheidungen. Gelten die Argumente für die Liberalisierung des Güterhandels ebenso in der erweiterten Globalisierung? Trotz mancher Bedenken, die z. B. auch in der neuen Welthandelsorganisation nach wie vor eine Rolle spielen, ist die Frage auch gerade aus beschäftigungspolitischer Sicht zu bejahen. Zwar ist nicht zu bestreiten, daß die asiatische Finanzkrise auch für die USA und Europa Gefahren beinhaltet (vgl. Krugman, 1996c und Hesse / Auria 1998) und es ist ebenfalls nicht zu übersehen, daß die Schuldenkrise z. B. der lateinamerikanischen Länder viele Probleme aufgeworfen hat; aber es könnte auch sein, daß die Finanzmärkte in Westeuropa, Japan und den USA die Warnzeichen nicht richtig einschätzten und aus ihren Versäumnissen lernen.

Seit geraumer Zeit hat in der Literatur wie in der Politik die strategische Handelspolitik Furore gemacht, wozu eine im Gegensatz zu früher weniger liberale US-amerikanische Politik und ein wachsender Hang zur Regionalisierung beigetragen haben. Anders als früher betont, haben im Zuge steigender Skalenerträge auch ökonomisch ansonsten kleinere Länder Möglichkeiten, Handelsvorteile zu erzielen, die allerdings meist zu Lasten anderer Länder und oftmals nicht geförderter Sektoren im eigenen Land ausgehen. Eine Wohlfahrtsverbesserung ist somit weder innerhalb der solche Strategien praktizierenden Länder noch weltweit zu erwarten.

Sicher ist unstrittig, daß wie schon bei reinen Handelsbeziehungen noch stärker im Zuge der weitergehenden Globalisierung Wettbewerbsverschärfungen zu erwarten sind, die für diejenigen Nachteile bringen, die bisher Vorteile aus Marktunvollkommenheiten ziehen konnten. Und es ist ferner zu erwarten, daß für diese u.U. langfristige Anpassungsprozesse oder sogar dauerhafte Wohlfahrtsverluste die Folge sind, insbesondere, wenn auch seitens der Wirtschaftspolitik erforderliche Umstellungen nicht in Angriff genommen werden. Aber das kann kaum als Argument für dauerhafte Wettbewerbsbeschränkungen dienen. Vielmehr sind die Kosten verstärkter Abhängigkeiten durch verbesserte Informationen und Mechanismen zur

Verringerung von Unsicherheiten, die aus Güter- und Finanzmärkten herrühren, zu verringern. Dies kann sicher durch die Flexibilität erhöhende nationalstaatliche Maßnahmen erleichtert werden, kann aber auch durch internationale Koordinierung von Strategien gefördert werden. Das bedeutet nicht, daß z. B. fiskal- oder sozialpolitische Politiken harmonisiert werden müssen. Obwohl die an Bedeutung gewinnenden Regionalisierungen die weltweite Liberalisierung nicht unbedingt fördern müssen, können sie trotz u. U. neuer monopolistischer Gefährdungen den Weg hierzu erleichtern. Dies ist auch ein Argument gegen die vielerorts nach wie vor bestehende Skepsis gegenüber der Europäischen Währungsunion.

V. Was folgt aus dem Gesagten für die Frage, ob nationale Beschäftigungspolitik in einer globalisierten Welt noch möglich erscheint? Man kann die Frage mit „ja" oder mit „nein" beantworten. Die zunehmende Globalisierung der Märkte führt dazu, daß die wirtschaftlichen Grenzen zwischen den Ländern durchlässiger werden; aber auch in anderen Feldern der Politik bedeutet das einen Verlust an Souveränität. Vor allem dort, wo bisher Märkte unter Friktionen und monopolistischen Verzerrungen gelitten haben, wird dies für die Beteiligten Einkommens- und Beschäftigungsverluste implizieren, die umso nachhaltiger sein werden, je weniger man bereit ist, sich dem internationalen Wettbewerb zu stellen. Man sollte aber auch nicht vergessen, daß größere Märkte einen Risikopool schaffen, der die Kosten hausgemachter Abhängigkeiten verringern kann. Im internationalen Rahmen sind Vorkehrungen gegen Instabilitäten anzustreben. Ob in einem System weitgehend flexibler Wechselkurse und größerer Zinsunterschiede nicht versucht werden sollte, rein spekulative Kapitalbewegungen – so man sie als solche identifizieren kann – einzudämmen, bleibt zu überlegen (Tobin-Steuer). Ob insoweit nicht nur regional, sondern auch weltweit Fiskal- und Geldpolitik besser koordiniert werden können, um zumindest Zielzonen für die Wechselkurse zu schaffen, ist zu fragen.

Auf jeden Fall ist ein Währungssystem mit stabileren Wechselkursen als in den letzten 25 Jahren wünschenswert. Trotz mancher Risiken ist in Europa die bevorstehende Europäische Währungsunion positiv zu werten.

Das „ja" auf die obige Frage ist eher angebots- als nachfrageorientiert begründet und setzt auf die von der Ökonomie eigentlich akzeptierte Vorstellung von der Effizienz des Wettbewerbs. Sicher ist diese kaum zu realisieren ohne ein Sicherheitsnetz einer möglichst länderübergreifenden Wettbewerbspolitik.

Die nationale Beschäftigungspolitik ist unseres Erachtens nicht von der Wachstums- und Wettbewerbspolitik zu trennen. Sie muß auf Produktivitätsfortschritte setzen, was nicht undifferenziert geschehen darf, sondern die Flexibilität der Märkte beachten muß. Daß alle, insbesondere aber die wirtschaftlich fortgeschrittenen Länder, zunehmende Dienstleistungsgesellschaften werden, ist mehr als bisher zu beachten.

Produktivitätssteigerungen sprechen nicht nur für die Liberalisierung der Güterströme, sondern auch der Faktorbewegungen. Trotz eines verständlichen Interesses an mehr Investitionen im Inland ist die Kritik an zunehmenden Auslandsinvestitionen kaum berechtigt.

Trotz unserer im wesentlichen auch angebotsorientierten Sichtweise sollte nicht verkannt werden, daß Verbesserungen der Angebotsbedingungen dann nicht ausreichen, wenn diese zu viel Zeit benötigen. Gerade die Interdependenz der Märkte verlangt auch, die Nachfrageseite im Auge zu halten. Gelingt beides, so müssen befürchtete Verteilungseffekte und soziale Konflikte nicht eintreten.

## Summary

National employment policy in a global world? Markets for commodities and factors have become more and more interdependent. This and the increasing importance of direct investments and international production mean that national economic policies are becoming more and more difficult. Even in the simple Keynesian world expenditure increases in one country may not succeed because of increasing propensities to import as a consequence of changing real exchange rates. Not only in a globalized world but also in a closed economy traditional macropolicies may fail and should be substituted by more efforts in improvements at the supply side. That means that markets should become more flexible than they still are and that the consequences of the increasing importance of services for the job markets have to be kept in mind. It cannot be denied that as a consequence of globalization the risks for entrepreneurs, investors and consumers may increase. The question is, whether there are possibilities to stabilize international financial markets for instance without reducing the efficiency of international cooperation. We do not believe that the chances ot the economy have decreased by international competition in the world market. The tasks of economic policy have become more difficult and better international coordination may support the markets for goods and assets.

The end of the Bretton Woods System and the change to flexible exchange rates have increased the danger of instability. Insofar capital movements do not follow differences in productivity but do react only to expectations on changes in exchange rates they are not efficient. The EMS and the ECU are helpful to overcome international destabilization.

## Literatur

*Filc,* Wolfgang (1997): Das Ende der Effizienzträume, Hamburger Jahrbuch für Wirtschafts- und Gesellschaftspolitik 42. Jg. S. 9 - 28. – *Forrester,* Viviane (1997): Der Terror der Ökonomie, dt. Übersetzung, Wien. – *Hauser,* Richard (1997) Beratung ohne Auftrag zum Abbau des Sozialstaats – zu den sozialpolitischen Reformvorstellungen des Sachverständigenrates, Hamburger Jahrbuch für Wirtschafts- und Gesellschaftspolitik 42. Jg. S. 159 - 182. – *Hesse,* Helmut und Laura Auria (1998): Die Finanzkrise in Südostasien – Ursachen und Auswirkungen auf die Weltwirtschaft. Vortrag beim Ibero-Amerika Institut für Wirtschaftsforschung der Universität Göttingen am 6. 2. 1998. – *Kromphardt,* Jürgen (1997): Direkt-Investitionen – Zerstören oder Erhalten von Arbeitsplätzen und internationaler Wettbewerbsfähigkeit in Zeiten der Globalisierung?, in Globalisierung – Ende nationaler Wirtschaftspolitik?, Kocheler Kreis – Friedrich-Ebert-Stiftung, Bonn, S. 13 - 28. – *Krugman,* Paul (1996 a), Competitiveness: A Dangerous Obsession, in Krugman, Pop Internationalism, Cambridge (Mass), S. 3 - 24. – *Krugman,* Paul (1996 b), Myths and Realities of US Competitiveness, ibid., S. 87 - 104. – *Krugman,* Paul (1996 c), The Myth of Asia's Miracle, ibid., S. 167 - 188. – *Martin,* Hans Peter u. Harald *Schumann,* (1996): Die Globalisierungsfalle, Reinbek bei Hamburg. – Sachverständigenrat zur Begutachtung der gesamtwirtschaftlichen Entwicklung (1996 f): Jahresgutachten der letzten Jahre.

# Global Macro Policies for Reducing Persistent High Unemployment Rates in OECD Countries

By Paul Davidson, Knoxville / Tennessee

The world unemployment situation is very grim. In most industrialized countries unemployment remains stubbornly high. The average unemployment rate in the EU was 11.3% in July 1996 (ILO, 1996). With the exception of the United States unemployment rates in OECD nations have reached or remained close to historical highs not seen since the Second World War. The 1997 Asian financial collapse implies higher unemployment rates for Europe, Japan, and the United States – and perhaps even Latin America in 1998. Does this dire trend mean that with the globalization of the market system, there is little or no hope of restoring full employment in most economies around the world?

I shall argue that reforming the world's international payments system combined with national macropolicies to expand aggregate demand internally is the only possible route that can restore a golden age of economic growth similar to what the global economy experienced between 1950 and 1973. This message is contrary to the conventional wisdom of mainstream economists who argue that the primary source of today's persistently high unemployment is labour market rigidities. The conventional wisdom, therefore, advocates micropolicies to loosen domestic labor markets to increase employment.

This belief in loosening labor mobility to create employment, I call "the laxative theory for curing unemployment". Even if such laxative policies were to succeed in increasing employment in any one country it can do so only by exporting part of this nation's unemployment to its trading partners. Institution of these laxative policies in many nations simultaneously will invoke a negative sum game that will unleash deflationary forces around the globe.

## I. The golden age of economic development

The Bretton Woods years of 1950 to 1973 were an era of unsurpassed economic global prosperity. Adelman (1991) has characterized the Bretton Woods period as a "Golden Age of Economic Development ... an era of unprecedented sustained economic growth in both developed and developing countries". *Table 1* provides the statistical evidence (augmented by more recent data) that Adelman used in reaching her conclusion about our economic golden age.

*Table 1*

**Real GDP (annualized growth rate)**

| Years | Real GDP per capita | | |
|---|---|---|---|
| | World | OECD Nations | Developing Nations* |
| 1700 - 1820 | na | 0.2% | na |
| 1820 - 1913 | na | 1.2% | na |
| 1919 - 1940 | na | 1.9% | na |
| 1950 - 1973 | na | 4.9% | 3.3% |
| 1973 - 1981 | na | 1.3% | na |
| 1981 - 1990 | 1.2% | 2.2% | 1.2% |
| 1991 - 1993 | – 0.4% | 0.6% | 2.6% |
| 1994 - 1995 | 1.3% | 2.3% | 2.9% |
| | Total real GDP | | |
| | World | OECD Nations | Developing Nations* |
| 1950 - 1973 | na | 5.9% | 5.5% |
| 1966 - 1973 | 5.1% | 4.8% | 6.9% |
| 1974 - 1980 | 3.4% | 2.9% | 5.0% |
| 1981 - 1990 | 3.2% | 3.1% | 3.3% |
| 1991 - 1993 | 1.2% | 1.2% | 4.6% |
| 1994 - 1995 | 2.8% | 2.6% | 4.7% |

* Excluding Eastern and Central Europe and Former Soviet Union.

Although reliable statistics on GDP per capita before 1700 are not available, it is probably true that from biblical times until the Renaissance the average standard of living in the world showed little improvement from year to year or even generation to generation. Improvement in economic living standards started with the development of merchant capitalism during the Renaissance period in Europe. Between 1700 and 1820 (see *Table 1)* per capita income increased at an average annual rate of 0.2 per cent. If the average person lived approximately 45 years, the person's standard of living increased less than 10 per cent from the time of birth to death.

Living standards started to increase substantially early in the $19^{th}$ century. The industrial revolution period was truly revolutionary. Between 1820 and 1913, living standards grew at 1.2 per cent per annum – much faster than in the previous century. Labor productivity increased 6.65 times greater than during the previous 100 years. Per capita income of the advanced nations more than trebled in less than 100 years. No wonder this period is often portrayed in Western literature as the era of growth of the common man. Moreover, during this period the volume of world exports grew thirty fold as a global trading economy and financial system developed with a fixed exchange rate under a gold-sterling-standard. By 1913, the degree of globalization, if measured by foreign ownership share of the world's stock of real capital, was equal to the degree of globalization today (Milberg, 1997, p. 305).

During the Golden Age of Bretton Woods, the growth rate was almost double the previous *peak* annual growth rate of the industrializing nations during the Industrial Revolution (from 1820 to 1913). Between 1950 and 1973 annual labor productivity growth was more than triple that of the industrial revolution and real GDP per capita in the developed (or OECD) nations grew 2.6 times faster than between the wars.

The resulting prosperity of the industrialized world was transmitted to the less developed nations through world trade, aid, and direct foreign investment. From 1950 - 73, annual growth in per capita GDP for *all* developing nations was 3.3 per cent, almost triple the growth experienced by the industrializing nations during the industrial revolution. GDP of the less developed countries (LDCs) increased at almost the same rate as that of the developed nations, 5.5 per cent and 5.9 per cent respectively. The higher population growth of the LDCs caused the lower per capita income growth.

*During this golden age, labor union power increased in all OECD nations. Simultaneously legislation increasing occupational safety environment was almost universally while the modern welfare state that provided historic protection for the poor reached its high-water mark adopted.* In other words, labour market rigidities increased and became commonplace during the "golden age".

Labor markets were much more flexible between the world wars. Moreover, since 1973 there has been a steady deterioration in labor union power and legislation regulating safety in the workplace. In most OECD nations the scope of the welfare state has been reduced substantially in the period since 1973. OECD growth since 1973 is approximately half of what it was during Bretton Woods and not much better than the experience of the $19^{th}$ and earlier $20^{th}$ century. Since 1973, OECD nations have suffered through persistently higher rates of unemployment, despite the fact that unions have lost power, social safety nets have been dismantled, and protective labor legislation has been relaxed.

The economic contrast for the LDCs is even more startling with average annual real income per capita declining in absolute terms since 1973. The best economic performances since the 1970s has been turned in by the newly developing nations along the Pacific rim, the Asian tigers. Nevertheless the "economic miracle"of the Asian tigers registered a significantly lower rate of economic growth than those experienced by the industrial nations during the golden age. Moreover, since the 1997 financial collapse of Asia's currencies, the hard-earned economic gains of these Asian tigers are at risk.

## II. The lesson that should have been learned

What can we conclude from these facts? First, fixed exchange rate systems are associated with better global economic performance than flexible rate systems. Second, during the post-war period until 1973 global economic performance was nothing short of spectacular despite increasing rigidities in national labor markets throughout the industrialized world. This unparalleled "golden age" experience required combining a fixed exchange rate system with another civilizing economic principle, namely that creditor nations (and/or institutions capable of providing sizable liquid foreign reserves) must accept a major share of the responsibility for solving persistent international payments imbalances and any flights of capital that may develop. Third, since the 1973 breakdown of Bretton Woods, the global economy has stumbled from one global economic crisis to another, e.g., stagflation in the 1970s, the Latin American and African Debt problems of the 1980s, and the international financial market crises of the 1990s. Global economic growth has slowed significantly while the growing global population threatens to reduce standards of living. The number of mouths to be fed are threatening to increase at a faster rate than global GDP. Economics has once more become the dismal science with its Malthusian overtones. Instead of bringing the utopian benefits promised by conservative economics, the post Bretton Woods system of flexible exchange rates and financial and labor market deregulation has generated a growing international monetary crisis. As early as 1986 New York Times columnist Flora Lewis noted that government and business leaders recognize that "the issues of trade, debt, and currency exchange rates are intertwined". Lewis warned that the world is on a course leading to an economic calamity, yet "nobody wants to speak out and be accused of setting off a panic ... the most sober judgment is that the best thing that can be done now is to buy more time for adjustments to head off a crash ... decision makers aren't going to take sensible measures until they are forced to by crisis". Is the Asian financial crisis the event that will finally galvanize public opinion in to the need for major international monetary institutional reforms?

The current international payments system does not serve the emerging global economy well. *The Financial Times* of London and *The Economist,* both previously strong advocates of today's floating rate system, have acknowledged that this system is a failure and was sold to the public and the politicians under false advertising claims[1]. Yet even today, no national leader is calling for a complete overhaul of an international payments system that is far worse than the one we abandoned in 1973. No one has the courage to speak out in public forums and suggest that the classical economic philosophy that has rationalized our economic affairs in recent decades is a formula for potential economic disaster at worst and modest global economic growth at best.

## III. The Post Keynesian explanation of persistently high OECD unemployment

Bretton Woods formed the basis of the immediate postwar international payments system. In large measure, this system was shaped by Keynes' thesis that flexible exchange rates and free international capital mobility are incompatible with global full employment and rapid economic growth in an era of multilateral free trade (cf. Felix, 1997 - 8). Operating until 1973 under an international trading system compatible with Keynes' "incompatibility thesis", OECD nations experienced unparalleled growth and prosperity.

In the 1960s, mainstream economists developed open economy models based on the classical axioms that Keynes had overthrown. These orthodox classical (supply-side) models "demonstrated" that Keynes' incompatibility thesis was wrong. Instead these classical models "demonstrated" that free trade and optimum global economic growth required a *laissez-faire* approach with flexible exchange rates, free international capital mobility and flexible domestic labor markets where those who experienced long term unemployment were naturally slated for the Darwinian dustbin. Those who called themselves Neoclassical Synthesis Keynesians had already adopted microfoundations that required these classical axioms for their closed economy models (Davidson, 1984). Consequently, these Old "Keynesians" were easy prey for the classical counterrevolution analysis of closed and open economies. Nevertheless, this successful academic resurrection of the classical system would have not been sufficient to alter the policy mix if it were not for events of the 1970s.

The 1973 oil price shock created huge international payments imbalances and unleashed inflationary forces in oil consuming nations. The resulting economic dislocation placed policy makers in a difficult position. Under the circumstances, politicians found irresistible the allure of the Panglossian siren song that "all is for the best in the best of all possible worlds provided we let well enough alone".

---

[1] The *Economist* magazine (January 6, 1990) indicated that the decade of the 1980s will be noted as one in which "the experiment with floating currencies failed". Almost two years earlier (February 17, 1987), the *Financial Times* admitted that "floating exchange rates, it is now clear, were sold on a false prospectus ... they held out a quite illusory promise of greater national autonomy ... [but] when macro policies are inconsistent and when capital is globally mobile, floating rates cannot be relied upon to keep the current accounts roughly in balance".

Without having to admit that they did not know what to do, policy-makers used the conclusions of the 1960s classical counter-revolutionary theories to justify their abandonment of any attempt to constrain international financial flows and fix exchange rates.

The resulting new international world of finance made the exchange rate itself an object of speculation. Utilizing new computer technology, financial capital could speed around the globe at the speed of light. Since the mid-1970s, international financial transactions have grown thirty times as fast as the growth in international trade (Felix, 1997 - 8). International financial flows now dominate trade payments. Exchange rate movements reflect changes in speculative positions rather than changes in patterns of trade.

Significant exchange rate movements affect the international competitive position of domestic vis-à-vis foreign industries and therefore tend to depress the inducement to invest in large projects with irreversible sunk costs. Since 1973, volatile exchange rates have made entrepreneurs more wary of undertaking large investment projects.[2] In an uncertain (nonergodic) world where the future cannot be reliably predicted from past and present price signals, volatile exchange rates undermine entrepreneurs' confidence in their ability to appraise the potential profitability of any large investment project. Every exchange rate increase not only threatens domestic industries with significant loss of export-market share but also home-market share loss as imports become less expensive. Managers realize that any upward blip in the exchange rate during the lifetime of any contemplated investment project can saddle their enterprises with irreversible costly idle capacity. Consequently, the marginal efficiency of investment is reduced.[3] The greater the uncertainty regarding future exchange rates, the less investment globally – just as Keynes (1936, ch. 17) analysis of liquidity preference and investment predicted. As a result, trade and real investment spending in open economies have become the tail wagged by the international speculative exchange rate dog.

It is not surprising, therefore, that when the free world changed from a fixed to a flexible exchange rate system, the annual growth rate in investment in plant and equipment in OECD nations fell from 6% (before 1973) to less than 3% (since 1973). Less investment growth means a slower economic growth rate in OECD nations (from 5.9% to 2.8%) while labour productivity growth declined even more dramatically (from 4.6% to 1.6%).

2 While, at the same time vastly increasing the liquidity demands of entrepreneurs, bankers, and ultimately central bankers in terms of foreign reserve holdings. The results are episodes of international liquidity crises.

3 Volatility increases the possibility of an uncertain future and encourages entrepreneurs to continually put off making investments. Hysteresis concepts have been used to explain why, when volatility occurs, even when conditions for profits brighten investors fail to undertake what would appear to be profitable investment projects under a more stable economic environment (Pindyck, 1991, p. 1134 - 5). Even in the long run, more volatility "implies a firm should hold less capital" (Pindyck 1991, p. 1139).

From a Post Keynesian perspective, the pre-1973 period was a golden age because both the international payments system *and* domestic fiscal and monetary policies tended to follow the policy prescriptions that Keynes' principle of effective demand suggests (Davidson, 1994, ch 16). Abandonment of the international monetary system that embedded Keynes' "incompatibility thesis" principle is one major factor in explaining why, since 1973, OECD economies have experienced slower economic growth, rising global unemployment, and increasing inequalities of income within each nation as well as between nations (Davidson, 1997).[4] Restoring a golden age of low unemployment, rapid economic growth and a stable international competitive structure that will allow nations to specialize in their comparative advantage industries requires reforming the international monetary system to embody the teachings of Keynes' effective demand principle while requiring each nation to be responsible for pursuing macropolicies to assure that domestic internal aggregate demand is close to full employment.

Since the 1970s, Tobin (1974) has been almost the only voice with significant visibility in the economics profession warning that "super-efficient" free capital markets with flexible exchange rates can have a "devastating impact on specific industries and whole economies" (Eichengreen, Tobin and Wyplosz, 1995). To avoid the real economic havoc brought by volatile exchange rates, Tobin advocates that governments constrain international financial flows via a "Tobin tax". Elsewhere I (Davidson, 1997) have suggested why a Tobin tax is too timid a marginal adjustment and why effective demand analysis suggests that a more fundamental reform of the international payments system is necessary.

## IV. Why the law of comparative advantage is inapplicable to our global economy

That most pop of pop economists, Paul Krugman has announced that the one universal economic truth that all economists can agree on is the "law of comparative advantage" which demonstrates that all nations gain from free trade. Unfortunately, from a Keynesian perspective, this law suffers from some severe logical weaknesses that make applying its teaching that suggests letting unregulated markets determine the nation's industrial specialization and international trade patterns can be misleading and dangerous.

The law of comparative advantage attempts to offer a proof that is irrelevant to the question at hand. To illustrate, assume there are two economies each employing 1000 workers. Under autarky, the 2000 workers produce (and presumably their em-

---

4 Recent studies by the ILO (1996) and the Luxembourg Income Study group (Gottschalk and Smeeding 1997a, 1997b) indicates widening inequalities are associated with increasing unemployment rates of OECD nations except where a sufficient social safety net has been maintained, e.g., Germany (and Italy until 1985).

ployers can sell) a global total of 350 bicycles and 55 computers. After trade, as each nation specializes in its comparative advantage, the same two thousand workers produce 400 bicycles and 70 computers. Ergo the world has gained a total of 50 bicycles (= 400 - 350) and 15 computers (= 70 - 55) by engaging in trade and each nation specializing in its comparative advantage (even if one nation has an absolute advantage in producing both bicycles and computers).

Unfortunately this analysis assumes that the hypothesized increase in supply automatically creates its own demand. (Wouldn't the multinational auto companies be glad to know that if they increase global productive capacity by siting plants in countries that have comparative advantage in auto assemblies, then they will sell (at a profit) all the cars they can produce? There can never be surplus capacity – as there seems to be today.)

The notion that supply creates in own demand is called Say's Law. Keynes noted that Say's Law implies "that there is no obstacle to full employment" Keynes' *General Theory* demonstrated that Say's Law could not be applied to money-using, entrepreneurial economies. Consequently, if there is anything economists should have learned since Keynes, it is that one cannot prove that there will be gains from trade that both economies will share unless one *assumes* that there is full employment in both economies both before and after trade.

That brings us to a second problem in applying the law of comparative advantage to the real world. The textbooks assume that the gains from trade due to the law of comparative advantage occurs only if neither capital nor labor are mobile across national boundaries. If capital is internationally mobile than the usefulness of this "law" in determining trade patterns is diminished. With free international capital mobility, a good will be produced where it is most profitable, i.e., where units labor costs are lowest. Thus in our two economy model if one country has an absolute advantage in that unit labor costs are lower for the production of both bicycles and computers, then that nation will attract enough foreign capital to produce all the bicycles and computers to meet global market demand. Production and employment in the other country will decline to zero. In sum, the use of comparative advantage analysis as a justification for letting free markets determine trade and international payments flows can be dangerous to the health of real world economies.

## V. Additional macroeconomic errors embedded in mainstream conventional wisdom

Another post 1973 conventional wisdom (based on the axioms of classical theory) has exacerbated the global depressing effect of volatile exchange rates, free international financial markets and a strong reduction in the "rigidity" of domestic labor markets. This classical homily is that government spending is *per se* undesirable and deficit spending designed to increase the point of effective demand employment is especially misguided. But "in a society where there is no question of direct investment under the aegis of public authority [because of a fear of deficits], the economic objects, with which it is reasonable for the government to be preoccupied, are the domestic rate of interest and the balance of foreign trade" (Keynes, 1936a, p. 335).

When however, volatile exchange rates depress global investment spending and deficits are precluded, then if the worldly wisdom of central bankers is that inflation can only be held in check by promoting the fear of "job insecurity" among workers (Uchitelle, 1997, p. C6), then the rate of interest will be used to perpetuate unemployment rather than promote prosperity. Subscribing to the conventional wisdom rationalized by natural rate theories, politicians and central bankers have foisted onto society a Hobson's choice that has devastating real effects on industry and the global economy.

I remind fellow economists of the wisdom of Keynes' (1936a, p. 349) dictum that "In truth, the opposite [of the conventional wisdom] holds good. It is the policy of an autonomous rate of interest, unimpeded by international preoccupations, and of a national investment programme directed to an optimum level of domestic employment which is twice blessed in the sense that it helps ourselves and our neighbors at the same time. And it is the simultaneous pursuit of these policies by all countries together which is capable of restoring economic health and strength internationally, whether we measure it by the level of domestic employment or by the volume of international trade".

## VI. Reforming the world's monetary payment system

Too often economic discussions on the requirements for a good international payments system have been limited to the question of the advantages and disadvantages of fixed vs. flexible exchange rates. Although this issue is very important, the facts of experience plus Keynes' revolutionary analysis indicate that more is required than simply choosing between fixed and flexible exchange rates if a mechanism is to be designed to resolve payments imbalances while simultaneously promoting full employment economic growth and a long-run stable international standard of value.

The post-war world has conducted several experiments with the international payments system. For a quarter of a century after the war, there was a fixed, but adjustable, exchange rate system (1947 - 1973) set up under the Bretton Woods Agreement. Since 1973, we have operated under a flexible exchange rate system. During the Bretton Woods epoch, free economies experienced unprecedented real economic growth. Moreover, during this period, there was "a much better overall record of price level stability" vis-à-vis either the post-1973 period or the earlier gold-standard fixed exchange rates (1879 - 1914) [McKinnon, 1990, p. 10].

The dismal post-1973 experience of recurrent unemployment and inflationary crises, slow growth in OECD countries, and debt-burdened growth and / or stagnation (and even falling real GNP per capita) in developing countries, and even the possibility of product price deflation contrasts sharply with the experience during the Bretton Woods period. As we have already noted, the free world's economic performance in terms of both real growth *and* price level stability during the Bretton Woods period was unprecedented. Moreover, even the record during the earlier gold standard-fixed exchange rate period was better than the experience during the 1973 - 1991 period of flexible exchange rates.

As we have already noted, several hundred years of experience support the thesis that a fixed exchange rate system provides an international environment that is more compatible with greater global real economic growth and price stability compared to what was experienced under a flexible exchange rate regime. The significantly superior performance of the free world's economies during the Bretton Woods fixed rate period compared to the earlier gold standard fixed rate period suggests that there must have been an additional condition besides exchange rate fixity that contributed to the unprecedented growth during the 1947 - 73 period. That additional condition had been spelled out by Keynes, in developing his proposals for an international payments scheme. To reduce entrepreneurial uncertainties and the possibility of massive currency misalignments Keynes recommended the adoption of a fixed, but adjustable, exchange rate system. More importantly, Keynes argued that the "main cause of failure" of any traditional payments system – whether based on fixed or flexible rates – was its inability to actively foster continuous global economic expansion when persistent current account imbalances among trading partners occurred. This failure, Keynes [1980, p. 27] wrote,

> "can be traced to a single characteristic. I ask close attention to this, because I shall argue that this provides a clue to the nature of any alternative which is to be successful. It is characteristic of a freely convertible international standard that it throws the main burden of adjustment on the country which is the *debtor* position on the international balance of payments – that is, on the country which is (in this context) by hypothesis the *weaker* and above all the *smaller* in comparison with the other side of the scales which (for this purpose) is the rest of the world".

Keynes (1980, p. 176) concluded that an essential improvement in designing any international payments system requires transferring "the *onus* of adjustment from the debtor to the creditor position", and aiming "at the substitution of an expansionist, in place of a contractionist, pressure on world trade". In other words, to achieve a golden era of economic development requires combining a fixed, but adjustable, rate system with a mechanism for requiring the surplus trading nation(s) or any nation receiving "hot money" (capital flight) inflows to restore liquidity to their trading partners without removing all discipline from the deficit trading partner.

After World War II, the economic recovery of the free capitalist world required the European nations to run huge import surpluses to feed their populations and rebuild their war-devastated plant and equipment. This implied that the United States would have to provide enormous credits to finance the required export surplus to Europe. The resulting European indebtedness would be so burdensome that it was unlikely that, even in the long run, the European nations could ever service this debt. Moreover, U.S. policy makers were mindful that reparation payments after World War I were financed by U.S. investors lending Germany foreign exchange and Germany never repaid these loans. Given this history and existing circumstances it was obvious that private lending facilities could not be expected to provide the credits necessary for European recovery.

Under the fixed exchange rate system of Bretton Woods, the only mechanism available for redressing this potentially lopsided global import-export trade flow was for the debtors to accept the main burden of adjustment by "tighten their belt" and reduce their demand for imports to what they could earn from exports[5]. The result would have been to depress further the standard of living of Western Europeans. This could have induced political revolutions in most of Western Europe. Instead the United States produced the Marshall Plan and other foreign grants and aid programs. The Marshall Plan provided $5 billion in aid in 18 months and a total of $13 billion in four years. (In 1997 dollars this is equivalent to almost $150 billion.)

Marshall plan transfers represented approximately 2 per cent per annum of the GNP of the United States. Yet no U.S. resident felt deprived of goods and services. Real GNP per capita in the United States during the first year of the Marshall Plan was still 25% larger than in the last peacetime year of 1940. Per capita GNP continued to grow throughout the 1950s.[6] There were no real sacrifice associated with this U.S. government unilateral transfers. The resulting exports were produced by employing what otherwise would have been idle resources. For the first time in its history, the United States did not suffer from a severe recession immediately after the cessation of a major war. The world experienced an economic "free lunch" as both the potential debtors and the creditor nation gained from this "give away".

By 1958, however, although the U.S. still had a goods and services export surplus of over $5 billion, U.S. governmental and military transfers exceeded $6 billion, while there was a net private capital outflow of $1.6 billion.[7] The post-war U.S. surplus position on current account was at an end. As the U.S. current account swung into deficit other nations began to experience current account surpluses. These nations converted a portion of their dollar current account surpluses into

5 The "scarce currency" clause of the Bretton Woods Agreement would permit European nations to discriminate against American imports. But this would not resolve the problem since there was no other major source of the goods necessary to feed and rebuild Europe.

6 Only in the small recessions of 1949 and 1957 did per capita GNP stop growing. But even during these brief periods, GNP never declined.

7 Figures obtained from *Statistical Abstract of the United States 1959,* U.S. Bureau of Census, Washington, 1959, p. 870.

gold. For example, in 1958, the U.S. lost over $2 billion in gold reserves to foreign central banks. This trend accelerated in the 1960s, partly as a result of increased U.S. military and financial aid responses to the construction of the Berlin Wall in 1961 and later because of the U.S.'s increasing involvement in Vietnam. At the same time, a rebuilt Europe and Japan became important producers of exports so that the rest of the world became less dependent on the U.S. exports.

The U.S. maintained a positive merchandise trade balance until the first oil price shock in 1973. More than offsetting this trade surplus during most of the 1960s, however, were foreign and military unilateral transfers plus net capital outflows. The Bretton Woods system had no way of automatically forcing the emerging surplus nations to step into the adjustment role that the U.S. had been playing since 1947. Instead they continued to converted some portion of their annual dollar surpluses into calls on U.S. gold reserves. The seeds of the destruction of the Bretton Woods system and the golden age of economic development were sown as surplus nations drained gold reserves from the United States.

When the U.S. closed the gold window and unilaterally withdrew from Bretton Woods, the last vestige of Keynes's enlightened international monetary approach was lost – apparently without regret or regard as to how well it served the global economy.

## VII. A Post Keynesian international payments system

The following proposal for an international payments system builds on Keynes' incompatibility thesis and Bretton Wood proposals that help explain the expansionist pressure on world trade and development during the 1947 - 73 period.

In an interdependent world economy, some degree of economic cooperation among trading partners is necessary. Our proposal, however, does not require the establishment of a Supranational Central Bank to create a Unionized Monetary System (UMS) – even if this is believed desirable on other grounds. Keynes' original "bancor" plan for the post World War II environment, was developed around the idea of a single Supranational Bank and a single international central bank money. At this stage of the evolution of world politics, however, a global UMS with a Supranational Central Bank is not feasible[8]. Our suggestion is a more modest one aimed at obtaining an international agreement that does not require either

[8] This does not deny that some groups of trading partners may wish to integrate their central banks and banking systems into a regional UMS common market. The Maastricht Treaty implies that ultimately there will be a single currency among all the European Community of Nations governed by a single Supranational Central Bank. If some nations were willing to develop an interregional UMS they would be free to develop their own UMS clearing mechanism which would operate as a single unit in the larger global clearing union proposed below.

surrendering national control of local banking systems or independent national fiscal policies.

Fifty years ago, Keynes [1980, p. 158] provided a clear outline of what was needed when he wrote:

> "We need an instrument of international currency having general acceptability between nations ... We need an orderly and agreed upon method of determining the relative exchange values of national currency units ... We need a quantum of international currency ... [which] is governed by the actual current [liquidity] requirements of world commerce, and is capable of deliberate expansion ... We need a method by which the surplus credit balances arising from international trade, which the recipient does not wish to employ can be set to work ... without detriment to the liquidity of these balances".

What is required is a *closed,* double-entry bookkeeping clearing institution to keep the payments score among the various trading regions plus some mutually agreed upon rules to create and reflux liquidity while maintaining the international purchasing power of the international currency. The eight provisions of the clearing system suggested in this section meet the criteria laid down by Keynes. The rules of our proposed system are designed [1] to prevent a lack of global effective demand[9] due to any nation(s) either holding excessive idle reserves or draining reserves from the system, [2] to provide an automatic mechanism for placing a major burden of payments adjustments on the surplus nations, [3] to provide each nation with the ability to monitor and, if desired, to control movements of financial capital[10], and finally [4] to expand the quantity of the liquid asset of ultimate international redemption as global capacity warrants.

Some elements of such a clearing system would include:

1. The unit of account and ultimate reserve asset for international liquidity is the International Money Clearing Unit (IMCU). All IMCUs are held *only* by central banks, not by the public.

2. Each nation's or UMS's central bank is committed to guarantee one way convertibility from IMCU deposits at the clearing union to its domestic money. Each central bank will set its own rules regarding making available foreign monies (through IMCU clearing transactions) to its own bankers and private sector residents[11].

---

9 Williamson recognizes that when balance of payments "disequilibrium is due purely to excess or deficient demand", flexible exchange rates *per se* can not facilitate international payments adjustments [Williamson, May 1987, pp. 200 - 204].

10 This provides as an added bonus by making tax-avoidance and profits from illegal trade more difficult to conceal.

11 Correspondent banking will have to operate through the International Clearing Agency, with each central bank regulating the international relations and operations of its domestic banking firms.

Small scale smuggling of currency across borders, etc., can never be completely eliminated. But such movement's are merely a flea on a dog's back – a minor, but not debilitating,

Since central banks agree to sell their own liabilities (one-way convertibility) against the IMCU only to other central bankers and the International Clearing Agency while they simultaneously hold only IMCUs as liquid reserve assets for international financial transactions, there can be no draining of reserves from the system. All major private international transactions ultimately clear between central banks on their own account within the international clearing institution.

3. The exchange rate between the domestic currency and the IMCU is set *initially* by each nation – just as it would be if one instituted an international gold standard. Since enterprises that are already engaged in trade have international contractual commitments that would span the change-over interval, then, as a practical matter, one would expect that the existing exchange rate structure (with perhaps minor modifications) would provide the basis for initial rate setting.

Provisions #7 and #8 *infra* indicate when and how this nominal exchange rate between the national currency and the IMCU would change in the future.

4. Contracts between private individual's will continue to be denominated into what ever domestic currency permitted by local laws and agreed upon by the contracting parties. Contracts to be settled in terms of a foreign currency will therefore require some announced commitment from the central bank (through private sector bankers) of the availability of foreign funds to meet such private contractual obligations.

5. An overdraft system to make available short-term unused creditor balances at the clearing house to finance the productive international transactions of others who need short-term credit. The terms will be determined by the *pro bono publico* clearing managers.

6. A trigger mechanism to encourage any creditor nation to spend what is deemed (in advance) by agreement of the international community to be *"excessive" credit balances accumulated by running current account surpluses.* These excessive credits can be spent in three ways: (1) on the products of any other member of the clearing union, (2) on new direct foreign investment projects, and / or (3) to provide unilateral transfers (foreign aid) to deficit members. Spending via (1) forces the surplus nation to make the adjustment directly by way of the balance on goods and services. Spending by way of (3) permits adjustment directly by the current account balance, while (2) provides adjustment by the capital accounts (without setting up a contractual debt that will *require* reverse current account flows in the future).

Consequently, proviso #6 provides the surplus country with considerable discretion in deciding how to accept the "onus" of adjustment in the way it believes is in

---

irritation. If, however, most of the residents of a nation hold and use (in violation of legal tender laws) a foreign currency for domestic transactions and as a store of value (e.g., it is estimated that Argentineans hold close to $5 billion U.S. dollars), this is evidence of a lack of confidence in the government and its monetary authority. Unless confidence is restored, all attempts to restore economic prosperity will fail.

its residents best interests. It does not, however, permit the surplus nation to shift the burden to the deficit nation(s) via contractual requirements for debt service charges independent of what the deficit nation can afford[12]. The important thing is to make sure that continual oversaving[13] by surplus nations can not unleash depressionary forces and / or a building up of international debts so encumbering as to impoverish the global economy of the 21 century.

In the unlikely event that the surplus nation does not spend or give away these credits within a specified time, then the clearing agency would confiscate (and redistribute to debtor members) the portion of credits deemed excess[14]. This last resort confiscatory action by the managers of the clearing agency would make a payments adjustment via unilateral transfer payments in the current accounts.

---

12 Some may fear that if a surplus nation is close to the trigger point it could short circuit the system by making loans to reduce its credit balance *prior* to setting off the trigger. Since preventing unreasonable debt service obligations is an important objective of this proposal, a mechanism which monitors and can restrict such pretrigger lending activities may be required.

One possible way of eliminating this trigger avoidance lending loophole is as follows: An initial agreement as to what constitutes sensible and flexible criteria for judging when debt servicing burdens become unreasonable is established. Given these criteria, the clearing union managers would have the responsibility for preventing additional loans which push debt burdens beyond reasonable servicing levels. In other words, loans that push debt burdens too far, could not be cleared though the clearing union, i.e., the managers would refuse to release the IMCU's for loan purposes from the surplus country's account. (I am indebted to Robert Blecker for suggesting this point.)

The managers would also be required to make periodic public reports on the level of credits being accumulated by surplus nations and to indicate how close these surpluses are to the trigger point. Such reports would provide an informational edge for debtor nations permitting them to bargain more successively regarding the terms of refinancing existing loans and / or new loans. All loans would still have to meet the clearing union's guidelines for reasonableness.

I do not discount the difficulties involved in setting up and getting agreement on criteria for establishing unreasonable debt service burdens. (For some suggestions, however, see the second paragraph of provision #8.) In the absence of cooperation and a spirit of goodwill that is necessary for the clearing union to provide a mechanism assuring the economic prosperity of all members, however, no progress can ever be made.

Moreover, as the current international debt problem of African and Latin American nations clearly demonstrates, creditors ultimately have to forgive some debt when they previously encourage excessive debt burdens. Under the current system, however, debt forgiveness is a last resort solution acceptable only after both debtor and creditor nations suffer from faltering economic growth. Surely a more intelligent option is to develop an institutional arrangement which prevents excessive debt servicing burdens from ever occurring.

13 Oversaving is defined as a nation persistently spending less on imports plus direct equity foreign investment than the nation's export earnings plus net unilateral transfers.

14 Whatever "excessive" credit balances that are redistributed shall be apportioned among the debtor nations (perhaps based on a formula which is inversely related to each debtor's per capita income and directly related to the size of its international debt) to be used to reduce debit balances at the clearing union.

Under either a fixed or a flexible rate system, nations may experience persistent trade deficits merely because their trading partners are not living up to their means – that is because other nations are continually hoarding a portion of their foreign export earnings (plus net unilateral transfers). By so doing, these oversavers are creating a lack of global effective demand. Under provision #6, deficit countries would no longer have to deflate their real economy merely to adjust their payment imbalance because others are oversaving. Instead, the system would seek to remedy the payment deficit by increasing opportunities for deficit nations to sell abroad.

7. A system to stabilize the long-term purchasing power of the IMCU (in terms of each member nation's domestically produced market basket of goods) can be developed. This requires a system of fixed exchange rates between the local currency and the IMCU that changes only to reflect permanent increases in efficiency wages[15]. This assures each central bank that its holdings of IMCUs as the nation's foreign reserves will never lose purchasing power in terms of foreign produced goods, even if a foreign government permits wage-price inflation to occur within its borders. Consequently, the rate between the local currency and the IMCU would change with inflation in the local money price of the domestic commodity basket.

If, however, increases in productivity lead to declining nominal production costs, then the nation with this decline in efficiency wages [say of 5 per cent] would have the option of choosing either [a] to permit the IMCU to buy [up to 5 per cent] less units of domestic currency, thereby capturing all (or most of) the gains from productivity for its residents while maintaining the purchasing power of the IMCU, or [b] to keep the nominal exchange rate constant. In the latter case, the gain in productivity is shared with all trading partners. In exchange, the export industries in this productive nation will receive an increasing relative share of the world market.

By altering the exchange rate between local monies and the IMCU to offset the rate of domestic inflation, the IMCU's purchasing power is stabilized. By restricting use of IMCUs to central banks, private speculation regarding IMCUs as a hedge against inflation is avoided. Each nation's rate of inflation of the goods and services it produces is determined solely by (a) the local government's policy towards the level of domestic money wages and profit margins vis-à-vis productivity gains, i.e., the nation's efficiency wage. Each nation is therefore free to experiment with policies for stabilizing its efficiency wage to prevent inflation. Whether the

---

15 The efficiency wage is related to the money wage divided by the average product of labor, it is the unit labor cost modified by the profit mark-up in domestic money terms of domestically produced GNP. At this preliminary stage of this proposal, it would serve no useful purpose to decide whether the domestic market basket should include both tradeable and non-tradeable goods and services. (With the growth of tourism more and more nontradeable goods become potentially tradeable.) I personally prefer the wider concept of the domestic market basket, but it is not obvious that any essential principle is lost if a tradeable only concept is used, or if some nations use the wider concept while others the narrower one.

nation is successful or not, the IMCU will never lose its international purchasing power. Moreover, the IMCU has the promise of gaining in purchasing power over time, if productivity grows rapidly more than money wages and each nation is willing to share any reduction in real production costs with its trading partners. Consequently, the IMCU becomes an ideal store of value medium for creditor nations.

Provision #7 produces a system designed to maintain the relative efficiency wage parities amongst nations. In such a system, the adjustability of nominal exchange rates will be primarily (but not always, see Provision #8) to offset changes in efficiency wages among trading partners. A beneficial effect that follows from this proviso is that it eliminates the possibility that a specific industry in any nation can be put at a competitive disadvantage (or secure a competitive advantage) against foreign producers solely because the nominal exchange rate changed independently of changes in efficiency wages and the real costs of production in each nation.

Consequently, nominal exchange rate variability can no longer create the problem of a loss of competitiveness due solely to the overvaluing of a currency as, for example, experienced by the industries in the American "rust belt" during the period 1982 - 85. Even if temporary, currency appreciation independent of changes in efficiency wages can have significant permanent real costs as industries abandon export markets and existing plant and equipment is cast aside as too costly to maintain.

Proviso #7 also prevents any nation from engaging in a beggar-thy-neighbor, export-thy-unemployment policy by pursuing an exchange rate devaluation that does not reflect changes in efficiency wages. Once the initial exchange rates are chosen and relative efficiency wages are locked in, reductions in real production costs which are associated with a relative decline in efficiency wages due to relatively grater improvements in productivity is the main factor (with the exception of provision #8) justifying an adjustment in the exchange rate.

Although provision #6 prevents any country from piling up persistent excessive surpluses this does not mean that it is impossible for one or more nations to run persistent deficits. Consequently proposal #8 *infra* provides a program for addressing the problem of persistent export-import deficits in any one nation.

8. If a country is at *full employment* and still has a tendency towards persistent international deficits on its current account, then this is *prima facie* evidence that it does not possess the productive capacity to maintain its current standard of living. If the deficit nation is a poor one, then surely there is a case for the richer nations who are in surplus to transfer some of their excess credit balances to support the poor nation[16]. If it is a relatively rich country, then the deficit nation must alter its standard of living by reducing its relative terms of trade with its major trading part-

[16] This is equivalent to a negative income tax for poor fully employed families within a nation. [See Davidson, 1987 - 88 for further development of this argument.]

ners. Rules, agreed upon in advance, would require the trade deficit rich nation to devalue its exchange rate by stipulated increments per period until evidence becomes available to indicate that the export-import imbalance is eliminated without unleashing significant recessionary forces.

If, on the other hand, the payment deficit persists despite a continuous positive balance of trade in goods and services, then there is evidence that the deficit nation might be carrying too heavy an international debt service obligation. The *pro bono* officials of the clearing union should bring the debtor and creditors into negotiations to reduce annual debt service payments by [1] lengthening the payments period, [2] reducing the interest charges, and / or [3] debt forgiveness[17].

If any government objects to the idea that the IMCU provisions provide governments with the ability to limit the free movement of "capital" funds, then this nation is free to join other nations of similar attitude in forming a regional currency union [UMS] and thereby assuring a free flow of funds among the residents of the currency union.

## VIII. Conclusion

Our suggested provisions for a new international payments system are not unalterable either in principle or for practical reasons. Instead they should provide the basis for the beginning of a sound analytical discussion of how to prepare for a 21st century international monetary system.

The problems facing the international payments system are not easily resolved. If we start with the defeatist attitude that it is too difficult to change the awkward system we are enmeshed in, then no progress will be made. We must reject such defeatism at this exploratory stage and merely ask whether these particular proposals for improving the operations of the international payments system to promote global growth will create more difficulties than other proposed innovations. The health of the world economic system will not permit us to muddle through!

Once we have reformed the international monetary payments system so that nations do not have to fear balance of payments problems, then the leaders of the major nations of the world can take steps to stimulate global demand without having to fear adverse economic consequences for their own nation. Then, and only then, we may restore a golden age of economic development to our planet.

---

17 The actual program adopted for debt service reduction will depend on many parameters including: the relative income and wealth of the debtor vis-à-vis the creditor, the ability of the debtor to increase its per capita real income, etc.

## References

*Adelman,* I.: "Long Term Economic Development", (Working Paper No. 589) California Agricultural Experiment Station, Berkeley California, March 1991. – *Arrow,* K. J. and *Hahn,* F. H.: General Competitive Equilibrium, San Francisco, Holden-Day, 1971. – *Davidson,* P.: "A Modest Set of Proposals For Solving The International Debt Crisis", Journal of Post Keynesian Economics, X, 1987 - 88. – *Davidson,* P.: "A Post Keynesian Positive Contribution to 'Theory'", Journal of Post Keynesian Economics, 13, Winter 1990 - 91. – *Friedman,* M.: "A Theoretical Framework for Monetary Analysis", in Milton Friedman's Monetary Framework: A Debate With His Critics, edited by R. J. Gordon. University of Chicago Press, 1974. – *Froot,* K. A. / *Kim,* M. and *Rogoff,* K.: "The Law of One Price Over 700 Years", NBER Working Paper, No. 5132, May 1995. – *Keynes,* J. M.: The Collected Writings of John Maynard Keynes, 14, edited by D. Moggridge. Macmillan, London, 1973. – *Keynes,* J. M.: The Collected Writings of John Maynard Keynes, 25, edited by D. Moggridge. Macmillan, London, 1980. – *McKinnon,* R. I.: "Monetary and Exchange Rate Policies for International Financial Stability: A Proposal", Journal of Economic Perspectives, 2, 1988. – *McKinnon,* R. I.: "Interest Rate Volatility and Exchange Rate Risk: New Rules For A Common Monetary Standard", Contemporary Policy Studies, 8, April 1990. – *Milberg,* W.: "Globalization and International Competitiveness" in Improving The Global Economy, edited by P. Davidson and J. A. Kregel. Elgar, Cheltenham, 1997. – *Thirlwall,* A. P.: "The Balance of Payments Constraint as an Explanation of International Growth Rate Differences", Banca Nazionale del Lavoro Quarterly Review, 1989. – *Williamson,* J.: "Exchange Rate Management: The Role of Target Zones", American Economic Review Papers and Proceedings, 77, May 1987a. – *Williamson,* J. and *Miller,* Marcus H.: Targets and Indicators: A Blueprint For The International Coordination of Economic Policy. Institute for International Economics, Washington, 1987b.

# International Direct Investment: Export of Headquarter Services or Export of Jobs?

By Henning Klodt, Kiel

## I. Introduction

In the public debate about economic issues, there is widespread concern that Germany is losing ground in global competition. It is feared that the attractiveness of the German economy for internationally mobile investors is declining and that Germany is converting from the world champion in exports of goods to the world champion in export of jobs. The central focus of this debate lies on the large and steadily increasing deficit in the German balance of foreign direct investment.

It is argued in this paper that the emphasis on the balance of foreign direct investment is misplaced for two reasons: first, the statistical reliability of foreign direct investment data is rather low. Second, and more important, outflows of foreign direct investment do not necessarily reflect an export of domestic jobs, but may also improve the labor market performance in the home country.

Nevertheless, it would be equally misguided to conclude that international investment flows were completely irrelevant for national labor markets. The increase in foreign direct investment reflects a rising integration of the world economy which eventually results in an international equalisation of factor prices. The paper is organized as follows: part II presents the development of the German balance of foreign direct investment by different statistical sources. Part III briefly surveys the theoretical background of multinational activities in the light of the new trade theory. Part IV discusses the regional and sectoral patterns of multinational activities of German firms. Part V concludes.

## II. Statistics on Foreign Direct Investment

### *The German Balance of Foreign Direct Investment by Different Statistical Sources*

The deficit in the German balance of foreign direct investment has significantly enlarged during the 1990s. Outflows from Germany increased to a level of 40 to

50 billion DM, whereas inflows from abroad are stagnating *(Figure 1)*. Many observers are interpreting this development as an indicator of a reduced attractiveness of the German economy for internationally mobile investors.

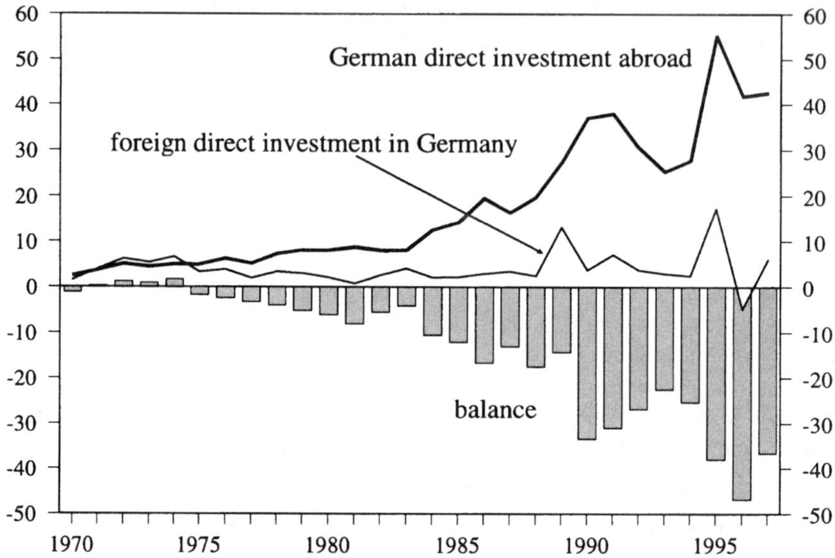


*Source:* Deutsche Bundesbank (a).

Figure 1: German Balance of Foreign Direct Investment (billion DM)

However, a closer look at the data casts some doubts on this interpretation. Data collectors at central banks are facing severe difficulties when separating foreign direct investment flows from other types of international capital movements. As a result, the data provided by the Deutsche Bundesbank significantly differ from the corresponding data of foreign central banks.

According to the German balance of payments, cumulated direct investment of German firms in foreign OECD countries amount to 226 billion DM for the period from 1984 to 1994, whereas cumulated direct investment from OECD countries in Germany amounts to 45 billion DM. By contrast. the OECD partner countries are reporting significantly different numbers for the same state of affairs. Summing up the inflows of foreign direct investment from Germany to OECD countries by their national balances of payments yields a cumulated value of 166 billion DM for the years 1984 to 1994; and outflows from OECD countries to Germany are reported as 139 billion DM. Hence, the cumulated German deficit reduces to 27 billion DM – as compared to the deficit of 181 billion DM according to the German balance of payments (Figure 2).

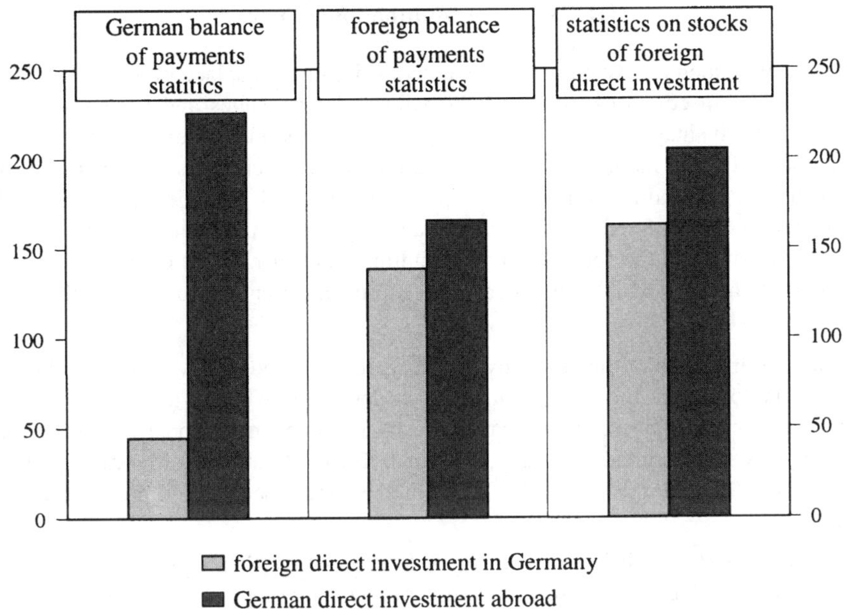


*Source:* Deutsche Bundesbank (1997a, 1997b); own calculations.

Figure 2: Cumulated German Balance of Foreign Direct Investment by Different Statistical Sources 1984 - 94 (billion DM)

A rather low German deficit also results from the statistics on the stocks of foreign direct investment. These data are also collected by the Deutsche Bundesbank, but they are not based upon balance of payments statistics but on balance sheets of multinational firms. From 1984 to 1994, the stocks of German direct investment in foreign countries increased by 205 billion DM and the stocks of foreign multinationals in Germany increased by 163 billion DM. Hence, the deficit amounts to about 40 billion DM, which is much closer to the deficit reported by foreign balances of payments than to the German balance of payments.

The large differences between cumulated flows from balance of payments statistics and changes in stocks from balance sheets may partly be explained by the fact that bank credits to affiliates from financial institutions of the host country are included in statistics on stocks, but do not show up in balances of payments, because they do not induce international capital transactions. As the German tax systems favors external over internal financing, this could explain why the growth of stocks of foreign direct investment in Germany exceeds the reported inflows of foreign direct investment. The large deficit of foreign direct investment in the German balance of payments can hence be regarded as a rather poor indicator of Germany's position in global competition.

## III. Theory of Multinational Firms

If businessmen are asked why they are considering to displace production activities to foreign countries, they usually point to lower wages and tax burdens or other cost advantages abroad. From an economist's point of view, these answers are not really convincing, because international cost differentials are no sufficient explanation for multinational activities. As international activities are associated with certain costs of control, supervision and organization, which do not accrue to local companies in the foreign country, multinational firms must dispose of specific cost advantages which are not accessible to independent competitors in the host country.

In the framework of the new growth theory, several models have been developed which try to picture the basic factors which determine whether a specific market will be dominated by multinational firms, by independent national producers, or by imports from abroad (see, e.g., Helpman 1984; Horstmann, Markusen 1992; Krugman 1983; Markusen 1984). These models are based upon three central assumptions:

(1) There exist two different types of scale economies. Plant-specific economies of scale, which may result from fixed capital requirements of production or other indivisibilities, can only be exploited at individual production sites. Firm-specific economies of scale, by contrast, can be transferred between different plants within firms and can also be utilized in foreign affiliates. This type of economies of scale result from so-called headquarter services such as research and development, global public relations activities, the establishment of brand names, or the development of managerial know-how which applies to the whole firm.

(2) Selling on export markets is associated with higher costs than selling in the domestic market. These additional costs may result from transport costs or from artificial trade barriers.

(3) Managing and monitoring of foreign affiliates give rise to additional costs which may result from geographical distance, from language and cultural barriers, or from unfamiliarity with foreign bureaucracies and institutions.

The relative importance of these three factors is crucial for the decision whether a domestic firm prefers to serve foreign markets by exports or by foreign production and for the competitive advantages and disadvantages of independent producers in the foreign country. The different constellation are illustrated in Figure 3.

$AC_d$ represents the average cost curve of the domestic firm. On the home market, its sales are represented by $00'$, which size depends on domestic demand conditions. If the foreign market shall be served by exports, average costs are given by $AC_e$, which consists of the sum of $AC_d$ and $t$, where $t$ represents the cost equivalent of trade barriers. The average costs of an independent foreign competitor ($AC_f$) are equal to the cost situation of the domestic firm in its home market (technologies are assumed to be identical), but the origin of $AC_f$ lies in 0′, because the foreign firm is not able to exploit firm-specific economies of scale. Finally, $AC_s$ represents average costs of the foreign subsidiary, which has to face lower fixed costs than the foreign competitor, because it is able to benefit from headquarter services provided by its parent company. On the other hand, the subsidiary has to bear additional costs of international production which are represented by z. Hence, the cost curve $AC_s$ is more convex than $AC_f$. Under such conditions, it depends on the size of the foreign market which producer will serve foreign demand. If the market size lies in a range of 0′ to $A$, the foreign market will be served by exports from the home country, because $AC_e$ is below the other two cost curves. With a market size larger than $B$, the independent foreign producer will dominate the market. In the area between $A$ and $B$, the cost advantage is with the foreign subsidiary of the domestic firm. Hence, foreign direct investment is encouraged if the importance of firm-specific scale economies rises, if trade barriers are increased, and if the costs of monitoring international production are declining.

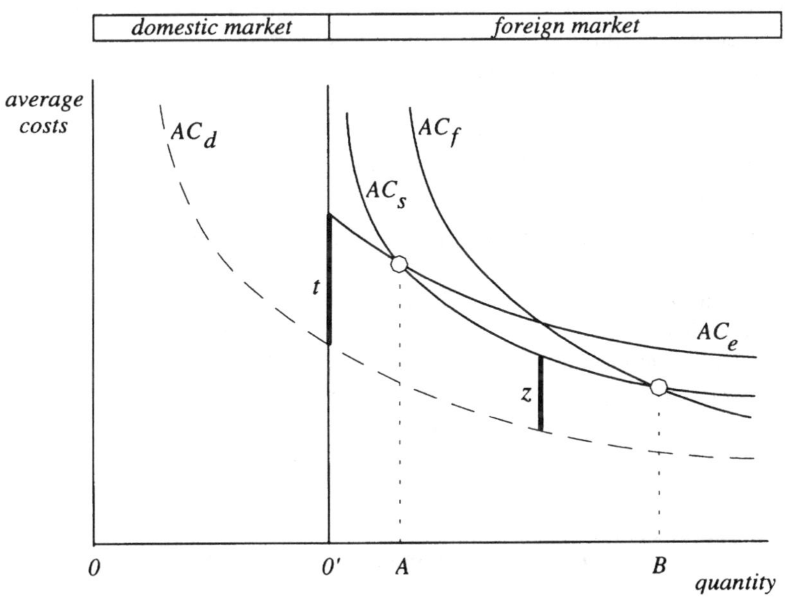


Figure 3: Determinants of Foreign Direct Investment (per cent)

Several conclusions can be drawn from this simple model:

A cost increase in the domestic country shifts $AC_e$ upwards and compresses the area $0'A$, where exports are dominant. Excessive wage increases or other cost disadvantages of the home country may induce foreign direct investment at the expense of domestic production, if the foreign market is smaller than $0'A$.

A reduction of trade barriers (for instance through superior transport technologies of through successful GATT / WTO negotiations) shifts point A to the right, which may give rise to less foreign direct investment and more exports.

*A* decrease of *z* (which may result from technological progress in information technologies and corresponding reductions of monitoring costs) shifts *A* to the left and *B* to the right and thus strengthens the cost advantages of multinational activities.

A rising importance of firm-specific economies of scale (which may reflect an increase of technological sophistication and product differentiation) shifts *B* to the right, because the upward shift of $AC_f$ exceeds the upward shift of $AC_s$. In consequence, production of independent foreign producers may be replaced by production of multinational subsidiaries. The point A is unaffected, because $AC_s$ and $AC_e$ are shifted upwards by the same amount.

All in all, there is no simple and unequivocal relationship between the number of jobs in foreign affiliates and in domestic production. Therefore, increased multinational activities are not necessarily associated with an export of jobs. In those cases where foreign subsidiaries are primarily competing with independent foreign producers, production at home may even be strengthened by foreign direct investment, because the improved exploitation of firm-specific economies of scale will stimulate the production of headquarter services in the home country. In this case, an expansion of foreign direct investment may even lead to an improved labor market performance in the home country.

A further point is worth to be noticed: In the model represented by Figure 3, there will be no multinational activities at all if there exist no firm-specific economies of scale. As the importance of headquarter services depends of the technological properties of production, there can be expected large sectoral differences in the relative importance of foreign direct investment. Multinationals will be prevalent in those industries were firm-specific economies of scale are large, i.e. in technology-intensive industries and in industries with a high degree of product differentiation.

## IV. Patterns of Foreign Direct Investment

As shown in the preceding section, the primary objective of foreign direct investment is to exploit firm-specific economies of scale. Multinational activities can be encouraged by (1) widening international cost differentials, (2) improved efficiency in monitoring internationally dispersed production networks or (3) a rising importance of headquarter services due to increased technological sophistication or product differentiation. It can be expected that actual investment decisions are influenced by all three factors to some extent. For an assessment of the global competitiveness of the German economy, however, it would be helpful to separate the importance of international cost differentials from the two other factors, because cost-induced foreign direct investment will be associated with a decline of jobs in the home country, whereas the two other types of foreign direct investment may even raise the number of jobs in the provision of headquarter services.

In the empirical literature on the determinants of foreign direct investment there is commonly distinguished between cost oriented and market oriented multinational activities. Virtually all studies confirm that international cost differentials can not be regarded as the major determinant of foreign direct investment. Investing abroad accompanies rather than substitutes export activities (UNCTC 1992; Greenaway 1993; Nunnenkamp, Gundlach, Agarwal 1994; Hummel et al. 1995; Narula 1996; Pfaffermayer 1996; Hoekman, Djankov 1996; Blomström, Fors, Lipsey 1997).

This view is supported by the fact that the main bulk of German foreign direct investment flows to other high-wage countries and not to typical low-wage regions (Table 1). The regional structural of German outward investment by and large reflects the structure of exports (cf. Klodt, Maurer 1996). If the exploitation of cost differentials were the dominant purpose, it should be expected that developing countries, the transformation countries and the Asian tigers would attract much more direct investment from Germany.

*Table 1*

**Regional Structure of German Foreign Direct Investment 1996**

| | Million DM | per cent |
|---|---|---|
| All countries | 41 824 | 100.0 |
| Industrial countries | 31 599 | 75.6 |
| European Union | 19 688 | 47.1 |
| United States | 8 907 | 21.3 |
| Japan | 1 934 | 4.6 |
| Other industrial countries | 1 070 | 2.6 |
| Transformation countries | 6 149 | 14.7 |
| South East Asian Emerging Economies | 2 172 | 5.2 |
| Developing countries | 1 904 | 4.6 |

*Source:* Deutsche Bundesbank (b).

Further evidence on the determinants of investment outflows can be derived from the sectoral structure of multinational activities. Direct investment flows are not dominated by those industries which are under strong cost pressure in Germany, but by industries which have stabilized or even expanded their domestic employment in the past decades (Figure 4). A prevalent strategy of exporting jobs from Germany to foreign locations should show up in high direct investment especially in those industries where domestic employment declines. As a matter of fact, ailing industries such as basic metals, leather, and apparel are hardly engaged in international investment activities.

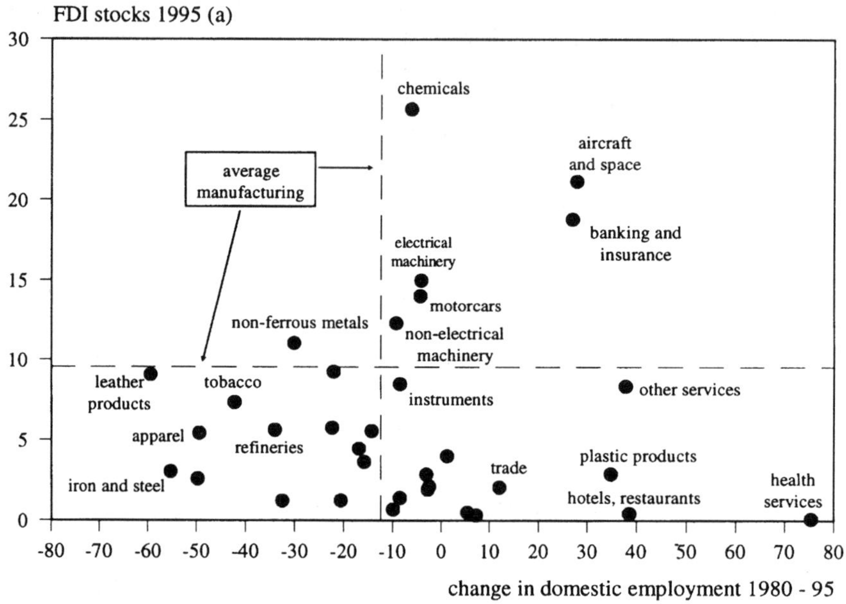


(a) As percentage of domestic gross capital stock.

*Source:* Deutsche Bundesbank (c); Statistisches Bundesamt (a); own calculations.

Figure 4: Stock of Foreign Direct Investment (a) and Change in Domestic Employment by Industry

Apparently, the international dislocation of jobs is not effected through foreign direct investment, but through other channels. For instance, if German shipyards are exposed to aggravated competition from South Korea, this does typically not lead to foreign direct investment of German shipbuilders and a corresponding displacement of jobs within firms. Instead, Korean-owned shipyards are expanding and German shipyards are shrinking. Such a development may be interpreted as an export of jobs, but there is no foreign direct investment involved. Where firms chose the strategy of foreign direct investment, for instance in the banking and insurance industry or in the motorcar industry, they basically aim at penetrating foreign markets which would not be accessible by exports alone.

## V. Conclusions

Theoretical reasoning as well as the empirical patterns of German foreign direct investment suggest that the widened deficit in the balance of foreign direct investment does not reflect a response to deteriorating economic conditions at home. The main objective of outward investment is to exploit economies of scale from an expanded provision of headquarter services. The decisions on these activities are surely affected also by cost considerations, but other determinants seem to be predominant. Therefore, statistics on foreign direct investment should not be misinterpreted as indicators of a country's position in global competition.The true challenge of foreign direct investment for the German economy is its contribution to the integration of the world economy. The large increase of direct investment flows over the past decades adds to the rising international mobility of capital, and rising capital mobility supports the tendency towards international factor price equalisation. As a result, the relative wages of low-qualified workers in Germany will come under pressure.

In addition, increased multinational activities are changing the structure of labor demand. If German firms are investing abroad, standardized production activities at home are reduced and headquarter services are expanded. The total number of jobs in Germany may remain unaffected or may even increase, but the qualification requirements of labor demand are raised. Corresponding structural change in the German labor market will be difficult to achieve, because low-qualified workers are already highly overrepresented in structural unemployment.

Hence, the conclusion that there is no reason to worry about the large deficit in the German balance of foreign direct investment should not be confused with the conclusion that there is nothing at all to worry about. Total unemployment in Germany is approaching five million people, and the group-specific unemployment rate for the low-qualified is more than twice as high as for qualified workers. It can be expected that future trends of globalization and future increases of international direct investment will tend to aggravate rather than mitigate this imbalance.

In the light of these considerations, it is not the rising gap between inflowing and outflowing capital which counts, but the rising integration of world capital markets and its implications for the sustainability of international factor price differentials. It would go far beyond the scope of this paper, however, to analyse how the German problem of structural unemployment could be solved.

## References

*Blomström,* M. / *Fors,* G. and *Lipsey,* R. E.: Foreign Direct Investment and Employment: Home Country Experience in the United States and Sweden. NBER Working Papers, 6205, October 1997. – *Deutsche Bundesbank* (1997a): Zur Problematik internationaler Vergleiche von Direktinvestitionsströmen. Monatsbericht 49 (5), S. 79 - 86. – *Deutsche Bundesbank* (1997b): Entwicklung und Bestimmungsgründe grenzüberschreitender Direktinvestitionen. Monatsbericht 49 (8), S. 63 - 82. – *Deutsche Bundesbank* (a): Monatsbericht. Frankfurt, lfd. Jgg. – *Deutsche Bundesbank* (b): Zahlungsbilanz nach Regionen. Statistische Sonderveröffentlichung 11. Frankfurt, lfd. Jgg. – *Deutsche Bundesbank* (c): Kapitalverflechtung mit dem Ausland. Statistische Sonderveröffentlichung 10. Frankfurt, lfd. Jgg. – *Helpman,* E.: A Simple Theory of International Trade with Multinational Corporations, in: Journal of Political Economy, Vol. 92 (1984), S. 451 - 471. – *Hoekman,* B., *Djankov,* S.: Intra-Industry Trade, Foreign Direct Investment and the Reorientation of East European Exports, CEPR Discussion Papers 1377, London 1996. – *Horstmann,* I., *Markusen,* J. R.: Endogenous Market Structures in International Trade, in: Journal of International Economics, Vol. 20 (1986), S. 225 - 247). – *Hummel,* M., et al.: Strukturbericht 1995, Ifo Institut für Wirtschaftsforschung, München 1995. – *Klodt,* H., *Maurer,* R. Internationale Direktinvestitionen. Determinanten und Konsequenzen für den Standort Deutschland, in: Kieler Diskussionsbeiträge, Nr. 284, Kiel 1996. – *Krugman,* P. R.: The "New Theories" of International Trade and the Multinational Enterprise, in: C. P. Kindleberger, D. B. Audretsch (Hrsg.), The Multinational Corporation in the 1980s, Cambridge 1983, S. 57 - 73. – *Markusen,* J. R.: Multinationals, Multi-Plant Economics, and the Gains from Trade, in: Journal of International Economics, Vol. 16 (1984), S. 205 - 226. – *Markusen,* A. J.: Venables, Multinational Firms and the New Trade Theory, NBER Working Paper Series 5036, Cambridge, Mass. 1995. – *Narula,* R.: Multinational Investment and Economic Structure, London 1996. – *Nunnenkamp,* P. / *Grundlach,* E. and *Agarwal,* J. P.: Globalisation of Production and Markets, Kieler Studien 262, Tübingen 1994. – *Pfaffermayr,* M.: Direktinvestitionen im Ausland, Heidelberg 1996. – *Statistisches Bundesamt* (a): Fachserie 18: Volkswirtschaftliche Gesamtrechnungen. Reihe 1.3: Konten und Standardtabellen. Stuttgart, lfd. Jgg. – *UNCTC* (United Nations Centre on Transnational Corporations): The Determinants of the Foreign Direct Investment. A Survey of Evidence, New York 1992.

# III. Financial Markets and Employment

# Monetary Conditions and Fiscal Policy – A Comparison over Various Business Cycles and Different Phases of the Business Cycle

By Alexander Juchems and Willi Leibfritz, München

## I. Unemployment and Business Cycle

A steady economic trend creates better conditions for strong growth and a high level of employment than a strongly fluctuating economy. This is especially the case for the German economy which in comparison to other national economies is marked by highly inflexible prices and wages. In an economy with flexible wages, negative shocks on the supply or demand side lead to a weakening of wages thus restoring the balance on the labour market.

A decline in the demand for labour as a consequence of an adverse shock is thus a result of inflexible wages; employment and production suffer. If the contraction is serious enough a recession results. The economic trend is then considerably weaker than its potential: physical capacities are not fully utilised and available human resources are not employed. The longer the knowledge and skills of the employed are not utilised, the larger the possibility that they will be lost forever: cyclical unemployment becomes structural unemployment and production potential drops.

The impact of recessions on unemployment in Germany in the past 25 years is seen in Figure 1. During each of the three last recessions, the unemployment rate rose sharply and was only slightly reduced in the following recovery periods. Consequently, there was a rise in structural unemployment.

Here, we will examine the influence of monetary conditions and fiscal-policy on the German economy during the last three business cycles. Special attention is given to the recession phases, as these obviously have a strong (negative) impact on employment.

## II. Monetary Conditions and Fiscal-Policy in the Overall Business Cycle

Of the numerous factors that influence the business cycle, we will focus on only the monetary conditions and on fiscal policy. Other important determinants such as endogenously generated real business cycles or other economic-policy areas, in particular wage policy, will not be taken into consideration. The Ifo Business Climate will be used to show the course of the business cycle.[1]

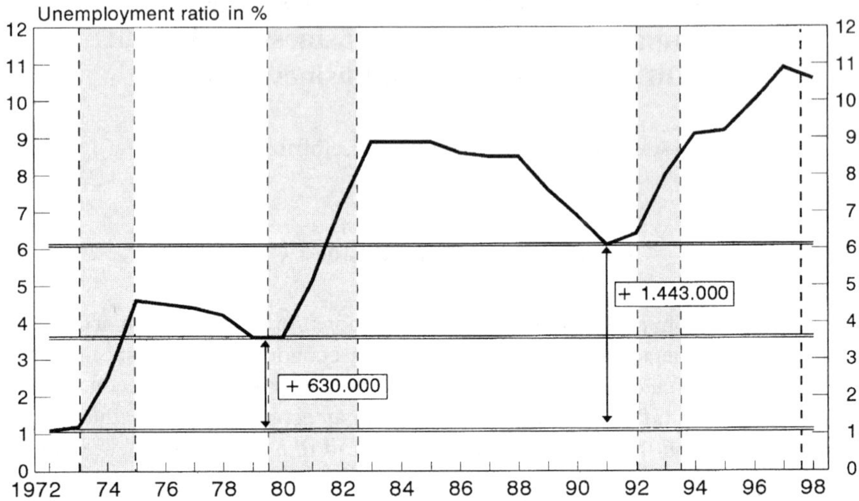


Figure 1: Development of the unemployment ratio in western Germany since 1972

## *1. Description of Indicators*

We will compare the business cycle not only with individual indicators but also with composite indicators. The indicator 'monetary conditions' consists of two individual indicators (interest rate spread, real exchange rate). The indicator 'fiscal policy' consists of only one time series (primary structural government budget balance). Bringing the indicators 'monetary conditions' and 'fiscal policy' together, a composite indicator of overall policy conditions results. Figure 2 shows the construction of different indicators surveyed in this study.

*Monetary conditions* are defined here as a composite indicator of the interest rate difference (interest rate for ten-year government bonds minus the three-month interest rate) and the real exchange rate of the D-Mark (vis-à-vis 18 industrial countries). With a decidedly positive yield spread, the conditions for an upswing are better than is the case for a less positive spread of even a negative. In the first case the Bundesbank keeps the short-term interest rates clearly below the long-

[1] The Ifo Business Climate Index has in general a very high correlation with the business cycle. As this study applies only monthly data, we have taken the survey-based Ifo-data because of it's monthly publication; against that, the GDP-data from the Federal Statistical Office are only published quarterly.

term market interest rates and thus helps provide favourable financing conditions which stimulate investors and private consumers. Also a higher real exchange rate (a real undervaluation of the D-Mark) can shore up an economic expansion since it enhances Germany's price competitiveness vis-à-vis other countries. Both indicators used here for monetary conditions and been tested frequently with regard to their quality for business-cycle and inflation forecasts with good results.[2]

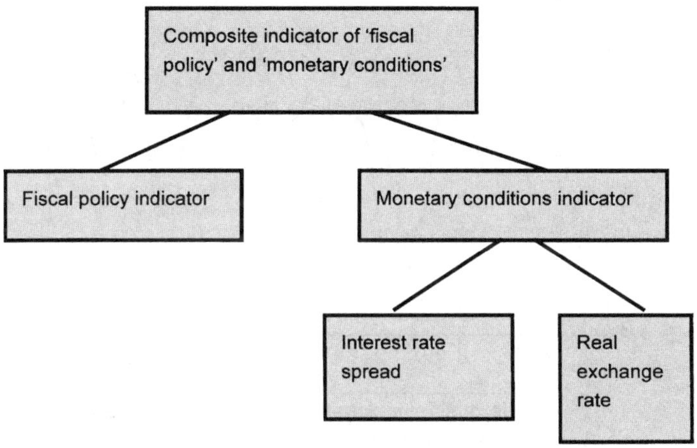


Figure 2: Combination of indicators

Figure 3 shows the two factors impacting the indicator for monetary conditions,[3] and it is evident that especially the yield spread has a very close relation to the economic situation. All three recessions – the shaded areas in the figures – are shown at an early stage by this indicator (about a year before the lower turning point of the cycle). Before the recessions the Bundesbank regularly raised short-term rates clearly above the level of the long-term rates – for various reasons as we will show in Section III – so that with a negative yield spread, the willingness to take on debts

2 Of the numerous investigations, those that analyze the German economy include: Estrella, Arturo / Hardouvelis, Gikas H.: The Term Structure as a Predictor of Economic Activity, in: The Journal of Finance, June 1991; Hu, Zuliu: The Yield Curve and Real Activity, in: IMF Staff Papers Dec. 1993, pp. 781 - 805; Döpke, Jörg / Langfeld, Enno: Indikatoren für die konjunkturellen Wirkungen der Geldpolitik, Kieler Arbeitspapiere, September 1993; Leibfritz, Willi (II): Internationaler Vergleich finanz- und geldpolitischer Indikatoren, in: K.H. Oppenländer, Konjunkturindikatoren, München Wien 1995, pp. 282 - 97; Juchems, Alexander / Nerb, Gernot: Indicators for Monetary Policy, in: Oppenländer, K.H. / G. Poser (eds.), Business Cycles Surveys: Forecasting Issues and Methodological Aspects, Aldershot 1996.

3 The times series presented in graphs 2, 3 and 4 are smoothed and normed. The smoothing is to achieve a clear depiction of an otherwise strongly 'fluttering' series. Norming is necessary for the joint graphic depiction of more than two differently scaled time series. In the subsequently carried-out regressions, the original data was used.

weakened with an accompanying cyclical decline. In upswing phases as well, there is a comparatively close dependency of the business cycle and the yield spread curve.

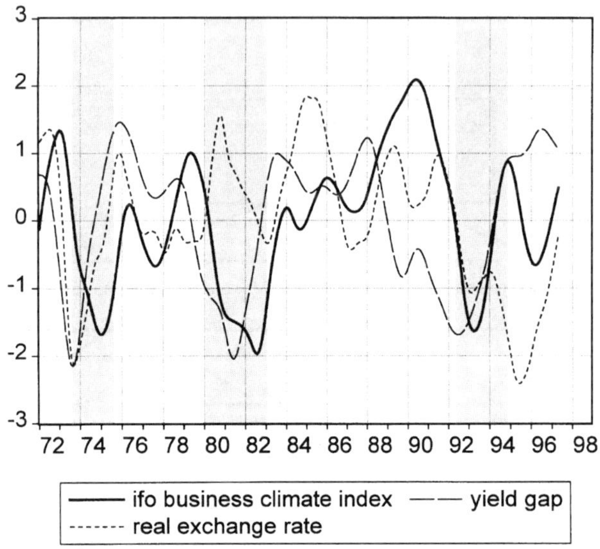


Note: Time series are normalised and smoothed; grey areas indicate recessions

Figure 3: Components of the indicator 'monetary conditions' and the business cycle

The course of the real exchange rate has a less close connection with the business cycle. To be sure, the 1974/75 recession was caused by the preceding, sharp appreciation of the D-Mark in the wake of the collapse of the Bretton Woods regime, but the ensuring recession was marked by a general erosion of confidence regarding Germany's economic performance, leading to a real depreciation of the D-Mark which supported the economy in this phase. In the 1992/93 recession, in contrast, the course of the business cycle and the real exchange rate were once more in accord: the economic downturn was caused in part by the sharp appreciation of the D-Mark in the summer of 1992. The not-so-close overall connection between the real exchange rate and the business cycle is not only seen in the non-recession phases: The strong dollar caused by the US policy mix between 1982 and 1985 did not have such an expansive impact on the economy, and also the extreme appreciation of the D-Mark in 1995 did not result in an immediate recession, as was actually shown by the status of the indicator.

By combining the two individual monetary indicators we obtain the indicator 'monetary conditions' (cf. Figure 4). The method of combination is explained in the Box below. The 'monetary conditions' indicator runs more closely parallel to the business cycle than the two individual monetary indicators. For example, the otherwise very reliable yield-spread indicator did not indicate the 'growth dip' in 1995. Against that, the monetary conditions indicator, which additionally captured the strong D-Mark appreciation in early 1995, moved downward at this time and thus in the same direction as the business cycle.

**Box: Construction of Composite Indicators**[4]

First, the time series are detrended if they have a trend (in our case, all time series were stationary).

Second, all time series are standardised (mean is set to zero, standard deviation to one).

Third, time series are combined:

- the optimum lag / lead of the individual indicators against the explained variable (here: ifo business climate index) is evaluated with the cross correlation method,
- a regression is run of the individual indicators on the target variable (here: ifo business climate index); in our case, the regression approach is as follows:

$$\text{IFOBUSINESSCLIMATE} = 92.5 + 3.3\ \text{YIELDSPREAD}_{t-12} - 1.5\ \text{REALEXCHANGERATE}_{t-4}\ ,$$

- the variables are added with the coefficients from the regression without any lead / lag; in our case, the composite monetary indicator is calculated as follows:

$$\text{monetary conditions} = 3.3\ \text{yield spread (normed)} - 1.5\ \text{real exchange rate (normed)}.$$

*Fiscal policy* is seen here as the primary structural budget balance of the government (budget balance, adjusted for the business cycle and interest payments). This concept can only approximate the actual impulses on business cycle that stem from fiscal policy. It cannot, for example, capture tax-policy disincentives such as a generally high tax burden or a growth-preventing tax structure. Nevertheless, as an approximate value for short-term government economic incentives this concept is standard practice[5] (although it must be kept in mind that there are fewer studies on suitable fiscal indicators than on the quality of monetary indicators). The fiscal policy indicator thus calculated is shown in Figure 4.

The fiscal policy indicator did not run closely parallel with the business cycle in all phases. In the 1974 / 75 recession expansive fiscal policy certainly hastened the end of the recession. Also in the ensuing upswing between 1975 and 1979 there was a close relationship between this indicator and the cycle. Thereafter, the fiscal policy brakes were abruptly applied, thus being primarily responsible for the long-lasting 1980 / 82 recession. At this time a paradigm shift in German fiscal policy

4 For more details of the technique of combining the individual indicators, see: Oppenländer, Karl-Heinrich / Poser, Günter: Handbuch der ifo Umfragen, Berlin 1989, Chapter 4.

5 See Leibfritz, Willi (II).

occurred, i.e. a turning from (putative) anticyclical fiscal policy à la Keynes to a consolidation policy aimed at a favourable incentive structure in the tax system. Between 1983 and 1988 the business cycle showed a moderately upward trend despite a restrictive fiscal policy (measured in terms of the government deficit). Between 1989 and 1992 once again fiscal policy was expansive; it artificially extended the reunification boom.[6] Fiscal policy brakes were strongly applied on into the following recession.

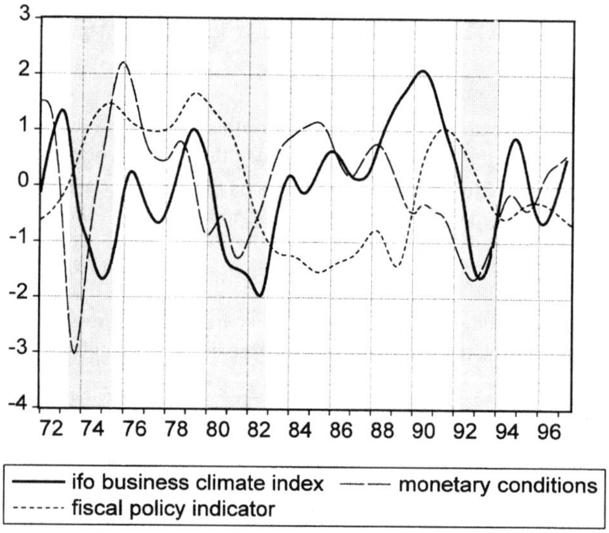


Note: Time series are normalised and smoothed; grey areas indicate recessions

Figure 4: Fiscal policy, monetary conditions and the business cycle

By combining the indicators of monetary conditions and fiscal policy, we obtain an *overall indicator of the monetary and fiscal environment* (see Figure 5). Of all the indicators examined here, this one seems to show the business cycle most accurately. At least one of the two underlying indicators almost always points in the same direction as the business cycle so that false readings of an individual indicator hardly bear any weight in the composite indicator.

6 This pro-cyclical pattern was caused by the strong increase in transfers to east Germany, which were financed by additional government debt, at the same time that the tax cuts in the tax reforms of 1986 / 88 / 90 took effect. See Leibfritz, Willi (I): Finanz- und Geldpolitik – zwei feindliche Schwestern?, in: HWWA-Wirtschaftsdienst 1994 / VII, pp. 345 - 51.

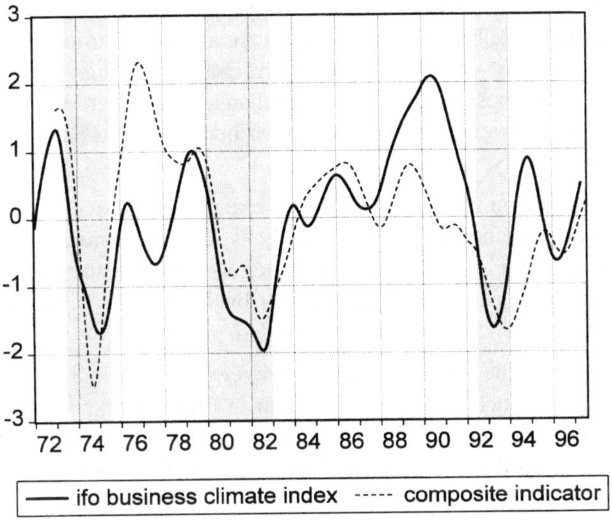


Note: Time series are normalised and smoothed; grey areas indicate recessions

Figure 5: Composite indicator and the business cycle

## 2. *Analytical Test of Indicator Performance*

A prerequisite of the following procedure is that all time series used here are stationary (indicators as well as the business cycle variable). Table 1 shows that time series are indeed stationary in their level form.

*Table 1*

**Augmented Dickey-Fuller-tests on time series**

| Variable | Specification | included lags | *t*-value | critical *t*-values on a 5%-level |
|---|---|---|---|---|
| Ifo business climate index | C | 4 | – 3,22 | – 2,87 |
| Real exchange rate | NC | 4 | – 3,19 | – 1,94 |
| Yield spread | NC | 4 | – 2,85 | – 1,94 |
| Monetary conditions | NC | 4 | – 2,73 | – 1,94 |
| Fiscal policy | NC | 4 | – 2,31 | – 1,94 |
| Composite indicator | C | 4 | – 3,43 | 2,87 |

Legend: C=Constant, NC=No constant because it is not significant.

Time series are monthly data running from 1: 1972 to 6: 1997.

Source: Calculations of the Ifo Institute.

A regression analysis shows that all employed indicators are able to contribute to an explanation of the business cycle: They are always significant – in individual or multiple regressions – and contain the correct algebraic sign. The monetary indicator leads the business cycle: the real exchange rate has a lead of four months and the yield spread twelve; the indicator used here for fiscal policy lags the business cycle by two years.

The close connection between the interest rate difference and the business cycle which was already demonstrated graphically is also confirmed analytically: this variable is not only highly significant in all regressions, but the quality (measured by the correlation coefficient) of an existing business-cycle prognostic approach increases strongly when this variable is included.

The superiority of the monetary indicator over the fiscal indicator in predicting the business cycle, which was already evident in Figure 4, is confirmed by the regression analysis: the correlation coefficient from the regression with the business cycle is 0.26 and thus three times higher than with the fiscal policy indicator.

*Table 2*

**Business-cycle prognosis with various indicators**

*Explained variable: German business cycle (measured by the Ifo Business Climate Index)*

| Name of indicator | Optimal lead (–) or lag (+) before / after the business cycle in months | C | RE | YS | FP | $R^2$ | Std. error of regression |
|---|---|---|---|---|---|---|---|
| *Real exchange rate* | – 4 | 92.5 (226.8) | 2.0 (4.9) | | | 0.08 | 7.0 |
| *Yield spread* | – 12 | 92.5 (242.4) | | 3.48 (9.0) | | 0.21 | 6.5 |
| *Monetary conditions* | – 12 | 92.5 (248.6) | 1.5 (4.0) | 3.3 (8.7) | | 0.26 | 6.3 |
| *Fiscal policy* | 24 | 91.9 (216.7) | | | 1.2 (4.9) | 0.08 | 7.0 |
| *Composite indicator* | 0 | 92.2 (240.9) | 1.7 (4.5) | 3.0 (7.5) | 0.8 (3.7) | 0.29 | 6.2 |

Legend: C=Constant, RE=Real exchange rate, YS=Yield spread, FP=Fiscal policy.

Time series are monthly data running from 1: 1972 to 6: 1997.

Note: Regressions are done here with unsmoothed time series; this gives a bias to low correlation coefficients. Regressions with smoothed time series gives much higher values for the correlation coefficients.

Source: Calculations of the Ifo Institute.

As already evident from a comparison of Figures 4 and 5, of all the indicators used in this study the composite indicator has the greatest explanatory power for the business cycle (correlation coefficient of 0.29). The areas of economic policy it contains, monetary and fiscal policies together, are thus 'cycle makers' that cannot be ignored.

When aggregating into a composite indicator, however, information is lost: the composite indicator can no longer identify the actual trigger of the recessions; it is also no longer as early an indication of the business cycle turning points. With a separate depiction of the individual indicators, however, the causes of the recession can be named. Thus, in the following, we will turn again to the individual indicators and examine the developments these show at the lower turning points of the business cycle.

## III. Monetary Conditions and Fiscal-Policy in Recessions

Figure 4 contains the individual indicators of 'monetary conditions' and 'fiscal policy' as well as the business cycle course. It is easily recognisable that shortly before or during a recession, a strong deterioration of one of the two indicators occurred: before the 1974/75 recession there was a significant worsening of the monetary conditions indicator; before or during the recessions of 1980/82 and 1992/93 both policy areas were affected. Table 3 shows the development of the individual indicators shortly before or during the recession.[7]

*Table 3*

**Changes in the economic-policy environment and recessions**

| | Recession of . . . | | |
|---|---|---|---|
| Increase of the degree of restriction . . ., | 1974/75 | 1980/82 | 1992/93 |
| . . . I. of the monetary conditions owing to a . . . | | | |
| . . . I.1 real appreciation of the D-Mark | X | | X |
| . . . I.2 reduction of the interest rate spread – or a negative spread – owing to monetary policy tightening by the Bundesbank because of . . . | | | |
| . . . I.2.a. a prior fiscal policy expansion | | X | X |
| . . . I.2.b. an oil price shock | X | X | |
| . . . II. of fiscal policy | | X | X |

7 In Table 3 monetary conditions are divided in the two individual indicators 'real exchange rate' and 'yield spread'. The reduction of the otherwise positive yield spread – or the turning into a negative spread – is particularly attributable to a tightening of monetary policy. Here again, primarily two main factors are responsible: either a strong prior fiscal-policy expansion or an oil price shock; the Bundesbank reacted to both developments by raising interest rates to avert inflation.

We attempted to set up rules indicating a recession. It turned out, that it was not possible to determine the probability of occurrence of a recession at the *level* of economic-policy indicators; only the *change* of the economic-policy indicators reliably announces recessions: Every time that the 'monetary conditions' or the 'fiscal policy' indicator – or both indicators – show strong and rapid worsening, a recession follows. For the past we have set up the following rule: when the monetary condition indicator worsens by two percent within six months and / or when the fiscal policy indicator worsens by 0.6 percent within six months, this was followed by or coincided with a recession.[8]

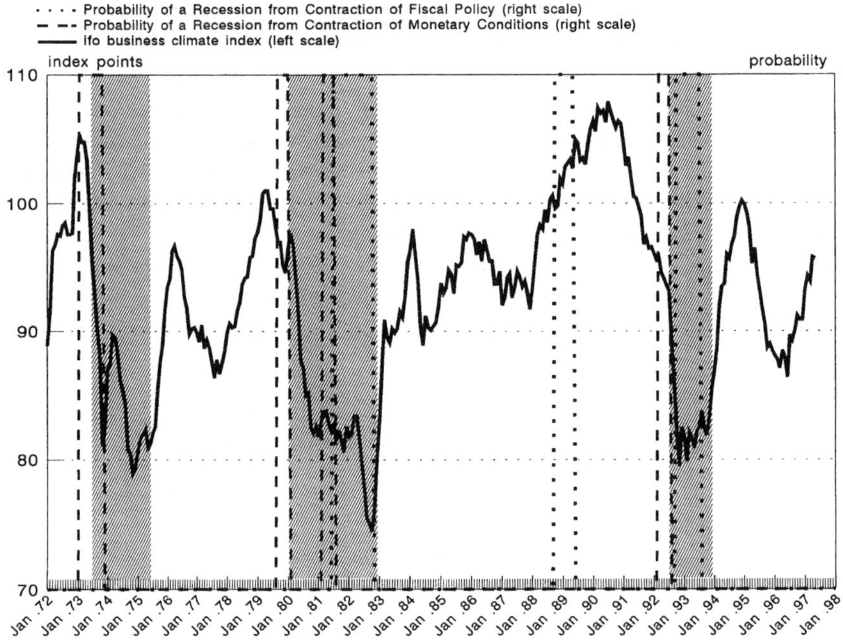


Figure 6: Likelihood of recessions from contraction of monetary conditions or fiscal policy

This relationship is shown in Figure 6. When one of the two indicator series develops in a poorer manner than described by the above rules, then the indicator that signals the probability of a recession jumps from 'zero' to 'one'. According to this rule, the individual indicators signal all recessions; it is clear that the monetary conditions lead the business cycle, even in the recession phases – as in the entire period under investigation; fiscal policy in the recession phase does not lag the

[8] '100' was added to each of the previously standardized series in order to achieve meaningful growth rates.

business cycle – as in the average of the entire period under investigation – but here it coincides with the business cycle. A 'false alarm' from the fiscal policy indicator came in 1989, but is 'excusable' because of the unusual circumstances just before reunification; at the time government revenues rose sharply (tax revenues from the purchases of then GDR citizens) and government spending was at a much lower level than after reunification.

## IV. Consequences for Economic Policy

The overall importance of monetary, exchange-rate and fiscal policy for the business-cycle and the labour market must not be overestimated. Our study showed that only about a third of the month-to-month business-cycle movements can be explained by the development of the above policy indicators. A sustainable increase in employment is achievable in particular by measures that effect the labour market directly such as the increase of flexibility on the labour market; in this way the cementing of originally cyclically caused unemployment into structural unemployment can be prevented.

These considerations show, however, that without the rapid worsening of the parameters 'fiscal policy' and 'monetary conditions' at least the gravity of the past recessions and therefore the sharp increase in unemployment could have been prevented. Accordingly, economic policy can be improved by the following measures:

1. Clear expansion of fiscal policy which regularly lead to an overheating of the economy – and then to a stabilisation recession – must be avoided.

2. The European Economic and Monetary Union (EMU) must be implemented on time and with the largest possible number of qualified member states so that the sharp appreciations of the D-Mark vis-à-vis the currencies of other European countries no longer occur.

3. After EMU is achieved, the exchange-rate fluctuations of the Euro against the Dollar and to a somewhat lesser extent against the Yen will continue to affect the German economy. The exchange rate decision-makers must participate in the discussion on measures to reduce fluctuations of world currencies instead of avoiding this discussion with the argument that such measures lead directly to an unacceptable exchange-rate orientation in monetary policy. In fact, a reduction of exchange-rate fluctuations between important currency blocks could indeed be achieved by greater transparency on currency markets. The Annex shows that there are measures for this that are in conformance with a market-oriented policy and not too restrictive. An exchange-rate oriented monetary policy or a foreign-exchange market tax, in our opinion, would be too strong an intervention or would not be in conformance with market principles, and thus should not be considered.

A side effect of the reduced DEM / USD-fluctuations is, that the fluctuations of commodity prices, mostly quoted in US-dollars, could be diminished; with reduced fluctuations in commodity prices, less drastic monetary policy reactions would be necessary.

4. A tightening of the monetary policy of the Bundesbank – and in future of the European Central Bank – must be done in appropriate doses. To be sure, the inflation potential touched off by a fiscal-policy expansion, high wage agreements or an oil price shock should not be nourished, but moderation is necessary. If the Bundesbank applies the brakes too sharply, as it did in the case of the fiscal-policy expansion of 1989 / 92, this can lead to a recession – as many observers at the time agree it did.[9] In case of a sharpening of the degree of restriction because of a rise in leading interest rates, the central bank must always take into consideration the consequence of a currency appreciation – and thus an additional worsening of monetary conditions. A more promising strategy is a moderate but early intervention of the central bank (pre-emptive strike) which would obviate more stronger subsequent reactions.

## Annex: Types of Currency Market Intervention

The table shows the options for currency market intervention with the goal of reducing exchange rate volatility.[10] The weaker interventions are at the top, with the degree of intervention increasing towards the bottom. There is however, no strict hierarchy among the various measures. The strength or weakness of the intervention depends on the extent of the individual measure, e.g. the volume of currency buyed / sold.

*Table 4*

**Kinds of foreign exchange market interventions**

| *Kind of foreign exchange market intervention* | *Example* | *Comment, suitability as an instrument to reduce EUR / USD-volatility* |
|---|---|---|
| *'Talking about the Currency'* | Bundesbank end of 1994 / beginning of 1995[11]. | More often used in recent times. Together with other measures, i.e. buying / selling foreign exchange by central banks, quite successful. |

[9] See Filc, Wolfgang: Bundesbank, Konjunktur und EWS, in: HWWA-Wirtschaftsdienst 1993 / IX, pp. 461 - 68.

[10] See also Juchems, Alexander: Schwachstellen des Weltwährungssystems und Möglichkeiten zu ihrer Beseitigung, in: ifo Schnelldienst 27 / 1994.

[11] For example: Deutsche Bundesbank: Press Release of 2 November 1994. Press release with the following text: 'Bundesbank President Dr. Hans Tietmeyer made the following comment this evening to the declaration of the US Secretary of the Treasury, Lloyd Bentsen: "I welcome the fact that the American currency officials have stressed their interest in a strong

| | | |
|---|---|---|
| *Increase of transparency at foreign exchange authorities*<br>• Publication of time and volume of forex interventions<br><br>• Publication of the records of meetings of the central bank council<br>• Publication of articles indicating the view of the central banks on the "fundamental value" of the exchange rate | <br><br>More and more since the beginning of the 90s in the USA<br>In the USA since the beginning of the 90s<br><br>Bundesbank since 1993[12] | <br><br>Quite successful according i.e. to a study of K. Dominguez / J.A. Frankel.[13] |
| *Enhancement of transparency at the banks*<br>• Increase of the collateral for forex transactions<br><br><br>• Obligation to publish foreign exchange transactions, divided by currency, trading partner and kind of transaction | | <br><br>The 'Bale committee on banking supervision' tries to set up international standards, see: Bank for International Settlements[14].<br>Up to now data on forex transactions are published by the BIS only every third year on a highly aggregated basis; it would be highly desirable to have more detailed and more up-to-date data |
| *Short-term interest rate variations* | In the EMS member states (except Germany) in summer 1992 to stabilise their currencies against the D-Mark | In the long-term only applicable if the interest rate variation "fits" into the home business cycle development. |
| *Foreign exchange buying / selling of central banks*<br>• Free interventions<br><br><br><br>• Institutionalised interventions | <br><br>From time to time to influence the DEM / USD-exchange rate<br><br>Regularly in the EMS | <br><br>Interventions to influence the EUR / USD-exchange rate may have the same prominence as interventions in the DEM / USD-foreign exchange market.<br>"Target zones" for exchange rates are necessary for obligatory interventions; applicable "target zones" for the EUR / USD are not very meaningful (a very large corridor would have to be set up); therefore obligatory interventions on the EUR / USD exchange rate are not very likeful. |

dollar and seek to shore this up with corresponding policies. This declaration should help lead to a market valuation of the dollar that is more in accord with the fundamentals".

12 Dominguez, Kathrin / Frankel, Jakob A.: Does Foreign Intervention Work?, Institute for International Economics, Washington 1994.

13 Deutsche Bundesbank: Entwicklung und Bestimmungsfaktoren des Außenwerts der D-Mark, Monatsbericht, November 1993; Deutsche Bundesbank: Gesamtwirtschaftliche Bestimmungsgründe der Entwicklung des realen Außenwerts der D-Mark, Monthly Report, August 1995.

14 Bank for International Settlements: Annual Report 1996, especially Annex 1, Activities of the Bank.

| *Kind of foreign exchange market intervention* | *Example* | *Comment, suitability as an instrument to reduce EUR/USD-volatility* |
|---|---|---|
| *Tax on foreign exchange transactions* | Not used | Goes back on an idea of J. Tobin;[15] has to be rejected as an artificial market distortion. |
| *Co-ordination of economic policy* | Tighter co-ordination of Irelands economic policy with the economic policy of continental Europe than with the economic policy of Great Britain since the mid-80s | Despite of many promises i.e. at G7-meetings only very modest progress of the G7-states towards more co-ordination; therefore co-ordination seems not to have a great chance as an instrument to 'manage' the EUR/USD-exchange rate. |

## References

*Bank for International Settlements:* Annual Report 1996, especially Annex 1, Activities of the Bank. – *Deutsche Bundesbank:* 'Entwicklung und Bestimmungsfaktoren des Außenwerts der D-Mark', Monatsbericht, November 1993. – *Deutsche Bundesbank:* Press Release of 2 November 1994. – *Deutsche Bundesbank:* 'Gesamtwirtschaftliche Bestimmungsgründe der Entwicklung des realen Außenwerts der D-Mark', Monthly Report, August 1995. – *Dominguez,* K. M./*Frankel* J. A.: Does Foreign Intervention Work? Institute for International Economics, Washington 1994. – *Döpke,* J./*Langfeld* E.: Indikatoren für die konjunkturellen Wirkungen der Geldpolitik, Kieler Arbeitspapiere, September 1993. – *Estrella* A./*Hardouvelis* G. A.: 'The Term Structure as a Predictor of Economic Activity', The Journal of Finance, June 1991. – *Filc* W.: 'Bundesbank, Konjunktur und EWS', HWWA-Wirtschaftsdienst 1993/IX, pp. 461 - 68. – *Hu,* Z.: 'The Yield Curve and Real Activity', IMF Staff Papers Dec. 1993, pp. 781 - 805. – *Juchems,* A.: 'Schwachstellen des Weltwährungssystems und Möglichkeiten zu ihrer Beseitigung', ifo Schnelldienst 27/1994. – *Juchems* A./Nerb G.: 'Indicators for Monetary Policy', in: Oppenländer, K. H./G. Poser (eds.), Business Cycles Surveys: Forecasting Issues and Methodological Aspects, Aldershot 1995. – *Leibfritz,* W.: (I) 'Finanz- und Geldpolitik – zwei feindliche Schwestern?', in: HWWA-Wirtschaftsdienst 1994/VII, pp. 345 - 51. – *Leibfritz,* W.: (II) 'Internationaler Vergleich finanz- und geldpolitischer Indikatoren', in: K. H. Oppenländer, Konjunkturindikatoren, München Wien 1995, pp. 282 - 97. – *Oppenländer,* K. H./*Poser* G.: Handbuch der ifo Umfragen, Berlin 1989, Chapter 4. – *Tobin,* J.: The New Economics One Decade Older, The Eliot Janeway Lectures in Honour of Joseph Schumpeter, Princeton University Press, Princeton 1974, pp. 88 ff.

[15] Tobin, Joseph: The New Economics One Decade Older, The Eliot Janeway Lectures in Honour of Joseph Schumpeter, Princeton University Press, Princeton 1974, pp. 88 ff.

# Financing Constraints, Output and Employment*

## Lessons from Theory and Empirical Evidence on the Micro and Macro Level

By Peter Winker, Mannheim

### I. Introduction

Recently, the impact of financial markets and potential financing constraints on real economic performance regained interest. This may be attributed to at least three more or less independent causes.

First, an increasing literature contributes to the empirical assessment of the existence, extent and effects of financing constraints at the firm level.[1] Although there is a vivid debate about the correct method, an outside observer might conclude that this phenomenon exists, at least at the micro level, and may be supposed to have real effects.

Second, the modeling of financing constraints in macroeconomics still lags far behind the theory and econometric modeling at the micro level. Nevertheless, a growing number of attempts has been undertaken to incorporate this aspect in aggregate models.[2] So far, however, it would be premature to speak of a standard or even unanimous theoretical framework. Either the approaches lack a stringent connection to the theory of firms and banks or they evade an empirical assessment. Nevertheless, some descriptive analysis based on the available modeling is possible.[3]

Finally, the recent experience with financing constraints, financial crises and economic problems in some south-east Asian countries could be a trigger for renewed research activities. At least, it represents a stylized fact which deserves attention in the context of macroeconomic reasoning.

---

* I am indebted to W. Franz and W. Smolny for helpful comments on a preliminary version of this paper. The usual disclaimer applies.

1 Cf. Winker (1996) for a recent literature survey.

2 Cf. Greenwald and Stiglitz (1990), Waller and Lewarne (1994), Fender (1995) and Blum and Hellwig (1996).

3 Cf. Mishkin (1996).

This paper aims to contribute to a better understanding of the importance of financing constraints in particular with regard to potential real effects and implications for macroeconomic policy. However, as macroeconomic theory and even more macroeconometric studies on this issue are still in an early stage of development, the results should be taken as report on work in progress. Instead of presenting final answers it will rather raise new questions and hint to areas of future research activities. Nevertheless, it cannot and should not be avoided to draw also at least some tentative conclusions.

The exposition starts with a short review of theory and evidence for financing constraints and their real effects at the firm level. In addition to previous work new estimation results for the financing constraint employment link are presented based on a unique firm panel for West Germany. Section III. is devoted to an aggregate view on loan markets. A simple model of the German credit market is sketched which is essentially based on the micro foundations provided by the standard approaches to model information asymmetries. While a partial analysis of the loan market seems also feasible empirically – some estimation results are provided – the model does not yet allow for a completely integrated analysis in a macroeconometric model. Instead a simpler version – similar to the theoretical framework proposed by Blum and Hellwig (1996) – is used in section III.3. for this purpose inside a macroeconometric disequilibrium model for West Germany. Using this model allows, e.g., to analyze the impact of the reinforcement of equity requirements following the Basle accords. Combining the available evidence at the micro and macro level in the final section some tentative conclusions on the relevance of these phenomena for the German economy and its employment problems are drawn.

## II. Financing Constraints at the Firm Level

### *1. Causes for Financing Constraints*

Arguments for the existence of financing constraints and their causes date back at least to the times of Adam Smith (1776).[4] They regained some interest in the context of the availability theory in the late 1940s as part of an alternative monetary transmission mechanism. The dominating aspect in the recent analysis, however, is asymmetric information.[5] If banks do not dispose of the same information as do firms, interest rates play a double role. First, they act as price for loans, and second, they influence the quality, i.e. the risk of a loan portfolio. An increase of interest will have a negative influence on the quality by adverse selection and mor-

---

4 "If the legal rate of interest [...] was fixed so high [...], the greater part of the money which was to be lent would be lent to prodigals and projectors, who alone would be willing to give this high interest. Sober people, who will give for the use of money no more than a part of what they are likely to make by the use of it, would not venture into the competition."

5 Cf. Jaffee and Stiglitz (1990) for an overview.

al hazard effects. Consequently, the interest level which maximizes banks' expected profits does not necessarily coincide with the market clearing price. Credit rationing can be a rational outcome of profit maximizing subjects.[6]

While the theoretical appraisal of the potential effects of asymmetric information on loan market does not differ substantially in the literature despite the differences in exposition and depth of the analysis, various approaches can be found for the empirical assessment of such phenomena. I will come back to aggregate approaches in the next section and concentrate on microeconometric studies for the moment.

The advantage of microeconometric approaches is that financing constraints could, at least in principle, be directly observed and other observable characteristics of the firms can be used to explain these constraints. However, the ifo firm panel data used in Winker (1996, 1998a) seems to be one of the rare data sets which include explicit statements on financing constraints. Consequently, the empirical research in general has to rely on approximations. The most common one is to study the influence of cash flow on real activities, e.g. investment, after controlling for other relevant factors. If investment exhibits a strong sensitivity on cash flow, this is taken as an indicator for financing constraints. In order to make these results more reliable and to obtain some information on the causes of financing constraints, mostly only differences in cash flow sensitivity between groups of firms or for different time periods are interpreted. However, an exogenous grouping of firms by size, stock market listing, stance of monetary policy or other indicators might not only be subjective but bias the results.[7]

The problem of finding suitable indicators for those firms, which, ceteris paribus, are more likely to face financing constraints, can be avoided using the ifo firm panel described in Schneeweis and Smolny (1997). In the questionnaire of the ifo survey on innovative activities, firms report directly whether they face constraints by missing internal and external funds. This information can be matched with other firm specific data to draw inference on the causes of such financial constraints. The empirical assessment supports the hypothesis that firms with a large number of employees are less likely to face financing constraints compared to small firms, while an expected improvement of business prospects increases the rationing probability. This second effect might seem contra intuitive at first glance. However, it is strictly in line with the theory of asymmetric information since firms expecting an improvement of their business situation are more likely to ask for a loan and hence, ceteris paribus, more likely to be rejected if the banks cannot differentiate between firms.[8]

6 Cf. Stiglitz and Weiss (1981) for the basic theoretical framework.

7 Cf. Faroque and Ton-That (1995) for a discussion of this effect, and the vivid debate between Kaplan and Zingales (1997) and Fazzari, Hubbard and Petersen (1995) on the right a priori grouping.

8 Cf. Winker (1998a) for a formal exposition of this effect.

To sum up the findings of empirical research on evidence for effects of asymmetric information at the firm level, it can be stated that most of the studies find significant effects either directly or via some proxy variables which are in line with the existence of financing constraints.[9] Furthermore, the applications show that small and young firms are more likely to face such constraints, while diversification, ongoing business relationships with banks and high collateral tend to reduce this risk. It is an obvious shortcoming of the indirect approaches that they can deliver only qualitative statements on the existence and indirect inference on the causes of financing constraints. Using the ifo firm panel avoids the latter shortcomming because direct inference on the causes of financing constraints is possible. However, the information on financing constraints is purely qualitative. Hence, statements on the share of firms facing financial constraints are possible, but it is not feasible to estimate the amount of excess demand for financing. A quantitative assessment of the extent of this phenomenon is beyond the scope of the microeconometric analysis at least up to date.

## 2. *Effects*

"There is apt to be an unsatisfied fringe of borrowers, the size of which can be expanded or contracted, so that banks can influence the volume of investment by expanding or contracting the volume of their loans, without there being necessarily any change in the level of bank-rate, in the demand-schedule of borrowers, or in the volume of lending otherwise than through the banks. This phenomenon is capable, when it exists, of having great practical importance."[10]

Once the existence of financing constraints is established, a natural question to ask is about their real effects. Again, firm level data lend themselves for a first assessment: if there are no real effects at the firm level, no aggregate effects can be expected. Indirect approaches towards the existence of financial constraints already answer the question partly. If financing constraints are implicitly defined by an excess sensitivity of investment on cash flow, real effects of financing constraints are imposed by definition. However, such indirect approaches do not allow for an estimate of the magnitude of these effects.

Again, the ifo firm panel data offer the advantage of direct information on financing constraints. A standard reduced form model of investment or innovation activities is easily augmented by a financing constraint dummy (*MF* if firm faces financing constraints). Table 1 summarizes some findings of pooled tobit estimates.[11]

---

9 A noteworthy exception is the study by Stöß (1996) based on the Deutsche Bundesbank's corporate balance sheet statistics.

10 Keynes (1930) I, S. 212.

11 All specifications include sectoral and firm size dummies.

*Table 1*

**Effects of Financing Constraints on R&D Expenditures and Investment**

| | Dependent variable: Share of | | | |
|---|---|---|---|---|
| | innovation expenditures | | investment | |
| | in sales | | | |
| | (1) | (2) | (3) | (4) |
| Constant | 0.0253<br>(1.782) | 0.0261<br>(1.825) | 0.0058<br>(0.356) | 0.0158<br>(0.958) |
| *MF* | – 0.0113<br>(– 4.787) | – 0.0106<br>(– 4.485) | – 0.0545<br>(– 3.806) | – 0.0545<br>(– 3.814) |
| $Q_{-1}^{100}$ | | | 0.0375<br>(4.190) | – 0.2441<br>(– 2.149) |
| $Q_{-1}^{100}/100 \times MF$ | | | 0.0631<br>(3.639) | 0.0646<br>(3.728) |
| sectoral and year specific mean of dependent variable | 0.0241<br>(2.549) | – 0.2553<br>(– 2.256) | – 0.0058<br>(– 0.057) | – 0.0165<br>(– 0.162) |
| changing business prospect dummies | without | with | without | with |
| $\sigma$ | 0.0629<br>(88.082) | 0.0626<br>(88.116) | 0.0697<br>(105.198) | 0.0695<br>(105.200) |
| Log-Likelihood | 4928.0 | 4952.3 | 6826.8 | 6844.5 |

*MF* dummy for financing constraints.
$Q_{-1}^{100}$ rate of capacity utilization.
*t*-statistics in parenthesis
*Source:* Winker (1998a)

Both for innovation expenditures and investment a significant negative impact of financing constraints appears. As the investment model incorporates the degree of capacity utilization which itself might have an impact on internal cash flow an interaction term is included in the investment equation. The estimates are in line with the interpretation that financing constraints are ceteris paribus less binding for firms with a high degree of capacity utilization.

To conclude the analysis of real effects at the firm level one might have a look at employment effects. Financing constraints may influence employment at least for two reasons. First, financing constraints may directly restrict the possibilities to pay wages before products are sold and, consequently, constrain employment even if expected demand and available capacities would allow an increase. Second, financing constraints reduce innovation expenditures, i.e. possibly employment in R&D, and investment. The employment effect of reduced investment is not clear a priori. If investments were undertaken to increase productive capacities due to an expected increase in demand, they probably would increase employment, whereas purely substitutive investments could also reduce employment at the firm level.

Empirical evidence of the financing employment link in the literature is rather limited. Nickell and Wadhwani (1991), Nickell and Nicolitsas (1995) and Funke, Maurer, Siddiqui and Strulik (1998) seem to be some of the few exceptions. While in Nickell and Wadhwani (1991) financial factors are considered only as additional explanatory variables, the other two papers aim directly at the financing employment nexus. All three studies find a significant impact of the debt ratio on employment. However, again no direct indicator of financial constraints is available in these studies. Funke et al. (1998) interpret a significant negative interaction term between sales and the share of external finance as evidence for a borrowing constraint effect which is expected to be more important for small firms (low sales).

Although the ifo firm panel includes information on the employment level, some other important variables for the modeling of employment at the firm level are missing including measures of the capital stock and wages. Hence, in order to get at least a first exploratory idea of potential employment effects, only the rate of change in employment is considered for the following empirical assessment which should be interpreted rather as descriptive. Besides the indicator variable for financial constraints in the previous period $(MF_{-1})$[12] and time dummies for all specifications, the following explanatory variables were used in different specifications: dummies for current and expected business situation, degree of capacity utilization in the previous period and sectoral dummies. While no significant impact could be found for the degree of capacity utilization, the other explanatory variables became significant at least in some specifications.

Besides pooled OLS-Regressions (OLS), fixed effect panel models (FE) were estimated for the complete unbalanced panel of available observations. Some more advanced and robust estimation techniques require balanced panel. However, eliminating firms with incomplete history could result in a severe selection bias. Finally, although fixed effect estimation eliminates all time constant firm specific effects such as management quality, product market characteristics or stock market listing, many observations are excluded implicitly due to missing variance of the explanatory variables. Hence, estimates of random effects (RE) specifications are also presented although these specifications are strongly rejected by a Hausman test against the alternative of fixed effects. Tables 2 and 3 summarize the results.

Although the negative impact of financing constraints on employment changes seems to be rather robust over the different specifications, it is not always significant at conventional levels. Furthermore, some test statistics indicate misspecification of the model. This is not surprising as basic explanatory variables are missing in the available data set. Finally, the ad hoc modeling of the financing constraints employment link does not allow for a structural interpretation of the results. In particular, the negative impact cannot be attributed solely to one of the potential transmission channels. Nevertheless, these estimates stress the potential impact of financing constraints on employment. Further research should be oriented towards

12 Note that this lag structure corresponds to the one chosen for investment.

an integrated modeling of the finance, investment and employment decision of the firm. This is clearly beyond the scope of the present analysis.

*Table 2*

**Effects of Financing Constraints on Employment Changes I**

| | Dependent variable: Rate of Employment Change | | | | | |
|---|---|---|---|---|---|---|
| | (1) | (2) | (3) | (4) | (5) | (6) |
| | (OLS) | (FE) | (RE) | (OLS) | (FE) | (RE) |
| Constant | 0.1252<br>(5.180) | – | 0.1311<br>(5.586) | 0.1175<br>(4.615) | – | 0.1241<br>(5.046) |
| *MF* | – 0.0237<br>(– 1.276) | – 0.0768<br>(– 2.781) | – 0.0393<br>(– 1.724) | – 0.0260<br>(– 1.211) | – 0.0759<br>(– 2.744) | – 0.0381<br>(– 1.671) |
| sectoral dummies | without | without | without | without | without | without |
| business situation dummies | without | without | without | with | with | with |
| Std. error of regres. | 0.5087 | 0.4481 | 0.5092 | 0.5084 | 0.4481 | 0.5090 |

*MF* dummy for financing constraints.
*t*-statistics in parenthesis.

*Table 3*

**Effects of Financing Constraints on Employment Changes II**

| | Dependent variable: Rate of Employment Change | | | | | |
|---|---|---|---|---|---|---|
| | (1) | (2) | (3) | (4) | (5) | (6) |
| | (OLS) | (FE) | (RE) | (OLS) | (FE) | (RE) |
| Constant | 0.0813<br>(2.887) | – | 0.0910<br>(3.107) | 0.0139<br>(0.177) | – | 0.010<br>(0.092) |
| *MF* | – 0.0332<br>(– 1.530) | – 0.0745<br>(– 2.693) | – 0.0420<br>(– 1.835) | – 0.0254<br>(– 1.167) | – 0.0759<br>(– 2.734) | – 0.0375<br>(– 1.636) |
| sectoral dummies | without | without | without | with | without | with |
| business situation dummies | with | with | with | with | with | with |
| firm size dummies | with | with | with | without | without | without |
| Std. error of regres. | 0.5078 | 0.4480 | 0.5083 | 0.5055 | 0.4497 | 0.5063 |

*MF* dummy for financing constraints.
*t*-statistics in parenthesis.

## III. An Aggregate View on Loan Markets

Turning now to an aggregate view on loan markets, again three different approaches to an empirical assessment of financing constraints can be distinguished. The first one is directed towards an analysis of interest rates on the loan market and their adjustment to risk free rates such as the interbank rates. The second approach uses a partial model of loan demand and supply to test for the existence of excess demand or supply. The third approach, finally, undertakes to incorporate the loan market, which might be in a situation of temporary disequilibrium, in a complete macroeconometric model.

### *1. Interest Rates*

Both theoretical and empirical results at the micro level indicate that the phenomena of adverse selection and moral hazard have some impact at least in some time periods for some segments of the loan market. Then, interest rates on this market segments will not react immediately to changes in other market rates. Osano and Tsutsui (1985) and Winker (1998b) conclude that these effects influence differently the optimal adjustment speed of loan and deposit rates with regard to changes of the interbank rate.

Unfortunately, at least for Germany, interest rates disaggregated by market segments are not available. In particular for the loan market, the availability of useful data is strictly limited. Consequently, only some tests of the adjustment processes at the aggregate level are feasible. The results show a different adjustment speed of deposit and loan rates with regard to changes of the interbank rate. This is in line with the theoretical reasoning. However, as for the microeconometric results this result cannot be used to draw conclusions about extent or effect of these phenomena at the aggregate level.

### *2. Partial Analysis*

The first shortcoming can be avoided by an analysis of loan demand and supply at the aggregate level. There exist a few contributions in the literature about this aspect. One of the first papers to be cited in this context is by Melitz and Pardue (1973). They give some theoretical reasoning for the determinants of loan supply and demand and present an empirical assessment though still under the assumption of market clearing. This assumption is removed in later studies, e.g., by Laffont and Garcia (1977), Sealey (1979) or Ito and Ueda (1981).[13] However, the theory is similar to that used by Melitz and Pardue. Consequently, rationing appears rather

---

13 For an extensive review of partial disequilibrium approaches see Winker (1996), pp. 180 ff.

ad hoc and is not derived from an explicit treatment of the decisions taken by the banking firm.

A further problem consists in the econonometric modeling of the disequilibrium situation. As neither loan supply nor loan demand can be directly observed, if the assumption of market clearing is removed, they have to be treated as latent variables. Identification of parameters is still possible if there exists some information about which market side is more likely to be constrained. The just cited approaches in the literature use the movement of the loan market interest rate as such an indicator. If interest rates rise, it is rather the demand than the supply side which is rationed and vice versa. However, taken the microeconomic foundations of credit rationing and the empirical results on the sluggish adjustment of interest rates seriously, it is questionable whether this approach is justified.

Thus, the task of an adequate partial modeling of the loan market is at least twofold. First, specifications of supply and demand functions have to be derived from models of bank and firm behaviour. At least for the banks the influence of adverse selection and moral hazard has to be admitted. Second, the estimation of such an disequilibrium model should not rely on assumptions which are not compatible with the theoretical framework.

The first task can be tackled using a model of a profit maximizing bank producing high and low risk loans, bonds and reserves based on deposits and equity as central input factors.[14] Using this model, supply functions for high and low risk loans can be derived. They depend positively on the own interest rate and equity and negatively on an alternative interest rate and the insolvency rate as a measure of default risk. The dependence of the high risk loan supply on the insolvency rate can be shown to be stronger. Consequently, under reasonable assumptions an increase in insolvency risk will lead to a shift of loan supply to low risk loans and to an overall shrinking of total loan supply. The same reaction results if only low risk loans experience an increase in default risk. An increase in the rate of return on alternative assets will, in contrast, lead to an increase of the share of high risk loans.

Unfortunately, this model cannot be estimated empirically as not only data on loan supply are missing, but even transacted volumes are not available disaggregated by risk category. The situation for interest rates is even worse as already mentioned in the previous subsection. Consequently, for the empirical assessment an aggregated version has to be used. The resulting loan supply function is

$$(1) \qquad \log L^s = \beta_0 + \beta_1 \log EQ + \beta_2 \log(1 + r^L) + \beta_3 \log(1 + cd) + \beta_4 \log(ir) + \varepsilon_S$$

with an error term $\varepsilon_S$ with expected value zero. $EQ$ denotes the share of equity in banks' balance volume. $r^L$ is the loan interest rate, $cd$ the costs of holding deposits and $ir$ the insolvency rate.

---

14 Cf. Winker (1996), pp. 148 ff.

Loan demand for this aggregate model is derived from expected real activity, the expected wage share ($ws$), nominal interest rates ($r^L$), and the inflation rate ($\hat{p}$). Expected real activity ($Y^a$) can be modeled by adaptive expectations; alternatively, explicit estimates of a macroeconometric disequilibrium model similar to the one described in section III.3. could be used. Then, loan demand is given by

$$(2) \quad L^d = \alpha_0 + \alpha_1 \log E(Y^a) + \alpha_2 \log(1 + r^L) + \alpha_3 \log \hat{p} + \alpha_4 \log ws + \alpha_5 \log bci + \varepsilon_D \ ,$$

where $\varepsilon_D$ is an error with expected value zero. The activity indicator variable $Y^a$ is instrumented by lagged values of production indices and expectations from business cycle surveys. Finally, *bci* covers additional business cycle effects through the use of some business cycle expectation indicator.

Given these loan supply and demand functions, the second task, namely the estimation of a disequilibrium model, has to be undertaken. The approach followed in the earlier contributions in the literature, namely to estimate a canonical disequilibrium model using interest movements as regime classification information, seems inadequate for the reasons mentioned above. One alternative is to estimate a canonical disequilibrium model without regime classification information. The results for West Germany and the time period 1975 to 1989 imply a significant amount of rationing of the loan demand approaching 10% in peaks around 1977 and 1985/86. However, the shortcomings of this approach seem obvious. First, the loan interest rate is treated as exogenous, and second, loan supply does not react to excess demand as equity also is assumed to be given exogenously.

An explicit treatment of the loan interest rates derived from the optimization problem of profit maximizing is also possible.[15] However, the incorporation in a disequilibrium framework leads to a highly complex maximum likelihood estimation problem which is difficult to solve using standard techniques. While the use of optimization heuristics could help to overcome this restriction, another aspect requires some further research and modeling effort, namely to model explicitely the reaction of banks to a persistent excess demand for loans. At this point one has to go a further step towards an explicit modeling of the banking firm.

### 3. *Total Analysis*

The last subsection may have given an idea about the manyfold problems for an adequate modeling of loan demand and loan supply. The obstacles are found not only in the econometric analysis but although in the theory of bank behaviour. Despite these open problems, a look at effects in a macroeconomic framework is reasonable as long as the results of partial analysis allow for the conclusion that relevant disequilibria may persist on the loan market.

---

15 Cf. Winker (1996).

Following the arguments and results of the previous section, it is loan supply which might affect real activity in a rationing context. Hence, the following analysis is concentrated on supply side considerations for the loan market. Blum and Hellwig (1996) use a small macroeconomic model to demonstrate that the introduction of equity requirements may increase instability after demand shocks to the economy. To do so they model loan supply depending on equity requirements as binding constraint and deposits if the equity constraint is not binding. To close the model, investment demand is assumed to depend on loan supply besides the usual factors.

As a completely integrated formulation in a macroeconometric model seems not possible due to the difficulties faced in the partial analysis, this reduced formulation of the loan market and its real effects is used in the macroeconometric disequilibrium model presented by Franz, Göggelmann and Winker (1998). This model is the result of ongoing research activity starting within the European Employment Programme.[16] It is beyond the scope of this paper to give a complete description of the model. Nevertheless, some short remarks might give an idea of its basic ingredients.

Perhaps the most striking difference to standard macroeconometric modeling consists in the explicit treatment of disequilibrium situations on goods, labour and loan market. For the goods and labour market disequilibria are modeled at the level of micro markets where the existence of either excess supply or excess demand can be justified. Through an explicit aggregation mechanism the aggregate model allows for the coexistence of excess supply and excess demand in the aggregate. Hence, for the labour market the contemporary presence of vacancies and unemployment is taken into consideration. A further advantage of this so called "smoothing by aggregation" aproach lies in the fact that changes between regimes of excess demand and excess supply take place continuously. This is not only more realistic but also eases the econometric estimation considerably.

The estimation of the model provides different notional series for goods, labour and loan market. Perhaps the most natural interpretation can be given to the labour market series. Besides labour supply, these series cover capacity employment ($L_{Y^c}$) and demand determined employment ($L_{Y^d}$). $L_{Y^c}$ denotes the amount of labour which can be employed using available capacities and technology, whereas $L_{Y^d}$ denotes the number of employees necessary to produce goods demand given technology. The mismatch between labour supply and labour demand is also estimated and allows to derive regime shares from these estimated labour market series. These regime shares can be interpreted as the share of micro markets or firms constrained in their employment decision by the three factors supply, available capacities and goods demand, respectively.

As the decision of firms on investment, employment and production is influenced by the prevailing regimes on their markets, the model will react differently to exogenous shocks, policy measures or influences from the financial markets de-

16 The results are published in Drèze and Bean (1990).

pending on the dominant regime. If, for example, a shortfall in expected goods demand makes firms reluctant to expand production capacities, financing constraints will have only a minor influence compared to a situation when existing capacities define the main constraint.

Unfortunately, this well developed framework cannot be applied directly to the loan market for two reasons. First, as already mentioned, a theory of the banking firm suitable for this purpose is not available yet. Second, even if bank loan supply could be modeled from a nice theory the coexistence of excess demand and excess supply can hardly be justified as, in contrast to goods and labour, financial assets can be shifted almost instantaneously and at low costs between different banks. Hence, the loan market is implemented only as a torso along the theoretical framework in Blum and Hellwig (1996).

Consequently, loan supply is modeled as minimum of two components. The first component is potential loan supply constraint by available equity which is given in log-linear form by equity, the rate of insolvencies, and the parameter $\lambda$. This regulatory parameter fixes the maximum loan supply to the multiple $\lambda$ of banks' equity. While $\lambda$ is an exogenous parameter, the development of equity and insolvencies had to be endogenized. In the current version of the model, this has been done by simple adaptive schemes. The second component mirrors available deposits. It depends on cumulated savings, which is an endogenous variable of the model, the loan interest rate and the rate of insolvencies to capture effects of risk on expected returns. The estimates of a canonical disequilibrium model[17] exhibit the expected signs and magnitudes. Under the equity constraint, loan supply raises almost proportionally with a raise in equity, while a raise of the multiple $\lambda$ has a smaller impact (0.73). The rate of insolvencies shows the expected negative sign in both regimes. In the deposit regime, the elasticity of loan supply to cumulated savings is significantly smaller than one (0.84), while the loan interest rate has the expected positive sign. Furthermore, the estimates imply that at least from 1983 on deposits were the limiting factor for loan supply up to 1990, while in the period 1991 to 1993 equity became the binding constraint. One reason is certainly that the stronger equity requirements following the Balse accord became effective in 1991 ($\lambda = 12.5$ instead of $\lambda = 18$).

The loan investment link is estimated by including the loan volume as additional explanatory variable in a standard investment function excluding investment in residential buildings and changes of inventories. Thereby, it was assumed that investment plans do not react to potential credit rationing prior to actually facing this constraint. A significant and strong impact is found supporting the microeconometric evidence and the theory.

Now, the complete model can be summarized by the schematic illustration in figure 1. It should be noted that parts of the model – including the loan market – are still subject of ongoing research.

---

17 Cf. Franz, Göggelmann and Winker (1998) for the details.

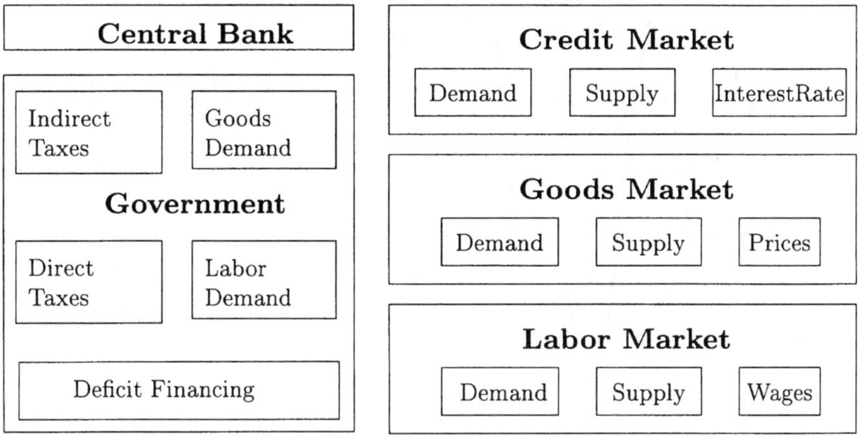


Figure 1: Central building blocks of the model

Most of the 29 stochastic equations of the model are estimated in error correction form, an obvious exception being the disequilibrium model for loan supply. The sample period is 1960 to 1994 with quarterly observations for West Germany. An extension of the sample period is aimed at. It has to include East Germany, as some aggregate data are provided only for Germany as a whole from 1995 on. Furthermore, the practical usefulness of a model for West Germany becomes more and more limited.

The central feature of the model, namely the endogenous determination of different regimes on labour, goods and loan market may be illustrated by figure 2. It shows the development of the different regimes on the labour market. Obviously, restrictions by labour supply were important in West Germany only up to the early seventies. The periods of recession after the two oil price shocks are mirrored by a sharp increase of the goods demand regime, while starting from the early eighties a growing importance of the capacity regime can be detected which hints towards an underinvestment problem during this period.

The sharpening of equity requirements following the Basle accords represents a kind of natural experiment for an empirical assessment of the transmission mechanism sketched in the Blum and Hellwig approach. Consequently, a straightforward simulation experiment using the macroeconometric disequilibrium model to assess the impact of financing constraints in a macroeconometric setting is to modify the restrictions imposed by the Basle accord. For the simulation, it is assumed that $\lambda$ decreases only down to 14.5 in 1991 instead of the actual figure of 12.5.

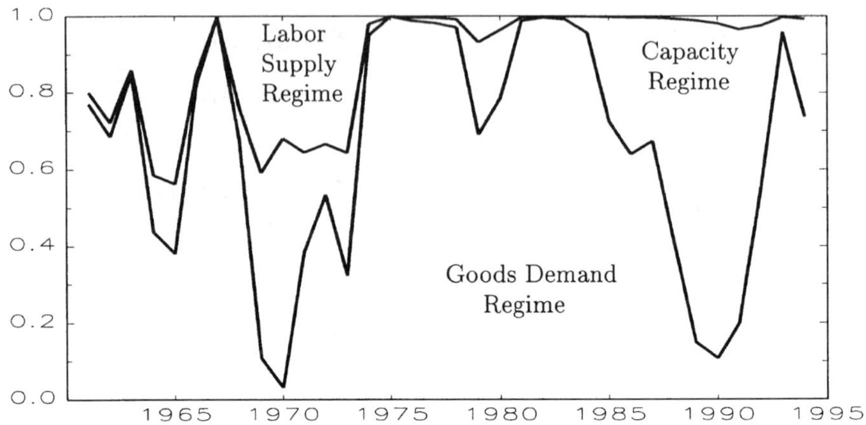


Figure 2: Regime shares

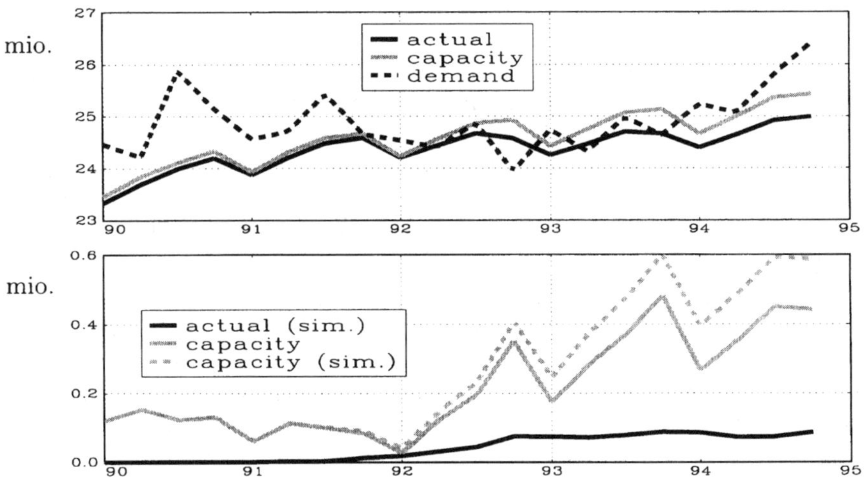


Figure 3: Employment effects (deterministic simulation)

Figure 3 summarizes some of the simulated effects on employment. The upper panel shows the baseline solution for actual employment $L^T$ as solid line together with capacity employment $L_{Y^c}$ (grey line) and demand determined employment $L_{Y^d}$ (dashed line). Up to the end of 1991 capacity employment mainly determines actual employment. This corresponds to the large regime share for the capacity regime for this period shown in figure 2. From 1992 to 1994 goods demand is a slightly stronger constraint to employment than available capacities, while from 1994 the capacity constraint becomes dominant again.

During the period, when equity was the binding factor for loan supply, i.e. from 1991 to 1993, the simulated lower equity requirements lead to a loan supply increase by up to 3 percent over the baseline solution. The resulting changes in investment in plants and equipments are reaching a peak of approximately 8 percent over the baseline solution in 1993, while the impact on output growth was more moderate with peaks around 0.4 percent. The resulting effect on employment is depicted in the lower panel of figure 3. The solid line shows the increase of actual employment over the baseline solution, whereas the solid grey line denotes the difference between capacity and actual employment for the baseline solution ($L_{Y^c} - L^T$) and the dashed grey line denotes the difference between capacity employment of the simulation experiment and actual employment of the baseline solution. Consequently, the difference between the two grey lines can be interpreted as the weakening of the capacity constraint on employment caused by more investment due to an increased loan supply. The total employment effect reaches 0.3 percent. While the deviations in loan supply, investment and output growth fall back to values close to zero in 1994 when the equity constraint was not binding any more in the baseline, the employment effect persists to the end of the sample in 1994.

## IV. Macroeconomic Effects?

The empirical evidence of the two preceeding sections implies that there might exist alternative monetary transmission mechanisms besides the standard interest rate and asset price (wealth) channels. In this section some of these alternative channels, which are more or less in line with the empirical findings, are sketched. Furthermore, some consequences for the impact of monetary policy are stressed.

Mishkin (1996) indicates three different alternative channels. First, if deposits are the limiting factor in banks' loan supply, a rise of money supply will have an impact on loan supply through an extension of deposits. This will ease financing constraints. The effect will be more important for small than for large firms as the estimation results in section II. suggest. Consequently, an expansionary monetary policy will not only have level but also distributional effects. This results comes as a direct consequence of the special role banks play in information processing. Second, a rise in money supply will lead to an increase in asset prices reducing adverse selection and moral hazard effects. In addition, a fall in short-term nominal interest rates could increase cash-flow. An overall easening of financing constraints will cause increased investment. Finally, an unexpected expansive monetary shock will lead to unexpected increases in the price level. Hence, the real value of loans outstanding will fall reducing again adverse incentive problems and lead ceteris paribus to more lending and to higher investment and output.

Besides these aspects the role of equity seems prominent, if the results of the previous section are taken into account. However, the question has to be answered why banks do not adapt their equity accordingly to expand supply in light of persistent excess demand.[18] This question has not been tackled so far extensively, probably as it can be answered only based on a solid theory of the banking firm which is missing. Assuming an exogenous negative shock to equity or an increase in the expected rate of insolvencies the following transition mechanism evolves. Both effects may have their causes in real phenomena such as a negative demand shock or they can be the result of changes in expectations which may become self fulfilling prophecies. Another reason for reduced loan supply is given by changes in banking regulation requiring a larger equity share. The reduced loan supply will lead to a cut back in investment, innovation expenditures and employment leading to or enlarging a negative demand shock. The consequence is an increase in loan defaults and the expected rate of insolvencies, a decrease in banks' profits and consequently in the banks' equity position.[19] If this process is amplified by a worsening of expectations or – as in the case of some south-east Asian countries – by imposing even stricter regulations on banks' equity and demand oriented policies a financial crisis results.[20]

What are the implications for monetary authorities? First, as long as there exist disequilibria situations on the loan market and taking into account the special role of banks in closing the information gap between lenders and firms, it is not adequate to describe and analyse the stance of monetary policy purely by the development of short-term interest rates. Second, other asset prices including the price of banks' equity are important indicators for the development of the financing situation. Third, the role of banks' equity can be crucial if it is the limiting factor of loan supply. Banking regulation has a direct impact on the loan volume. In particular, in situations when it is expensive or impossible to raise additional equity negative information shocks may lead to a vicious circle resulting in a strengthening of financing constraints or even a financial crisis. Finally, as under these conditions money does not matter only for the level of economic activity but also for its distribution between small and large firms, it may have even stronger impact on innovation activities and employment.

## V. Conclusions

What does this study contribute to the analysis of causes and potential cures for the German unemployment problem? Neither does it treat the labour market expli-

---

18 Of course, the same questions have to be asked with regard to the situation mentioned above when banks were limited by available deposits.

19 In such a situation it is nearly impossible for banks to increase equity by issuing new shares. Potential investors will take it as a negative signal and fear moral hazard. Cf. Greenwald and Stiglitz (1990).

20 Of course, this argument does not imply that imposing equity constraints on banks' lending cannot improve the stability of the financial sector in the long run.

citely, nor is it mainly concerned with demand or supply side effects from the goods market. Instead, the potential impact of disequilibrium situations on the loan market is analyzed.

The first finding is that the theoretical reasons for the existence of financing constraints at the firm level including the case of credit rationing are strong and robust to changes in the underlying models and assumptions. Furthermore, the empirical results on the micro level seem to support in their overwhelming majority the existence of such phenomena at least for some market segments and time periods both in the U.S. and Germany, as well as in some other industrialized countries.

Second, as financing constraints at the micro level do matter as they influence, e.g. quite heavily the innovative activities, investment and employment, real effects on the aggregate level cannot be precluded a priori.

Third, the available theoretical macroeconomic models for spillovers from financial markets to goods and labour markets do not lend themselves easily to an empirical analysis. This might be the cause for the fact that empirical studies on existence, extent and effects of financing constraints at the macro level are still in their infancies. The results presented in this paper may give a hint that there might be some relevant effects to be confirmed by a deeper analysis. However, it is too early to give more than a tentative conclusion on their qualitative or even quantitative impact on employment.

Finally, the findings suggest that the impact of monetary policy and developments on financial markets is probably not restricted to interest rate and asset price effects. Consequently, aiming at low real interest rates in order to promote investment might be only one of several instruments which monetary authorities can contribute to reduce unemployment.

## References

[1] *Blum,* J. and *Hellwig,* M.: Die makroökonomischen Wirkungen von Eigenkapitalvorschriften für Banken. in: D. Duwendag (Ed.). Finanzmärkte, Finanzinnovationen und Geldpolitik. Schriften des Vereins für Socialpolitik 242, Duncker&Humblot, Berlin 1996, 41-71. – [2] *Drèze,* J. H. and *Bean,* C. (Ed.): Europe's Unemployment Problem. MIT Press, Cambridge, MA, 1990. – [3] *Faroque,* A. and *Ton-That,* T.: Financing Constraints and Firm Heterogeneity in Investment Behaviour: an Application of Non-Nested Tests. Applied Economics 27,3 (1995), 317-326. – [4] *Fazzari,* S. M./ *Hubbard,* R. G. and *Petersen,* B. C.: Financing Constraints and Corporate Investment: Response to Kaplan and Zingales. NBER working Paper No. 5462, Cambridge, MA, 1995. – [5] *Fender,* J.: A Simple Macroeconomic Model with Endogenous Credit Rationing. Annales d'Économie et de Statistique 37/38 (1995), 215-235. – [6] *Franz,* W./ *Göggelmann,* K. and *Winker,* P.: Ein makroökkonometrisches Ungleichgewichtsmodell für die deutsche Volkswirtschaft 1960 bis 1994: Konzeption, Ergebnisse und Erfahrungen, in: U. Heilemann and J. Wolters (Eds.), Gesamtwirtschaftliche Modelle in der

Bundesrepublik Deutschland: Erfahrungen und Perspektiven. Schriften des Rheinisch-Westfälischen Instituts für Wirtschaftsforschung 61, Duncker & Humblot, Berlin 1998, 115 - 165. – [7] *Funke,* M./ *Maurer,* W./ *Siddiqui,* S. and *Strulik,* H.: The Employment – Financing Nexus: Evidence from a Panel of West German Firms. Small Business Economics, forthcomming 1998. – [8] *Greenwald,* B. C. and *Stiglitz,* J. E.: Macroeconomic Models with Equity and Credit Rationing. in: R. G. Hubbard (Eds.). Asymmetric Information, Corporate Finance, and Investment. University of Chicago Press, Chicago 1990, 15-42. – [9] *Ito,* T. and *Ueda,* K. Tests of the Equilibrium Hypothesis in Disequilibrium Econometrics: An International Comparison of Credit Rationing. International Economic Review 3 (1981), 691-708. – [10] *Jaffee,* D. M. and *Stiglitz,* J.: Credit Rationing. in: B. M. Friedman and F. H. Hahn (Eds.).Handbook of Monetary Economics, Vol. 1. Elsevier, Amsterdam 1990, – [11] *Kaplan,* S. N. and *Zingales,* L.: Do Investment-cash Flow Sensitivities Provide Useful Measures of Financing Constraints? Quarterly Journal of Economics 112 (1997), – [12] *Keynes,* J. M.: A Treatise on Money. MacMillan&Co. Ltd., London 1930. – [13] *Laffont,* J.-J. and *Garcia,* R.: Disequilibrium Econometrics for Business Loans. Econometrica 45, 5 (1977), – [14] *Melitz,* J. and *Pardue,* M.: The Demand and Supply of Commercial Bank Loans. Journal of Money, Credit and Banking 5 (1973), 689-702. – [15] *Mishkin,* F. S.: The Channels for Monetary Transmission: Lessons for Monetary Policy. NBER Working Paper No. 5464, Cambridge, MA, 1996. – [16] *Nickell,* S. and *Nicolitsas,* D.: How Does Financial Pressure Affect Firms? Centre for Economic Performance Discussion Paper No. 266, London 1995. – [17] *Nickell,* S. and *Wadhwani,* S.: Employment Determination in British Industry: Investigations Using Micro-Data. Review of Economic Studies 58 (1991), 955-969. – [18] *Osano,* H. and *Tsutsui,* Y.: Implicit Contracts in the Japanese Bank Loan Market. Journal of Financial and Quantitative Analysis 20,3 (1985), 211-229. – [19] *Schneeweis,* T. and *Smolny,* W.: Das ifo Unternehmenspanel 1980-92. Discussion Paper No. 32, CILE, Konstanz 1996. – [20] *Sealey,* C. W.: Credit Rationing in the Commercial Loan Market: Estimates of a Structural Model Under Conditions of Disequilibrium. The Journal of Finance 34, 3, 689-702. – [21] *Smith,* A.: The Wealth of Nations. A. A. Knopf, New York 1991 (First Edition 1776). – [22] *Stiglitz,* J. E. and *Weiss,* A.: Credit Rationing in Markets with Imperfect Information. American Economic Review 71 (1981), 393-410. – [23] *Stöß,* E.: Die Finanzierungsstruktur der Unternehmen und deren Reaktion auf monetäre Impulse. Discussion Paper 9/96, Econonomic Research Group, Deutsche Bundesbank, Frankfurt 1996. – [24] *Waller,* C. J. and *Lewarne,* S.: An Expository Model of Credit Rationing. Journal of Macroeconomics 16,3 (1994), – [25] *Winker,* P.: Rationierung auf dem Markt für Unternehmenskredite in der BRD. Mohr&Siebeck, Tübingen 1996. – [26] *Winker,* P.: Causes and Effects of Financing Constraints at the Firm Level: Some Microeconometric Evidence. Small Business Economics (1998a) forthcoming. – [27] *Winker,* P.: Sluggish Adjustment of Interest Rates and Credit Rationing. Applied Economics (1998b), forthcoming.

## Summary

Recently, the potential fragility of financial systems and resulting real effects on output and employment regained interest due to the developments in some south-east Asian countries.

This contribution is directed towards reviewing and supplementing existing empirical evidence on financial constraints and their role in the transmission mechanism. Special attention is given to the German case. Furthermore, besides the more common microeconometric approaches, also some approaches of modeling the mechanisms of interest at the aggregate level are considered. This aggregate approaches include the estimation and simulation of a macroeconometric disequilibrium model for West Germany.

The empirical findings are analyzed with respect to the actual and the potential impact of financing constraints on employment both at the firm and the aggregate level.

# The Informational Efficiency of Financial Markets and Macroeconomic Equilibrium

By Michael Frömmel and Lukas Menkhoff, Aachen

## I. Introduction

When compared with the goal of achieving macroeconomic equilibrium, particularly that of a high level of employment, financial market efficiency would appear to be a mere marginality. The financial sector directly employs relatively few people and nevertheless some still ask the question whether these are not too many (similarly Tobin 1984). In Germany, for example, only approximately 4% of all employed work within the financial services sector and although the trend in this service sector segment has to date been positive, this development could for the time being come to an end with the announced reduction in banking staff.

The significance of the financial sector, therefore, hardly stems from its role as an employer. Rather more it is the economic functions in a decentrally organised monetary economy which are of interest. We call to mind just two central tasks:

- Financial intermediaries are of great importance with respect to the choice of investment projects and thus also with respect to the allocation of capital.
- The interest rate (or the spectrum of interest rates) influences intertemporal allocation, as do exchange rates with respect to international allocation.

Accordingly price formation in financial markets is of great importance for allocation and therefore in the long run also for economic growth. Changes in financial market prices, in this case especially the interest rate and the exchange rate, in addition directly affect the trend in economic activity and the stability of an economy. Even if in some theories the inherent tendency to economic equilibrium is assumed to be relatively rapid, this does not alter the fact that changes of financial market prices, at least for a certain period, have real economic effects (stated clearly, e.g., in Neumann 1997).

Therefore, since financial market prices and their changes give rise to macroeconomic effects, it may be assumed that "wrong" financial market prices have damaging consequences for the economy. The necessary evaluation involved here of such prices will only be considered in the following analysis at the microeconomic level. The theoretical framework, within which microeconomic efficiency is usually discussed, is the concept of informationally efficient markets (Fama 1970 and 1991; more widely defined concepts of efficiency are to be found, e.g., in Filc 1997 or Tobin 1984).

In this paper different approaches and empirical studies on this subject will be presented and analysed by way of example for foreign exchange markets. The results vary as might perhaps be expected in the case of an academically controversial issue. However, if the studies are arranged according to their respective time horizons a pattern ensues such that in the very short term and in the long run – that is, looked at in terms of hours or several years respectively – efficiency would appear to be more likely to exist than it does in the short and medium term. However, when looking at the economy as a whole and at employment, the way in which financial market prices develop over a time period which ranges from a daily basis up to that of one or two years should not be neglected. The idea of generally informationally efficient financial markets, which almost always deliver the correct price signals, does not appear to hold at least for the case of currencies.

In section II the hypothesis of informationally efficient markets and above all the starting point for an empirical analysis hereof regarding foreign exchange markets will be dealt with in more detail. Following this, in section III one of these methods, that of direct questionnaire survey, will by way of example be considered more closely whilst drawing upon our own analyses. Finally, economic policy options will be addressed in section IV.

## II. On the testing of informationally efficient financial markets

### *1. The concept of informational efficiency*

Although the origins of the efficient market hypothesis can be traced back to the beginning of this century, the now classic study by Fama (1970) was seminal in this field. Fama coined the phrase of an informationally efficient market with respect to a given amount of information: "A market in which prices always 'fully reflect' available information is called 'efficient'".

Depending on the amount of information under consideration he thereby distinguishes between the degree of efficiency based on the type of information which is available to economic agents:

- In the presence of *weak informational efficiency* the actual price reflects the historic development of a price trend. It is, therefore, in particular not possible using an analysis of previous prices to gain additional information, which goes beyond the information incorporated in the current price.
- In the event that a market exhibits *semi-strong efficiency,* then one price reflects all "publicly available information".

- In the case of *strong informational efficiency* the price reflects all information, that is, it also includes "private information". This implies, therefore, that even insider information is contained within the market price and thus knowledge thereof does not carry any advantage.

Obviously the existence of an efficient market as defined by Fama has remarkable consequences. If prices completely reflect the prevailing information this infers that all economic agents have access to all information, or are able to observe its effects on the market directly. There exists, therefore, a perfect flow of information via which all market participants may simultaneously be reached. Efficiency in Fama's sense hence assumes not only an efficient, i.e., immediate and "correct" processing of all information, but also its availability and be it only in an aggregated form of prices. However, since every one has access to the same information at the same time, all economic agents, to the extent that they behave rationally, must exhibit absolutely synchronous behavior.

Certainly this interpretation is an idealistic model removed from reality, not least because it is unclear how the transformation of information to prices should occur. Thus it would be impossible to gain an informational advantage via analysis, irrespective of whether the analysis involved is based on past price trends or on fundamental economic data. This would be a clear contradiction to the postulated efficiency. For this reason the original premise is nowadays extended to the effect that the (marginal) costs of information search are taken into consideration.

Another modification extends the three degrees of informational efficiency to a spectrum of efficiency concepts and their respective methodology (cf. Menkhoff 1995, pp. 33). *Table 1* represents an extension of this kind with seven concepts of efficiency, which are ordered in accordance with Fama's original notion. The results of empirical tests (in the far-right-hand column of the table) show, however, that it does not necessarily make sense to arrange the individual concepts in a logically strict super and subordinate system to one another respectively. The individual concepts of informational efficiency are dealt with below, whereby section II.3 looks more closely at the basic aspect of efficient use of past prices (point 3 in Table 1).

### *2. Measuring informational efficiency*

A special role amongst those concepts included in Table 1 is assigned to *arbitrage efficiency* tests, where efficiency is tested under certainty. Empirical tests show independently of the type of arbitrage chosen that when transaction and opportunity costs etc. are taken into account this elementary form of efficient information processing in financial markets is satisfied (compare, e.g., Frankel and Rose 1995 or Taylor 1995).

*Table 1*

**Degrees of Informational Efficiency on Financial Markets**

| Kind of efficiency | Typical kind of test | Tendency of results | Efficiency? |
|---|---|---|---|
| 1. arbitrage efficiency | test of covered interest rate parity | quite strong result of efficiency | (+) |
| 2. efficient information processing | tests for systematic price expectation bias; further investigation on expectation | systematic expectation biases etc. | (−) |
| 3. efficient use of past prices | time series analysis; profitability of chartism? | many hints for price pattern and chartism profitability | (−) |
| 4. efficient statistical use of fundamentals | statistical optimization of adjusted exchange rate models | vague hints for unexploited information | (+/−) |
| 5. efficient use of news | event study methodology | consistent price reaction although possibly complicated pattern | (+) |
| 6. efficient use of structural models | test of exchange rate models | long-term power of purchasing power parity and monetary model | (+/−) |
| 7. efficient use of private information | profitability of insiders' decisions | weak tendency towards efficiency | (?) |

The way in which *information is processed* deserves more detailed consideration. Here the opportunity is given to analyse not only the results of information processing, that is, price expectations, but also the mechanisms involved in their formation (*Figure 1*). Price expectations can be dealt with in the light of distortions or implausibilities as well as with respect to the inclusion of relevant information (a survey of pioneering studies can be found, e.g., in Takagi 1991).

This last aspect at the same time makes the connection to the analysis of expectation formation mechanisms (cf. Figure 1 bottom). If the argumentation using the fundamentalist approach is adopted, then fundamentals alone serve as the only and exhaustive basis of information. Sources of information which deviate from this ideal, in particular those such as technical analysis, opinion leaders and market makers that rest on market events themselves, should hence provide some understanding about the type and extent of potential inefficiencies (cf., e.g., Goodhart 1988, Taylor and Allen 1992, Menkhoff 1995). A further starting point for research is the way of information processing, which involves on the one hand concepts from

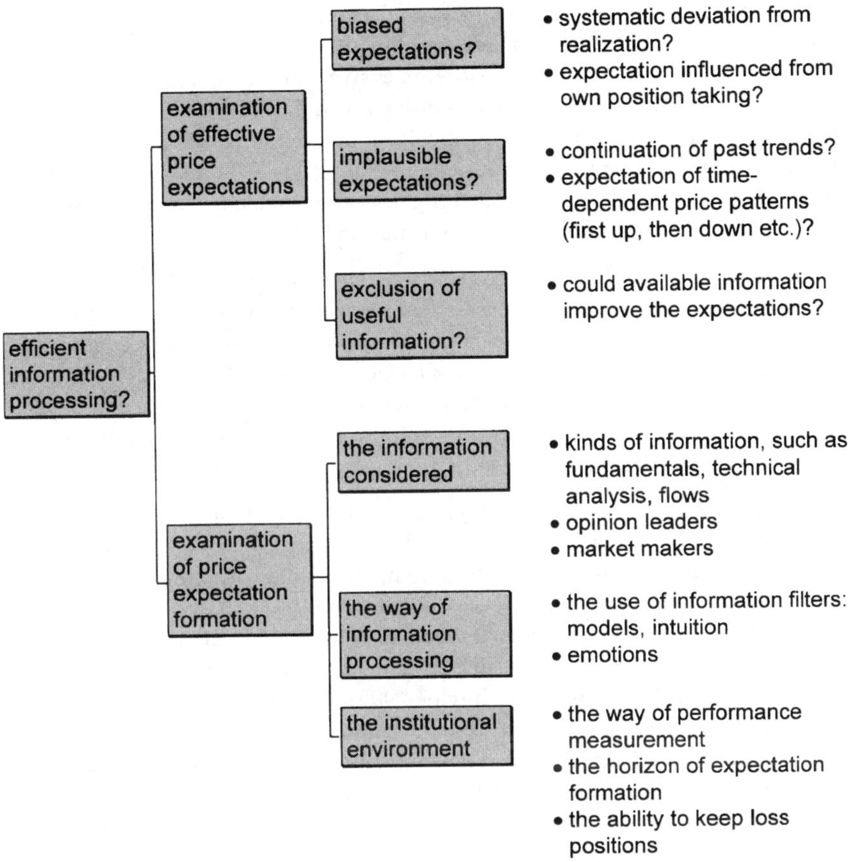


see e.g. Menkhoff (1995), p. 177

Figure 1: Testing the efficiency of information processing

behavioral finance and on the other hand concepts from models of interacting, heterogeneous agents (e.g., Kirman 1993 or Lux 1995). There are also some research approaches which take the influence of institutional framework conditions into consideration, as for example the noise trading approach (e.g., Schleifer and Summers 1990), or the herding concept (Froot, Scharfstein and Stein 1992). The results provide strong evidence of inefficiencies.

This also applies in tendency to the purely *statistical analysis of fundamentals*. In essence this category represents a cross between traditional technical analysis, in which usually only past price data form the basis for the analysis, and traditional fundamental analysis, in which fundamentals are analysed within the framework of structured theoretical notions. Meese (1990), for example, who examines the statistical correlation between individual fundamental variables and exchange rates without being able to find a clear relationship at this level, may be regarded as a simple approach in this direction. More extensive, for example, are the neuronal networks or approaches, in which the coefficients of the structural models are optimised on a variable time basis (e.g., Schinasi and Swamy 1989). The latter approaches tend to find explanatory strength in their models, but have the substantial problem that there is no theoretical bridge between fundamentals and exchange rates – the models live of complicated statistics and not explanatory content.

*Event studies* come off well in comparison. They analyse the short-run reaction of market prices to news. In the case of efficient information processing it is assumed that news, such as the announcing of macroeconomic data or central bank decisions, quickly lead to price adjustments. Goodhart's work (1988), which investigates reactions to the Bank of England's interest rate policy resolutions, is mentioned as example. The results of event studies in general confirm the efficient processing of unexpected news (see also, e.g., Hogan, Melvin and Roberts 1991).

The introduction of flexible exchange rates between large industrial countries at the start of the 70s was actually associated with the expectation that unrestricted market price formation would lead to a comprehensible orientation towards economic fundamentals. However, Meese and Rogoff (1983) showed very early and in devastating clearness that *fundamental structural models* cannot explain actual exchange rate movements out of sample. This result must nowadays be regarded as extremely well documented (cf. Taylor 1995). The only "ray of hope" among these, from an economic point of view, disappointing test results can be found when the high level of standards is relaxed and long-term relationships are considered. Then, however, it can indeed be shown that something like a tendency towards fundamentally-determined exchange rate levels exists (with regard to purchasing power parity Rogoff 1996; with regard to the relevant monetary model, e.g., MacDonald and Taylor 1993).

Testing for excessive volatility represents a side aspect of this direction of research. Whilst early studies would appear to provide confirmation of inefficiency, reservations exist with regard to the methodology and it is therefore doubtful whether excessive volatility really does exist (Bartolini and Bodnar 1996). In any event the regime dependency of volatility, which shot up following the abolition of Bretton-Woods exchange rate band widths for nominal and real values, is worth noting (Flood and Rose 1995).

The efficient use of *private information* on stock markets is accepted as having been confirmed (Fama 1991). In this context "insiders" are regarded as those with access to private information, that is analysts, portfolio managers and in particular the decision makers within firms. With regard to foreign exchange markets the question arises as to who the potential insiders with access to superior information might be. Basically the central banks, which with respect to interest rate policies are at an advantage compared with other market participants, would mainly appear to be relevant. At any rate a study for the US Federal Reserve Bank shows that profits have been made via intervention (Leahy 1995) and this could be regarded as a weak indicator for the efficient use of insider information.

### *3. Are past prices used efficiently?*

The use of past prices for decisions in financial markets should in the context of market efficiency be an absurdity, since prices are determined by fundamental news. To the extent that such news is interrelated, a potential for prognosis arises, which under efficiency should be exploited and contained within the price. In brief: the taking into account of past prices is ruled out and would, should it occur, indicate inefficiency. Two testable implications derive from this view of informational efficiency. Firstly, exchange rate time series should not exhibit properties which permit price forecasts, and secondly, technical analysis should be neither profitable nor used by rational agents.

The rapid development of time series analysis in recent years is reflected in the wealth of different research approaches (*Figure 2*). *Linear price dependencies* constitute here the older methodological approach. Autocorrelation and spectral analysis methodology can indeed be used to demonstrate serial correlations, but the results are not very clear. Furthermore, empirical studies are able to identify short-run changes in financial market prices as being leptocurtic (cf. Boothe and Glassmann 1987, Hsieh 1987), that is, very small and very large changes occur overproportionately often. As a result of this considerable deviation from the normal distribution caution is necessary when interpreting autocorrelation. If the distribution is unknown, then it is not possible to name critical thresholds for the values of the autocorrelation function. A second methodological objection is to be found in the fact that serial correlations are not necessarily caused by exchange rate deviations from the equilibrium price, but are possibly the result of changes in the underlying fundamental factors. In addition it must be considered that autocorrelations associated with different lags are not independent of one another, since at any one time the same variables for all lags enter the equations, which are not very robust with respect to outliers. On the whole the results of autocorrelation analysis, which frequently indicate linear price correlations and hence inefficiency, should not be overvalued.

The mean reversion property is also included in linear dependencies. This appears to represent an observable medium and long run phenomenon. However, it is precisely for such time horizons that the data basis is correspondingly small so that statistical substantiation of the mean reversion property is difficult. Furthermore, as with the results of linear structures in general, it cannot be discounted that the observed property is not so much a result of market inefficiency as of a corresponding movement in the fundamentals (Fama 1991).

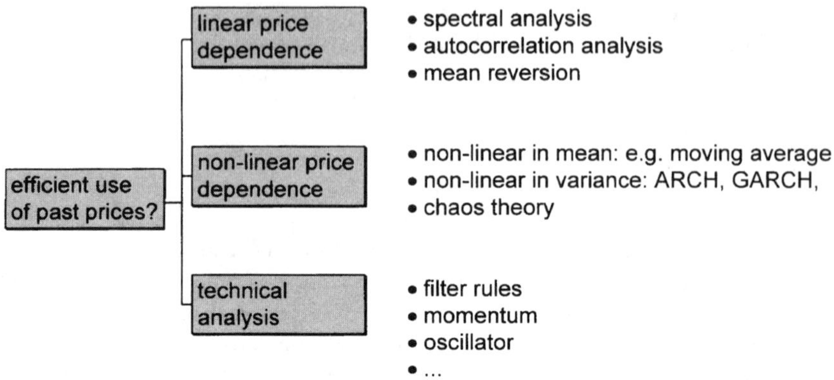


Figure 2: Testing efficient use of past prices

Thus, in recent times it has been the *non-linear structures* of financial market time series which have been the focus of interest (for a survey cf. Campbell, Lo and McKinley 1997). The number of non-parametric models is extremely large and at the same time heterogeneous. Non-linear structures are investigated with respect to mean and variance. In particular ARCH models (= Autoregressive Conditional Heteroscedasticity), in which the variance at every point in time is expressed as a random variable, have, since they were first introduced by Engle (1982), been at the centre of attention. Owing to the temporally fluctuating time series variance it is possible to model the effect, familiar from financial markets, of a strong clustering of extreme price changes, which alternate with periods of relative tranquillity. In addition on account of the leptocurtic (unconditional) distribution a further empirically confirmed financial market characteristic can be traced. Extensions of the model such as the GARCH model (Generalized ARCH) have in recent years also been the subject of extensive studies (e.g., Bollerslev 1992).

All in all the study of non-linear dependencies would thus also seem to speak against financial market efficiency. If the variance correlation to past realisations is seen as the convergence towards expectation formation within markets (cf. Engle 1982), then it would appear that expectations do indeed depend on past events occuring in these same markets. The efficient processing of actual information hence seems to be questionable (Filc 1997).

By comparison non-linear models, which are not based on stochastic processes, have increased in importance. This includes the results deriving from chaos theory. Chaos theory, which goes back to the pioneering study by Lorenz (1963), has over the last few years increasingly been the subject of detailed studies (e.g., DeGrauwe et al. 1993, Hsieh 1993, Reszat 1993). Here, however, the question must be asked as to whether the results tend to support the concept of efficient markets to the extent that they reveal an efficient but also extraordinarily complicated type of information processing, or whether chaotic behavior does indeed contradict efficiency as it is understood in theory.

A further direction of empirical work attempts to show the *profitability of technical algorithms* in simulations. A methododological problem arises to the extent that whilst it is possible to carry out an analysis for any arbitrary period of time, a surplus yield attained during this period cannot, however, be systematically identified using this sample. Nevertheless studies carried out frequently show results, which make it reasonable to suppose that the use of technical algorithms on average allows surplus yields to be achieved. This applies moreover with respect to very different technical analysis methods (cf., e.g., Levich and Thomas 1993 or Osler and Chang 1995) as well as for different data frequencies. Here in recent years, above all in the case of foreign exchange markets, attention has increasingly been directed towards the area of high frequency data (e.g., Curcio et al. 1997) in keeping with the important role accorded there to the short-run (cf. section III). It is in addition worth noting that the existence of surplus yields frequently observed in these studies, when compared with the buy-and-hold strategy, is apparently of lengthier duration, which is not to be expected should the efficient market hypothesis be valid (cf. Menkhoff and Schlumberger 1995).

When interpreting these results there are essentially two directions to be considered: either methodological objections can be made, in particular doubt can be cast on whether the risk premium is adequately measured (Kho 1996) such that efficiency need not be questioned, or risk-adjusted profitability is accepted, which begs the question regarding the compatibility with rational behavior.

### *4. Interim summary*

Overall the results of the different approaches can be summarised with the consequence that doubt can be reasonably cast on the informational efficiency of financial markets (see also Filc 1997). Whilst with respect to news processing in the very short run, as well as to the long run tendency towards purchasing power parity clear fundamental influences can be recognised, in the large intermediate time period there are rather price movements, which seem not to be fundamentally determined (cf. Frankel and Rose 1995).

Certainly there should be no jumping to conclusions with regard to irrational behavior, since on the one hand arbitrage efficiency – as an indicator of rationality – would appear to be completely fulfilled, and on the other hand the test approaches suffer from joint hypothesis difficulties: are foreign exchange markets inefficient, or is it more the case that the underlying model is not relevant? In order to escape from this logically unsolvable problem it might be advisable to analyse the behavior of market participants more directly.

## III. Implications of informational efficiency and surveys on behavior

### *1. Questionnaire approach methodology*

Questionnaire surveys aimed at systematically recording the behavior of financial market participants are a comparatively recent item. The pioneer in this respect is probably Robert Shiller, who – in 1987 – was the first to conduct financial market surveys on a larger scale and with a scientific interest, that is, at the time of the sharp fall in prices on the stock market.

From the point of view of methodology this represents an innovation to the extent that this instrument is otherwise typically used within the framework of other social sciences, such as psychology, sociology and political sciences, but not in economics. One of the main reasons for this is probably the fact that economics confidently attaches great significance to the concept of a homo oeconomicus, whereas related sciences tend only to be acquainted with controversial notions such as a homo sociologicus devised by Ralf Dahrendorf. However, if the view is held that it is possible to derive the agents' behavior on an abstract basis, then this is an automatic obstacle to direct questionnaire surveys.

There is also the fact that questionnaires, owing to the methodology, do not yield absolutely clear-cut results. While exact models are obtained if the well-known rational calculation and certain simplifications of the problem in question are used, the results of questionnaires are never completely unambiguous. Rather the answers usually exhibit deviation and are sensitive to the context and formulation of the questions. In this respect, it is precisely economists who are loath to permit such ambiguity in their argumentation. It is not only out of persistence that they insist on the traditional instruments, but rather on quite reasonable grounds. If the precise concept of an economic agent is given up, costs arise in the form of less precise derivations. These should be weighed up against the possibly better novelty value. Here again the question of a trade-off between the "exact but possibly irrelevant", on the one hand, and the "imprecise but possibly more meaningful" on the other hand arises.

His uneasiness about the traditional interpretation of reality found in economic theory could indeed have been the trigger for Shiller's innovation. It was as early as 1984 that he wrote a widely-heeded article on the social dynamics of financial markets, that is, on influencing factors, which are not usually covered by an economic model. The abrupt worldwide decline of prices on the stock markets in the autumn of 1987, which cannot be traced back to perceivably larger changes in economic fundamental data, almost inevitably gave rise to doubts about traditional explanation patterns including the concept of the homo oeconomicus. Thus Shiller carried out several surveys on financial market agents in order to learn about their behavioral motives. When his results are summarised in one hypothesis it postulates that the crisis on the financial markets is not attributable to changes in economic data, but rather that it is self sustaining. It is a matter of a speculative bubble as the agents react to one another or to past price changes but not to fundamental data changes.

This is the crucial point: according to Shiller's surveys professional agents on financial markets behave like "ordinary" people and not like ideal people, which has consequences for the quotation of financial market prices. Although a small crash, such as the one in 1987, can always be rationalised with the aid of unknown risk premia if necessary, there arises the question as to the benefit of such explanations, which arouse the suspicion of immunisation. Looked at from this point of view in our opinion a questionnaire approach appears to be scientifically rewarding because it brings out potential stylised facts, which in a second step may then be incorporated into models, as has been done in many different ways.

### *2. The concrete questioning of foreign exchange market participants*

After these introductory remarks about the controversial questionnaire methodology for investigating behavior, some important results concerning the three fields of investigation specified in the second section (see the lower part of Figure 1) shall be presented in the following, that is, with respect to the kind of information considered, on how the information has been processed, and with regard to the institutional set-up involved. The underlying survey used in all cases is that from Menkhoff (1995). Approximately 500 professional foreign exchange market participants in Germany were questioned by means of a uniform questionnaire and about 200 responses were obtained. The target group includes agents who are allowed to take up open currency positions on their own responsibility. These are for the major part foreign exchange dealers, who in general have variously high limits at their disposal depending on their seniority, as well as international fund managers, who have room to maneuver with respect to the weighting of foreign currency positions.

The explanatory power of such a survey critically depends on the response rate, on the degree to which the respondents are representative, and on whether the incoming answers are reliable. All the three aspects can be tested, to some extent directly, but also indirectly. See *Table 2* for a comparison of the different testing possibilities. By way of example this shall be explained for the response rate. It amounted here to roughly 40%, which in itself does not say very much. Compared with the figures drawn from past experience in market research it would appear to be a large figure. Compared with the study of Taylor and Allen (1992), who achieved 60%, or with Wolgast (1997, p. 231), who reached 64%, it seems to be a low figure. In fact it depends on the exact circumstances of the survey, because they strongly influence the response rate. If the sender is well-known, like the Bank of England in the case of Taylor and Allen, or, as with respect to some of the questionnaires returned here, like the Association of Public Sector Banks ("Bundesverband Öffentlicher Banken Deutschlands"), it increases the response rate considerably (in the case of the Association to 64%). The same applies to other incentives, used by Wolgast, such as the promise to make the evaluation available to all respondents, or calling on non-respondents by telephone. For the actual comparable case of returning a questionnaire without further incentives Shiller achieved, for example, an average of 33% for all his different initiatives. This figure corresponds to the result of this study of 34% for questionnaires or, which is strictly speaking more applicable, a figure of 45% for institutions respectively. In contrast to the other surveys quoted here, institutions were sent several questionnaires each. Frequently, however, they did not complete all questionnaires (cf. Menkhoff 1995, pp. 128). To this extent it can be concluded that this response rate – with respect to to the procedure used – is above rather than below average, which as a tendency speaks well for the surveys' quality.

*Table 2*

**Quality check of the questionnaire response**

| kind of check<br>criteria | direct checks | indirect checks |
|---|---|---|
| response rate | • "normal" response rate according to method | • comparison with other similar questionnaires |
| representativeness | • selection of target group<br>• structure of response compared to target group (age, position, education etc.) | comparison to intensive interviews and the questionnaire results of Taylor and Allen (1992) |
| reliability | • cross-checks between several answers<br>• cross-checks between subsamples | |

### *3. The type of information considered*

As foreign exchange market professionals well know, economic agents here do not only use economic fundamental information to form their expectations. It was Frankel and Froot (1986), who probably first drew attention to this fact in an academic article and pointed out its potential relevance for market rates. The first extensive study on the significance of the most important non-fundamental information, that is technical analysis, is probably that of Taylor and Allen (1992, first published in a different context in 1989). There it is stated that technical analysis has a major impact on expectation formation. As shown in *Figure 3,* this result can be confirmed in our own study, which some years later was carried out in a different place with an extended question and a larger target group. Technical analysis is a second major source of information after fundamentals and before flows. Up to this level of investigation, however, it is possible to deny the practical importance of technical analysis on the basis of numerous objections. Even if this may appear almost absurd to practitioneers, science has generally kept clear of technical analysis because an analysis that solely relies on past movements of rates cannot be serious from the point of view of the efficient market hypothesis. If these doubts about the relevance of technical analysis were to be put into a more concrete form, then there exist several starting points, three of which are specified below:

- Technical analysis is always only a secondary instrument in the analysis and forecasting of exchange rates.
- Those who use technical analysis are younger and thus less experienced than other market participants.
- Users of technical analysis reach senior positions less frequently than other professionals.

The attempt can be made in a second procedure to test the potential shortcomings of the first survey, which would suggest an overestimation of the average

Question: "Please evaluate the importance of the three following information types for your typical decision making, by distributing a total of 100 points. For information types which you do not use, please give 0 points."

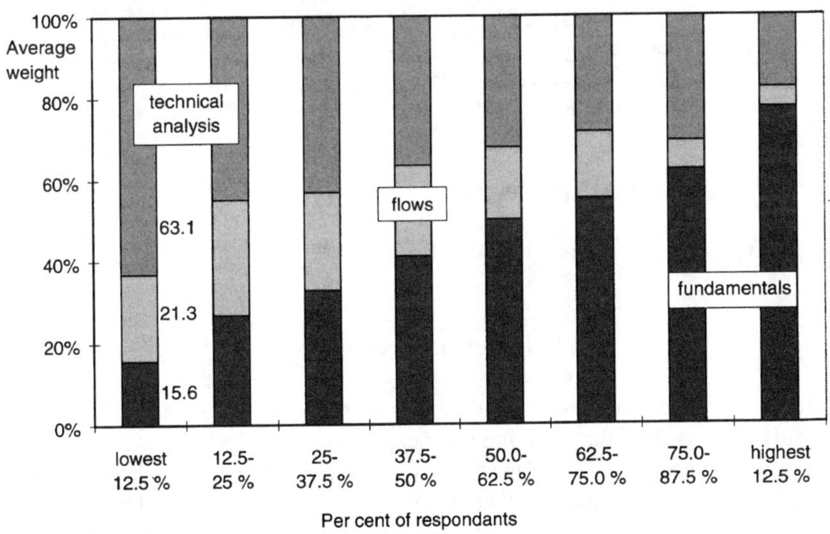


(read for example: the 12.5 % of the respondents which use fundamentals least extensive put an average weight of 15.6 % to fundamentals, of 21.3 % to flows and of 63.1 % to technical analysis)

Figure 3: Information types

values shown. Through our own survey it has become apparent that technical analysis cannot simply be dismissed as being unimportant (Menkhoff 1997). This shall be illustrated with the help of a further argument. It would not appear implausible to assume that it requires a qualified economic education to use fundamental information, whereas technical analysis does not. In this respect the latter might be the substitute instrument for those market participants with a lower level of education, a view which was sometimes expressed in interviews. This hypothesis is, however, not systematically supported by the survey: those who prefer technical analysis do not have a lower level of education than others, that is, are not less qualified market participants (cf. *Figure 4*).

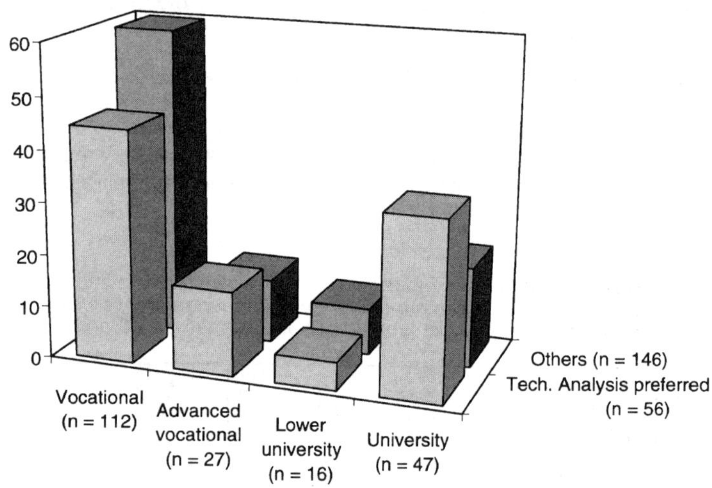


Pearson $\chi^2$ = 6.483 (0.090)

Figure 4: Technical analysis and education

*4. The way of information processing*

Just a few discussions with professionals working on foreign exchange markets are sufficient to show that deriving price expectations on the basis of a strict model orientation is obviously not a matter of course. For all that, a model is not to be understood in the conventional theoretical sense, but solely as a stable complex of thoughts, in which new parameter values lead to the corresponding adaptations of expectations. Numerous market participants tend to prefer instead procedures which would more be called intuitive, that is, new information is assessed according to what the "market feeling" and / or experience advise. One further variant, that of renouncing independent price expectations and limiting activities to arbitrage transactions as well as exploiting the advantages of diversification, which might be anticipated on account of the efficient market hypothesis, appears to be not too popular. See *Figure 5* for the concrete statements of the persons answering.

Question: "How do you process the different kinds of information?"

- O I rely on my intuition and feelings (intuition).
- O I do not believe to be able to forecast exchange rates more accurately than the market and act in a defensive way (market efficiency).
- O I strictly rely on my own fundamental considerations, technical analysis or flows (analytical framework)

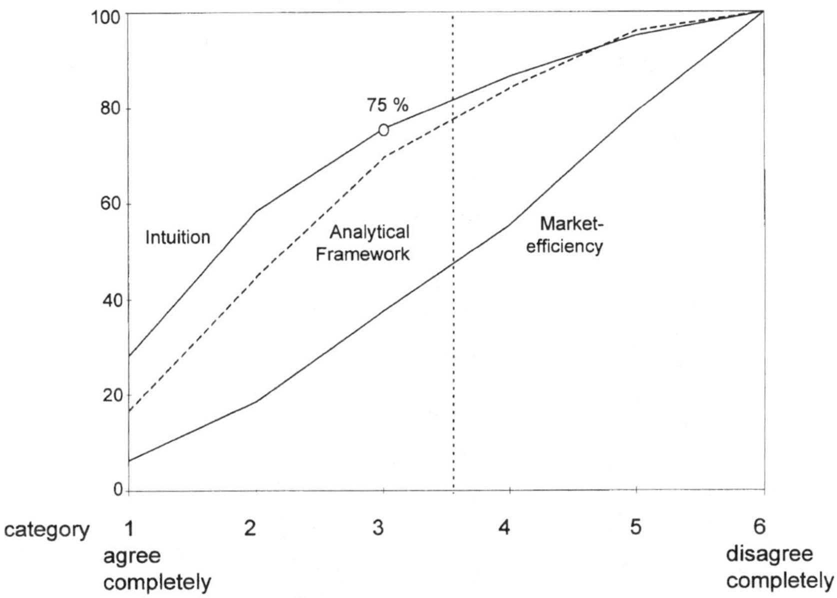


cumulated answers per category from complete agreement to complete disagreement (read e.g.: 75 % of respondents rather agree than disagree to process information via intuition)

Figure 5: Different ways of information processing

Certainly good reasons exist which explain observed behavior, such as the time pressure under which decisions have to be taken. Besides, the complexity of the context plays an important role. It depends on the actual environment whether a rise of the interest rate leads to a rise or a fall in exchange rates and this is difficult to generalise in a model. However, also in the case of technical analysis the impression seems to prevail that the conditions and, therefore, the optimum procedure will change over time.

*5. The institutional environment*

The third area, to be discussed here, deals with the institutional environment, in which expectations are formed and decisions made. In economic theory this area is practically not taken into consideration because the level of abstraction is so high that it is assumed that systematic influences do not emanate. However, the environment is actually very important for the agents' behavior. This can be shown, for example, for the ability to endure loss positions, which is noticeably associated with to the functions of a foreign exchange dealer or fund manager (cf. *Figure 6)* but not, for example, with respect to the use of fundamental information versus other information (Menkhoff 1998).

Question: "How long do you believe you can afford to hold on to loss positions? After how much time and after what amount of loss do you in general close your loss positions?"

O within one day
O only after a few weeks
O only after 2-6 months or later
O only after 6 months or later

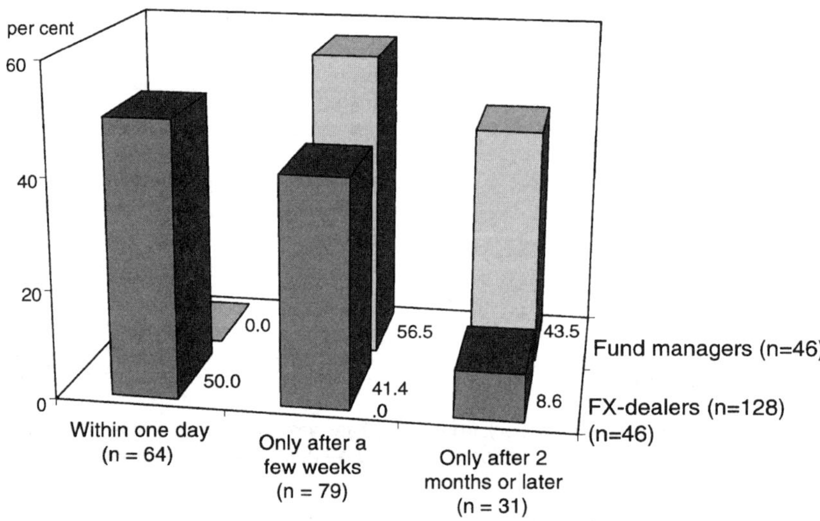


FX-dealers vs. fund managers:
Mann-Whitney-U: Z = -6.877 (0.000)

Figure 6: Endurance of market participants

The same applies to the anticipation horizon regarding possible price influences. Here there are no variables with a clear influence with the exception of the respondents' occupational field (cf. *Figure 7)*. Furthermore it is interesting that both, anticipation horizon and the endurance in absolute values are over within days for most of the foreign exchange dealers and after a few months for fund managers. This certainly does not correspond to the ideal type of an efficient market with an indefinite horizon and an ultimate preponderance of fundamentally active market participants relative to noise traders (cf. also Menkhoff 1998).

Question: "How far in advance do you take into account possible influences on the exchange rate when opening a position (<u>1 answer</u>)?"

| | | | |
|---|---|---|---|
| O | < 1 day/intra-day | O | a few days |
| O | a few weeks | O | 2-6 months |
| O | 6-12 months | O | > 12 months |

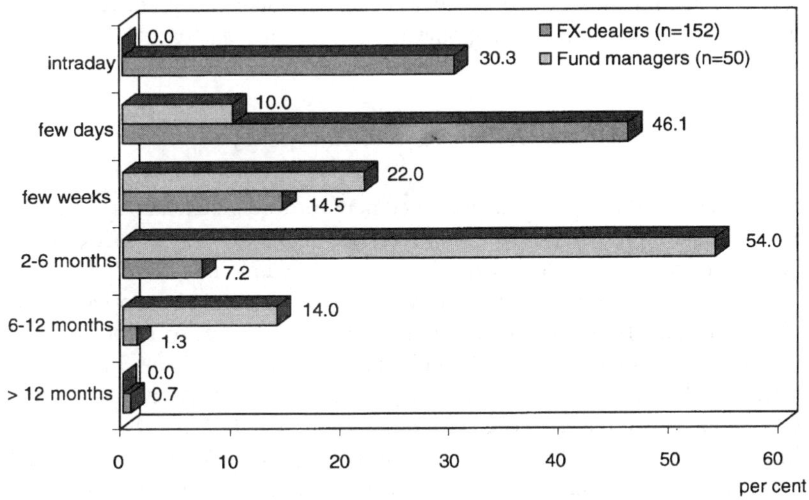


Pearson $\chi^2 = 90.147$ (0.000) (FX-dealers vs. fund managers)

Figure 7: Anticipation horizon of dealers and fund managers

## *6. Interim summary*

The concrete survey of the behavior of foreign exchange market participants, parts of which were reproduced here, does not conform well with the (implicit) picture of informationally efficient markets. This was shown with respect to the following aspects:

- Besides economic fundamentals other influential factors, such as technical analysis and flow information, are important to take decisions.

- The theoretically unexpected importance of technical analysis cannot be traced back to a correspondingly lower level of education among its respective users.
- The processing of information is strongly influenced by intuition.
- The endurance of the respondents tends to be low.
- The anticipation horizon of those responding to the questionnaire is – from a theoretical point of view – unexpectedly short and, like the endurance, depends on the field of occupation.

Summing up, it is difficult to talk about a process of expectation formation, which relies on fundamentals, is determined by rationality and adheres to decisions on the longer run, irrespective of market movements. On the contrary, non-fundamental information, non-rational influences and short-term factors play an important part (see also Wolgast 1997). In so far it cannot be expected that the result of the price formation process might always and instantaneously converge towards the ideal of the efficient market hypothesis.

## IV. Options for economic policy

If it is accepted that the results presented here for foreign exchange markets may essentially also be transferred to other financial markets, such as stock and bond markets, and there is indeed not much to be said against this, then the economic policy is faced with a problem. On the one hand, it is clear that the price formation on financial markets is not always informationally efficient or to put it in Filc's words (1997) "an end to dreams of efficiency is required" ("Das Ende der Effizienzträume"), so that sensible action may follow. On the other hand, it is not obvious in which way market efficiency may be improved. After all, the market is not inefficient throughout, the state not omniscient and market intervention not for free. Against this background four perceivable alternatives to the status quo are discussed, which relate best to the foreign exchange markets discussed extensively above (cf. Menkhoff 1995, pp. 217):

- state interventions in the process of price formation
- cooperation in the area of economic policy making
- transaction taxes
- quality assurance of speculation.

To begin with *state interventions,* it seems that the knowledge requirements and the costs of potential mistakes are particularly high. Indeed until now nobody has made such proposals for stock markets, whereas the official fixing of foreign exchange rates has numerous protagonists owing to presumptions of high externalities. Experience has shown that states have similar difficulties to markets with a rational exchange rate policy. Without being able to give reasons in detail, the

Bretton Woods agony of the 70s, the EMS definitely in the year 1992 and even current crises in newly industrialised countries (NICs) countries, such as in South-East Asia in 1997/98, are good examples for a remarkable failure of economic policy on the one hand and of the cleansing effect of market-induced currency crises on the other hand. In this respect, increasingly globalised financial markets exert a beneficial disciplinary effect in favor of a stability-oriented economic policy of national states (cf. e.g. Hesse 1998, Menkhoff 1997a).

However, this stability promoting effect is not the same as stabilisation itself. On the contrary, there are also indications that stability emanating from markets is accompanied by stabilisation costs (cf., e.g., Hesse 1998). In the three above-mentioned cases overshooting phenomena emerged:

- This has already been mentioned with regard to the transition from the Bretton Woods System to flexible exchange rates, which was simultaneously a transition to higher real exchange rate volatility without there being an increase in the volatility of the fundamentals (Flood and Rose 1995).
- In the case of the EMS criteria the devaluations of 1992, for example, roughly corresponded inflation differentials, whereas the devaluation pressure of 1993 also included destabilising elements.
- In the still recent South-East Asia crisis a deferred necessity to devalue existed, however, both overshooting and herd instinct could be diagnosed.
- Finally, even the gold standard was an example for a high volatility of economic activity and prices (cf. Jarchow and Rühmann 1997, pp. 48).

For the case of a *cooperation-oriented economic policy* the problem is ultimately similar. It is not sufficient that the advantages of cooperation can be demonstrated in order to convince the participants to follow this strategy reliably. This applies to the national monetary, financial and income policy (cf. Filc 1997, Köhler 1996, Krupp and Cabos 1996) and to the international cooperation of countries. The requirements involving participants' rational conduct tend to be even higher than in the case of official rate pegging because cooperation is a permanent process, which can only be formalised and regulated to a limited extent. In this respect, not too much hope should be placed in making gains from cooperation, and in particular the costs of misdirected cooperation should not be underestimated.

These problems are at least partly avoided by *transaction taxes* mainly because they must be fixed only once (cf. Tobin 1978, with respect to the discussion cf. e.g. Menkhoff and Michaelis 1995). However, there arise the direct costs of an allocation distortion, for example in the case of a currency transactions tax in the form of a barrier to foreign trade. Nevertheless, two aspects should not be disregarded: On the one side the transaction tax would appear to deal better than other instruments with the above mentioned pricing problem on financial markets by acting as a brake on the short-term dynamics. On the other side, it does not assume a superior knowledge of the policy makers with respect to the "correct" prices, but leaves price formation jointly to the markets and the institutions of economic policy, such as monetary policy. Ideally, therefore, it can be said transaction taxes correct pricing distortions on financial markets.

Finally the minimum intensity of intervention, which has been called the *quality assurance of speculation,* must be considered. The approach taken here is not that of internalising external costs but disclosing actual costs (such as risks) of the foreign exchange speculation. Too many many market participants do not behave in such a rational way as it could be expected given the available information (cf. e.g. Glaum 1992 for the foreign exchange management of enterprises or Wolgast 1997 for currency dealing). While this might still be considered their own problem, economic costs arise if the unnoticed losses of these participants form the financial feeding ground in the redistribution process of speculation, which in turn leads to unwelcome prive movements (cf. e.g. Shleifer and Summers 1990). The instruments of a genuine profit and risk disclosure naturally belong to the realms of business economics.

*Table 3*

**Comparison of political options**

| political options | evaluation categories | | | | |
|---|---|---|---|---|---|
| | required knowledge of states (1) | required rational behavior of administration (2) | opportunity costs (3) | inherent risk Σ (1+2+3) | potential of improvement |
| fixed (regulated) asset prices | – | – | – | – – | ++ |
| approach of cooperation | – | – – | + | – | + |
| transaction taxes | + | (-) | (-) | (+) | (+) |
| quality approach of speculation | +/– | (-) | + | + | (+) |

+ favorable, – unfavorable

In conclusion it may be said that the two initially mentioned economic policy options offer the larger potential for increases of welfare as compared to the final two but also the greater risk in the event of failures (cf. *Table 3).* Given that financial markets are not desperately inefficient and governments not miraculously efficient we tend to prefer gradual measures in order to improve the financial markets' contribution to achieving macroeconomic equilibrium.

## References

*Bartolini* Leonardo and *Bodnar,* Gordon M. (1996): "Are Exchange Rates Excessively Volatile? And What Does 'Excessively Volatile' Mean, Anyway?", IMF Staff Papers, 43:1, 72 - 96. – *Bollerslev,* Tim P. (1992): "Price Volatility, Spread Volatility and the Role of Alternative Market Mechanisms", Review of Futures Markets, 10:1, 78 - 102. – *Boothe,* Paul and *Glassmann,* Debra (1987): "The Statistical Distribution of Exchange Rates", Journal of International Economics, 22:3 / 4, 297 - 319. – *Campbell,* John Y. / *Lo,* Andrew W. and *MacKinley,* A. Craig (1997): "The Econometrics of Financial Markets", New Jersey: Princeton University Press. – *Curcio,* Riccardo / *Goodhart,* Charles / *Guillaume,* Dominique and Payne, Richard (1997): "Do Technical Trading Rules Generate Profits? Conclusions from the Intra-Day Foreign Exchange Markets", International Journal of Finance & Economics, 2:4, 267 - 280. – *DeGrauwe,* Paul and *Dewachter,* Hans (1993): "A Chaotic Model of the Exchange Rate: The Role of Fundamentalists and Chartists", Open Economies Review, 4, 351 - 379. – *Engel,* Charles and *Hamilton,* James D. (1990): "Long Swings in the Dollar: Are They in the Data and Do Markets Know it?", American Economic Review, 80, 689 - 713. – *Engle,* Robert F. (1982): "Autoregressive Conditional Heteroscedasticity with Estimates of the United Kingdom Inflation", Econometrica, 50:4, 987 - 1007. – *Fama,* Eugene F. (1970): "Efficient Capital Markets: A Review of Theory and Empirical Work", Journal of Finance, 25, 383 - 417. – *Fama,* Eugene F. (1991): "Efficient Capital Markets: II", Journal of Finance, 46, 1575 - 1617. – *Filc,* Wolfgang (1997): "Das Ende der Effizienzträume", Hamburger Jahrbuch für Wirtschafts- und Gesellschaftspolitik, 42, 9 - 28. – *Flood,* Robert P. and *Rose,* Andrew K. (1995): "Fixing Exchange Rates, A Virtual Quest for Fundamentals", Journal of Monetary Economics, 36, 3 - 37. – *Frankel,* Jeffrey A. and *Froot,* Kenneth A. (1986): "The Dollar as an Irrational Speculative Bubble: A Tale of Fundamentalists and Chartists", Marcus Wallenberg Papers on International Finance, 1, 27 - 55. – *Frankel,* Jeffrey A. and *Rose,* Andrew K. (1995): "Empirical Research on Nominal Exchange Rates", in: Gene Grossman and Kenneth Rogoff (eds.), Handbook of International Economics, Vol.III, Amsterdam et al.: North-Holland, 1689 - 1729. – *Froot,* Kenneth A. / *Scharfstein,* David S. and *Stein,* Jeremy C. (1992): "Herd on the Street: Informational Inefficiencies in a Market with Short-term Speculation", Journal of Finance, 47, 1461 - 1484. – *Glaum,* Martin (1994): "Informationseffizienz der Devisenmärkte und unternehmerisches Wechselkursrisiko-Management", Kredit und Kapital, 27, 67 - 99. – *Goodhart,* Charles A. E. (1988): "The Foreign Exchange Market: A Random Walk with a Dragging Anchor", Economica, 55, 437 - 460. – *Hesse,* Helmut (1998): "1998 – Ein schwieriges Wirtschaftsjahr", Deutsche Bundesbank, Auszüge aus Presseartikeln, No. 4, 8 - 15. – *Hogan,* Ked / *Melvin,* Michael and *Roberts,* Dan J. (1991): "Trade Balance News and Exchange Rates: Is There a Policy Signal?", Journal of International Money and Finance, 10, 90 - 99. – *Hsieh,* David A. (1993): "Implications of Nonlinear Dynamics for Financial Risk Management", Journal of Financial and Quantitative Analysis, 28, 41 - 64. – *Hsieh,* David A. (1987): "The Statistical Properties of Daily Foreign Exchange Rates", Journal of International Economics, 24, 129 - 145. – *Jarchow,* Hans-Joachim and *Rühmann,* Peter (1997): "Monetäre Außenwirtschaft, II. Internationale Währungspolitik", Göttingen: Vandenhoek & Ruprecht, 4. Ed. – *Jorion,* Phillipe and *Sweeney,* Richard J. (1996): "Mean Reversion in Real

Exchange Rates: Evidence and Implications for Forecasting", Journal of International Money and Finance, 15:4, 535 - 550. – *Kho,* Bong-Chan (1996): Time Varying Risk Premia, Volatility and Technical Trading Rule Profits: Evidence from Foreign Currency Futures Markets, Journal of Financial Economics, 41:2, 249 - 290. – *Kirman,* Alan (1993): "Ants, Rationality, and Recruitment", Quarterly Journal of Economics, 108:1, 137-. – *Köhler,* Claus (1996): Preisstabilität und Vollbeschäftigung in einer globalen Wirtschaft, München, Landsberg: Olzog. – *Krupp,* Hans-Jürgen and *Cabos,* Karen (1996): "Geldpolitik und Beschäftigung", in: Bernhard Gahlen, Helmut Hesse and Hans-Jürgen Ramser (eds.): Arbeitslosigkeit und Möglichkeiten ihrer Überwindung, Tübingen: Mohr, 363 - 387. – *Leahy,* Michael P. (1995): "The Profitability of US Intervention in the Foreign Exchange Market", Journal of International Money and Finance, 14:6, 823 - 844. – *Levich,* Richard M. and *Thomas,* Lee R. (1993): "The Significance of Technical Trading-Rule Profits in the Foreign Exchange Market: A Bootstrap Approach", Journal of International Money and Finance, 12, 451 - 174. – *Lorenz,* E. (1963): "Deterministic Aperiodic Flow", Journal of Atmospheric Sciences, 20, 130 - 141. – *Lux,* Thomas (1995): Herd Behaviour, Bubbles and Crashes, Economic Journal, 105: 3, 881 - 196. – *MacDonald,* Ronald and *Taylor,* Mark P. (1993): "The Monetary Approach to the Exchange rate:rational expectations, long-run equilibrium and forecastimg", IMF Staff Papers, 40:1, 89 - 107. – *Meese,* Richard A. (1990): "Currency Fluctuations in the Post-Bretton Woods Era", Journal of Economic Perspectives, 4, 117 - 134. – *Meese,* Richard A. and *Rogoff,* Kenneth (1983): "Empirical Exchange Rate Models of the Seventies: Do They Fit Out of Sample?", Journal of International Economics, 14, 3 - 24. – *Menkhoff,* Lukas (1995): "Spekulative Verhaltensweisen auf Devisenmärkten", Tübingen: J.C.B. Mohr. – *Menkhoff,* Lukas (1997): "Examining the Use of Technical Currency Analysis", International Journal of Finance & Economics, 2:4, 263 - 334. – *Menkhoff,* Lukas (1997a): "Steuerung der Zinsen bei globalen Finanzmärkten?", in: Bernhard Gahlen, Helmut Hesse and Hans-Jürgen Ramser (eds.), Finanzmärkte, Schriftenreihe des Wirtschaftswissenschaftlichen Seminars Ottobeuren, Vol.26, 299 - 322. – *Menkhoff,* Lukas (1998): "The Noise Trading Approach – Questionnaire Evidence from Foreign Exchange", Journal of International Money and Finance, forthcoming. – *Menkhoff,* Lukas and *Michaelis,* Jochen (1995): "Ist die Tobin-Steuer tatsächlich 'tot'?", Jahrbuch für Wirtschaftswissenschaften, 46:1, 34 - 54. – *Menkhoff,* Lukas and *Schlumberger,* Manfred (1995): "Persistent Profitability of Technical Analysis on Foreign Exchange Markets?", BNL Quarterly Review, 48:193, June, 189 - 216. – *Neumann,* Manfred J. M. (1997): "Geldpolitik und Stabilisierung", in: Jürgen von Hagen, Paul J. J. Welfens and Axel Börsch-Supan (eds.), Springers Handbuch der Volkswirtschaftslehre 2, Berlin et al.: Springer, 81 - 121. – *Osler,* Carol L. and *Chang,* P. H. Kevin (1995): "Head and Shoulders: Not just a Flaky Pattern", Federal Reserve Bank of New York Staff Reports, No.4, August. – *Reszat,* Beate (1993), "Zur Systemdynamik chaotischer Devienmärkte", Kredit und Kapital, 26:4, 516 - 532. – *Rogoff,* Kenneth (1996): "The Purchasing Power Parity Puzzle", Journal of Economic Literature, 34:2, 297 - 319. – *Schinasi,* Garry J. and *Swamy,* P. A. V. B. (1989): "The Out-of-sample Forecasting Performance of Exchange Rate Models when Coefficients are Allowed to Change", Journal of International Money and Finance, 8, 375 - 390. – *Shiller,* Robert J. (1984): "Stock Prices and Social Dynamics", Brookings Papers on Economic Activity, No.2, 457 - 498. – *Shiller,* Robert J. (1989): "Market Volatility", Cambridge, London: MIT Press. – *Shleifer,* Andrei and *Summers,* Lawrence (1990): "The Noise Trader Approach to Finance", Journal of Economic Perspectives, 4, 47 - 66. – *Takagi,* Shinji (1991): "Exchange Rate Expectations, A Survey of Survey Studies", IMF Staff Papers, 38:1, 156 - 183. – *Taylor,* Mark P. (1995): "Exchange Rate Economics", Journal of Economic Literature, 33:1, 13 - 47. – *Taylor,* Mark P. and *Allen,* Helen (1992), "The Use of Technical Analysis in the Foreign Exchange

Market", Journal of International Money and Finance, 11, 304 - 314. – *Tobin,* James (1978): "A Proposal for International Monetary Reform", Eastern Economic Journal, 4, 153 - 159 . – *Tobin,* James (1984): "On the Efficiency of the Financial System", Lloyds Bank Review, No.153, 1 - 15. – *Wolgast,* Michael (1997), Deviseneigenhandel der Geschäftsbanken, Devisenspekulation und nichtfundamentale Wechselkursbewegungen, Berlin: Duncker & Humblot.

## Summary

Within the framework of a classification of different research directions we present in more detail two approaches in order to examine the hypothesis of informationally efficient financial markets: the statistical analysis of time series focuses on the result of information processing, and the questionnaire analysis approach deals with the actual way in which information is treated. Our own empirical work on the nature of information processing in foreign exchange markets does not support the efficiency hypothesis. For this reason it must be supposed that disturbances to macroeconomic equilibrium will ensue. Taking into account the, as a whole, varying results on informational efficiency, we prefer economic policy measures which are a remedy more for the causes than for the effects of inefficiency on foreign exchange and financial markets respectively.

## Zusammenfassung

Im Rahmen einer Einordnung verschiedener Untersuchungsrichtungen zur Überprüfung der Hypothese informationseffizienter Finanzmärkte stellen wir zwei Richtungen näher vor: Auf das Ergebnis der Informationsverarbeitung zielt die statistische Analyse von Kurszeitreihen und auf die tatsächliche Art der Informationsverarbeitung der Befragungsansatz. Eigene empirische Arbeiten zur Art der Informationsverarbeitung auf Devisenmärkten stützen die Effizienzhypothese nicht unbedingt. Deshalb muß man vermuten, daß hiervon Störungen des makroökonomischen Gleichgewichts erfolgen. Unter Berücksichtigung der insgesamt uneinheitlichen Ergebnisse zur Informationseffizienz bevorzugen wir wirtschaftspolitische Maßnahmen, die Ursachen und weniger Auswirkungen der Ineffizienz der Devisen- bzw. Finanzmärkte möglichst direkt kurieren.

# IV. Country Studies and Country Comparisons

# Labour Market Dynamics in Western Europe and the USA

By Lothar Funk, Trier

> "Unemployment is such a complex and serious problem that we cannot afford the 'luxury' of not using all potentially useful policy instruments to combat it. Wishful thinking and ideological hang-ups should not be allowed to prevent the broad package of policy actions that is needed today to win the battle against high and persistent unemployment."
>
> *Assar Lindbeck, 1995, p. 15*

## I. Introduction

Unemployment is Europe's number one problem. Over the past twenty-five years it has moved – in contrast to the U.S.-experience with a long-run average rate of 6 per cent – relentlessly upwards, meanwhile to about 11 per cent. European Unemployment is mainly involuntary from the point of view of the individual unemployed because many job-searching people in general do not get a job even if they try to supply labour for less than the going wage (in their skill-category). An increasing number of such involuntary unemployed people leads to rising social costs in term of social exclusion (in particular for the so-called long-term unemployed with a duration of unemployment of more than one year) and the resulting problems, for example a higher rate of illness in comparison to the employed. From an economic point of view a lower than potential real product is to be expected at present and also in the future because inactive people lose their skills leading to a societal loss of human capital. Furthermore, it is mostly recognized that unemployment in Western Europe in general and especially in Germany is mainly institutional or structural in nature whereas the cyclical component is at the most 25 per cent nowadays.

The persistence of the high and rising unemployment in Europe raises doubts about the prospects for a return to full employment or a halving of the number of unemployed in Europe to 9 million within the next five years which is sometimes demanded by politicians or the European Commission. If unemployment is mainly involuntary, as is often argued, economic policy has to be changed considerably in order to solve that problem. Merely to wait until the problem fades away somehow in the future would be the wrong policy conclusion and most likely wishful thinking. As stated by Assar Lindbeck in the quotation at the outset, a lot in the present institutional framework and many incentives have to be changed to solve the problem of high and persistent unemployment in Europe successfully. It seems to be the case that the right medicine has been found already in some countries, even in Europe.

It is very likely misleading to claim that the higher unemployment level is curiously unique to special conditions in Europe, because not every country in Europe has experienced this same persistence of higher unemployment rates after a shock. Besides some very small countries like Luxembourg with long-term low unemployment, especially Britain and the Netherlands have officially achieved results much better than some of their neighbour countries[1]. This was possible, however, only after their own experience of high unemployment, financial pressures and thereafter comprehensive reforms to lower the unemployment rate by several percentage points to about 5 - 6 per cent again, which is much lower than the European average rate.

The irony is that the latter two economies belong to two alternative variants of capitalism with very different features, the so called Anglo-Saxon and Rhineland models, respectively, with Germany belonging to the latter group.

The Anglo-Saxon model countries, in particular the United Kingdom (UK) and the United States of America (USA), are characterised by a coordination mainly by markets, little government involvement and aim at short-term results. The countries with a variant of the Rhineland-model, like the Netherlands and Germany, are

[1] I do not discuss the other seemingly 'success countries' which have recorded a remarkable decline in the unemployment rate, i.e. New Zealand and Denmark. This is for several reasons. First: "Although during the 1990s New Zealand has achieved a marked improvement in its labour market situation, the period is still too short to reach an unequivocal conclusion on the sustainability of this development. This is even more the case with Denmark, where in addition the statistical basis is rather patchy" (German Economic Research Institutes: Unemployment Trends in Selected Industrialised Countries, Economic Bulletin, No. 11, 1997, p. 18). Secondly, I do not discuss the case of New Zealand although the effects of this policy have very likely been favourable for the labour market (cf. Kasper, Wolfgang: Right to work: Job creation New Zealand style, in: Intereconomics, No. 6, 1997), because the "policy conspiracy for free market reforms" which made the changes possible (cf. Wallis, Joe: Conspiracy and The Political Process: A Case Study of the New Zealand Experiment, in: Journal of Public Policy, No. 1, 1997) seem to be completely unthinkable in present Germany and most of the other European countries. Thirdly, I do not look deeper into the seemingly successful, partly market-oriented but mainly interventionistic reforms, of Denmark because such a policy – if not more market oriented in the future – will not be sustainable in the medium term, "as it will be impossible to maintain a high living standard while having an increasing proportion of the work force on public transfers" (Anderson, Torben M.: Structural Changes and Barriers in the Danish Labour Market, in: Siebert, Horst (ed.): Structural Change and labor market flexibility: experience in selected OECD economies, Tübingen 1997, p. 147). The European economies need more profitable jobs, mainly more jobs in the public sector do not have such effects. Cf. the resulting problems of the Swedish case with a mainly public sector job growth Lindbeck, Assar: The Swedish Experiment, Journal of Economic Literature, Vol. 35, 1997, pp. 1273 - 1319.

characterised by relatively more government involvement and tripartism (in differing degrees) as a coordinating device, concertation is used instead of conflict, long-term investments are preferred, but the mixture and degree are different in the affected countries.[2]

Empirical evidence for the industrial countries confirms that neither a fast increase in labour productivity nor a large expansion of the labour force necessarily create unemployment in a long term perspective.[3] The Netherlands and the UK seem to demonstrate that persistent high unemployment is no necessity and that it is reversible also in European countries. At least in principle both models of capitalism are able or can be reformed in such a way to be able to adapt successfully to the present economic and societal changes and challenges. This means: The Anglo-Saxon model and a reformed Rhineland model (e.g. the Dutch example) can both process a lower economy-wide unemployment rate than the traditional Rhineland model variant still existing in Germany which has been malfunctioning for some years. Successful models imply a structural change compatible with a low degree of persistent unemployment and they are in the main neutral with regard to unemployment in the medium-term (not in the short-term, however).

What can be the conclusion for other European countries tormented with rising and persistent unemployment? My answer: If the lower unemployment rates in Britain and the Netherlands are not only the "result of a beggar-my-neighbour-policy" at the cost of their European neighbours or the "result of pure coincidence of exceptional positive external factors" then one could try to develop a "masterplan"[4] for the German economy (and adapted to their own special circumstances for the other West-European countries) to move in one of the two directions to fight the unemployment problem, the Anglo-Saxon-model or a reform of the German variant of the Rhineland model into the Dutch direction. Furthermore, one could try to use the best features of the different models in order to devise a new third way. This has to be done, however, with care and is certainly not without risk (but to change nothing or not reforming enough might even be riskier and social welfare-reducing[5].

---

2 cf. CPB (Netherlands Bureau for Economic Policy Analysis): Challenging Neighbours. Rethinking German and Dutch Economic Institutions, Berlin et al. 1997, p. 268 ff., Delsen, Lei. / Jong, Eelke de: The German and Dutch Economies. Who follows whom?, Heidelberg 1998, p. 4.

3 Lindbeck, Assar: The Unemployment Problem, Stockholm, Working Paper, mimeo 1995, p. 1.

4 I am aware that the law of unintended consequences runs riot. But careful evaluation of the empirical evidence in other countries might help to implement a sensible economic policy package.

5 There is very often a bias against social welfare improving reforms because in assessing institutional reforms "it is often not the actually relevant alternatives that are compared against one another, rather: present endowments and entitlements are regarded as being sure, even though they are not in fact ... in the evaluation of institutional reforms, it is always the future effects of institutional arrangements – under alternative assumptions of both with and

The article is organized as follows. In sections II to IV I will use the USA as an Anglo-Saxon benchmark model against the European Union, mainly consisting of more regulated countries with more government involvement, to see the comparative economic performance. I will also ask if the US economic measures to fight successfully a persistent rise in unemployment are a valuable lesson for Continental Europe. Special features are a comparison and evaluation of the performance in the following fields: unemployment and employment growth (section II), labour productivity, real labour costs and capital-intensity developments, the role of demand-side factors (section III), and interactions between the demand- and the supply-side and the determinants for a successful demand-side policy (section IV). Moreover, in section V I will discuss the effects of the different policy packages in the Netherlands and in the United Kingdom, especially their common economic rationale but different equity and efficiency implications. A judgement about the relative merits of the Anglo-Saxon model and a reformed Rhineland model is partly a question of differing economic efficiency results, partly of political economy considerations and (re-)election chances in societies with different cultures, and partly of value-judgements concerning trade-offs e.g. between equity and efficiency. Value-judgements cannot be answered by economists in an objective way. The implications of different ways of reforms can be shown, however. Furthermore, one can propose a plan for an implementation of reforms in Germany that, based on certain sensible assumptions, seems to be efficiency- and employment-enhancing and moreover politically feasible. I will do that in my conclusions where I will finally discuss some possible reform options for Germany to better master future adjustment pressures (section VI).

## II. Different paths of economic development in the U.S. and Western Europe: The stylized facts of unemployment and employment growth

The main characteristic of European unemployment is the inability of unemployment rates to return to the pre-shock level in the years after major supply and demand shocks. This is completely different to the U.S.-experience. Typical for European unemployment and the basic employment problem there is the weak net hiring of labour during business upswings. Unemployment rates in West Europe have varied less within business cycles than across them for more than two decades and the capacity to create jobs is small. Since the early 1970s the aggregate unem-

without reform – that must be compared to one another. The 'losers' under a particular reform are often – properly viewed – only alleged losers: that is, the losers, are viewed relative to the current situation projected into the future, without factoring in the consequences of 'continuing on', which are in themselves even more annoying. The ability to consent to an institutional reform is therefore absolutely consistent with a worsening in relation to the present, insupportable status quo". Quoted from Soltwedel, R.: Competition, responsibility and solidarity – the social market economy ensuring success in the global economy, Gütersloh 1997 (I), pp. 77 f.

ployment rate in Western Europe has been on a rising ratchet-like trend from about 3 percent to about 11 per cent as stated above[6], whereas the employment rate for people of working age fell from 65 to about 58 per cent[7].

In the United States the unemployment rate has basically fluctuated with little, if any, upward trend – the "normal" rate of unemployment has fluctuated cyclically around a horizontal line of 6 per cent since 1970[8] in the USA – although immigration was comparatively high and the employment rate for the working-age population has increased considerably over the last 25 years from 68 to about 75 per cent.[9] This means that irrespective of labour supply developments the end of the cycle in the USA typically sees unemployment reverting to something like its starting rate.

If we look at the USA and the main European Community countries they have roughly similar-sized labour forces. "Yet over the last 20 years the US economy has created just over 40 million new jobs, of which nearly 90 per cent have been in the private sector. Europe over the same period has created fewer than 6 million net new jobs; and until a few years ago more than all of these had been in the public sector – private-sector employment actually declined"[10].

Since the mid-1970s, unemployment durations have been much higher in Western Europe than in the U.S. Increases in unemployment have been associated with more long-term unemployment compared to the USA – some five times higher.[11] This is a serious problem because as a rule the longer people are unemployed, the lower are their chances of re-employment.

The burden of unemployment is concentrated especially among unskilled people, partly among the young and among women in Western Europe.[12] In general, unemployment rates are also higher for blue-collar workers than for white collar workers. In comparison to the USA redistributive programs in Europe do spread, however, the costs of unemployment more broadly within the European economies – in a financial sense and by spreading the increases in unemployment more broadly across workers of different skill-levels. But mainly the long-term unemployed are at a comparative disadvantage. For a long time, however, the European

6 cf. Blanchard, Olivier / Katz, Lawrence F.: What we know and do not know about the natural rate of unemployment, in: Journal of Economic Perspectives, No. 1, 1997, pp. 51 - 72, here: p. 67.

7 cf. Lindbeck, A.: The West European Employment Problem, in: Weltwirtschaftliches Archiv, No. 4, 1996 (I), pp. 609 - 637, here: p. 609 f.

8 cf. Mankiw, N.Gregory.: Principles of Macroeconomics, Orlando 1998, p. 569.

9 cf. Welfens, Paul J. J. et al.: Technological Competition, Employment and Innovation Policies in OECD Countries, Berlin et al. 1998, p. 21, appendix I, cf. also Lindbeck 1996 (I).

10 Llewellyn, John: Tackling Europe's competitiveness, in: Oxford Review of Economic Policy, Vol. 12, No. 3, 1996, p. 91.

11 Llewllyn 1996, p. 91.

12 cf. Wolf, Martin: Europe's real insiders, in: Financial Times, November 18, 1997, p. 16.

approach has hindered an even harder concentration of adjustment costs on a particular group of workers like in the USA and with less relief provided by public transfer programs than in Europe, partly explaining the higher crime rates in the USA.[13]

That the economic capacity to adjust to shocks in the West-European economies has decreased and / or especially that the shocks and new trends with a given adjustment capacity have increased becomes clear if we compare the 1950s and 1960s with the time since the 1970s. Over the former time period, the average unemployment rate in West-Europe was much below that in the U.S. In the latter time-period, however, the average European unemployment rate has significantly exceeded the rate in the USA. The reason seems to be a worse ability of the traditional Rhineland model to deal with the new kind of structural change to a service society, hence institutional reforms are necessary.

## III. The role of the demand side: Is hysteresis or are institutional rigidities mainly responsible for persistent European unemployment?

Since the mid-1970s the real GDP in the European Community has grown by almost the same amount as in the USA – between 1973 and 1995, 2.3 per cent on average for the EC, 2.4 for the USA. As stated above, the employment and unemployment results differed considerably in spite of the similar real demand growth. To say it with the words of J. Llewellyn[14]: The "observations suggest that, while faster European growth, aided perhaps by a less tight macroeconomic policy and a more flexible, less inflation-prone economy, would almost certainly have seen somewhat faster employment growth, nevertheless, a significant part of the unemployment in Europe is structural. And this is likely to be particularly so if, or to the extent that, a significant part of Europe's inflation proneness is itself due to structural rigidities".

The noteworthy empirical regularities shown above represent a challenge to theorizing about unemployment. A theory of unemployment should be able to explain

---

[13] cf. Blank, Rebecca M.: The Misdiagnosis of Eurosclerosis, in: The American Prospect,, No. 1, 1997, pp. 81 - 85. The USA seem to have a displacement problem especially for low-skilled unemployed, and even neoclassical economists argue for some kind of intervention like subsidizing retraining or employment. It is argued that "the worsening situation of the less skilled is a legitimate cause for concern. There has been a steady decrease in demand for such workers and markets are clearing! Allegations that the great American job machine has created too many bad jobs now seems off the mark; rather, the point is that there is a surplus of unskilled labor in a market that seemingly requires more higher level skills than ever", Addison, John T.: The U.S. Labor Market: Structure and Performance, in: Siebert, Horst (ed.): Structural Change and labor market flexibility: experience in selected OECD economies, Tübingen 1997, pp. 187 - 222, p. 214.

[14] Llewellyn 1996, p. 91.

these stylized facts in order to be a sensible foundation for policy conclusions.[15] The factors taken together until now suggest that especially institutional impediments on the supply side are the main problem in Europe. If one scrutinizes the most relevant theories[16] for European unemployment, the theory of hysteresis and mainly macroeconomic mistakes on the one hand and persistence theories of unemployment due to institutional rigidities on the other hand, they seem to be observationally equivalent in many respects. Looking more deeply at plausibility and empirical evidence, however, supply-side institutional rigidity theories seem to win the battle. But this view is controversial.

The common starting point of both theories is that aggregate unemployment increases after massive shocks. Unemployment rose in three abrupt steps in Western Europe in 1973 - 75, the end of the 1970s and the start of the 1980s and the early 1990s. These stepwise increases were initiated by major macroeconomic shocks connected with the oil-price hikes in the mid- and late 1970s and restrictive economic policies designed to fight inflation, reduce budget deficits and sustain fixed exchange rates.[17] The question is why unemployment remained high in western Europe after the shock subsided and although there was an upswing (leading to a lower decrease of unemployment than the rise of unemployment was due to the previous shock). The supporters of the hysteresis school[18] argue that this is due to wrong macroeconomic management, the supporters of the persistence school argue that a low employment intensity of an upswing mainly results from wrong microeconomic and institutional incentives.

Hysteresis theories mainly stress the loss of human capital and real capital due to deep and prolonged recessions as the cause of (long-term) unemployment. Since prolonged unemployment will lead to a deterioration of the skills of the unemployed vis-a -vis the skills of the employed, there will be human capital deprecia-

---

15 cf. Snower, Dennis J.: Evaluating unemployment policies: what do the underlying theories tell us?, in: Oxford Review of Economic Policy, No. 1, 1995, pp. 110 - 135, here: p. 110.

16 Standard macroeconomic theories are not very helpful in this context. Snower 1995, pp. 111 ff. discusses the deficiencies of the traditional Keynesian theory, the natural rate theory, the new classical and the real business cycle theories, the efficiency-wage theory and of trade union theories in explaining the evolution of the problem of persistent unemployment. He concludes that these theories are not very much suited to develop appropriate policy measures. Cf. another survey also Funk, Lothar / Knappe, Eckhard: Der Beitrag des Neukeynesianismus zur Erklärung der Arbeitslosigkeit in Europa, in: Hamburger Jahrbuch für Wirtschafts- und Gesellschaftspolitik, Vol. 41, 1996, pp. 43 - 57. Cf. also Knappe, Eckhard: Einige Irrtümer in der Arbeitsmarktdebatte, in: Knappe, Eckhard / Berthold, Norbert (eds.): Ökonomische Theorie der Sozialpolitik. Bernhard Külp zum 65. Geburtstag, Heidelberg 1998, pp. 168 - 193.

17 cf. Knappe, E.: The Aims and Effects of Technology, in: Dobers, H. / Nieuwenhuijze, V. (eds.): The Technological Era – Continuity and Change in the Arab and European Societies, St. Augustin 1985, cf. also Lindbeck, Assar: 1996 (I).

18 cf. e.g. Spahn, Heinz-Peter: Makroökonomie. Theoretische Grundlagen und stabilitätspolitische Strategien, Berlin et al. 1996, pp. 173 ff.

tion with long-run consequences. As far as the real capital stock tends to depreciate during deep and prolonged recessions it may be too small in a subsequent business upswing to employ the entire labour force. Real capital shortage would be responsible for unemployment persistence. To say it in the words of some proponents: "A long period of high actual unemployment leads to an increase in the proportion of long-term unemployed. If the long-term unemployed either lose skills or become less effective in their search, their effect on bargaining will decrease, leading to a higher natural rate"[19].

However, seen from the perspective of the institutional rigidity school such explanations are incomplete in the following sense: sufficiently large moderation of real wages for the workers concerned would overcome the problem – at least concerning involuntary unemployment.[20] Thus, both theories have to assume that workers or unions resist wage moderation. If one compares the different approaches of resistance to wage moderation to explain aggregate unemployment, most of them have severe deficiencies.[21] The insider-outsider theory of unemployment seems to have the best prognostic power.[22] It focuses attention on labour turnover costs as a source of unemployment and argues as follows: Labour turnover costs which have to be paid by the firms give market power to the experienced, incumbent employees, the insiders, because they know that their employers would find it costly to replace them. The insiders use their power to improve their wages. Firms are discouraged from firing their current insiders on the one hand, high insider wages discourage, on the other hand, the hiring of new entrants. This means that the strategic behaviour of insiders can yield a bidding up of the insider wages so that it is not profitable for firms to hire an outsider even if the value of the marginal product of an outsider exceeds the reservation wage.

This model can explain quite convincingly many empiricial regularities in the real world, for example:

1. The persistence of unemployment in Europe is its major feature. Especially striking is the fact that there was no large decrease of unemployment once the effects of the crises (e.g. oil) had been reversed. A central implication of this theory is that it is very difficult for unemployment to disappear as long as mainly workers with jobs are able to influence wage demands. Hence, the empirical development of real wage increases in Europe can be explained by the insider-outsider approach. Normally, when market conditions are good, wages adjust upward, because those who are employed stop fearing about losing their job. This prevents the unem-

19 Blanchard / Katz 1997, p. 68 f.

20 cf. Funk, Lothar / Knappe, Eckhard: Neue Wege aus der Arbeitslosigkeit, in: Montada, Leo (ed.), Beschäftigungspolitik zwischen Effizienz und Gerechtigkeit, Frankfurt a.M. and New York 1997, pp. 80-97, here: p. 87.

21 cf. Lindbeck, Assar: Microfoundations of Unemployment Theory, in: Labour, No. 3, 1991, pp. 5 ff.

22 cf. Snower 1995.

ployed from benefitting fully, for example, from the upturns of the cycle in order to get a job. Wage moderation is only possible in the case of a threat of unemployment for employed workers, it is not when cuts are necessary to increase net job creation. This argument is not in contradiction with a tendency to negotiate wage cuts in order to avoid unemployment (some years ago an example was Volkswagen; a recent example is payment lower than union bargained minimum wages in the new eastern Länder in many firms in Germany at present). In Continental Europe, a core of insiders has succeeded to resist the pressure of competition imposed on the labour markets by the gradually developing stock of outsiders. This helped them to keep upward pressures on wages, despite the seemingly endless rise of unemployment.

The reason for the insider's possibility to influence wages in such a way as described above are the relatively high labour turnover costs. They result mainly from the bargaining of still relatively powerful trade unions and are due to government regulations concerning minimum standards in collective bargaining and social security but also due to unavoidable firm-specific investments and costs of hiring and firing etc. These labour turnover costs are relatively high in Europe in comparison to the USA. In Continental Europe they often insulate the insiders from becoming unemployed. Consequently, high unemployment has little effect on wage bargaining. This is especially true for high long-term unemployment, because one can distinguish two types of outsiders: those who have been unemployed for a long time and those who have just lost their jobs.[23] It is likely that the jobless who have just entered the pool of the unemployed are the first to be rehired because employers regard them as better qualified to fill positions. Then insiders will in spite of high long-term unemployment easily move from firm to firm. Wage bargaining results will all the same remain at a high level, insofar as employed workers' fears of unemployment will never be such as to make them accept wages that would be compatible with hiring all the jobless because effective competition is low.

2. Insider-outsider problems do not only occur in European countries but also in the Anglo-Saxon economies,[24] but with a much less damaging effect on aggregate unemployment at least in the USA, although there are negative distributional side-effects because "in the United States new hires pay the price for higher wages of insiders, since tenure profiles are relatively steep".[25] This is because there are a lot of counteracting factors in the USA which are missing in many European countries. One secret of success is that the United States kept putting pressure on the em-

---

23 Blanchard, Olivier / Diamond, Peter: Ranking unemployment duration and wages, in: Review of Economic Studies, Vol. 61, 1994, pp. 417 - 434.

24 cf. Broeder, Corina den: Institutions at work. Commitment and flexibility on the German and Dutch labour markets, Research Memorandum No. 131, Centraal Planbureau, Den Haag 1996, p. 92.

25 Broeder 1996, p. 92.

ployed to leave room for the unemployed. Wages are more responsive to unemployment there, whereas labour turnover costs tend to be considerably lower on average. As a result we see the return to a "full-employment unemployment rate" in the USA after shocks. This has implications also for medium and long-term real wage developments: "A great deal of labour market adjustment in the U.S. seems to take place without systematic real wage movement".[26] But what is the reason for that pressure in the U.S.? Institutional differences can explain this quite well: The pressure of competition in the market and due to the system of social security in the United States forces workers to take a job, whatever the wage. The result is a wide disparity of earnings due to the decline of unions or the lack of really binding minimum wages.[27] In comparison to Continental Europe real wages are more flexible downwards, unemployment benefits less generous, job security legislation less strict, and unions less strong. An effective deregulation of product and capital markets seems to be very important to curb local insider power in the USA. "In unionized firms with market power significant wage markups exist. In contrast, unionmark-ups are small for firms that encounter fierce product market competition".[28]

The insider-outsider approach is also compatible with the following important differences between the U.S. and Europe in long-term adjustment of average growth of labour productivity, real wage and kind of capital-investment.[29] Let me quote, for example, a study by the IMF:[30]

"The increase in real GDP in the United States and in the European Union since 1970 has been remarkably similar, as has the increase in the capital stock. The growth of employment, on the other hand, has been very different. ... A plausible explanation ... for high employment and low productivity growth in the USA and the opposite in Europe ... can be found in the types of investment in the two regions. In Europe, investment was capital *deepening* as indicated by the sharp rise in the capital-labour ratio. With more capital for each worker, the increase in output came about primarily through higher labour productivity rather than through higher employment. In this sense, investment appears to have been primarily directed towards substituting increases in capital for increases in employment. In the United States, on the other hand, the growth of the capital-labour ratio was much

26 Krueger, Alan B. / Pischke, Jörn-Steffen.: Observations and Conjectures on the U.S. Employment Miracle, NBER Working Paper 6146, Cambridge, MA, 1997, p. 20.

27 "Perhaps as many as 40 percent of the workers who qualify for the minimum wage are paid less than that". Quoted from Borjas, George J.; Labor Economics, New York et al. 1996, p. 167.

28 Broeder 1996, p. 92.

29 cf. Matthes, Heinrich / Todd, Douglas: 'Unemployment in Europe', in: Sautter, Hartmut (ed.), Wirtschaftspolitik in offenen Volkswirtschaften, Göttingen 1994, Larsen, Flemming: Comments, OECD (ed.): Macroeconomic Policies and Structural Reform 1996, Lindbeck 1996 (I), pp. 618 f.

30 IMF 1997: Germany – Selected Issues, IMF Staff Country Report No. 97/01, 1997, Washington, p. 32.

more modest, indicating that investment was more capital *widening*. ... The much larger increases in the capital-labour ratio and in labour productivity in Europe were reflected in only modest gains in employment that did not keep pace with the growth in labour supply."

In the words of Assar Lindbeck:[31]

"The relatively fast rate of labour productivity in Western Europe is partly a *result* of rapidly rising product wages. The brisk increase in real product wages in Western Europe has favoured both capital-intensive sectors and the use of capital intensive technologies within various sectors. The rapid rise in real product wages has also forced low-productivity plants and firms out of business – indeed faster than other firms have been able to reemploy 'redundant' workers. In a medium-term perspective, these developments have not only boosted aggregate productivity growth, but also contributed to the slow expansion of aggregate employment. The mirror image in the United States is that stagnating real product wages have retarded productivity growth and contributed to expanding aggregate employment".

Here is the interpretation of these facts by the Insider-Outsider theory: In countries where labour turnover costs are very high, hoarding will be stopped in deep prolonged recessions and firing will be started. Firms will be comparatively slow to rehire this labour in a subsequent recovery, because they have to face further firing costs in the case that the recovery does not materialize. This can explain why investment in labour-saving equipment may then take the place of new employment.

Differences in labour turnover costs can explain why U.S. unemployment has been more variable than European unemployment and why there has been more decoupling of employment and production in Europe than in the USA with generally lower labour turnover costs. Last but not least, this model can explain why unemployment rates in Europe were significantly lower than in the USA in the 1950s and 1960s. At this time business cycles were mild and short-lived which had the following implication: With comparatively high labour turnover costs it was in Western Europe intertemporally optimal not to hire and to fire in the medium term after full-employment was reached, hoarding labour in the slumps and bringing it back into use in the booms.

Moreover, it is possible to interprete reasonably why in many European economies wages in the traditional manufacturing sectors have not fallen with a shrinking demand. The reason is significant labour turnover costs in these sectors mainly due to trade-union policy. This may explain why employment in manufacturing in the European Union dropped significantly whereas in the USA "the absolute numbers employed in manufacturing have remained roughly constant since 1970, alongside a large increase in total civilian employment".[32]

---

31 Lindbeck, A.: Full Employment and the Welfare State, The Industrial Institute for Economic and and Social Research, Working Paper No. 469, Memphis (1996 (II), p. 618.

The insider-outsider theory can also explain why much service sector employment and temporary employment is rising in comparison with industrial employment. The reason is that it is associated with relatively low turnover costs.

Furthermore, the approach can explain the resistance against a market-oriented wage-differentiation in systems of collective wage bargaining. Because this would imply "the sacrifice of the interests of those insiders with similar characteristics as the relevant outsiders" (unskilled and / or older workers, for example).[33] This is all the more so if an unemployment insurance system allows long periods of low-intensity job search.

The insider-outsider approach can in conjunction with e.g. human capital depreciation (increasing with a rising duration of unemployment) also interprete the lasting outward shift in the unemployment-vacancy (UV) relation observed for Europe (implying that a given level of vacancies is then associated with higher unemployment) and the not lasting one for the USA.[34] Some additional arguments to support the idea that the effective labour force in Europe declined and equilibrium real wages have risen are that firms will respond to deteriorating skill levels associated with lengthy unemployment by creating fewer jobs in the future. Furthermore, workers will give up searching in such a situation and rely on unemployment insurance benefits.[35]

Supporters of macroeconomic hysteresis theories of unemployment, e.g. the German Institute for Economic Research[36], have, however, sharply criticized this kind of analysis of stylized facts. They argue:

"... the only example of lasting success that remains is the USA. It is often claimed that this is due to the fact that real wages and productivity there have grown less strongly than in Europe, that the USA has 'chosen' a path of economic development oriented towards job creation and less toward realising income opportunities to the detriment of the unemployed. This 'choice', it is argued, is possible because labour markets in the USA react much more 'flexibly' to economic challenges than those in Continenatal Europe. In the view of the DIW, however, this position cannot be squared with the facts".[37]

---

32 Ramaswamy, Ramana / Rowthorn, Robert: Deindustrialisation: Causes and Implications, IMF Working Paper, WP / 97 / 42, Washington 1997, p. 14.

33 cf. Paqué, Karl-Heinz: From Miracle to Crisis? The German Economy at the End of the Twentieth Century, Institute for German Studies Discussion Paper, University of Birmingham 1996, pp. 12 f.

34 cf. Kösters, Wim / Belke, Ansgar: Slow Adjustment to Shocks or True Hysteresis? Lessons from the Different Labour Market Performances in Western Europe and the USA, Intereconomics, No. 3, 1996, pp. 107 - 121, here: pp. 111 ff., Sneessens, Henri R.: Lessons for Employment and growth in Western Europe, in, Giersch, H. (ed.), Fighting Europe's unemployment in the 1990's, Berlin et al. 1996, pp. 183 - 211, here: p. 186 and pp. 194 f.

35 cf. Welfens, Paul J. J. et al. 1998, p. 44.

36 German Economic Research Institutes: Unemployment Trends in Selected Industrialised Countries, Economic Bulletin, Vol. 34, No. 11, November 1997, pp. 25 f.

But such a position must be explained with plausible arguments. So what are the arguments? Firstly, they say that "nominal wages set by pay bargainers exerted far less pressure on productivity during the 1980s in Germany than in the USA. Yet because prices increased more rapidly in the USA than in Germany, real wages in the USA grew slower".[38] Secondly, they argue that "between 1984 and 1990 the volume of working hours increased and unemployment fell in West Germany, so that it cannot be claimed that real wages exerted pressure on productivity growth in this period". Thirdly, it is argued that the approach above must be wrong because the evidence in Britain shows that nominal wages "did not drive productivity growth, as would be supposed on the basis of the theory of the substitution of labour by capital".[39]

The problems with the above arguments are simply that they only refute theories that nobody of e.g. the insider-outsider theory proponents uses and the latter can quite plausibly explain the evidence with their models. One can explain, for example, the U.S. experience as follows: American firms will speculate that nominal wage increases will translate into higher product prices so that firms' resistance to nominal wage claims exceeding real productivity growth could be rather weak. This means: If firms are rational to some extent they anticipate higher prices so that ex post the wage-price ratio will increase less strongly than nominal wages. Furthermore, it can be seen that in the period 1984 - 1990 just the effects occured which are expected by the neoclassical school of thinking: employment increased due to wage-moderation.[40] The period of wage moderation was, however, not long enough to solve the unemployment problem before the next shock occured. The British example is also misleading because real wages are again not taken into account, implying an irrational firms' behaviour. Even more misleading is the following statement: "One cannot seriously talk of a simple 'choice' between real wage and employment and the trends in Great Britain can in no way be explained with reference to movements in real wages there."[41] It is curious that the DIW does not take into account macroeocomic factors (and severe problems of the British supply side which we will analyse later) that are important explanations for the British developments which are accepted by the modern neoclassicals. Even if it is right that for the second half of the 1980s real wages in the UK were growing by substantially less than the productivity growth rate in manufacturing this does, even from a neoclassical-monetarist perspective not necessarily lead to more employment and less unemployment in the medium term if other shocks counter this effect. The answer from the British economist[42] to what seems to be the puzzle of

---

37 DIW (German Institute for Economic Research): Unemployment Trends in Selected Industrialised Countries – A different opinion, Economic Bulletin, No. 11, 1997, p. 25.

38 DIW 1997, p. 25.

39 DIW 1997, p. 25.

40 cf. Lapp, Susanne / Lehment, Harmen: Lohnzurückhaltung und Beschäftigung in Deutschland und in den Vereinigten Staaten, in: Die Weltwirtschaft, No. 1, 1997, pp. 67 - 83.

41 DIW 1997, p. 26.

the British rise of unemployment at the beginning of the 1990s is "that owing to our tragic errors in monetary policy we had to hit on the head an economy which otherwise could have remained on a sustained growth path of some 3 percent. ... In short it was recession, not the trends of a poorly-performing labour market, that delivered us this apparent ratchet effect".[43]

Some commentators of the hysteresis school would go so far as to question whether structural problems really are any more serious in Europe than elsewhere. Hence, they plead for a more expansionary monetary policy even if there is not much slack in the labour market and see no need to make comprehensive institutional reforms. Standard hysteresis models therefore imply that the unemployment rates "could just as easily ratchet downward as upward under appropriate conditions. For example, a prolonged economic expansion that steadily reduced unemployment would over time lower the "equilibrium" unemployment rate. However, while examples of countries getting stuck in high unemployment are not uncommon, examples of countries moving hysteretically into low unemployment equilibria are scarce".[44] Furthermore, even the proponents of such an approach argue that "the empirical case for hysteresis is far from tight".[45]

There is, however, a great danger if the diagnosis of the hysteresis school that does not take account of the supply-side arguments mentioned before is in fact inappropriate. Then it could be that a more expansionary monetary policy[46] without additional reforms or an additional incomes policy would give trade unions an incentive to press for strongly rising wages. An accommodating monetary policy could then lead to rather high inflation rates and a stabilization crisis with higher unemployment to bring inflation down again. To summarize the counter-arguments: "It may be dangerous to over-stimulate (beyond the natural unemployment rate), because it inevitably invites inflation. We have seen many episodes of this kind in the last three decades, sometimes mistaking the level of the natural unemployment rate, or sometimes deliberately taking advantage of a short-run boom".[47]

---

42 Minford, Patrick: Deregulation and Unemployment – The UK Experience, in: Swedish Economic Policy Review, Vol. 1, pp. 113 - 141, here: p. 134.

43 It is quite funny that even some principles of economics textbooks do include easily such macroecomic shock effects into an aggregate labour market analysis wich is not in contradiction to the insider-outsider theory or our stylized facts analysis. Cf. e.g. Parkin, Michael / Powell, Melanie / Matthews, Kent: Economics, New York 1997, pp. 612 ff.

44 IMF: Germany – Selected Issues, IMF Staff Country Report No. 97 / 01, October 1997, p. 15.

45 Blanchard, Katz 1997, p. 69.

46 We do not discuss explicitly fiscal policies here. Cf. the limits and benefits of fiscal policies e.g. Lindbeck 1995 and Lindbeck, Assar: Full Employment and the Welfare State, The Industrial Institute for Economic and Social Research, Working Paper No, 469, Memphis, 1996 (II).

47 Ito, Takatoshi: Commentary: The Role of Demand Management in Reducing Unemployment, in: Federal Reserve Bank of Kansas City (ed.): Reducing Unemployment: Current Issues and Policy Options, Jackson Hole 1994, pp. 139 - 154, here: p. 144. Even Andrew

A speeding-up of monetary expansion could be justified[48], however, on the one hand "if we could be sure that the expansion really had its full effect on output and would not fuel inflation. For this, a voluntary wage pause is needed, a consensus not to raise wages in response. Wage restraint, on the other hand, needs to be coupled with an expansionary policy package in order to produce its full employment effect".[49]

---

Glyn: Internal and External Constraints on Egalitarian Policies in Europe, in: International Politics and Society, No. 2, 1997, pp. 172 - 183, who is clearly a left-wing Post-Keynesian economist, argues as follows: "Unless the expansion left the unemployment rate above the pre-existing non-accelerating inflation rate of unemployment (NAIRU), or was accompanied by measures to reduce the NAIRU, accelerating inflation would develop". The main message of his article is that it is mostly domestic constraints (competing claims) which impair the sustainablity of egalitarian policies. With slow economic growth, all egalitarian policy options (e.g. a Keynesian demand management policy) intensify distributional conflicts, which must be resolved politically if the policies are to be sustainable. But high growth eventually also generates inflationary struggle over distribution unless there are wage bargaining institutions capable of containing it.

48 At present, the monetary policy in Europe does not seem to be restrictive, however. A more expansionary course of monetary policy would very likely require more incentive-compatible structural reforms to be helpful to sustainably reduce average unemployment in the aggregate. "It is often stated that the persistently high unemployment in Europe is due to a – supposedly – restrictive monetary policy, while unemployment in the United States was reduced quickly in the 1990s because the Fed stimulated economic activity strongly. The available indicators suggest, however, that monetary policy has been on an expansionary course for some time in Europe. Real short-term interest rates in Germany are substantially lower than the historical average. In the United States, policy has been on a neutral course; real money market rates are close to their average for three years already. Similarly, the term spread in the United States has been near the average for three years now while it is substantially higher in Germany and in France, also indicating that monetary policy is expansionary in Europe. Furthermore, if monetary policy in Europe really had been overly restrictive one should observe that inflation had been reduced by more than in the United States. This is, however, not the case: Since 1990, inflation rates in Europe and in the United States have come down by about the same amount. Also, the reduction of inflation in the United Kingdom was more pronounced than in Germany or in France; at the same time, unemployment in the latter countries continued to increase, while it declined markedly in the United Kingdom. All these indicators suggest that monetary policy in Europe has not been an impediment to the improvement of economic activity and of unemployment", cf. Gern, Klaus-Jürgen et al.: Kräftiger Aufschwung in den Industrieländern, in: Die Weltwirtschaft, No. 3, 1997, pp. 229 - 263, here: p. 261 f. As a general rule, if an expansionary policy package lacks during times of structural reforms then there is the danger of only slow investment in the short run and the incentive changes due to these reforms is weak only.

49 Giersch, Herbert: Openess for Prosperity. Essays in World Economics, 1993, p. 132. The position of Stanley Fischer seems to be appropriate in our view: "Central banks should not be alarmed by growth that looks high by the standards of the last decade. Rapid growth by itself would not be a good reason to reduce money growth or raise interest rates. Rather, central bankers should judge the supply potential of the economy by the behaviour of the inflation rate – and they should be prepared to tighten policy when inflation threatens", Fischer, Stanley: Commentary: The Role of Demand Management Policies in Reducing Unemployment, in: Federal Reserve Bank of Kansas City (ed.): Reducing Unemployment: Current Issues and Policy Implications, Kansas City, 1994, pp. 133 - 137, here: p. 137. Cf. Filc,

Hence, an expansionary policy package can help to increase employment and fight unemployment on the one hand. A flanking, more expansionary monetary policy can make market-oriented reforms more credible and therefore more politically feasible in the medium-term on the other hand.[50] It has become quite clear now that a more expansionary demand policy in the product market generates a strong supply and labour demand response only if there is a very elastic supply side in the medium- and longer term and, in particular if labour supply reacts elastically. An important question therefore is, how to increase the aggregate supply elasticity in order to achieve better non-inflationary results of demand management?

## IV. The interaction between demand- and supply-side policies

One precondition for non-inflationary results of demand management is that private agents must not interpret expansionary economic policy as the start of a process of an increase of inflation. Hence one has to look for mechanisms that prevent that a more expansionary demand-side policy leads to a wage-price spiral.

The underlying motivation to analyse this further is to provide a plausible account of how demand management policies and other aggregate demand changes can affect employment over a period longer than the short-term, i.e. a period long enough for prices to be flexible and for price surprises to be no more important. There are various channels whereby these longer-term effects may occur and at least two approaches that deal with these interactions more deeply.[51]

From the perspective of the Lindbeck / Snower-approach one has to distinguish between a situation where capital is roughly constant and there are diminishing returns to labour, and a situation in which the capital stock adjusts fully, the long run. The most important aspect of this theory lies in showing that the ability of any given type of product demand to shift the labour demand curve depends on whether a limited number of transmission channels from product demand to demand for labour are open. Particularly important in this regard are the entry and exit of firms and the productivity-enhancing effects of infrastructure investment. From a policy-oriented perspective this means that supply-side policies such as the removal of

---

Wolfgang: Geldpolitik im Rahmen eines beschäftigungsorientierten Gesamtkonzepts, in: Reader zum Fachkongress "Innovation, Beschäftigung, Wachstum und Wettbewerb", Berlin 28. / 29. 4. 1997, pp. 243 - 246.

50 cf. Bertola, Giuseppe / Ichino, Andrea: Crossing the river. A comparative perspective on Italian employment dynamics, in: Economic Policy, No. 2, 1995, pp. 361 - 415.

51 cf. Lindbeck, Assar / Snower, Dennis J.: How are product demand changes transmitted to the labour market?, in: The Economic Journal, Vol. 104, 1994, pp. 386 - 398, Snower 1995, p. 120 ff., Lindbeck, Assar: New Keynesianism and aggregate economic activity, The Economic Journal, Vol. 108, No. 1, 1998, pp. 167 - 180 on the one hand, Krueger, Alan. B. / Pischke, Jörn-Steffen: Observations and Conjectures on the U.S. Employment Miracle, NBER Working Paper 6146, Cambridge, MA, 1997 on the other hand.

barriers to the entry and exit of firms might strengthen the longer-term impact of demand-side policies on employment. Moreover, government investment spending on infrastructure should have a bigger impact on employment than increased transfer payments or tax reductions.

These results are in general confirmed by a recent analysis of Krueger and Pischke[52] who argue as follows: The demand curve for labour becomes more elastic if constraints on capital or other factors of production are decreased. This results from Marshall's third law of derived demand – the elasticity of demand for labour is lower if the supply of other factors of production, e.g. capital, is less elastic.[53]

This means that the effective labour demand curve becomes less steep the lower the constraints in the capital and product markets and on entrepreneurs in bringing new products to markets or in starting new enterprises are, because then the supply of these resources is more elastic. The main difference of a West-European country like Germany to the USA then can be described in the following way:[54] The effective demand curve for labour (in Germany for example) is quite steep because resource and product market constraints cause the demand curve to become inelastic. Then a lowering of a factual wage floor has only a modest impact on employment as the demand constraint causes the effective demand curve to become more elastic. Therefore, rigidities may arise from outside the labour market with an important effect in lowering labour demand. The implication is that in many European countries "both supply-side constraints (e.g. wage floors and social insurance programs) and demand-side constraints (e.g., restrictions on entrepreneuer and product market regimes) are important".[55]

The analysis until now seems to suggest that the high labour intensity of growth in the USA in the last years can be explained because this economy is already (as opposed to many Western European countries) characterised by an extremely flexible supply side (avoiding tensions with a rising inflation rate) so that an expansionary monetary policy has its full effect on output.[56] The USA might in its cur-

52 Krueger / Pischke 1997.

53 cf. Filer, Randall K. / Hamermesh, Daniel S. / Rees, Albert E. (1996), The Economics of Work and Pay, 6th ed., New York 1996, p. 156.

54 cf. Krueger / Pischke 1997, pp. 23 ff.

55 Krueger / Pischke 1997, p. 26.

56 cf. Horn, G. A.: Beschäftigungswachstum in den USA – ein erklärbares Wunder, in: DIW-Wochenbericht, No. 9, 1998, pp. 173 - 180, Kramer, Charles F. / Li, Yutong: Job Uncertainty, Unemployment, and Inflation in the United States, in: Finance and Development, December 1997, pp. 30 - 32, Krueger / Pischke 1997. In this sense a statement of the German Council of Economic Experts is at least incomplete, may be misleading: "Governments should be aware that a lax monetary policy will do nothing to stimulate the growth of employment". Quoted from German Council of Economic Experts: Growth, Employment, Monetary Union – Guidelines for the Future, Annual Report 1997 / 1998, Wiesbaden 1997, p. 19.

rent expansion even represent a possible case where there has been a downward drift in the natural rate of unemployment due to a hysteretical move into a low unemployment equilibrium.[57]

Hence, a policy-mix including deregulation (and appropriate reregulation respectively) and a more expansionary monetary policy seems to be economically and also from the viewpoint of political-economy a sensible strategy as wage pressures will decline and the chances for success of structural reforms will improve.

There are, however, trade-offs between flexibility and efficiency[58] which have to be taken into account before implementing the policy proposals we just mentioned. Therefore, let us have a look at the two European success models that brought official unemployment down considerably in the last decade before making appropriate reform proposals for Germany.

## V. Lessons from the United Kingdom and the Netherlands for Germany

In the discussion there has been in particular one argument to explain the high and persistent (long-term) unemployment in industrial countries: skill-biased technical progress.[59] It is argued that technical progress – such as arising from the computer revolution amplified by rising internationalisation[60] – has accelerated and is increasingly in favour of skilled labour to the disadvantage of unskilled labour. This showed up in widening differentials between skill groups either of earnings or of employment and unemployment rates. This depended on whether collective agreements and welfare state provisions allowed for increasing wage differentiation or not. In general, in Continental Europe unemployment of low-skilled workers and long-term unemployment in particular increased disproportionally, the U.S. showed the other picture of an extremely rising wage differentiation. Two special cases are Germany and the United Kingdom. As has been pointed out by Stephen Nickell[61], low skilled workers in West Germany earn more than twice as much as equivalent workers in the US and yet their unemployment rates are much the same, partly because elderly and long-term jobless are not counted as unemployed in the German unemployment statistics. The United Kingdom is special as it "to some

57 IMF 1997, p. 15.

58 cf. Walwei, Ulrich: Flexibility of Employment Relationships: Possibilities and Limits, IAB-topics, Institute for Employment Research, No 22, Nürnberg 1997, cf. also Delsen / Jong 1998, pp. 159 ff.

59 cf. e.g. Koesters / Belke 1996, Nickell, Stephen: Structural Changes and the British Labour Market, in: Siebert, Horst (ed.), Structural Change and Labor Market Flexibility. Experience in Selected OECD Economies, Tübingen 1997, pp. 3 - 28.

60 cf. IMF 1997, pp. 53 ff.

61 Nickell, Stephen (1996), The Low-Skill Low-pay Problem: Lessons from Germany for Britain and the US, Policy Studies, Vol. 17, pp. 7 - 21.

extent combined the worst of both worlds: a disproportionate increase of unemployment of low-skilled workers and a widening of wage differentials, though not yet a real wage decline of low-paid workers".[62]

Therefore, one should see that there is not only skill-biased technical change per se but an important role for labour market and social institutions to shape earnings inequality and unemploment.[63] Especially in the USA and in Britain the decline of trade unions and the fall in the real value or the abolishment of the minimum wage has contributed to rising inequality.[64] In Britain the Thatcherite reforms led wage formation towards a decentralised market process. The power of trade unions was reduced by law, membership declined by more than 4 million to 9 million in the mid-nineties, and bargaining became less coordinated. Employment legislation was weakened, job security provisions have been reduced or abolished, and wage councils were eliminated. Benefit replacement rates declined and the benefit system was tightend: since 1979, welfare benefits have been made much less generous. Furthermore, there was a switch away from payroll taxes towards commodity taxes. The results: "The unemployment rate has fallen since the mid-eighties but it still remains high ...".[65] The main change has been, indeed, an increase in earnings dispersion since the mid-eighties, certainly not only due to a secular trend of technical change but exacerbated by institutional changes. "But despite the flexibility in relative wages which is all or more than many advocates of the policy wanted, the predicted reduction in unemployment that was supposed to be associated with this wage flexibility has not happened".[66] The annual entry rate into work for unemployed did not increase, large numbers of people have become inactive. In particular less educated men are not bothering to search for work but are accepting long-term sickness or semi-enforced retirement.[67] Paul Gregg and Alan Manning[68] summarise the problems of the British Conservative Party approach as follows:

62 Paqué, K.-H.: Structural Unemployment in Europe – a Bird's Eye View, in: Addison, John T. / Welfens, Paul J. J. (eds.): Labor Markets and Social Security. Wage Costs, Social Security Financing and Labor Market Reforms in Europe, Berlin et al. 1998, pp. 17 - 43, here: p. 28.

63 Cf. the following analysis especially Owen Smith, Eric / Funk, Lothar: A Comparison of German and British Macroeconomic Performance, Institute for German Studies Discussion Paper, University of Birmingham, forthcoming 1998.

64 cf. Freeman, Richard .B.: Labor Market Institutions and Earnings Inequality, New England Economic Review, No. 3, 1996, Gregg, Paul / Manning, Alan: Labour market regulation and unemployment, in: Snower, Dennis J. / Dehesa, Guillermo de la (eds.), Unemployment policy: government options for the labour market, Cambridge 1997, pp. 39 - 424, Heise, Arne: Deregulation and employment in Britain and Germany, Anglo-German Foundation for the Study of Industrial Society, London, Nickell 1997.

65 Siebert, Horst: Labor Market Rigidities: At the Root of Unemployment in Europe, Journal of Economic Perspectives, No. 3, 1997, pp. 37 - 54

66 Gregg / Manning 1997, p. 410.

67 cf. also Simonazzi, Annamaria / Villa, Paola: Employment, growth and income inequality: some open questions, Discussion Paper, University of Rome, mimeo 1996

68 Gregg / Manning 1997, p. 415.

"The agenda of de-regulation ... undermines the position of the weak but makes no assault on the sources of the bargaining power of more privileged workers. As such, it will serve to raise inequality in society, but not efficiency". Even if such an interpretation were exaggerated, it seems that the supply-side cannot easily be made more elastic with the Thatcherite reforms alone, and only with severe, undesirable side-effects.

From a German perspective, the aim is to find reform proposals which try to protect the economic favourable aspects of the German model but give enough scope for more flexibility and (relative) lower labour costs to improve the labour market outcomes. Besides the aspects of economic theory and empirical evidence one has to take into account in this dicussion political economy aspects. The challenging task is to devise not only effective but also politically feasible policies for fighting unemployment. Furthermore, they should foster egalitarian aims as globalisation has an anti-egalitarian bias. Egalitarian aims can also lead to efficiency gains:[69] "Social disintegration is not a spectator sport – those on the sidelines also get splashed with mud from the field. Ultimately, the deepening of social fissures can harm all".[70]

Labour market rigidities mainly benefit well organized insiders at the expense of badly organized and politically marginalized outsiders.[71] These outsiders exist in the UK and in Germany, one time they are (mainly) the low wage earners, the other time they are the unemployed, mainly the long-term unemployed. To repeat: The English labour market since Thatcher offers one particular solution to the distribution of labour's share of national income. By driving down the wage rates of substantial parts of the labour force, employment opportunities can be created if the macroeconomic environment is stable. But this approach makes a dramatic widening of the distribution of income necessary. Unemployment is kept relatively low, and the distributional consequences have to be carried by those whose real wages are forced down.

By contrast, in the Continental European experience of the past 20 years the distributional costs have essentially been incurred by the unemployed. As argued earlier, a system of social relationships has been built up which enables those in employment to operate as a cartel, and to appropriate the proceeds of economic growth, to the exclusion of the unemployed. The evidence seems to point to the rapid increase in real wages together with the rise in capital intensity which seems to be the most important reason for the modest rise in German employment. "Ra-

---

69 cf. Fitoussi, Jean-Paul / Zoega, Gylfi: Wage Distribution and Unemployment, in: Baldassari, Mario / Paganetto, Luigi / Phelps, Edmund S. (eds.): The 1990s Slump. Causes and Cures, London et al. 1996, pp. 157 - 172, Freeman 1996.

70 Rodrik, Dani: Has Globalization gone too far?, California Management Review, No. 3, pp. 29 - 53, here: p. 34.

71 Saint-Paul, Gilles: High unemployment from a political economy perspective, in: Snower, Dennis J. / Dehesa, Guillermo de la (eds.), Unemployment policy: government options for the labour market, Cambridge 1997, pp. 54 - 73.

pid real wage growth encouraged capital deepening which raised labour productivity by substituting increases in the capital stock for increases in employment."[72]

In the British and the German cases the burden of adjustment is put upon new hires, wheras e.g. in the Netherlands, insiders and new hires share much more the risks of cyclical variations. This gives potential outsiders a better position, as risks are shared, and they are only 'semi-outsiders'.[73] Such a solution is likely a "better" – more efficient and fairer – solution at the present time than the pure Anglo-Saxon or the traditional Rhineland model. The UK needs a more appropriate re-regulation after the market excesses with its undesirable side effects. Only some catch phrases to show the directions to steer have to suffice:[74] programmes targeted on the long-term unemployed and on the unskilled, improving education and training for the bottom half of the ability range, reforming the benefit system, and the encouragement of employer co-ordination, which can be very helpful in holding down inflation when the labour market is tight. This is not to say that all labour market regulation will lead to an improvement in labour market performance. There is some optimal level and form of regulation, primarily because there are likely to be monopolistic elements for those groups of workers who are most prone to unemployment. "The important point is that the optimal bargaining power of workers in search and matching models is not zero, so that complete labour market deregulation should not be expected to lead to efficiency".[75] General principles are for example as follows: Increasing labour costs reduce incentives for firms to recruit, invest and hiring. But this increases on the other side the incentives of workers to undertake activities like job search, investment in human capital and acceptance of rotation of jobs when necessary due to structural change.

Germany needs more flexibility induced by organized de- and reregulation to solve the problem of high and persistent unemployment and low growth. Because the insiders are a quite stable political majority against radical market oriented changes of the labour market one has, however, to assume that radical reforms do not have a good chance in the German political system (at best after a long period of "learning by suffering" which is not desirable). Hence, one has to find more intelligent solutions which try to combine economic and political rationality.[76] Let us therefore have a deeper look at the Dutch example[77] to possibly learn for reforms in Germany.

---

72 Larsen, F.: Comments, OECD (ed.): Macroeconomic Policies and Structural Reform, pp. 231 f.

73 Broeder 1996

74 cf. Nickell 1996

75 Gregg / Manning 1997, p. 417

76 cf. Funk, L.: Institutionell verhärtete und politisch rationale Arbeitslosigkeit in der Bundesrepublik Deutschland, doctoral dissertation at the University of Trier 1996, Münster: Lit, forthcoming 1998

77 cf. an overview Funk, Lothar / Winkler, Albrecht: Konsensmodell Niederlande: Ein sozial- und beschäftigungspolitisches Vorbild für die Bundesrepublik Deutschland?, in:

In the 1980s, the Netherlands had one of the highest unemployment rates in the EU, Germany one of the lowest. Today, the reverse is true. How can this be explained? Now the Dutch have an interesting new configuration in which the advantages of competitive and coordinated capitalism are combined with a modernised form of the welfare state. To reduce the high labour costs, including very high payroll taxes, the Netherlands focused on achieving general wage moderation through centralised bargaining and tax reductions, lowering minimum wages, in particular for young workers, and scaling back payroll taxes, especially on low-wage groups. Furthermore, the incentives for part-time employment were improved. Thus, the fall in unemployment there coincided with a considerable expansion in the number of part time workers (more than 37% part-time employment rate, Germany 16%, UK 24%). Also after correcting the Dutch figures of employment growth for the shortening of working hours due mainly to the rise of part-time work this still leads to a very fast growth. The reforms made have typically affected very broad groups in the labour market, including the insiders. Why were such reforms necessary?

Throughout normal conditions of the past structural change until 1973 the 'European model' or Rhineland model of collective bargaining plus welfare state worked quite well, in some cases remarkably well. This model was, however, in many countries and for a long time unable to cope with the long-term consequences of more dramatic waves of de-industrialisation. "Such waves appear to leave structural traces in the labour market that call for adjustments which go beyond the capacity of the system"[78]. With such a kind of structural change and the costs of reunification (with the aim of equalizing living standards at the greatest possible speed) the German system of labour market regulation and its sophisticated system of fiscal equalization has been put under considerable strain. According to some commentators a "cosy corporatist sort of division of labour" is no longer sustainable.[79] In the eyes of these commentators cosy corporatism is defined by the following division of labour: the employers' associations and the unions are concerning themselves with wages (promoting high wages, good working conditions and solving social problems in a cooperative manner, maxim 'equal pay for equal work'), the government concerns itself with the employment problems generated by the non-market clearing employment costs set by collective agreements.

For neoliberal economists the results are easy to recognize: "The outcome of this tightly knit web of regulation is a spiral of intervention: non-market clearing employment costs have been encouraged; government intervention has helped enforce contractual wages as minimum wages (by declaring collective agreements compulsory for all employers in the relevant industry), thus prevent efficient underbidding

Knappe, Eckhard / Winkler, Albrecht (eds.): Sozialstaat im Umbruch. Herausforderungen an die deutsche Sozialpolitik, Frankfurt a.M. / New York 1997, pp. 151 - 186.

78 Cf. Paqué 1996, p. 34.

79 cf. Soltwedel, Rüdiger: Social Engineering in Europe: A German Perspective, in: Addison, John T. / Siebert, W. Stanley (eds.), Labour Markets in Europe. Issues of Harmonization and Regulation, London, 1997 (II), pp. 177 - 190.

by outsiders; and labour market policies and early retirement schemes have been designed to buy out labour at existing wages in order to reduce excess labour supply. In addition, rather generous income support schemes have implied considerable individual moral hazard. All this has enhanced labour market rigidity and caused a marked insider-outsider segmentation, as well as a substantial drain on taxpayers' money".[80]

There are certainly deficiencies of the German 'cosy corporatism' in an increasingly competitive product market, and the evidence seems to be in favour of the competitive model when comparative evidence is provided. W. Stanley Siebert argues for example[81] that, firstly, the more regulated a country is, the slower its private sector employment growth, and the lower its level of average earnings / incomes seem to be. Secondly, income inequality in the European labour markets seems to be not correlated with the degree of regulation. "Finally, as regards unemployment inequality, we found that unskilled relative unemployment had increased during the 1980s in all four countries examined ( the UK, the USA, France and West Germany), with no obvious advantage for more regulated such as West Germany or France"[82].

As the case of the Netherlands shows, however, not only the overall degree of regulation is relevant, but the kind of regulation which can also lead to more or less desirable results concerning either income inequality or unemployment rates. When looking at the Dutch model one has to scrutinize how the employment miracle was possible. By now more than two thirds of Dutch employment is in the service sector. The (rising) female labour force is heavily concentrated in the service sector. Part-time work occurs mostly in trade and other services and in the public sector. One could conclude that the increased participation of women has been made possible by the growth of the service sector. Conducive to the increasing participation rate of women seems to be the general Dutch policy of wage restraint, because a higher female labour supply is a way to achieve a higher target family income than otherwise possible.

In terms of wage determination, there can be no doubt that the corporatist structure of collective bargaining in the Netherlands is conducive to wage restraint, and therefore helps to make the supply-side more elastic. In the Netherlands the regime with mandatory extension does not generate the highest wage levels: they are realised under company agreement. Collective bargaining with the existence of escape routes and the potential vulnerability of established positions of trade unions[83] sets

80 Soltwedel 1997 (II), p. 178.

81 Siebert, W. Stanley: Overview of European Labour Markets, in: Addison, John T., Siebert, W. Stanley (eds.), Labour Markets in Europe. Issues of Harmonization and Regulation, London, Dryden 1997, pp. 229 - 241, here: p. 240.

82 Siebert, W.S., p. 240.

83 To explain: When an employer signs a contract with a single union, this contract automatically applies to all its employees, other unions are then left out; entry is free to new

minimum wage levels more compatible with higher employment (as it was also the case in the more successful times of the Soziale Marktwirtschaft concerning unemployment) and can lead to a more equal wage distribution in the economy.[84] The Dutch welfare state and labour market system is a model in the sense that it is a highly coupled system with checks and balances. As the wage distribution is fairly equal and wage differentials across occupations are not large one might wonder why mobility is still at normal levels in the Netherlands, fully comparable with other OECD countries. The explanation might be differences in employment opportunities across occupations or for that matter regions can be sufficient to stimulate mobility especially in such a small country.

That insiders and new hires share the risks of cyclical variations is possible because the institutional incentives are shaped in a way that the social partners perform the necessary policy of wage restraint to avoid the genesis of new outsiders or to integrate them again in the labour market (although sometimes only as part-time semi-outsiders – but that seems to be preferable to long-term unemployment). Collective bargaining in the Netherlands has enough escape clauses to maintain a wage bargaining system with a relatively high union density and collective bargaining coverage without persistent high and stepwise rising unemployment. The Dutch system of wage formation encompasses both more centralized and more decentralized elements, both of which are employment enhancing:

"Sectoral trade unions have more power to raise wages than decentralized trade unions because the sectoral level eliminates competition between firms. However they are less inclined to do so if the degree of centralisation sufficiently guarantees that bargaining units internalize external effects. Hence, the greater reliance on tripartite overt coordination is a strong element of Dutch wage formation, because it moderates wage claims of trade unions. ... the Dutch system also features more decentralized elements, as a larger number of firms bargain at the firm-level. This allows greater flexibility to adjust wages to firm-specific shocks,

---

unions; when employers demand concessions in harsh times, it sometimes occurs that one union agrees, and that the others can only follow suit, their protest notwithstanding.

84 The case of the Netherlands shows that a possibility for the state to declare collective bargaining agreements legally binding for all worker can be an effective instrument to support wage restraint and a more equal income distribution, if used in a responsible way. "... the Minister of Social Affairs and Employment has the authority to declare collective bargaining agreements legally binding for all workers and employers in a certain branch of industry, whether they are unionized or not. This provision remains a treasured policy instrument and is crucial for securing economy-wide wage restraint. It also implies the power to declare (parts of) collective agreements not generally binding. ... the Minister has the right to refuse a request for extension when the content of the agreement is not in line with policy interests. ... Employing a so called 'shadow of hierarchy' (Fritz W. Scharpf), governments have been effective in encouraging labour and capital to reach agreements that concur with their central policy goals". Quoted from Hemerijk, Anton / Kersbergen, Kees van: A Miraculous Model? Explaining the New Politics of the Welfare State in the Netherlands, in: Acta Politica, No. 2, 1997, pp. 258 - 280, here: p. 268.

which is particularly relevant for firms that are exposed to a volatile economic envirnment".[85]

But problems remain which all point to severe disincentives, which might need more market oriented reforms even with a widening of the wage structure, e.g. a cut off at the bottom by a still too large minimum wage to solve the unemployment problem by markets alone, a small number of annual working hours, large amounts of part time work, very large rates of early retirement, and high rates of inactivity as indicators of the discouragement of the labour supply. These problems can be solved, however, in the next years when the political entrepreneurs remain as brave as in the last years and as they will have to become in Germany.[86]

Although nowadays the continental European countries' consensus based model has often come to be seen as inferior to the more competititve and decentralised system of the Anglo-American countries, one has not only to take into account the costs (high and persistent unemployment) of this model but also its (possible) advantages, e.g. the higher relationship-specific investments and the curbing of local insider power by consensus-building at a centralized level, all potentially leading to an elastic aggregate supply reaction to aggregate demand increases. Moreover, social insurance not only has an influence on equity, but insures investments in firm-specific human capital and can support job search.[87] Furthermore, the question of fairness is answered in different ways in the existing two systems: in the United States and the UK the burden of adjustment to the risks of cyclical variations is put upon new hires mainly through downward wage flexibility (but also some long-term displacement from the labour market through discouragement), in the existing more consensus based model it is mainly the risk of long term unemployment.

---

85 Broeder 1996, p. 96.

86 Although there are still difficulties with the Dutch results, the main argument for this model is that it made change possible: "Wheras the popular opinion of the Social Market Economy shifted from a superior form of capitalism to an example of institutional rigidity, an opposite development took place for the Netherlands. Dutch disease turned into the Delta model, delta representing both the geographical position of the Netherlands in the Rhinedelta and the mathematical symbol for change ... The Delta model is said to combine the positive features of the Anglo-American model and the Social Market Economy: flexibility and solidarity", quoted from CPB 1997, p. 8.

87 These are important reasons why the wage dispersion and the necessary more incentive-compatible reconstruction and reduction of social security systems should not be exaggerated in Germany. An increase in the wage structure as the main policy option to increase employment might "for example, undercut the attractiveness to young people of investing in lower-level apprenticeships, thus increasing the pool of low-paid unskilled labour in the economy", quoted from Soskice, David et al.: Wage bargaining, Labour Markets and Macroeconomic Performance in Germany and the Netherlands, in: Delsen, Lei / Jong, Eelke de (eds.), The German and Dutch Economies. Who follows whom?, Heidelberg 1998, pp. 39 - 51, here: p. 50.

In contrast to the German Tarifautonomie (autonomous collective wage bargaining at the sectoral level) in the Dutch system the government may directly intervene into the collective bargaining process. This possibility is conducive to a policy of general wage restraint. Although the right for wage interventions has not been exercised, "quite recently (in 1993) the threat of government intervention had the impact of restricting the scope of bargaining".[88]

Another pillar of the supply side corporatism in the Netherlands is a substantial reconstruction of the social security system by attacking both the employee and the employers side to distribute adjustment costs as symmetrically as is possible in an efficiency enhancing policy. Besides changes in the organisational structure of the social insurance systems (abolishing the social insurance administration by the Industry Associations to lower moral hazard problems) the basic replacement ratios for unemployment, sickness and disability were lowered and a stronger rationing at the entry level took place to reduce the incentives for insurance consumption by employees.[89] The supplementary employment costs could be reduced considerably due to this and other reforms. Furthermore, the employers became directly liable for wages of sick employees from 1994 onwards. These changes had been necessary as the disability benefit recipients exploded relative to similar countries in the 1980s due to the following reasons: a combination of a generous benefit scheme, generous and fuzzy eligibility criteria and a governance structure that was not conducive to restraint. All of this made disability a very attractive exit route.

Besides the legalized possibilities to increase the flexibility of employers with part-timers and temporary workers (generally with lower rights and therefore lower labour costs relative to productivity than the insiders), there are a number of employment service programmes of subsidies and direct job creation which in particular concentrate on helping the problematic unemployed with low probability of finding a suitable job.

---

88 Broeder 1996, p. 84.

89 Let me quote Siebert, H. 1997, p. 42: "Between 1985 and 1987, the government benefits for unemployment, sickness and disability were scaled back from 80 to 70 percent of the previous wage. More restrictive definitions of disability were put in place in 1993. In 1994, employers were made directly liable for wages of sick employees in their first weeks off the job, rather than those costs being born by government, and employer contributions for sick leave were for the first time tied to the sickness record of the firm". The average social security tax rate was in 1994 31.9% for employees and 7.9% for employers (in Germany 19.3% for each of them), cf. Mayer, Thomas / Grillet-Aubert, Laurent: The New Dutch Model – A Blueprint for Continental Europe, Goldman Sachs, Frankfurt 1997, p. 4. The percentage change between 1991 and 1996 for real compensation per employee was -0.6 in the Netherlands and 9.0 in Germany (ibidem p. 3). Furthermore (ibidem p. 4): Income tax 1994 in the Netherlands (top rate 60.0%, entry rate 7.0%) and in Germany (top rate 57,0% and entry rate 27.8%). The corporation tax rate in the Netherlands was 40% for the first Gld 100,000 profit and 35% over that amount, Germany 45%. VAT rates Netherlands 6%-17.5 and Germany 7%-15%.

With adequate reforms (without destroying the corporatist system) the Dutch have managed to have a very fast growth of jobs especially in the low-productivity segment of the economy, faster even than the United States. The employment growth turned the Netherlands from a high- into a low unemployment economy by European standards. This proves: With adequate reforms the main disadvantage of the German model, the high unemployment problem, can be solved without sacrificing its main benefits, if the Dutch approach is not only a beggar-my-neighbour policy (meaning that the Dutch 'miracle' would not be successful if also used in a similar way by other European countries as well).

It is sometimes argued that the Dutch success can only be explained by a real depreciation of the Dutch guilder mainly due to real wage increases below the employment-neutral productivity growth but with practically fixed nominal exchange rates vis-a-vis its trading partners.[90] The argumentation goes on that, then, the Netherlands should not and cannot be a role model for Germany and other countries because "the decline in unit labour costs throughout Europe will, in the longer term, lead to falling prices i.e. to a deflation, as goods prices will react flexibly to the lower costs".[91]

But are these arguments really convincing? I am not quite sure. On the one hand, the economic policy rationality for the Netherlands alone is as follows: The Dutch monetary policy has been completely linked to the German Bundsbank policy. With a monetary policy similar to the German one, the Dutch made it possible to restore profitability, to make growth more labour intensive, and to export more by mainly a general policy of wage moderation.[92] Employment increased, however, mainly in the non-tradeable service sector in the Netherlands and not in the international sector. The named effects have overpowered the lacking positive contribution of higher wages to consumer demand stabilisation in the Netherlands.

Does this result really change significantly if many countries try to implement a strategy of wage moderation without jeopardising moderate wage increases in the aggregate? Theoretical and empirical analysis suggests that it does not. Such a general policy of wage moderation would also be possible for Germany and, parallel, in other countries with high and persistent unemployment as long as GDP per head does not fall by more than the increase in employment. Lower real labour cost increases than the rise in employment-neutral productivity growth would indeed not generate much foreign demand for the implementing countries but would in general, if the main incentives for the private actors in the economies are right, lead to more room for lower interest rates for the central banks which would boost invest-

90 cf. DIW 1997, p. 25, p. 29.

91 DIW 1997, p. 29.

92 Cf. the positive effects of such a policy on employment Drèze, Jacques H.: Employment in Europe, in: Gual, Jordi: The Social Challenge of Job Creation. Combatting Unemployment in Europe, Cheltenham, Brookfield 1996, pp. 29 - 54, here: p. 35 and German Council of Economic Experts 1997.

ment, consumption etc. and finally employment.[93] Empirical analysis shows that in the European Union since the 1960s the course of the growth rates of consumption and employment is quite closely parallel and that even the cutting of governments' budget deficits in the Western Europe in the last decade did not have negative effects on private consumption and the hereof resulting employment.[94] Hence, the picture of the DIW seems to be too pessimistic. The same applies in general to the thesis of a great danger of deflation, although one must certainly not underestimate the dangers if it really happened.

Deflation is a persistent fall in the general price level. If some prices fall this is not deflation. It is monetary policy that determines general inflation or deflation, not structural factors such as global competition. If e.g. the prices of imported products decline, then so long as the money supply continues to grow at the same rate, spending on other goods and therefore their prices should increase. Hence, I agree with the following statement concerning wage moderation and deflation: "there is no danger of such a policy leading to a deflationary process as long as the European Central Bank sticks to its inflation targets".[95] This implies the following kind of policy if there seems to be a danger of inflation: If one has to expect that supply did seriously exceed demand, the central bank should above all cut interest rates early enough.

There is, however, some truth in the argument that the successes from the Netherlands (and the United Kingdom) are partly (although not mainly as claimed by the DIW) due to devaluations that boosted employment in the tradables sector. This had prolonged real effects in the labour market because nominal wages did not catch up immediately after the devaluations. This can indeed be explained, for example, if devaluations occur in a situation of high unemployment and a threatening of even higher unemployment especially in the tradeables sector.

"Under such circumstances, insiders and labour union leaders in the tradables sector may occasionally accept lower real (product and consumption) wages via higher output prices (in domestic currency) in order to reduce the employment risks. In this way, a devaluation may speed up the transition to a sustainable ('equilibrium') employment level. This experience is quite consistent with Keynes's celebrated assertion that workers and their unions are often willing to accept real wage reductions via inflation, though not by nominal wage cuts (or even cuts in the rates of nominal wag increases)."[96]

Exchange rate devaluations were certainly a "trigger" that made the other structural reforms to increase supply-side flexibility politically feasible but were not the

---

93 cf. Bovenberg, Lans: Dutch employment growth: an analysis, CPB Report, No. 2, 1997, pp. 16 - 24, here: p. 23.

94 cf. Pauer, Wolfgang: Budgetkonsolidierung, privater Konsum und Beschäftigung in Europa, in: Wirtschaftspolitische Blätter, No. 1, 1998, pp. 74 - 84.

95 German Economic Research Institutes with the exception of the DIW 1997, p. 22.

96 Lindbeck 1998, pp. 1310 f.

main effect to enhance employment in the Netherlands or in the UK.[97] This kind of policy is not available for all West European countries concerned. But this policy experience is certainly a valid argument for a central bank to support appropriate supply-side reforms (leading to a threat of even higher short-term unemployment than prevailing) by a more expansionary monetary policy in order to become more growth- and employment-creating.

Sometimes it is reasoned that the Dutch successes will not be sustainable.[98] It is correct that the problem of cyclical unemployment cannot be abolished by successful reforms of the supply-side. The problem of a ratchet-like upward trend can, however, be turned around which would already be a great success. Moreover, there does not seem to be a fairer and more efficient alternative to the approach suggested by the Dutch model as the other alternative would be very likely the Anglo-Saxon model, as shown now.

It is often argued that above all the deregulatory bias of globalisation will result in the perverse outcome of the worse performing Anglo-American model of capitalism outcompeting the formerly better performing German model. Suitably de- and reregulated to the future necessities, the German model might indeed lead to better results than the Anglo-Saxon model. In comparison to the present German model the Anglo-American model seems to be, however, better adapted to master the new kind of structural change from high paying industry jobs to service sector jobs partly with low market wages and partly with high wages (depending on the intensity of human capital and the market forces without a persistent rise in unemployment). There is indeed the danger that procrastination of necessary reforms of the hitherto system in Germany will eventually render the existing structures in the German model countries unsustainable and induce market forces finally to sweep them away. The 'disorganization thesis' of collective bargaining argues for example that industrial change is expected to cause a shift from non-market governance institutions to the market. There are certainly interest groups that prefer such a change. There are, however, also interest groups that prefer a suitable reform of the present system of collective bargaining and social security i.e. with a streamlined system based on consensus and cooperation when faced with the alternative of a decentralized system of economic organization along the lines of the Anglo-American countries. Such a streamlined consensus based model might lead to more employment, less unemployment and higher efficiency without necessarily sacrificing the degree of social security to similar low standards as in the Anglo-American system. Economists must try to find new means of providing sound social protection while allowing markets to work more efficiently. Furthermore they should search for the political economy preconditions for sensible reforms. Both of these aspects must be discussed (e.g. social security accounts, a targeted negative income tax, new proposals of incomes policy[99]. But the acceptance of the following is vital

---

97 Cf. German Economic Research Institutes 1997, pp. 18 ff.

98 cf. e.g. Delsen / Long 1998, pp. 168 ff.

in my opinion: "reconciliation with neo-liberalism" in order to have less of a dramatic adjustment to make in Germany and save more of the institutionalist agenda as in the Anglo-Saxon economies. Necessary is the implementation of "social neo-liberalism" instead of neo-liberalism without a social-cushion. The implication is that one has to accept (at least partly) the following statement: "Nothing can be done about the markets (ever); we must help our people adapt to their requirements".[100] This means: "pressing the role of social policy in support of adaptations to the markets, seeking amendments to the rougher edges of finance-driven capitalism, maximizing the importance of education".[101]

## VI. Some concluding reform proposals for Germany

To summarize the arguments until now: Western Europe's poor unemployment and employment performance, relative to the USA, cannot be blamed on insufficient demand growth (alone) as real GDP growth was similar. Nor can it be attributed to capital shortage as the expansion of the capital stock was also similar. The evidence seems to show that the rapid increases in real wages together with the rise in capital intensity seem to be the principal reasons for the modest rise in European employment. Rapid real wage growth encouraged capital deepening which raised labour productivity by substituting increases in the capital stock for increases in employment. In the U.S., investment was more capital widening in nature, generating much less an increase in the capital-labour ratio but permitting significant job creation.

An important lesson seems to be as follows: "Whichever social modalities it activates, whether it be straight laissez-faire or centralizing corporatism, a procedure is efficient if it eradicates unemployment at the base and 'forcibly' (through market or institutional forces) reintegrates workers as soon as they lose their jobs. After a latency period, reentry becomes a much more painful process. ... Which side should one choose: laissez-faire , or corporatism? Neither way is easy".[102]

This evaluation is appropriate in my view. Both models are in principle able to master the current and future trends with a considerably lower unemployment rate than in present Western-Europe. But blind deregulation would not be the best option for Western Europe and especially Germany. The supply-side can be made much more flexible also with measured-out deregulation and appropriate reregulation to secure the best of both worlds. Concerning labour market policies and wel-

---

99 cf. Funk 1996.

100 Crouch, Colin: The Terms of the Neo-Liberal Consensus, in: The Political Quarterly, No. 4, 1997, pp. 352 - 360, here: p. 359.

101 Crouch 1997, p. 359.

102 Cohen, Daniel: The Misfortunes of Prosperity. An Introduction to Modern Political Economy, Cambridge, London 1996, p. 54.

fare state reform I agree perfectly with Henri R. Sneessen's[103] following evaluation:

"... defects should be remedied. This, of course, does not mean cutting blindly and dismantling the welfare state, which would be unlikely to lead back to full-employment in the near future. The negative effects of unemployment schemes should not be exaggerated. The right balance has to be found between creating incentives and alleviating unemployment hardships. Full-employment is not a policy objective per se; the objective is welfare maximization, which requires taking into account the tradeoff between economic efficiency and income equality. In such contexts, second best policies may imply wage rigidities and unemployment."

Moreover, one must not forget macroeconomic policy. Especially the sad English experience of European exchange rate mechanism membership in 1990 - 92 where slumping Britain thought it were forced to follow Bundesbank monetary stringency, mainly designed to cool Germany's boom teaches us: A combination of good macroeconomic and good structural policies will be necessary. The latter is absolutely vital because there is an asymmetry which policymakers should always take into account: "Good macroeconomic policy cannot guarantee good economic performance, but bad macroeconomic policy almost invariably produces bad economic performance".[104]

On the assumption that aggregate demand policies under EMU constraints will not be available because the union's rules constrain monetary and fiscal policy, there will be, in order to reap the possible benefits of the European Union[105], a need for Germany (as for the other European countries) to reform. Germany will have to improve the flexibility of the labour market, the social security and the tax system, fiscal federalism responsibilities etc.[106] to counter the possibly adverse effects of the underlying trends (e.g. demographic trends, skill-intensive structural change etc.). All the same it will be important to look at both the supply and the demand side, which results, for example, from the simple labour market model of Krueger / Pischke who summarize as follows [107]:

"A neglected concern is that restrictions on entrepreneurs and product market regulations and institutions may distort labour demand, causing the labour demand

103 Sneessens 1996, p. 208.

104 Llewellyn 1996, p. 90.

105 cf. Filc, Wolfgang: Wenn Maastricht scheitert, droht das Ende des Binnenmarktes, in: Welt am Sonntag, 5. 11. 1995, p. 60, Hesse, Helmut: Neues auf dem Weg zur Europäischen Wirtschafts- und Währungsunion, in: Deutsche Bundesbank (ed.): Auszüge aus Presseartikeln, No. 16, 1998, pp. 11 - 17.

106 German Council Economic Experts 1997, Funk 1996, Jackman, Richard: EU Labor markets inside and outside the monetary union, in: Welfens, Paul J. J. (ed.): European Monetary Union. Transition, International Impact and Policy Options, Berlin et al., 1997, pp. 297 - 300.

107 Krueger / Pischke 1997, p. 26.

curve to shift in and become more inelastic. In this scenario, providing additional wage flexibility would generate more wage dispersion but possibly little additional employment. Just as sharpening one blade of a scissor will not greatly enhance performance if both blades are dull, reducing wages without relaxing constraints on the demand curve may be less effective than is commonly expected".

Similar arguments follow from an "insider-outsider" perspective.[108] Proponents of this model argue that many different types of policy actions are needed to reduce unemployment substantially. The labour market needs, in this perspective, lenient type policies like e.g. employment subsidies and transfer payments to low productivity workers or retraining but also harsh policies to get a well-functioning labour market where wages and labour flows respond to skill differentials and relative shortages of workers without jeopardising moderate wage increases in the aggregate, which reduces, in combination with a monetary policy that sticks to its inflation targets, deflationary dangers. The harsh policies also include an encouraging of limited greater downward flexibility of real wages in response to higher unemployment, and a wider dispersion of wages among people with different skills and less job security legislation to lower labour turnover costs.

Such a mix of policies is partly necessary because their repercussions concern different time perspectives, some are particularly favourable in the long run (e.g. training policies), others have speedier effects (e.g. wage differentiation and wage moderation). In addition to labour market changes, a mix, including product and capital market deregulation and a parallel more expansionary demand management would be extremely helpful (and possible without unjustified dangers) because firms need to be stimulated to increase their demand of labour, especially because there is a great uncertainty about the effects of each policy action. This shows that the risk that the overall policy will fail is dramatically reduced if many proper actions are taken simultaneously.

Germany has three options: Firstly, a non-strategy of learning by suffering if procrastination of or delayed and too weak reforms prevail. If this does not seem to be sensible one can try to learn some lessons from successful individual country experiences, which would lead into different distributive directions but would both be employment creating. The second strategy would be one of a massive wage differentiation like e.g. in the United Kingdom leading to a lower unemployment rate but also to a concentration of adjustment costs to the low-skilled and weak, and is not necessarily efficiency-enhancing in the German kind of capitalism. Therefore, these things have to be changed with great care. A third more egalitarian strategy was followed by the Netherlands and seems to be more compatible with the German political and corporatist system. Necessary will be, in particular, an expansion of the service industry which offers flexible and specialized services at low prices, especially in Germany. "The argument that the percentage of services jobs in Germany – disregarding whether such jobs are in industry or in specialized firms – are

---

108 cf. Lindbeck 1996 (I) and (II), Snower 1995.

similar is not addressing the point. Namely that only explicit outsourcing of services brings specialization gains and allows the opportunity to provide innovative and relatively cheap services as valuable inputs to industry, which therefore, can more easily continue to grow in absolute terms"[109].

Even if one follows the Dutch strategy this would mean quite a radical reform for Germany and such a great change seems to be possible only in a strategic way to secure reelection chances of the implementing political parties. The idea would be to partly include and partly exclude the social partners as their incentives are not conducive to accept the radical reforms necessary to cut unemployment decisively and efficiently by creating profitable jobs in the private sector and to return to a situation much closer to full-employment. I have made the following proposal, only sketched here:[110]

The goal is a dismantling of employment-hampering roadblocks by inducing co-operation on wage restraint by making the alternative worse. The members of the pact (state, social partners, implicitly the Central Bank) would have to attribute to an employment creation aim, e.g. one or two million new profitable jobs after 5 years (depending on political courage). The instrument should be the positive incentive for social partners to be a member of an alliance to fight unemployment. This has to be supplemented, however, by a parallel reduction of state involvement in the market (tax, social security, fiscal federalism reforms etc.) and a credible threat of harsher measures by legislation in the case of failure to reach the employment goal (maybe to be scrutinized by the independent German Council of Economic Experts). The market-oriented measures (e.g. separation of social security from the working contract, right to opt out of an industry wage agreement by law etc.) would have to be legislated as early as at the announcement of the dual-track decision approach. The sanctions could begin automatically in the case of failure. This could enhance the interest of social partners to increase the speed of reforms in the common interest directed by themselves (by a more general wage moderation in sectors where necessary and more wage differentiation where it would be sensible, and by a general opt out of an industry wage agreement, if workforce and employers at the firm level do agree etc.). For a market-oriented political entrepreneur who binds his career on this proposal, this could also be a successful strategy in elections.

---

109 Welfens, Paul J. J. / Jungmittag, André: Political Economy of EMU and Stabilization Policy, in: Welfens, Paul J. J. (ed.): European Monetary Union. Transition, International Impact and Policy Options, Berlin et al., 1997, pp. 331 - 392, here p. 363. Outsourcing is important for an increase of employment if some workers' wages include a share of monopoly rents that are being earned by firms in protected product or service markets. The outsourcing of such work will likely squeeze out these wage rents, most likely in the highly unionized segments of the manufacturing sector that face increased competition.

110 cf. Funk 1996.

## References

*Addison,* John T.: The U.S. Labor Market: Structure and Performance, in: Siebert, Horst (ed.): Structural Change and labor market flexibility: experience in selected OECD economies, Tübingen 1997, pp. 187 - 222. – *Anderson,* Torben M.: Structural Changes and Barriers in the Danish Labour Market, in: Siebert, Horst (ed.): Structural Change and labor market flexibility: experience in selected OECD economies, Tübingen 1997, pp. 124 - 149. – *Bean,* Charles R.: The Role of Demand Management Policies in Reducing Unemployment, in: Federal Reserve Bank of Kansas City (ed.): Reducing Unemployment: Current Issues and Policy Implications, Kansas City 1994, pp. 99 - 132. – *Bertola,* Giuseppe / *Ichino,* Andrea: Crossing the river. A comparative perspective on Italian employment dynamics, in: Economic Policy, No. 2, 1995, pp. 361 - 415. – *Blanchard,* Olivier / *Diamond,* Peter: Ranking unemployment duration and wages, in: Review of Economic Studies, Vol. 61, 1994, pp. 417 - 434. – *Blanchard,* Olivier / *Katz,* Lawrence F.: What we know and do not know about the natural rate of unemployment, in: Journal of Economic Perspectives, No. 1, 1997, pp. 51 - 72. – *Blank,* Rebecca M.: The Misdiagnosis of Eurosclerosis, in: The American Prospect, No. 1, 1997, pp. 81 - 85. – *Borjas,* George J.: Labor Economics, New York et al. 1996. – *Bovenberg,* Lans: Dutch employment growth: an analysis, CPB Report, No. 2, 1997, pp. 16 - 24. – *Broeder,* Corina den: Institutions at work. Commitment and flexibility on the German and Dutch labour markets, Research Memorandum No. 131, Centraal Planbureau, Den Haag 1996. – *Cohen,* Daniel: The Misfortunes of Prosperity. An Introduction to Modern Political Economy, Cambridge, London 1996. – *CPB* (Netherlands Bureau for Economic Policy Analysis): Challenging Neighbours. Rethinking German and Dutch Economic Institutions, Berlin et al. 1997. – *Crouch,* Colin: The Terms of the Neo-Liberal Consensus, in: The Political Quarterly, No. 4, 1997 pp. 352 - 360. – *Delsen,* Lei / *Jong,* Eelke de (eds.): The German and Dutch Economies. Who follows whom?, Heidelberg 1998. – *DIW* (German Institute for Economic Research): Unemployment Trends in Selected Industrialised Countries – A different opinion, Economic Bulletin, No. 11, 1997, pp. 23 - 32. – *Drèze,* Jacques H.: Employment in Europe, in: Gual, Jordi: The Social Challenge of Job Creation. Combatting Unemployment in Europe, Cheltenham, Brookfield 1996, pp. 29 - 54. – *Filc,* Wolfgang: Wenn Maastricht scheitert, droht das Ende des Binnenmarktes, in: Welt am Sonntag, 5. November 1995, p. 60. – *Filc,* Wolfgang: Geldpolitik im Rahmen eines beschäftigungsorientierten Gesamtkonzepts, in: Reader zum Fachkongreß "Innovation, Beschäftigung, Wachstum und Wettbewerb", Berlin 28. / 29. 4. 1997, pp. 243 - 246. – *Filer,* Randall K. / *Hamermesh,* Daniel S. / *Rees,* Albert E.: The Economics of Work and Pay, 6th ed., New York et al. 1996. – *Fischer,* Stanley: Commentary: The Role of Demand Management Policies in Reducing Unemployment, in: Federal Reserve Bank of Kansas City (ed.): Reducing Unemployment: Current Issues and Policy Implications, Kansas City 1994, pp. 133 - 137. – *Fitoussi,* Jean-Paul / *Zoega,* Gylfi: Wage Distribution and Unemployment, in: Baldassari, Mario / Paganetto, Luigi / Phelps, Edmund S. (eds.): The 1990s Slump. Causes and Cures, London et al. 1996, pp. 97 - 132. – *Freeman,* Richard B.: Labor Market Institutions and Earnings Inequality, New England Economic Review, No. 3, 1996, pp. 157 - 172. – *Funk,* Lothar: Institutionell verhärtete und politisch rationale Arbeitslosigkeit in der Bundesrepublik Deutschland, doctoral dissertation at the University of Trier 1996, Münster: Lit, forthcoming 1998. – *Funk,* Lothar / *Knappe* Eckhard: Der Beitrag des Neukeynesianismus zur Erklärung der Arbeitslosigkeit in Europa, in: Hamburger Jahrbuch für Wirtschafts- und Gesellschaftspolitik, Vol. 41, 1996, pp. 43 - 57. – *Funk,* Lothar / *Knappe,* Eckhard: Neue Wege aus der Arbeitslosigkeit, in: Montada, Leo (ed.), Beschäftigungspolitik zwischen Effizienz und Gerechtigkeit, Frankfurt a.M. / New York 1997, pp. 80 - 97. – *Funk,* Lothar / *Winkler,* Albrecht: Konsensmodell Niederlande: Ein sozial- und beschäftigungspolitisches Vorbild für die Bundesrepublik Deutschland?, in: Knappe, Eckhard / Winkler, Albrecht (eds.): Sozialstaat im Umbruch. Herausforderungen an die deutsche Sozialpolitik, Frankfurt a.M. / New York 1997, pp. 151 - 186. – *German Council of Economic Experts:* Growth, Employment, Monetary Union – Guidelines for the Future, Annual Report 1997 / 98, First Chapter, Wiesbaden 1997. – *German Economic Research Institutes:* Unemployment Trends in Selected Industrialised Countries, Economic Bulletin, No. 11, 1997, pp. 13 - 23 (This part of the evaluation of the economic situation is not supported by the DIW.). – *Gern,* Klaus-Jürgen. / *Schatz,* Klaus-Werner / *Scheide,* Joachim / *Schlie,* Markus / *Solveen,* Ralph: Kräftiger Aufschwung in den Industrieländern, in: Die Weltwirtschaft, No. 3, 1997, pp. 229 - 263. – *Giersch,* Herbert: Openness for Prosperity. Essays in World Economics, Cambridge, London 1993, p. 132. – *Glyn,* Andrew: Internal and External Constraints on Egalitarian Policies in Europe, Politik und Gesellschaft / International Politics and Society, No. 2, 1997, pp. 172 - 183. – *Gregg,* Paul / *Manning,* Alan: Labour market regulation and unemployment, in: Snower, Dennis J. / Dehesa, Guillermo de la (eds.), Unemployment policy: government options for the labour market, Cambridge 1997, pp. 395 - 424. – *Heise,* Arne: Deregulation and employment in Britain and Germany, Anglo-German Foundation for the Study of Industrial Society, London 1997. – *Hemerijk,* Anton / *Kersbergen,* Kees van: A Miraculous Model? Explaining the New Politics of the Welfare State in the Netherlands, in: Acta Politica, No. 2, 1997, pp. 258 - 280. – *Hesse,* Helmut: Neues auf dem Weg zur Europäischen Wirtschafts- und Währungsunion, in: Deutsche Bundesbank (ed.): Auszüge aus Presseartikeln, No. 16, 1998, pp. 11 - 17. – *Horn,* Gustav A.: Beschäftigungswachstum in den USA – ein erklärbares Wunder, in: DIW-Wochenbericht, No. 9, 1998, pp. 173 - 180. – *IMF* (International Monetary Fund): Germany – Selected Issues, IMF Staff Country Report No. 97 / 01, Washington 1997. – *Ito,* Takatoshi: Commentary: The Role of Demand Management in Reducing Unemployment, in: The Federal Reserve Bank of Kansas City (ed.): Reducing Unemployment: Current Issues and Policy Options, Jackson Hole 1994, pp. 139 - 154. – *Jackman,* Richard: EU Labor markets inside and outside the monetary union, in: Welfens, Paul J. J. (ed.): European Monetary Union. Transition, International Impact and Policy Options, Berlin et al. 1997, pp. 297 - 323. – *Kasper,* Wolfgang: Right to work: Job creation New Zealand style, in: Intereconomics, Vol. 32, No. 6, 1997, pp. 293- 300. – *Knappe,* Eckhard: The Aims and Effects of Technology, in: Dobers, H,, Nieuwenhuijze, V. (eds.) The Technological Era – Continuity and Change in the Arab and European Societies, St. Augustin 1985, pp. 112 - 124. – *Knappe.* Eckhard: Einige Irrtümer in der Arbeitsmarktdebatte, in: Knappe, Eckhard / Berthold, Norbert (eds.): Ökonomische Theorie der Sozialpolitik. Bernhard Külp zum 65. Geburtstag, Heidelberg 1998, pp. 168 - 193. – *Knappe,* Eckhard / *Funk,* Lothar: 'Irritationen über den Zusammenhang zwischen Arbeitsproduktivität und Beschäftigung', in: List Forum für Wirtschafts- und Finanzpolitik, No. 1, 1997, pp. 65 - 81. – *Kösters,* Wim / *Belke,* Ansgar: Slow Adjustment to Shocks or True Hysteresis? Lessons from the Different Labour Market Performances in Western Europe and the USA, in: Intereconomics, No. 3, 1996, pp. 107 - 121. – *Kramer,* Charles F. / *Li,* Yutong: Job Uncertainty, Unemployment, and Inflation in the United States, in: Finance and Development, No. 4, 1997, pp. 30 - 32. – *Krueger,* Alan B. / *Pischke,* Jörn-Steffen: Observations and Conjectures on the U.S. Employment Miracle, NBER Working Paper 6146, 1997, Cambridge, MA. – *Lapp,* Susanne / *Lehment,* Harmen: Lohnzurückhaltung und Beschäftigung in Deutschland und in den Vereinigten Staaten, Die Weltwirtschaft, No. 1, 1997, pp. 67 - 83. – *Larsen,* Flemming: Comments, in: OECD (ed.): Macroeconomic Policies and Structural Reform, Washington, D.C. 1996, pp. 229 - 235. – *Lindbeck,* Assar: Microfoundations of Unemployment Theory, in: Labour, No. 3, 1991, pp. 3 - 23. – *Lindbeck,* Assar, The Unemployment Problem, Working Paper, Stockholm 1995, mimeo. – *Lindbeck,* Assar: The West European Employment Problem, in: Weltwirtschaftliches Archiv, No. 4, pp. 609 - 637, 1996 (I). – *Lindbeck,* Assar: Full Employment and the Welfare State, The Industrial Institute for Economic and and Social Research, Working Paper No. 469, Memphis 1996 (II). – *Lindbeck,* Assar: The Swedish Experiment, Journal of Economic Literature, No. 4, 1997, pp. 1273 - 1319. – *Lindbeck,* Assar: New Keynesianism and aggregate economic activity, in: The Economic Journal, No. 1, 1998, pp. 167 - 180. – *Lindbeck,* Assar / *Snower,* Dennis J.: How are product demand changes transmitted to the labour market?, in: The Economic Journal, Vol. 104, 1994, pp. 386 - 398. – *Llewellyn,* John: Tackling Europe's competitiveness, in: Oxford Review of Economic Policy, No. 3, 1996, pp. 87 - 96. – *Mankiw,* N. Gregory: Principles of Macroeconomics, Orlando 1998. – *Matthes,* Heinrich / *Todd,* Douglas: 'Unemployment in Europe', in: Sautter, Hartmut (ed.), Wirtschaftspolitik in offenen Volkswirtschaften, Göttingen 1994, pp. 177 - 204. – *Mayer,* Thomas / *Grillet-Aubert,* Laurent: The New Dutch Model – A Blueprint for Continental Europe?, Goldman Sachs, Frankfurt 1997. – *Minford,* Patrick: Deregulation and Unemployment – The UK Experience, in: Swedish Economic Policy Review, No. 1, 1994, pp. 113 - 141 . – *Nickell,* Stephen: The Low-Skill Low-pay Problem: Lessons from Germany for Britain and the US, Policy Studies, Vol. 17, 1996, pp. 7 - 21. – *Nickell,* Stephen: Structural Changes and the British Labour Market, in: Siebert, Horst (ed.): Structural Change and Labor Market Flexibility. Experience in Selected OECD Economies, Tübingen 1997, S. 3 - 28. – *Owen* Smith, Eric / *Funk,* Lothar: A Comparison of German and British Macroeconomic Performance, Institute for German Studies Discussion Paper, University of Birmingham, forthcoming 1998. – *Paqué,* Karl-Heinz: From Miracle to Crisis? The German Economy at the End of the Twentieth Century, Institute for German Studies Discussion Paper, University of Birmingham 1996. – *Paqué,* Karl-Heinz (1998): Structural Unemployment in Europe – a Bird's Eye View, in: Addison, John T. / Welfens, Paul J. J. (eds.): Labor Markets and Social Security. Wage Costs, Social Security Financing and Labor Market Reforms in Europe, Berlin et al. 1998, pp. 17 - 43. – *Parkin,* Michael / *Powell,* Melanie / *Matthews,* Kent: Economics, 3rd. ed., New York et al. 1997. – *Pauer,* Wolfgang: Budgetkonsolidierung, privater Konsum und Beschäftigung in Europa, in: Wirtschaftspolitische Blätter, No. 1, 1998, pp. 74 - 84. – *Ramaswamy,* Ramana / *Rowthorn,* Robert: Deindustrialisation: Causes and Implications, IMF Working Paper, WP / 97 / 42, 1997, Washington D.C. . – *Rodrik,* Dani: Has Globalization gone too far?, California Management Review, No. 3, 1997, pp. 29 - 53. – *Saint-Paul,* Gilles: High unemployment from a political economy perspective, in: Snower, Dennis J. / Dehesa, Guillermo de la (eds.): Unemployment policy: government options for the labour market, Cambridge 1997, pp. 54 - 73. – *Schnabel,* Claus: Arbeitsmarktinstitutionen im Wandel: Perspektiven der kollektiven Lösung arbeitsmarktpolitischer Probleme, in: List Forum für Wirtschafts- und Finanzpolitik, Vol. 23, 1997, pp. 107 - 128. – *Siebert,* Horst: Labor Market Rigidities: At the Root of Unemployment in Europe, in: Journal of Economic Perspectives, No. 3, 1997, pp. 37 - 54. – *Siebert,* W. Stanley: Overview of European Labour Markets, in: Addison, John T. / Siebert, W. Stanley (eds.), Labour Markets in Europe. Issues of Harmonization and Regulation, London 1997, pp. 229 - 241. – *Simonazzi,* Annamaria / *Villa,* Paola: Employment, growth and income inequality: some open questions, Discussion Paper, University of Rome 1996, mimeo. – *Sneessens,* Henri R.: Lessons for Employment and growth in Western Europe, in, Giersch, Herbert (ed.): Fighting Europe's unemployment in the 1990's, Berlin et al. 1996, pp. 183 - 211. – *Snower,* Dennis J.: Evaluating unemployment policies: what do the underlying theories tell us?, in: Oxford Review of Economic Policy, No. 1, 1995, pp. 110 - 135. – *Soltwedel,* Rüdiger: Competition, responsibility and solidarity –

the social market economy ensuring success in the global economy, Gütersloh 1997 (I). – *Soltwedel,* Rüdiger: Social Engineering in Europe: A German Perspective, in: Addison, John T. / Siebert, W. Stanley (eds.), Labour Markets in Europe. Issues of Harmonization and Regulation, London, 1997 (II), pp. 177 - 190 . – *Soskice,* David / *Hancké,* Bob / *Trumbull,* Gunnar / *Wren,* Anne: Wage bargaining, Labour Markets and Macroeconomic Performance in Germany and the Netherlands, in: Delsen, Lei / Jong, Eelke de (eds.), The German and Dutch Economies. Who follows whom?, Heidelberg 1998, pp. 39 - 51. – *Spahn,* Heinz-Peter: Makroökonomie. Theoretische Grundlagen und stabilitätspolitische Strategien, Berlin et al. 1996. – *Wallis,* Joe: Conspiracy and The Political Process: A Case Study of the New Zealand Experiment, in: Journal of Public Policy, No. 1, 1997, pp. 1 - 29. – *Walwei,* Ulrich: Flexibility of Employment Relationships: Possibilities and Limits, IAB-topics, Institute for Employment Research, No 22, Nürnberg 1997. – *Welfens,* Paul J. J. / *Audretsch,* David / *Addison,* John T. / *Grupp,* Hariolf: Technological Competition, Employment and Innovation Policies in OECD Countries, Berlin et al. 1998 . – *Welfens,* Paul J. J., Jungmittag, André: Political Economy of EMU and Stabilization Policy, in: Welfens, Paul J. J. (ed.): European Monetary Union. Transition, International Impact and Policy Options, Berlin et al. 1997, pp. 331 - 392. – *Wolf,* Martin: Europe's real insiders, in: Financial Times, November 18, 1997, p. 16.

# Micro and Macro Determinants of Unemployment

## A Comparison of Trends in the United States and Germany

By Michael Heise and Mathias Moersch, Frankfurt a. M.

### I. Introduction

Rising unemployment has for years been the dominant and most pressing economic policy problem in most of the industrialised countries. The relentless intensification and globalisation of competition in labour and technology-intensive sectors has presented the employment policy of the established industrial economies with enormous challenges (Berthold / Heise, 1998).

That is especially true for Germany and most of the member states of the European Union. Their jobless rate has been trending upwards for a quarter of a century now, and presently more than 18 million people are officially without work in Europe. For many employees, especially the low-skilled, the chance of finding another job in the event of losing the one they hold is extremely low. This means that the proportion of long-term unemployed is constantly rising, and now accounts for almost half the jobless total.

The public debate frequently seeks to qualify these figures. It is objected that a significant number of the jobless only register as unemployed in order to enjoy access to generous state transfer payments. On the other hand though, the official statistics need to be augmented by the large number of people who are not registered as employed, but who are effectively underemployed because they either work part-time, are undergoing job training or retraining programs, have taken early retirement, or are in a state-subsidised job. In Germany, according to estimates by the government's national expert panel of economic advisers, there are around 1.9 million people in this category. It is therefore simply not possible to argue away the threatening scale of the unemployment problem.

In terms of employment growth, the United States of America currently provide the most positive example. Over the decades, the U.S. economy has succeeded in creating the highest number of new jobs; today the labour force is 65 percent larger than in 1970. Total employment in West Germany has increased by just five percent over the same period. In the age of benchmarking, it seems desirable to analyse the causes of this employment dynamism in the U.S. and to see what lessons can be drawn for Germany's labour market.

Section 2 of the paper demonstrates that the American jobs miracle cannot be attributed to the higher long-term rates of economic growth relative to Germany. However, America's growth has been significantly more jobs-intensive and the question is why. Section 2 also seeks to show that the U.S. experience casts doubts on the at times popular theory that unemployment in Germany is the result of demographical changes. Virtually no other industrial country has seen its labour supply expand on the same scale as the U.S., and yet there has been no increase in unemployment.

Section 3 goes on to describe structural differences between the German and U.S. labour markets which are important in explaining the jobs-intensive growth and the absence of demographic unemployment in the United States. These structural components are largely microeconomic factors; section 4 therefore examines macroeconomic – or macropolicy – attempts to explain the different evolutionary trends of the respective labour markets. Specifically, the influence of wage policy and monetary policy is discussed. Section 5 concludes.

## II. High unemployment in Europe is not due to slower growth or demographic changes

Germany and most other European countries have for years been faced with a situation where the unemployment numbers fail to fall even when the economy is growing satisfactorily, and where unemployment instead increases from one economic cycle to the next. (Figure 1).

The same phenomenon cannot be observed in the United States. Although the economy has not grown significantly faster in the U.S. than in Germany over the the last three decades (Figure 2), a vastly greater number of jobs has been created.[1] There are now 50 million more jobs in the United States than in 1970, implying an increase of around 65 percent. By comparison, the number of persons gainfully employed in the West German economy at present is just 1 million or 5 percent higher than in 1970 (Figure 3).

It is generally assumed that the employment success of the American economy can be attributed to an increase in jobs in the service sector. Indeed, employment in the service sector has doubled since 1970, while only increasing by 50 percent in West Germany (Figure 4). There is an additional factor however, namely that the United States has also been able to approximately hold constant over the dec-

1 Without the inclusion of East Germany beginning in 1990, there is a slightly bigger growth differential in favour of the United States. However, this difference pales in comparison to the relative employment performance.

**Figure 1: Unemployment Rate**

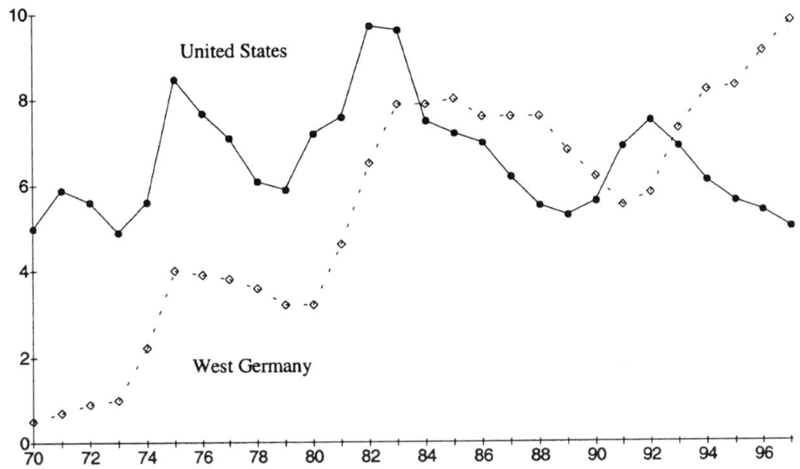


**Figure 2: Real GDP Growth**

1970 = 100

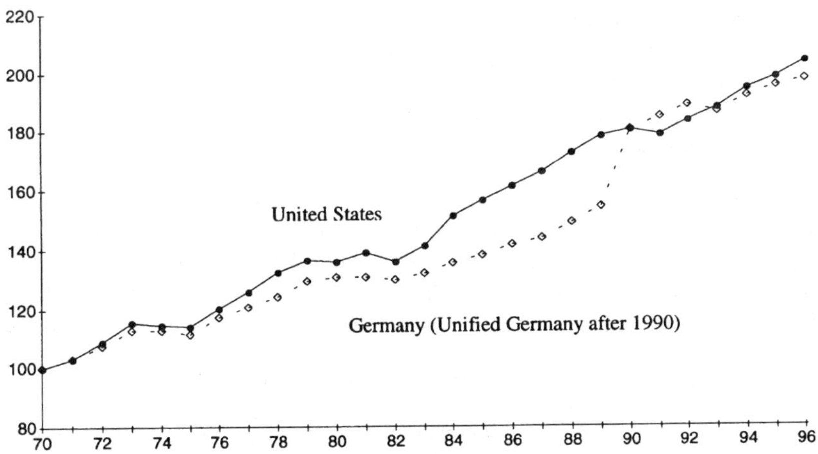

**Figure 3: Total Employment**

1970 = 100

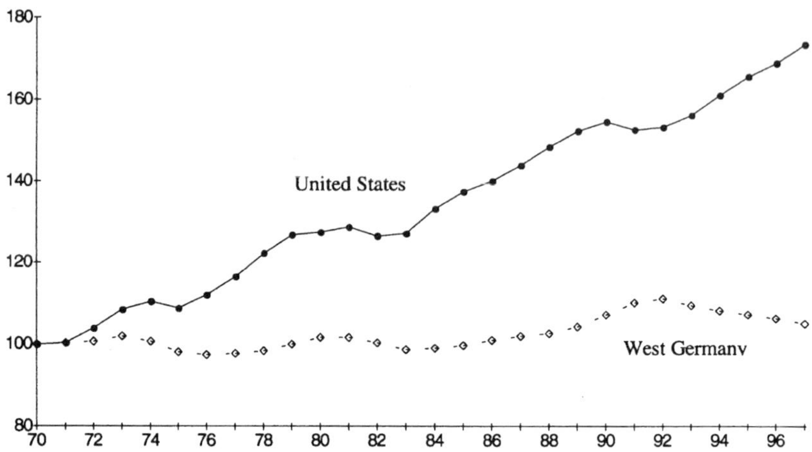


ades employment in the manufacturing sector. In West Germany in contrast, employment in the manufacturing sector has fallen by 25 percent since 1970, from 13 million to 9.8 million jobs (Figure 5). If Germany had succeeded in maintaining the number of jobs in the manufacturing sector while increasing employment in the service sector, 3 million more jobs would be available today.[2] Germany's employment problem cannot therefore be explained purely by reference to inadequate tertiarisation of the economy, in other words too small an expansion of service sector employment. Rather, a crisis of employment in industry was a substantial contributing factor in this development.

There is inevitably a downside to the fact that employment in the American economy has increased significantly faster than in Germany while achieving similar growth rates in output; namely a slower rise in labour productivity in the U.S. relative to Germany. Macroeconomic labour productivity is nothing more than the arithmetic relationship between gross domestic product and the total number em-

2 For statistical reasons, any comparison of the relative shares of employment accounted for by the manufacturing and service sectors is fraught with problems. DIW (1997) for instance points out that German industry provides a much higher proportion of the services they require in-house than their American counter-parts (e.g., engineering, planning, marketing and distribution services etc.). If the relative proportions of the service and manufacturing sectors are surveyed with reference to the actual work done by employees, the DIW's findings show that the proportion of total employment accounted for by services is approximately as high as in the United States. Still, it seems clear with regard to economic policy that Germany's jobless problem can only be eliminated if the negative trend in manufacturing employment is successfully turned around and employment in the sector is stabilized.

**Figure 4: Employment in Manufacturing**

1970 = 100

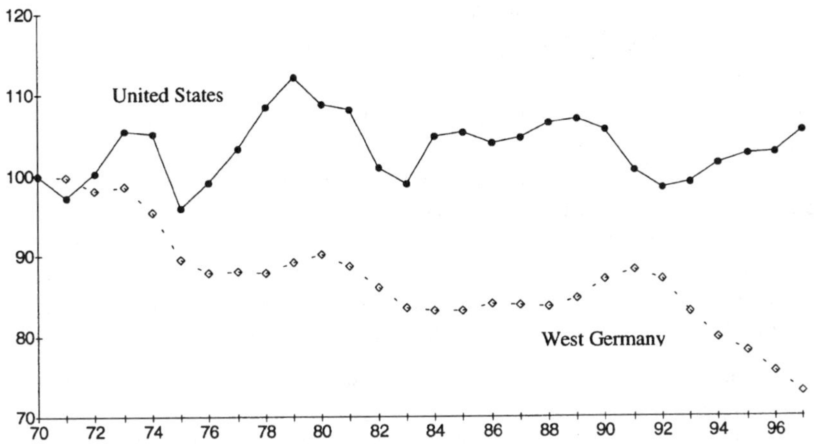


**Figure 5: Employment in Services**

1970 = 100

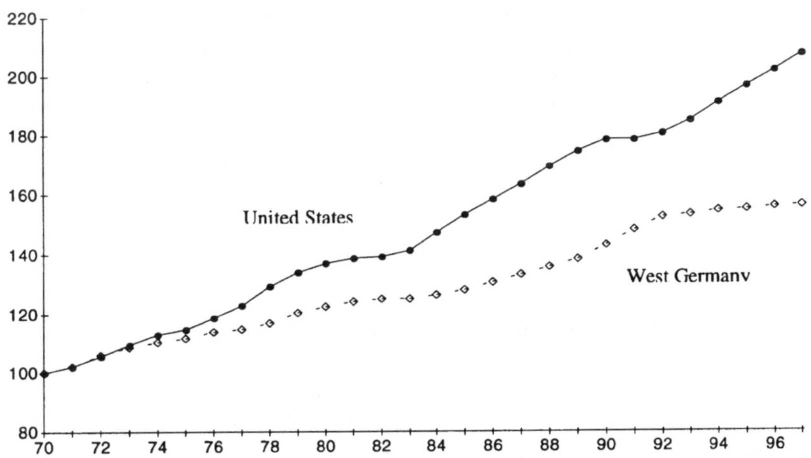

ployed (although calculations may also occasionally be based on total hours worked). The smaller rise in labour productivity in the United States is reflected in a slower increase in labour income. Behind these developments lies the slow growth of the capital stock in the U.S. and a weaker trend to capital intensification relative to Germany. We will return to this subject and to the role of wage policy in section 4.

The fact that the jobless rate in the U.S. does not exhibit an upward trend over the decades (unlike in Germany and most other European countries) is even more impressive considering that the U.S. labour supply has expanded on a scale which virtually no other industrialised country can match. Since 1970, i.e. in a little more than a quarter century, the labour supply has increased by 50 million people (Civilian Labor Force, aged 16 and older). The labour force participation rate, defined as total employment divided by the working age population, is with 80 percent also higher in the U.S. than in Germany with 70 percent (OECD, 1997a).

Thus the labour market in the U.S. has absorbed a rise in the supply of labour with much less friction than in Germany or the rest of Europe. This calls into question the hypothesis of "demographically induced unemployment" which has a strong following in Germany, especially during periods of high immigration. In the end, pointing to an increase in the labour supply without reference to exceptional structural characteristics relating to skill levels, age or other features, can only provide a superficial explanation of unemployment. In functioning labour markets (in conjunction with the goods markets), an increase in supply will be converted into extra employment. Certainly there can be integration problems which result in a temporary increase in unemployment. This was the case in Germany at the start of the nineties when a sudden wave of immigrants from eastern Europe and elsewhere, for a variety of reasons related to language and skills, could not be absorbed into the labour market in the short term. In the long term however, an increase in supply to the labour market cannot be cited as the causal factor for a rise in unemployment; rather it is necessary to explain why the market has failed.

## III. Structural differences

### *1. Wage differentiation and mobility of the labour force*

An important reason for the more labour-intensive growth process in the United States is the greater degree of wage differentiation in that country. A comparison of compensation growth in the two countries does show greater differentiation in the U.S.; Germany shows more of a leveling out. Whereas in Germany wages in the lower income groups have increased considerably, especially in the period since 1984, in the U.S. they have fallen in real terms (Figure 6). Those at the top of the income distribution have enjoyed lower levels of increases in Germany than low-wage groups, while exactly the opposite was the case in the U.S. Empirical

**Figure 6: Relative Real Wage Growth**

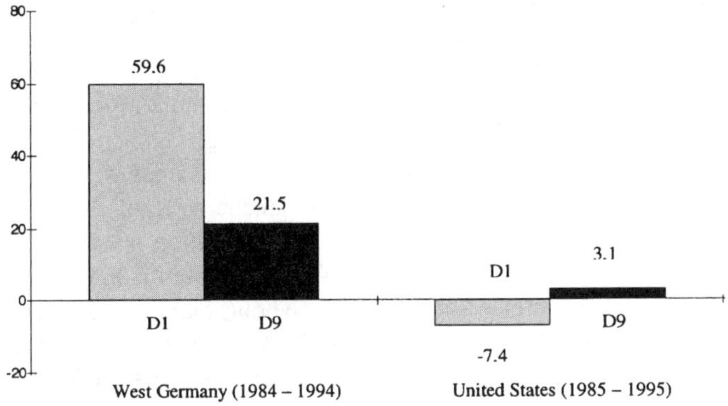


Note: D1 = 10-percentile of the income distribution.
D2 = 90-percentile of the income distribution.
Source: OECD, 1997a, p.7.

studies have attributed the poor growth of wages in the lower income groups in the United States primarily to the low density of unionisation and to the lowering of the minimum wage in real terms. (Gottschalk / Smeeding, 1997).

The problem with wage equalization in Germany is that it is accompanied by an increase in unemployment among the less qualified. According to Ifo (1995), of the 4.8 million people registered unemployed in Germany, around 50 percent had no vocational training. Their chances of finding another job are extremely low. Germany is attempting to address the problem of underemployment in this market segment through supporting actions such as state training and employment programmes. The bridging function of these programmes, which are intended to smooth the path back to regular work, has yet to be proven in practice, however. What can be said is that long-term unemployment is continuing to rise at undiminished speed.

It is therefore no wonder that discussions about labour market policies run along diametrically opposed lines in the United States and Germany. While Germany debates whether the increasing unemployment of the low-skilled is not too high a price to pay for the desired equality of incomes, criticism in the U.S. is focused on the degree of income inequality and the increase in low-paid jobs (Council of Economic Advisers, 1997). Which policy-mix a country adopts is ultimately a matter of political and social choice. However, the basis for decision-making should be clearly identified. A high degree of income equality through raising the income levels of low-paid groups can only be achieved at the price of reduced regular employment in these segments and thus higher state transfer payments.

A second aspect plays an important role in this regard. The higher the degree of regional, sectoral or vocational mobility in the labour force of an economy, the lower is the need for wage differentiation between individual segments of the market. In a highly mobile environment, imbalances in labour sub-markets are corrected through migration of the labour force. High rates of wages in certain regions or for certain skills attract labour while low wages promote an exodus of labour. This mobility tends over time to equalise wages through the action of the market mechanism. In Germany however, mobility of this kind is underdeveloped in terms of both regional migration and job-switching (Blanchard / Katz, 1992, Decressin / Fatas, 1994). It follows that the need for wage differentiation is greater. The higher mobility of labour in the United States relative to Germany is evidenced not only by migration statistics but also by numerous labour market indicators, e.g. the shorter average duration of unemployment spells, the lower average length of employment with a single employer or the higher percentage of lay-offs.

### *2. Collective wage bargaining systems – less organisation and centralisation, less corporatism in the U.S.*

Systems of wage setting and collective bargaining differ considerably across countries. The German system is characterised by a high level of union influence, widespread coverage by collective agreements, a medium to high degree of centralisation, and strong consensus elements (Berthold / Fehn, 1996).

In a direct comparison with the Unites States, these characteristics become particularly clear. The degree of union organisation and the wide applicability of collective agreements ("bargaining coverage") are both significantly higher in Germany than the U.S. It is well known that wage bargaining in the U.S. is decentralised and that coordination between unions is low. This is confirmed by the findings of the OECD (1997a, p. 71).

In the European context, the specific characteristics of the German system are less distinct. Together with Austria, Germany is outstanding for its degree of coordination. What is meant by this is the systematic consensus approach pursued by both unions and employers. The settlements reached in the first wage round in Germany (pilot agreements) have a huge influence on subsequent settlements. Germany does not rank particularly high among European countries on unionisation density and bargaining coverage; however, the labour market throughout Europe is much more strongly regulated than in the U.S.

What do these differences tell us about the evolution of employment and labour markets? A hypothesis put forward by Calmfors / Driffill (1988) states that both decentralised, competition-intensive systems and highly centralised systems can produce favourable employment outcomes; what is disadvantageous are hybrid systems such as Germany's. Briefly, the argument runs as follows: in decentralised wage setting systems the bargaining partners at the plant level are subject to the risk that if they agree to excessive wage increases, they put jobs in jeopardy. If a non-monopolistic enterprise attempts to roll over wage increases which exceed advances in productivity, it will suffer severe penalties in lost sales (assuming its competitors' wage rates are unchanged). This competition effect is reduced where the degree of centralisation is higher (as in the case of Germany's industry-wide agreements). Generous wage settlements affect one's domestic competitors as much as oneself so that the terms of competition remain the same. It follows that the incentive to agree to higher wage settlements is greater than in decentralised bargaining systems.

On the other hand, centralised wage setting systems take more of the external effects of one's own wage settlement on other sectors or the economy as a whole into account. While it has virtually no relevance to decision makers in sector-level wage bargaining systems if other industries follow one's agreement even at the cost of lost jobs or if generous wage settlements reduce purchasing power by raising prices across the board, centralised systems need to pay greater attention to the general interest. In completely centralised wage negotiations winners and losers coincide. For this reason such systems have to pay particular attention to the potentially negative employment effects of excessive wage settlements.

The empirical evidence for these hypotheses is not conclusive, however. According to OECD (1997a), it cannot be shown that highly centralised or even highly decentralised systems will produce better employment outcomes than the hybrid forms. One reason for this is presumably that centralised systems have a greater ability to roll over adjustment burdens at the workplace onto the state and thus to escape discipline. There are, however, clear indications that highly organised, centralised and coordinated systems of wage setting decrease the extent of wage dispersion. As was discussed earlier, this can generate employment problems in individual segments of the labour market.

Such insights have in recent years led to the belief that the relatively low degree of wage differentiation in Germany – at least in a global comparison – constitutes an employment policy problem. The consequence has first been a trend towards a decentralisation of the collective bargaining system, which has first manifested itself through increasing numbers of companies withdrawing from their industry associations. This move, however, will only increase their flexibility in the long term, since association agreements for contractual reasons will continue to be binding for them for some years. Second, the increasing number of exemptions included in collective agreements permits more flexible wage setting arrangements, plus what are known as plant-level "location safeguarding agreements." With such agreements, the workforce accepts additional working hours, which are often unpaid, in order to secure jobs.

The reform of Germany's national wage bargaining system is therefore clearly moving in the direction of decentralisation. Globalisation has made the advantages of centralised collective bargaining less significant (Danthine / Hunt, 1994). The equalisation of national competition which a wage agreement can produce becomes less significant for the participants as foreign competition increases. Another feature of industry-level bargaining, which is to keep redistribution conflicts away from the plants and move them to the collective level, has also lost significance over the years. A survey of German small and medium sized enterprises by DG BANK in 1996 showed that companies no longer see this argument as very important. The reason is presumably that the representatives of labour feel more willing to seek agreement at the plant level than before, since many employees perceive widespread underemployment and job insecurity as threats.

If the German industry-level collective bargaining system fails to provide scope for enhancing differentiation in the near future, it will probably be seen as increasingly failing to respond to the interests of workers or the competitive needs of companies. The effective consequence of this would be a further undermining of the system through the actions of the participants in it.

### *3. Business dynamism and venture capital markets*

A crucial factor in the employment succes of the United States seems to be the greater business dynamism, i.e. the higher rates of company start-ups and closures. OECD (1997b) has confirmed that the business start-up and closure process operates at a vastly higher speed in the U.S. than in Germany. One indication of this phenomenon is that the average life of businesses is shorter in the U.S. The OECD cites studies which show that only 50 percent of new U.S. companies are still in existence five years after their formation, compared to 63 percent in Germany. The OECD also puts numbers on the employment gains resulting from start-up activities. Whereas in the U.S. between 1984 and 1991 around 7 percent of all jobs were created by new start-ups and only 4 percent by the expansion of existing enterprises, in Germany by contrast job creation was primarily attributable to business expansion (6.5 percent) while new start-ups only contributed 2.5 percent of the total. On the other hand, more jobs were lost in Germany through the selective cutting of the existing workforce than through business closings.

There are numerous reasons for the greater dynamism of business in the United States. First, there is a more favourable framework for company formation, including fewer regulations and a lighter tax burden. Second, there is also a different enterprise culture, characterised by the importance attached in the U.S. to standing on one's own feet; business success is rewarded with social prestige and business failure does not by itself imply a personal failing; it is seen as an inevitable part of the market process.

A third reason for this corporate dynamism is probably the fact that fast-growing companies in America can finance themselves through highly developed capital markets. For many years, the equity market has been the fastest-expanding market for corporate financing. Despite the sharply rising trend in Germany, venture capital still plays a much greater role in the U.S. Venture capital is also supported by an institutional structure in the U.S., which helps to absorb the funds. Namely pension funds, which manage considerable pools of money are in search of diversified investment opportunities. Also, venture capital has been boosted by the formation of new capital markets – specifically NASDAQ. These capital markets provide an outlet for selling the matured equity stakes. In other words, it is easy for venture capitalists to realise the capital gains on successful investments.

## IV. Macroeconomic analysis of unemployment

### *1. Wage development and labour intensity of the growth process*

From a macroeconomic perspective, one immediately striking difference in the evolution of the German and U.S. labour markets is the development of labour productivity and capital intensity. Since the growth of the U.S. economy has been significantly more employment-intensive, average labour productivity has risen more slowly than in Germany over the last two and a half decades. Figure 7 shows that the German economy has recorded impressive labour-productivity gains (measured as real GDP relative to total employment) because the capital component per worker has increased sharply over time, significantly faster than in the U.S.

**Figure 7: Labour Productivity**

1970 = 100

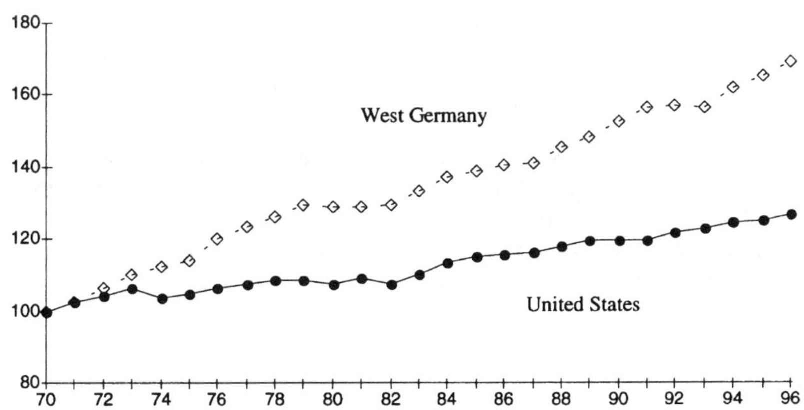

A much higher gain in real wages is compatible with this. And indeed, whereas real wages (measured as the average per-capita earnings, adjusted for inflation by the cost of living index) have risen by around 25 percent in the U.S. since 1970, in Germany they have increased by 60 percent in the last two decades (Figure 8).

**Figure 8: Real Wage Growth**

1970 = 100

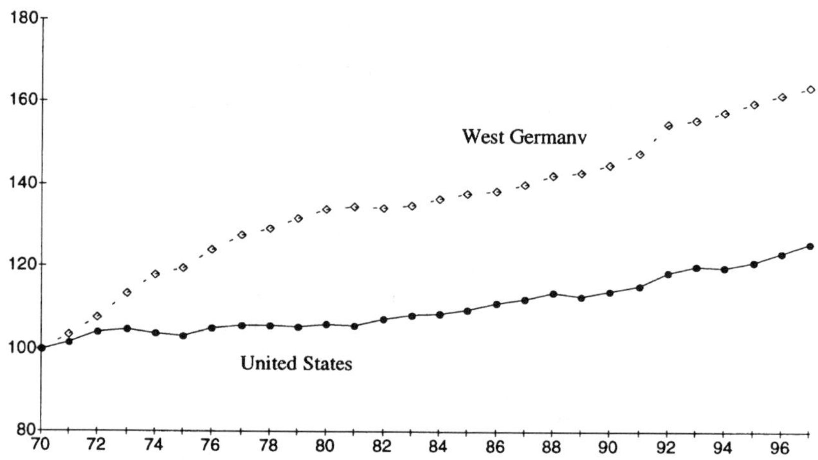


However, high real wage increases as a consequence of high labour-productivity will lead to additional pressure on firms to substitute capital for labour. Whether companies structure their production more capital-intensively or more labour-intensively and thereby achieve greater or smaller increases in labour productivity depends crucially on relative factor prices. If wage increases are high, as they have been in Germany, there is a strong incentive to economise on labour and produce capital-intensively (Siebert / Heise, 1995) (Figure 9).

These relationships make it clear that a moderate pay policy is a central element of a strategy for fighting unemployment. Although there is no question that low wage settlements cannot possibly generate full employment on their own, it is equally certain that without them there will not be any significant progress in fighting unemployment.

**Figure 9: Capital-Labour Ratio**

1970 = 100

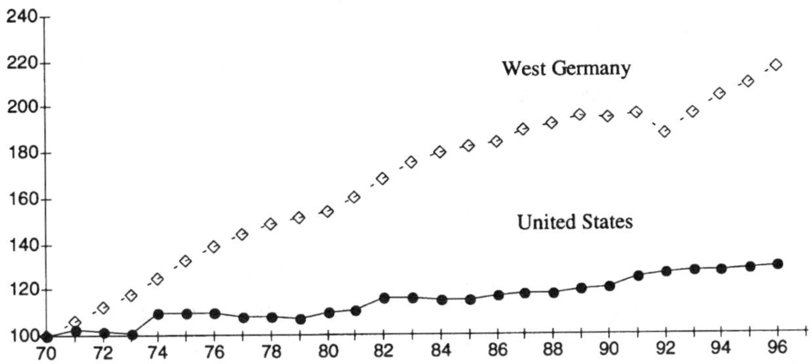


*2. Employment effects of monetary policy*

In the preceeding sections it was argued that the flexibility of labour-markets is an important determinant of the dissimilar relative employment performance in Germany and the United States. This section argues that these microeconomic differences should also be taken into account when comparing monetary policies and their employment effects in the two countries.

a) The natural rate

According to Taylor (1997, p. 233), the absence of a long-term trade-off between inflation and unemployment is one of the five key principles that define "a core of practical macroeconomics" that is widely shared by the profession. It follows from this position that monetary policy should primarily concern itself with maintaining price stability. Price stability in turn is a prerequisite for growth in real output and employment.

This does not mean, however, that employment effects of monetary policy are ruled out in this framework. Market imperfections, incomplete information or uncertainty about the transmission mechanism of monetary policy can produce employment effects in the short run.

A crucial component in this framework is the existence of a natural rate of capacity utilization. Targeting this rate will lead to the optimal level of output growth, while still maintaining price stability. An overly expansionary monetary policy, on the other hand, will move the economy past this natural rate and merely result in higher inflation. While theoretical models are mostly concerned with the NAIRU, the non-accelerating inflation rate of unemployment, the idea is not restricted to the labour force but applies equally to the capital stock. Overstepping the available capacity constraints creates inflation via the prices for these production factors. Wages and other input prices are bid up, as firms compete for increasingly scarce resources and these price increases are channeled to the consumer price level.

### b) Monetary policy

A large literature has developed concerning the problems that arise from the well-documented phenomenon of long and variable time-lags between the implementation of policy and its effect on output. In this context, suffice is to say that the Federal Reserve Bank of the United States and the German Bundesbank follow different approaches. Still, neither scheme absolves the central banks from taking the level of resource utilization into consideration when formulating monetary policy. The Federal Reserve Bank currently follows a multi-indicator approach, where all available macroeconomic variables are evaluated for useful information. In this context, capacity utilization rates of capital and labour are important indicators that provide direct evidence about the state and direction of the economy.

In the German context of an intermediary target in the form of a monetary aggregate, the degree of factor utilization also plays a role – even though it may be smaller than in the American case. In order to determine the growth potential of real output, which, besides an inflation goal and an estimate about velocity, is required for the quantity theory, the availability of productive resources must be considered.

What makes the policy process even more complex is the fact that the natural rate is not a constant, but varies over time. This variability should not be seen as invalidating the usefulness of the theoretical framework, which still makes the important point that trying to push the economy past a certain resource-constraint will lead to inflation. This constraint defines an upper limit to growth and reminds us of the limitations of monetary policy. It allows the formulation of a pragmatic policy approach, which is also the baseline in the following analysis: The overriding goal of monetary policy is price stability, but given this constraint, real growth should be fostered.

The variability of the natural rate does however make monetary policy more complex, since it obviously makes it harder to hit the target. Underestimating the amount of available resources results in an inappropriately tight monetary policy, which risks losses in output (Stevenson, 1996). Overestimating the resources at the same time risks an undesirable build-up in inflation.

It is exactly the variability of the binding output constraint that leads to an additional complication in a comparison of German and American monetary policy. While the NAIRU is estimated relatively precisely in the United States, estimates for Germany vary widely. But since the danger of over- or under-estimating the natural rate and thus committing a policy mistake increases with the variability of this band, German policy makers should pursue a less expansionary monetary policy relative to the United States, all other things equal.

Estimates of the NAIRU in the United States show some variation, but except for the most recent years, six percent appears to be a good point estimate (Gordon, 1997). In Germany on the other hand, estimates of the NAIRU differ much more widely. For example during the eighties, Franz / Hoffmann (1990) estimate the NAIRU at 5,5 percent, while Funke (1991) concludes that the NAIRU was closer to 9 percent during that period. The situation with regard to the capital stock is less well documented, but overall it appears that its relationship with inflation is reasonably well behaved in both countries. Garner (1994) argues that the link between capacity utilization and inflation in the United States is stable, but Emery / Chang (1997) find indications for a weakening of this link since the mid-eighties. Franz / Gordon (1993) find that in Germany the capacity utilization – inflation nexus is stable.

The extreme uncertainty about the exact location of the binding capacity constraint in the German labor market implies a problem for German policy makers. The larger variability implies that the policy maker should be less agressive in attempting to use the marginal capacities to generate growth. The reason is simple: he runs a much higher risk of generating inflation than his counterpart, who has much more precise information about the location of the capacity constraint. In general, the point that must be borne in mind in a comparative analysis is that even with identic loss functions, which penalize a build-up in inflation, the policymaker who has less precise information about the capacity constraint will be forced to follow a less expansionary monetary policy as the economy moves closer to this constraint.

The role that uncertainty about the availability of productive resources plays in the policy process is illustrated well by the discussions over the recent years in the FOMC, the body responsible for monetary policy in the United States. After a long period in which the NAIRU in the United States was estimated to be relatively stable at 6%, evidence mounted that it had fallen below this value during the last few years. The actual rate of unemployment has been lower than this since mid-1994 and is currently less than 5%. Nevertheless, no negative reaction of prices was observable.

The initial response of the authorities to this undershooting of the NAIRU in 1994 was to adopt a restrictive monetary policy. However, the Federal Reserve Bank subsequently allowed a somewhat more expansionary monetary environment during 1995 and 1996, even though the rate of capacity utilisation in the labor market continued to rise. As the minutes of the FOMC meetings reveal, this policy is by no means uncontroversial and individual committee members have demanded a tighter policy. As the minutes show, panel member Broaddus justified his dissent from the no-change policy in May 1997 by reference to the high rate of capacity utilization in the economy. The other members were also aware of this risk but felt the costs of a wait-and-see approach were not excessive, especially in view of the lack of immediate inflationary pressure.

### c) Implications for the country comparison

What can be concluded from this for the question of monetary policy effects on employment and the comparative study of the United States and Germany? First, it is assumed throughout that pragmatic monetary policy will attempt to use all available resources, given that the overriding goal of a low and constant inflation rate is not violated. It appears that the recent experience of the Federal Reserve is a good example of such a strategy.

Second, as the economy comes closer to its resource constraint, such a policy becomes riskier, since any "overuse" of resources will lead to inflation. This also is manifest in the discussions at the FOMC meetings. The risk of such a policy will also increase with uncertainty about the location of the capacity constraint.

Third, this uncertainty appears to be considerably greater in Germany than the United States. Additionally, it seems that the capacity constraint in Germany has moved rightward, implying a higher NAIRU, while it has moved to the left in the U.S. (Gordon, 1997). Even assuming identical preferences of the two central banks, it would therefore be optimal for the German policy maker to pursue a less expansionary policy than his American counterpart.

Fourth, the increased uncertainty about the location combined with a bias towards a higher NAIRU in Germany may well be due to the structural problems discussed earlier. The lack of wage differentiation and low mobility of the labor force as well as strong real wage growth have probably contributed both to the increase of the NAIRU and the greater uncertainty concerning its location. These factors prevented the return towards equilibrium and instead contributed to the build-up of long-term unemployment. Indirect support for this position is found in Gordon (1997, p. 30) who explains the inward movement of the NAIRU in the U.S. by saying that "the 1990s have been a time of labor peace, relatively weak unions, a relatively low minimum wage and a slight decline in labour's income share." An extreme interpretation of this, helpful to sharpen the argument, would be that U.S. monetary policy is currently reaping the rewards of the considerable structural reforms of the eighties, which liberalized goods and factor markets.

## V. Summary

Using a country comparison with the U.S. as our tool, we have investigated a series of possible explanations for the poor performance of the German labour market. In particular, we looked closely at microeconomic structural differences, wage policy and monetary policy.

There is considerable evidence that more flexible pay structures, coupled with higher labour force mobility and a moderate rise in the average wage level, have contributed to the more labour-intensive growth in the U.S. The influence of monetary policy on the labour market cannot be viewed in isolation from the debate about the microstructure. A comparison of the impact of monetary policy on employment is considerably complicated by the different initial conditions applying in the two countries. The U.S. benefits from the fact that functioning factor markets can on balance support monetary policy in following a more accomodating policy stance. This does not deny a possible role of monetary policy for fostering employment, but reinforces the impression that addressing the structural problems is the most pressing issue in fighting unemployment in Germany.

## References

*Berthold,* Norbert and *Fehn,* R. (1996): "Evolution von Lohnverhandlungen – Macht oder ökonomisches Gesetz?" in Zohlnhöfer, W. (ed.) Die Tarifautonomie auf dem Prüfstand, Schriften des Vereins für Socialpolitik, N. F., Band 244, 57 - 94. – *Berthold,* Norbert and *Heise,* Michael (1998): "Rahmenbedingungen der Arbeit im internationalen Wettbewerb," in von Stein, Johann and Siebertz, Paul (eds.) Handbuch Banken und Personal. – *Blanchard,* Olivier and *Katz,* Laurence (1992): "Regional Evolutions," Brookings Papers on Economic Activity, 1 - 75. – *Board of Governors of the Federal Reserve System* (1997): "Minutes of the Federal Open Market Committee Meeting held on May 20, 1997," Federal Reserve Bulletin, 773 - 779. – *Calmfors,* Lars and *Driffill,* John (1988): "Bargaining Structure, Corporatism and Macroeconomic Performance," Economic Policy, 14 - 61. – *Council of Economic Advisers* (1997): Economic Report of the President, 1997. – *Danthine,* J.-P. and *Hunt,* J. (1994): "Wage Bargaining Structure, Employment and Economic Integration," Economic Journal, 528 - 541. – *Decressin,* J. and *Fatas,* A. (1994): "Regional Labour Market Dynamics in Europe," CEPR Discussion Paper No. 1085. – *DG BANK* (1996): "Mittelstandsumfrage Herbst 1996" Konjunktur und Kapitalmarkt, Dezember. – *DIW* (1997): "Rückstand beim Anteil der Dienstleistungstätigkeiten aufgeholt," DIW Wochenbericht, 34 - 97, 613 - 617. – *Emery,* Kenneth and *Chang,* Chih-Ping: (1997): "Is there a stable relationship between capacity utilization and inflation?" Federal Reserve Bank of Dallas Economic Review, First Quarter, 14 - 20. – *Franz,* Wolfgang and *Gordon,* Robert (1993): "German and American wage and price dynamics," European Economic Review, 719 - 762. – *Franz,* Wolfgang and *Hofmann,* Thomas (1990): "Eine Schätzung der inflationsstabilen Arbeitslosenquote mit Hilfe von Preiserwartungen des Ifo-Konjunkturtests," Ifo-Studien, 211 - 227. – *Funke,* Michael (1991): "Das Hysteresis Phänomen," Zeitschrift für Wirtschafts- und Sozialwissenschaften, 527 - 551. – *Garner,* Alan (1994): "Capacity utilization and the U.S. inflation," Federal Reserve Bank of

Kansas City Economic Review, Fourth Quarter, 1 - 21. – *Gordon,* Robert (1997): "The time-varying NAIRU and its implications for economic policy," Journal of Economic Perspectives, 11 - 32. – *Gottschalk,* Peter and *Smeeding,* Timothy (1997): "Cross national comparisons of earnings and income inequality," Journal of Economic Literature, 633 - 687. – *Ifo* (1995): Strukturbericht des Ifo-Instituts für Wirtschaftsforschung, München. – *OECD* (1997a): Employment Outlook, Paris: OECD. – *OECD* (1997b): Economic Survey United States, Paris: OECD. – *Siebert,* Horst and *Heise,* Michael (1995): "Lohn-Zins Relation und Kapitalintensität," WiSt, 361 - 364. – *Stevenson,* Richard W. (1996): "It's heresy at Fed, but critics say: Step on the gas," New York Times, June 7, Chicago ed., 15. – *Taylor,* John (1997): "A core of practical macroeconomics," American Economic Review, 233 - 235.

# Unemployment in Germany and Britain – A Question of Micro-Rigidities or Macro-Obstruction?*

By Arne Heise, Düsseldorf

## I. An introduction to deregulation and flexibility

Mass unemployment is the phenomenon, deregulation the cure. This seems to be the simple but almost undisputed orthodoxy regarding employment policy today.[1] Deregulation is not seen as an end in itself, but the means to greater flexibility and, as a corollary, labour market clearance and lower unemployment. In today's *zeitgeist,* deregulation and flexibility represent more than this: they stand for a mobile and dynamic society; they are almost a synonym for modernity. Whoever is unable, or unwilling, to adapt to rapidly changing market conditions is lost in the new global capitalism at the end of the 20th century.

In addition, deregulation is used by policy makers as a proof of their willingness to fight unemployment: policy is restricted to facilitating the freedom which the markets supposedly requires in order to achieve optimum results – a general equilibrium. This is all part of neo-classical policy assignment in which the central bank facilitates price stability, the social partners are responsible for employment levels and policy makers enshrine flexibility into the legal system.

Finally, deregulation not only epitomises today's *zeitgeist* but is also substantiated by a well established theoretical consensus. In this guise, deregulation does not attempt to destroy socio-economic relations and collective agreements, which seek to reduce a variety of economic uncertainties (see Standing 1997:8 f.), but is a device to break up such institutions and regulations, which shelter particular interest groups, and to restore the market clearing capacity of the price mechanism.

Policy that affects price flexibility in the labour market should be evaluated with regard to the following (see Berthold / Fehn 1996):

- Social security may inhibit the downward fexibility of wages by effectively setting reservation wages.

---

* I would like to thank Paul Selden for his very instructive help. The usual disclaimer apply.

1 "A substantially better employment performance remains a chimera without greater efforts at liberalizing the labor market." Berthold / Fehn 1996:594

- Employment protection against unfair dismissal may increase the power of insiders ('rent seeking').
- The autonomy of collective bargaining (*Tarifautonomie* in Germany) limits the possibility of policy interventions.
- The structure of trade unions and employer associations (in terms of their degree of centralisation or cooperation) and their respective strength (in terms of membership, coverage rates, etc.) influence their ability to promote particular interests.

The clear inference to be taken from these tenets of mainstream economics is that the inhibition of wage flexibility in the labour market by existing institutions and regulations will lead to higher unemployment, particularily after exogenous shocks to market equilibrium (such as the oil price shocks of the mid-1970s and early 1980s). Consequently, mainstream economists and neo-liberal policy advisers persistently challenge the existence of these institutions and regulations.

## II. Britain and Germany: Prototyps of flexibility and sklerosis?

At the beginning of the 1980s several industrialised countries experienced a political turnaround: in the USA, Britain and Germany governments took office which promised to tackle the twin-problems of unemployment and inflation from a neo-liberal perspective. In Germany, Kohl renounced interventionist macro-policies and promised sound public finances as prerequisite for more growth and employment, while Reaganomics was based on the monetarist desire for price stability and the magic of the so-called 'Laffer-curve', i.e. the promised (though never realised) twin achievements of tax redemption for higher income groups and, at the same time, a reduction of public deficits. In Britain, Margaret Thatcher promised no less than a radical break with the post-World-War-II welfare state, the privatisation of much of the public sector and the renewal of industrial relations, regarded as the major cause of what had become known as the 'British desease'.

Recent economic studies have been based on a comparison of the US and the German employment performance (see Schettkat 1992, Paqué 1995, Werner 1997, Birk / Gries 1997, Gaß / Schmidt 1997).[2] This paper takes the British experiences as a point of reference for two reasons: on the one hand, the Thatcher and Major administrations have not only shifted policy attention from demand to supply oriented measures, as in the USA and Germany, but started a micro-economic re-

2 There are also many studies that use the method of multi-country comparison by way of cross-country regression – see e.g. Kormendi / Meguire 1985; Bean / Layard / Nickell 1996; Rowthorn / Glyn 1991; Barro 1991. As Levine / Zervos (1993) have pointed out, the 'believability' of many such multi-country studies is greatly impaired due to the low robustness of parameters with respect to the specification of the regression – which is why I prefer the lucidity of a two-country comparison.

structuring of the British economy (precisely in a way often proposed to Germany since the beginning of the 1990s). On the other hand, in terms of size, industrial fabric, degree of openess and industrial culture, Britain and Germany seem far more comparable than the US and Germany.

Institutional change in Germany and Britain during the past two decades are often regarded as converse: Britain as the prototype of a flexible economy and Germany as an example of what has become known as 'Eurosclerosis' (see OECD 1994 for Britain and Giersch / Paqué / Schmieding 1994 and Berthold / Fehn 1996 for Germany). Indeed, Germany shows a high degree of institutional stability: (1) the degree of unionisation and the degree of coverage of collective agreements, taking account of cyclical fluctuations, remains surprisingly stable; (2) co-determination and dismissal legislation is – despite initiatives by the junior partner in the ruling government in the mid-1980s (see Wood 1997) – basically unchanged; (3) legislation on strike activities and collective bargaining has undergone only marginal alterations (see Zachert / Bobke 1987:360 ff.); (4) social legislation influencing the labour market has been only moderately weakened.

This assessment of institutional stability, although not unchallenged (see Keller / Seifert 1997), is certainly comparatively true when considering the dramatic changes in British institutions and regulations over the past two decades: (1) in various 'Employment Acts', the 'Social Security Act' and the 'Trade Union Reform and Employment Right Act' the capacity and legal rights to strike of trade unions have been substantially curtailed; (2) with the 'Employment Protection Act' unfair dismissal protection has been reduced and the burden of evidence reversed; (3) eligibility for income related unemployment benefits has been progressively circumscribed until finally replaced by the job seekers allowance (JSA) which is independent of previous income and contingent on actively seeking employment; (4) the degree of unionisation is at a historically low level and the coverage rate of collective agreements (which are not binding, anyway) has dropped below 50 percent; (5) the firm level, being predominant already during the 1960s and 1970s, has become the main focal point of trade union activity due to the privatisation policy during the Thatcher-era and the abandoning of the central level of collective bargaining in the public sector; (6) the 'closed shop' and the 'wages councils' – central elements of British industrial relations in the 1970s – have been abrogated.

Despite this 'impressive' record of political achievements of the Thatcher and Major administrations, 'deregulation' does not accurately describe the direction of institutional change in Britain: abandoning the principle of 'non-intervention' started a process of *de jure* regulating formerly uncodified industrial relations which increased the *density* of regulations (i.e. the number of codified rules), yet diminished the *level* of regulation (i.e. the restrictions on enterpreneurial options). This, of course, had a negative impact on the options of trade unions and their representatives at the firm level – from their point of view, the level and density of regulations had increased. 'Deregulation', therefore, does not mean the 'unfettering' of market forces, as is most often suggested, but the reconstruction of the British economy as an 'entrepreneurial society' (see Jessop 1991:135).

## III. Testing neo-liberal hypotheses

In this chapter, I will assess some common neo-liberal hypotheses by means of an Anglo-German comparison. However, as raw data cannot be controlled for all such factors which may have direct or indirect effects on the variables under investigation (external influences of various kinds or the parallel deregulation of commodity or service markets), there will never be a reliable method of falsification in the Popperian sense. We will, therefore, take another approach: we will try to explain the comparative labour market performance from a purely macro-economic perspective which may, if successfull, leave no room for neo-liberal reasoning.

*1st neoliberal hypothesis: the breaking up the 'cartellisation' of the labour market will result in a better consideration of macro-economic requirements by the wage setting system (wage moderation).*

It is not the outcome of elaborate reasoning but the *a priori* assumption of the mainstream market clearing model that any divergence from market equilibrium (i.e. involuntary unemployment) must be rooted in a lack of price flexibility[3], which, itself, is caused by the cartellisation of the market in question. Considering the drastic institutional change of British labour (market) relations in the 1980s and 1990s, one would expect a marked increase in wage moderation compared to the 1970s, in Britain and Germany throughout this period of relative institutional stability.

An empirical inquiry into such an assumption forcefully rejects this line of argument (see table 1): (1) both economies experienced a moderation in nominal wages – parallel to the increase in unemployment – as compared to the 1970s, but nominal wage moderation was not only higher in Germany, the reduction of the average annual growth rate was also more pronounced here (– 58,8%) than in Britain (– 46,2%) during the 1980s, despite lower unemployment rates (as a determinant of wage moderation) and a lower annual growth rate, as a starting point, in the 1970s. Even during the first half of the 1990s – despite the distorting effect of German unification – this picture has not been reversed, although the divergence in nominal wage increases has been narrowed.

Of course, the evolution of nominal wages is not exclusively determined by the labour market performance and institutional structure, but also by the (expected) conduct of monetary policy or, to be more precise, inflation tolerance of the central

3 "One of these axioms is that prices constitute the sole source of information on which decisions (of purchases or sales) are based, so that the allocation of resources between different uses is solely determined by prices." (Kaldor 1996:5)

bank. Therefore, higher nominal wage increases may also reflect a higher willingness to accommodate on the part of the Bank of England which is evident in a comparison of the inflation records of both economies.

*Table 1*

**Growth performance in Britain and Germany**

| | Germany | | | UK | | |
|---|---|---|---|---|---|---|
| | 71 - 80 | 81 - 90 | 91 - 94 | 71 - 80 | 81 - 90 | 91 - 94 |
| GR nominal wages | 8,5 | 3,5 | 4,0 | 16,0 | 8,6 | 5,5 |
| GR price deflator | 5,3 | 2,8 | 3,1 | 14,0 | 6,5 | 4,2 |
| GR real wages | 3,2 | 0,7 | 0,9 | 2,0 | 2,1 | 1,3 |
| GR labour productivity (hours) | | 2,5 | 2,4 | | 2,7 | 1,9 |
| GR labour productivity (employees) | 2,6 | 1,5 | 1,7 | 1,7 | 2,1 | 2,4 |
| Unemployment rate | 2,2 | 6,0 | 6,1 | 3,8 | 9,7 | 10,5 |

Note: GR: rate of change of a variable; nominal wages: monthly nomnal wages in Germany (Tariflöhne), hourly nominal wages in the UK; price deflator: price deflator GDP

Source: Europäische Wirtschaft, Nr. 54, 1993; Butcher / Hart 1995; IAB-Zahlenfibel 1995; WSI-Tarifhandbuch 1997, Eurostat – Labour Force Survey on CD ROM

The neo-liberal market clearing model maintains that the *real* wage rate is more important than the *nominal* wage rate. (2) Although real wage growth cannot directly be targeted by the 'social partners' as it is an endogenously determined variable, proponents of the neo-liberal market clearing model presuppose the possibility of a parallel determination of nominal and, *uno actu,* real wages by a 'rule of thum'[4]. However, changes in real wages do not support the neo-liberal hypotheses either: in the 1980s, and during the first half of the 1990s, real wage growth in Germany was well below real wage growth in the 1970s, and below the corresponding growth rates in Britain where they accelerated after the Thatcher revolution in the 1980s.

However, real wage growth has limited significance without correlation with labour productivity. At this point, we need to define 'full employment' labour productivity as opposed to of labour productivity measured in reality (i.e. ex post), in order to preclude the possibility of factor substitution. As the determination of such a category depends crucially upon the identification of a reference year of full employment and the acceptence of traditional postulates of factor substitution, ex post realised growth rates of labour productivity will be used as a sufficient standard. (3) During the 1980s, as well as the first half of the 1990s, markedly less of the distributional margin (i.e. productivity growth plus inflation compensation) has

[4] For this 'rule of thum' see Siebert 1994:92; Lehment 1993, for a critique see Heise 1996a:166 f.

been converted into real wage increases (and working time reduction – the difference between labour productivity per hour and labour productivity per worker) in Germany than in Britain, or to put it differently: real wage moderation was clearly higher in Germany than in Britain over the past one and a half decades.

As we can see from table 2, there is less evidence of 'insider behaviour' in collective bargaining in Germany than in Britain: the impact of the *rate of change* of unemployment (as opposed to the *level* of unemployment) on nominal wage levels is insignificant in the case of Germany. However, it is stronger and statistically significant in the case of Britain, i.e. nominal wages not only start to increase when the unemployment level approaches full employment but also when the rate of change becomes negative (i.e. when unemployment starts to fall).

*Table 2*

**Insider behaviour in the UK and Germany**

$\Delta w = a\Delta UNR + b\Delta UNR(-1)$

| | $a$ | $b$ | $R$-square | $F$ | $DW$ |
|---|---|---|---|---|---|
| D | 0,037 | – 0,0049 | 0,18 | 1,8 | 0,62 |
| GB | 0,168 | – 0,0103 | 0,45 | 7,13 | 0,79 |

Notes: F:F-test, DW: Durbin-Watson-test; ΔUNR: rate of change of the unemployment rate; a and b: coefficients of regression

Source: Europäische Wirtschaft, Nr. 56, 1995

The first neo-liberal hypothesis must, therefore, clearly be rejected on grounds of this Anglo-German comparison.[5] Indeed, the corporatist reasoning seems to be much more cogent in this area (see Calmfors / Drifill 1988; Soskice 1990): a more centralised system of collective bargaining results in a greater wage moderation because 'encompassing institutions' (Mancur Olson) are more willing to take the macro-economic effects of their actions into account (internalising external effects), than fragmented institutions that only care for particular interests. The latter is exemplified in Britain by the tendency of employed insiders, at the firm level, to maximise short-term real wages instead of deferring to internal career opportunities and upward income mobility. Finally, in case of 'local pushfullness' (see Soskice 1990) of strong trade unions at the firm level, an internalisation of external effects of wage increases cannot be expected.

*2nd neo-liberal hypothesis: in order to force a stronger consideration of intersectoral, regional and qualificatory requirements in the process of wage bargaining, the cartellisation of the labour market has to be dismantled.*

---

5 This result is confirmed by a recent study comparing Germany, France and the USA; see Flassbeck 1998.

The neo-liberal model is an allocation model by character, i.e. it describes the optimum allocation of initial endowments (of commodities, services or factors) by considerations of scarcity. The degree of scarcity is reflected by relative prices. In the case of the labour market, this means that real wages have to reflect the relative scarcity of the factors of production in terms of regional, sectoral and qualificatory characteristics in order to guarantee an optimum allocation. An overall increase in unemployment should be accompanied by an increased variance in unemployment rates, and subsequently wage dispersion, on a regional, sectoral and qualificatory basis. This is evident in both Germany and Britain.

Whether or not a completely flexible wage structure is considered a precondition for full employment, wage dispersion has to set incentives for mobility and adjustment procedures. In other word, changes in sectoral, regional and qualificatory wage differentiation must reflect changes in relative scarcity, if the signalling function of the wage structure is not to be impaired. In a number of studies (see Zweimüller / Barth 1994, Freeman 1988, Appelbaum / Schettkat 1996) the degree of centralisation, or co-operation, of collective bargaining systems has been inversely related to the degree of wage dispersion, because centralised collective bargaining systems, or co-operative trade unions ('encompassing institutions' in Mancur Olson's terms), conduct their wage policy according to the egalitarian principles of 'solidarity' or 'fair wages' (as in the efficiency wage theory), unlike decentralised bargaining systems, company based systems or crafts unions.

Figure 1 shows that wage dispersion – measured by the ratio of the highest / lowest income decile to the median income decile – is higher in Britain, and increased markedly during the 1980s, whilst, in Germany it remained stable and even slightly diminished at the lower end. In fact, wage dispersion in Britain has reached a level comparable to *Victorian times*. At a closer look, this difference between Britain and Germany is almost entirely explained by the higher qualificatory wage differentiation in Britain (there are only minor differences in the levels of regional and sectoral wage dispersion).[6]

Although wage dispersion between skilled and unskilled labour has, contrary to conventional wisdom, actually increased in Germany (see Heise 1997b), it is far lower and much more stable than in Britain.[7] We can, therefore, conclude that the higher degree of centralisation, or co-operation, of the supply side of the German labour market has resulted in a more egalitarian wage structure with respect to qualifications, than the more decentralised supply side of the British labour market.

6 For regional wage dispersion see Hyclak / Johnes 1992 and Johnes / Hyclak 1989, for sectoral wage dispersion see Möller / Bellmann 1996 and Elliot / White 1993, for a summary see Heise 1997a.

7 As skill classifications are not entirely comparable, the levels of differentiation cannot easily be compared. However, the ratio between skilled and unskilled labour changed between 15,5% (wholesale / retail) and 80,2% (chemical industries) in Britain and 11,2% (technical white collar workers in manufacturing and services) and 11,7% (commercial white collar workers in manufacturing and services) in Germany since 1970.

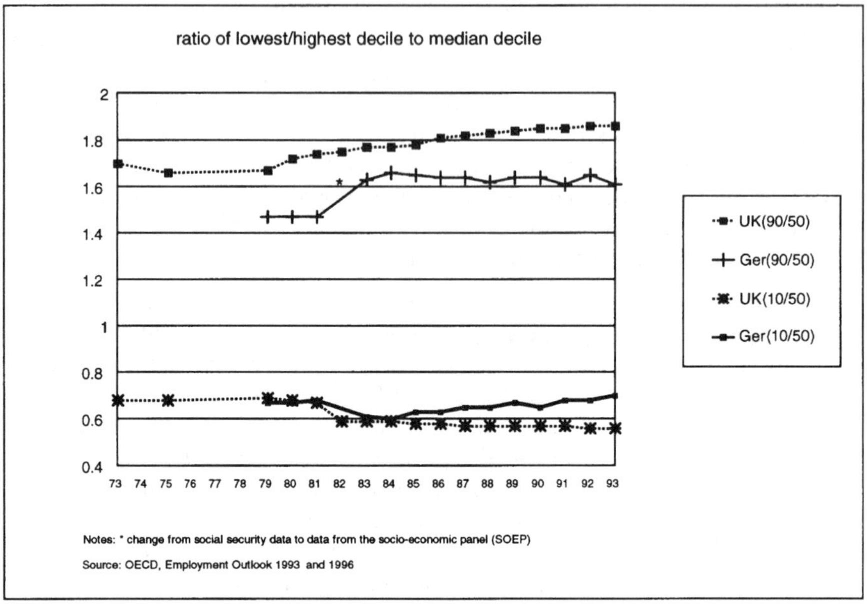


Figure 1: Wage dispersion

*3rd neo-liberal hypothesis: wage moderation is the precondition for a positive employment performance.*

Wage moderation – so often called in by neoliberal economists and politicians alike – is not regarded as an end in itself, but as a precondition for more employment growth. When empirical data is used to support this supposition the possibility of co-determination of two unrelated variables is ignored, and the exogeneity and controllability of the real wage[8] is assumed. We will now test the hypothesis form a comparative perspective: we have already seen that wage moderation was higher in Germany than in Britain, despite the greater degree of 'cartellisation' of the German labour market. But has this sacrafice, which is possibly the unintentional result of macro-economic developments, been rewarded by comparative employment gains?

Table 3 shows that this was not the case: even if the unparalleled cyclical downturn at the beginning of the 1980s in Britain or the 'extra-boom' of the German unification at the end of the 1980s is not controlled for, Britain still experienced a better employment performance. If the period under investigation is shortened to exclude these anomalies, it becomes even more evident that lower wage moderation in Great Britain was coincidental with higher annual employment growth.

---

8 I critically commented on both issues; see Heise 1995.

*Table 3*

**Employment performance in the UK and Germany (in %)**

| | 81 | 82 | 83 | 84 | 85 | 86 | 87 | 88 | 89 | 90 | *81-90* | *82-89* |
|---|---|---|---|---|---|---|---|---|---|---|---|---|
| UK | – 3,9 | – 1,8 | – 1,2 | 2,6 | 1,3 | 0,1 | 2,1 | 3,3 | 3,0 | 0,7 | *0,6* | *1,2* |
| Ger | – 0,1 | – 1,2 | – 1,4 | 0,2 | 0,7 | 1,4 | 0,7 | 0,8 | 1,5 | 3,0 | *0,5* | *0,3* |

Source: Europäische Wirtschaft, Nr. 54, 1993

*4th neo-liberal hypothesis: wage dispersion enhances structural change and improves the employment prospects of low skilled labour.*

In some recent studies (see Appelbaum / Schettkat 1996; Paqué 1995) the need for higher wage dispersion to help smooth the process of structural change towards a service economy and, in particular, to enhance the employability of unskilled labour, has been argued from an allocative perspective. Low productivity growth of (particular low skilled) services and the assumption of a high price elasticity of demand for such services produce what has been labelled the 'cost desease of services' (see Scharpf 1992) under an egalitarian wage regime. Besides these assumptions, the complete neglect of income effects (i.e. income elasticities of demand by different wage earner groups; see Heise 1998) and the negative impact of a growing wage dispersion on the propensity to invest (see Alesina / Perotti 1996, Persson / Tabellini 1994) should be noted and, if taken into account, leave employment and structural effects indetermined.

*Table 4*

**Sectoral employment performance in the UK and Germany (rate of change of share in total employment in percent)**

| | UK | | Germany | |
|---|---|---|---|---|
| | 70 - 80 | 80 - 90 | 70 - 80 | 80 - 90 |
| Agriculture | 0,0 | – 0,4 | – 3,3 | – 1,7 |
| Energy / mining | – 0,5 | – 1,1 | – 0,2 | – 0,2 |
| Manufacturing | – 8,5 | – 7,9 | – 4,9 | – 2,6 |
| Construction | – 0,4 | – 1,0 | – 0,9 | – 1,3 |
| Wholesail / Retail | + 0,3 | + 1,8 | + 1,1 | + 0,5 |
| Transp. / Comm. | – 0,2 | – 0,7 | + 0,3 | – 0,5 |
| Banking / Insurance | + 1,5 | + 6,8 | + 0,7 | + 0,5 |
| Other Services | + 6,9 | + 2,2 | + 5,5 | + 4,5 |
| Public Sector | + 0,9 | + 0,2 | + 1,4 | + 0,0 |
| Organ. without business character | | | + 0,3 | + 0,3 |
| *Sum (absolute value)* | *19,20* | *22,10* | *18,6* | *12,10* |

Source: UK: Employment (and Productivity) Gazette, various years, Germany: Stat. Bundesamt, Stat. Jahrbuch 1993; own calculations

Table 4 shows the rate of growth of employment of traditionally classified industries[9]. Structural change appears to have accelerated in Britain and retarded in Germany. However, this deduction depends very much on the classifications used and neglects intra-sectoral structural change. Data on job-turnover – which measures the total amount of job re-allocation – points to a higher dynamic in the case of Germany (see Cramer / Koller 1988, Blanchflower / Burgess 1994, Heise 1997a). Evidence on the dynamics of structural change is, at best, inconclusive.

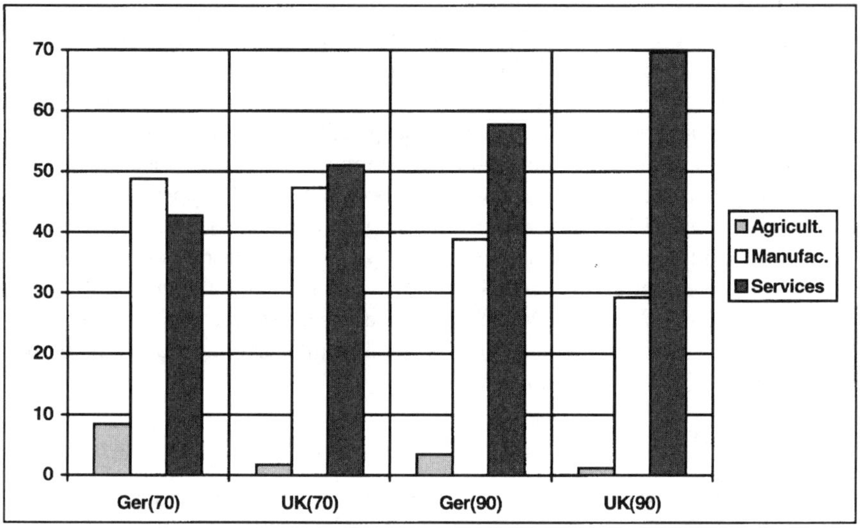


Source: Stat. Bundesamt, Sta. Jahrbuch 1993 und Employment (& Productivity Gazette), various years

Figure 2: Employees in industries in the UK and Germany (share in %)

Figures 2 and 3 reveal the often lamented weakness of the German services industry (see e.g. Krupp 1987). However, this weakness has not exacerbated since the 1970s: in both economies employment in the service sector grew almost identically: 42% in the case of Germany, 44% in the case of Britain. In addition, differences in the development of certain sectors of both economies – e.g. 'banking / insurance', 'other services' – can in large part be explained by differences in categor-

9 At this point, we have to mention the problem of international comparison of structural change which stems from differences in national definitions of classifications and the problem of employment being measured according to sectoral classification rather than occupations.

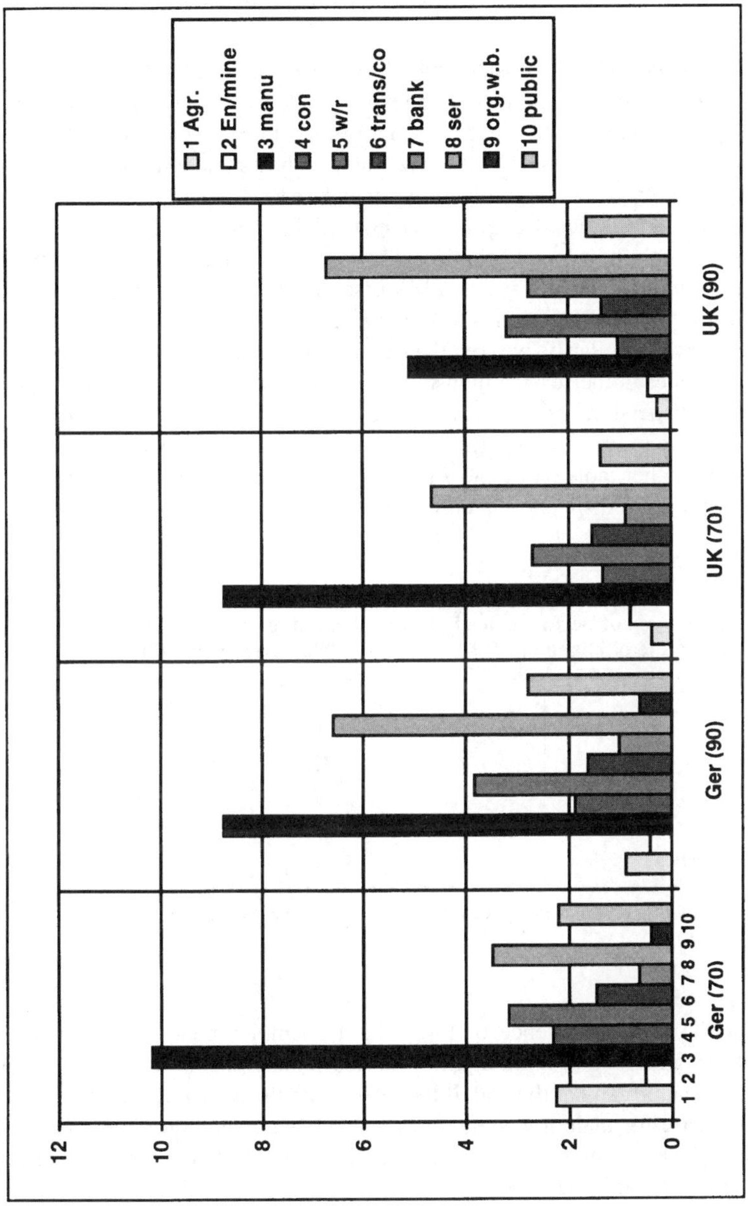


Source: see figure 2

Figure 3: Employees in industries (in mio)

isation – e.g. business services are classified under 'other services' in Germany, while they are included in 'banking / insurance' in the UK classification – and the process of outsourcing of services from manufacturing companies (see Ochel / Schreyer 1988: 161 ff.)

We have demonstrated considerable differences in wage dispersion between Germany and Britain, particularily with respect to skills, and we will now ascertain whether sectors using a relatively high proportion of low and unskilled labour profited from high wage dispersion in the UK. Table 5 shows that employment dropped drastically in low skilled manufacturing industries. This confirms conventional wisdom about the restricted employment potentials of low skilled manufacturing industries in highly developed countries. However, it should be noted that Britain's performance in this respect was actually worse than that of Germany, despite higher qualificatory wage dispersion. The overall performance of Britain's manufacturing industry was similarily weaker than that of Germany. As the wage share of turnover is higher in the service industries, than in manufacturing industry, qualificatory wage dispersion should be able to overcome the 'cost desease' of service industries and so promote comparative employment growth. However: it cannot be deduced from either table 6 or table 7 that low skilled labour profited from a higher qualificational wage dispersion in either Britain or Germany.[10]

*Table 5*

**Employment performance in low skilled manufacturing industries (rate of change in %; UK: 1980 - 1990, Ger: 1980 - 1989)**

| | Ger | UK |
|---|---|---|
| Textiles | – 28,7 | – 53,9 |
| Leather | – 38,1 | – 31,6* |
| Paper | – 7,7 | – 44,5 |
| Glas | – 11,9 | |
| rubber and plastics | + 28,2 | + 1,5 |

Source: Employment (& Productivity) Gazette, various years; Stat. Bundesamt, Stat. Jahrbuch 1993

* 1980 - 1985

Table 8 shows the incidence of low skilled unemployment as correlated with qualifications and gender. Although low skilled female unemployment is lower in Britain than in Germany at the end of the 1980s – contrary to a decade earlier – this was not the case for male low skilled unemployment. In addition, the ratio of low skilled to high skilled unemployment is not only higher in Britain than in Germany for both sexes, its incidence even increased.

10 Due to the small number of testable branches and problems with comparability of data, this result must be interpreted with cautiousness.

*Table 6*

**Employment performance in various service branches (rate of change in %)**

| | Ger | UK |
|---|---|---|
| | low share of low skilled labour | |
| Education | + 26,0 | + 1,0 |
| | medium share of low skilled labour | |
| Banking | + 29,1 | + 45,2 |
| Insurance | + 12,0 | + 0,7 |
| Business services | + 82,2 | + 195 |
| Health | + 35,8 | + 11,0 |
| Wholesale / retail | + 10,0 | +17,3 |
| | high share of low skilled labour | |
| Hotel / restaurants | + 69,3 | + 50,7 |
| Household | + 30,5 | + 18,9** |
| Cleaning services | + 30,7* | + 13,3 |

Note: Classification of 'low skill' as in O'Mahony / Wagner / Paulssen 1994

Source: Employment (& Productivity) Gazette, various years, StaBu, FS 1, R. 4.1.1, various years; *: 1983 - 90, **: 1985 - 91

*Table 7*

**Rank correlation between qualification and employment performance**

| | *R*-square | *t*-test |
|---|---|---|
| Ger | – 0,028 | – 0,883 |
| UKB | – 0,071 | – 0,683 |
| DiffUK / Ger | – 0,135 | – 0,221 |

*Table 8*

**Qualification-specific unemployment figures**

| | | Unemployment rates by increasing qualification First quartile | last quartile | ratio |
|---|---|---|---|---|
| Germany | | | | |
| Men | 1978 | 3.6 | 1.7 | 2.12 |
| | 1987 | 11.0 | 4.2 | 2.64 |
| Women | 1978 | 4.4 | 3.5 | 1.24 |
| | 1987 | 12.5 | 8.1 | 1.54 |
| Britain | | | | |
| Men | 1979 | 5.9 | 1.9 | 3.14 |
| | 1990 | 11.6 | 2.2 | 5.30 |
| Women | 1979 | 6.1 | 4.1 | 1.47 |
| | 1990 | 7.6 | 3.7 | 2.04 |

Source: OECD, OECD Jobs Study – Part 1, Paris 1994, p. 40

## IV. Macroeconomics of comparative labour market developments

To date, comparative labour market developments in the UK and Germany cannot be substantiated by neo-classical modelling based on the allocative functioning of unfettered markets. Therefore, we will employ a macro-economic perspective in the following.

Figure 4 demonstrates the strong correlation between developments in unemployment[11] and levels of investment. This is also confirmed by econometric testing (table 9). There is a definite correlation between hours worked and net investment which can be taken as additional (or entreprise) investment while the difference between gross and net investment can be regarded as 'defensive' investment (see Lamfalussy 1963): more than 80 per cent of the number of hours worked in both economies are deducible from net investment in equipment and buildings – and the lag structure hints on the direction of causation. Therefore, levels of employment as well as unemployment[12] can to a large extent be explained by changes in investment demand.

Source: Europäische Wirtschaft, Nr. 54, 1993

Figure 4: Gross fixed capital formation and unemployment

[11] The unemployment rate is taken as a proxy for 'labour market disequilibrium'.

[12] In economies showing a rather stable supply of labour – like Germany and Britain – both variables are closely interrelated.

*Table 9*

**Determinants of labour market developments**

| | $a^*$ | $b^*$ | $c^*$ | $D^*$ | $e$ | $F$ | $R$-square |
|---|---|---|---|---|---|---|---|
| 1: $UNR = aINV + bINV(t-1) + cINV(t-2) + e$ | | | | | | | |
| UK | | – 0,538 | – 0,459 | | 15,729 | 65,82 | 0,89 |
| | | (– 3,961) | (– 3,377) | | (19,48) | | |
| Ger | – 0,297 | – 0,604 | | | 12,395 | 30,746 | 0,79 |
| | (– 0,835) | (– 1,697) | | | (9,708) | | |
| 2: $Hour = aINV(t-1) + bINV(t-2) + e$ | | | | | | | |
| UK** | 1,091 | – 0,242 | | | 687,34 | 25,73 | 0,88 |
| | (5,976) | (– 1,326) | | | (27,81) | | |
| Ger | 54,49 | 0,58 | | | 24246 | 51,52 | 0,83 |
| | (5,66) | (0,059) | | | (22,18) | | |
| 3: $INR = aProf + bProf(t-1) + cProf(t-2) + dProf(t-3) + e$ | | | | | | | |
| UK | | 0,594 | – 0,116 | 0,626 | – 0,820 | 5,52 | 0,56 |
| | | (1,982) | (– 0,330) | (2,241) | (– 0,171) | | |
| Ger | – 0,919 | 0,914 | – 0,304 | 0,256 | 19,297 | 1,533 | 0,34 |
| | (– 2,252) | (1,608) | (– 0,605) | (0,745) | (3,072) | | |
| 4: $INV = aPro + bPro(t-1) + cPro(t-2) + e$ | | | | | | | |
| UK | – 0,463 | 0,544 | 0,054 | | 4,945 | 0,937 | 0,16 |
| | (– 1,007) | (0,796) | (0,113) | | (0,823) | | |
| Ger | – 0,479 | 1,153 | | | – 2,799 | 18,502 | 0,69 |
| | (– 2,189) | (5,266) | | | (– 1,290) | | |
| Ger | | 0,028 | 0,864 | | – 4,137 | 27,136 | 0,78 |
| | | (0,148) | (4,595) | | (– 2,611) | | |

Notes: * standardised coefficients (t-values in brackets); ** hours work per week; INR: gross fixed capital formation INV: net fixed capital formation; UNR: standardised unemployment rates; Hour: hours worked; Prof: gross operating surplus / gross capital stock in private sector; Pro: net returns on net capital stock – total economy

Source: UNR: Europäische Wirtschaft, Nr. 54, 1993; INR and INV: OECD, National Accounts, various years, SVR-Jahresgutachten 1996, EC (1993), own calculations; Hour: Butcher / Hart (1995), IAB-Datensatz; Prof: Europäische Wirtschaft, Nr 50, 1990; Pro: European Commission data base; own calculations

Wage policy (or, rather, wage moderation) plays only a minor role: I have shown in a different context (see Heise 1993) that the extent of wage moderation has no significant impact on investment and, furthermore, in econometric modelling (see Heilemann 1991: 83 f.), the demand component greatly dominates the wage- or unit-labour-cost-component. In addition, the indirect impact of wage moderation on investment via the level of profitability does not prove to be significant. Figure 5 reveals only a weak correlation between the (gross) investment performance and the gross rate of return on capital in both economies: for example, the restoration of profitability in Germany after 1982 did not result in an augmentation of investment for well over five years until the 'boom of double unification' – the European common market and German unification – altered the economic landscape. Similarily, in the UK the cyclical upturn in investment demand at the end of the 1980s[13] had not been preceded by an improvement in the profitability of capital. Consequently, the econometric test (table 9; equation 3) demonstrates this weak – and statistically insignificant in the case of Germany – correlation between investment and profitability. Testing net investment performance against net profitability seems – in the case of Germany – to establish a much closer link (table 9; equation 4). But the 'believability' of this result is only week as the significance of the parameters depends crucially on the specification of the regression; i.e. the lacking robustness of the parameters suggests a rejections of the indicated relation.

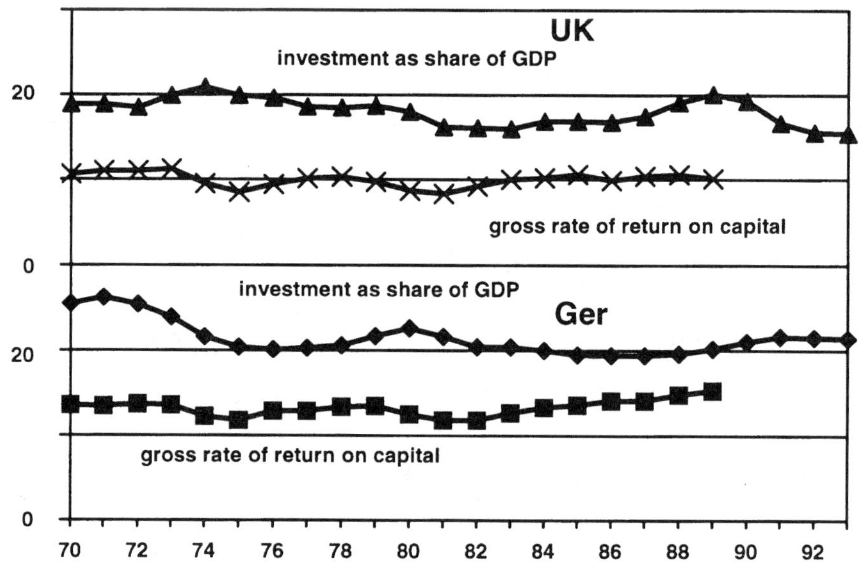


Quelle: Europäische Wirtschaft, Nr. 54, 1993 und Europäische Wirtschaft, Nr. 50, 1990

Figure 5: Investment and profitability

The question is whether the comparative labour market performances of both countries can be explained by macro-economic and macro-political determinants without reference to the process of institutional change. Figure 6 shows the difference between standardised unemployment rates (Eurostat definition) of both economies and it is evident that labour market disequilibrium was not only more acute in Britain than in Germany over the whole period under investigation but that British comparative labour market developments became even worse during the

13 Which was particularily spured by wealth effects of financial deregulation ('Big Bang') in 1986 "... together with the willingness of those in the personal sector to get themselves into debt on a quite unparalleled scale." (Wells 1993:94)

1980s and early 1990s. Our hypothesis is that this difference can be attributed to the differences in investment demand, exchange rate changes and contrasting monetary and fiscal policy.

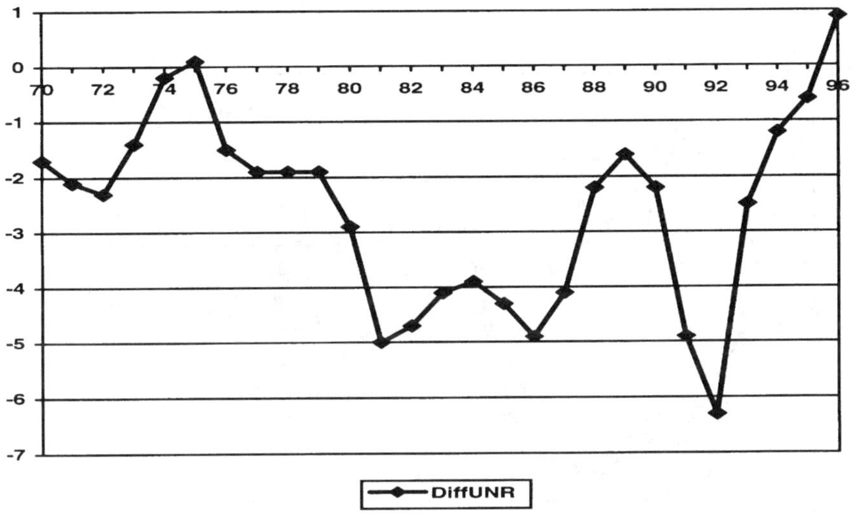


Note: a positive value means: UNR is higher in Germany, a negative value means: UNR is higher in the UK

Source: see foregoing tables and figures and Eurostat: Arbeitslosigkeit in der europ. Union, Luxemburg 1996

Figure 6: Comparative labour market development

The significance of investment demand in relation to unemployment has already been established. We will now concentrate on other determinants. The respective changes in the level of exchange rates (fig. 7) reveals long spells of deviation from the purchasing power parity[14], i.e. over- or undervaluation of a currency.[15] The change in the valuation of the Sterling, from being strongly undervalued at the end of the 1970s, to being slightly overvalued at the beginning of the 1980s, is particularly marked. During this time the reverse took place in Germany: a period of severe overvaluation after the failure of the system of Bretton Woods was followed by a period of marked undervaluation after the establishment of the European Monetary System (EMS) in 1979. Comparative exchange rate levels gave strong

14 The purchasing power parity (PPP) is that exchange rate which levels out differences in national price level movements; see Turner / Van't dack 1993:72 ff.

15 A currency is overvalued (undervalued) if the real exchange rate shows a positive (negative) value. The real exchange rate is the (weighed) nominal exchange rate (against 26 – in the case of Britain – or 18 – in the case of Germany – countries) deflated by the (weighed) consumer price index.

competitive advantages to Britain in the 1970s. This situation was reversed at the beginning of the Thatcher-era. However, after the disturbing effect of the discovery of North Sea oil and the overshooting of exchange rate movements due to expectations in the new government, Sterling became undervalued again giving Britain a competitive edge over Germany.

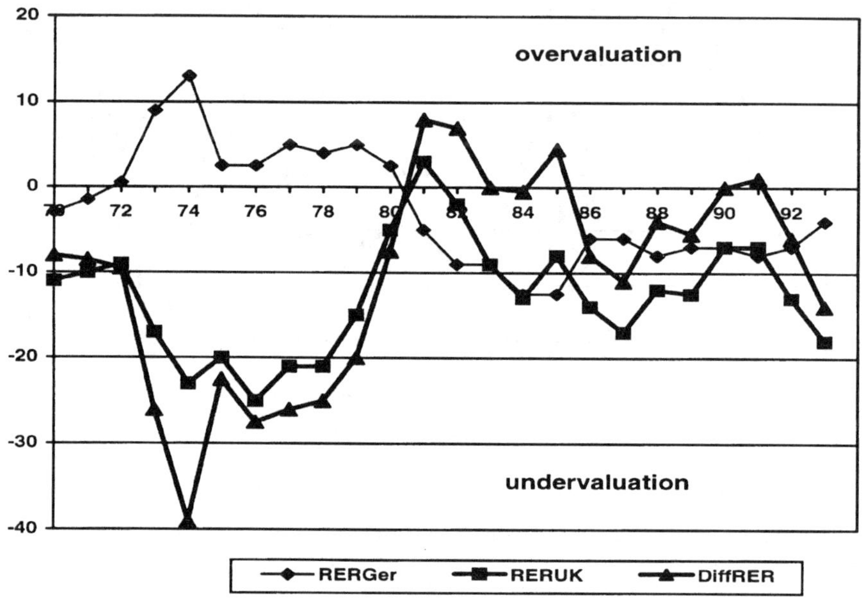


Source: calculations according to Turner / Van 't dack (1993) and Flassbeck (1995)
Note: RER: real exchange rate

Figure 7: Comparative exchange rate performance

The conduct of fiscal policy in both economies is depicted in figure 8: net public borrowing (or lending respectively) – after being controlled for cyclical impacts[16] – is monitored here. The elimination of 'automatic stabilisers' provides a clearer picture of the fiscal policy stance of both economies. It is evident that fiscal policy was more restrictive during the 1980s than during the 1970s – however, this was more the case in Germany than in Britain: after drastic restrictions on fiscal policy by the incoming Thatcher administration (see Minford 1988; Healey 1993), a more expansionary policy orientation clearly helped the recovery of growth and employment at the end of the decade. It should also be noted here, that overall net public

16 The process of adjustment for cyclical movements has been elaborated by the European Commission; see European Economy, No.60, 1995.

borrowing in Britain at the end of the 1980s – i.e. including the cyclical component – is close to balance (1988: +0.1; 1989:–0.1). A comparison of fiscal policy in both countries shows a clearly less restrictive orientation in the case of Britain – even under the Thatcher-administration – than the German authorities were willing to pursue.

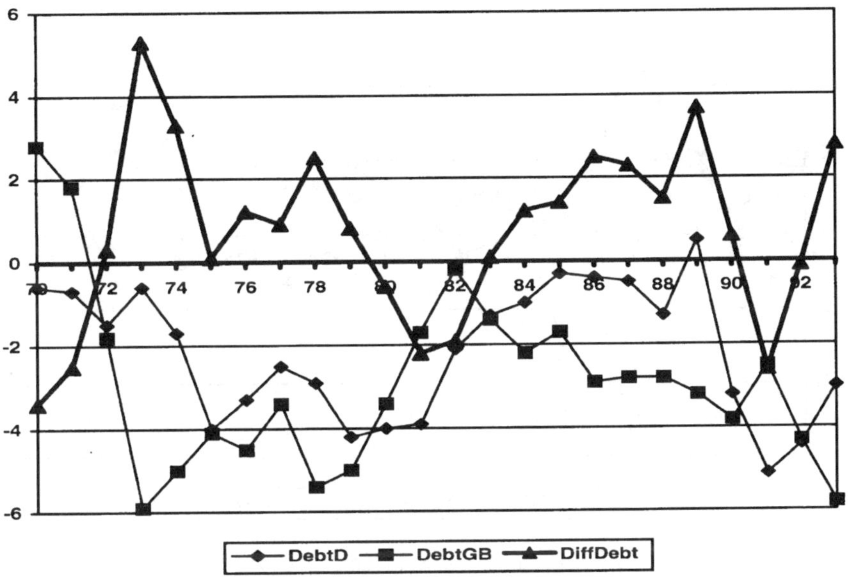


Source: Europäische Wirtschaft, Nr. 60, 1995

Figure 8: Comparative fiscal policy

Finally, some light must be shed on the monetary policy stance of both economies. The short term restrictive effect of monetary policy on output and employment growth is largely undisputed (see Heise 1996, Ragnitz 1994, Spahn 1988). Disputed, however, are long term effects (see Kaehler / Korn 1995): on the one hand, the transmission mechanism from short term- to long term interest rates is still obscured, on the other hand, modelling of expectations plays a crucial role in the transmission process. The latter is vitally important in the case of Britain as the structural break in monetary policy orientation which occured in the UK with the incoming Thatcher-government (see Minford 1988, Healey 1993) ought to have altered long term expectations of economic agents concerning the tolerated inflation rate and the prospective conduct of the Bank of England. This kind of expectation effect, however, renders the investigation of long term interest rates – which are most important for the investment-, employment- and growth performance – much more difficult: the decisive variable in this respect – the *real* interest rate –

has to be constructed by deflating *nominal* long term interest rates with the *expected* inflation rate. But, although the determination of inflation expectations is a most intricate task under any circumstances (for some attempts see Kaehler / Korn 1995 and Alogoskoufis / Smith 1991), it is impossible to achieve in the presence of structural breaks without the need to rely on arbitrary settings.

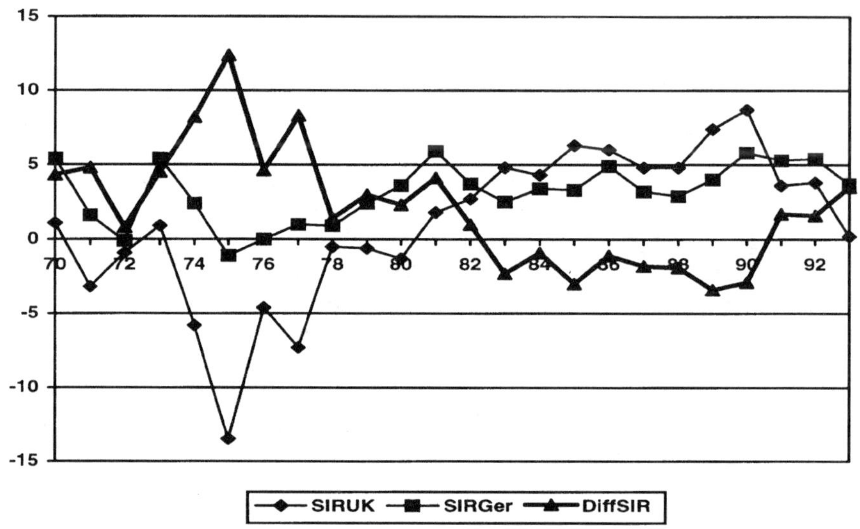


Quelle: SVR-Jahresgutachten 1996; Europäische Wirtschaft, Nr. 54, 1993

Note: SIR: short term real interest rate: short term nominal interest rate / deflator private consumption

Figure 9: Comparative monetary policy

For an appraissal of monetary policy orientation, the short term interest rate is a more appropriate indicator anyway. In addition, it is not flawed by the above-mentioned caveats as the approximation of the expected (short term) inflation rate by the actual level of inflation can readily be accepted. Figure 9 shows several features: (1) both economies experienced a more restrictive policy stance during the 1980s as compared to the 1970s – whereby the shift was stronger in the UK although it came later. (2) Half way through the 1980s both economies saw a parallel slackening in monetary conditions in reaction to the stock exchange crash in 1987 and as consequence of Britain's *de facto* entry to the EMS ('shadowing the Deutschmark'). (3) Monetary tightening in reaction to German unification in the early 1990s was at first followed by the UK under aggravated conditions. When the British labour market collapsed – unemployment doubled in two years only – the UK left the EMS (in 1993) and pursued an independent, considerably less restrictive monetary policy stance.

*Table 10*

**Determinants of comparative labour market development**

1: Diff*UNR* = *a* Diff*INV* + *e*

| *a* | *e* | *F* | *DW* | *R*-square |
|---|---|---|---|---|
| – 0,718<br>(– 4,371) | – 3,011<br>(– 11,61) | 19,106 | 0,783 | 0,51 |

2: Diff*UNR* = a Diff*INV* + b Diff*DEBT* (*t* – 1) + *c* Diff*RER* (*t* – 1) + *d* Diff*SIR* + e

| *a* | *b* | *c* | *d* | *e* | *F* | *DW* | *R*-square |
|---|---|---|---|---|---|---|---|
| – 0,565<br>(– 5,103) | – 0,273<br>(– 2,727) | – 0,321<br>(– 1,845) | 0,402<br>(2,648) | – 3,668<br>(– 19,50) | 28,40 | 1,318 | 0,89 |

3: Diff*UNR* = *a* Diff*INV* + *b* Diff*INV* (*t – 1*) + *c* Diff*DEBT* + *d* Diff*DEBT* (*t* – 1) + *e* Diff*RER* + *f* Diff*RER* (*t* – 1) + *g* Diff*SIR* + *h*

| *a* | *b* | *c* | *d* | *e* | *f* | *g* | *h* | *F* | *DW* | *R*-sq. |
|---|---|---|---|---|---|---|---|---|---|---|
| – 0,53<br>(– 2,8) | 0,15<br>(1,0) | 0,27<br>(1,6) | – 0,31<br>(– 2,8) | 0,23<br>(0,8) | – 0,49<br>(– 2,3) | 0,41<br>(1,9) | – 4,72<br>(– 5,1) | 17,5 | 1,582 | 0,92 |

Note: DW: Durbin Watson test statistics

Source: see foregoing tables and figures

At this point, we want to close the circle and estimate whether the macro-economic developments just described are able to explain and predict the comparative labour market changes. Table 10 indicates that this is, indeed, the case to a very considerable extent: around 90 percent of the differences in (standardized) unemployment rates can be attributed to the differences in monetary and fiscal policy, investment levels and exchange rate changes. Taking into consideration that comparative labour market developments are also influenced by various other variables such as consumption demand growth (which has risen much stronger in the UK after the deregulation of financial markets – the 'Big Bang' – than in Germany) or participation rates (i.e. the supply side of the labour market), not much room is left for a reasoning on the lines of the neo-liberal model.

## V. Conclusions

This study has found little empirical evidence to support the neo-liberal claim, so prominently featured in the political and academic discussions today, that deregulation of the labour market (as a mean) will increase wage moderation and flexibility (as an intermediate end) and, as is promised by the proponents of such a policy, consequently produce a reduction in unemployment.[17] Rather, we have seen that changes in the labour market can be correlated with patterns of private and public investment behaviour[18] and macro-policy behaviour:

(1) The dramatic increase in unemployment in Britain in the early 1980s and in Germany in the early 1990s, can be attributed to a fatal policy mix of monetary restriction, fiscal consolidation and exchange rate appreciation.

(2) The performance of the UK economy during the second half of the 1980s also provides support for the view that unemployment can be reduced by as much as 50 per cent if macro-policy initiates and support a cyclical upturn. The essential investment boom of that period was initiated and fostered by an expensionary macro-policy, but was also facilitated by autonomous factors such as the 'extra-boom' of European integration after the Single European Act and the 'Lawson boom' after financial deregulation (Big Bang) in the UK.

(3) Macro-policy should, however, be carefully gauged: too great a macro push will lead inevitably to monetary restriction (i.e. stop-go economics), if capacity growth does not match demand growth and a profit- and income inflation will result. The economic performance of both Britain and Germany between 1989 and 1993 exemplifies badly gauged and unco-ordinated macro-policy.

(4) Current economic performance shows a lower unemployment rate in the UK for the first time since 1975. This is consistent with the above reasoning: fiscal policy (structural public deficts of between 4.0 and 5.8 percent of GDP in Britain and 2.0 and 2.2 percent in Germany, despite the huge financial burden of unification), as well as monetary policy (after the UK left the exchange rate mechanism of EMS) was clearly less restrictive in Britain than in Germany, and was reinforced by the depreciation of Sterling and the appreciation of the Deutschmark (the anchor currency of the crumbling EMS), which undermined Germany's export performance.

Like Britain in the early 1980s, Germany in the early 1990s suffered from a similarily restrictive monetary and fiscal policy in preparation for European Monetary Union. This was aggravated by exchange rate distortions, unlike in the early 1980s when the undervaluation of the Deutschmark offset the cyclical downturn. It is only the current weakness of the Deutschmark since autumn 1996, foreshadowing the European Monetary Union, and the parallel strength of Sterling (accompanying the US-dollar) which altered the picture and triggered off a reciprocal movement of the business cycle of both countries.

---

17 Which does not imply that institutional change in Britain was without consequences: on the one hand, it aggravated poverty problems (and the situation of the 'working poor'; see Leslie/Pu 1996 and Glyn/Miliband 1994), on the other hand, it enhanced productivity growth; see table 1.

18 At this point, we should not forget to mention that the public investment share has dropped by half during the past two decades.

While the importance of monetary and fiscal policy has been made clear, exchange rate strategy is less straightforward. On the one hand, the 'policy of undervaluation' is played on the backs of the trading partners and may therefore cause similar reactions on their part. On the other hand, the valuation of a currency may be altered due to changing conditions – quite independently of the general policy: i.e. the hegemonic currency of an exchange rate system with fixed parities, such as the EMS until 1993, is *undervalued* in principle, while the hegemonic currency of an exchange rate system with floating parities, such as the EMS since 1993, is *overvalued* in principle (see Heise 1994). This, of course, sheds a particular light on the shaping of exchange rate arrangements and, especially in the case of a regionally hegemonic currency like the Deutschmark, the necessity of European Monetary Union.

In the light of the aforementioned I would like to propose the following: that the negligence of macro-policy or, put another way, its replacement by monetarist austerity, undermines the welfare system of highly developed economies and creates an environment where the deregulation of markets and the downsizing of social security seems inevitable. Firstly, this is done under the 'war-cry' of 'supply-side economics' in order to restore the rate of return on capital. Later, when supply-side policy has lost its appeal, globalisation helps to keep the pressure up on labour in order to permanently maintain high capital profitability. Once this policy has become dominant, Keynesian style demand management may possibly see a revival – although without mention – in order to create labour market success, which serves as proof for the superiority of deregulation.

## Literature

*Alesina,* A., *Perotti,* R.: Income distribution, political instability, and investment; in: European Economic Review, Vol. 40, No.6, 1996, pp. 1203 - 1228. – *Alogoskoufis,* G., *Smith,* R.: The Phillips Curve, the Persistance of Inflation, and the Lucas Critique: Evidence from Exchange-Rate Regimes; in: American Economic Review, Vol. 81, 1991, pp. 1254 - 1275. – *Appelbaum,* E., *Schettkat,* R.: Das Ende der Vollbeschäftigung? Zur Wirtschaftsentwicklung in Industrieländern; in: Wirtschaftsdienst, Heft 4, 1994, pp. 193 - 202. – *Appelbaum,* E., *Schettkat,* R.: The Importance of Labor Market Institutions for Economic Development; in: Gerlach, K., Schettkat, R. (Hrsg.), Beiträge zur neukeynesianischen Makroökonomie, Berlin, 1996. – *Barro,* R. J.: Economic Growth in a Cross-section of Countries; in: Quarterly Journal of Economics, Vol. 106, 1991, pp. 407 - 443. – *Bean,* C. R., *Layard,* P. R. G., *Nickell,* S. J.: The Rise in Unemployment: A Multi-country Study; in: Economica, Vol. 53, Supplement, 1986, pp. S1 – S22. – *Berthold,* N., *Fehn,* R.: The Positive Economics of Unemployment and Labor Market Inflexibility; in: Kyklos, Vol.49, Fasc.4, 1996, pp. 583 - 613. – *Birk,* A., *Gries,* Th.: Amerikanisches Job-Wunder versus deutsches Produktivitätswunder – Ein Vergleich der Arbeitsmarktstrategien; in: Wirtschaftsdienst, No.1, 1997. – *Blanchflower,* D. G., *Burgess,* S. M.: Job Creation and Job Destruction in Britain: 1980 - 1990, CEPR Discussion Paper No.912, 1994. – *Bruno,* M., *Sachs,* J. D.: The Economics of Worldwide Stagflation, Cambridge (Mass.), 1985. – *Butcher,* S., *Hart,* D.: An analysis of working time 1979 - 1994; in: Employment Gazette, (May) 1995, pp. 211 - 231. – *Calmfors,* L., *Drifill,* J.: Bargaining structure, corporatism and macroeconomic performance; in: Economic Policy, Heft 1, 1988. – *Cramer,* U., *Koller,* M.: Gewinne und Verluste von Arbeitsplätzen in Betrieben – der 'Job-Turnover'-Ansatz; in: Mitteilungen aus der Arbeitsmarkt- und Berufsforschung, Heft3, 1988. – *Elliot,* R., *White,* M.: Recent Developments in the Industrial Wage Structure of the UK; in: Cambirdge Journal of Economics, Vol. 17, 1993, pp. 109 - 129. – *Flassbeck,* H.: Deutschland – kein Standort für Investitionen?; in: WSI-Mitteilungen, Heft 11, 1995, pp. 699 - 704. – *Flassbeck,* H.: Reallöhne und Arbeitslosigkeit – Eine einfache empirische Widerlegung der neoklassischen Beschäftigungstheorie; in: WSI-Mitteilungen, Heft 4, 1998, pp. 233 - 241. – *Fourastié,* J.: Le Grand Espoir du XXe Siecle, Paris 1949. – *Freeman,* R,: Labor Market Institutions and Economic Performance; in: Economic Policy, Vol. 6, 1988, pp. 63 - 80. – *Gaß,* G., *Schmid,* A.: Lohn- und Arbeitsmarktentwicklung in den USA – Einige Anmerkungen zu neueren Tendenzen; in: WSI-Mitteilungen, Heft 5, 1994, pp. 290 - 299. – *Giersch,* H., *Paqué,* K.-H., *Schmieding,* H.: The fading miracle, Cambridge, 1992. – *Glyn,* A., *Miliband,* D. (eds.): Paying for Inequality. The Economic Cost of Social Injustice, London, 1994. – *Healey,* N. M.: The Conservative Government's 'Fight against Inflation': Ten Years without Cheers; in: Healey, N. M. (ed.); Britain's Economic Miracle. Myth or Reality?, London 1993, pp. 127 - 148. – *Heilemann,* U.: Das RWI-Konjunkturmodell; in: RWI (Hrsg.), Arbeit mit ökonometrischen Modellen, Essen, 1991, pp. 77 - 220. – *Heise,* A.: Lohnzurückhaltung, Arbeitszeitverkürzung und Beschäftigung: einige Anmerkungen; in: WSI-Mitteilungen, Heft 1, 1993, pp. 30 - 34. – *Heise,* A.: Haben wir ein Wechselkursproblem?; in: Wirtschaftsdienst, Heft 1, 1994, pp. 30 - 34. – *Heise,* A.: Lohnzurückhaltung und Beschäftigung – wider den unkritischen Empirismus; in: Wirtschaft und Gesellschaft, Heft 2, 1995; pp. 235 - 245. – *Heise,* A.: Arbeit für Alle – Vision oder Illusion?, Marburg 1996. – *Heise,* A.: Deregulation and employment in Britain and Germany, Anglo-German Foundation Report, London 1997a. – *Heise,* A.: Wage Differentials between Skilled and Unskilled Workers; in: Jahrbücher für Nationalökonomie und Statistik, Vol. 216, No. 3, 1997b, pp. 368 - 372. – *Heise,* A.: Ungleichheit und Beschäftigung aus makroökononischer Perspektive; in: Heise, A. (ed.); Renaissance der Makroökonomik, Marburg 1998. – *Hyclak,* Th., *Johnes,* G.: Regional Wage Inflation and Unemployment Dynamics in Great Britain; in: Scottish Journal of Political Economy, Vol. 39, No.2, 1992, pp. 188 - 200. – *Jessop,* B.: Thatcherism and Flexibility: The White Heat of a Post-Fordist Revolution; in: Jessop, B., Kastendieck, H., Nielsen K., Pedersen, O. K. (eds.); The Politics of Flexibility. Restructuring State and Industry in Britain, Germany and Scandinavia, Aldershot 1991, pp. 135 - 161. – *Johnes,* G., *Hyclak,* Th.: Wage Inflation and Unemployment in Europe: The Regional Dimension; in: Regional Studies, Vol. 23, No.1, 1989, pp. 19 - 26. – *Kaehler,* J., *Korn,* O.: Wirkungszusammenhänge zwischen Zinsen und makroökonomischer Aktivität, Baden-Baden, 1995. – *Kaldor,* N.: Causes of Growth and Stagnation in the World Economy, Cambridge 1996. – *Keller,* B., *Seifert,* H.: Eine Zwischenbilanz der Deregulierung; in: WSI-Mitteilungen, Heft 8, 1997, pp. 522 - 531. – *Kormendi,* R., *Meguire,* P.: Macroeconomic Determinants of Growth: Cross-Country Evidence; in: Journal of Monetary Economics, Vol. 16, 1985, pp. 141 - 163. – *Krupp,* H. J.: Gibt es in der Bundesrepublik einen Rückstand in der Entwicklung von Dienstleistungen?; in: Allgemeines Statistisches Archiv, Vol. 71, 1987, pp. 56 - 75. – *Lamfalussy,* A.: The United Kongdom and the Six, London 1963. – *Lehment,* H.: Bedingungen für einen kräftigen Beschäftigungsanstieg in der Bundesrepublik Deutschland – Zur Tarifpolitik der kommenden Jahre; in: Die Weltwirtschaft, Heft 3, 1993, pp. 302 - 310. – *Leslie,* D., *Pu,* Y.: What Caused Rising Earnings Inequality in Britain? Evidence from Time Series; in: British Journal of Industrial Relations, Vol. 34, No. 1,

1996, pp. 111 - 136. – *Levine,* R., *Zervos,* S. J.: What We Have Learned About Policy and Growth from Cross-Country Regressions; in: American Economic Review, Vol. 83, No. 2, Papers & Proceedings, 1993, pp. 426 - 430. – *Minford,* P.: Mrs. Thatcher's Economic Reform Programme – Past, Present and Future; in: Skidelsky, R. (ed.); Thatcherism, London 1988, pp. 93 - 106. – *Möller,* J., *Bellmann,* L.: Qualifikations- und industriespezifische Lohnunterschiede in der Bundesrepublik Deutschland; in: ifo-Studien, No.2, 1996, pp. 235 - 272. – *Newell,* A., *Symons,* J.: Corporatism, Laissez-faire and the Rise in Unemployment; in: European Economic Review, Vol. 31, 1987, pp. 567 - 614. – *Ochel,* W., *Schreyer,* P.: Beschäftigungsentwicklung im Bereich unternehmensorientierter Dienstleistungen: USA – Bundesrepublik im Vergleich; Beiheft der Konjunkturpolitik No. 35, Berlin, 1988, pp. 139 - 173. – *OECD:* Economic Survey – United Kongdom, Paris 1994. – *Olson,* M.: The Rise and Decline of Nations, New Haven, 1982. – *Olson,* M.: The varieties of Eurosclerosis: the rise and decline of nations since 1982; in: Crafts, N., Toniolo, G. (Hrsg.), Economic Growth in Europe since 1945, Cambridge, 1996, pp. 73 - 94. – *O'Mahony,* M., *Wagner,* K., *Paulssen,* M.: Changing Fortunes: an industry study of British and German productivity growth over three decades, WZB discussion paper FS I 94 - 304, Berlin, 1994. – *Paqué,* K.-H.: Why the 1950s are not the 1920s? Olsonian and Non-Olsonian interpretations of two decades of German economic history; in: Crafts, N., Toniolo, G. (Hrsg.), Economic Growth in Europe since 1945, Cambridge, 1996a, pp. 95 - 106. – *Paqué,* K.-H.: Flexibilität und Differenzierung der Lohnstruktur; in: Wirtschaftswissenschaftliches Studium, Heft 3, 1996b, pp. 112 - 118. – *Persson,* T., *Tabellini,* G.: Is Inequality Harmful for Growth?; in: American Economic Review, Vol. 84, 1994, pp. 600 - 621. – *Ragnitz,* J.: Zinsstruktur und Wirtschaftswachstum; in: Kredit und Kapital, H.1 / 1994, pp. 11 - 29. – *Rowthorn,* B., *Glyn,* A.: The Diversity of Unemployment Experience since 1973; in: Marglin, S., Schor, J. B. (eds.), The Golden Age of Capitalism, Oxford, 1991, pp. 218 - 264. – *Scharpf,* F. W.: Structures of Postindustrial Societies or Does Mass Unemployment disappear in the Service and Information Economy?; in: Appelbaum, E., Schettkat, R. (eds.); Labor Market Adjustments to Structural Change and Technological Progress, New York 1990, pp. 17 - 35. – *Schettkat,* R.: The Labor Market Dynamics of Economic Restructuring. The United States and Germany in Transition, New York 1992. – *Siebert,* H.: Geht den Deutschen die Arbeit aus?, München 1994. – *Soskice,* D.: Wage Determination: The Changing Role of Institutions in Advanced Industrialised Countries; in: Oxford Review of Economic Policy, Vol. 6, No.4, 1990. – *Spahn,* H-P.: Bundesbank und Wirtschaftskrise, Regensburg, 1988. – *Standing,* G.: Globilazation, Labour Flexibility and Insecurity: The Era of Market Regulation; in: European Journal of Industrial Relations, Vol. 3, No. 1, 1997, pp. 7 - 37. – *Turner,* Ph., *Van 't dack,* J.: Measuring International Price and Cost Competitiveness, BIS Economic Papers No. 39, 1993. – *Wells,* J.: The Economy after Ten Years: Stronger or Weaker?; in: Healey, N. M. (ed.), Britain's Economic Miracle. Myth or Reality?, London, New York, 1993, pp. 91 - 108. – *Werner,* H.: Die Arbeitsmarktentwicklung in den USA – Lehren für uns?; in: Mitteilungen aus der Arbeitsmarkt- und Berufsforschung, No. 3, 1997, pp. 585 - 600. – *Wood,* S.: Weakening Codetermination? Works Council Reform in West Germany in the 1980s, WZB discussion paper FS I 97 - 302. – *Zachert,* U., *Bobke,* M. H.: Koalitions-, Tarif- und Arbeitskampfrecht; in: Kittner, M. (Hrsg.), Gewerkschafts-Jahrbuch 1987, Köln 1987, pp. 336 - 373. – *Zweimüller,* J., Barth, E.: Bargaining structure, wage determination, and wage dispersion in 6 OECD countries; in: Kyklos, Vol. 47, 1994, pp. 81 - 93.

# Reducing Unemployment in an Era of Low Inflationary Expectations

By Derek Hum*, Wayne Simpson, and Norman Cameron, Winnipeg / Manitoba

## I. Introduction

Throughout the 1990s Canada pursued a policy of low inflation. In 1993, the federal government and the Bank of Canada jointly announced that inflation would be kept within a range of one to three per cent per annum between 1995 and 1998. This has been achieved, since inflation (excluding indirect taxes) has remained stable near two per cent or lower since 1994. The present target range for inflation has just been extended for a further three years and many wonder whether such success in fighting inflation has not come at too great a cost in terms of high unemployment. Indeed, the Governor of the Bank of Canada himself posed the question, albeit rhetorically, asking "... whether the Bank's focus on low inflation leads to a monetary policy that fails to support the growth of incomes and employment in our economy" (Speech to Toronto Board of Trade, 6 November 1996). Combined with the reduction of government expenditures (federal and provincial) and the success of the federal government in eliminating its budget deficit, an announced target of price stability by the Central Bank should prolong the current era of low inflationary expectations.

Macroeconomists generally believe that any rate of inflation is consistent with the natural rate of unemployment in the economy. Since lower inflation is presumed to be better – better for investment, better for resource allocation, better for productivity, better for employment and real incomes, etc. – many maintain that zero inflation is the proper goal. According to this view, the Bank of Canada, with the approval of the federal government, should set monetary policy to achieve absolute price stability as its long-term objective.[1] On the other hand, detractors argue that achieving zero inflation is not costless and that the costs likely outweigh

* We would like to thank Robert Amano and Advin Pagtakhan of the Bank of Canada for making the settlements data available to us. The viewpoints, interpretations, and errors in this paper are the responsibility of the authors.

1 Allowance must be made for the inflationary bias inherent in the Consumer Price Index. Erwin Diewert (1998) examines the bias associated with US index number measures. In private conversation he "guesses" the bias in the Canadian CPI to be "about 1% upwards". Since the Canadian CPI is rising at 1% or less, Canada has effectively achieved zero inflation.

any benefits compared to moderate and steady inflation (Lucas, 1989). For example, Fortin (1991) argues that the unemployment cost of achieving and maintaining zero inflation is underestimated and, if properly calculated, would far exceed any benefits from further inflation reduction. Moreover, the major benefits of low inflation – increased productivity growth – have not been clearly established (Cameron, Hum and Simpson, 1996).

Those who argue that the costs of very low inflation are significant generally appeal to wage and price rigidities or some other cause of hysteresis effects in the natural rate of unemployment. Several recent papers have pointed to evidence that workers resist pay cuts. Fortin (1996) examines Canadian wage settlements involving 500 or more workers for 1992 - 94 and finds that most settlements are zero, some settlements are positive, but negative settlements are noticeably absent. Similar evidence from the U.S. supports the idea of effective resistance to nominal wage reductions over a longer period for both union and nonunion workers. Akerlof, Dickens and Perry (1996,8) argue that the "data show a pronounced asymmetry; the part of the tail of the distribution of wage changes below zero is almost completely truncated."

The implications of resistance to nominal wage reductions for resource allocation, employment and output growth could be important. A recent study of private salaries in the U.S. over a forty-year period found that the variation in wage adjustments among occupations declined significantly when inflation fell below 4%, (Groshen and Schweitzer, 1996). During periods of low inflation, the economy loses the "grease" that permits relative wage adjustments to occur across occupations without any nominal pay cuts. Could this account, to some extent, for the weak performance of the Canadian economy in the 1990s and provide a warning against a low inflation policy?

This paper investigates the idea of resistance to nominal wage reductions – pay cuts for short- as a factor causing higher unemployment in an era of low inflationary expectations. Not surprisingly, this idea has received little attention to date. When inflation is high, fairly large real and relative wage declines are possible without pay cuts.[2] Hence, the consequences for employment and output of resistance to pay cuts are minimal until the inflation rate is quite small. The 1990s, with their low inflation, offer the first episode in recent decades where clear evidence of resistance to pay cuts could be expected. Therefore, it should now be possible to detect any impact of such resistance on employment, and assess the costs of a policy which we term hypoinflation.

---

[2] Productivity growth also plays a role in this equation. If, for example, the mean real wage settlement equals the rate of productivity growth, and that growth is rapid, then there will be considerable room for variation in real and relative wages about the mean settlement without any group of workers being forced to accept pay cuts. Thus, high productivity growth during earlier periods of low inflation should have limited the importance of pay-cut resistance. In any case, the productivity growth rate is now quite low and, to simplify the exposition, we have ignored this effect in our discussion.

The next section uses microdata to elaborate on Fortin's evidence for Canada for both union and nonunion workers. Since this data shows considerable evidence of resistance to pay cuts, we discuss the ramifications of this behaviour for wage bargaining. We next estimate the effect of this pay cut resistance on wages and employment. In particular, we estimate the extent to which the jobless recovery since 1993 may be attributed to pay-cut resistance as low inflation reduced the room for bargaining over real and relative wages without cutting pay. We conclude by discussing the implications of our findings for future policy.

## II. Do Canadians Resist Pay Cuts during Low Inflation?

We first summarize the evidence from the Canadian settlements data for bargaining units of 500 or more workers. We focus on the first year of each agreement, since many agreements do not extend beyond one year.[3] Moreover, the first year of multiyear agreements is likely to be the most responsive to economic conditions. Table 1 presents the distribution of total agreements into pay cuts, pay freezes (zero settlements), and pay increases for each year from January, 1978 to August, 1995.

The incidence of pay cuts is very low until 1994. When inflation is high during the 1978 - 81 period, there are virtually no zero settlements, let alone pay cuts. With high average nominal settlements, there is considerable negotiating room for substantial real and relative wage cuts without cutting nominal wages. When inflation declines during the 1983 - 86 recession, pay cuts are more frequent but, except for 1983, still less than 1% of all settlements. Of course, inflation never falls below 4% in this period, still providing room for up to a 4% real wage decline without a pay cut. During the recovery from 1987 to 1990, when inflation rises to 5%, pay cuts virtually disappear again. But when inflation falls again during the 1990s, the room to negotiate over real and relative wages without cutting pay virtually disappears for the first time in decades. In 1994, with inflation at 0.2%, 13.8% of settlements involve pay reductions and, perhaps even more significantly, 61.3% of all settlements are pay freezes. In 1993 and 1995, with inflation at about 2%, 60% of all settlements are pay freezes while only about 2% involve pay cuts.

The distribution of settlements for each of these episodes is presented in Figures 1 and 2. Figure 1 shows the distributions during the two episodes of higher inflation, 1978 - 81 and 1987 - 90. In each case the distribution approximates a normal distribution about a modal settlement of 10% in 1978 - 81 and 5% in 1987 - 90. There is, however, a noticeable spike at 0% for 1987 - 90, effectively truncating the distribution at that point.[4] This truncation at 0% is more prominent when we

[3] In some cases there is provision for salary renegotiation in each year of an agreement.

[4] The upper category includes all settlements exceeding 20%. The spike at this point for 1978 - 81 reflects truncation introduced by the authors. The distribution may have a positive skew for this period.

*Table 1*

**Incidence of Pay Cuts, Pay Freezes, and Pay Increases in Canadian Wage Settlements, 1978 - 95**

| Year | Unemp. Rate | Inflation Rate | % Pay Cuts | % Pay Freezes | % Pay Increases |
|---|---|---|---|---|---|
| 1978 | 8.3% | 7.2% | 0.1% | 0.3% | 99.6% |
| 1979 | 7.4 | 9.7 | 0.0 | 0.2 | 99.8 |
| 1980 | 7.5 | 11.3 | 0.0 | 0.2 | 99.8 |
| 1981 | 7.5 | 12.0 | 0.0 | 0.2 | 99.8 |
| 1982 | 11.0 | 9.3 | 0.2 | 0.6 | 99.2 |
| 1983 | 11.8 | 4.5 | 2.7 | 7.7 | 89.5 |
| 1984 | 11.3 | 4.4 | 0.9 | 25.7 | 73.4 |
| 1985 | 10.5 | 3.9 | 0.6 | 19.0 | 80.5 |
| 1986 | 9.6 | 4.2 | 0.2 | 18.1 | 81.8 |
| 1987 | 8.9 | 4.4 | 0.0 | 9.4 | 90.6 |
| 1988 | 7.8 | 4.0 | 0.4 | 4.1 | 95.6 |
| 1989 | 7.5 | 5.0 | 0.0 | 3.8 | 96.2 |
| 1990 | 8.1 | 4.8 | 0.0 | 0.8 | 99.2 |
| 1991 | 10.4 | 5.6 | 0.5 | 20.3 | 79.2 |
| 1992 | 11.3 | 1.5 | 0.8 | 13.6 | 85.6 |
| 1993 | 11.2 | 1.8 | 2.5 | 58.6 | 38.9 |
| 1994 | 10.4 | 0.2 | 13.8 | 61.3 | 24.9 |
| 1995[a] | 9.6 | 2.2 | 2.5 | 60.7 | 36.8 |

Note: [a] Data for 1995 is from January to August

Source: Wage settlements in unions with 500 or more workers from Labour Canada; unemployment and inflation rates from the *Bank of Canada Review*

look at the distributions during episodes with lower settlements, 1983 - 86 and 1993- 95, in Figure 2. The pattern in 1983 - 86 is similar to 1987 - 90 because the inflation rates are comparable.[5] In 1993 - 95, however, the pay freeze category dominates all settlements, as Fortin (1996, 779) illustrated. Instead of a distribution of settlements along the negative half of the horizontal axis, we have virtually no pay cuts and a plethora of pay freezes.

The above evidence refers only to base rate settlements of large bargaining units. Nickell (1997) notes that union wage negotiations determine the wages of many other workers who are not part of union bargaining. He presents a "coverage index" to capture the structure of wage determination for different countries. On a three point scale, Canada receives a value of 2, representing 25 - 70% of workers deemed covered by union bargaining. Germany is assigned a value of 3, represent-

[5] During 1983 - 86 the average unemployment rate is close to 11%, putting greater downward pressure on wages than during 1987 - 90 when the average unemployment rate is 8%.

ing more than 70% covered. We examined two other Canadian data sets to determine whether the distribution of wage increases for more broadly defined groups is comparable with that for workers in large bargaining units in recent years. The 1989 - 90 Labour Market Activity Survey (LMAS) is a longitudinal microdata file, and the 1993 Survey of Labour and Income Dynamics (SLID) is a panel design, with only the first wave reported.

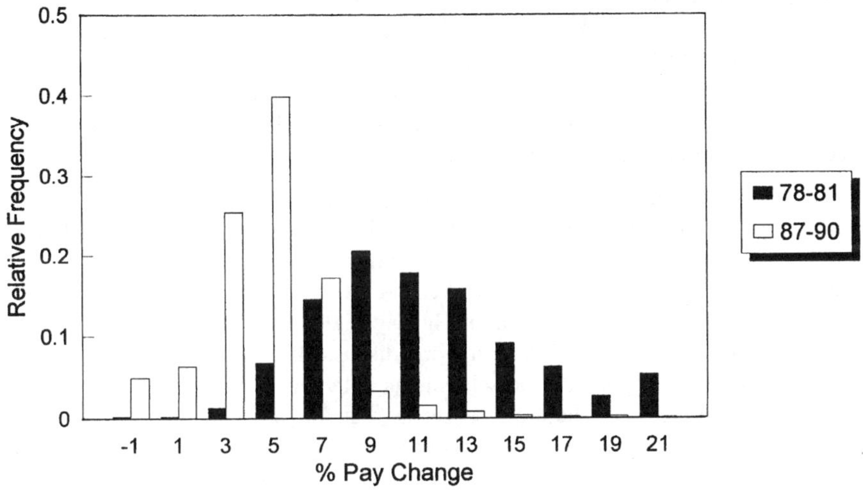


Figure 1: Settlements Distribution – High Inflation

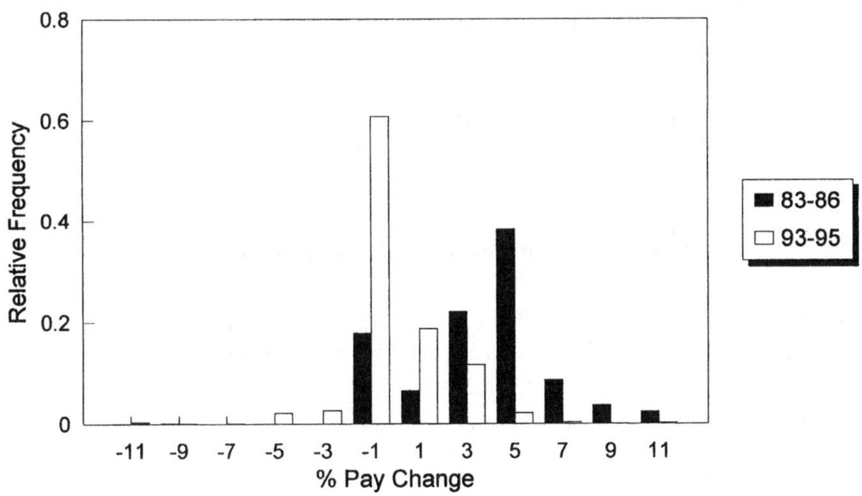


Figure 2: Settlements Distribution – Low Inflation

For the LMAS we chose workers who held the same job in 1989 and 1990, whose job was full-time, and who were paid hourly. The LMAS provided 1085 workers who were covered by a collective agreement and 1099 uncovered workers. The measure of wage rate changes differs from the settlements data because it reflects wage changes from all sources, including career increments and undetected promotions and demotions, not just base salary increases.[6] Perhaps more importantly, there may also be more measurement error, generating spurious changes in wage rates, judging from other experiences with longitudinal microdata (e.g., Hammermesh, 1987; Bjorklund, 1989; Bound and Krueger, 1991). Akerlof, Dickens and Perry (1996, 12 - 17) estimate that more than half of the pay rates in the U.S. Panel Study of Income Dynamics are reported inexactly and that, for union workers, up to 85% of reported pay cuts are spurious. In other words, we can expect much more noise in this type of data.

The 1993 SLID is an even better source, since it reflects the more recent period when inflation is under 2% and provides little room for real wage adjustments without pay cuts. Moreover, the sample is larger for SLID, involving 4,028 covered workers and 5,856 uncovered workers. Although the SLID is not yet longitudinal, it provides a starting and ending hourly rate for paid workers who had the same job throughout 1993. The limitations discussed above in comparing annual individual wage changes with the settlements data also hold for the SLID results, however. Much the same picture emerges as that for the settlement data; furthermore, the distribution of pay changes is very similar for both covered and uncovered workers and that there is a concentration around zero.[7]

In sum, there is evidence of resistance to pay cuts in the data we examined. The distribution of wage increases during low inflation is generally truncated at zero rather than spread symmetrically over a range of pay cuts. This pattern is particularly clear in the union settlements data for 1993 - 95 (Figure 2). Moreover, the microdata indicate that the distribution of pay changes is comparable between union and non-union workers, suggesting that resistance to pay cuts is widespread across the Canadian economy. But what is the consequence of such resistance on unemployment?

## III. Can Pay Cut Resistance Affect Employment?

Standard economic analysis concludes that the effect of wage bargaining on employment is ambiguous when contracts are efficient (McDonald and Solow, 1981).

6 The LMAS and SLID treat promotions, demotions and transfers as a job change unless they are undetected. The proportion of such job changes is small, however, suggesting that many of them may be unreported.

7 For space reasons, we omit presentation of these data. The results are available from the authors on request.

We argue that resistance to a pay cut, which has not been considered in these models, modifies this conclusion. When a pay cut is resisted, and an efficient contract is struck, the effect is always to reduce employment below what it would have been if the pay cut had been accepted. We then ask what the implications are for employment growth across sectors of the economy. The next section tests these implications.

The conventional bargaining model starts by describing the preferences of workers and the firm for real wages and employment. For the firm, the implied trade-offs between wages and employment are derived from profit maximization. For any real wage rate, there is a profit-maximizing level of employment which defines a point on the downward-sloping demand curve for labour; at a higher wage rate, the firm will always choose a lower level of employment if it can, thereby resulting in more unemployment. The model then demonstrates that an efficient bargain (a bargain which exploits available gains from trade and which cannot be improved upon without making one of the parties worse off) implies a level of employment that is higher than that implied by the demand curve for labour. This remarkable result, which has empirical support (e.g., MacCurdy and Pencavel, 1986), refutes the negative trade-off between employment and wages implied by the demand curve for labour. Unions may be able to bargain for higher wages and higher employment; in any case, they can normally do better than the trade-off implied by the demand curve for labour.

In this type of bargaining model, the pay cut resistance observed in the previous section can be described in terms of a preference by workers to oppose pay cuts regardless of the consequences for job security and employment. For unionized workers, this could reflect a median voter with sufficient job security who is willing to accept lower real wages in order to protect the employment of more junior co-workers, but only up to a point. When the nominal settlement must decline to maintain employment, the median voter opts for a pay freeze rather than a pay cut regardless of the employment consequences. This means that the indifference curves describing union preferences for wages and employment must be flat (when employment is on the horizontal axis and real wages is on the vertical axis) in the vicinity of a pay freeze. When unions protect wages in this fashion, however, the efficient bargain is no longer distinct from the demand curve for labour. The firm will choose the level of employment that maximizes profits along the downward-sloping demand-for-labour curve. In the vicinity of a pay freeze, there must therefore be a negative trade-off between pay and employment, and pay cut resistance can only be achieved by permitting employment to be lower than it would have been if a pay cut had been accepted.[8]

[8] Moreover, since other bargains involve higher levels of employment than are implied by the demand-for- labour curve, the trade-off between employment and wages must be worse in the vicinity of a pay freeze than for bargains at higher wage levels. That is, prevention of a \$1 pay cut requires larger employment sacrifices than attainment of an additional \$1 pay increase. Further discussion is given in the appendix.

The implications of this result are that the employment effects of wage bargaining will differ depending upon the level of inflation. Compare, for example, the circumstances during earlier business cycles (in the late 70s and mid-80s) with those of the most recent cycle (the mid-90s). Even at the troughs of the earlier cycles inflation remained relatively high, never falling below 4%. Such rates of inflation provide considerable room for real wage adjustment without pay cuts. During the most recent cycle, however, inflation declined nearly to zero. What can we expect to happen to wages and employment in these different circumstances? When inflation is sufficiently high, as it was during earlier cycles, no clear relationship between wages and employment can be predicted. As output contracts, employment may be protected through modest settlements which permit inflation to erode real wages.[9] During the current cycle, however, modest settlements will not reduce real wages. Even pay freezes will only reduce real wages marginally. But pay cuts can only be resisted at the expense of employment loss (the magnitude of which would depend on the slope of the firm's demand curve for labour). Whereas a great deal of employment could be protected during earlier recessions without pay cuts, this is not possible in the hypoinflation of the 1990s. If pay cuts are generally resisted, as the evidence suggests, then employment must decline more sharply than in earlier cycles.

## IV. Evidence on the Employment Effects of Pay Cut Resistance

The effects of the business cycle on wage bargaining and employment differ across sectors of the economy and, within each sector, across firms. Some sectors scarcely notice a recession that hits other sectors hard, and some firms in sectors hit hard fare much better than others. In terms of bargaining, this means that wage settlements and their employment implications will differ across sectors and across firms within a sector.

Our main interest is to see if pay cut resistance has an impact on employment growth, particularly during periods of low inflation, as suggested by the previous section. Our strategy is to use data on employment and output by sector (two-digit SIC) available from Statistics Canada along with the settlements data (aggregated to the same two-digit SIC level) to analyze the effect of pay resistance on employment for different episodes of inflation. Firms that are forced by (unobserved) circumstances specific to the sector and / or the firm to entertain pay cuts will, when pay cuts are resisted, be expected to reduce employment. Thus, when more settlements that involve pay freezes and pay cuts are observed in a sector, we would expect lower employment growth. To account for other cyclical differences across sectors, we use the output growth rate.

---

9 In actual fact, real wages appear to be only weakly procyclical at best. For a recent review of the issues and evidence, focussed on the U.S. economy, see Abraham and Haltiwanger (1995).

*Table 2a*

**Mean Values of Sectoral Data**

| | Employment Growth | % Pay Freezes or Cuts | Output Growth |
|---|---|---|---|
| 1978 - 81 | 2.65% | 0.32% | 2.61% |
| 1983 - 86 | 2.12% | 20.55% | 5.37% |
| 1987 - 90 | 2.21% | 6.10% | 2.72% |
| 1993 - 95 | 0.82% | 54.97% | 2.79% |
| All periods | 2.15% | 14.61% | 3.67% |

Sources: Employment growth and output growth by 2-digit SIC calculated from Statistics Canada series (Cansim matrices 9639 and 7916 and cat. no. 72 - 202); % pay freezes or cuts from Labour Canada wage settlements data. Calculations by authors.

Note: Means are weighted by the number of settlements in each sector.

Table 2a presents the mean values for employment growth, the incidence of pay freezes or cuts, and output growth by time period weighted by the number of settlements in each sector. The time periods are the same as those used in section 2. They represent different inflation and unemployment episodes recently experienced by the Canadian economy. The periods are long enough to permit a sufficient number of settlements to occur, but not so long that inflation conditions change dramatically. These periods of fairly steady inflation should permit firms and unions to predict inflation moderately well and incorporate those expectations into their negotiating behaviour.

The incidence of pay cuts or freezes rises as employment growth declines over these time periods, as depicted in Figures 1 and 2 earlier. Incidence is much higher during the slower employment growth periods of 1983 - 86 and, especially, 1993 - 95. These two periods illustrate the "jobless recovery," although output growth was larger during the 1983- 86 recovery. In both recoveries, there was substantial excess labour capacity, hoarded during the recession, to work off. An important difference is that the inflation rate was higher in 1983 - 86, leaving more room for real wage reductions (where necessary) without pay cuts. In 1978 - 81 and 1987 - 90, the ratio of employment growth to output growth is roughly 1 to 1; for 1993 - 95 it is only about 0.3 and for 1983 - 86 it is only about 0.4. To what extent are these jobless recoveries, particularly the one in 1993 - 95, related to resistance to pay cuts as inflation declines?

Table 2b presents ordinary least squares regression results to explain employment growth by sector in terms of the incidence of pay freezes or cuts in the sector and output growth in the sector for the four inflationary episodes.[10] In effect, this allows

10 Wage settlements and employment growth are jointly determined by changes in the incidence of pay cut resistance and output growth in our model. In effect, we are estimating a reduced-form employment growth equation to assess the impact of pay cut resistance. Thus, ordinary least squares regression should provide consistent estimates.

us to assess the impact of pay cut resistance on employment growth in different inflationary conditions after accounting for differences in output growth across sectors. This will permit us to disentangle the employment effects of pay cut resistance from the employment effects of output growth during each of these periods.

The effect of pay cut resistance, measured by the incidence of pay freezes or cuts, is negative for each period as expected and significant at the 5% level in every period except 1983 - 86. The results confirm that a sector with a high incidence of pay freezes or cuts experiences a lower rate of employment growth after adjusting for differences in output growth across sectors. The very large coefficient estimate for 1978 - 81 is surprising, but it is based on a very small number of observed pay freezes and cuts.[11] The effect of output growth is positive and significant in every period as expected. The coefficient estimate drops sharply in 1993 - 95 from earlier periods, reflecting the jobless recovery experience observed in the aggregate data in Table 2a.[12]

*Table 2b*

**Regression Results to Explain Employment Growth Across Sectors by Inflation Episode**

| Variable | 1978 - 81 | 1983 - 86 | 1987 - 90 | 1993 - 95 |
|---|---|---|---|---|
| Constant | 2.440 | 0.293 | 0.250 | 1.359 |
| | (31.49) | (3.09) | (4.23) | (4.87) |
| % Pay Freezes or Cuts | – 93.19 | – 0.087 | – 2.36 | – 1.881 |
| | (13.74) | (0.30) | (4.73) | (4.56) |
| Output Growth | 0.196 | 0.344 | 0.775 | 0.178 |
| | (11.61) | (35.30) | (52.59) | (7.39) |
| $R^2$ | 0.188 | 0.342 | 0.558 | 0.187 |

Note: Regression is weighted by the number of settlements for each sector; dependent variable is employment growth by sector; t-values are in parentheses.

11 During 1978 - 81, only one settlement involves a pay cut (food industries) and four settlements are pay freezes (two in clothing and two in paper). These settlements are correlated with big declines in employment in those sectors during that period. The correlation may be largely spurious from our perspective, given the high inflation rate and the substantial room to bargain without cutting pay during this period.

12 We also pooled the data to assess the effect of resistance to pay cuts across all periods. The pooled results show the effect of output growth to be positive and significant, and the effect of the incidence of pay freezes or cuts to be negative and significant, as expected. To investigate the differential effect of the 1993 - 95 period of low inflation, the intercept is allowed to differ for each period and the effects of the incidence of pay freezes or cuts and output growth on employment growth are allowed to differ for 1993- 95. The results are again as one might expect. The negative impact of pay cut resistance is significantly greater for the 1993 - 95 period than for all other periods combined while the positive effect of output growth is smaller. The results suggest that the jobless recovery of 1993 - 95 is a product both of a smaller response of employment growth to output growth during that period and a greater effect of resistance to pay cuts as low inflation reduces the room for bargaining over real wages without cutting pay.

So how much has employment growth been affected by resistance to pay cuts? Our results can be used to estimate the impact by comparing actual mean employment growth with the estimated mean employment growth that would have occurred without pay freezes or cuts. These results are presented in Table 2c for each period (using results from Table 2b) and for all periods (using pooled results not reported here). Not surprisingly, the biggest effect occurs during the 1993 - 95 period. The effect of resistance to pay cuts is estimated to reduce the mean employment growth rate across sectors from 1.85% to 0.82%, or by more than half. This translates into an impact on unemployment as follows: At an unemployment rate of 10%, the ratio of unemployed to employed is 1/9, so 1% reduction in those employed is equivalent to a 9% increase in the pool of job seekers, or about a 1% increase per annum in the unemployment rate as a result of pay cut resistance.

*Table 2c*

**Estimated Effect of Pay Cut Resistance on Employment Growth**

| | Mean Employment Growth | Estimated Growth With No Pay Cut Resistance | Difference |
|---|---|---|---|
| 1978 - 81 | 2.65% | 2.95% | 0.30% |
| 1983 - 86 | 2.12% | 2.14% | 0.02% |
| 1987 - 90 | 2.21% | 2.35% | 0.14% |
| 1993 - 95 | 0.82% | 1.85% | 1.03% |
| All periods | 2.15% | 2.56% | 0.41% |

Source: Calculations by Authors

## V. The Impact of Pay Cut Resistance on Unemployment

There is another way to examine the effect of pay cut resistance using the settlements data. If there were no pay cut resistance, what would the distributions of wage settlements in Figures 1 and 2 look like? We saw in section 2 that resistance to pay cuts virtually eliminated the negative portion of those distributions. For example, the distribution for 1978 - 81 in Figure 1 is roughly normally distributed because high inflation makes pay cuts and freezes unnecessary. But, staying with Figure 1, slide the settlements distribution to the left (toward lower mean settlements) for the 1987 - 90 period as inflation falls. Pay cut resistance effectively censors the distribution at zero, where we observe a spike in place of a distribution of negative settlements. If we shift to Figure 2 and continue to slide the distribution to the left, the censoring increases. A sprinkling of pay cuts are observed, although we argue that these cuts may be smaller than one would observe in the absence of resistance to pay cuts. Thus, we combine pay freezes and pay cuts as in section 4 and consider them to be potentially censored data. What would the average settlement have been in the absence of pay cut resistance?

In the absence of pay cut resistance, the distribution of settlements might be expected to look like the distribution in 1978 - 81 during all periods. The mean distribution would shift as economic conditions change. In particular, the wage distribution would shift to the left (lower mean) as the rate of inflation in the economy falls and as the unemployment rate increases. We observe these movements of the distribution in the actual settlements, but the distribution is censored because of pay cut resistance. Maximum likelihood regression, in the form of the standard Tobit model (Tobin, 1958), permits us to estimate the underlying distribution of settlements that would have emerge without the censoring, depending on the prevailing economic conditions (inflation and unemployment rates).

The unemployment rate and the rate of inflation are standard determinants of wage settlements in the Phillips curve literature. Higher unemployment generates pressure on real wages to fall, leading to a distribution of settlements with a lower mean for a given inflation rate. Similarly, a 1% reduction in inflation can be expected to reduce the mean settlement by roughly the same amount to maintain a real wage consistent with a given inflation rate. Our measure of settlements continues to be the rate of change in pay during the first year of each agreement.

What is the implied effect of pay cut resistance from these models? We can use the Tobit results (as well as the standard OLS results) to predict settlements each month.[13] Table 3 summarizes these results for the different inflation / disinflation episodes discussed earlier. The Tobit model consistently predicts settlements to be lower than the actual or OLS predicted settlements after 1978 - 81 – that is, once inflation begins to fall and pay cut resistance is evident. The difference is fairly small through the 1980s when inflation is running at 4% or more, but the 1990s are another story. As the inflation rate falls to the 2% range and pay cut resistance is evident in the number of pay freezes among all settlements, the Tobit model predicts that settlements in the absence of pay cut resistance would be very much lower. For 1991 - 2, the model predicts that settlements would have been 2.43% instead of 3.37%. For 1993 - 95, settlements would have averaged -0.11% rather than 0.56%. In other words, pay cut resistance is estimated to raise average settlements by 0.94% in 1991 - 2 and 0.67% in 1993 - 5, generating higher labour costs and lower employment as lower inflation targets are pursued.

What increase in the unemployment rate in the short run would be required to reduce settlements by 0.94% in 1991 - 2 and 0.67% in 1993 - 5 to offset the estimated effect of pay cut resistance? If we ignore pay cut resistance by reverting to

---

13 These results are available from the authors on request. The coefficient estimate for the unemployment rate is negative and that for the inflation rate is positive (and near one) as expected, and each is highly significant. The effect of the unemployment rate and inflation rate is greater for the Tobit estimates than for the OLS estimates, reflecting the fact that wages are more responsive to labour market conditions in the absence of pay cut resistance. For example, when the inflation rate falls and the unemployment rate rises in the 1990s we expect settlements to fall more sharply under the Tobit model, which assumes there is no resistance to pay cuts.

the OLS model, the model predicts that the unemployment rate would have had to be 2.9% higher during 1991 - 2 and 2.1% higher during 1993 - 95.[14] If settlements in the economy are typical of the settlements analyzed here, the unemployment cost of pay cut resistance exceeds 2% throughout the 1990s. The effect of further disinflation meeting similar pay cut resistance would be expected to be larger still.

*Table 3*

**OLS and Tobit Predictions of Settlements, 1978 - 95**

| Period | Settlements | OLS Prediction | Tobit Prediction | % Difference: OLS vs. Tobit | Inflation Rate | Unempt Rate |
|---|---|---|---|---|---|---|
| 78.01 - 81.12 | 11.08% | 10.95% | 11.07% | -0.09% | 9.7% | 7.7% |
| 82.01 - 82.12 | 11.42 | 11.08 | 11.06 | -3.15 | 10.7 | 11.0 |
| 83.01 - 86.12 | 3.87 | 4.06 | 3.67 | -5.17 | 4.6 | 10.8 |
| 87.01 - 90.12 | 4.94 | 4.93 | 4.70 | -4.86 | 4.6 | 8.1 |
| 91.01 - 92.12 | 3.37 | 2.89 | 2.43 | -27.89 | 3.6 | 10.8 |
| 93.01 - 95.08 | 0.56 | 0.47 | -0.11 | -119.64 | 1.4 | 10.5 |
| 78.01 - 95.08 | 5.59 | 5.52 | 5.26 | -5.90 | 5.4 | 9.4 |

## VI. Is Hypoinflation Worth the Unemployment Cost?

Resistance to pay cuts, as a specific form of wage rigidity, should be a consideration in determining inflation targets, especially if a policy of hypoinflation is pursued. Our findings corroborates earlier evidence for Canada and the U.S. that resistance to pay cuts may be a significant factor as inflation approaches zero. This evidence should be updated, as the period of low inflation is extended, to see if pay cut resistance will decline in the longer term.

The evidence to date seems sufficient to cause some concern. We provide two models to assess the effect of pay cut resistance and its impact on the unemployment rate in the short term. The first model is a standard bargaining model which implies that from 1993 to 1995 employment growth has been about 1% lower per year, and hence the unemployment rate has been about 1% higher per year as a result of pay cut resistance. The second model is a Phillips curve model of wage settlements which treats pay freezes and cuts as censored data. It estimates that settlements were 0.9% higher in 1991 - 2 and 0.7% higher in 1993 - 5 because of pay cut resistance, which would require an unemployment rate increase of more than 2% to correct. Whether these estimates will hold up to further scrutiny, and

14 That is, 0.94% / 0.325 and 0.67% / 0.325, respectively. We use the OLS model because it estimates the actual wage settlement process; the Tobit model estimates the hypothetical settlement process in the absence of pay cut resistance, which provided us with the estimates of the effect of pay cut resistance on settlements.

whether they suggest that the costs of further disinflation are too large or not, we feel that they are compelling enough to receive further attention in research and policy discussions.

## References

*Abraham,* Katherine and *Haltiwanger,* John (1995): "Real Wages and the Business Cycle," Journal of Economic Literature 33 no.3, 1215 - 64. – *Akerlof,* George / *Dickens* , William and *Perry,* George (1996): "The Macroeconomics of Low Inflation," Brookings Papers on Economic Activity no.1, 1 - 76. – *Bjorklund,* Anders (1989): "Potentials and Pitfalls of Panel Data," European Economic Review 33, 537 - 46. – *Bound,* John, and *Krueger,* Alan (1991): "The Extent of Measurement Error in Longitudinal Earnings Data: Do Two Wrongs Make a Right?" Journal of Labor Economics 9 no.1, 1 - 24. – *Cameron,* Norman / *Hum* , Derek and *Simpson,* Wayne (1996) "Stylized Facts and Stylized Illusions: Inflation and Productivity Revisited," Canadian Journal of Economics XXIX no.1, 152 - 162. – *Diewert,* Erwin W. (1998): "Index Number Issues in the Consumer price Index" Journal of Economic Perspectives 11, no.1, 47- 58. – *Fortin,* Pierre (1991): "Innis Lecture: the Phillips curve, macroeconomic policy, and the welfare of Canadians," Canadian Journal of Economics XXIV no.4, 774 - 803. – *Fortin,* Pierre (1996): "Presidential Address: The Great Canadian Slump," Canadian Journal of Economics XXIX no.4, 761 - 87. – *Groshen,* Erica and *Schweitzer,* Mark (1996): "The Effects of Inflation on Wage Adjustments in Firm-Level Data: Grease or Sand?" Federal Reserve Bank of New York Staff Reports no.9, January. – *Hammermesh,* Daniel (1987): "Why do fixed-effect models perform so poorly? The case of academic salaries," Working Paper No. 2135, National Bureau of Economic Research, New York. – *Lucas,* R. F. (1989): "The Bank of Canada and Zero Inflation: A New Cross of Gold?" Canadian Public Policy 15 no.1, 84 - 93. – *MacCurdy,* Thomas and *Pencavel,* John (1986): "Testing Between Competing Models of Wage and Employment Determination in Unionized Markets," Journal of Political Economy 94 no.3, pt.2, S3-S39. – *McDonald,* Ian, and *Solow,* Robert (1981): "Wage Bargaining and Employment," American Economic Review 71 no.5, 896 - 908. – *Nickell,* S. (1997): "Unemployment and labor Market Rigidities: Europe versus North America." Journal of Economic Perspectives 11 no 3, 55 - 74. – *Tobin,* James (1958): "Estimation of relationships for limited dependent variables," Econometrica 42 24 - 36.

## Appendix: A Bargaining Model with Pay Cut Resistance

Although models which incorporate real or nominal wage rigidity have been developed (e.g., McDonald and Solow, 1981; Akerlof, Dickens and Perry, 1996) specific resistance to a pay cut has received little attention. Union resistance to pay cuts implies that the indifference curves of the union must flatten in the vicinity of a zero settlement because the marginal utility of employment approaches zero. This pattern is represented in Figure 3 in terms of real wages, $w$, and employment, $N$ for representative indifference curves $U_0U_0'$, $U_1U_1'$ and $U_2U_2'$. Suppose that the previous settlement occurred at point $A$ at real wage $w_0$. This is an efficient bargain on the contract curve $CC'$ and above the marginal revenue product (labour demand) curve $VV'$ where the union indifference curve $U_0U_0'$ is tangent to the firm's isoprofit curve $P_0P_0'$. Then, if the inflation rate is $\pi$, a zero settlement requires that the real wage floor be $w_f = w_0(1 - \pi)$. Thus, union indifference curves become progressively flatter as prospective bargains approach $w_f$, which represents a pay freeze in real terms. When indifference curves are flat in the vicinity of $w_f$, isoprofit curves can only be tangent to them at their peaks along the labour demand curve. Hence, this pattern of indifference curves necessitates a contract curve whose (negative) slope increases in the vicinity of $w_f$. That is, if the preferences of the union and the profit situation of the firm remain unchanged, subsequent bargains could occur at $B$ on the contract curve $CC'$ above $w_f$ or at some point such as $C'$ in the vicinity of $w_f$ along the labour demand curve $VV'$. Pay freezes such as $C'$, as opposed to a pay cut at point $D$, must forego employment to maintain nominal wages because the labour demand curve $VV'$ slopes downward.[15]

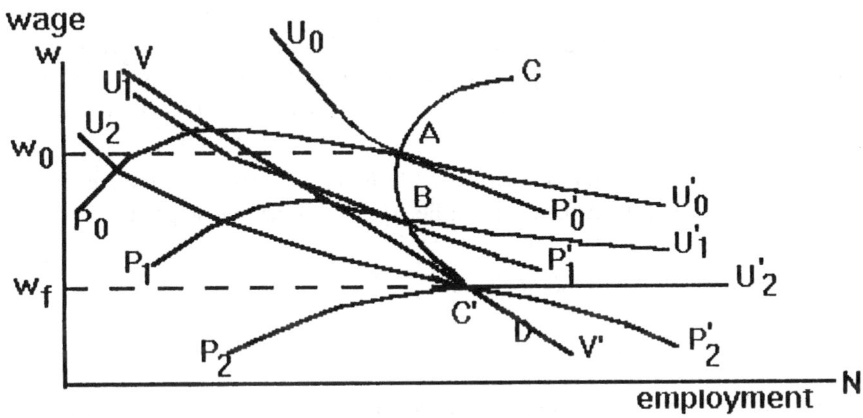


Figure 3: Bargaining with pay cut resistance

More formally, suppose that the firm maximizes a standard short-run profit function of the form

$$P = R(N) - wN \tag{1}$$

where $R(N)$ is the standard concave revenue function ($R_N > 0$, $R_{NN} < 0$) depicted in Figure 3. We depart from McDonald and Solow in assuming that union preferences are described by a general additive utility function of the form

15 McDonald and Solow (1981) derive a similar utility function with a wage floor which yields utility equivalent to the nonunion wage plus the disutility of union work, but their contract curve is vertical in the vicinity of the wage floor, implying no employment reductions. This seems unrealistic in our view.

(2) $$U = \frac{\beta_1}{\alpha_1}\left(\frac{w - w_f}{\beta_1}\right)^{\alpha_1} + \frac{\beta_2}{\alpha_2}\left(\frac{N}{\beta_2}\right)^{\alpha_2}$$

where $0 < \alpha < 1$ and $\beta_j > 0$ $(j = 1, 2)$. The general additive utility function has the advantage of being a fairly general utility function which captures the idea of a wage floor, $w_f$, as in Figure A.[16] We can now find the slope of the isoprofit and isoutility functions by differentiating (1) and (2)

(4) $$\frac{dw}{dN} = \frac{R_N - w}{N} \quad \text{for the firm's isoprofit curves}$$
$$= -\frac{\left[\frac{w-w_f}{\beta_1}\right]^{1-\alpha_1}}{\left[\frac{N}{\beta_2}\right]^{1-\alpha_2}} \quad \text{for the union's indifference curves}$$

The firm's isoprofit curves slope upward (rise with increasing $N$) until $w = R_N(N)$ on the labour demand curve $VV'$ in Figure A; it falls thereafter. The union's indifference curves slope downward but at a declining rate as $w$ approaches $w_f$. At $w = w_f$ the slope is zero, implying that the marginal utility of employment is zero.

The equation for the contract curve $CC'$ in Figure A is given by the tangency of the isoprofit and indifference curves or the equality of the two slopes given in (3):

(5) $$w - R_N(N) = k(w - w_f)^{1-\alpha_1} N^{\alpha_2},$$
$$\text{where } k = -\frac{\beta_2^{1-\alpha_2}}{\beta_1^{1-\alpha_1}} > 0$$

Equation (4) implies that the efficient bargains normally involve a settlement on the contract curve to the right of the labour demand curve $R_N$ (McDonald and Solow, 1981, or MacCurdy and Pencavel, 1986). At $w = w_f$, however, the contract curve lies on the labour demand curve. To find the slope of the contract curve we differentiate equation (4) to obtain

(5) $$\frac{dw}{dN} = \frac{R_{NN}(N) + k\alpha_2 N^{\alpha_2 - 1}[w - w_f]^{1-\alpha_1}}{1 - k(1-\alpha_1)[w - w_f]^{-\alpha_1} N^{\alpha_2}}$$

As $w$ approaches $w_f$, the slope of the contract curve approaches $R_{NN}$, the slope of the labour demand curve, from above. This implies that the contract curve lies above the labour demand curve, with a smaller negative or even positive slope, as

16 The utility function contains the Stone-Geary and CES utility functions as special cases. McDonald and Solow adopt a simpler utility function, but it contains the undesirable property that the contract curve is vertical in the vicinity of their wage floor. This implies no trade-off of employment for wages in the vicinity of the wage floor. If union workers are going to resist pay cuts, we suspect that they must sacrifice employment.

depicted in Figure 5. That is, contracts at or near the wage floor, $w_f$, which resist a pay cut (along portion $BC'$ of the contract curve in Figure 5) will involve a greater reduction in employment than contracts above $w_f$ (along portion $CAB$ of the contract curve $CC'$). Indeed, if the contract curve is positive over some portion, as shown in Figure 5 over portion $AC$, then higher wage settlements may be associated with higher employment; this is not possible, however, in the vicinity of the wage floor.

Over time the contract curve will shift as the objective functions of the firm and union change. Following McDonald and Solow, union preferences are stable but the firm's revenue function shifts over the business cycle according to a business cycle parameter $B$. Thus, $R = R(N, B)$, $R_B > 0$, $R_NB > 0$, such that $B$ increases both total revenue and marginal revenue product at all levels of employment. Now the equation for the contract curve is given by

$$w - R_N(N,B) = k[w - w_f]^{1-\alpha_1} N^{\alpha_2} \tag{6}$$

and we can ask how wages and employment evolve over the business cycle and as inflation adjusts the wage floor, since $w_f = w_0(1 - \pi)$.

Consider the troughs of two business cycles, one occurring at high inflation where $w_f << w_0$, such that there is considerable room for real wage adjustment without pay cuts, and another cycle (such as the one we are now experiencing) where inflation is low and $w_f \approx w_0$. What can we expect to happen to wages and employment? Differentiating (6) we find

$$\begin{aligned} \frac{dw}{dB} &= \frac{R_{NB}(N,B)}{1 - k(1-\alpha_1)[w - w_f]^{-\alpha_1} N^{\alpha_2}} \\ \frac{dN}{dB} &= -\frac{R_{NB}(N,B)}{R_{NN}(N,B) + k[w - w_f]^{1-\alpha_1} \alpha_2 N^{\alpha_2 - 1}} \end{aligned} \tag{7}$$

Neither expression is easily signed but, as $w$ approaches $w_f$, $dw/dB$ approaches $R_NB$, which is positive, and $dN/dB$ approaches – $R_NB/R_NN$, which is also positive. Thus, in the vicinity of a pay freeze, as $B$ is falling, real wages and employment will also be falling. We can also see how employment responds to the movement of the wage floor, which depends on the prevailing inflation rate:

$$\frac{dN}{dw_f} = -\frac{k(1-\alpha_1)[w - w_f]^{-\alpha_1} N^{\alpha_2}}{R_{NN}(N,B) - k[w - w_f]^{1-\alpha_1} \alpha_2 N^{\alpha_2 - 1}} < 0 \quad \text{if} \quad \frac{dN}{dB} > 0 \tag{8}$$

This expression is negative if we assume $dN/dB$ is generally positive (employment is procyclical) in equation (7), as would be expected[17]. That is, when the

[17] McDonald and Solow (1981) assume that employment is procyclical, which implies that the denominators in equation (7) and (8) are positive.

wage floor at the trough of the business cycle is higher as a result of a lower inflation rate (our current circumstances), there will be a greater (negative) employment response of a disinflation policy.

# V. Macroeconomic Policy Designs to Regain High Employment

# Effects of a Change in Policy Rules on the Growth of the Economy

## Temporary versus Permanent Effects

By Attiat F. Ott, Worcester

> "It may be a little late in the day to say this, but I wish we could agree to define as a contribution to growth *anything* that increases potential output in a permanent way. Then it would be possible to say, in good conscience, that any policy that induces an increase in the fraction of GDP invested is a policy that promotes growth. It may not make any permanent change in the growth rate; the point is that asking for that is asking too much and unnecessarily. It is no mean achievement to shift the steady-state growth path upward, parallel to itself."
>
> Robert Solow (1996)

### I. Introduction

After decades of neglect, macroeconomics have rediscovered growth. More significant perhaps is their inquiry about the effects of macro policy on the *long run* growth rate of the economy to be distinguished from short run stabilization policy. The Great Depression and Keynes' General Theory had a unification effect on economists' thinking about the structure of the economy and the role of the economist as an advisor to policy makers. Most if not all macroeconomists of the 50's and 60's vintage believed in that structure as well as in their ability to charter the path of the economy. Fine tuning the economy was then the prescribed conduct for macropolicy.

The 1980 decade played havoc with that framework of analysis. Research in this decade have cast a doubt on the validity of the macromodel in general and on the relationship between policy and economic performance in particular. Recent research on growth give more scope for policy to influence the long-run growth rate of the economy. By making the determination of long-run growth endogenous, within the model rather than by some exogenously growing variable (technical progress), policies that impact these variables have the potential to influence growth.

My paper takes the view that understanding the facts about growth is essential for the design of macropolicy for long term growth. It adopts the "Solow" premise that any policy that increases potential output in a permanent way makes a contribution to economic growth. The paper is organized as follows: I begin with stylized facts of growth. This is followed by a brief description of basic growth models and their quantitative predictions. Next, I address the question: What are the implications of growth theories for macro policy? The final section presents some empirical findings.

## II. Stylized Facts of Growth

One hallmark of modern macroeconomics is its emphasis on empirical analysis. Recent work on economic growth have relied on international data to test growth theories, the "old" and the "new" and examine systematically the differences between countries that have experienced rapid growth and those who have not. The literature on economic growth is quite vast, although the findings are still inconclusive.

To organize our thinking about the outcome of this research, it is perhaps useful to begin with the growth accounting. From Solow (1957) representation of the neoclassical growth model, output growth ($g_y$) can be decomposed as

$$g_y = ag_n + bg_k + z \tag{2.1}$$

where

$g_y$: growth rate of labor productivity
$g_k$: growth rate of capital
$a$: share of labor in output, $0 < a < 1$
$b$: share of capital in output, $0 < b < 1$
$z$: the residual, or multifactor productivity growth
and $(a + b) = 1$.

Rewriting (2.1) to express growth per man hour

$$(g_y - g_n) = (b/a)(g_k - g_y) + (1/a)z \tag{2.1$'$}$$

According to (2.1)$'$ the rate of growth of output per man hour depends on the rate of growth of the capital-output ratio and on the Solow residual.[1] Existing measure of capital in the US and other industrialized economies suggest that $(g_k - g_y)$ is close to zero. This finding implies a positive Solow residual. The growth rate of output (or labor productivity growth) is determined by multifactor productivity growth, which is exogenous in the neoclassical model. Hence, this growth account-

[1] Although Solow's name is associated with the residual, the discovery of the residual belongs to Copeland and Martin (1938). Tinbergin (1942) using Cobb-Douglas production function provided a measure of this residual (calling it a measure of technical efficiency) for Germany, Great Britain, France and US. For a historical review see Griliches (1996).

ing can neither explain sources of growth of multifactor productivity and / or why the residual is higher in some countries than in others or during one period or another.

To address the weakness of this framework, an alternative decomposition has been suggested derived from models of endogenous growth (Benhabib and Spiegel [1997], Lau and Kim [1994]). A key feature of the endogenous growth model is the absence of diminishing returns to the factors that can be accumulated. This tendency is eliminated by assuming that knowledge creation is a side product of investment (Romer [1986]). A firm that increases its physical capital "learns" how to produce more efficiently. In other models such as 'AK model,' the absence of diminishing returns to capital is attributed to the broadening definition of capital to include human capital.

Benhabib and Spiegel offer two versions of growth accounting. The first decomposition assumes a Cobb-Douglas technology and introduces human capital as a separate argument.

$$g_y = g_A + ag_n + bg_k + \gamma g_H \tag{2.2}$$

$a, b, \gamma$ are the productivity function's parameters, $g_A$ rate of technological progress, $g_n, g_k$ are growth rates of labor and capital respectively and $g_H$ is the growth rate of human capital.

This decomposition (assuming $\gamma$ is positive) reduces the size of the residual. Moreover, since human capital accumulation can be influenced by policy parameters, it incorporates, albeit indirectly policy in the growth framework.

Again, assuming a Cobb-Douglas production function the second decomposition is given by

$$g_y = g_{A(h)} + ag_n + bg_k \tag{2.3}$$

$g_{A(h)}$ captures the relationship between human capital and technology.

Alternative growth decomposition frame the question for empirical research: Is productivity growth largely exogenous? If not, what are the sources accounting for productivity growth? A related question is the significance of the "endogenous" variables to the growth process. The vast empirical literature amassed since the early 1980's does not answer these questions to everyone's satisfaction. On the basis of findings in independent studies, these are the "stylized" facts of growth:

- Technical progress is the most significant source of economic growth for the developed countries in the post-war period. The average growth rate of total factor productivity is 1.7% per annum. In developing countries the rate is quite small, about 0.7% per annum (Maddison [1982, 1992], Abramovich [1986], Baumol and Wolff [1988], Lau and Kim [1994], Nehru and Dhareshwar [1994], de Long [1996] and Lau [1996]).

- Technical progress can be purely capital augmenting or human augmenting (Kim and Lau [1992], Hulten [1992], Stiroh and Jorgenson [1995]).[2]
- Capital accumulation (physical and human) explains most if not all of the growth in NIC of East Asia (Young [1995], Krugman [1994], Nehru and Dhareshwar [1994]).
- Externalities generated by human capital accumulation (R&D, learning by doing, knowledge) contribute to growth. Economies that are accumulating human capital (knowledge) rapidly and utilizing this knowledge to build and operate physical capital achieve a high rate of growth (Grossman and Helpman [1991], Lucas [1988], and Barro [1991], Benhabib and Spiegel [1994]).[3]
- More open economies have experienced faster productivity growth (Edwards [1997]).

Until recently the focus of empirical research has been on identifying those "ancillary" variables such as openness, political stability, income distribution, government investment in human capital, and financial development, which impact the growth rate of labor productivity.[4] Recent studies began analyzing the relationship between these explanatory variables and total factor productivity. These efforts notwithstanding, the residual, or "technical change" still remains a "measure of our ignorance." As Griliches puts it, much observed growth remains unexplained.[5]

Another pocket of ignorance has to do with the neoclassical growth model's prediction of convergence. The literature on convergence to date reflects three waves of research: The first tested for convergence among group of countries where the group was either broad enough to encompass the entire world economy (Barro [1991], Barro and Sala-i-Martin [1995], Mankiw, Romer and Weil [1992], De Long [1996]), or significantly narrow as to restrict the test to a group of like economies (Maddison [1982], Abramovich [1986], Baumol [1986], Dorwick and Nguen [1987, 1989]). The second wave is characterized by the search for "sources" accounting for convergence. This wave of research not only offers a more rigorous test of the convergence hypothesis (testing for data bias, sample selection bias, a historical period bias and so on) but also makes the distinction between conversion of per capita income or labor productivity and levels of total factor productivity.

---

2 This finding is consistent with the endogenous growth model where the production function is of the form $Y = F(K\beta(t), L)$, $\beta(t)$ is an index of technology, $\dot{\beta}(t) \geq 0$. This production function is called capital augmenting because technical improvements increase production in the same way as an increase in the stock of capital.

3 Human capital can be incorporated in the production function as suggested by VonNeumann (1937). Knight (1944) introduced the idea that diminishing returns might not apply if the definition of capital is broadened. Capital with externalities is attributed to Romer (1986, 1987). Jorgenson (1996) on the other hand, defines technology as knowledge whose returns are appropriated by the investor.

4 Edwards (1993).

5 Griliches (1996), p. 1329. The expression is attributed to Abramovich.

The most recent research challenges the findings on conversion on technical grounds (Cellini [1997] and Evans [1997]). Since conversion (or lack thereof) is a test of the appropriateness of the growth frameworks, we sketch below a neoclassical growth model (old) and an endogenous growth model (new) and compare their predictions with actual experiences.

## III. Growth Models and their Quantitative Predictions

What derives national growth rates is a question that has eluded historians and macroeconomists throughout human history. If it were possible to explain the varying experiences of world economies, we would have by now discovered the "recipe for making miracles" (Lucas [1993]). Still growth theories, the old and the new, is where one has to start to find "partial" answers to the growth question. Not only is there a need for understanding why some countries grow faster than others but also whether public policy (macro and micro) have a role, even a modest one in influencing the growth rate of the economy. The importance of identifying the sources of long term growth is self evident. By almost any standard, differences in real per capita income across countries is staggering and the gap between rich and poor, rather than narrowing is getting even bigger (Charts A.1 and A.2).

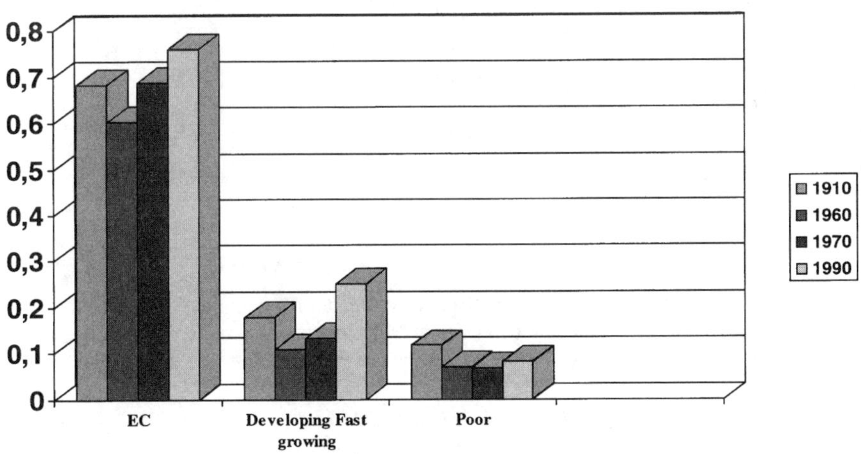


Chart A.1: Changing Fortunes
(per capita income relative to US)

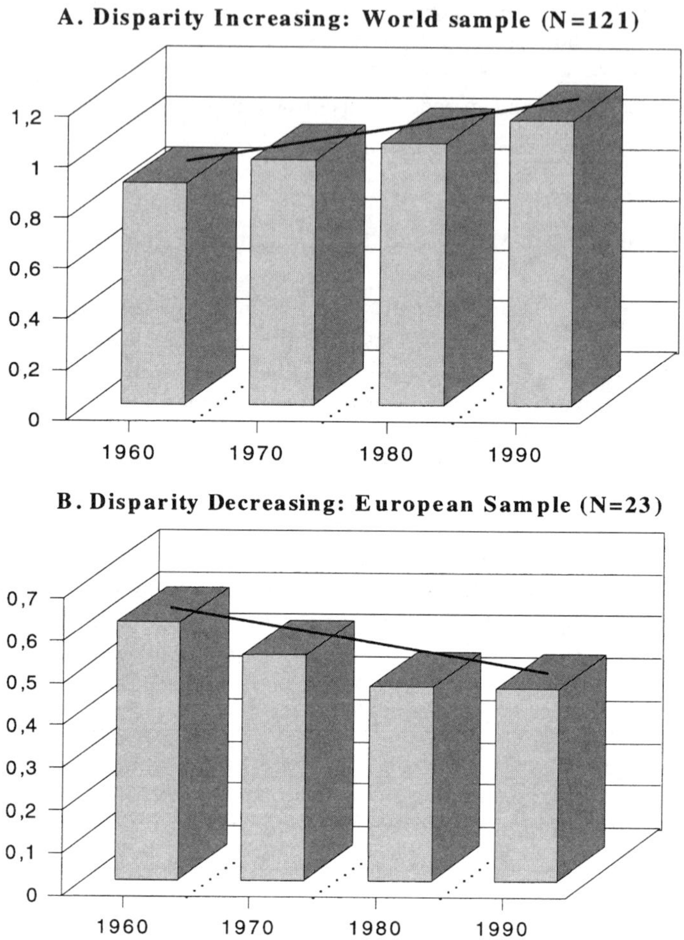


Chart A.2: Income Disparities: Standard Deviation
(per capita income real GDP in 1985 International prices)

### *1. The Neoclassical Model*

The starting point in growth analysis is the neoclassical model of capital accumulation. The most basic version is the Solow (1956)-Swan (1956) model. The model's foundation is rooted in its characterization of the production function. This neoclassical function satisfies the following conditions: Constant returns to scale, diminishing returns to both labor and capital and the Inada condition. Knowledge or technology enters the production function as labor-augmenting.

(3.1) $$Y = F(K, AL)$$

where $Y$ is output, $K$ is capital, $L$ is labor and $A$ is technology. $AL$ is referred to as effective labor. Under the assumption of constant returns to scale (3.1) can be written

(3.1)′ $$y = f(k)$$

where $y = Y/AL$ and $k = K/AL$ and $f(k) = F(K, 1)$. Equation (3.1)′ expresses output per unit of effective labor as a function of capital per effective labor. A specific example of the production function is the Cobb-Douglas:

(3.2) $$F(K, AL) = K^a (AL)^b, \qquad 0 < a < 1$$

and

(3.2)′ $$f(k) = k^a$$

In equation (3.2)′, a captures the degree of diminishing returns to capital. The larger a is, the lower are the returns to increasing the stock of capital. The evolution of inputs into production are given as

$$\dot{L} = nl$$
$$\dot{A} = gA$$
$$\dot{K} = s(Y) - \delta k$$

The rate of growth of labor $n$ and technology g are exogenous parameters. The stock of capital accumulates over time through net investment where $s(Y)$ is investment and $\delta$ is the rate of depreciation. The model takes the division of output between consumption and investment as exogenous and constant.

The key equation of the model then is

(3.3) $$\dot{k} = sf(k) - (n + g + \delta)k$$

According to equation (3.3), the rate of change of the capital stock per unit of effective labor is the difference between two terms: Actual investment per unit of effective labor and break even investment, that amount that must be made to keep $k$ at the existing level. $\dot{k}$ is zero when the two terms are equal. The value of $k$ at this point is referred to as the steady state value or $k^*$. The evolution of the capital stock may be expressed as

(3.4) $$\dot{k} = \dot{k}(k)$$

If $k$ is initially less than $k^*$, actual investment exceeds the break-even investment and $\dot{k}$ is positive; if $k$ is above $k^*$, $\dot{k}$ is negative and when $k = k^*$, $\dot{k}$ is zero. Thus, regardless of the initial condition, where $k$ starts, it converges to $k^*$, its steady state value.

The neoclassical model give rise to the following predictions:

1. In the long run, the economy approaches (converges towards) a steady state independent of the initial conditions. Both output per effective labor and capital per effective labor are constant.
2. With no change in technology, total income and the capital stock grow at the same rate as the rate of population growth. Per capita values will not exhibit growth.
3. With technical progress, per capita income (and capital stock) grow at a rate that is proportional to the rate of technical change.
4. The steady state level of income depends on the rate of saving / investment and population growth. While these variables impact the long-run income of a country they have no effect on growth.
5. Countries with the same production technology, similar saving / investment rates should converge to similar steady state levels of per-capita income. The convergence hypothesis implies that a poorer country, starting with a low capital labor ratio will grow faster during the transition to the steady state as it catches up to the rich country.

The empirical research seems to focus on the conversion property of the neoclassical model. As discussed below two hypothesis of conversion have been tested.

## 2. *Convergence: Absolute and Conditional*

The notion that per capita income in poorer countries / regions tend to grow faster than per capita income in rich countries / regions without "conditioning" is referred to as absolute conversion.[6] Thus, if a group of countries were alike (have same steady state position, i.e. $s, n, \delta$ and $f(\cdot)$) but differed only in their starting values of the capital labor ratio $(k)$, then poorer countries will catch up with rich countries as rates of growth of $k$ in the poorer countries will be higher than those of the rich. Convergence is "mean reverting."[7]

---

[6] Baumol (1986), Barro and Sala-i-Martin (1991), Abramovich and David (1996) and others.

[7] See Barro and Sala-i-Martin (1995) for a comparison of statistical measures of conversion.

A simple test of absolute conversion is obtained by regressing average annual growth rate of GDP per capita over a period of time against the starting position. A typical cross countries regression is of the form:

$$\ln(Y/N)_{it} - \ln(Y/N)_{i0} = a + b[\ln(Y/N)_{i,0}] + \varepsilon_i$$

$\ln(Y/N)$ is log per capita output, $\varepsilon$ is an error term, $i$ indexes countries, $t$ is the terminal period and 0 the initial period. A value of $b = -1$ corresponds to perfect convergence – higher initial level of income on average lowers subsequent growth one-to-one. A value of $b = 0$ implies that growth is uncorrelated with initial level of income and thus no convergence. Given $b$, the rate at which economies or regions converge towards the steady state can be calculated as

$$\beta = 1 - (1 + bT)1/T$$

where $T$ designates length of period. From this equation, it is clear that convergence is more rapid, the more negative $b$ is.

Evidence of convergence would be expected for a sample consisting of homogenous economies like OECD. On the other hand for a heterogeneous sample like the world sample, the data may not support absolute conversion.[8] In effect the empirical evidence seem to support convergence for the OECD sample and for a sample consisting of the 48 states of the US, but reject the hypothesis for samples that include diverse economies such as African countries, Latin America, East Asian countries along with industrialized countries.[9]

Lack of convergence in the world sample does not refute the neo-classical model predictions unless all sources of heterogeneity was controlled for. Accounting for heterogeneity among countries, that is by allowing for different values of $s, n, \delta$ and $f(\cdot)$, the neoclassical model predicts that "each country will converge to its own steady state". That is poor countries and rich countries will converge to their *own* steady state defined by the values of their parameters. This concept is referred to as conditional convergence.

How quickly output per capita converges to its steady state value–how rapidly $k$ approaches $k^*$ (speed of conversion) can be ascertained from the equation describing the evolution of $k$ (equation (3.4)). A first order approximation of $(k)$ around $k = k^*$ yields

$$\dot{k} \approx \left( \frac{\partial \dot{k}(k)}{\partial k} |_{k=k^*} \right) (k - k^*) \tag{3.4$'$}$$

---

8 Evans (1997) shows that unless control variables are included in the estimating equation, the estimation will yield inconsistent conversion rate.

9 Doubt is still voiced about the robustness of this conclusion. See Dowrick and Quiggin (1997).

Differentiating equation (3.3) with respect to $k$ and evaluating the result at $k = k^*$ we get

$$\frac{\partial \dot{k}(k)}{\partial k}\Big|_{k=k^*} = [\alpha + 1](n + g + \delta) \ , \text{ or}$$
$$= -[1 - \alpha](n + g + \delta) \ .$$

Substituting in (3.4)′

$$\dot{k}(t) \approx -[1 - \alpha](n + g + \delta)(k - k^*) \tag{3.4''}$$

Equation (3.4)″ says that, in the vicinity of the steady state capital per effective labor converges towards $k^*$ at a speed proportional to its distance from $k^*$.

Setting $\beta = (1 - \alpha)(n + g + \delta)$, implies

$$\dot{k} \approx -\beta\big(k(t) - k^*\big) \tag{3.5}$$

The growth rate of $\big(k(t) - k^*\big)$ is constant and equal to $-\beta$. The path of $\big(k(t) - k^*\big)$ or $\big(y(t) - y^*\big)$ is therefore given by

$$\begin{aligned}\big(y(t) - y^*\big) &\approx e^{-\beta t}\big(y(0) - y^*\big) \text{ or} \\ &\approx e^{-(1-\alpha)(n+g+\delta)t}\big(y(0) - y^*\big)\end{aligned} \tag{3.6}$$

The speed of convergence $\beta$ is determined from the steady state parameters and the capital share.[10] Given the values of $n + g + \delta$, $\beta$ depends on the value of \alpha , the capital share. Note that as $\alpha \to 1$, $\beta \to 0$.[11]

Barro, Sala-i-Martin, Mankiw, Romer and Weil as well as others have estimated cross countries regression equation of the form

$$1/T \log(y_{it}/y_{i0}) = a - \big[(1 - e^{-\beta t})/T\big] \log(y_{i0}) + u_{i0,T} \tag{3.7}$$

$y_{i0}, y_{it}$ per capita income at the beginning and the end of the interval, $u_{i0,T}$ the average of the error terms between date 0 and $T$ and the intercept in (3.7), a, is the steady state position. The coefficient on initial income declines with the length of the interval $T$, for a given $\beta$. In other words as the interval increases, the effect of the initial position on the average growth rate declines. The reason being that over a large time span, the growth rate combines more of the future small growth rates

10 The time it takes for $(y - y^*)$ with a constant negative growth rate to fall is approximately equal to 70 divided by its growth rate in percent. These results are derived from Taylor series expansion and the steady state. More exactly half life, $t^*$, is the solution to $e^{-\beta t^*} = 0.5$. Taking logs of both sides, $t^* = -\ln(0.5)/\beta \approx 0.69\lambda$.

11 This case is discussed in the context of the endogenous growth model.

with the initially large rates. As $T \to \infty$, the coefficient approaches 0 and it tends to $\beta$ as $T$ approaches 0.

Barro (1991), Barro and Sala-i-Martin (1995), Mankiw, Romer and Weil (1992), and Levin and Renelt (1992) among others have tested for conditional conversion by regressing growth rate of per capita income on initial income and including variables to control for determinants of the steady state. The empirical evidence reported in Barro, Sala-i-Martin (1995) suggests a convergence rate of about 2 percent per year for the 48 US states for nine subperiods 1980 - 1990; 1.25 percent to 3.1 percent for Japanese prefectures for seven subperiods 1930 - 1990 and about 2 percent across European regions for four subperiods 1950 - 1990, 1.4 percent for a world sample (Mankiw, Romer and Weil) for the time period 1960 - 1985. On the other hand Cellini (1997) found no evidence of convergence and Evans (1997) believes the reported conversion rate for the 48 US states to be quite low[12].

Mankiw (1995) believes that the low conversion rates found in the literature (almost 2% or less) is a source of "trouble" for the neoclassical model. At a rate of 2 percent per year a country moves half-life towards its steady state in 35 years. Using data for the US, Mankiw calibrated equation (3.3) to estimate the rate of conversion implied by the model. The exercise yielded a value of 4% per year. At this rate the US economy will go half way towards its steady state in 17 $^1/_2$ years.[13]

### *3. Endogenous Growth*

A viable alternative to the neoclassical growth model is a model that offers a framework of analysis capable of explaining two fundamental questions: The persistence of growth and convergence. To do so, the model has to "discard" a growth framework that fails to provide an explanation for the "steady state". In the neoclassical model, long term growth is independent of savings and investment; the steady state is determined by the exogenous rate of the technological progress. Since the characterization of the production process in the neoclassical model derives the model's predictions, the point of departure in every endogenous model is an alternative characterization. Endogenous growth models offer several production processes.

The most common versions of the model are: The AK model (Rebelo [1991]), AK model with human capital (Rebelo; Mankiw, Romer, and Weil [1992], Kremer and Thomson [1994]), and growth with externalities and spillovers (Romer [1986, 1990], Grossman and Helpman [1991]).[14] The models presented here are one sec-

---

12 Evans (1997), p. 223.

13 Mankiw (1995), p. 285.

14 Jorgenson (1996) offers an endogenous growth model that retains the neoclassical framework but treats technology (knowledge) as endogenous which enters the model as a form of capital.

tor growth models. Endogenous models with more than one sector are given in Lucas (1988), Mulligan and Sala-i-Martin (1993).

*The AK model*

Consider the production function

(3.8)
$$Y = AK, \text{ and}$$
$$dY/dK = Y/K = A$$

A reflects the level of technology assumed to be a positive constant. From equation (3.8) this production process rules out diminishing returns to capital. In contrast to the neoclassical model, the capital share is set equal to 1. Since capital share, in the neoclassical model is less than one (empirically around 1 / 3 in the industrialized countries), the AK model may be viewed as a limiting case of the neoclassical model. To see the implication of the AK model for growth, examine the accumulation equation:

(3.9)
$$\dot{k} = sf(k) - (n + \delta)k$$

Since technology is assumed to be fixed, and setting $n = 0$,

(3.9)′
$$\dot{k} = sy - \delta k$$

Together with equation (3.8), we have

(3.10)
$$\dot{y}/y = \dot{k}/k = sA - \delta$$

An economy described by the AK model can grow forever as long as $sA > \delta$. The model yields positive growth even in the absence of technical progress ($\dot{A} = 0$). Another model result is the dependence of the growth rate $\dot{y}/y$ on behavioral parameters of the model, i.e. the saving rate. Hence anything, including public policy which raises the savings rate will permanently raise the rate of growth.

If one accepts the AK model characterization of the production process then the model delivers the following predictions: First, large differences in saving rates across countries give rise to increasingly large differences in income over time. Secondly, the absence of diminishing returns to capital means that disparities in capital and income across countries will persist without inducing capital to move. Also, the constancy of marginal and average product of capital rules out conversion.

Although the AK model offers the requisite framework for explaining persistence, it fails in predicting conversion (absolute or conditional). Aside from this failure, the model does not offer a precise interpretation of what $K$ stands for. In other words what are the elements of $K$ that do not exhibit diminishing returns.

This task has been taken up in subsequent development of the endogenous growth framework.[15] In some models broadening the concept of capital is delivered by human capital while other models treat knowledge as a type of capital which is distinct from human capital.

*The AK model with human capital*

In this model the production process, assuming a Cobb-Douglas is:

$$Y = AK^a H^b \qquad a > 0;\ b > 0 \text{ and } (a+b) = 1 \tag{3.11}$$

Equation (3.11) exhibits constant returns to scale in $K, H$. $K$ is physical capital and $H$ is human capital. Output allocation:

$$Y = C + I_k + I_H$$

$C$ is consumption and $I_k$ and $I_H$ are gross investment in physical and human capital. Net stocks are

$$\dot{K} = I_k - \delta K$$
$$\dot{H} = I_H - \delta H$$

From consumers and firms maximization conditions, the growth rate of consumption and the equality of the net marginal product of human capital and physical capital are obtained. The equality of the marginal products means that the ratio of the two capital stocks is given by the ratio of the production parameters, that is

$$H/K = b/a$$

Substitute into the production function, equation (3.11) becomes

$$Y = AK(b/a)^b \tag{3.11$'$}$$

The model given by equation (3.11)′ is essentially the same as the AK model, hence the decomposition of $K$ did not add much to the theoretical framework. In other words the predictions of the AK model still hold for the augmented model.

---

15 It is worth noting that the theoretical literature on endogenous growth models is cast in terms of dynamic optimization. The model usually assumes infinitely lived households choose consumption and saving to maximize their dynamic utilities subject to intertemporal budget constraint. Most models start with the Ramsey growth model (1928). Models with infinite lives, overlapping generation models are given in Diamond (1965).

*Endogenous Growth with Knowledge*

Romer (1986) offers a growth model which utilizes Arrow's (1962) knowledge creation hypothesis to eliminate diminishing returns to the accumulating factors in the production process. According to Romer, knowledge should be treated as a "side product" of investment. That is, a firm that increases its physical capital learns simultaneously how to produce more efficiently. This positive effect is referred to as "learning by investing" or alternatively as "learning by doing." Using a neoclassical production function with labor augmented technology, Romer expresses the production function of firm i as

$$Y_i = F(\phi k_i, \phi Ai, \phi x_i) \qquad \phi \leq 1 \tag{3.12}$$

$k_i, x_i$ are conventional input; $A$ is the index of knowledge. The analysis of this production process proceeds along several lines. One line is to assume that knowledge is produced by individuals (private good). But since newly produced knowledge cannot be kept secret for long, the production of output does not depend only on private knowledge but also on the economy's stock of knowledge. And, because knowledge and inventions are developed by profit maximizing firms, the economy may underinvest in these forms of capital. Combining learning by investing with knowledge spillovers equation (3.12) becomes

$$Y_i = F(K_i, K, L_i) \tag{3.12$'$}$$

Note that in $(3.12)'$ as $K_i$ expands, $K$ rises providing spillovers to other firms.

The model thus leaves room for policy to affect the growth rate by providing incentives (tax and / or subsidies) to firms to eliminate diversion between private benefits and social benefits.

Endogenous growth models, in short, provide explanation for sustained economic growth and persistent difference across countries in living standards and growth rates. In its simplest version, the endogenous growth model lacks any transitional dynamics, hence, growth rates do not exhibit the convergence property. As empirical evidence tend to support conditional conversion, variants of the basic model were developed in which the convergence property holds. This was accomplished by modifying production technology to reintroduce diminishing returns to capital. The modification suggested by Jones and Manuelli (1990) is to rewrite the production function as[16]

$$Y = F(K, L) = AK + \Omega(K, L) \tag{3.13}$$

$AK$ delivers endogenous growth $(A > 0)$
$\Omega(K, L)$ generates diminishing returns, the convergence behavior.

---

[16] Barro, Sala-i-Martin offers examples using Cobb-Douglas and CES production functions.

Several problems still vex the endogenous growth model. Data problems–how to measure knowledge, how knowledge is accumulated, the time framework for knowledge accumulation and diffusion, etc., renders the model "untestable". More importantly the fact that the model sheds little light on the sources of sustained growth, an issue that has rekindled the interest in growth.

Data problems notwithstanding, several endogenous growth models were estimated to test for conditional convergence, and to determine the role of human capital, knowledge accumulation and diffusion of technology as well as the role of a host of ancillary variables in the growth process.

To summarize the empirical debate about the "validity" of the growth framework, I present in Table 1 some findings on conversion (absolute and conditional).[17] Table 2 lists those variables that were positively or negatively associated with growth. Findings reported in Table 2 shed some light on the role of policy in the growth process.

## IV. Policy Rules and Economic Growth

Policy, whether macro or micro refers to all these actions taken by governments (including the Central Bank) to achieve a desired target or a multiple targets. Macro policy often referred to as stabilization policy are designed to achieve a stable rate of inflation and to reduce if not eliminate *short run* fluctuations in output and employment. As such it has often been described as discretionary act to be distinguished from automatic or built in stability associated with policy parameters. Early on in the macro literature, an alternative policy to that which involves discretion was specified. The Friedman 3 percent money rule or the balanced budget rule were examples for a policy action that once set rules out discretion. The discretion being the setting up of a value of a policy type in *response* to the state of the target. Today the notion of a policy rule encompass the discretionary aspect of policy. That is, a policy rule can be fixed such as the Friedman rule or a feedback rule where money supply or the tax rate responds to changes in employment or inflation. In this paper I adopt this broader interpretation of policy rules. This is consistent with Taylor (1979) findings that in the design of policy feedback rules dominates rules with fixed value for the instruments.

17 Studies testing for conversion in the endogenous growth framework test a variant of the model that allows for transitional dynamics. Ortigueira and Santos (1997) provide a theoretical framework for calculating the speed of convergence for an endogenous model with human capital. Rather than estimating a regression equation they use a set of numerical computations to test for variables affecing the rate of conversion.

*Table 1:* **Conversion Findings: A Summary**

| Study | Sample | | Conversion | | Variable |
|---|---|---|---|---|---|
| | Country | Period | Absolute | Conditional | |
| Conversion: Labor Productivity | | | | | |
| Baumol (1986) | 16 industrialized countries | 1970 - 1979 | b = – 0.995 (0.094) | | Per capita real income |
| DeLong (1988) | 23 countries | 1970 - 1979 | b = – 0.566 (0.144) | | Per capita real income |
| Baumol / Wolf (1984) | several samples | Several periods | $b < 0$ and $b > 0$ | | Per capita real income |
| Barro and Sala-i-Martin (1995)[a)] | 48 US States | 1980 - 1990 | | $\beta$ =0.017 to 0.0222 (0.0013) (0.002) | Per capita personal income |
| Barro and Sala-i-Martin (1995)[a)] | 47 Japanese prefectures | 1930 - 1990 | | $\beta$ =0.0125 to0.0312 (0.003) (0.004) | Per capita personal income |
| Barro and Sala-i-Martin (1995)[a)] | 90 regions in 8 European countries | 1950 - 1990 | | $\beta$ =0.019 to 0.018 (0.002) (0.003) | Per capita personal income |
| Mankiw, Romer and Weil (1992)[a)] | 98 countries | 1960 - 1985 | | $\beta$ =0.0142 (0.0019) | Per capita real income |
| DeLong (1996) | World Tables and other dataset | 1870 - 1993 | b = 1.542 (0.145)<br>b = 0.621 (0.126)<br>b = 1.252 (0.305) | | Per capita income full sample<br>Rich half sample<br>Poor half sample |
| Gapinski (1996)[b)] | World Tables and other dataset | 1850 - 1990 | B = – 0.129[e)] [-2.652] | | Labor productivity |
| Cellini (1997)[d)] | Four countries, 1960 - 1988 (US, France, Italy, Japan) | 1960 - 1988 | $B = 0$ | | Per capita output |

| | | | | |
|---|---|---|---|---|
| Conversion: Labor productivity and TFP | | | | |
| Dowrick / Nguyan (1989) | | 1950 - 1985 | $B < 0$ for OECD<br>$b = 0$ for large sample.<br>Evidence of catch up | Relative level of labor productivity<br>Relative TFP |
| Bernard and Jones (1996) | 14 OECD countries | 1970 - 87 | b = – 0.298<br>(0.0052)<br>b = – 0.0262<br>(0.0147)<br>b = – 0.226<br>(0.0056)<br>b = – 0.0146<br>(0.0132) | Labor productivity All industry<br>Labor productivity in manufacturing<br>total factor productivity all industries<br>total factor productivity in manufacturing |
| Dowrick and Quiggin (1997) | 17 OECD countries | 1980 and 1990 | B = – 0.145<br>[– 1.57]<br>b = – 0.186<br>[– 2.14] | GDP per capita prices measured by ICP index<br>GDP per capita prices measured in AFRIAT Index |

*Note:* terms in ( ) below the coefficients is the standard error. T values are in [ ].

a) Evans / Karras (1996) dispute these findings.

b) The model differs from the Solow model in that it features heterogeneous capital. Technical progress is embodied and augments capital and also disembodied and augments labor.

c) Evans (1997) cast doubt on the empirical estimates reported in the literature. He shows that the conventional approach produces inconsistent estimate of conversion as they fail to account for all cross countries heterogeneity. He offers an alternative approach to obtain consistent estimates. With the alternative method the conversion rate was 5.89% for the 48 countries sample and 15.50% for the US state sample.

d) Cellini shows labor productivity must be considered as stochastic. Tests for unit root and cointegration cast doubt on the validity of neoclassical model.

e) There is no evidence of convergence in manufacturing at 10% level. Similar results are found for mining sectors whether the conversion regressions were for labor productivity or TFP.

*Table 2:* **Explaining Growth in Cross Countries Regression: Summary of Findings**
(Dependent variable: Growth rate of real GDP per capita)

| Study | Basic data / period | Variable of interest | Findings |
|---|---|---|---|
| Feder (1983) | 31 semi industrialized countries 1964 - 73 | **dX / X** | Change in export rate (+) |
| Ram (1986) | World tables 1960 - 80 | **dG, G / GDP, dG / GDP** | Growth in government size and spending (+), G / GDP (–) |
| Kormandi-Mcguire (1985) | 47 countries, 1950 - 77 | **G, G / GDP** | Supply of public goods (+), size of government G / GDP (–) |
| Romer (1990) | World tables, 1960 - 85 | **H, I / GDP, Gc** | Ratio of investment to GDP (+), Literacy rate (+), government consumption (–) |
| Levine and Renelt (1992) | World tables, 1960 - 85 IMF, 1960 - 85 | **H, G / GDP, I / GDP, POL, G** | Human capital, rate of investment, political stability (+), government expenditure (–) |
| Mankiw, Romer, and Weil (1992) | World tables, 1960 - 85 | **H** | Human capital has a positive contribution |
| King and Levine (1993) | 80 countries, 1960 - 1989 | **FV** | Financial variables have positive effect (+) |
| Barro and Sala-i-Martin (1995) | World tables, 1965 - 75, 1975 - 85 | **H, I / GDP, Gc, POL** | All except Gc have positive effect (+) Gc (–) |
| Ott and Ott (1996) | World tables, 1973 - 92 | **Gc, POL** | Government consumption Gc (–), political democracy (+) |
| Gapinski (1996) | World tables, 1950 - 90 | **E, M, POL** | Education (+), high mortality and reduced liberties (–) |
| Benhabib / Spiegel (1997) | 92 countries, 1960 - 1985 | **H, dL / L, dK / K** | Human capital (–), growth in labor and capital (+) |

*Note::* Variables definition: dX / X is rate of growth of exports, dG – rate of change in government expenditure, G / GDP – size of government , Gc- Government consumption. H or E refer to education. I / GDP share of investment in GDP, POL political variables measured by democracy (+) or civil unrest (-), M- mortality rate. Not all variables used as control variables are reported in the table. For details see individual studies.

There is a general agreement today that macro policy impact the *short run* behavior of macro variables such as output and the inflation rate. In the short run if output is below potential, a policy rule can "temporarily" increase output. The effect of policy rules on the *long run* path of the economy is less certain. In the context of the natural rate of unemployment models, in the long run, the economy returns to the level of output that is consistent with the "natural rate of unemployment" (NAIRU). In essence the NAIRU framework defines limits of policy.[18] Once the economy reaches that level of unemployment, i.e. NAIRU, potential output cannot be increased. This leads to the logical conclusion: For policy rules to have permanent effects on the economy, a link has to be established between the growth in productivity and NAIRU.[19] Search theories such as those by Lucas and Prescott (1974), Pissarides (1992) imply a negative relation as the advancement of knowledge would lead to job destruction and higher rate of job turnover. The opposite finding is reported in studies by Caballero (1993), Aghion-Howitt (1992, 1994). In a recent paper Berman, Bound, Jaffe and Machin (1997) examined the implication of skill-biased technical change on employment in OECD. Their empirical evidence suggests that this type of technology has a destructive effect on less skilled workers and job creation effect for skilled workers.[20]

Given these conflicting evidence, a less ambitious task would be to uncover a link between policy and productivity growth. One may approach this question in two ways: Examine the effect of a policy rule that is designed to affect the short-run behavior of a macro variable, say the level of output and investigate its effects on tong-term growth. Alternatively investigate the effects of a change in the policy rule on productivity growth. The first route was followed by Taylor (1996). The second can be investigated within the framework of an endogenous growth model.

## *1. Policy Rules: Feedback Versus Fixed Rules*

Shocks to the economy generate information which could be useful for formulating policy responses. A policy maker following a fixed rule (passive mechanism) will steer the course regardless of the "wind direction." A feedback rule, in contrast, "leans with the wind." That is, the new information is fed back into the planning mechanism and through this policy.

Phillips (1954) discusses several types of feedback rules: Proportional, integral and derivative, all of which affect the "temporal" movement of output. The simple feedback rule is the proportional rule. Suppose that the path of the economy de-

---

18 Recent discussion of NAIRU and its instability are given in several articles in the Journal of Economic Perspectives (Winter 1997). Of particular interest is Galbraith's article.

19 In their 1983 paper Grubb, Jackman and Layard attributed 1.3% of extra unemployment in the OECD to the decline in productivity growth (p. 28).

20 Aghion-Howitt (1994) theoretical framework show that higher growth rates has two effects: Job destruction and job creation.

viated from its optimal path, i.e. $Y_t < Y^*$, where $Y_t$ is output at time $t$ and $Y^*$ is the natural rate. Assume that budget policy (government spending $(G)$, taxes $(T)$) is the policy of interest. Under a passive or a fixed rule the budget balance is set equal to a constant, zero or some percent of $Y$. In this case budget posture $(G - T)$ would remain unchanged. Under a feedback rule, budget balance would be sacrificed–Policy would be set in response to deviation of $Y$ from $Y^*$.

Let policy at time t be set with reference to the gap between $Y_t - 1$ and $Y^*$. A proportional feedback rule:

$$G_t - T_t = \lambda(Y_{t-1} \text{ and } Y^*)$$

Suppose that $G$ is set according to needs

$$G_t = \overline{G}$$

Policy maker would then set $T_t$ on the basis of (4.1)

(4.2) $$T_t = \lambda y + \overline{G} \qquad \lambda < 0$$

where $\lambda$ is the proportionality factor and $y$ is the deviation between $Y$ and $Y^*$.

A fixed rule implies $G_T - T_t = a$ constant and $\lambda = 0$. The following table gives a particular example of a feed back rule for budget policy.

**A budget rule: An illustration**

| Variable | Values (percent) | | | | |
|---|---|---|---|---|---|
| $y$ = Output deviation from trend | − 5 | − 4 | − 3 | − 2 | − 1 |
| with $\lambda = 0.5$ | | | | | |
| $(Gt - Tt)$ = Budget deficit | − 2.5 | − 2 | − 1.5 | − 1 | − 0.5 |
| with $\lambda = 0.3$ | | | | | |
| $(Gt - Tt)$ = Budget deficit | − 1.5 | − 1.2 | − 0.9 | − 0.6 | − 0.3 |

The choice of $\lambda$ depends on objectives of policy makers. The higher $\lambda$ the more weight is attached to output and employment level, the lower $\lambda$ the more weight is attached to the budget posture.

### 2. *Transitory and Permanent Effects*

Suppose that the government believes that a rise in $G$ (for example to increase spending on R&D or education), a tax cut (for example the corporate tax), or a reduction in the deficit (to raise national saving) would enhance economic growth.

Would such a policy exert a permanent or temporary effect on output. If the policy were to permanently raise potential output (trend value), then such a policy is according to Solow conducive to growth. On the other hand, if the policy had a temporary effect, the economy or the level of output would be trend-reverting.[21]

To test for persistence vector autoregression models (VAR) can be utilized. After estimating the VAR model, a shock equal to one standard deviation (of the error term) is given to the policy variable. The VAR model:

$$Y_t = c_1 + \alpha_1 \text{ time } + \sum_{i=1}^{n} \beta_{1i} Y_{t-i} + \sum_{i=1}^{n} \gamma_{1i} G_{t-i} + \rho_1 u_{t-i} + \varepsilon_1$$

$$G_t = c_2 + \alpha_2 \text{ time } + \sum_{i=1}^{n} \beta_{2i} Y_{t-i} + \sum_{i=1}^{n} \gamma_{2i} G_{t-i} + \rho_2 u_{t-i} + \varepsilon_2$$

$G$ is the policy variable, $u$ is an exogenous variable, $\varepsilon$ error term and $n$ is the order of the autoregression.

## *3. Budget Policy and Productivity Growth*

As outlined earlier growth in labor productivity or per capita real output is *exogenous* in the neoclassical model. It is determined by the "exogenous" rate of technical progress. Policy plays no role in determining the steady state position of the economy $(Y^*)$. If we take $Y^*$ as the natural rate of output, then $Y^*$ is given by $n, \delta, g$ all of which are exogenous parameters. In this framework, policy can have only short run effect, it cannot affect the natural rate.

If we drop the neoclassical framework in favor of the *endogenous* model framework, then the choice of one model versus another will depend on the model explanation of sources of growth. The AK model with human capital and endogenous technology gives room for budget policy to affect growth.

Normally we think of budget policy (or fiscal policy) as consisting of $\Delta G$, $\Delta T$ or a combination of the two. In the growth model framework, I would like to redefine budget policy in terms of changes in budget allocation. That is budget policy would focus on the allocation function rather than the stabilization function of the public sector. The hypothesis is that a shift from government consumption to government investment will increase accumulation of human capital or knowledge. Since government investment is nonrival in nature, externalities would be generated. Using Mankiw, Romer and Weil characterization of the production process

21 Nelson and Plosser (1982), Cambell and Mankiw (1987) and Campell (1994) investigated the effects of shocks to output. The effects of shocks in these studies, whether temporary or permanent were not clear cut. The results depend on large measure on the characteristics of the time series for output as well as what is assumed about the shock.

(4.3.1) $$Y(t) = K(t)^{\alpha} H(t)^{\gamma} \left[A(t)L(t)\right]^{1-\alpha-\gamma} \qquad \alpha > 0,\ \gamma > 0,\ \alpha + \gamma < 1$$

$H$ is the stock of human capital. The specification of the production function in (4.3.1) implies a constant return to scale to $K, H$ and $L$ together. Assuming the usual dynamics of $K$ and $L$, the dynamics of $H$ can be specified

(4.3.2) $$\dot{H}(t) = G_H G(t) \qquad 0 < G_H < 1$$

where $G_H$ is the fraction of budget resources devoted to human capital or knowledge accumulation.

Since $G$ is a fraction of $Y$, equation (4.3.2) may be written as

(4.3.2)′ $$\dot{H}(t) = S_{Hg} Y(t)$$

$S_{Hg}$ is a multiplicative term reflecting the share of output devoted to government purchases and the portion of government purchases devoted to investment in human capital.[22] To test for the role of policy, growth equations may be estimated. One method is to relate the policy parameters to the growth rate of labor productivity or to relate it to growth rate of the residual, i.e., first estimate

(4.3.3) $$(y - p)_i = -\delta(\ln Y_i) + b(l_i - p_i) + ak_i + \varepsilon_i$$

where

$y$: growth rate of labor productivity
$p$: growth rate of population
$l$: growth rate of labor
$k$: growth rate of capital per worker
$\varepsilon_i$: residual, or total factor productivity
$\ln Y_i$: logarithm of initial income

From equation (4.3.3), the residual (TFP) would then be regressed on policy parameters.

(4.3.4) $$\left(\frac{dTFP}{TFP}\right)_i = TFP_i^0 + b\left(\frac{dIg}{Ig}\right)_i + cx + \varepsilon_i$$

where

$TFP_i^0$: initial value of total factor productivity
$Ig$: government investment
$x$: a vector of other variables

$\varepsilon$ is the error term.

22 This formulation is similar to these in the empirical literature. See for example Dorwick and Duc-Tho Nguyen (1989).

## V. Empirical Analysis

In the preceding section the hypothesis was advanced: For policy to have permanent effects on the economy a link has to be established between the natural rate of unemployment and productivity growth. For a start, one needs to look at the data. Given that we do not observe the natural rate of unemployment, one way around this problem is to compare the average growth in productivity with the average unemployment rate. According to Fisher (1996), NAIRU can be approximated by mean value of the unemployment rate over 5 years period. Chart 1 plots average unemployment rate and average growth in per capita income over the period 1960 - 1992 for 10 European countries. Chart 2 shows the relationship between average productivity growth and average unemployment over 5 years period for four EC countries: Belgium, Germany, Italy and the UK. The choice of four countries was made for ease of presentation and because they exhibit divergence in the relationship over time.

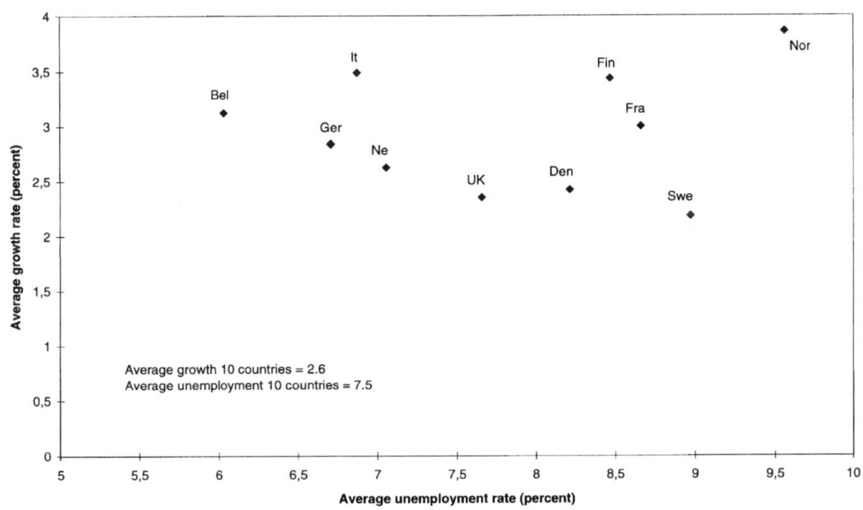


Chart 1: Real per capita income growth and unemployment, 1960 - 1992

Focusing on averages over the entire period for the 10 countries one finds no "unidirectional" pattern between growth and unemployment. Italy, Finland, France and Norway have average growth rates of GDP in excess of 3% (or above average for the 10 countries). Yet the average unemployment rate in both Finland and Norway were 1 to 2 percentage points above the average. Belgium, Germany and Netherlands had about average GDP growth and lower average unemployment while UK, Denmark and Sweden had both low productivity growth than the aver-

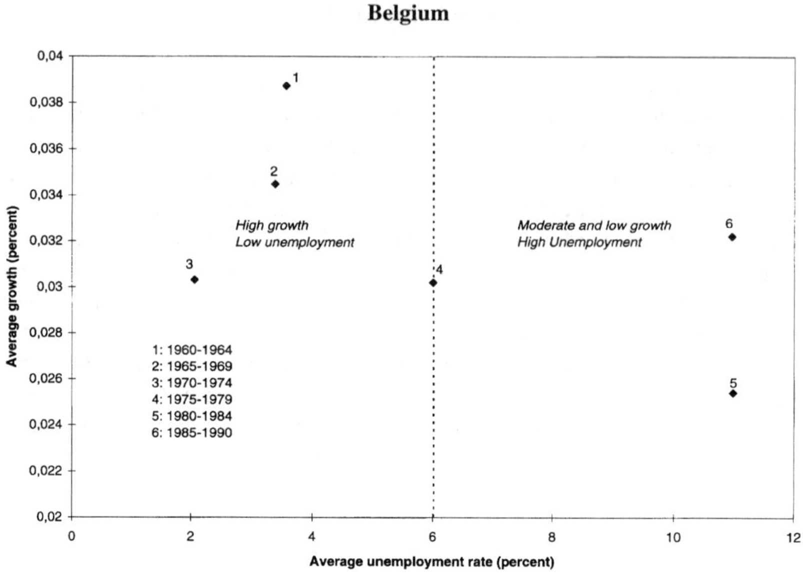


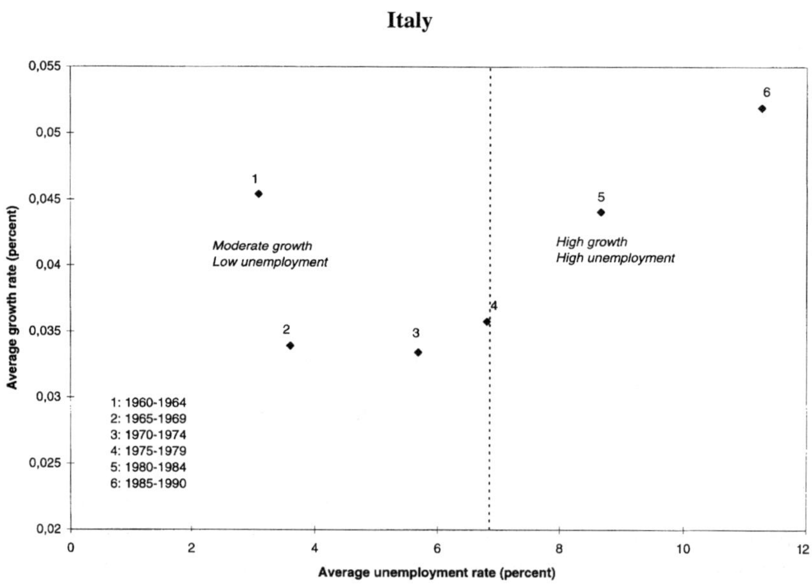


Chart 2: Real per capita income growth and unemployment:
Average by 5 years (1960 - 1990)

**Germany**

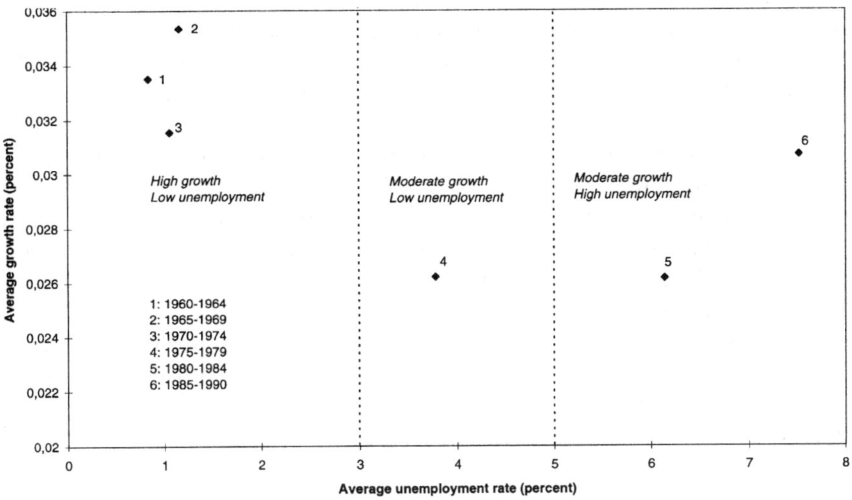
0,036
0,034
0,032
0,03
0,028
0,026
0,024
0,022
0,02
Average growth rate (percent)
0
1
2
3
4
5
6
7
8
Average unemployment rate (percent)
High growth
Low unemployment
Moderate growth
Low unemployment
Moderate growth
High unemployment
1: 1960-1964
2: 1965-1969
3: 1970-1974
4: 1975-1979
5: 1980-1984
6: 1985-1990

**UK**

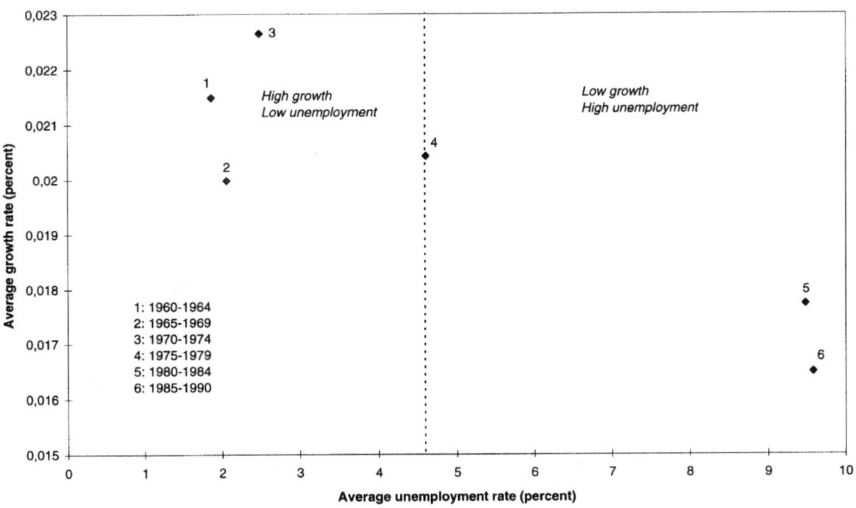
0,023
0,022
0,021
0,02
0,019
0,018
0,017
0,016
0,015
Average growth rate (percent)
0
1
2
3
4
5
6
7
8
9
10
Average unemployment rate (percent)
High growth
Low unemployment
Low growth
High unemployment
1: 1960-1964
2: 1965-1969
3: 1970-1974
4: 1975-1979
5: 1980-1984
6: 1985-1990

age and unemployment around or above the average. The data in Chart 2 are more instructive. First of all, one notice a break in unemployment growth trend centering around 1975 - 1979. From 1960 to the mid 1970, productivity growth and low unemployment were not uncommon. In the later periods, from 1975 on and especially since 1980 the relationship seems to have broken down. High unemployment and lower productivity growth are evident in the UK (1980 - 85 and 1985 - 90), Belgium and Germany (1980 - 85) although Italy experienced both high unemployment and high growth. If the pattern observed in these countries fell short of establishing a relationship between high growth and low unemployment, it clearly points out to the disturbing phenomenon of a rising natural rate of unemployment independent of the trend in productivity growth. Charts 3 and 4 are presented to uncover an association between a fiscal variable the tax rate and economic growth. Chart 3 presents the data for a sample of 10 European countries over the period 1972 - 1992 while data in Chart 4 plots average growth rates of labor productivity for 1975 - 80 and 1980 - 87 and average tax rates over the same period for the four countries.

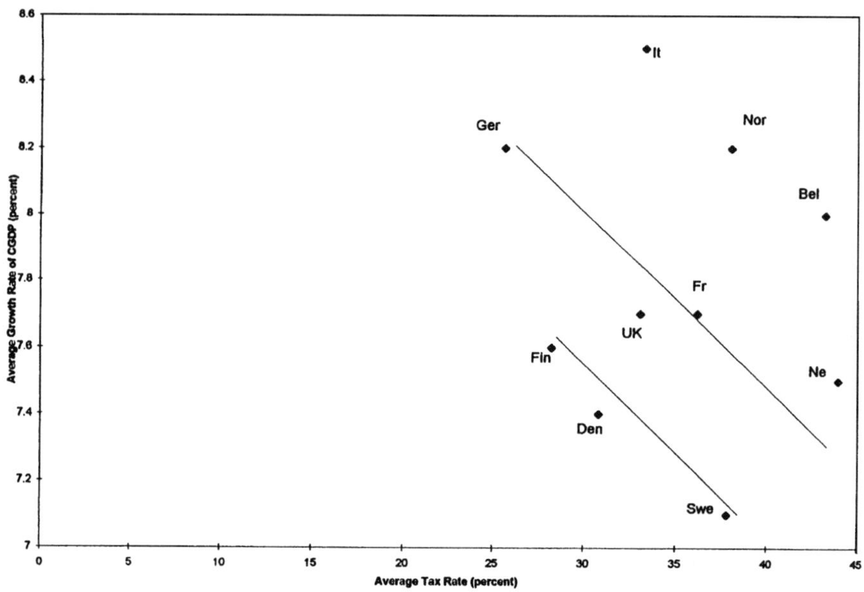


Chart 3: Average Growth Rate of Real per capita income (CGDP) and Average Tax Rate (T/GDP)

The relationships exhibited in Chart 3 are not robust. Although over 1972 - 92 one discerns a negative relationship between high tax rates (T / GDP) and the growth rate of per capita income, two countries, Belgium and Norway, have higher tax rates and high growth rate of GDP compare to the ten country average. Between 1975 - 80 and 1980 - 89 average growth rates for the four countries, Belgium, Germany, Italy and the UK have fallen by 33 percent while the average tax rates have risen by over 8 percent. On a country by country basis there is no coherent trend that can be detected. A fall in the growth rate experienced by Belgium and Germany was accompanied by a rise in the tax rate; the opposite is true for Denmark and UK. To further shed light on the role of policy in the growth process one has to rely on growth models' prediction about the determinants of productivity growth.

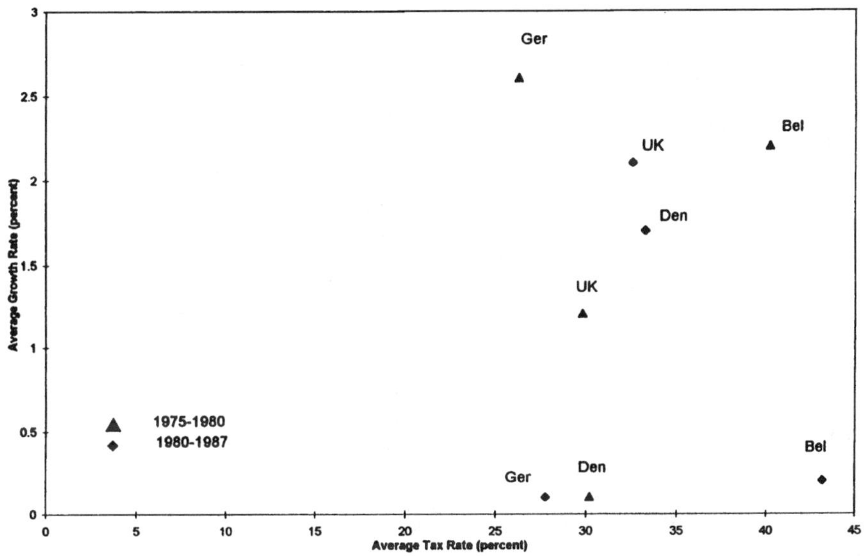


Chart 4: Average Growth Rate of Labor Productivity and Average Tax Rates

Empirical findings derived from growth models estimation is somewhat contradictory and limited in their scope to be useful for deriving conclusions about the long-run association between policy parameters and growth trends. On the basis of the evidence presented earlier (Table 2), it is neither profitable or useful to undergo yet another experimentation with the data. Almost all recent studies have utilized one set of data, the Heston-Summors' World Tables. Because of the small number of data points on key fiscal variables such as the share of government investment in total investment,[23] total level of government spending (a measure of public goods or government size) as well as labor productivity and capital per worker,

23 This variable is derived from a set of variables relating the share of private investment in total investment.

sample size utilized by researchers is usually limited to a few countries, the time span to two or three decades.

Since my interests lie in exploring the relationship between public sector parameters and long run economic growth, an attempt was made to construct data points for the relevant variables for our European sample. Unfortunately the World Tables data on the share of government investment could not be reconciled with data on capital expenditures of the public sector obtained from national budget. From the World Tables, a dataset containing fiscal variables were compiled for 6 European countries over the period 1975 - 1987. This clearly is not a long enough period to test for long term association between policy parameters and growth.

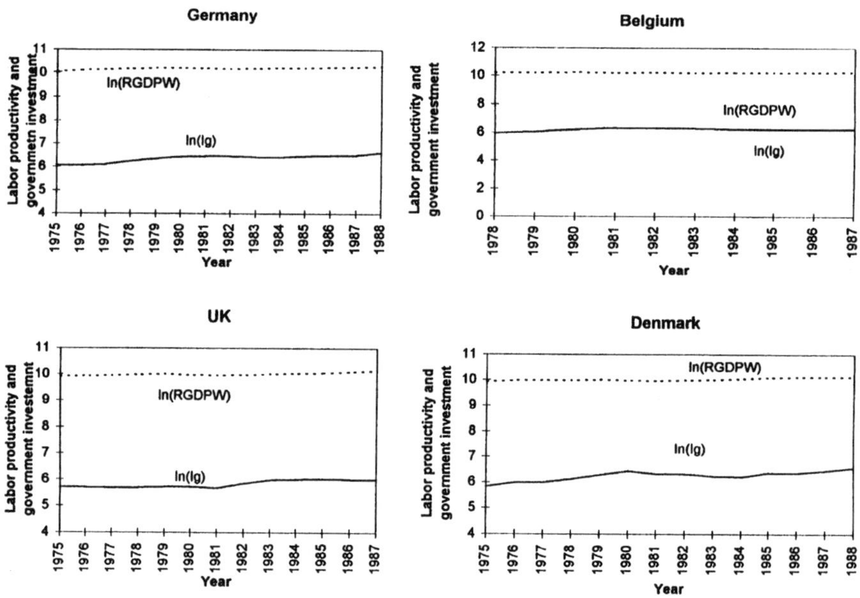


Chart A.3: Labor Productivity and government investment (in logs: 1975 - 1987)

### *The Impact of Changes in the Policy Rule*

Another way of looking at the relationship between policy and growth is to test for Granger causality between policy parameters and economic growth. If the causality were to run from fiscal parameters to economic growth (uni-directional) one can then proceeds to simulate the effects of a change in the policy rule on the path of output. If the effect is transitory, then fiscal parameters exert no long term effect. On the other hand if the effect was permanent, then policy rules can play a role in the growth process.

For illustrative purposes two countries were selected: Germany and the UK. The data is quarterly data from 1957 - 1991. Since economic time series have been known to contain a unit root, we use Dickey-Fuller statistic to test for the presence of unit roots in nominal government spending, nominal government deficit, and nominal gross national product. We consider the null hypothesis

(5.1) $$Y_t = u + \rho Y_{t-1} + e_t$$

and the alternative

(5.2) $$Y_t = u + \beta(t - T/2) + \rho Y_{t-1} + e_t$$

where $Y_t$ denotes the variable of interest, $u$ is drift, $e_t$ is a zero mean serially uncorrelated and mutually independent disturbance term, and under the null hypothesis $\rho = 1$, and $\beta = 0$, i.e. $Y_t$ is integrated of order one or $Y_t \sim I(1)$. Under the alternative hypothesis $\rho < 1$, we estimate the regression

(5.3) $$\Delta Y_t = u + \beta t + \gamma Y_{t-1} + \sum_{i=1}^{q} \lambda_i \Delta Y_{t-i} + v_t$$

where $\gamma = (\rho - 1)$, and compare the $t$-ratio on the estimated $\gamma$ with MacKinnon (1991) critical values. The results of this test (the cointegration test) are reported in Table 3. The choice of the value of q is dictated by the rejection of the serial correlation among the residuals ($v_t$) of equation (5.3).

To establish stationarity of the residuals, the following cointegration regression was estimated

(5.4) $$GNP = \hat{a}_0 + \hat{a}_1 G_t + \hat{u}_t$$

$G$ is government expenditures. Since the deficit (surplus) series is stationary, cointegration test was not performed.

Next we test for causality using the Granger approach. The two policy variables chosen are: total government expenditures and the budget deficit. The Granger-causality test results based on data for government expenditures and deficits or surplus for Germany and the UK are summarized in Table 4. As indicated in the table, unidirectional causality was found from GNP to government expenditures in Germany but the pattern was bidirectional for the UK. For both countries, a bidirectional causality-from surplus to GNP and from GNP to surplus-was discovered. The lag structure was however much longer for the UK than for Germany. Given this pattern of causality, the VAR model can be used to ascertain the effect of a change in the policy rule on GNP and for how long. (The VAR model dependent variable is GNP. Endogenous variables are GNP and the surplus. Government expenditures and the unemployment rate are the exogenous variables.) After

*Table 3*

**Engle-Granger cointegration test results**

| Country / Series | | U Root | Statistic |
|---|---|---|---|
| *Germany* | | (T, 2) | |
| Cointegration vector | | | |
| GNP | | 1.0000 | |
| Government expenditures | | – 4.5178 | |
| Trend | | – 8.649 | |
| Dickey-Fuller t-statistic | | | – 3.7069 |
| MacKinnon critical values | 1% | | – 4.43385 |
| | 5% | | – 3.8485 |
| | 10% | | – 3.5472 |
| *UK* | | (T, 12) | |
| Cointegration vector | | | |
| GNP | | 1.0000 | |
| Government expenditures | | – 3.9470 | |
| Trend | | 780529 | |
| Dickey-Fuller t-statistic | | | – 3.8233 |
| MacKinnon critical values | 1% | | – 4.4551 |
| | 5% | | – 3.8585 |
| | 10% | | – 3.5547 |

*Table 4*

**Direction of causality: Granger-causality test results**

| Description | Lag | F-stat. | Prob. |
|---|---|---|---|
| *Germany* | | | |
| 1. Unidirectional | | | |
| G $\not\Rightarrow$ GNP, but | 4 | 1.7524 | 0.1423 |
| GNP $\Rightarrow$ G | 4 | 2.3505 | 0.575 |
| 2. Bidirectional | | | |
| S $\Rightarrow$ GNP, and | 4 | 2.1575 | 0.0773 |
| GNP $\Rightarrow$ S | 4 | 3.1999 | 0.0152 |
| *UK* | | | |
| 1. Bidirectional | | | |
| G $\Rightarrow$ GNP, and | 12 | 1.9767 | 0.0342 |
| GNP $\Rightarrow$ G | 12 | 2.4912 | 0.0068 |
| 2. Bidirectional | | | |
| S $\Rightarrow$ GNP, and | 12 | 3.8941 | 0.0001 |
| GNP $\Rightarrow$ S | 12 | 4.5962 | 0.0001 |

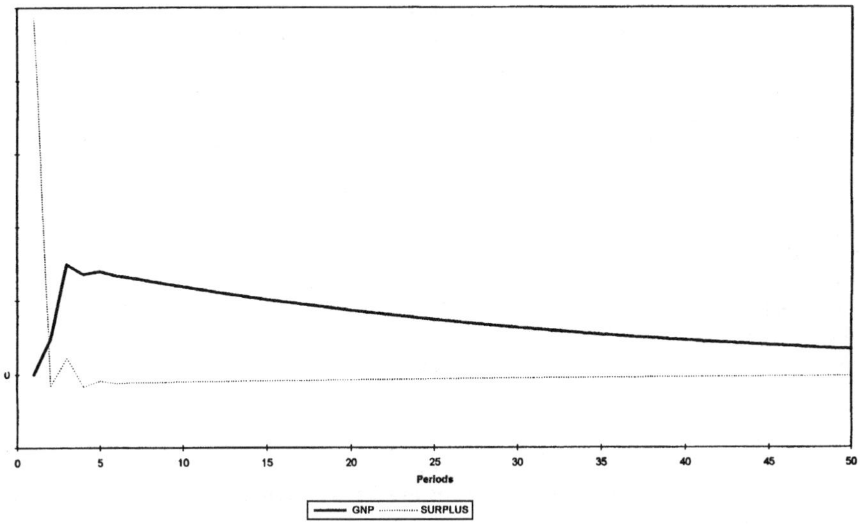


Chart 5: Germany: Response to One Standard Deviation Shock of Surplus

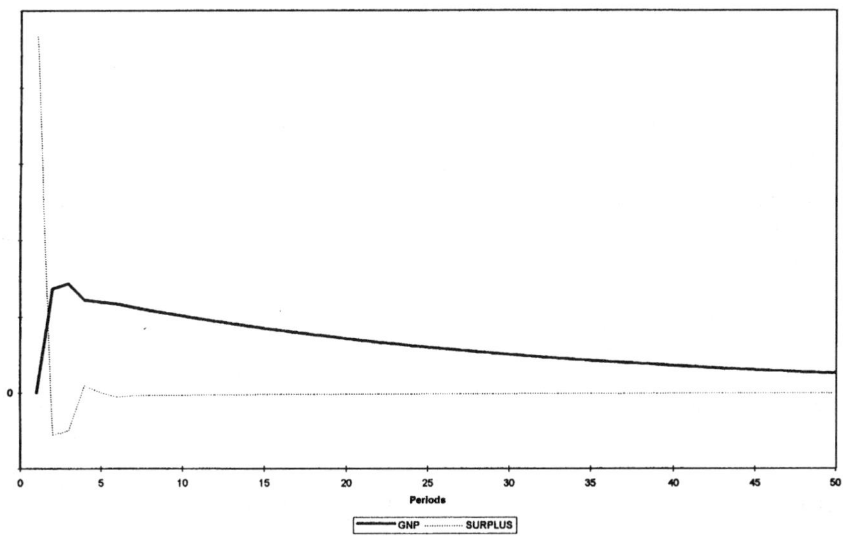


Chart 6: UK: Response to One Standard Deviation Shock of Surplus

*Table A.1*

**Average Annual Growth Rate of Real per capita Income, Alternative Measures**

(in percent: 1960 - 1992)

| Country | RGDPW | RGDP | CGDP |
|---|---|---|---|
| Belgium | 2.68 | 2.72 | 7.90 |
| Denmark | 1.76 | 2.11 | 7.34 |
| Finland | 2.91 | 3.04 | 7.33 |
| France | 2.74 | 2.65 | 7.76 |
| Germany, West | 2.54 | 2.48 | 8.10 |
| Italy | 3.41 | 3.05 | 8.29 |
| Netherlands | 2.03 | 2.32 | 7.44 |
| Norway | 2.42 | 3.37 | 7.84 |
| Sweden | 1.65 | 1.9 | 6.84 |
| UK | 2.00 | 2.07 | 6.94 |

*Table A.2*

**Engle-Granger cointegration test results**

| Country / series | lag | Statistic |
|---|---|---|
| *Belgium* | | |
| Ig | 3 | |
| RGDPW | 3 | |
| Trend | | |
| Dickey-Fuller *t*-statistic | | – 5.149 |
| MacKinnan critical values 5% | | – 5.769 |
| 10% | | – 4.807 |
| *Denmark* | | |
| Ig | 3 | |
| RGDPW | 3 | |
| Trend | | |
| Dickey-Fuller *t*-statistic | | – 2.0956 |
| MacKinnon critical values 5% | | – 4.1116 |
| 10% | | – 3.5691 |
| *Germany* | | |
| Ig | 3 | |
| RGDPW | 3 | |
| Trend | | |
| Dickey-Fuller *t*-statistic | | – 3.958 |
| MacKinnon critical values 5% | | – 4.024 |
| 10% | | – 3.510 |
| UK | | |
| Ig | 3 | |
| RGDPW | 3 | |
| Trend | | |
| Dickey-Fuller *t*-statistic | | – 3.591 |
| MacKinnon critical values 5% | | – 4.112 |
| 10% | | – 3.5691 |

*Notes:* Ig: per capita government investment, RGDPW Labor productivity per worker; RGDP: Real per capita Income in 1985 international prices; CGDP: Real per capita Income in current international prices.

estimating the VAR model, using quarterly data (1957 - 1992), a shock equal to one standard deviation (of the error term) is given to the endogenous variable in each equation at some time period $t$. Then the model is simulated to determine the dynamic effect on all the model variables in the time interval $t$ to $[t+n]$. In the simulation, for both countries, a shock to the budget surplus (an increase in the deficit), at time $t$ causes the path of GNP to rise rapidly for 4 quarters then decreases slowly over time (Charts 5 and 6). After 25 quarters the effect is still 50% of the initial impact, after 50 quarters, the effect of the shock still persists, around 10 percent.

From the behavior of the model outlined here, it appears that a fiscal stimulus is likely to raise the level of GNP and that such an effect is likely to persist over a long span of time. A word of caution however. Because the data is in nominal terms, no robust conclusion can be derived as to the effect of fiscal stimulus on the growth rate of output. To do so one need to decompose the rise in GNP induced by a change in fiscal policy into inflation component and a real component. This can only be done in the context of a structural model linking the natural rate of output and the inflation rate, a task outside the scope of this paper.

## References

*Abramovich,* M. (1986): "Catching up, Forging ahead, and Falling behind." Journal of Economic History 46: 385 - 406. – *Abramovich,* M. and *David,* P. (1996): "Convergence and Deferred Catch up: Productivity Leadership and the Waning of American Exceptionalism." The Mosaic of Economic Growth Ed. Taylor, T. and Gavin Wright. Stanford: Stanford U. Press: 21 - 62. – *Aghion,* P. and *Howitt,* Peter (1994): "Growth and Unemployment." Review of Economic Studies 61: 477 - 494. – *Aghion,* P. and *Howitt,* Peter (1992): "A Model of Growth through Creative Destruction." Econometrica 60, 2: 323 - 351. – *Arrow,* K. (1962): "The Economic Implications of Learning by Doing." Review of Economic Studies 29: 155 - 173. – *Barro,* R. (1991): "Economic Growth in a Cross Section of countries." Quarterly Journal of Economics 106, 2: 407 - 443. – *Barro,* R. and *Sala-i-Martin,* X. (1991): "Convergence across States and Regions." Brookings Papers on Economic Activity 1: 107 - 182. – *Barro,* R. and *Sala-i-Martin,* X. (1995): Economic Growth New York: McGraw Hill, Inc. – *Baumol,* W. (1986): "Productivity Growth, Convergence and Welfare: What the Long-Run Data Show." American Economic Review 76, 5: 1072 - 1085. – *Baumol,* W. and *Wolff,* E. N. (1988): "Productivity Growth, Convergence, and Welfare: Reply." American Economic Review 78, 5 (December): 1155 - 1159. – *Benhabib,* J. and *Spiegel,* Mark (1994): "The Role of Human Capital in Economic Development: Evidence from Aggregate Cross Country Data." Journal of Monetary Economics 34: 143 - 173. – *Benhabib,* J. and *Spiegel,* Mark (1997): Cross Country Growth Regression Processed. – *Berman,* E. / *Bourd,* John and *Machin* (1997): Implications of Skill-Biased Technological Change: International Evidence Boston: Boston University Institute for Economic Development Discussion paper series, 78. – *Bernard,* A. and *Jones,* C. (1996): "Comparing Apples and Oranges: Productivity Convergence and Measurement across Industries and Countries." American Economic Review 85, 5: 1216 - 1238. – *Buckhanan,* J. and *Yoon,* Yong J. eds. (1994): The Return to Increasing Returns Ann Arbor:

University of Michigan Press. – *Caballero,* J. and *Santos,* Manuel (1993): "On Endogenous Growth with Physical and Human Capital." Journal of Political Economy 101, 6: 1042 - 1067. – *Campell,* J. (1994): "Inspecting the Mechanism: An Analytical Approach to the Stochastic Growth Model." Journal of Monetary Economics 33: 463 - 506. – *Cambell,* J. and *Mankiw,* Gregory (1987): "Are Output Fluctuations Transitory?" Quarterly Journal of Economics 102: 857 - 880. – *Cellini,* R. (1997): "Implications of Solow's Growth Model in the Presence of a Stochastic Steady State." Journal of Macroeconomics 19, 1: 135 - 153. – *Diamond,* P. (1965): "National Debt in a Neoclassical Growth Model." American Economic Review 55, 5: 1126 - 1150. – *Dorwick,* S. and *Nguen,* Duc Tho (1987): Australia's Post-War Economic Growth: Measurement and International Comparison Canberra: Center for Economic Policy Research, Australia National University, Discussion paper 160. – *Dorwick,* S. and *Nguyen,* Duc Tho (1989): "OECD Comparative Economic Growth 1950 - 85: Catchup and Convergence." American Economic Review 79, 5: 1010 - 1030. – *Dowrick,* S. and Quiggin, John (1997): "True Measures of GDP and Convergence." American Economic Review 87.1: 41 - 64. – *Edwards,* S. (1993): "Openness, Trade Liberalization, and Growth in Developing Countries." Journal of Economic Literature 31, 3: 1358 - 1393. – *Edwards,* S. (1997): Openness, Productivity and Growth: What Do We Really Know? NBER working paper No. 5978. – *Evans,* P. (1997): "How Fast Do Economies Converge?" Review of Economics and Statistics 2: 219 - 225. – *Feder,* G. (1983): "On Exports and Economic Growth." Journal of Development Economics 12, 1: 59 - 73. – *Fisher,* S. (1996): Why Are Central Banks Pursuing Long-Run price Stability? A symposium sponsored by the Federal Reserve Bank of Kansas City: 7 - 34. – *Galbraith,* J. (1997): "Time to ditch the NAIRU." Journal of Economic Perspectives 11, 2: 93 - 108. – *Gapinski,* J. (1996): "Heterogeneous Capital, Economic Growth, and Economic Development." Journal of Macroeconomics 18, 4: 561 - 585. – *Grilliches,* Z. (1996): "The Discovery of the Residual: A Historical Note." Journal of Economic Literature 34, 3: 1324 - 1330. – *Grossman,* G. and *Helpman,* Elhanan (1991): Innovation and Growth in the Global Economy Cambridge, MA: MIT Press. – *Grubb,* D. / *Jackman,* R. and *Layard,* R. (1983): European Economic Review 21(1/2): 11 - 39. – *Hulten,* C. (1992): "Growth Accounting when Technical Change Is Embodied in Capital." American Economic Review 82, 4: 964 - 980. – *Jorgenson,* D. (1996): "Technology in Growth Theory." Technology and Growth Federal Reserve Bank of Boston Conference Series No. 40: 45 - 77. – *King,* R. and *Levine,* R. (1993): "Finance, Entrepreneurship and Growth Theory and Evidence." Journal of Monetary Economics 32: 513 - 542. – *Knight,* F. (1944): "Diminishing Returns from Investment." Journal of Political Economy 52: 26 - 47. – *Kormendi,* R. and *Meguire,* P. (1985): "Macroeconomic Determinants of Growth: Cross Country Evidence." Journal of Monetary Economics 16: 141 - 63. – *Kremer,* M. and *Thomson,* J. (1994): Young Workers, Old Workers and Convergence NBER working paper No. 4827. – *Krugman,* P. (1994): "The Myth of Asia's Miracle." Foreign Affairs: 62 - 78. – *De Long,* J. B. (1988): "Productivity Growth." American Economic Review 78, 5: 1138 - 1154. – *De* Long, J. B. (1996): "Cross-Country Variations in National Economic Growth Rates: The Role of Technology." Technology and Growth Federal Reserve Bank of Boston Conference Series No. 40: 127 - 150. – *Lau,* L. (1996): "The Sources of Long-Tern Economic Growth: Observations from the Experience of Developed and Developing Countries." The Mosaic of Economic Growth Ed. Landan, R., T. Taylor and G. Wright. Stanford: Stanford U. Press: – 63 - 91. – *Lau,* L. and *Kim,* Jong-il (1994): "The Sources of Economic Growth of the East Asian Newly Industrialized Countries." Journal of the Japanese and International Economies 8: 235 - 271. – *Levin,* R. and Renelt, D. (1992): "A Sensitivity Analysis of Cross-Country Growth Regressions." American Economic Review 82, 4: 942 - 963. – *Lucas,* R. (1988): "On the Mechanics of Economic

Development." Journal of Monetary Economics 22: 3 - 42. – *Lucas,* R. (1993): "Making a Miracle." Econometrica 61, 2: 251 - 272. – *Lucas,* R. and Prescott, E. (1974): "Equilibrium Search and Employment." Journal of Economic Theory 7: 188 - 209. – *Maddison,* M. (1982): Phases of Capitalist Development Oxford: Oxford University Press. – *Maddison,* M. (1992): "A Long-Term Perspective on Saving." Scandinavian Journal of Economics 94, 2: 181 - 196. – *Mankiw,* G. (1995): "The Growth of Nations." Brookings Papers on Economic Activity 1: 275 - 310. – *Mankiw,* G. / *Romer,* D. and *Weil,* D. (1992): "A Contribution to the Empirics of Economic Growth." Quarterly Journal of Economics 107, 2: 407 - 437. – *Mulligan,* C. and *Sala-i-Martin,* Xavier (1993): "Transitional Dynamics in Two-Sector Models of Endogenous Growth." Quarterly Journal of Economics 108, 3: 737 - 773. – *Nehru,* V. and *Dhareshwar,* A. (1994): New Estimates of Total Factor Productivity Growth for Developing and Industrial Countries Policy Research Working Paper 1313, The World Bank. – *Nelson,* C. and Plosser, C. (1982): "Trends and Random Walks in Macroeconomic Time Series: Some Evidence and Implications." Journal of Monetary Economics 10: 139 - 162. – *Ortiguira,* S. and *Santos,* M. (1997): "On the Speed of Convergence in Endogenous Growth Models." American Economic Association 87, 3: 303 - 399. – *Ott,* A. and *Ott,* D. (1996): "Are Authoritarian Regimes Compatible with Development." Middle East Business and Economic Review 8, 2: 10 - 30. – *Phillips,* A. (1954): "Stabilization Policy in a Closed Economy." Economic Journal 64: 290 - 305. – *Pissarides,* C. (1992): "Loss of Skill during Unemployment and the Persistence of Employment Shocks." Quarterly Journal of Economics 107, 4: 1371 - 91. – *Ram,* R. (1986): "Government Size and Economic Growth: A New Framework and some Evidence from Cross-Section and Time Series Data." American Economic Review 76, 1: 281 - 284. – *Ramsey,* F. (1928): "A Mathematical Theory of Saving." Economic Journal 38: 543 - 559. – *Rebelo,* S. (1991): "Long Run Policy Analysis and Long Run Growth." Journal of Political Economy 99, 3: 500 - 521. – *Romer,* P. (1986): "Increasing Returns and Long Run Growth." Journal of Political Economy 94, 5: 1002 - 1037. – *Romer,* P. (1987): "Growth Based on Increasing Returns due to Specialization." American Economic Review 77, 2: 56 - 62. – *Romer,* P. (1990): "Endogenous Technical Change." Journal of Political Economy 98, 5 Part 2: S. S71 - S102. – *Solow,* R. (1956): "A Contribution to the Theory of Economic Growth." Quarterly Journal of Economics 70,1: 65 - 94. – *Solow,* R. (1957): "Technical Change and the Aggregate Production Function." Review of Economics and Statistics 39: 312 - 320. – *Swan,* T. (1956): "Economic Growth and Capital Accumulation." Economic Records 32: 334 - 361. – *Stiroh,* K and *Jorgenson,* D. (1995): "Computers and Growth." Economics of Innovation and New Technology 3: 295 - 316. – *Taylor,* J. (1979): "Staggered Wage Setting in a Macromodel." American Economic Review 69: 108 - 113. – *Taylor,* J. (1996): "Stabilization Policy and Long-Term Economic Growth." Mosaic of Economic Growth Ed. Landan, R., T. Taylor and G. Wright. Stanford: Stanford University Press: 129 - 149. – *VonNeumann,* J. (1937): Trans. K. Menger. "A Model of General Equilibrium." Review of Economic Studies (1945) 13: 1 - 9. – *Young,* A. (1995): "The Tyranny of Numbers: Confronting the Statistical Realities of the East Asian Growth Experience." Quarterly Journal of Economics 109, 3: 641 - 680.

# Does Structure Matter?
# The Macroeconomics of Unbalanced Growth

By Loek Groot and Ronald Schettkat, Utrecht

## I. Introduction

In perfect-market models (like in new-classical economics) economic structure is unimportant, because – by assumption – the economy is in equilibrium representing the optimum. If external shocks occur, instantaneous price reactions will bring the economy back to equilibrium, whatever the underlying structure is. However, structural models gained importance in economics in general as in work on adjustment processes (e.g., Pasinetti 1983, Leonard 1996, Schettkat 1992), on unbalanced productivity growth (e.g., Baumol 1967, 1996, Appelbaum / Schettkat 1997), or in work on the relation between inter-country and / or interindustry employment and productivity growth patterns (e.g., Freeman 1988, Appelbaum / Schettkat 1995). These papers are not the first discussions of the impact of industry structure on economic growth patterns. The history dates back as far as to Adam Smith and includes more recent authors like Schumpeter, Rehn / Meidner, Salter, and Kaldor. The last five authors were mainly concerned with the improvement of average productivity growth through structural economic dynamics, i.e. their emphasize was on the causes of and conditions for the expansion of the industries with the highest productivity levels and growth rates. Baumol (1967) turned the emphasize to the impact of unbalanced productivity growth on the industries with the lowest productivity levels and growth rates, predicting a cost disease of many service industries.

In this paper, we first briefly discuss some models of unbalanced productivity growth. We then present some simple simulation studies, which relate to the models discussed. We elaborate on the underlying assumptions and consequences for economic structure, and growth and we close the paper with some remarks on further research and policy implications.

## II. Brief discussion of some unbalanced productivity growth models

Probably the most influential structural economic model is the Rehn-Meidner model, which is not only a theoretical model but which was applied for economic policy formulation in Sweden. The core of the Rehn-Meidner model is the so-called solidaristic wage policy, which was thought to influence economic structure and average productivity growth. Solidaristic wages were actually equilibrium wages as they would occur in prefect markets, i.e. wages depending on skills (individual productivity) but not on industry. Compensatory wage differentials would, of course occur. However, setting wages at such an 'equilibrium' (average may be a better word) puts industries (and firms) with low productivity levels and growth rates under pressure. These industries either improve their productivity or they disappear from the market and thus increase average productivity of the (remaining) economy. Industries with high productivity levels and growth rates, on the other hand, would face lower wage costs than their productivity would allow them to pay. I.e., compared to wages oriented on industry-specific productivity (ability to pay, which is often labeled a "flexible wage policy") these industries have under the solidaristic wage policy lower wage costs, which allows for price reduction and a stronger expansion of demand for the products of these industries. Again this effect increases average productivity. As a consequence employment would decline in industries with low productivity and expand in industries with high productivity (see Figure 1).[1] The underlying relation between employment and productivity growth in the Rehn-Meidner model thus is positive as described as characteristic for industrial development by Salter (1960).

Salter emphasized technological change as the main source for productivity growth and hence changes in relative prices and demand. Industries which experience technological progress can lower their (relative) prices and expand more than technological stagnant industries where relative prices are rising, given similar wage trends. This is exactly the same reasoning as behind the Rehn-Meidner model, but Salter emphasizes technological progress rather than wage policy. Indeed, Salter showed that prices in technological progressive industries fell relative to prices in technological stagnant industries and this result was confirmed for later years (Appelbaum / Schettkat 1995).

Another model consistent with a positive correlation between industry-specific productivity growth and employment growth is Kaldor's model of cumulative growth. Whereas Salter's model may be described as a supply-side model, Kaldor (1966) strongly emphasized the demand side. Demand expansion leads to productivity growth mainly through economies of scale, which improve income and this leads to an even higher demand in the second round, this way creating a cumulative (or positive feedback effect) process of economic growth. However, demand and e.o.s. are unevenly distributed across industries and in Kaldor's paper it is the manufacturing sector, which is the 'engine of growth'. Since productivity growth is highest in manufacturing industries, all three models predict employment expan-

---

1 The only problem Rehn and Meidner identified was the mobility of workers between shrinking (low productivity) and expanding (high productivity) industries for which they designed the Swedish labor market policy.

sion in manufacturing. A development which is confirmed by an analysis of Singh (1988), who found that manufacturing employment culminated in the industrialized countries in the late 1960s or early 1970s.

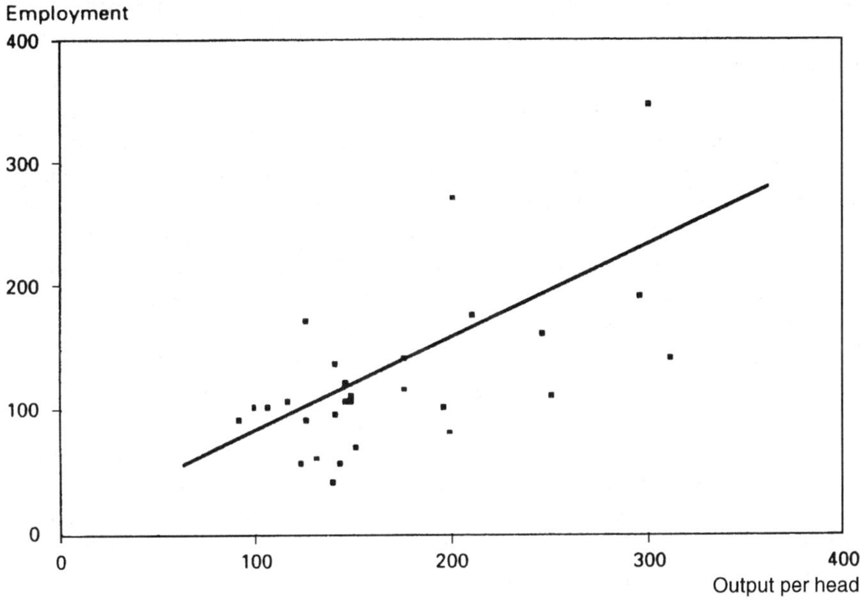


Figure 1: The relationship between changes in employment and in output per head across industries in Britain according to Salter, 1924 - 1950 (1924 = 100)

Kaldor obviously discussed a full-employment situation because he saw the availability of labor as the main growth constraint for high-productivity manufacturing industries. Other growth constraints as emphasized by Schumpeter (1934) (stemming, for example, from product demand, lack of innovations, saturation) were not discussed, which fits very well the 1950s and 1960s when a slowdown of economic growth was not an issue. However, all three models are based on unbalanced productivity growth and all three models focus on the expansion of high-productivity industries, which expand forever because possible growth constraints on the demand side were not integrated into the models (Schettkat 1997).

With a specific demand function in mind, Baumol (1967) emphasized the effects of unbalanced productivity growth on the technological stagnant industries. Assuming similar growth of real demand in technologically stagnant (services)[2] and

[2] To be clear, we do not believe that services are unproductive in the sense that they do not contribute to economic wealth. In this respect they are not different from manufacturing goods. Many services, however, are produced at lower productivity levels (although the initial level of productivity is in a sense arbitrary because it depends on the initial value (the

technologically progressive (manufacturing) industries and thus a constant ratio of real output of these two sectors, Baumol predicted a cost disease of technologically stagnant services.[3] Baumol assumed aside from growth rates of real demand for technological progressive and stagnant industries being identical that wages rise at the same rate in all industries, which is obviously the case at full-employment. Under these conditions prices in the technological stagnant industries as well their share in nominal GDP and employment will rise.[4]

The advantage of Baumol's model is the introduction of a demand constraint but his assumption on the demand function is a bit arbitrary. Baumol simply assumed that real demand for the two sectors grows proportional to real income. This assumption, however, requires that the income elasticities are equal to one and price elasticities are equal to zero (i.e. that prices do not matter), or that the income elasticity for the technological progressive industries is smaller than one but enhanced by the price elasticity (relative prices in these industries fall). For the technological stagnant industries this requires that the income elasticity is larger than one but reduced by the price elasticity (here relative prices will rise). In other words, income and price effects need to cancel (for a discussion Appelbaum / Schettkat 1997). In a long-run analysis Baumol et al. (1989) actually found the ratio of real output in technologically stagnant industries (services) to real output of the technologically progressive industries (manufacturing) to be constant up to the mid 1970s. For the 1970s and 1980s, however, there is evidence that this ratio is rising, i.e. that the output of technological stagnant industries (services) is growing in real terms more than proportionally (Appelbaum / Schettkat 1997).

However, 'Baumol's cost disease' is obviously dominating discussions on the costs of services with a general feeling that especially public services are getting

---

wage) assigned to certain activities) and most important at lower productivity growth rates. This is especially the case with personal services.

Some personal services, like shoeshine or household cleaning, may be regarded as less valuable work, because the professional shoeshine-man does not work at a (much) higher productivity than everybody else. There are hardly any specific skills necessary and specialization hardly delivers efficiency gains. However, if one buys cleaning services, one may gain leisure time. The latter, however, makes only sense, if one's own net wage is higher than the service provider's gross wage (if one does not especially dislike cleaning). Therefore, wage differentials (including overhead costs, taxes and contributions) are important. The higher the wage differential between consumer and producer, the more attractive the substitution. The higher the taxes and contributions to be paid (the wedge) the less attractive it is to buy services, the more attractive is 'do-it-yourself' (Scharpf 1980).

3 Later (1985) Baumol et al. made a more realistic classification of industries according to their technological capacities, which is, however, not important to develop the basic arguments.

4 The ratio of nominal output of the technological stagnant ($s$) to the technological progressive sector ($p$) is equal to the ratio of employment. With $P = \frac{W}{\pi}$ where $P$ = price, $W$ = wage, $\pi$ = productivity, $Q$ = quantity produced (real output), $Y$ = nominal output, $P = \frac{W * E}{Q}$, $W_p = W_s$, one gets $\frac{Y_p^{n,t}}{Y_s^{n,t}} = \frac{E_p^t}{E_s^T}$; if $\dot{\pi}_p > \dot{\pi}_s$ it follows that $E_p^t$ declines relative to $E_s^t$.

too expensive and many governments actually tried to revise the trend of an ever expanding public share in GDP. In a more recent paper (1993) William Baumol pointed out that there is no principle problem with unbalanced productivity growth. As long as average productivity in the economy increases, consumers as group can afford more of everything, more technologically stagnant services and more technologically progressive goods. True, this is actually the full-employment assumption easily made in theory but reality seems to be bit more complicated as Baumol (1993), of course, observes.

Under the condition of full-employment (and a constant labor force) Baumol's constant ratio of real output of the technological stagnant industries to real output of the technological progressive industries requires a continuous shift of workers from the technological progressive to the technological stagnant industries. The former is still growing in real output terms but employment declines. However, if real output in the technological progressive industries stagnates, Baumol's condition of a constant real output ratio requires stagnating output and employment in the technologically stagnant industries and thus falling overall employment levels (i.e., unemployment) because with stagnating output in the technological progressive industries but positive productivity growth employment in these industries will fall.[5]

Is there any reason to believe that demand for products of technological progressive industries stagnates? Technology progressive industries are mainly (although not only) manufacturing industries and employment in these industries started to decline in the early 1970s in almost all industrialized countries, i.e., productivity growth was higher than output growth, these markets became saturated[6]. The 'engine of growth' lost speed and one may explain the substantially lower rates of income (and productivity)[7] growth since 1970s compared to earlier periods by this development. In the 1970s and 1980s one can also observe a negative correlation

---

5 From the assumption $\dot{Q}_p = \dot{Q}_s$ and the definition of productivity as $\pi = \frac{Q}{E}$ one can approximate the growth rates by $\dot{\pi}_p + \dot{E}_p = \dot{\pi}_s + \dot{E}_s$ , which gives us together with the assumption of $\dot{\pi}_s = 0$ under full employment ($\dot{E}_p = -\dot{E}_s$) the result that employment in $s$ must grow as long as productivity growth in $p$ is not totally compensated by a decline in $p's$ employment. I.e., as long as real output in $p$ grows less than the rate of productivity growth in $p$, employment in $s$ can expand.

6 Saturation, of cause, means partial saturation for certain goods. It does in no way mean that all (material) human needs are satisfied, as it is obviously not the case in a worldwide context and not in the industrialized countries. However, food is in the industrialized countries obviously available in abundance (the market is saturated) but the needs for food in parts of the third world are obviously not sufficient to initiate transfers. Needs become only effective if they are market demand.

7 Productivity and income per capita are not the same thing actually. Only with full employment and a constant employment rate both grow with the same rate. With rising employment rates income per capita may grow even if productivity growth is zero. On the other hand, positive productivity growth may lead to stagnating or even falling income per capita if the employment rate falls (for a more systematic discussion Schettkat 1992).

between industry-specific productivity growth and employment growth (i.e., employment in industries with less than average productivity growth (and levels) expands, Appelbaum / Schettkat 1995), which is the reverse of the 'industrial model' and sometimes labeled as 'de-industrialization' (post-industrial society, post-fordism are other labels).

To summarize, the models of Kaldor, Salter, Rehn and Meidner emphasized different means to improve average productivity growth but they did not include any other growth constraints than labor supply. Thus the technological progressive industries could expand and only Kaldor emphasized full-employment (labor supply) as a growth constraint explicitly. Also Baumol seems to assume full-employment but he introduces demand constraints on the technological progressive industries. However, if in the Baumol model output in the technological progressive industries stagnate this will also lead to a stagnation of output in technological stagnant industries and thus to a decline in overall employment, i.e. unemployment. Wage differentiation, however, may overcome the 'cost disease'. To capture the stylized features of the models discussed we develop simple simulation models in the next section.

## III. Simulation models

We use two types of models, one model in which product demand may be characterized as price-driven and another in which product demand maybe characterized as income-driven. We assume an economy with two sectors, for convenience labeled as a technological progressive (goods) sector ($p$) and a technological stagnant (service) sector ($s$). For each model we implement three different versions of wage-setting and we run versions imposing full-employment as well as versions which relax the full-employment assumption. The structure of the models is summarized in Boxes 1 and 2. The three versions of each model may be characterized as follows:

A: perfect-labor-market or solidaristic-wage-policy model
Wages in both sectors are identical and change with average productivity.
Full-employment is assumed.

B: wage-dispersion (according to industry-specific productivity) or flexible-wage model
Wages in the sectors develop according to industry-specific productivity trends.
Full-employment is assumed.

C: nominal average wage increases
Nominal wages develop according to average productivity growth.
Full-employment condition relaxed.

**Box 1: The structure of model I (price-driven)**

Basic structure

| | | |
|---|---|---|
| | (1) $P_p = k\frac{W_p}{\pi_p}$ | (5) $P_s = k\frac{W_s}{\pi_s}$ |
| | (2) $Q_p = \frac{1}{b_p}(a_p - P_p)$ | (6) $Q_s = \frac{1}{b_s}(a_s - P_s)$ |
| | (3) $L_p = \frac{Q_p}{\pi_p}$ | (7) $L_s = \frac{Q_s}{\pi_s}$ |
| | (4) $Y_p = Q_p P_p$ | (8) $Y_s = Q_s P_s$ |

Variants

| | | |
|---|---|---|
| **I-A:** | (9) $W_p = W_s$ | (10) $L_0 = L_p + L_s$ |
| **I-B:** | (9) $\dot{W}_{p,r} = \dot{\pi}_p$ | (10) $L_0 = L_p + L_s$ |
| **I-C:** | (9) $W'_{p,n} = \bar{\pi}' W^0_{p,n}$ | (10) $W'_{s,n} = \bar{\pi}' W^0_{s,n}$ |

where:

$P$ = price, $W$ = nominal money wage, $\pi$ = labor productivity, $Q$ = real output, $L$ = employment level, $Y$ = nominal output and $L_0$ = labor force, employment.

This is a model with ten equations, and ten endogenous variables:

$$P_p, Q_p, W_p, L_p, Y_p, P_s, Q_s, W_s, L_s, Y_s$$

Exogenous parameters are $a_p = 1.5; a_s = 2.0; b_p = 0.01; b_s = 0.02; k = 1;\ L_0 = 100;$ $\pi_s = 1.0$. The $\pi_p$ is variable in simulation. The values of the exogenous parameters are chosen to get simple values for the endogenous variables (see the upper rows of the model outcomes) in the first run ($\pi_p = 1.0$).

According to equation (1) and (5), prices of goods ($p$) and services ($s$) are determined by unit labor costs (assuming the mark-up to be constant and unitary). Equations (2) and (6) express negatively sloped product demand curves ($P = a - bQ$, with $b > 0$). Equations (3) and (7) determine labor demand in both sectors, dependent on product demand and labor productivity. Substitution of (1) into (2) and subsequently into (3) gives a negatively sloped labor demand curve, with labor demand dependent on the wage level. From (1) and (3) can be derived that $P_pQ_p = W_pL_p$, and from (5) and (7) that $P_sQ_s = W_sL_s$. Nominal outputs are defined in (4) and (8).

**Box 2: The structure of model II (income-driven)**

Basic structure

(1) $P_p = k\frac{W_p}{\pi_p}$ (6) $P_s = k\frac{W_s}{\pi_s}$

(2) $C_p = Caut_p + \beta Y_r - \delta Y_r^2$ (7) $C_s = Caut_s + \beta Y_r - \delta Y_r^2$

(3) $C_p = P_p Q_p$ (8) $C_s = P_s Q_s$

(4) $L_p = \frac{Q_p}{\pi_p}$ (9) $L_s = \frac{Q_s}{\pi_s}$

(5) $Y_p = Q_p P_p$ (10) $Y_s = Q_s P_s$

(11) $Y_r = P_p^0 Q_p + P_s^0 Q_s$

Variants

**II-A:** (12) $W_p = W_s$ (10) $L_0 = L_p + L_s$

**II-B:** (12) $\dot{W}_{p,r} = \dot{\pi}_p$ (10) $L_0 = L_p + L_s$

**II-C:** (12) $W'_{p,n} = \bar{\pi}' W^0_{p,n}$ (10) $W'_{s,n} = \bar{\pi}' W^0_{s,n}$

Where $C_{aut}$ is autonomous consumption.

This is a model with thirteen equations, and thirteen endogenous variables:

$$P_p, Q_p, W_p, L_p, Y_p, P_s, Q_s, W_s, L_s, Y_s, C_p, C_s, Y_p$$

The values of the exogenous parameters are chosen to obtain smooth outcomes in the first run: $Caut_p = 40$; $Caut_s = -20$; $\beta = 0.4$; $\delta = 0.001$; $k = 1$; $L_0 = 100$; $\pi_s = 1.0$ and $\pi_p$ is the variable in simulation.

The results of the simulations are summarized by the ratio of real output in $p$ (the technologically progressive sector) over real output in $s$ (the technologically stagnant sector) and total real income in Figures 2-A and 3-A. In Figures 2-B and 3-B we present the ratio of nominal output in $p$ to nominal output in $s$ and the ratio of employment in $p$ over employment in $s$ (the complete variables are displayed Tables 2 and 3 in the Appendix).

In Model I-A real wages increase with average productivity growth and are identical in both sectors (perfect labor market). Prices are developing accordingly. They fall in the technological progressive sector and rise in the technological stagnant sector. As long as the price elasticity of product demand in the technological progressive sector is greater than one ($\eta_p > 1$), employment in this sector ($L_p$) increases together with nominal output. If $\eta_p < 1$, then employment in the technological progressive sector ($L_p$) falls (i.e., the labor saving effect of productivity growth outweighs the product demand effect). The full-employment assumption requires that resources not used in the technological progressive sector will be shifted to the stagnant sector. Therefore, the ratio $L_p/L_s$ declines as soon as the Labor saving effect dominates. Given equal wages in both sectors with constant $\pi_s$ implies that relative prices of services increase. This can be easily seen from equations (1) and (5): $\dot{P}_p < 0$ if $\dot{W}_p < \dot{\pi}_p$ ; $\dot{P}_s > 0$ if $\dot{W}_s > \dot{\pi}_s$ . Model I-B allows for wage dispersion, and nominal wages in $s$ decrease. Relative wages in $s$ drop substantially because wages in $p$ rise with productivity.

Comparing model I-B (flexibile wage model) with model I-A (perfect market, equal wage model) is particularly interesting because in I-B service employment is boosted by downward flexible wages. At the same time, wages in the technological progressive sector are upward flexible and thus reducing the expansion of this sector compared to the 'perfect-labor-market' model (I-A). This is the mechanism Linda Bell and Richard Freeman (1985) emphasized. The impact of (downward) wage flexibility on output and employment in the technological stagnant industries is positive but, at the same time, (upward) wage flexibility in the technological progressive industries has a negative impact on sector output and employment. Flexible wages oriented on industry-specific productivity trends thus have a labor enhancing effect in the low-productivity industry but also a labor reducing effect in high-productivity industries. Thus the overall employment impact depends on the relative strength of the two effects. As long as there are no demand constraints on the technological progressive industries, low wage differentials are favorable for overall productivity and overall income in the economy (the Rehn-Meidner model). The rise in real income (and overall productivity) in the simulations (see Figure 2-A and Table 2 in the Appendix) is only 38% in the 'flexible wage model' but 50% in the 'perfect-market model'. Full employment is (by assumption) retained in both models but in case of wage dispersion the outcome is sub-optimal. Too many workers are employed in the low productive service sector. On the other hand, however, higher wages in the technological progressive industries maybe necessary to attract workers away from the technological stagnant industries, which

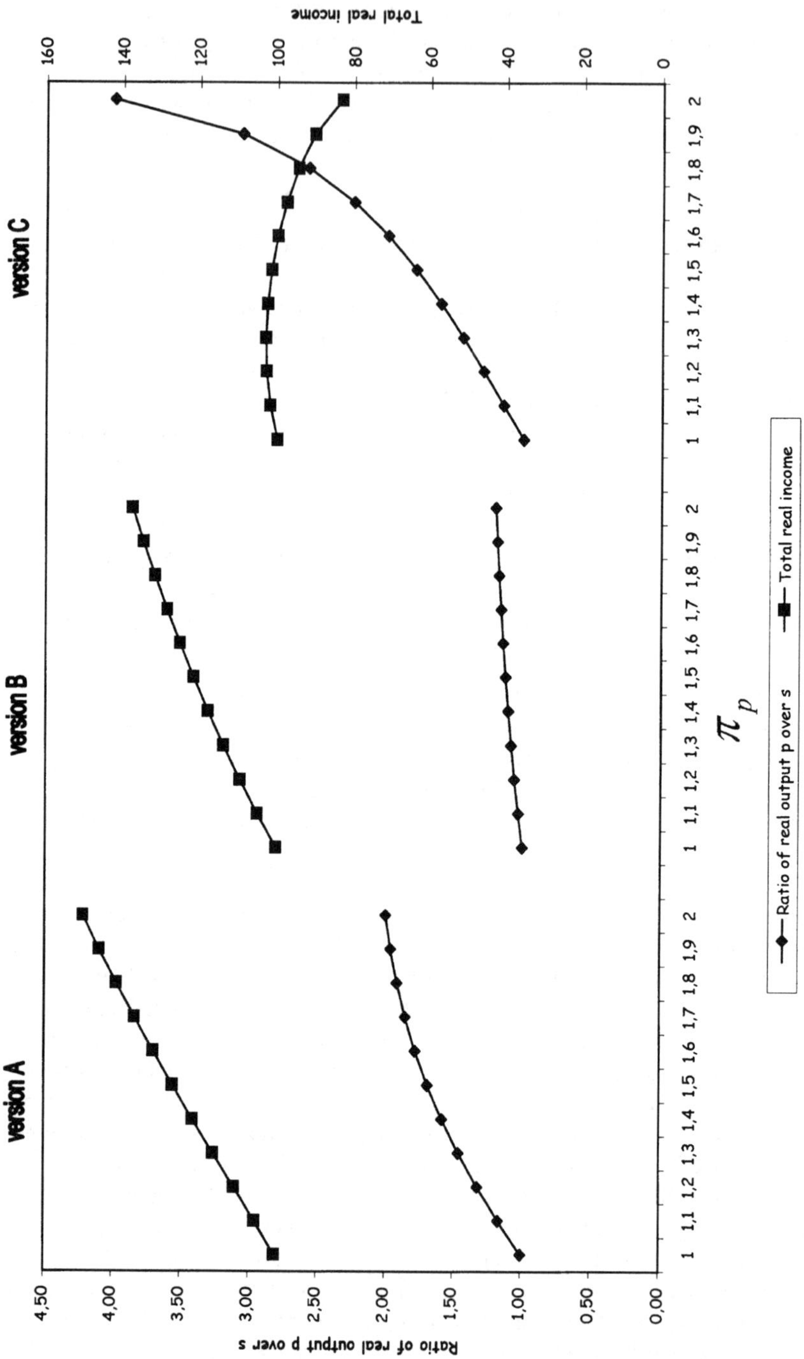


Figure 2-A: Model I: Ratio of real output in $p$ over real output in $s$ and total real income

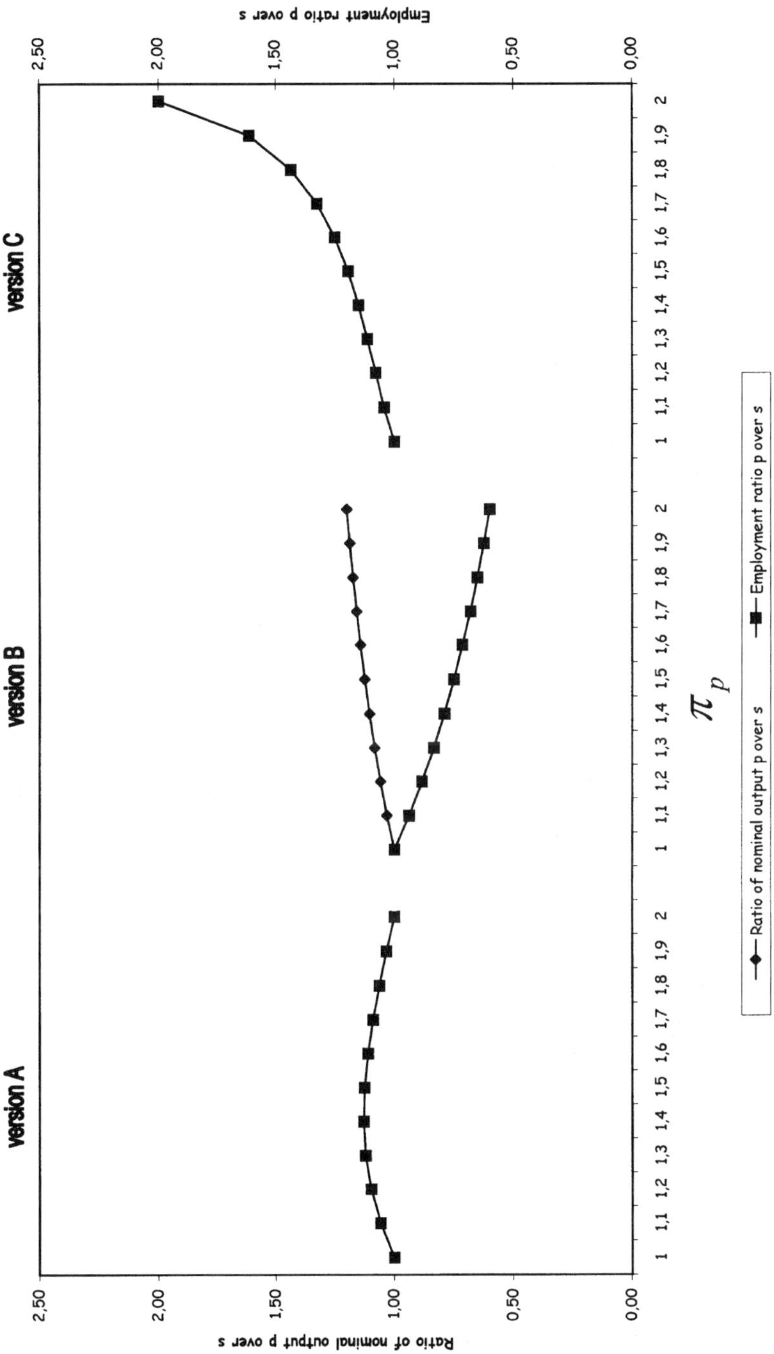


Figure 2-B: Model I: Ratio of nominal output in $p$ over nominal output in $s$ and employment ratios $(L_p/L_s)$

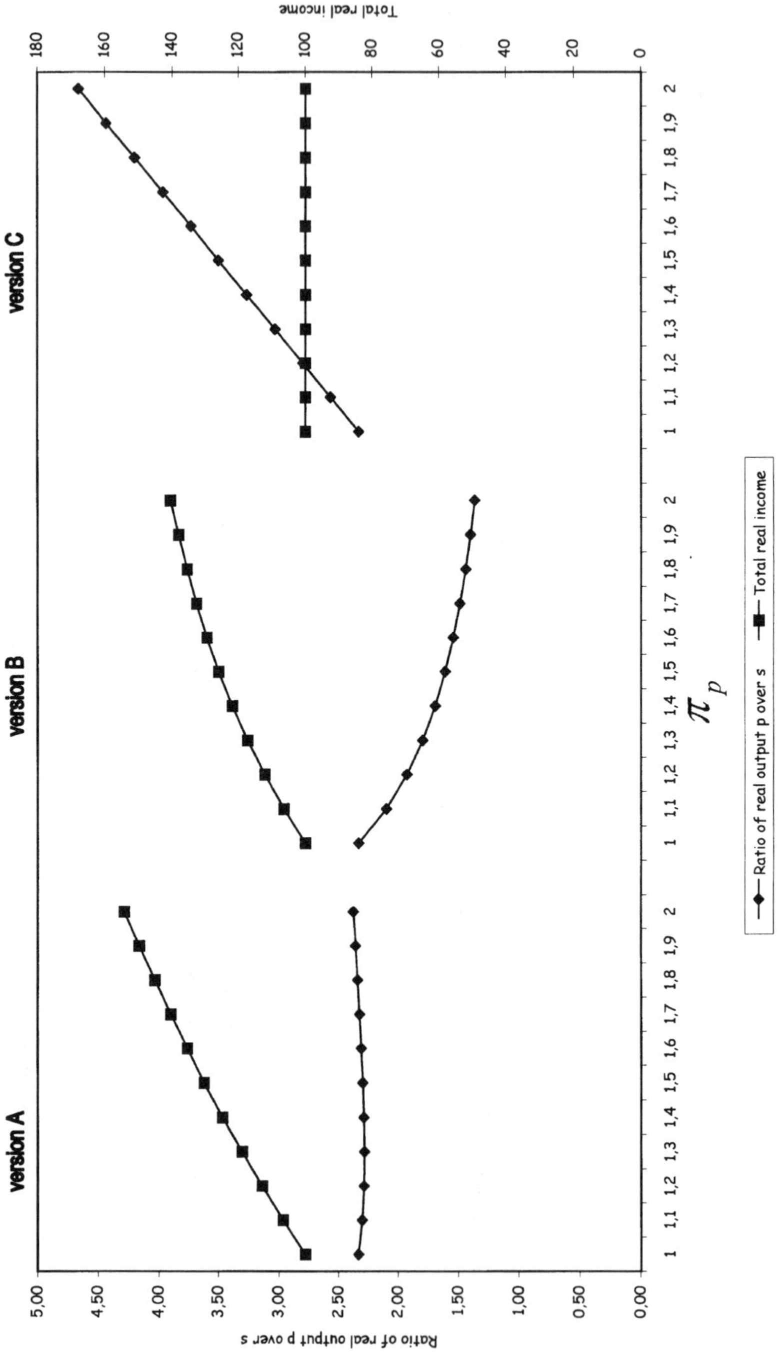


Figure 3-A: Model II: Ratio of real output in $p$ over real output in $s$ and total real income

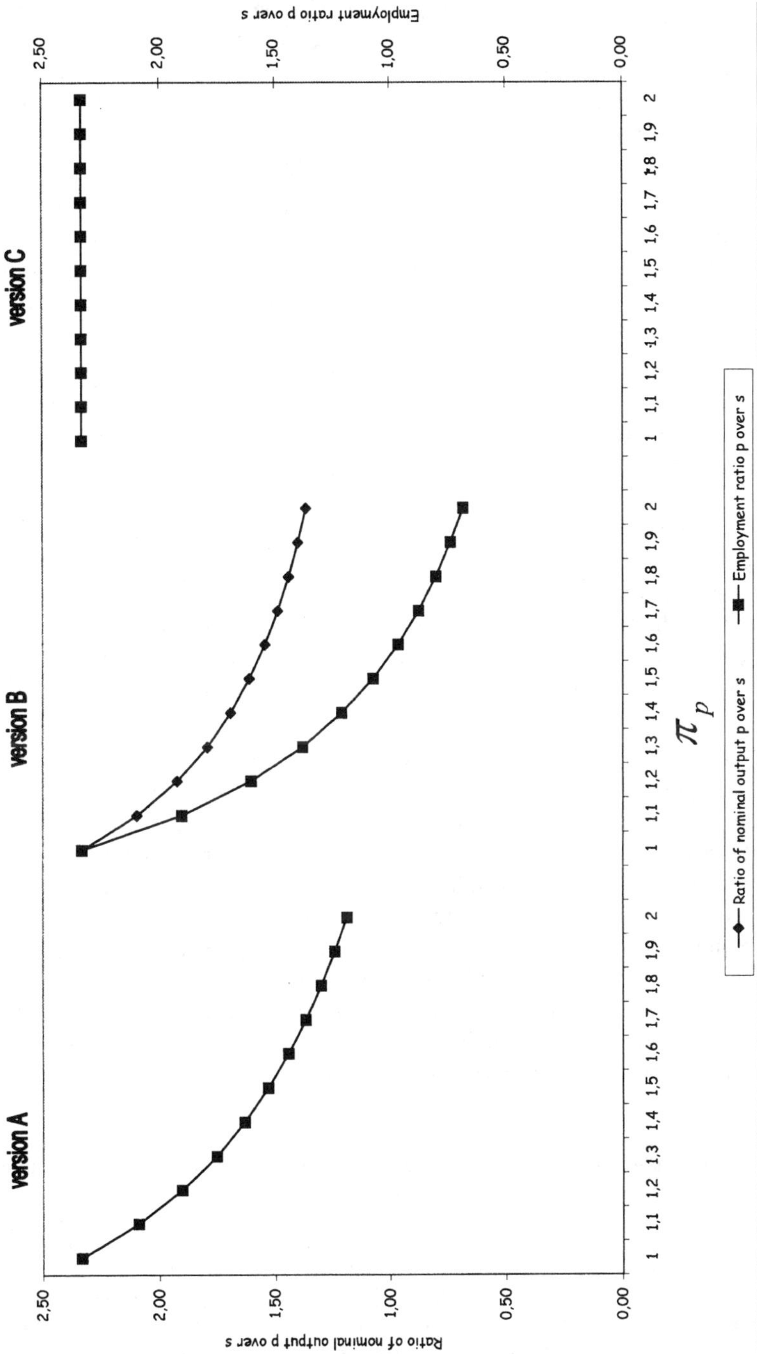


Figure 3-B: Model II: Ratio of nominal output in $p$ over nominal output in $s$ and employment ratios $(L_p/L_s)$

was (under the full-employment condition) Kaldor's concern. To the extent that wage differentials are necessary to induce labor mobility they are functional but overly large (and persistent) wage differentials between industries (which can only persist in imperfect labor markets) may lead to sub-optimal productivity, and income results (Bell / Freeman 1985).

Model II may be characterized as income driven because demand for the two sectors depends on income rather than on price elasticities. We assume the income elasticities for the technologically progressive industries to be lower than one, but for the technological stagnant industries to be greater than 1. The general lines of the simulations of this model are similar to the simulations with the price-driven model above (Figures 3-A and 3-B)

Although these models do not replicate Baumol's assumptions exactly (we do not investigate the version of a constant real output ratio), version II-A illustrates Baumol's point very well. Service productivity does not increase at all but nevertheless consumers as a group can get more of everything. As long as productivity in one sector grows the overall labor necessary to produce a certain output is declining and resources are freed to produce a higher output. Òverall costs' are declining, society gets richer. "Even if it were true that productivity in the stagnant services was not increasing one iota, their rising prices could still not put them beyond the reach of the community; on the contrary, it would remain true that society could afford ever more of them, just as it has in fact been getting ever more of the health care and education that seem to grow steadily toward becoming too expensive to afford" (Baumol, 1993, 23).

In model II-A, the quantities of both goods and services rises with more than 50% despite the fact that the relative price of services doubles. This requires that inputs (labor) must be transferred from the progressive to the stagnant sector. Although the real share of manufacturing products in GDP remains constant, their nominal share decreases sharply. Nominal output growth of $p$ is mitigated by lower prices, and is therefore smaller than the growth in nominal output of services where price and quantity increase.[8] Whereas service employment started at a level of 30% of the labor force in the simulations, it increases to almost 50%, i.e. it will absorb almost half of GDP.[9] The paradox is that although the nominal price of services increases sharply (+43%), and the relative price doubles, the real costs (measured in terms of labor input) of services do not increase.

---

8 Because the income elasticity is less than one for $p$ but greater than one for $s$, growing real income leads to a less than proportional increase in the nominal output of $p$ and a more than proportional increase in the nominal output of $s$.

9 This is Baumol's main concern. If services (health care, education, police services, etc.) are mainly provided by the government, then "... the threat lies in the prospect that more than half of the value of the economy's total output will have to be devoted to services whose funding derives predominantly from the public sector. The consequences of so enormous an increase in the share of GDP that will have to flow through government channels rather than the private sector of the economy are hardly an attractive prospect" (Baumol 1993, 26).

In both full employment models (II-A and II-B), aggregate real income increases at a rate equal to overall productivity growth (which, is less than productivity growth in *p*). It is no surprise that employment in p declines but if redundant workers from p are hired in s, no employment problem occurs.

In models I-C and II-C the full employment assumption is relaxed, i.e. it is no longer guaranteed that the society will fully use its resources. Labor dismissed in *p* is no longer automatically transferred to *s*. In this model nominal wages increase with average productivity growth and thus given the industry-specific productivity trends prices in *p* are falling, whereas they rise in *s*. Nominal output remains constant but real output rises in *p* and falls in *s*. Rising prices in *s* lead to declining product demand in *s* and consequently falling employment in *s*. Again, trends are more or less similar in the price-driven model (I-C) and in the income-driven model (II-C).

## IV. Concluding summary

As long as full-employment is assumed (that is that society uses resources fully), demand stagnation and shrinking employment in the technologically progressive industries are no problem. Furthermore, without growth constraints for product demand in the technological progressive sector, a wage policy which narrows or diminishes wage differentials is most favorable for productivity and income trends. A flexible wage policy, in the sense that wages are developing with industry-specific productivity favors the technologically stagnant industries but harms technologically progressive industries and is under the full-employment condition sub-optimal. Too many resources are used in less productive activities, a concern the Kaldor as well as the Rehn-Meidner model share.

However, one may come to different conclusions if the full-employment condition is dropped. Of course the expansion of highly productive activities is most favorable with respect to average productivity but given unused resources also an expansion of the less productive activities would increase income (although it would lower average productivity). Therefore, if there are growth constraints for the technological progressive industries it is from the social viewpoint better to expand demand and employment in technologically stagnant industries rather than to accept unused resources, i.e. unemployment.

Kaldor and Rehn-Meidner identified labor scarcity as a growth constraint for the technological progressive industries, which fits the full-employment situation of the 1960s very well. However, there may be other growth constraints than labor supply, such as saturation in product markets.

Saturation is a 'no-word' in economics although discussions of this phenomenon date back to Adam Smith (1776), who predicted saturation for agricultural products, a quite remarkable position two centuries ago! However, Smith could not imagine saturation in markets for manufacturing products, a quite realistic view for the $18^{th}$ century which turned to be true for about two centuries. Nevertheless, there were always periods of slow growth, and economic development seems to undergo waves (Schumpeter 1934). At the end of the $20^{th}$ century there are some signs that manufacturing products reached saturation in the highly developed OECD countries as was predicted by Clark (1957). Market-penetration levels with consumer goods like appliances, cars, tv-sets reach the almost 100% (Table III). Manufacturing employment peaked in the late 1960s / early 1970s and declines since then in almost all industrialized countries (Singh 1987, Appelbaum / Schettkat 1995) and this process is driven by shifts in final demand rather by than outsourcing (Russo / Schettkat 1998).

*Table 1*

**Telephones, tv-sets and passenger cars per 1,000 inhabitants**

| | Telephones | Tv-sets | Cars |
|---|---|---|---|
| USA | 560 | 815 | 570 |
| Japan | 460 | 614 | 299 |
| Germany | 440 | 558 | 587 |

Source: OECD (1996).

Baumol (1993) argues that the ‘cost-disease’ of technological stagnant industries is no ‘real’ problem for consumers as a group. Even if productivity in services does not increase at all, society as a whole can afford more of everything if average productivity increases. The ‘social planner’ could still transfer workers dismissed in manufacturing to services. This however would result in a declining ratio of real output in the technological progressive industries to real output in the technological stagnant industries.[10] Whether this will happen without the ‘social planner’ crucially depends on consumers’ reaction to price and / or wage trends. If rising prices of products from the technological stagnant industries lead individual consumers to hesitate buying these products, then idle resources may not automatically shift to these activities. Unemployment may result, which is irrational from the societal viewpoint but, as we know, it nevertheless exists. There is no ‘end of work’, many needs are not satisfied but there is a problem of creating demand for unsatisfied needs. To make potential demand effective demand seems to be the most challenging task for economic policy.

[10] This process actually occurred in Sweden through expansion of public services and in the US through downward flexibility of relative wages in the technological stagnant industries (Appelbaum / Schettkat 1994).

*Table 2:* **Results of simulations Model I**

| $\pi_p$ | Pp | Qp | Wp | Yp | Ps | Qs | Ws | Ys | Lp | Ls | Yt,n | Wp,r | Ws,r | Yp,r | Ys,r | Pt | $\pi_t$ | NSp | RSp | Yt,r | Prel | elap | elas |
|---|---|---|---|---|---|---|---|---|---|---|---|---|---|---|---|---|---|---|---|---|---|---|---|
| A: perfect-labor-market or solidaristic-wage-policy model | | | | | | | | | | | | | | | | | | | | | | | |
| 1 | 1 | 50 | 1 | 50 | 1 | 50 | 1 | 50 | 50 | 50 | 100 | 1 | 1 | 50 | 50 | 1 | 1 | 0.5 | 0.5 | 100 | 1 | 2 | 1 |
| 1.1 | 0.935 | 56.54 | 1.028 | 52.84 | 1.028 | 48.6 | 1.028 | 49.96 | 51.4 | 48.6 | 102.8 | 1.051 | 1.051 | 56.54 | 48.6 | 0.978 | 1.051 | 0.514 | 0.538 | 105.1 | 0.909 | 1.653 | 1.058 |
| 1.2 | 0.872 | 62.79 | 1.047 | 54.76 | 1.047 | 47.67 | 1.047 | 49.89 | 52.33 | 47.67 | 104.7 | 1.105 | 1.105 | 62.79 | 47.67 | 0.947 | 1.105 | 0.523 | 0.568 | 110.5 | 0.833 | 1.389 | 1.098 |
| 1.3 | 0.813 | 68.7 | 1.057 | 55.85 | 1.057 | 47.15 | 1.057 | 49.84 | 52.85 | 47.15 | 105.7 | 1.159 | 1.159 | 68.7 | 47.15 | 0.912 | 1.159 | 0.528 | 0.593 | 115.9 | 0.769 | 1.183 | 1.121 |
| 1.4 | 0.758 | 74.24 | 1.061 | 56.24 | 1.061 | 46.97 | 1.061 | 49.82 | 53.03 | 46.97 | 106.1 | 1.212 | 1.212 | 74.24 | 46.97 | 0.875 | 1.212 | 0.53 | 0.613 | 121.2 | 0.714 | 1.02 | 1.129 |
| 1.5 | 0.706 | 79.41 | 1.059 | 56.06 | 1.059 | 47.06 | 1.059 | 49.83 | 52.94 | 47.06 | 105.9 | 1.265 | 1.265 | 79.41 | 47.06 | 0.837 | 1.265 | 0.529 | 0.628 | 126.5 | 0.667 | 0.889 | 1.125 |
| 1.6 | 0.658 | 84.21 | 1.053 | 55.4 | 1.053 | 47.37 | 1.053 | 49.86 | 52.63 | 47.37 | 105.3 | 1.316 | 1.316 | 84.21 | 47.37 | 0.8 | 1.316 | 0.526 | 0.64 | 131.6 | 0.625 | 0.781 | 1.111 |
| 1.7 | 0.613 | 88.65 | 1.043 | 54.39 | 1.043 | 47.85 | 1.043 | 49.91 | 52.15 | 47.85 | 104.3 | 1.365 | 1.365 | 88.65 | 47.85 | 0.764 | 1.365 | 0.521 | 0.649 | 136.5 | 0.588 | 0.692 | 1.09 |
| 1.8 | 0.573 | 92.75 | 1.031 | 53.1 | 1.031 | 48.47 | 1.031 | 49.95 | 51.53 | 48.47 | 103.1 | 1.412 | 1.412 | 92.75 | 48.47 | 0.73 | 1.412 | 0.515 | 0.657 | 141.2 | 0.556 | 0.617 | 1.063 |
| 1.9 | 0.535 | 96.52 | 1.016 | 51.62 | 1.016 | 49.2 | 1.016 | 49.99 | 50.8 | 49.2 | 101.6 | 1.457 | 1.457 | 96.52 | 49.2 | 0.697 | 1.457 | 0.508 | 0.662 | 145.7 | 0.526 | 0.554 | 1.033 |
| 2 | 0.5 | 100 | 1 | 50 | 1 | 50 | 1 | 50 | 50 | 50 | 100 | 1.5 | 1.5 | 100 | 50 | 0.667 | 1.5 | 0.5 | 0.667 | 150 | 0.5 | 0.5 | 1 |
| B: wage-dispersion (according to industry-specific productivity) or flexible-wage model | | | | | | | | | | | | | | | | | | | | | | | |
| 1 | 1 | 50 | 1 | 50 | 1 | 50 | 1 | 50 | 50 | 50 | 100 | 1 | 1 | 50 | 50 | 1 | 1 | 0.5 | 0.5 | 100 | 1 | 2 | 1 |
| 1.1 | 0.968 | 53.23 | 1.065 | 51.51 | 0.968 | 51.61 | 0.968 | 49.95 | 48.39 | 51.61 | 101.5 | 1.1 | 1 | 53.23 | 51.61 | 0.968 | 1.048 | 0.508 | 0.508 | 104.8 | 1 | 1.818 | 0.938 |
| 1.2 | 0.938 | 56.25 | 1.125 | 52.73 | 0.938 | 53.13 | 0.938 | 49.8 | 46.88 | 53.13 | 102.5 | 1.2 | 1 | 56.25 | 53.13 | 0.938 | 1.094 | 0.514 | 0.514 | 109.4 | 1 | 1.667 | 0.882 |
| 1.3 | 0.909 | 59.09 | 1.182 | 53.72 | 0.909 | 54.55 | 0.909 | 49.59 | 45.45 | 54.55 | 103.3 | 1.3 | 1 | 59.09 | 54.55 | 0.909 | 1.136 | 0.52 | 0.52 | 113.6 | 1 | 1.538 | 0.833 |
| 1.4 | 0.882 | 61.76 | 1.235 | 54.5 | 0.882 | 55.88 | 0.882 | 49.31 | 44.12 | 55.88 | 103.8 | 1.4 | 1 | 61.76 | 55.88 | 0.882 | 1.176 | 0.525 | 0.525 | 117.6 | 1 | 1.429 | 0.789 |
| 1.5 | 0.857 | 64.29 | 1.286 | 55.1 | 0.857 | 57.14 | 0.857 | 48.98 | 42.86 | 57.14 | 104.1 | 1.5 | 1 | 64.29 | 57.14 | 0.857 | 1.214 | 0.529 | 0.529 | 121.4 | 1 | 1.333 | 0.75 |
| 1.6 | 0.833 | 66.67 | 1.333 | 55.56 | 0.833 | 58.33 | 0.833 | 48.61 | 41.67 | 58.33 | 104.2 | 1.6 | 1 | 66.67 | 58.33 | 0.833 | 1.25 | 0.533 | 0.533 | 125 | 1 | 1.25 | 0.714 |
| 1.7 | 0.811 | 68.92 | 1.378 | 55.88 | 0.811 | 59.46 | 0.811 | 48.21 | 40.54 | 59.46 | 104.1 | 1.7 | 1 | 68.92 | 59.46 | 0.811 | 1.284 | 0.537 | 0.537 | 128.4 | 1 | 1.176 | 0.682 |
| 1.8 | 0.789 | 71.05 | 1.421 | 56.09 | 0.789 | 60.53 | 0.789 | 47.78 | 39.47 | 60.53 | 103.9 | 1.8 | 1 | 71.05 | 60.53 | 0.789 | 1.316 | 0.54 | 0.54 | 131.6 | 1 | 1.111 | 0.652 |
| 1.9 | 0.769 | 73.08 | 1.462 | 56.21 | 0.769 | 61.54 | 0.769 | 47.34 | 38.46 | 61.54 | 103.6 | 1.9 | 1 | 73.08 | 61.54 | 0.769 | 1.346 | 0.543 | 0.543 | 134.6 | 1 | 1.053 | 0.625 |
| 2 | 0.75 | 75 | 1.5 | 56.25 | 0.75 | 62.5 | 0.75 | 46.88 | 37.5 | 62.5 | 103.1 | 2 | 1 | 75 | 62.5 | 0.75 | 1.375 | 0.545 | 0.545 | 137.5 | 1 | 1 | 0.6 |
| C: nominal average wage increases | | | | | | | | | | | | | | | | | | | | | | | |
| 1 | 1 | 50 | 1 | 50 | 1 | 50 | 1 | 50 | 50 | 50 | 100 | 1 | 1 | 50 | 50 | 1 | 1 | 0.5 | 0.5 | 100 | 1 | 2 | 1 |
| 1.1 | 0.956 | 54.45 | 1.051 | 52.03 | 1.051 | 47.45 | 1.051 | 49.87 | 49.5 | 47.45 | 101.9 | 1.051 | 1.051 | 54.45 | 47.45 | 1 | 1.051 | 0.511 | 0.534 | 101.9 | 0.909 | 1.755 | 1.108 |
| 1.2 | 0.92 | 58.02 | 1.104 | 53.37 | 1.104 | 44.81 | 1.104 | 49.46 | 48.35 | 44.81 | 102.8 | 1.104 | 1.104 | 58.02 | 44.81 | 1 | 1.104 | 0.519 | 0.564 | 102.8 | 0.833 | 1.585 | 1.232 |
| 1.3 | 0.891 | 60.92 | 1.158 | 54.27 | 1.158 | 42.1 | 1.158 | 48.75 | 46.86 | 42.1 | 103 | 1.158 | 1.158 | 60.92 | 42.1 | 1 | 1.158 | 0.527 | 0.591 | 103 | 0.769 | 1.462 | 1.375 |
| 1.4 | 0.867 | 63.29 | 1.214 | 54.88 | 1.214 | 39.3 | 1.214 | 47.71 | 45.21 | 39.3 | 102.6 | 1.214 | 1.214 | 63.29 | 39.3 | 1 | 1.214 | 0.535 | 0.617 | 102.6 | 0.714 | 1.37 | 1.544 |
| 1.5 | 0.848 | 65.19 | 1.272 | 55.29 | 1.272 | 36.39 | 1.272 | 46.3 | 43.46 | 36.39 | 101.6 | 1.272 | 1.272 | 65.19 | 36.39 | 1 | 1.272 | 0.544 | 0.642 | 101.6 | 0.667 | 1.301 | 1.748 |
| 1.6 | 0.833 | 66.67 | 1.333 | 55.56 | 1.333 | 33.33 | 1.333 | 44.44 | 41.67 | 33.33 | 100 | 1.333 | 1.333 | 66.67 | 33.33 | 1 | 1.333 | 0.556 | 0.667 | 100 | 0.625 | 1.25 | 2 |
| 1.7 | 0.823 | 67.71 | 1.399 | 55.72 | 1.399 | 30.05 | 1.399 | 42.04 | 39.83 | 30.05 | 97.76 | 1.399 | 1.399 | 67.71 | 30.05 | 1 | 1.399 | 0.57 | 0.693 | 97.76 | 0.588 | 1.215 | 2.328 |
| 1.8 | 0.817 | 68.25 | 1.471 | 55.79 | 1.471 | 26.43 | 1.471 | 38.89 | 37.92 | 26.43 | 94.68 | 1.471 | 1.471 | 68.25 | 26.43 | 1 | 1.471 | 0.589 | 0.721 | 94.68 | 0.556 | 1.198 | 2.784 |
| 1.9 | 0.819 | 68.12 | 1.556 | 55.78 | 1.556 | 22.22 | 1.556 | 34.56 | 35.85 | 22.22 | 90.34 | 1.556 | 1.556 | 68.12 | 22.22 | 1 | 1.556 | 0.617 | 0.754 | 90.34 | 0.526 | 1.202 | 3.501 |
| 2 | 0.833 | 66.67 | 1.667 | 55.56 | 1.667 | 16.67 | 1.667 | 27.78 | 33.33 | 16.67 | 83.33 | 1.667 | 1.667 | 66.67 | 16.67 | 1 | 1.667 | 0.667 | 0.8 | 83.33 | 0.5 | 1.25 | 5 |

*Table 3:* **Results of simulations Model I**

| $\pi_p$ | Pp | Qp | Wp | Yp | Ps | Qs | Ws | Ys | Lp | Ls | Yt,n | Wp,r | Ws,r | Yp,r | Ys,r | Pt | $\pi_t$ | NSp | RSp | Yt,r | Prel | elyp | elys |
|---|---|---|---|---|---|---|---|---|---|---|---|---|---|---|---|---|---|---|---|---|---|---|---|
| A: perfect-labor-market or solidaristic-wage-policy model | | | | | | | | | | | | | | | | | | | | | | | |
| 1 | 1 | 70 | 1 | 70 | 1 | 30 | 1 | 30 | 70 | 30 | 100 | 1 | 1 | 70 | 30 | 1 | 1 | 0.7 | 0.7 | 100 | 1 | 0.286 | 2 |
| 1.1 | 0.958 | 74.41 | 1.054 | 71.31 | 1.054 | 32.35 | 1.054 | 34.1 | 67.65 | 32.35 | 105.4 | 1.068 | 1.068 | 74.41 | 32.35 | 0.987 | 1.068 | 0.676 | 0.697 | 106.8 | 0.909 | 0.279 | 1.921 |
| 1.2 | 0.921 | 78.69 | 1.105 | 72.45 | 1.105 | 34.43 | 1.105 | 38.04 | 65.57 | 34.43 | 110.5 | 1.131 | 1.131 | 78.69 | 34.43 | 0.977 | 1.131 | 0.656 | 0.696 | 113.1 | 0.833 | 0.271 | 1.862 |
| 1.3 | 0.887 | 82.83 | 1.153 | 73.46 | 1.153 | 36.29 | 1.153 | 41.83 | 63.71 | 36.29 | 115.3 | 1.191 | 1.191 | 82.83 | 36.29 | 0.968 | 1.191 | 0.637 | 0.695 | 119.1 | 0.769 | 0.262 | 1.817 |
| 1.4 | 0.856 | 86.85 | 1.199 | 74.35 | 1.199 | 37.97 | 1.199 | 45.5 | 62.03 | 37.97 | 119.9 | 1.248 | 1.248 | 86.85 | 37.97 | 0.96 | 1.248 | 0.62 | 0.696 | 124.8 | 0.714 | 0.252 | 1.782 |
| 1.5 | 0.828 | 90.74 | 1.242 | 75.13 | 1.242 | 39.5 | 1.242 | 49.06 | 60.5 | 39.5 | 124.2 | 1.302 | 1.302 | 90.74 | 39.5 | 0.954 | 1.302 | 0.605 | 0.697 | 130.2 | 0.667 | 0.242 | 1.753 |
| 1.6 | 0.802 | 94.53 | 1.284 | 75.83 | 1.284 | 40.92 | 1.284 | 52.53 | 59.08 | 40.92 | 128.4 | 1.354 | 1.354 | 94.53 | 40.92 | 0.948 | 1.354 | 0.591 | 0.698 | 135.4 | 0.625 | 0.231 | 1.73 |
| 1.7 | 0.779 | 98.2 | 1.323 | 76.45 | 1.323 | 42.23 | 1.323 | 55.9 | 57.77 | 42.23 | 132.3 | 1.404 | 1.404 | 98.2 | 42.23 | 0.942 | 1.404 | 0.578 | 0.699 | 140.4 | 0.588 | 0.219 | 1.711 |
| 1.8 | 0.757 | 101.8 | 1.362 | 77 | 1.362 | 43.46 | 1.362 | 59.19 | 56.54 | 43.46 | 136.2 | 1.452 | 1.452 | 101.8 | 43.46 | 0.938 | 1.452 | 0.565 | 0.701 | 145.2 | 0.556 | 0.207 | 1.694 |
| 1.9 | 0.736 | 105.2 | 1.399 | 77.49 | 1.399 | 44.61 | 1.399 | 62.4 | 55.39 | 44.61 | 139.9 | 1.499 | 1.499 | 105.2 | 44.61 | 0.933 | 1.499 | 0.554 | 0.702 | 149.9 | 0.526 | 0.194 | 1.68 |
| 2 | 0.717 | 108.6 | 1.435 | 77.91 | 1.435 | 45.69 | 1.435 | 65.54 | 54.31 | 45.69 | 143.5 | 1.543 | 1.543 | 108.6 | 45.69 | 0.93 | 1.543 | 0.543 | 0.704 | 154.3 | 0.5 | 0.181 | 1.669 |
| B: wage-dispersion (according to industry-specific productivity) or flexible-wage model | | | | | | | | | | | | | | | | | | | | | | | |
| 1 | 1 | 70 | 1 | 70 | 1 | 30 | 1 | 30 | 70 | 30 | 100 | 1 | 1 | 70 | 30 | 1 | 1 | 0.7 | 0.7 | 100 | 1 | 0.286 | 2 |
| 1.1 | 0.988 | 72.16 | 1.086 | 71.27 | 0.988 | 34.4 | 0.988 | 33.98 | 65.6 | 34.4 | 105.2 | 1.1 | 1 | 72.16 | 34.4 | 0.988 | 1.066 | 0.677 | 0.677 | 106.6 | 1 | 0.279 | 1.923 |
| 1.2 | 0.978 | 73.93 | 1.174 | 72.31 | 0.978 | 38.39 | 0.978 | 37.55 | 61.61 | 38.39 | 109.9 | 1.2 | 1 | 73.93 | 38.39 | 0.978 | 1.123 | 0.658 | 0.658 | 112.3 | 1 | 0.272 | 1.869 |
| 1.3 | 0.97 | 75.41 | 1.261 | 73.18 | 0.97 | 41.99 | 0.97 | 40.74 | 58.01 | 41.99 | 113.9 | 1.3 | 1 | 75.41 | 41.99 | 0.97 | 1.174 | 0.642 | 0.642 | 117.4 | 1 | 0.265 | 1.829 |
| 1.4 | 0.964 | 76.66 | 1.35 | 73.9 | 0.964 | 45.25 | 0.964 | 43.62 | 54.75 | 45.25 | 117.5 | 1.4 | 1 | 76.66 | 45.25 | 0.964 | 1.219 | 0.629 | 0.629 | 121.9 | 1 | 0.258 | 1.799 |
| 1.5 | 0.959 | 77.71 | 1.438 | 74.51 | 0.959 | 48.2 | 0.959 | 46.21 | 51.8 | 48.2 | 120.7 | 1.5 | 1 | 77.71 | 48.2 | 0.959 | 1.259 | 0.617 | 0.617 | 125.9 | 1 | 0.25 | 1.776 |
| 1.6 | 0.954 | 78.61 | 1.527 | 75.03 | 0.954 | 50.87 | 0.954 | 48.56 | 49.13 | 50.87 | 123.6 | 1.6 | 1 | 78.61 | 50.87 | 0.954 | 1.295 | 0.607 | 0.607 | 129.5 | 1 | 0.243 | 1.757 |
| 1.7 | 0.951 | 79.38 | 1.616 | 75.47 | 0.951 | 53.31 | 0.951 | 50.68 | 46.69 | 53.31 | 126.1 | 1.7 | 1 | 79.38 | 53.31 | 0.951 | 1.327 | 0.598 | 0.598 | 132.7 | 1 | 0.237 | 1.742 |
| 1.8 | 0.948 | 80.05 | 1.706 | 75.85 | 0.948 | 55.53 | 0.948 | 52.61 | 44.47 | 55.53 | 128.5 | 1.8 | 1 | 80.05 | 55.53 | 0.948 | 1.356 | 0.59 | 0.59 | 135.6 | 1 | 0.23 | 1.73 |
| 1.9 | 0.945 | 80.64 | 1.795 | 76.18 | 0.945 | 57.56 | 0.945 | 54.38 | 42.44 | 57.56 | 130.6 | 1.9 | 1 | 80.64 | 57.56 | 0.945 | 1.382 | 0.584 | 0.584 | 138.2 | 1 | 0.224 | 1.719 |
| 2 | 0.942 | 81.15 | 1.885 | 76.47 | 0.942 | 59.42 | 0.942 | 55.99 | 40.58 | 59.42 | 132.5 | 2 | 1 | 81.15 | 59.42 | 0.942 | 1.406 | 0.577 | 0.577 | 140.6 | 1 | 0.218 | 1.71 |
| C: nominal average wage increases | | | | | | | | | | | | | | | | | | | | | | | |
| 1 | 1 | 70 | 1 | 70 | 1 | 30 | 1 | 30 | 70 | 30 | 100 | 1 | 1 | 70 | 30 | 1 | 1 | 0.7 | 0.7 | 100 | 1 | 0.286 | 2 |
| 1.1 | 0.973 | 71.96 | 1.07 | 70 | 1.07 | 28.04 | 1.07 | 30 | 65.42 | 28.04 | 100 | 1.07 | 1.07 | 71.96 | 28.04 | 1 | 1.07 | 0.7 | 0.72 | 100 | 0.909 | 0.286 | 2 |
| 1.2 | 0.95 | 73.68 | 1.14 | 70 | 1.14 | 26.32 | 1.14 | 30 | 61.4 | 26.32 | 100 | 1.14 | 1.14 | 73.68 | 26.32 | 1 | 1.14 | 0.7 | 0.737 | 100 | 0.833 | 0.286 | 2 |
| 1.3 | 0.931 | 75.21 | 1.21 | 70 | 1.21 | 24.79 | 1.21 | 30 | 57.85 | 24.79 | 100 | 1.21 | 1.21 | 75.21 | 24.79 | 1 | 1.21 | 0.7 | 0.752 | 100 | 0.769 | 0.286 | 2 |
| 1.4 | 0.914 | 76.56 | 1.28 | 70 | 1.28 | 23.44 | 1.28 | 30 | 54.69 | 23.44 | 100 | 1.28 | 1.28 | 76.56 | 23.44 | 1 | 1.28 | 0.7 | 0.766 | 100 | 0.714 | 0.286 | 2 |
| 1.5 | 0.9 | 77.78 | 1.35 | 70 | 1.35 | 22.22 | 1.35 | 30 | 51.85 | 22.22 | 100 | 1.35 | 1.35 | 77.78 | 22.22 | 1 | 1.35 | 0.7 | 0.778 | 100 | 0.667 | 0.286 | 2 |
| 1.6 | 0.888 | 78.87 | 1.42 | 70 | 1.42 | 21.13 | 1.42 | 30 | 49.3 | 21.13 | 100 | 1.42 | 1.42 | 78.87 | 21.13 | 1 | 1.42 | 0.7 | 0.789 | 100 | 0.625 | 0.286 | 2 |
| 1.7 | 0.876 | 79.87 | 1.49 | 70 | 1.49 | 20.13 | 1.49 | 30 | 46.98 | 20.13 | 100 | 1.49 | 1.49 | 79.87 | 20.13 | 1 | 1.49 | 0.7 | 0.799 | 100 | 0.588 | 0.286 | 2 |
| 1.8 | 0.867 | 80.77 | 1.56 | 70 | 1.56 | 19.23 | 1.56 | 30 | 44.87 | 19.23 | 100 | 1.56 | 1.56 | 80.77 | 19.23 | 1 | 1.56 | 0.7 | 0.808 | 100 | 0.556 | 0.286 | 2 |
| 1.9 | 0.858 | 81.6 | 1.63 | 70 | 1.63 | 18.4 | 1.63 | 30 | 42.94 | 18.4 | 100 | 1.63 | 1.63 | 81.6 | 18.4 | 1 | 1.63 | 0.7 | 0.816 | 100 | 0.526 | 0.286 | 2 |
| 2 | 0.85 | 82.35 | 1.7 | 70 | 1.7 | 17.65 | 1.7 | 30 | 41.18 | 17.65 | 100 | 1.7 | 1.7 | 82.35 | 17.65 | 1 | 1.7 | 0.7 | 0.824 | 100 | 0.5 | 0.286 | 2 |

## Appendix

**Legenda:**

| | |
|---|---|
| $P_t = (P_p Q_p + P_s Q_s)/(Q_p + Q_s)$ | Overall price level |
| $Y_{t,n} = Y_p + Y_s$ | Total nominal income |
| $W_{p,r} = W_p/P_t$ | Real wages in p |
| $W_{s,r} = W_s/P_t$ | Real wages in s |
| $Y_{p,r} = Y_p P_p^0$ (at $\pi_p = 1.0$) | Real output $p$ evaluated at $P^0$ |
| $Y_{s,r} = Y_s P_s^0$ (at $\pi_p = 1.0$) | Real output $s$ evaluated at $P^0$ |
| $Y_{t,r} = Y_{p,r} + Y_{s,r}$ | Total real output evaluated at $P^0$ |
| $\pi_t = (L_p \pi_p + L_s \pi_s)/(L_p + L_s)$ | Overall productivity level |
| $NSp = Y_p/Y_{t,n}$ | Nominal share of $p$ |
| $RSp = Y_{p,r}/Y_{t,r}$ | Real share of $p$ |
| $Prel = P_p/P_s$ | Relative price |
| $elap = \eta_p = -(dQ_p/dP_p)(P_p/Q_p) = P_p/(b_p Q_p)$ | price elasticity $p$ |
| $elas = \eta_s = -(dQ_s/dP_s)(P_s/Q_s) = P_s/(b_s Q_s)$ | price elasticity $s$ |
| $elyp = -(dC_p/dY_{t,r})(Y_t, r/C_p)$ | income elasticity $p$ |
| $elys = -(dC_s/dY_t, r)(Y_{t,r}/C_s)$ | income elasticity $s$ |

## Bibliography

Appelbaum, E. / *Schettkat,* R. (1995): "Employment and Productivity in Industrialized Countries." International Labour Review 134(4 - 5): 605 - 623. – *Appelbaum,* E. / *Schettkat,* R. (1996): The Increasing Importance of Institutions for Employment Performance, in: Schmid, G. et al., International Handbook of Labor Market Policy and Policy Evaluation, London 1996: Edward Elgar, 791 - 810. – *Appelbaum,* E. / *Schettkat,* R. (1997): Are Prices Unimportant? The Changing Structure of the Industrialized Economies, Working Paper 97 / 10, The Netherlands School for Economic and Social Research, Utrecht, The Netherlands. – *Baumol,* W. (1967): "Macroeconomics of Unbalanced Growth: The Anatomy of the Urban Crisis." American Economic Review *57:* 415 - 426. – *Baumol,* W. (1993): Health care, education and the cost disease: A looming crisis for public choice, Public Choice, Vol, 77, pp. 17 - 28. – *Baumol,* W. / *Blackman,* S. / *Wolff,* E. (1985): Unbalanced growth Revisited: Asymptotic Stagnancy and new Evidence, American Economic Review, vol. 75, 806 - 817. – *Baumol,* W. / *Blackman,* S. / *Wolff,* E. (1989): Productivity and American Leadership: The Long View. Cambridge, Mass: MIT Press. – *Bell,* L. / *Freeman,* R. (1985): Does a flexible wage structure increase employment? The US experience, NBER working paper No. 1604, Cambridge Ma.: National Bureau of Economic Research. – *Clark,* C. (1957): The conditions of economic progress, London-Ann Arbor: Macmillan. – *Kaldor,* N. (1966): Causes of the Slow Rate of Economic Growth of the United Kingdom. Cambridge, Cambridge University Press. – *Pasinetti,* L. (1981): Structural Change and Economic Growth: A Theoretical Essay on the Dynamics of the Wealth of Nations, Cambridge, Cambridge University Press. – *Russo,* G. / *Schettkat* R.

(1998): Are structural economic dynamics a myth? Changing industrial structure in the final-product-demand concept, Utrecht University. Working paper 7 / 98, The Netherlands School for Economic and Social Research. – *Salter,* W. (1960): Productivity and Technical Change. Cambridge, Cambridge University Press. – *Scharpf,* F. W. (1990): Structures of Post-Industrial Society – or – Does Mass-Unemployment Disappear in the Service and Information Economy?, in: Appelbaum, E. / Schettkat, R. (eds.), Labor Market Adjustments to Structural Change and Technological Progress, New York, Westport, London: Praeger Publishers, 17 - 35. – *Schettkat,* R. (1992): The Labor Market Dynamics of Economic Restructuring, The United States and Germany in Transition, Praeger, New York, Westport, London. – *Schettkat,* R. (Hrsg.) (1996): Flow Analysis of Labor Markets. International Perspectives, London / New York: Routledge. – *Schettkat,* R. / *Wagner,* M. (1989): Technologischer Wandel und Beschäftigung, Duncker und Humblot, Berlin. – *Schumpeter,* J. (1934): Theorie der wirtschaftlichen Entwicklung. – *Schumpeter,* J. (1942): Capitalism, Socialism and Democracy, New York: Harper & Brothers, deutsche Übersetzung, Kapitalismus, Sozialismus und Demokratie, Tübingen: A. Francke 1950. – *Singh,* A. (1988): Manufacturing and de-industralization. The New Palgrave, McMillan, London. – *Smith,* A. (1976): An Inquiry into the Nature and Causes of the Wealth of Nations, 1976 edition, Oxford: Clarendon Press.

# The Role of Macroeconomic Policy in Overcoming Slow Economic Growth

## International Comparisons and Policy Perspectives*

By Ewald Nowotny, Wien

### I. Economic Growth and Labour Markets in Europe

A fundamental point of this paper is, that – given existing structures (!) – the persistent problem of high unemployment in Europe cannot be attributed to tendencies in "jobless-growth" but is mainly caused by the fact that GDP-growth has been – and is still too low. This argument is first based on the pronounced cyclical reagibility of employment and unemployment. A first glance at Figure 1 immediately reveals this cyclical reagibility of European labour-markets – which is, however combined with "hysteresis-effects", thus creating a tendency of increasing long-term unemployment. In the next section the question as to why growth-rates in the 80s and 90s were much lower than compared to the 60s and 70s will be studied. The connections between employment and economic growth will be discussed in more detail in section 3 of this paper.

### II. The Growth Perspective – the Central Role of Interest Rates

Economic growth is, of course, the result of many factors. From a macroeconomic perspective the following factors can be seen as relevant to the low economic growth of the last decade:

- Exchange rate developments:

  The successful stabilisation of exchange rates from 1979 to 1992 was followed by a period of more or less flexible exchange rates in Europe. Due to increased uncertainty for investors and corresponding high risk premiums this resulted in substantial GDP-losses. According to estimates by the EU-Commission (1996) the exchange rate turbulences in 1995 lowered EU-GDP by about 1 / 2 percen-

* For their valuable help with the empirical data I am grateful to Markus Marterbauer and Martin Zagler.

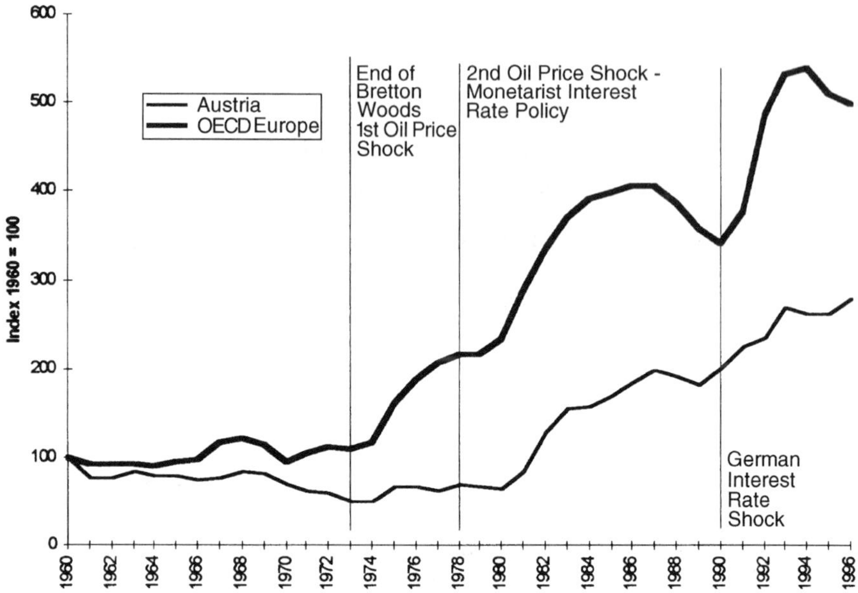


Source: OECD Labour Force Statistics, WIFO Datenbank

Figure 1: Unemployment in Europe

tage point (Germany 1 percentage point). Avoiding these exchange rate instabilities will create one of the major growth effects of EMU.

- Overvaluation:

  For many European currencies, especially those of the DM-bloc, there was a substantial overvaluation against the US-Dollar for a long period of the 80s and 90s. The reversal of this trend had an immediate impact on European export performance. This has been the major single factor for higher European growth rates in recent years.

- Fiscal policy:

  The recession of 93 and the fiscal impact of high interest rates resulted in budgetary deficits that in many European countries clearly were not sustainable. The provisions of the Maastricht Treaty thus only underlined an already existing need for fiscal consolidation. The dampening effect on European aggregate demand was however substantially increased by the simultaneous occurrence of restrictive fiscal policy in practically all European countries and by the high speed of fiscal consolidation. In 1995 net-lending of the public sector in EU-states was about 5% in average. Reaching the 3% goal meant – certeris paribus – a dampening effect on GDP of about 3% to 4% in two years (Marterbauer, 1996, p. 8).

When considering macroeconomic relationships between economic growth and fiscal policy it is important to pay special attention to flow-of-funds-effects – which unfortunately are often neglected in supply-side oriented analyses. As will be later shown, a policy of high interest rates will lead to a decrease in investment-rates and thus to a reduction in net-lending of the enterprise sector of an economy. Given stable (or in some European economies even increasing) rates of private savings and constant (or due to revaluation effects) declining external balances the lower net-lending of the enterprise sector "automatically" has to be balanced by higher net-lending of the public sector. The higher net-lending of the public sector thus essentially was – via automatic stabiliser effects – the effect and not the cause of the slow growth of European GDP.

Seen the other way round this means that a permanent and substantial fiscal consolidation in Europe will only be possible if sufficiently high rates of economic growth will be achieved again over a longer period. The American experience is a good illustration of this point.

It may be argued that lower public deficits enable central banks – and the markets – to lower interest rates, thus contributing to higher growth as well as helping with fiscal consolidation. The latter is obviously true. Given an average public debt stock of 73,2% of GDP (EU-15, 1996) an interest rate reduction of two percentage points results in lower public expenditures and lower net-lending by about 1% of GDP. The basic assumption of a causality chain lower deficits – lower interest rates – higher growth is however problematic from the point of view of flow-of-funds-analysis. If lower deficits ceteris paribus via lower aggregate demand lead to lower growth this will eventually result in lower interest rates – but the path for adjustment will be long and costly in terms of employment losses.

These costs can only be avoided if the negative demand effects of the public sector are compensated by positive effects in other sectors of the economy. This e.g. was the case in the Netherlands, where higher economic growth was achieved via increased external balance surpluses, based on a devaluation of the real (not the nominal) exchange rate, which in turn was achieved by substantially lower wage increases relative to important foreign-trade partners (especially Germany)[1]. It is obvious that this kind of strategy would result in a "beggar-my-neighbour"-policy if it were followed by all EU-members. A growth-creating effect for all EU-countries is only to be expected by an increase in foreign-trade balances vis-à-vis third countries. This happened recently due to the devaluation of most European currencies vis-à-vis the US-Dollar. As the events in South-East-Asia have shown, relying on external surpluses however cannot be a stable policy-strategy on a global scale and cannot be a permanent substitute for internal demand management.

---

1 From 1992 to 1998 the Dutch current account surplus increased from 2,3% of GDP to 6,9%. For total EU the current account deficit of – 1,1% of GDP in 1992 turned into a surplus of 1,3% of GDP in 1998.

- Monetary policy:

  There are two basic neo-classical propositions which are largely reflected in practical policy statements by (European) central-banks:

  - Central banks have only direct influence on short-run nominal interest rates. Long-run real interest rates can only be influenced in an indirect way by lowering inflationary expectations.
  - Real investment decisions are based on long-run interest rates. Central banks thus have no direct influence (and responsibility) with regard to the real sector of the economy. This view is e.g. reflected in the provisions of the European System of Central Banks (ESCB), where price-stability is stipulated as the sole policy objective.

  Although widely accepted in the field of practical monetary policy this neo-classical position is not undisputed in economic theory discussions. In this paper I would like to refer to a systematic, empirically tested counter-position in the tradition of " Keynesian" aggregate demand analysis[2]. The main points of this position can be summarised in the following way:

- The largest part of financial liabilities of the enterprise sector of an economy consists of bank-credits with variable (!) interest rates[3]. These interest rates (e.g. the "prime rate") show much larger variations as compared to the typical long-run interest-rate on government bonds. Via the refinancing costs of the banking sector these enterprise-related interest rates are directly linked with central-bank monetary policy.

  As can be seen from Figures 2 and 3 there is a strong – although not always direct – connection between short-run and long-run[4] interest rates. Comparing German and US data the dramatic extent of the German "interest rate shock" of 1990 also becomes visible, as well as the generally more stable trend of US monetary policy.

- Variations of the variable "prime rate" not only influence the costs of new investments but have a direct effect on the total financing costs of the accumulated (credit-financed) debt of the enterprise sector. Total financing costs are thus subject to the effects of an "interest rate accelerator". If, for instance, all financial liabilities of an enterprise consist of bank credits with flexible interest rates, an

---

2 These reflections are largely based on several studies by the Austrian economist Stephan Schulmeister (1996).

3 In Germany (and Japan) about 85% of total financial liabilities of the enterprise sector consist of bank-credits and "other liabilities" (trade obligations), in the US this percentage is about 70% (Schulmeister, 1996, p. 46). Although the role of capital market – financing and increased profit shares have recently reduced the role of bank credits in financing the enterprise sector, bank credits still remains by far the most important form of external financing in Germany.

4 For long-run interest rates long-run treasury bill rates are used. For direct use of "prime-rates" see S. Schulmeister (1996).

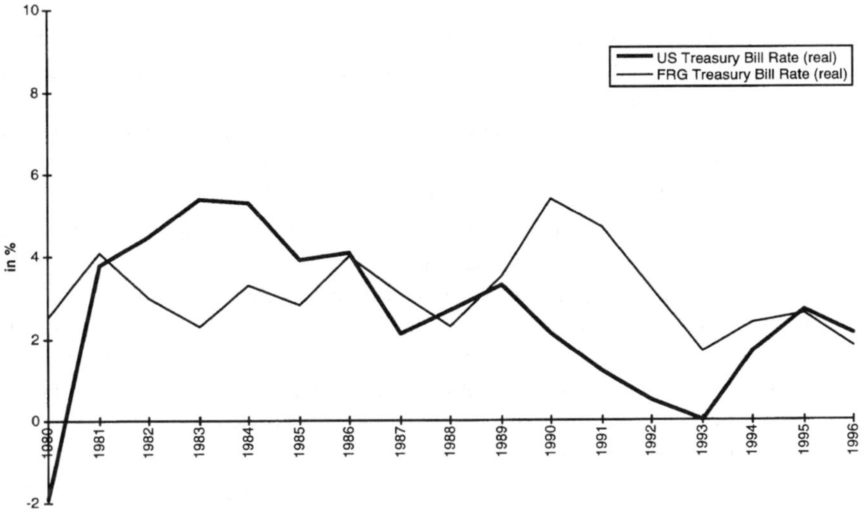


Source: OECD Financial Indicators, Paris 1997

Figure 2: Short Run Real Interest Rates

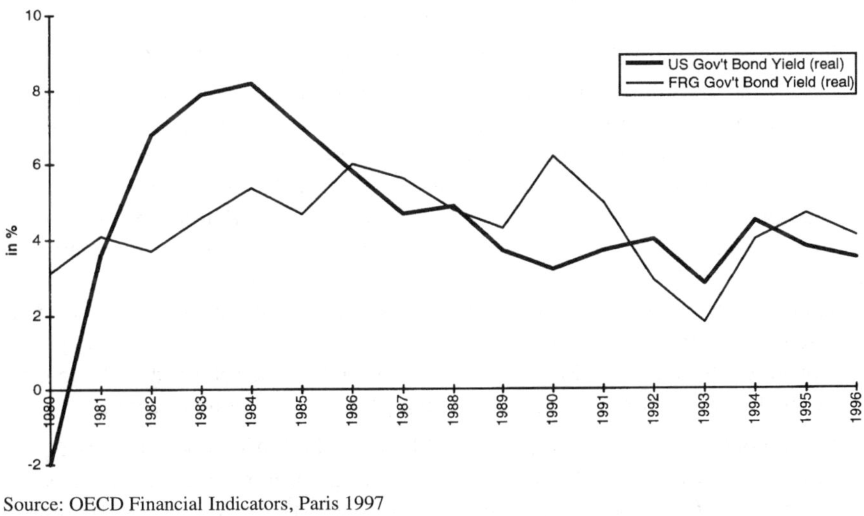


Source: OECD Financial Indicators, Paris 1997

Figure 3: Long Run Real Interest Rates

increase in the interest rate from 5% to 6.5% means an increase in interest payments of 30%. This means that a larger share of the operating surplus will have to be used for interest payments, resulting in a profit squeeze of the enterprise sector of the economy.

- Enterprises cannot react immediately to changes in their cost – and financing – structures. Empirically after about two years higher interest rates will result in lower investment and employment. In a following recession the flow-of-funds deficit of the enterprise-sector would decline (due to lower investments). As has been shown before, automatic stabiliser effects, ceteris paribus, will lead to increasing budgetary deficits[5]. Again an increase in interest rates has to be seen not as the result but as the cause of public deficits.
- Eventually the recession would also induce monetary authorities to follow a more expansionary policy which would be reflected in lower interest rates. With strong fluctuations in credit interest rates the rate of return on real investment, however, becomes more uncertain, causing increasing risk-premiums and in general leading to higher attractivity of financial investments as compared to real investments. Thus also in a climate of low credit-interest rates and – due to the credit accelerator – fast rising profits, it may take quite a long time for a substantial increase in private investments to occur.
- For a medium and long term perspective the dynamic budget constraints for stabilising the debt / income relationship are essential. Here the relationship between interest rates and rates of GNP-growth has a decisive effect. If the rate of interest lies above the rate of growth, enterprises – as well as the government-sector – will have to run primary surpluses for stabilising their debt / income-relationship. Their net-deficits (net debt-increase) have to be smaller than the amount of interest payments on the total debt (Blanchard et al, 1990).

One of the most important reasons for the slow economic growth of the last decade can be seen in the structural changes with regard to the interest-growth-differential. This interest-growth-differential was negative in the 50s and 60s and has been positive since the late 70s. Although in the 90s in particular there was a sharp rise in profits, this did not lead to an increase in real investments. Enterprises rather used this for a reduction in their net-borrowing. The changing interest-growth differential also made financial investments more attractive, resulting in a fast growth of the financial assets of the "non-financial" business-sector of the economy. All this contributed to the substantial (and continuing!) reduction in enterprise net-lending as is demonstrated for Germany in Table 1. As has been discussed above, this "automatically" had to be balanced by higher net-lending shares of the public sector.

In the context of the preparation for EMU over the last number of years a substantial harmonisation – both of short-run and long-run European interest rates has been observed. Combined with the lowering of interest-rates which mainly reflects the effects of Europe's severe recession, this tendency may offer the opportunity that an EMU-regime of monetary policy may be able to reach a more favourable interest growth-differential. In general, a large relatively closed economy (such as the US or the EMU), where exchange-rates are of no major policy-concern, offers

[5] This, of course, also works the other way round as can be observed at present in the USA.

better chances for growth-oriented monetary policy as compared to small open economies. Also the deflationary tendencies connected with the recent Asian crises in this context may be a blessing-in-disguise, as it will allow the future ECB to engage in a policy of low interest rates without risking "reputation-dangers" for the new European currency.

*Table 1*

**Sectoral Financial Balances**

Net surplus / net deficit in % of GDP

| | 1973 | 1975 | 1992 | 1994 | 1995 | 1996 | 1997 |
|---|---|---|---|---|---|---|---|
| **Germany** | | | | | | | |
| Private housholds | 7,9 | 9,4 | 7,0 | 7,6 | 7,5 | 7,6 | 7,5 |
| Enterprise sector | – 7,8 | – 2,7 | – 4,0 | – 6,2 | – 4,9 | – 4,4 | – 4,4 |
| Public sector | 1,2 | – 5,7 | – 2,3 | – 2,4 | – 3,6 | – 3,8 | – 3,2 |
| External balance[a)] | – 1,3 | – 1,0 | – 0,7 | 1,0 | 1,0 | 0,6 | 0,1 |
| **Austria** | | | | | | | |
| Private househoulds | 4,7 | 6,2 | 7,9 | 6,3 | 6,4 | 5,4 | 4,9 |
| Enterprise sector | – 6,3 | – 3,8 | – 5,9 | – 2,5 | – 3,2 | – 3,6 | – 4,2 |
| Public sector | 1,3 | – 2,5 | – 2,0 | – 4,8 | – 4,9 | – 3,8 | – 2,6 |
| External balance[a)] | 0,3 | 0,1 | 0,1 | 0,9 | 1,8 | 2,1 | 1,8 |

[a)] External balance: Current account with reversed sign.

*Source:* E. Nowotny (1996, p. 602), Österr. Institut f. Wirtschaftsforschung, Germany 1996/97: Gemeinschaftsgutachten der Wirtschaftsforschungsinstitute

These monetary policy perspectives are in agreement with proposals, for instance by W. Filc (1998), to take interest rates as the relevant (intermediate) policy target of a future European monetary policy. Technically this refers to short-run interest rates, which according to Filc (1998, p. 32) should only be slightly above the rate of inflation. As has been discussed above international experience demonstrates that such a policy has positive effects on economic growth without risking inflation. Obviously a policy of lower interest rates can and will be no cure for all aspects of low European growth-rates. But interest rate policy is indeed a very powerful tool because it effects four strategic fields of economic policy. Thus lower interest rates would help with regard to the following:

- higher real capital investment,
- preventing an overvaluation of the Euro,
- lowering public expenditure on interest payments and thus leading to a reduction of public net-lending without negative demand – and thus labour-market effects,

- lower macroeconomic (employment) costs of securing price-stability. Higher degrees of capacity-utilisation and the lower direct cost effects of interest payments mean decreasing average costs in production. Given the competition-effects of the Single European market this will be translated directly into lower price-increases. It has to be added that this perspective has to be complemented by a stability (i.e. productivity-) oriented wage policy on the macroeconomic level, as will be discussed later.

## III. Economic Growth and Employment

### *1. General View*

A basic proposition of this paper is, that there is a strong connection between the dynamics of employment / unemployment and macroeconomic growth. In addition to Figure 1 this is also demonstrated in Table 2. This basic connection is however modified by a large number of additional macroeconomic as well as structural factors. In the context of this paper only some macroeconomic aspects will be looked at.

As can be seen from Table 2 there are very few European countries which have managed to retain a relatively low rate of unemployment or even reduce it. Countries, where one can observe a very strong and pronounced link between economic growth and unemployment dynamics are – on the positive side – Norway, Ireland, Portugal and – to a certain extent – Great Britain. Examples for substantial increases in unemployment combined with low rates of growth of GDP are for instance Italy and Sweden. There are, however, countries, where this relationship between economic growth and unemployment is modified by a higher "employment intensity" of economic growth rates. This does not only refer to the well-known example of the US, but for instance also to the Netherlands, Denmark and to a certain extent also Austria. It is therefore of interest to discuss these "special cases". A first explanation may refer to the specific role of supply – side measures on the labour-markets in each of these countries. In the Netherlands this took the form of a vast increase in part-time work, in Denmark a reduction of labour-supply was achieved by the introduction of special forms of "sabbaticals" for professional training and for child-care. The case of Austria will be examined later.

### *2. Wage Shares, Wage Flexibility and Employment*

In addition to the general picture given above a specific marcroeconomic aspect may be of interest. This refers to the connection between wage flexibility and employment – a connection which is central to proposals from the side of the OECD (1994) and the EU. The relevant question here are the macroeconomic aspects of wage flexibility – not the structural effects of wage policy, e.g. with respect to wage differentials. To reduce unemployment economists recommend (real) wage increases that are below the increase of labour-productivity. This would induce forms of technological substitution between capital and labour, thus directly creating increased labour demand. Indirectly lower rates of labour-productivity-growth would increase the "employment-intensity" of economic growth.

*Table 2*

**Unemployment Rates and Economic Growth**

| | 1979 - 97 | | 1990 - 97 | | |
|---|---|---|---|---|---|
| | Change in Rates of Unemployment[a)] | Growth Rate of GDP[b)] | Change in Rates of Unemployment[a] | Growth Rate of GDP[b] | Unemployment Rate (1997) |
| Australia | 2,6 | 2,9 | 1,7 | 2,6 | 8,7 |
| Austria | 4,4 | 2,1 | 1,4 | 1,7 | 6,1 |
| Belgium | 5,1 | 1,7 | 3,9 | 1,2 | 12,7 |
| Canada | 1,7 | 2,3 | 1,0 | 1,6 | 9,2 |
| Switzerland | 5,0 | 1,4 | 4,8 | 0,0 | 5,3 |
| Germany | 8,2 | 2,4 | 5,2 | 2,7 | 11,4 |
| Denmark | 1,7 | 1,9 | – 1,7 | 2,2 | 7,9 |
| Spain | 13,0 | 2,3 | 5,3 | 1,5 | 21,0 |
| Finland | 8,6 | 2,2 | 11,1 | 0,6 | 14,6 |
| France | 6,6 | 1,8 | 3,5 | 1,2 | 12,4 |
| Great Britain | 2,4 | 1,9 | 1,0 | 1,5 | 6,9 |
| Greece | 8,6 | 1,5 | 3,5 | 1,4 | 10,5 |
| Ireland | 3,4 | 4,2 | – 2,6 | 4,9 | 10,3 |
| Island | 3,4 | 2,4 | 2,0 | 1,7 | 3,8 |
| Italy | 6,6 | 1,8 | 3,2 | 1,0 | 12,3 |
| Japan | 1,3 | 2,8 | 1,3 | 1,4 | 3,4 |
| Korea | – 1,3 | 7,2 | 0,1 | 6,3 | 2,5 |
| Luxembourg | 3,0 | 4,2 | 2,4 | 4,2 | 3,7 |
| Mexico | – 0,6 | 2,4 | 1,4 | 2,4 | 4,1 |
| Netherlands | 2,2 | 2,1 | – 0,2 | 2,1 | 5,8 |
| Norway | 2,0 | 3,0 | – 1,3 | 3,4 | 3,9 |
| New Zealand | 4,9 | 2,1 | – 1,1 | 1,9 | 6,7 |
| Portugal | – 1,4 | 2,5 | 2,1 | 1,7 | 6,8 |
| Sweden | 6,0 | 1,4 | 6,5 | 0,7 | 8,1 |
| Turkey | – 2,6 | 4,1 | –1,9 | 3,7 | 6,1 |
| USA | – 0,8 | 2,3 | –0,6 | 2,0 | 5,0 |

a) In percentage points
b) Average annual growth rate of real GDP
Source: OECD Main Economic Indicators

This kind of policy has in fact been followed in Germany and also in Austria, as can be seen from the declining wage-shares of GNP (Figure 4). But although there is a permanent tendency of declining wage-shares since the 1980s this has not prevented a substantial rise in unemployment. Rather the decline in the growth of real wages has led to an increase in the profit share of GNP. A macroeconomic policy of restricted wage-increases thus has not induced higher demand for labour, nor has it resulted in higher real investments (at least not in Germany or Austria). This development has, of course, to be seen in connection with the tendency of rising interest rates discussed above. This tendency contributed to a shift from real to financial investments. The structural effects of the opening of Eastern Europe, globalisation, etc. also have to be taken into account.

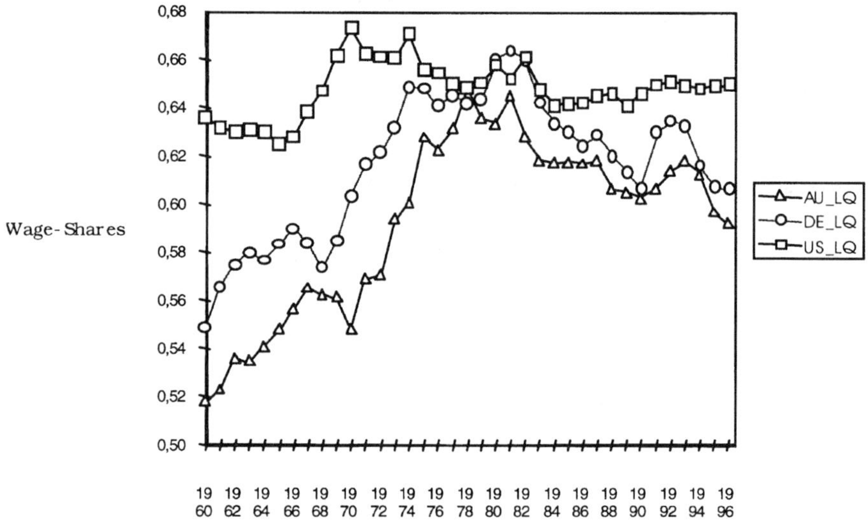


*Source:* H. Walther (1997, p. 122)

Figure 4: Wage-Shares US, Germany, Austria

It is of interest to compare these developments with the experience of the USA. Compared with Germany and Austria the US wage share is not only higher but also much more stable. As there also have been substantial decreases in the rate of growth of real wages (especially!) in the US, the constant wage-share means that in this case wage-restriction has in fact led to an increase in employment and also to a decrease in the rate of growth of labour-productivity.

There are many factors to explain this phenomenon (comp. e.g. R. B. Freeman, 1997, H. Walther, 1997). One institutional aspect will be discussed in the next section of this paper. Other factors may be insider-outsider effects, different qualification structures etc. In this paragraph one factor of special macroeconomic interest will be discussed. This is the aspect of macroeconomic flexibility of real wages.

Table 3 gives an overview of estimations for the direct impact of unemployment on wage increases and of the long-run elasticity of real wages[6]. It can be seen that both indicators show substantially higher values for Germany and most European countries as compared to the US – with Austria showing by far the most flexible wage-policy.. When seen in a macroeconomic context this result may give rise to several interesting considerations: In periods of low growth there is no clear and direct connection between macroeconomic wage flexibility and employment performance. For small open economies such as Austria and the Netherlands downward wage flexibility may serve as a way to devaluing the real exchange rate – as long as this is not neutralised by exchange-rate effects of rising interest rates. For the whole EU such a policy would only result in beggar-my-neighbour-effects.

*Table 3*

**Impact of Unemployment on Wage Increases**

| Country | Direct Effect | Longrun Elasticity of Real Wages |
|---|---|---|
| Belgium | – 0.90 | 1.18 |
| Denmark | – 0.90 | 1.11 |
| Germany | – 0.65 | 0.89 |
| Greece | – 0.55 | 1.24 |
| Spain | – 0.88 | 1.86 |
| France | – 0.90 | 1.27 |
| Ireland | – 0.48 | 0.71 |
| Italy | – 0.95 | 1.44 |
| Netherlands | – 0.95 | 1.42 |
| Austria | – 1.60 | 2.53 |
| Portugal | – 0.64 | 1.45 |
| Great Britain | – 0.50 | 0.74 |
| Finland | – 0.75 | 1.28 |
| Sweden | – 1.10 | 1.83 |
| USA | – 0.50 | 0.55 |
| Japan | – 2.50 | 3.47 |

*Source:* Roeger, W., in't Veld, J. (1997)

6 The parameters in Table 3 are obtained from the QUEST II-Model of the EU-Commission. See also Institut für Höhere Studien (1998).

There is, however an interesting second aspect with regard to international differences in wage-flexibility. This aspect refers to the reaction of wage increases in periods of an economic upswing. A high "upward mobility" of wages means that inflationary pressures and thus "preemtive measures" by central banks will occur at a much earlier stage of an economic upswing, thus contributing to a higher "structural" base of unemployment. This may (partially) explain the different attitudes especially of the US and the German central bank.[7]

The present US discussion about "New Age-Economics" is basically about the question as to whether the observable low "inflation propensity" of the present strong US economy is only a matter of delays or indicates a new structural phenomenon. Analytically this means that "old", well-established (short-run) Phillips-curve relationships, on which central-bank policies were oriented[8], may have changed.[9] This proposition has to be seen however against the background of the already relatively low extent of US macroeconomic wage-flexibility, as demonstrated in Table 3. From a policy point of view a tendency of decreasing "upward" wage flexibility in Europe, too, would allow the European Central Bank to engage in a more expansionary policy as compared towards former national central banks. Such a tendency can in fact be expected by larger and thus in real terms more flexible European markets for labour and products.

### *3. Productivity and the Service Sector*

As has been indicated above there are a number of structural aspects connecting macroeconomic growth, labour productivity and employment. In this section one institutional aspect will be studied which is of special importance for explaining the fact why high wage flexibility has so little employment effects in Europe. This refers to the role of the service sector in an economy. In contrast to the industrial sector the service sector may be characterised by a substantially higher wage-elasticity of labour demand. The small employment-effect of wage flexibility, especially in Germany and Austria, has thus to be seen in connection with the share of the service sector in these countries – as compared to the US, the Netherlands and the UK (compare Table 4). To a large extent this reflects differences in economic structures (compare e.g. the different employment shares of finance and business services!). To a certain extent these differences however indicate different institutional policy options – with very direct employment effects.

---

[7] According to H. Walther (1997, p. 125) in Germany in the period of 1961 - 1995 already an employment increase of more than 0.5% led to an increase of real per-unit labour costs in the next year. For the US this employment increase had to be 2%.

[8] See e.g. A. S. Blinder (1997, p. 39).

[9] For a critical discussion of the "Nirvana perspective" see A. S. Lown, R. W. Rich (1997).

*Table 4*

**Role and Structure of the Service Sector, 1994**

(Contribution to Employment in % of Total Employment)

| | Total Service Sector | Producers of Government Services | Community, Social and Personal Services |
|---|---|---|---|
| Germany | 59,1 | 15,9 | n.a. |
| Austria | 63,2 | 21,8 | 5,5 |
| Netherlands | 70,4 | 12,7 | 17,1 |
| France | 69,7 | 28,0 | 7,2 |
| Sweden | 69,9 | 32,0 | 8,2 |
| U.K. | 70,2 | 19,4 | 11,8 |
| U.S. | 73,1 | 14,5 | 17,5 |

*Source:* OECD in Figures, Paris 1997

In the US, community, social and personal services (such as e.g. education and health care) are organised in a private or semi-private way, whereas in European welfare states, such as in Germany and Austria, they are provided by different levels of government. The way of provision has different allocative and distributive effects which will not be discussed here. It is however obvious, that these kinds of services are subject to increasing demand and – due to their low productivity – show a large growth potential for employment. The realisation of this services-related growth potential contributed in a big way to the positive US employment performance. For the European welfare-states however this growth potential could not be realised due to institutional – political rigidities. As these services – to a large extent with good distributional reasons – are publicly financed in Europe an expansion of this sector and thus of public expenditure would lead to higher shares in public revenues. In fact, however, in most European countries the share of real public expenditure declined due to budgetary restrictions. The alternative to public provision would be to allow for private suppliers of relevant social services. Many European countries have however chosen a third way with negative employment effects: For political reasons no private supply of these services was allowed, but on the other hand it proved also politically not possible to provide public financing for an expansion of these services. Being unable to take one of these options meant the loss of vast opportunities for economic growth and for new employment.

## IV. The Austrian Experience – Macroeconomic Perspectives

In the final section of this paper Austria will be brievly discussed as a case-study of a small open economy that has managed to keep unemployment-rates remarkably low for a long period of time (see Table 5). With the exception of the last few years employment figures have also been more dynamic when compared to the rest of Europe, participation rates are relatively high and rising.[10] A major cause for the differences between European, particularly also the German labour-market performance and the results for Austria can be seen in structural differences (e.g. the higher employment share of the service-sector in comparison with Germany). Such structural differences both on the supply and the demand side of labour markets are also to be observed among the different regions of large countries. These kinds of differences may be the prime explanation for the large – and rather stable – regional variation of unemployment rates for instance in Germany.

*Table 5*

**Austria: Economic Growth, Employment and Unemployment**

| | 1970/80 | 1980/90 | 1990/95 | 1995/98[c)] |
|---|---|---|---|---|
| Real GDP-growth[a)] | | | | |
| Austria | 3,4 | 2,3 | 2,1 | 2,1 |
| OECD-Europe | 3,0 | 2,5 | 1,8 | 2,7 |
| Employment[a)] | | | | |
| Austria | 0,7 | 0,2 | 0,6 | 0,1 |
| OECD-Europe | 0,5 | 0,7 | – 0,3 | 0,7 |
| Unemployment[b)] | | | | |
| Austria | 1,9 | 4,4 | 6,2 | 7,0[d)] (4,25)[e)] |
| OECD-Europe | 4,0 | 8,2 | 9,4 | 6,1 |

a) Average annual percentage changes
b) absolute percentage
c) forcast
d) national definition
e) OECD-definition

*Source:* ÖSTAT / WIFO DB

Considering the case of Austria it can be expected however that macroeconomic factors are also of relevance for the explanation of differences in labour market dynamics. Without attempting a general analysis[11] special attention will be given to the connection between cyclical volatility of unemployment and the levels of unemployment because in this respect Austria is indeed a special case in Europe.

10 Participation rates (labour force as percentage of total population between 15 - 65 years) 1995; Austria: 59.4%, Germany: 57.7%, EU 15: 55.2%.

11 For more general discussions see e.g. E. Walterskirchen (1997), E. Nowotny (1997).

For a number of theoretical reasons (e.g. when assuming a non-linear short run Phillips-Curve) it can be expected that a lower cyclical volatility of unemployment ceteris paribus will be connected with lower levels of unemployment. In a comparison of various European small open economies (Table 6) for the period 1970 - 1996 Austria in fact shows the lowest average rate of unemployment and by far the lowest variability of unemployment rates.

*Table 6*

**Cyclical Volatility of Employment and Unemployment**

| | A | Dk | Nl | S | CH |
|---|---|---|---|---|---|
| Average rate of unemployment 1970 - 1996 | 4,90 | 7,70 | 7,70 | 4,30 | 1,50 |
| Variability of unemployment rates 1979 - 1996 | 0,35 | 1,10 | 1,02 | 0,84 | 0,47 |
| Variability of output[a] | 1,79 | 1,92 | 1,55 | 1,73 | 2,57 |
| Employment-reaction[b] | | | | | |
| 1979 - 1996 | 0,47 | 0,62 | 0,52 | 0,77 | 0,67 |
| 1979 - 1983 | 0,33 | 0,81 | 0,49 | 0,40 | 0,70 |
| 1984 - 1996 | 0,87 | 1,20 | 1,00 | 1,40 | 0,93 |
| Labour-supply reaction[c] | | | | | |
| 1979 - 1996 | 0,83 | 0,26 | 0,12 | 0,51 | 0,85 |
| 1979 - 1983 | 0,55 | 0,25 | 0,03 | 0,49 | 0,94 |
| 1984 - 1996 | 0.93 | 0,26 | 0,20 | 0,51 | 0,66 |

a) Standard deviation of first differences.

b) Coefficient b in a regression connecting 'employment deviation from trend' and 'output deviation from trend'.

c) Coefficient b in a regression connecting 'labour supply deviation from trend' and 'employment deviation from trend'.

*Source:* IHS (1998, p. 32).

It has to be noted that the differences in the variability of unemployment rates are much more pronounced than the differences in output-variability. The lower cyclical volatility of unemployment in Austria thus cannot be explained by lower cyclical variations of GNP. At first sight this is in contradiction to the position stressed in section 1 of this paper, that unemployment dynamics basically is determined by the dynamics of GNP-growth. It has to be noted however that one has to distinguish between the basic connection between GNP-growth and employment / unemployment and the modifications of this basic connection due to structural and policy influences. This can be seen in more detail looking at the reaction of employment to output deviations from trend and the reaction of labour supply to employment deviation from trend. In the first case Austria shows much lower, in the second case Austria shows much higher values than compared to the other countries, analysed in Table 6.

Lower cyclical reactions of employment to output changes, i.e. procyclical variations of labour-productivity could be an indicator of "labour hoarding" in periods of cyclical downswings and of anticyclical government employment policies (promoting part-time work, employment projects, etc.). In fact in Austria these kinds of strategy played a substantial role in the 70s , using e.g. the (then) nationalised industries and public investment programmes as instruments of employment policy (E. Nowotny, 1982). There have also been however additional factors of cyclical employment stabilisation, such as the higher flexibility of real wages discussed in section 3.2 and the effects of a larger service sector of the economy.

Unemployment dynamics is also affected by the reaction of labour supply to changes in labour market conditions. Procyclical changes in labour supply have a dampening effect on cyclical variations of the rate of unemployment. The strong labour supply elasticity in Austria is due to procyclical reactions concerning labour-immigration (also in Switzerland), but is also due to policy-induced effects concerning the retirement age and female work-force participation (e.g. by creating opportunities for additional maternity-leave). It has to be noted however that participation rates are relatively high in Austria, which indicates that the main long-run effect of these measures was not a permanent reduction in the labour-supply but rather substitutions-effects for instance in favour of youth employment.

It is of special interest to observe that in all countries shown in Table 5 there has been a dramatic change between reactions in the 70s and in the 80s and 90s. For 1984 - 1996 coefficients close to 1 indicate that now variations of output almost directly translate into cyclical reactions in employment. Next to Sweden[12] Austria exhibits the most dramatic change in employment reactions. This can be interpreted as indicating the end of a specific "Austrian way" of "active" employment policy. This development was brought about by several factors: One was the negative effects of the European steel-crisis on Austria's nationalised industry, leading to (partial) privatisation and intensive restructuring. In a more general way due to increasing debt-ratios and – later – in the process of preparation for EMU-membership public net deficits were reduced rapidly[13]. This did not only weaken general demand but it also had an immediate negative effect on the important role of the public sector as the "direct employer of last resort"[14].

---

[12] The coefficient of larger than 1 in Sweden can be seen as indicating the "explosion" of an "employment bubble".

[13] Between 1995 and 1998 total public sector net deficits (as % of GDP) were reduced from 5,1% to 2,7%.

[14] From 1987 - 1996 employment in Austria increased by 210 000 persons, 140 000 of which were added to the public sector workforce (including health and education).

Even if there has been a structural change in Austria's labour-markets, unemployment in the country in recent periods has also been much lower and has been increasing more slowly as compared to other European countries. There has been some increase in the form of "passive" labour market policy (increased rates of early retirement, etc.), but there are two main factors which are also of general relevance:

- The active macroeconomic and structural policies of fighting unemployment already at an early stage of employment problems prevented a high level of "structural unemployment" (and especially long-term "hysteresis"-unemployment). Of course a small open economy is not able to isolate itself permanently from rising European (and for Austria particularly German) unemployment. But it pays "to fight as long as you can". As can be seen from Figure 1, since the 1980s the development of unemployment in Austria closely followed the European pattern – but as can be seen from Table 5 at a much lower level. This means that the specifically employment-oriented active macroeconomic fiscal policy of the 70s could not be followed permanently – but the positive results of this policy did not get lost in later periods. Macroeconomic policies to prevent large economic fluctuations and a rocketing of unemployment in recessions not only have short-run but also positive long-run effects.
- Such an employment-oriented macroeconomic policy has to be based on a close co-operation between fiscal, monetary and incomes policy. This was – and largely still is – the case in Austria. The system of "Social-Partnership" leads to the relatively high real wages flexibility, discussed in section 3. By taking care of aspects of "distributional fairness" the system of "Social-Partnership" also enables a stability oriented fiscal policy without social turmoil. The role of monetary policy is restricted due to the strategy of following a "hard currency" policy of a fixed exchange rate with the DM. But within this context the Austrian Central Bank tries to support an employment-oriented policy by the government and the social-partners. This co-ordination is helped by the fact that the social partners (trade unions and associations of industry, commerce and agriculture) are also (minority) share holders of the Austrian Central Bank and are directly represented in its decision-making body.[15] The experience of Austria thus underlines the benefits of policy co-ordination and the importance of the integration of monetary policy into such a system of policy co-ordination.

## Literature

*Blanchard,* Oliver / *Chouraqui,* Jean-Claude / *Havemann,* Robert and *Sartor,* Nicola: The Sustainability of Fiscal Policy: New Answers to an Old Question. OECD Economic Studies,

15 This latter provision had to be changed in the course of Austria's preparations for EMU-membership.

Vol. 15, 1990, pp. 7. – *Blinder,* Alan. S.: A Core of Macroeconomic Beliefs? In: Challenge, July / August 1997, pp. 36. – *EG:* Jahreswirtschaftsbericht 1996, Europäische Wirtschaft, Brüssel 1996 (61). – *Filc,* Wolfgang: Wirtschaftswachstum durch gestaltete Finanzmärkte. Nationaler Verhaltenskodex und internationale Kooperation. In: Internationale Gesellschaft und Politik, 1 / 1998, S. 22 ff. – *Freeman,* Richard: Arbeitsplatzbeschaffung und Einkommensbildung in Europa und den USA. Wien 1997. – *Freeman,* Richard: The Limits of Wage Flexibility to Curing Unemployment. In: Oxford Review of Economic Policy, Vol. 11(1), 1995, pp. 63 - 72. – *IHS* (Institut für Höhere Studien): Mittelfristige Prognose der österreichischen Wirtschaft 1998 - 2002, Wien 1998. – *Lown,* Cara. S. and *Rich,* Robert.W: Is there an Inflation Puzzle? In: Federal Reserve Bank of New York Economic Policy Review, Vol. 3(4), Dec. 1997, pp. 51 - 69 – *Marterbauer,* Markus: Perspectives for an Effective Employment Policy, Austrian Institute for Economic Research Paper, Vienna 1997. – *Nowotny,* Ewald: Der öffentliche Sektor, 3. Auflage, Berlin-Heidelberg 1996. – *Nowotny,* Ewald:. Nationalized Industries as an Instrument of Stabilization Policy. The Case of Austria. In: Annuals of Public and Co-operative Economy, Vol. 51 (1982), pp. 41. – *Nowotny,* Ewald: Wirtschaftsvergleiche USA-Europa-Österreich. Über einige sinnvolle und einige weniger sinnvolle Schlußfolgerungen. In: R.B. Freeman (1997). – *OECD:* The OECD Jobs Study. Paris 1994 ff. – *Roeger,* William: in't Veld, John, Quest II. A Multy Country Business Cycle and Growth Model, EU-DG II, Economic Papers 123, Brussels, Oct. 1997. – *Schulmeister,* Stefan: Zinssatz, Investitionsdynamik, Wachstumsrate und Staatsverschuldung. Österr. Institut für Wirtschaftsforschung, Wien 1996. – *Walterskirchen,* Ewald: Austria's Road to Full Employment, WIFO-Working Paper, Vienna, 1997. – *Walther,* Herbert: Lohnpolitik und Beschäftigung. In: R. B. Freeman (1997).

# Economic Policy Targeting, Policy Mix and (Un-)Employment

By Carl-Ludwig Holtfrerich, Berlin

Exploring Germany's and Europe's unemployment problem from a macroeconomic perspective is the aim of this conference. I will start with the following hypotheses:

1. The still rising unemployment problem cannot be solved unless economic growth is speeded up.
2. Supply-side measures by the government and collective bargaining partners are not sufficient to raise the growth rate of the economy enough to solve the unemployment problem.
3. Under the constraints of the Maastricht Treaty, fiscal policy has been pro-cyclical and has deepened the recession.
4. The key to more economic growth and less unemployment lies in a different policy mix, especially between monetary and fiscal policies.

I will deal with these issues in turn.

## I. Okun's Law

Arthur Okun has shown empirically for the U.S. economy that only a growth rate of more than 2.5 percent lowers the unemployment rate and that each percentage point of more economic growth lowers the unemployment rate by 0.5 percentage points. Empirical studies for Germany have shown similar results.[1] That a one-percentage point of growth lowers the unemployment rate by only half the amount is due to the following. When economic growth and the demand for labor accelerates, employers at first tend to more fully occupy their existing staff instead of hiring more workers. The second explanation is that when growth accelerates, more persons enter the labor market who previously had given up looking for a job.

---

1 Hans Joachim Schalk / Jörg Lüschow / Gerhard Untiedt: Wachstum und Arbeitslosigkeit – Gibt es noch einen Zusammenhang?, in: Ifo Schnelldienst 1997, No. 17 - 18.

Had politicians in Germany been aware of Okun's Law, they would have known that cutting the unemployment rate of 10.4 percent in 1996 in half by the year 2000 would have required an average annual growth rate of more than 5 percent and even considerably more when they still proclaimed that goal in 1997. If Germany's growth rate would only attain the more realistic American average growth rate of 3.5 percent in the 1980s and again in the last few years, our unemployment rate would drop by only 0.5 percent per year. It would last 13 years to cut the current 12.6 percent of unemployment (February 1998) down to 6.3 percent. Our present economic growth rate of around 2.3 percent is more than eaten up by labor productivity growth. Hence we have still rising unemployment rates.

## II. Supply-side measures

The German government's "Program for More Growth and Employment" of early 1996 and its "Initiative for Employment" in East Germany of 1997 have both failed to show results. These and other measures increased the flexibility on the labor market, deregulated the capital market, lowered and abolished some business taxes etc. Labor displayed a remarkable wage restraint and took real wage cuts in the past few years. Nevertheless economic growth remained low and unemployment kept rising. Being an economic historian, this came as no surprise to me. The Great Depression in the U.S. lasted until 1939, when the beginning of the Second World War prompted the U.S. government to strongly increase its armaments expenditures and the Fed to serve the credit needs of the government and of private business on relatively easy terms.[2] During the 1930s the tax burden, social security contributions, the level of regulation, and the pressure of wage demands had all been so low that employers today would not even dare to dream of it, let alone demand it. Nevertheless, the American economy did not find its way out of the depression until the War. Therefore – in my view – even the Great Tax Reform, as necessary as it is for better-allocation and equity reasons, would not have much to contribute to a solution of our unemployment problem in Germany.

## III. Fiscal policy under the Maastricht Treaty

The deficit criterion and the debt ceiling of the Maastricht Treaty forced the German and other European governments to pursue a pro-cyclical fiscal policy just after the economy had turned on a recessionary course. They saved vigorously on public expenditures, while increasing revenue through generally higher taxes and social security contributions. This might have served the fulfillment of the Maas-

[2] Milton Friedman / Anna J. Schwartz: A Monetary History of the United States, 1867 - 1960, Princeton 1963, pp. 552 - 565.

tricht criteria. But these restrictive fiscal policies were poison for economic growth and employment. It resembled the policy course that the Brüning government pursued even more strongly from 1929 to 1932. Today's effects are similar in that unemployment did not diminish, but increase, in East Germany to about the same level as during the Great Depression of the 1930s.

It was a big policy mistake in the Maastricht Treaty not to differentiate between structural and cyclical deficits. Most of Germany's overall public deficit of around 3 percent is of a cyclical nature. Because the economy is not operating on the full-employment level, however defined, there is a great shortfall in tax revenue and social security contributions, while the expenditure side of the budget is burdened with huge amounts for social expenditure and subsidies for businesses that the government wants to keep alive for employment reasons. It has been estimated for Germany that each 1 million unemployed persons contribute 35 to 40 billion DM to the total government deficit. Therefrom it is easy to calculate that the current public sector deficit of about 102 billion DM in 1997 would, *ceteris paribus,* totally disappear, if 2.6 to 2.9 million of all the 4.8 million officially unemployed in Germany would get a job, i.e. if the unemployment rate could be cut by a little more than half.

Had the Maastricht deficit criterion been defined in terms of a figure for the structural deficit only, fiscal policy would not have been deprived of its leeway for counter-cyclical stabilization measures. Much of the pro-cyclical behavior of the German and other European governments in the 1990s would have been unnecessary. For instance, tax rates could have been cut to stimulate the economy instead of increasing them, as has been done. The expenditure share of public investment could have seen increases instead of the cuttings that actually took place.

The effect of the Maastricht Treaty in practice was that the government definitely gave up its responsibility for stabilizing the business cycle, although it is still committed to play this role by the Law for the Promotion of the Stability and Growth of the Economy ("Stabilitätsgesetz") of 8 June 1967. I regard it as a case for the Supreme Court to examine whether the government's and parliament's consent to the Maastricht Treaty was not in violation of Germany's constitution, because it disabled the government to shoulder the responsibility that it is being charged with by the "Stabilitätsgesetz" that still remains in force.

The result of the restrictions put on the German government by the Maastricht Treaty was that the government left the stabilization function to the Bundesbank's monetary policy alone. The Bundesbank – in my view – behaved overly restrictive during the 1990s, and, in contrast to the Fed, strove for total price stability alone and disregarded the real effects of its monetary policy on growth and employment. As Juchems / Leibfritz do for Germany in their contribution to this conference, Flassbeck et al. have used the interest rate structure between long- and short-term rates as an indicator for the restrictiveness of monetary policies in Europe as compared to the U.S. "If the spread is inverted with short rates higher than longer rates, monetary policy is restrictive and vice versa. ... If we compare the whole period, 1982 to 1996, monetary policy was restrictive in three quarters in the U.S., but in more than thirty quarters in Europe."[3] The Bundesbank thus contributed to the high deficits in the public budgets and almost wrecked EMU in making Germany and – on account of its actual role as a central bank for Europe as a whole – other European countries as well almost fail the fulfillment of the Maastricht deficit and debt ceiling criteria. Of course, the Bundesbank did and would always have to deny that it did this on purpose. But its aversion to EMU is well known. And an intent would well be in line with what the bureaucratic theory of public choice in government agencies predicts.

In any case, the governments were forced to counteract the deficit-augmenting effects of the Bundesbank's excessive restrictions on top of the consolidation task that the unification deficits required in Germany anyway. They did so by the strongly pro-cyclical policy measures already mentioned. Thus the Bundesbank aggravated the recession not only directly through its monetary policy resulting in excessively high real interest rates, but also indirectly in forcing the governments into even more drastic fiscal restrictions than would otherwise have been necessary.

## IV. Policy mix and policy results

As to all domestic economic policy goals, the results were better during the period of West Germany's "economic miracle" in the 1950s and 1960s than from the 1970s to today. This is not only true for Germany, but world-wide. Economic growth was much higher up to 1973 than thereafter.[4] Unemployment was a comparatively small problem up to 1973. Even price stability in Germany was on average greater in the 1950s and 1960s than in the decades thereafter. When we take a look at what in American parlance is called the "misery index" (the inflation rate plus the unemployment rate), the different performance of the pre- and post-1973 periods becomes even more visible (Figure 1).

The relative price stability in the early period was not the result of a moderate growth of the money supply. From the end of 1951, after the Korea boom, to the end of 1959, M3 grew at an average annual rate of 15.5 percent, while the average inflation rate was only 1.2 percent. 7.5 percent p.a. went into real economic growth.[5] Throughout the 1960s, M3 still grew at 10.7 percent p.a. on average,

---

3 Heiner Flassbeck / Brian Henry / Pierre Jacquet / Robert Levine: Unemployment in Europe and the U.S.: Macroeconomics is the Key, in: Internationale Politik und Gesellschaft / International Politics and Society 1997 / 4, p. 421.

4 Angus Maddison: The World Economy in the 20th Century, Paris 1989, p. 85 - 104. Ludger Lindlar: Das mißverstandene Wirtschaftswunder. Westdeutschland und die westeuropäische Nachkriegsprosperität, Tübingen 1997, p. 17 - 18.

5 The growth of the money supply that was not absorbed in the real economic growth rate plus the inflation rate went into the "refilling" of monetary assets, prompted by their destruc-

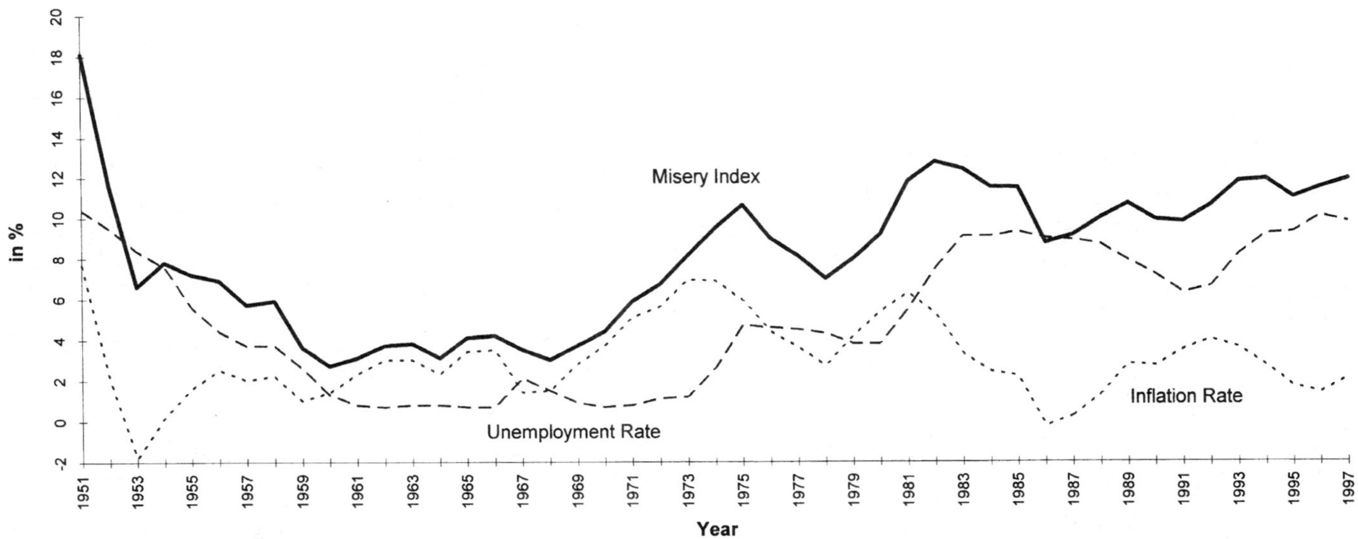


*Annotation:* The unemployment rate and the inflation rate are those of West Germany up to 1997. From 1962 the inflation rate is based on the cost-of-living index of all private households. For the years up to 1961 it is the cost-of-living index of a four-persons household with medium income.

*Sources:* Deutsche Bundesbank (ed.), 40 Jahre Deutsche Mark: Monetäre Statistiken 1948 - 1987, Frankfurt am Main 1988, p. 4 und 7. Institut der deutschen Wirtschaft (ed.), Zahlen zur wirtschaftlichen Entwicklung der Bundesrepublik Deutschland, Köln 1993, Tables 27 und 55, 1997, Tables 21 und 51.

Figure 1: Misery Index 1951 - 1997

while the inflation rate was only 2.5 percent p.a. and real economic growth 5.1 percent p.a.[6] The high growth rates of the money supply did not primarily fuel inflation, but overwhelmingly real growth and employment. Since 1974 a lower growth rate of the money supply was targeted at by the monetarist policies of the Bundesbank. M3 increased on average at a rate of 7.1 percent p.a. 1974 - 89 and 6.0 percent 1991 - 97.[7] If one takes into account that a rising share of Germany's money stock is circulating abroad since the fall of communist regimes in Eastern Europe, the growth rate of the money supply in the 1990s that fuels the German economy alone becomes even smaller.[8] Since 1974, when the growth rate of the money supply was reduced, economic growth slowed and unemployment started its long-term rise to 12.6 percent (February 1998), more than the level from which the West German economy had started out into its "economic miracle" in 1950.

Did something happen to the economic policy mix around 1973? In the fifties and sixties, the Bundesbank's monetary policy had always been closely coordinated with fiscal policies, while unit labor costs remained fairly stable, relative to abroad.[9] High nominal and real wage increases were compensated for by almost equally high labor productivity growth rates resulting from the entrepreneurs' strong investment activity in combination with the then very high marginal efficiency of capital.

There were several institutions, in which monetary and fiscal policies were closely coordinated. There was, first, the Central Bank Council, in whose meetings cabinet members often participated, especially the ministers of finance and of the economy. Even Chancellor Adenauer was occasionally present in the fifties, mainly to prevent discount rate increases, although unsuccessfully, as it turned out. In 1955 the Erhard ministry initiated the creation of the "Stabilization Policy Council" ("konjunkturpolitisches Gremium"), in which the ministers of finance and of the economy met with the president of the board of management of the central bank. They, in turn, instituted the important "committee of department heads" ("Abteilungsleiterausschuß"), which discussed and coordinated monetary, fiscal and other stabilization policy measures between the Bundesbank and the govern-

---

tion by the currency reform of 1948. For details see Wolfgang Stützel: Banken, Kapital und Kredit in der zweiten Hälfte des 20. Jahrhunderts, in: Fritz Neumark (ed.): Strukturwandlungen einer wachsenden Wirtschaft, vol. 2, Berlin 1964, pp. 527 - 575.

6 Data from Carl-Ludwig Holtfrerich: Geldpolitik bei festen Wechselkursen (1948 - 1970), in: Deutsche Bundesbank (ed.): Fünfzig Jahre Deutsche Mark. Notenbank und Währung in Deutschland seit 1948, München 1998, pp. 350 - 352: Tables 1 and 3.

7 Deutsche Bundesbank (ed.): 40 Jahre Deutsche Mark. Monetäre Statistiken 1948 - 1987, Frankfurt/M. 1988, p. 16, and further information from the Bundesbank.

8 See Franz Seitz: Der DM-Umlauf im Ausland (= Diskussionspapier 1/1995 der Volkswirtschaftlichen Forschungsgruppe der Deutschen Bundesbank), Frankfurt/M. 1995. Der DM-Bargeldumlauf im Ausland, in: Monatsberichte der Deutschen Bundesbank, July 1995.

9 Ludger Lindlar/Carl-Ludwig Holtfrerich: Geography, exchange rates and trade structures: Germany's export performance since the 1950s, in: European Review of Economic History, vol. 1 (1997), p. 233, 235.

ment in advance.[10] In addition, the so-called "economic cabinet" had existed since 1951 and performed coordinating functions. It consisted of a broader segment of cabinet members and met almost monthly with the president of the Bundesbank until 1969. It is symptomatic for the breakdown of stabilization policy coordination thereafter that since 1970 the "economic cabinet" met only once a year, merely to discuss the annual economic report ("Jahreswirtschaftsbericht") of the federal government.[11]

The Bundesbank Law, as did its forerunner, guarantees Germany's central bank's independence of "directives by the federal government". But it commits the Bundesbank to support the general economic policy of the government, albeit under the condition that its functions remain unimpaired. The wording of the Bundesbank Law defines the "safeguarding of the currency" as the Bundesbank's main function without mentioning the other economic policy goals. But what most people, including the decision-makers in the Central Bank Council, haven't kept in mind is the intent and the interpretation of this clause by the government that initiated the bill and by the legislator.

The reasons ("Begründung"), with which the Federal Government introduced the Bundesbank Bill in parliament on 18 October 1956, explicitly stated that the stability of the domestic purchasing power of money would be "- it is true – of outstanding importance". Nevertheless the other economic policy goals (stability of foreign purchasing power, i.e. of exchange rates, full employment and steady economic growth) would also have to be important goals of the Bundesbank. "Therefore, in recognition of all circumstances it will sometimes be necessary to find the optimal compromise for the 'general interest' or 'welfare of the country'". At the same time, the government and other institutions would also have to bear responsibility for the realization of economic policy goals including the "safeguarding of the currency". "Therefore a good cooperation between all authorities carrying such responsibilities, including the central bank, would be no less important than their ... independence of the other authorities."

The report with which the federal parliament's "Committee on Money and Credit" on 28 June 1957 sent the final bill to the Bundestag for the vote, stated explicitly that the responsibility for the "safeguarding of the currency" not only rested with the Bundesbank, but "even primarily" with the Federal Government and with the legislator and also with the collective bargaining partners. A contemporary expert, Friedrich Wilhelm von Schelling, long-term president of Hamburg's central bank, published recently that the parliamentary Committee on Money and Credit was concerned until the end of its proceedings on the Bundesbank Law that the

10 Helge Berger: Konjunkturpolitik im Wirtschaftswunder. Handlungsspielräume und Verhaltensmuster von Bundesbank und Regierung in den 1950er Jahren, Tübingen 1997, pp. 220 - 231.

11 According to information from the chancellor's office on the dates of the meetings. The minutes of all meetings since 1951 are still not open for research.

Bundesbank might "develop into a state within the state in a similiar way as allegedly the German army under General von Seekt had done during the Weimar Republic."[12]

The Law for the Promotion of the Stability and Growth of the Economy ("Stabilitätsgesetz") of 8 June 1967 made it even more explicit than the Bundesbank Law in which economic-policy fields the Bundesbank is obliged to support the general economic policy goals of the government. It commits all public corporations, including the Bundesbank, to conduct their policy measures in such a way "that they contribute at the same time to the stability of prices, a high employment level, external balance, and a steady and reasonable growth."

In pursuit of these goals, the Federal Government and the Bundesbank did, indeed, cooperate closely until the end of the sixties. In shaping its monetary policy, the Bundesbank took into consideration the goals of promoting employment and economic growth. The fiscal policy of the Federal Government made substantial contributions to the safeguarding of price stability, especially in the fifties, when budget surpluses led to the "Juliusturm" of money withdrawn from circulation up to a maximum of 7.5 billion DM in September 1956 (= 3.7 percent of West Germany's GNP in 1956). This was more than double the amount that the Bundesbank had reined in by way of increasing its minimum reserve requirements (about 2.5 billion DM) and through open-market operations (0.9 billion DM).[13]

This close cooperation and the sharing of responsibilities between the Federal Government and the Bundesbank for all economic policy goals broke down in the early seventies. On the one hand, it was observed that the Federal Government was no longer willing to let its fiscal leeway be narrowed by an orientation at the price stability goal. It left this task to the Bundesbank alone.[14] On the other hand, the Bundesbank's room for maneuver in conducting its monetary policy had much increased after the breakup of the Bretton Woods System. It was no longer obliged to intervene in the foreign exchange markets to defend a fixed

---

12 Friedrich Wilhelm von Schelling: Episoden eines Notenbanklebens, in: Ansprachen anläßlich des Empfangs zum 90. Geburtstag von Herrn Friedrich Wilhelm von Schelling im Hause der Landeszentralbank Hamburg am 6. Mai 1996, als Manuskript gedruckt von der LZB Hamburg 1996, p. 24. Already in 1975 the same author had criticized the "absolutism", "command power", and the "*carte blanche*" that the imprecise definition of the Bundesbank's functions in the wording of the Bundesbank law had given to West Germany's independent central bank. Friedrich Wilhelm von Schelling: Die Bundesbank in der Inflation. Plädoyer für eine neue Geldverfassung. Frankfurt / M. 1975, pp. 25 - 33, 58.

13 Carl-Ludwig Holtfrerich: Geldpolitik bei festen Wechselkursen (1948 - 1970), in: Deutsche Bundesbank (ed.), Fünfzig Jahre Deutsche Mark. Notenbank und Währung in Deutschland seit 1948, München 1998, p. 429.

14 Artur Woll / Gerald Vogl: Geldpolitik, Stuttgart 1976, S. 145.

15 David Marsh: The Bundesbank. The Bank that Rules Europe, London 1993, p. 26: "The shift towards a policy giving unambiguous priority to maximising price stability came only towards the end of the Bretton Woods System, when the commitment to steady exchange rates was necessarily downgraded."

DM-Dollar parity.[15] In 1974 the Bundesbank shifted to monetary growth targeting and specialized on fighting domestic inflation alone. This had been recommended by the "Sachverständigenrat", the German equivalent of the U.S. Council of Economic Advisers, in its annual report for 1974/75.[16] It had demanded that monetary policy should largely free fiscal policy from its business-cycle stabilization function. Those in charge of fiscal policy did, indeed, retreat from serving this function.

In the early seventies, fiscal policy started its long-term expansionary course, the consequences of which has made it so difficult to meet the Maastricht criteria. The best indicator of the structural break in fiscal policy is the ratio of public debt to GDP in Germany. From 1950 to the early seventies it held steady at a little under 20 percent on average, while in the decades thereafter until today it has more than tripled. Similar structural breaks at around the same time are visible in the equivalent time series of other industrial countries. This leads to the conclusion that the phenomenon was caused by an international event common to all countries, namely the breakdown of the Bretton Woods System.[17]

The new monetarist orientation of the Bundesbank's policy resulted in, on average, higher nominal and real interest rates in the last 25 years than during West Germany's "economic miracle" in the fifties and sixties. As we all well remember, they have been kept much higher in the 1990s than the growth rate of the economy. This also holds true for parts of the 1970s and for most of the 1980s (See Figure 2a for the comparison of nominal rates and Figure 2b for real rates). This is – in my view – the main reason, why the trend line of the development of unemployment in Germany since 1973 has steadily risen despite the many supply-side reform measures of the Federal Government, following, for instance, the change from the SPD- to the CDU-led government in 1982 and more recently the "Program for More Growth and Employment" of the spring of 1996, and despite the remarkable wage restraint of the collective bargaining partners in recent years.

We were taught in neoclassical macroeconomics ("the golden rule of accumulation") that, in equilibrium, the growth rate of the economy equals the interest rate. When the central bank keeps the interest rate persistently higher than the economic growth rate, it creates a disequilibrium by slowing economic activity and increasing unemployment. Vice versa, it can move an underemployed and staggering economy back to its equilibrium path by keeping the interest rate below the economic growth rate for a while.[18] This is what the Bundesbank could and should contribute to promote growth and employment. In my view, lower real interest

16 Paragraph 364 sequitur.

17 That this institutional break can also explain the shift to more aggressive wage policies that we have observed in the 1970s on a world-wide scale has been argued by Carl-Ludwig Holtfrerich: Wechselkurssystem und Phillips-Kurve, in: Kredit und Kapital, Vol. 15 (1982), pp. 65 - 89.

18 The old Wicksellian model of monetary policy was already based on the same reasoning.

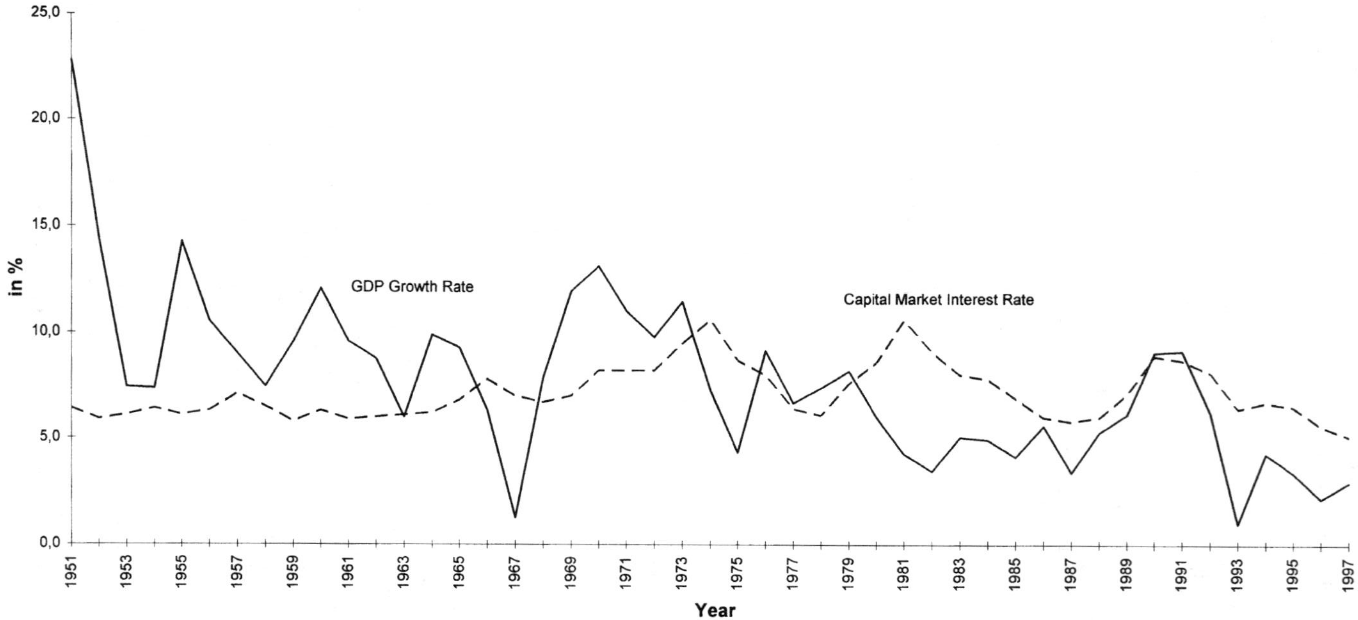


*Annotation:* The GDP growth rate is that of West Germany only up to 1997. The capital market interest rate is what the Bundesbank publishes as "Umlaufrendite festverzinslicher Wertpapiere inländischer Emittenten" (yield on domestic fixed-interest securities).

*Sources:* Deutsche Bundesbank (ed.). 40 Jahre Deutsche Mark: Monetäre Statistiken 1948 - 1987. Frankfurt am Main 1988, p. 226. For the period before 1955 capital market interest rates from: Markus Morawietz, Rentabilität und Risiko deutscher Aktien- und Rentenanlagen seit 1870: unter Berücksichtigung von Geldentwertung und steuerlichen Einflüssen, Wiesbaden 1994, p. 334. All other data directly from the Bundesbank.

Figure 2a: GDP Growth Rate and Capital Market Interest Rate 1951 - 1997
(both in nominal terms)

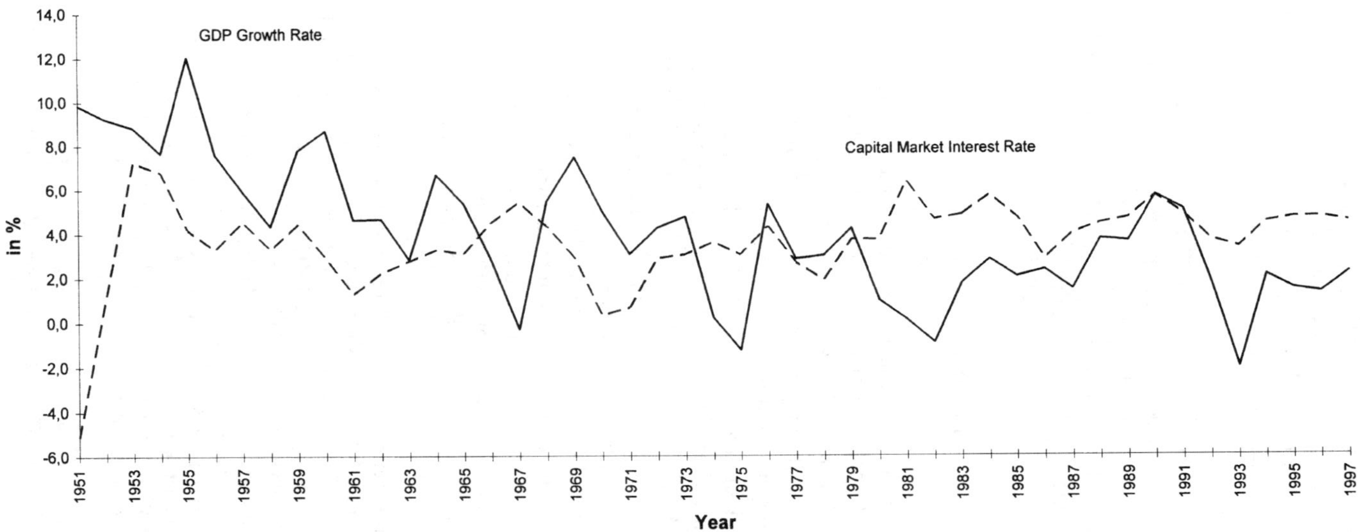


*Annotation:* The GDP growth rate is that of West Germany only up to 1997. The capital market interest rate is what the Bundesbank publishes as "Umlaufrendite festverzinslicher Wertpapiere inländischer Emittenten" (yield on domestic fixed-interest securities). The real capital market interest rate was calculated from the nominal one by substracting the rate of change of the GDP deflator.

*Sources:* Deutsche Bundesbank (ed.). 40 Jahre Deutsche Mark: Monetäre Statistiken 1948-1987. Frankfurt am Main 1988, p. 226. For the period before 1955 capital market interest rates from: Markus Morawietz, Rentabilität und Risiko deutscher Aktien- und Rentenanlagen seit 1870: Unter Berücksichtigung von Geldentwertung und steuerlichen Einflüssen, Wiesbaden 1994, p. 334. All other data directly from the Bundesbank.

Figure 2b: GDP Growth Rate and Capital Market Interest Rate 1951-1997
(both in real terms)

rates would have been and will be the key to more growth and employment. They would also have worked through lower exchange rates for the DM, i.e. lower interest rate parities, and thus through a higher international competitiveness of the German economy, as we now witness after the DM has depreciated somewhat from its earlier extremely high level.

The core problem – it seems to me – results from the "new assignment" of economic policy function upon the breakdown of the Bretton Woods System in the early seventies[19] and from the lack of the previously intensive cooperation and sharing of responsibilities for all economic policy goals since then, especially between those in charge of monetary and fiscal policies.[20]

## V. Conclusions

Monetary policy in the U.S., the dominant economy in the postwar world, targeted low real interest rates to promote growth and employment from the end of the War until the monetarist Volcker era began at the end of the seventies. Monetary policy of the Fed, which still today is explicitly obliged by law "to promote effectively the goals of maximum employment, stable prices, and moderate long-term interest rates" was relatively loose into the 1970s, while fiscal policy was restrictive until the early 1970s. Then fiscal policy turned loose, resulting in the inflationary speed-up of the 1970s, until Volcker's monetarist brakes broke the tide of inflation in the early 1980s, at the price of producing the deep recession of 1981 / 82. The American economy got out of it due to Reagan's expansionary fiscal policies, contributing to high real interest rates in the U.S., which sucked into the U.S. the savings of the world and contributed to high real interest rates abroad.[21] Because fiscal policy in the U.S. was more expansionary than in Europe, there was relatively high growth in America, while Europe showed the symptoms of "Eurosklerosis". The costs to America of its boom in the 1980s, however, was the change

[19] Norbert Kloten / Karl-Heinz Ketterer / Rainer Vollmer: West Germany's Stabilization Performance, in: Leon N. Lindberg / Charles S. Maier (eds.): The Politics of Inflation and Economic Stagnation, Washington, D.C. 1985, p. 392, 395; Norbert Kloten / Hans-J. Barth / Karl-Heinz Ketterer / Rainer Vollmer: Zur Entwicklung des Geldwertes in Deutschland. Fakten und Bestimmungsgründe, Tübingen 1980, p. 77 - 86.

[20] In his most recent publication, Claus Köhler sees the lack of coordination between the different economic-policy fields as the major cause of our unsatisfactory economic performance and demands more cooperation between monetary, fiscal, and incomes policy makers as well as more coordination internationally. Claus Köhler: Beschäftigung erhöhen, Arbeitslosigkeit verringern. Geld- und Währungspolitik vor dem Hintergrund der Bekämpfung der Arbeitslosigkeit, in: Arthur F. Utz (ed.): Die massive Arbeitslosigkeit und die Wirtschaftsordnung, Berlin 1998, pp. 91 - 92.

[21] Carl-Ludwig Holtfrerich: Reaganomics und Weltwirtschaft, in: Manfred Knapp (ed.): Transatlantische Beziehungen. Die USA und Europa zwischen gemeinsamen Interessen und Konflikt, Stuttgart 1990, pp. 37 - 61.

from its international creditor status to that of a debtor, i.e. a loss of wealth from its one-time spending spree.[22]

The U.S. boom of the 1990s rested on a more solid foundation. Monetary policy under Greenspan was not only independent of the government, but also free of the monetarist ideology. It turned relatively loose, which resulted in relatively lower real interest rates in the U.S. than in Europe. This weakened the dollar exchange rate and thereby improved the international competitiveness of U.S. producers. At the same time, this stimulus to the American economy helped the U.S. government to succeed in getting the deficit problem under control. It did so much more than the spectacular budget compromises that the White House negotiated with the majority leaders in Congress.

The Bundesbank's policies as those of the Fed were – it is true – independent of directives by the government. But the Bundesbank, in contrast to the Fed, lacked freedom of action over long periods. In the period of fixed exchange rates until the end of the early 1970s, monetary policy in Germany was constantly forced to be expansionary, as monetary restrictions were undermined by inflows of capital. Because the Bundesbank was obliged to defend the DM-Dollar parity, it had to soak up the inflowing foreign exchange and thus to expand the money supply at the rates that I mentioned for the 1950s and 1960s. When Bretton Woods broke up in the early 1970s and the Bundesbank for the first time since the *de-facto* convertibility of the DM in the mid-1950s was free to choose its monetary strategy, it opted for monetarism and a relatively scarce supply of money. This resulted in more stable prices and wages in Germany than abroad.[23] But the previous benefit of thereby improving the international competitiveness of the German economy was more than taken away by the flexibility of exchange rates, namely the revaluation of the DM. Even after all other important central banks had given up the monetarist strategy, after realizing its bad effects on growth and employment in the 1980s and early 1990s, the Bundesbank remained a prisoner of this ideology and is even trying to impose it on the future European Central Bank. With this rigidity it proves itself again unfree to serve more than the interests of the rentiers of Germany and Europe, namely those of the businessmen and labor, on the one hand, and the government in its dire financial straits, on the other, as well.[24]

In sum, economic growth and employment is much better served by a policy mix of loose monetary and restrictive fiscal policies, the recipe of Germany and the U.S. in the 1950s and 1960s, than by expansive fiscal and restrictive monetary

---

22 Carl-Ludwig Holtfrerich / Hans Otto Schötz: Vom Weltgläubiger zum Weltschuldner: Erklärungsansätze zur historischen Entwicklung und Struktur der internationalen Vermögensposition der USA, Frankfurt / M. 1988.

23 Ludger Lindlar / Carl-Ludwig Holtfrerich: Geography..., pp. 233, 235.

24 This conclusion is strongly supported by the results of the much broader study by John Smithin, Macroeconomic Policy and the Future of Capitalism. The Revenge of the Rentiers and the Threat to Prosperity, Cheltenham UK 1996.

policies, the recipe that Germany applied from 1974 to today and that other important countries also tried for a while during that period. The logic behind it is simple. Economic growth and employment is a function of the investment activity. The latter in turn is a function of the returns on productive investment in relation to the monetary price of capital. High interest rates resulting from tight monetary and loose fiscal policies might serve the safeguarding of price stability, but tend to dampen investment activity. The same effect on price stability can be achieved by loose monetary and tight fiscal policies. Economic growth and employment is much better served by this latter sort of policy mix. Relatively lower interest rates then promote investment activity and thus economic growth and employment.[25]

If not the Bundesbank, the future European Central Bank should dare to take the first step into this direction. It would serve the "general interest or welfare" of Europeans better by following the example of the Fed than that of the Bundesbank.

---

[25] Jürgen Kaehler / Olaf Korn: Wirkungszusammenhänge zwischen Zinsen und makroökonomischer Aktivität. Eine Untersuchung zu den binnen- und außenwirtschaftlichen Effekten der deutschen Geldpolitik, Baden-Baden 1995.

# Central Bankers, Games and Markets

## A Critical Assessment of the Microeconomic Optimization Approach in the Theory of Macroeconomic Stabilization

By Heinz-Peter Spahn[1], Stuttgart

### I. A heyday of the theory of monetary policy?

The time inconsistency model presented by Barro and Gordon in 1983 now exerts an equally strong influence on the theory of monetary policy as Phillips' famous article did on the general debate in macro policy. It is hardly possible to have an overall view of the quantity and varieties of monetary policy models based on that new classical approach. As the academic field of macroeconomics generally is not considered to be very practice-oriented, it may seem gratifying that research activities are not confined to theoretical analysis but are put into action in institutional economic policy reforms. With respect to the aim of designing an efficient constitution of central banks the remote country of New Zealand encounters much attention.[2] Do we observe a new attempt to resurrect the "outdated" macroeconomics?

Appearances are deceiving however. Actually the focus is not on market *processes* and *impacts* of monetary policy; rather the analysis is centred on the field of monetary policy *decisions* which has been discovered as a new area of application for game-theoretic reasoning and microeconomic optimization procedures.[3] It has become usual nowadays to explain macroeconomic facts by resorting to institutional features, political preferences and strategies. Persistent inflation is regarded as a consequence of low reputation of monetary policy, and a lowering of inflation as the successful implementation of a new central bank constitution. Some puzzles however remain unsolved:

- More than once German money growth exceeded the Bundesbank's target without causing inflationary expectations and actual inflation, which is what should

---

1 Helpful remarks by Rüdiger Dragendorf, Peter Kühnl, Thomas Schmid-Schönbein and Wolfgang Schröder are gratefully acknowledged.

2 Cf. Walsh (1995a).

3 This rather narrow interpretation of a "theory of monetary policy" already has a formative influence on economic textbooks (in Germany see e.g. Illing 1997).

happen according to monetarist theory. The violation of the "rules of the game" seems to launch a punishment in an unpredictable way.

- If then preserved monetary stability is explained by means of the famous "stability bonus" attributed to the Bundesbank, the pronounced costs of disinflation in terms of employment remain a matter of concern.
- Inflation came down in nearly all countries regardless of prevailing "stability culture" and/or institutional reforms in the field of monetary policy. In Italy, current inflation hardly exceeds 1,5%.

Many years ago, Keynesian concepts were criticized for a wide-spread belief in the ability to "manage" the economy.[4] In the meantime, however, the monetarist approach likewise has cultivated a scientific common sense which puts macroeconomic results down to economic policy making, i.e. to its institutional framework and to (the speculation on) its strategies. In a way, this is a revived postulate of the power of economic policy which is hardly persuading irrespective of whether the policy goal is full employment or monetary stability. Raising interest rates remains the most important instrument in a "strategy" of fighting inflation. Low inflation is the result of mass unemployment on a world scale. This cannot be captured by new classical models as they do not know what involuntary unemployment is. On the other hand, it is doubtful that inflation would rise again if optimal contracts which have been set up between government and central bankers were abolished.

The following section describes the analytical and historical background of the Barro-Gordon model. It is argued that this approach treats a macroeconomic scenario of full employment which hardly bears any resemblance to the current situation. The next section shows that game-theoretic reasoning which predominates in modern theory of monetary policy is limited in its importance by the fact that the peculiarities of the transmission process preclude the realization of a "surprise inflation". Moreover, this strategy makes no sense from a vote-maximizing point of view, particularly if a left-wing party wishes to stay in office.

The history of inflation is briefly analyzed in the following section. The pattern of origin and decline of inflation does not seem to fit with the story of a Barro-Gordon game. Inflation mostly was driven from the supply side whereas central banks differed in their attitude to accommodate. Thus their behaviour in some cases was characterized by weakness and inability to resist to inflationary pressures – but not by strategic choices in order to fool the public. It is then shown that the problems of monetary policy making are better captured by envisaging a game against "nature" (not against the private sector) in which central banks face the risks of either allowing an inflationary boom or causing the outbreak of a recession because a fine tuning of the economy aiming at a stable equilibrium path is unattainable. The basis for monetary policy decisions are uncertain because of shocks and endogenous feedback mechanisms between the utilization and production of

---

4 Cf. Sievert (1979).

resources. The key information problem is not a lack of knowledge about central bankers' preferences on the part of private market agents but rather the uncertainty on the part of both policymakers and market agents how to interpret market signals and to assess their medium and long run relevance.

The final section emphasizes that a substantial risk of anti-inflation policies is the emergence of persistent unemployment. There is however no "structural" unemployment which can be defined without making any reference to the stance of effective demand. This terms confuses the macroeconomic employment issue with the microeconomic topic of efficiency. Hence, monetary policy can increase employment if firms are compensated for the efficiency loss which accrue when low qualified workers are hired. If a rise of overall employment is on the political agenda, demand policies cannot be substituted by mere devices for promoting the flexibility of labour markets.

## II. The macroeconomic policy framework of the Barro-Gordon model

In his famous "Presidential Address" of 1968 Friedman argued that expansive monetary policy beyond a state of full employment (defined with some allusion to a Walrasian approach) would not yield permanent employment gains but rather start a process of accelerating inflation. This hardly could be assessed as a new message because Keynes himself had emphasized this point thirty years before.[5] Following the "discovery" of the Phillips curve, however, a debate emerged in which (among others) Samuelson and Solow demonstrated a trade-off between unemployment and inflation which could be exploited by economic policy.[6] What is striking in a retrospective view is the lack of a precise definition of a labour market equilibrium. Most probably the participants in that debate made implicit references to an equilibrium *corridor* comprising some "structural" unemployment. The reduction of that unemployment was part of a comprehensive social policy program against poverty in the U.S.

Friedman's analysis of that goal in a macroeconomic context then should have made clear that trading in price stability for lower unemployment simply meant

5 "As effective demand increases, employment increases, (...) until a point comes at which there is no surplus of labour available at the then existing real wage (...) unless money-wages rise (...) *faster* than prices. (...) After this point a unit of labour would require the inducement of the equivalent of an increased quantity of product, whereas the yield from applying a further unit would be a diminished quantity of product. The conditions of strict equilibrium require, therefore, that wages and prices, and consequently profits also, should all rise in the same proportion as expenditure, the 'real' position, including the volume of output and employment, being left unchanged in all respects. We have reached (...) a situation in which the crude quantity of money (...) is fully satisfied; for output does not alter and prices rise in exact proportion to *MV* [i.e. money in circulation]" (Keynes 1936: 289, cf. Friedman 1968; insertions in square brackets by the author).

6 Samuelson / Solow (1960).

*excess demand* on the labour market. It is astonishing that Keynesian writers held on to the concept of exploiting the Phillips curve and thus were forced to defend their case by resorting to dubious arguments, e.g. by assuming money illusion.[7] In the ensuing discussion, therefore, neoclassical economists had an easy job and were able to perfect their position by developing the idea of rational expectations which undoubtedly marked a substantial progress of economic thought.[8] Finally, they were able to demonstrate that demand policies aiming at an unemployment rate below the NAIRU would end up in a high-inflation equilibrium without any long-run gains in employment if rational expectations are assumed. Quite naturally this prompted the claim to abolish the scope for discretionary demand management altogether.[9]

This claim then was qualified by taking into account the occurrence of randomly distributed shocks. In addition the abolition of the assumption of perfect information about the policymakers' preferences complicated the game-theoretic setup of the analysis. Then an appealing solution seemed to be found by the idea of appointing a "conservative" central banker who differed from the representative agent by a relatively high preference for price stability.[10] In case of central bank *independence,* however, society no longer can control its actions which lead to the demand for making the central bank *responsible* for maintaining price stability; this could be achieved by designing optimal contracts which match the individual central banker's interest with social welfare.[11] But how can we be sure that the government – which was introduced as inflation prone at the beginning of the debate – will punish deviations from that contract? The conclusion is that optimal contracts do not solve the problem of time inconsistency but merely shift it to another level of the process of policy making.[12]

Throughout the discussion the basic premise was kept up: by initiating a surprise inflation the policymaker aims at an *excess* employment, relative to the NAIRU level which is not accepted as socially optimal. The reasons given for that assessment are hardly persuasive (the only sensible argument, the persistence effect which renders the NAIRU to be dependent from the state and path of actual employment, for a long time had no role to play in the dispute):

In the first place an allocative public finance problem was raised which has no direct links to the issue of macroeconomic stabilization: the "natural" labour market equilibrium may exhibit a level of employment which is too low from a welfare-theoretic point of view. Private households' labour supply is adversely affected by income taxes and unemployment benefits. But the individual calculus

7 Cf. e.g. Rothschild (1971).

8 Cf. Lucas (1972). For a critical assessment see Blinder (1987).

9 Cf. Kydland / Prescott (1977), Barro / Gordon (1983).

10 Cf. Rogoff (1985).

11 Cf. Walsh (1995b).

12 Cf. McCallum (1995), (1997).

ignores that each member of society profits from a higher employment level, e.g. because of tax-financed public goods. Thus external effects can justify employment-enhancing policies.[13] If however the government takes into account that in the long run a Barro-Gordon game produces nothing but inflation, additional public goods could only be financed in a not reliable way by the inflation tax.

A more obvious foundation of an easy money policy is given by the argument that aggressive wage policies would establish a too high real wage so that unemployment ensues.[14] It is questionable whether this constellation can be interpreted as an equilibrium in terms of Friedman's Phillips curve analysis; the unemployment may be accompanied by stable prices, but is not "natural" in any sense. Moreover one may ask why economic policy should be inclined to change the situation by expansive demand management. The traditional answer is that an incumbent "labour" government would run such policies in order to preserve and increase the approval of its supporters.

This line of argument lacks a solid political logic. An analysis of interests of all parties involved in the game reveals that the majority of employed workers will prefer the maintenance of the status quo. As wage competition on the part of outsiders obviously has to role to play (otherwise we could not speak of an equilibrium), the jobs of the employed appear to be secure and real income is relatively high. A "labour" or left-wing government then might try to improve the market conditions for the unemployed, but from a vote-getting point of view this does not seem to be a promising strategy:

- The transition to the "fooling solution" in the Barro-Gordon model allows inflation to attack real wages of the employed work force which will lower their approval of the policy of the party in office.
- The "wealthy" will increase their resistance against the incumbent government because inflation tends to devalue financial assets.

The straightforward conclusion is that the chances of the governing party to be re-elected will decline. Therefore we cannot expect that a policy of running a surprise inflation will be pursued. Rather we have to confirm the result of the *political* game-theoretic literature: here a scenario of unemployment and price stability proves to be an equilibrium from a vote-maximizing and from an economic policy point of view which is unlikely to be given up by an elected policymaker.[15]

An evaluation of the arguments given so far thus leads to the general conclusion that the relevant *economic* game-theoretic literature attributes to the policymaker an objective which is not rational in itself but only serves the purpose of *establishing* a scenario which is plagued by the risk of an inflation bias. "The role of this

13 Cf. Barro / Gordon (1983).

14 Cf. Canzoneri (1985).

15 Cf. Scharpf (1988).

employment target in the analysis is to introduce [sic!] a benefit from a surprise inflation."[16] The Barro-Gordon model treats a non-existing problem by looking at the wrong side of the Phillips curve. As the main topic it picks the case of excess demand which has lost its relevance for Western industrialized countries since the 1970s. Keynesian economists played a deplorable role throughout the debate as none of their school of thought but rather a leading advocate of neoclassical General Equilibrium analysis exposed the main flaw of new classical Monetarism. Already in 1982 Frank Hahn wrote: "It is puzzling to find it put forward as a discovery that a higher inflation rate will not increase the full-employment level of employment: Keynes and Keynesians would not have claimed otherwise. (...) The Lucasians, by denying the possibility of involuntary unemployment – indeed, they profess not to know what it means – have given no reason why anyone should be interested in their trade-off even if it existed. In fact, the world that they describe quite plainly needs no macro-policy. Keynesians were concerned with the problem of pushing the economy to its natural rate, not beyond it. If the economy is already there, we can all go home."[17]

## III. Central bankers on the problem of time inconsistency

Central bankers do not seem to share the same view on the game-theoretic approach in the analysis of monetary policy. On the one hand, Issing regards it to be the most important contribution of monetary theory to the problem of stabilization; on the other, Blinder stresses that during his time in office as vice-president of the Fed he never met a colleague who showed some susceptibility to the temptation to run a surprise inflation strategy. "I firmly believe that this theoretical problem is a nonproblem in the real world because central bankers have found simple, practical ways to solve it." For fighting inflation central bankers do not need neither rules nor optimal contracts. "Instead, they brought inflation down dramatically by purely discretionary policy decisions. As in the Nike commercial, they just did it." The new classical message that an expansive course of monetary policy at a given endowment of resources leads to nothing but inflation is trivial from a practical central banker's point of view. "That's why we don't do it."[18] Goodhart takes the same line and – by looking at new classical economics in general and time inconsistency models in particular – complains about a growing alienation "between state-of-the-art macro-theory and practical policy analysis"; it is doubtful "how far those in charge of monetary policy followed the finer points of this analysis".[19]

---

16 Svensson (1997: 100).

17 Hahn (1982: 74 - 5).

18 Blinder (1997: 13 - 4), cf. Issing (1997).

19 Goodhart (1989: 296 - 7).

A comprehensible temptation to run a surprise inflation only appears in the one-shot game variant. In a long-run view it is immediately clear that the employment gain can be preserved only for a short time period whereas the ensuing inflationary expectations may be kept up for a time span of indeterminate length. The high-inflation equilibrium thus can only be superseded if these inflationary expectations are dissolved by a stabilization crisis, i.e. when the central bank has to resurrect its reputation by demonstrating its willingness to bear high economic costs in order of a return to monetary stability. The idea that a central bank envisaging these prospects would take the first step to an easy money policy "seems inherently nutty, because the Central Bank itself *knows* from the outset that, if it plays this way, it will *fail* to improve employment and will just generate inflation, so that it must be a stupid game for it to play at all."[20]

The temptation to gain from a short-term increase in employment depends on a sufficiently high time preference on the part of the policymaker. The impression is that such a time preference rate is simply postulated intentionally in order to prove the case of a time inconsistency problem. By applying this ad-hoc assumption the economist attributes a low rationality on the part of central bankers compared to the private sector's strategic abilities. In contrast to this modelling practice, however, it is quite easy for the central banker to grasp the economic consequences of his decisions. "All that is needed for avoidance of the inflationary bias (...) is for the central bank to recognize the futility of continually exploiting expectations that are given 'this month' while planning not to do so in the future, and to recognize that its objectives would be more fully achieved on average if it were to abstain from attempts to exploit these temporarily given expectations."[21]

The derivation of a time inconsistency problem with respect to monetary policy is attained by way of an inappropriate research strategy: when modelling a certain institution – in this case: note-issuing central banks – some crucial characteristics are left out so that consequently a "defect" emerges. Banks however always exhibited a relatively high reputation with respect to financial stability simply because in their everyday business they were dependent on the confidence of their customers. Therefore, as Blinder remarks, the Rogoff solution tends to be already established in practical central banking. "Central bankers have typically been regarded as having a positive bias against monetary expansion and as willing to implement monetary policies tied to much longer-run considerations, even if these are politically costly for the government in the short run. This may be due, in part, to a greater degree of objectivity on matters relating to economic policy associated with an apolitical institution. It may also reflect the natural desire for monetary stability and low inflation on the part of the financial community from which the central bank derives much of its power".[22]

---

20 Goodhart (1994a: 106).

21 McCallum (1995: 208).

The basic intention of accounting for an inflationary demand policy by making use of a game-theoretic approach finally fails because of its ignorance of the basic mechanisms of the transmission process. For reasons of "convenience" new classical models use the rate of inflation both as a target and the *instrument* of monetary policy. "To a practical central banker, [this] seems downright silly, for it assumes away most of the uncertainties that define everyday life."[23] It is undoubted that the short-term rate of interest is the basic tool of policy making. Not even the quantity of money how ever defined can be controlled directly and perfectly as an intermediate target. This helps to recognize the importance of time lags in the process of monetary policy.[24] Two lines of transmissions have to be distinguished; the first captures a movement *on* and the second a shift *of* the Phillips curve:

- A lowering of short-term interest rates supports demand by way of altering the exchange rate and the capital-market interest rate; this leads to price increases if supply constraints show up on the labour market or in the firms' endowments of productive capacities (*market channel).*
- The (announcement or expectation of) lower interest rates may induce inflationary expectations and thus act directly on wage and price formation (*expectation channel).*

Following the market-channel, inflation will set in much later compared to the expectation-channel effect. But it is market-channel inflation which may be a by-product of a rise of employment. A surprise inflation then may occur only if decisions about interest rate changes go unnoticed. Moreover, it may happen only once. If learning is not precluded on the part of private agents, repeated attempts to inflate the economy would trigger off inflationary expectations and thus neutralize the employment effect. The possible argument of nominal wages being fixed in collective-bargaining settlements is not convincing:

- The period of validity of these settlements most probably is shorter than the time of the monetary transmission process.[25]

---

22 Blackburn / Christensen (1989: 32), cf. Blinder (1997). The idea that central bankers are maximizing welfare functions containing macroeconomic variables is rejected by Milton Friedman. He comments on the presentation of the Barro-Gordon approach in Stanley Fischer's survey as follows: "The major comment is the omission of what I have increasingly come to regard as Hamlet on this issue [rules versus discretion], namely the public choice perspective. To illustrate, (...) you talk about a loss function for 'the policymaker' that includes solely inflation and the deviation of real output from a target level. If we bring this down to earth, these are likely to be only very indirectly related to the real objectives of the actual policymakers. From revealed preference, I suspect that by far and away the two most important variables in their loss function are avoiding accountability on the one hand and achieving public prestige on the other. A loss function that contains those two elements as its main argument will I believe come far closer to rationalizing the behavior of the Federal Reserve over the past 73 years than one such as you have used" (quoted in Fischer 1990: 1181n).

23 Blinder (1997: 7).

24 Cf. Blinder (1997), Goodhart (1994a), (1994b).

– The argument seems fundamentally flawed because inflation in the Barro-Gordon model actually will start through a rise of wages which is passed on to the goods market (for otherwise the firms could not obtain additional labour services in a full-employment situation). If however workers are able to modify the time span or substance of labour market contracts in case of a change of the demand-supply ratio, they should do likewise in the case of new inflationary expectations.

If thus wage earners can react in time to an imminent inflation even an employment-oriented central bank will lose its incentive to pursue expansive policies simply because the time span in which an employment gain could be realized will be zero.[26] In turn, the consequence is that private agents do not need to build precautionary inflationary expectations; it is sufficient to observe interest rate policies. This implies that the inflation bias which is the cornerstone of the Barro-Gordon approach has disappeared.

## IV. Looking at the facts: Causes of and policies against inflation

The Barro-Gordon model seems to suggest a course of events where – starting from a full-employment equilibrium with low, stable inflation – a monetary demand shock is initiated which after bringing about some temporary employment gains finally ends up in a high-inflation equilibrium. This approach may have some merits in explaining the onset of inflation in the 1960s. The inflation history since 1970 has been coined by the two oil price shocks. Only in some countries a further, but relatively weak rise of inflation could be observed in the end of the 1980s which might have had direct monetary causes (figure 1).

The courses of short-term interest rates and of inflation in general exhibit a similar pattern. A norm (to avoid the notion of a "rule") for monetary stabilization

25 The Bundesbank (1992) estimates the lag between changes in the quantity of money and changes in prices to amount to 20 months.

26 This can be demonstrated by using a simple new classical model where the quantity of money $m$ as the intermediate target responds with a lag to changes in the primary instrument $i$. The central bank minimizes a loss function where the (over-)employment target is represented by $k$. In the Lucas supply function $p^e$ denotes the expected price level and $y^*$ equilibrium output. Demand depends on autonomous items $g$ and on real balances.

$$L = \beta(y^* + k - y)^2 + p^2$$
$$y = y^* + \alpha(p - p^e)$$
$$y = \delta g + \sigma(m - p)$$
$$m = \overline{m} - \mu i_{-1}$$

Already in the first moment when monetary policy becomes effective on the goods market we have $y = y^*$ and $p = \alpha\beta k$. The central bank cannot even in the short run realize an employment gain because market agents are "warned" by the lowering of interest rates and adjust their price expectations in turn.

might include the device of raising (lowering) interest rates when inflation is increasing (decreasing) so that appropriate movements of the *real* short-term rate help to stabilize the macro economy. Looking at the time of the first oil crisis we find – using this indicator – that particularly Switzerland, Japan, Belgium, Italy and the U.K. failed to apply sufficiently restrictive interest-rate policies to combat inflation. Note that inflation was surging already before the oil price shock when national monetary policies were hindered in their room for manoeuvre because of the Bretton Woods system.

After the second oil price shock only in France, Italy and the U.K. real interest rate increases were postponed. In general we observe restrictive monetary policies which however were not able to prevent a temporary acceleration of inflation. Note that interest rates were raised although in many countries unemployment figures following the deep recession of 1975 had hardly improved (figure 2). As the possibility of a *shifting* NAIRU was not yet conceivable[27] a substantial part of overall unemployment had to be interpreted as demand determined. Thus, monetary policy turned restrictive although the economy's position was on the *right* of the (contemporary) Phillips curve.

At the end of the 1980s renewed inflationary tendencies showed up in the Netherlands, the U.S. and particularly in Germany and Switzerland. The two last mentioned countries had suffered from a previous dollar depreciation in 1986/87 which had inflation brought down to zero and even below. In order to correct the non-intentional real interest rate increase money supplies in both countries were allowed to overshoot the self-chosen targets. When reflation reached 1% and 2%, respectively, the German and the Swiss central bank initiated a U-turn.[28] Real interest rates rose, but the cyclical demand boom continued in both countries. Whereas the Swiss monetary policy could permit itself to break off the stabilization campaign in 1990, the Bundesbank – ignoring critique at home and abroad – stuck to its course of a stepwise increase of interest rates because the German currency union provided for an extra demand stimulus. The policy stance changed shortly after the first EMS crisis in 1992 when the German rate of inflation had passed its peak.[29]

If we summarize so far, only those two episodes of monetary expansion sketched above seem to come close to the Barro-Gordon model. What is puzzling however is that the two central banks involved exhibit an outstanding reputation and are said to set an example with respect to monetary stability.

For methodological reasons it may seem futile to use *empirical* arguments in an assessment of the *logic* of a theoretical model. The Barro-Gordon approach does

---

27 Some hints, however, can already be found in Samuelson / Solow (1960), Phelps (1972: 77-8) and Tobin (1972: 238). See also Pohl (1979) and Hargreaves Heap (1980) as some of the first papers dealing with the hysteresis phenomenon.

28 Cf. Frowen / Karakitsos (1997), Rich (1997).

29 Cf. Spahn (1997a).

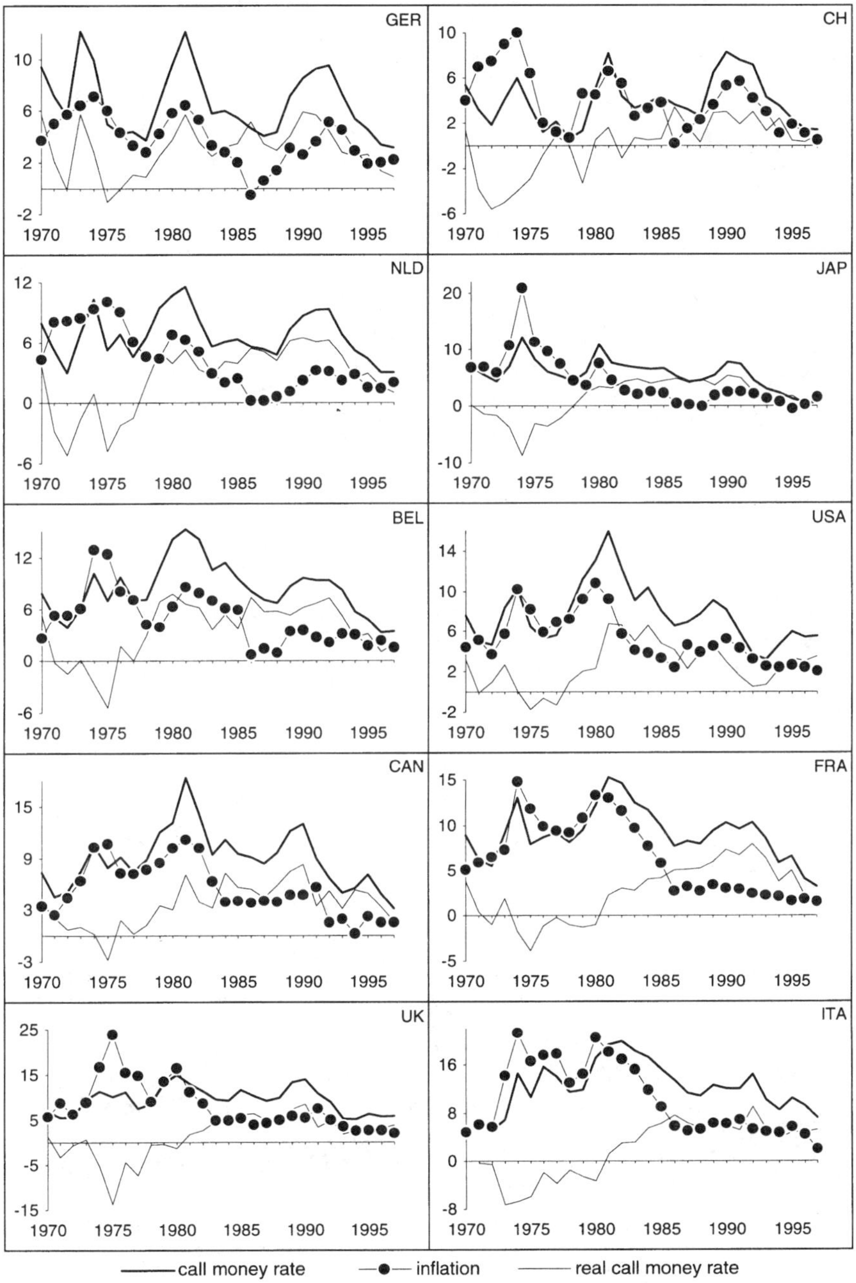


Figure 1: Inflation and interest rates in selected countries (data source: OECD)

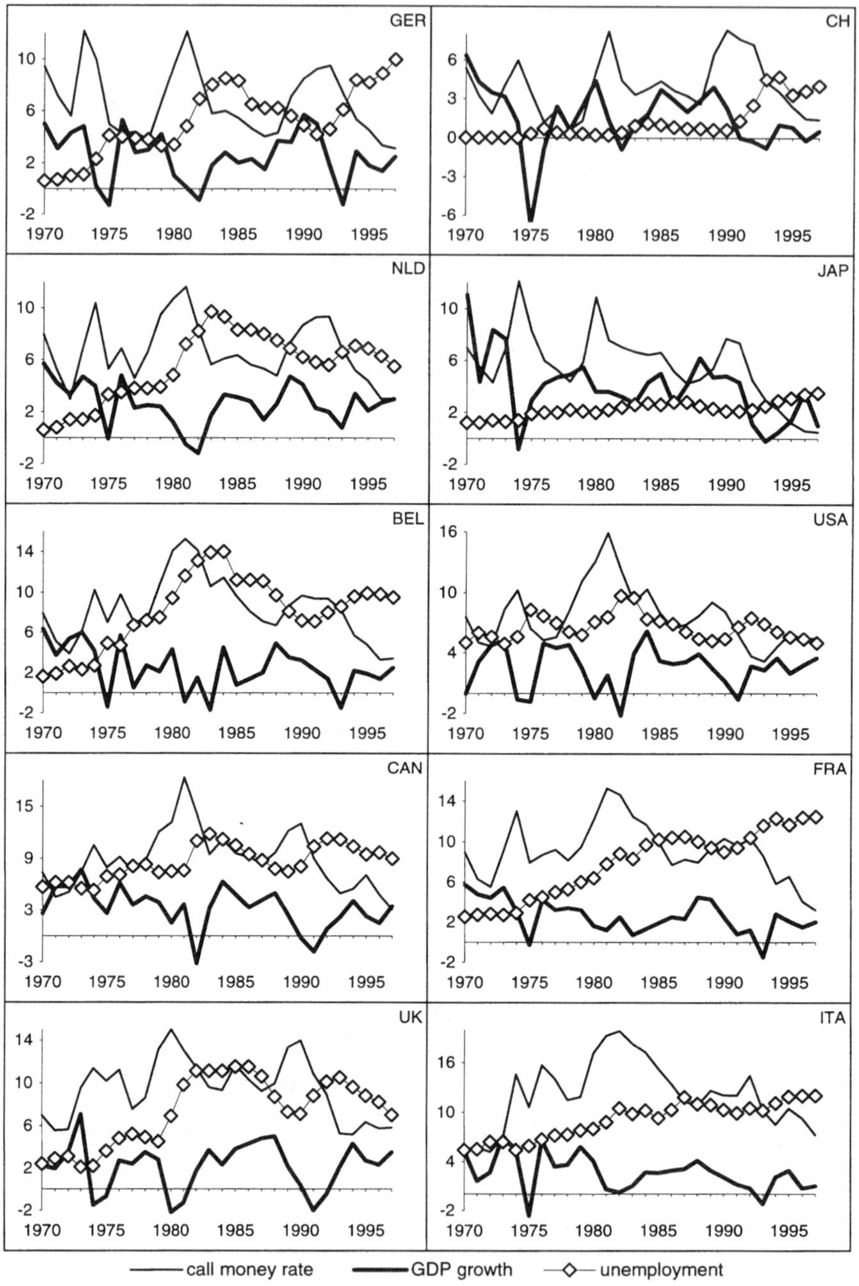


Figure 2: Interest rates, growth and unemployment in selected countries (data source: OECD)

not claim to give an account of a stylized course of an inflation process. Accordingly, it is not confined to a scenario of inflation which is driven by monetary factors. On the other hand, the process of learning and expectation building of market agents in the – actually prevailing – case of inflation initiated by a supply shock is more ambiguous compared to the standard game. Supply shocks cannot be perfectly neutralized by monetary policy and will lead to unemployment in the first place. In that case, markets agents will correctly attribute the incipient rise in prices to an exogenous factor. If then the central bank starts attacking inflation by raising interest rates, the impression might nevertheless spread that efforts to stabilize the economy are insufficient (although unemployment will persist); but private agents hardly will hit upon the idea that the central bank – following an optimization calculus – has triggered off and maintained a surprise inflation in order to support employment. In fact, no one is surprised that inflation prevails after a supply shock.

If therefore monetary policy is not regarded to be alone responsible for inflation, the standard hypothesis prevalent in the time inconsistency approach that a slow and costly disinflation process should be explained by a low credibility of the central bank's anti-inflationary measures loses much of its persuasiveness. It has to be stressed that, particularly after the second oil price shock, monetary policy strongly demonstrated in nearly all countries that in order to reduce inflation high and rising unemployment rates were to be tolerated. These rates were higher than the estimated NAIRU figures. It is true that these estimates were revised upwards in subsequent studies so that – according to an ex-post assessment – monetary policy only contributed to the realization of a macro equilibrium. A judgement of the central bank's readiness to combat inflation, however, has to be based upon the contemporary set of informations.

It is debatable whether a cold-turkey strategy of disinflation is preferable compared to gradualism.[30] But the remarkable high employment costs of disinflation especially in countries with a highly reputable central bank show that choosing the optimal response to an inflationary supply shock is not equivalent to the solution of a time inconsistency problem. Recently, the puzzle of high disinflation costs was explained by the argument that a regime of credible monetary policy supports entering into long-term contracts denominated in fixed nominal terms; as a consequence a change in the nominal quantity of money brings about real economic effects. However, if it became necessary in such a regime to contain inflationary pressure at all, we should experience a shortening of contract length or contents, particularly if restrictive policy measures are announced in time. It is not the flattened *slope,* but rather the lacking downward *shift* of the Phillips curve which causes disinflation costs.[31]

---

30 Cf. Fischer (1985), Ball (1995).

31 Cf. Walsh (1995c), Jordan (1997), Spahn (1997b).

## V. How to cope with supply constraints and unemployment

By using more or less refined rules of thumb central banks try to estimate the path of nominal demand which is compatible with productive capacities. This cannot be envisaged as solving a microeconomic optimization problem in "logical" time, but rather as a process of trial and error where policies permanently have to be calibrated to cope with unforeseen shocks. There is no "passive" way of policy making. The monetarist prohibition of fine tuning therefore cannot be realized:

- An attempt to keep the quantity of money fixed even in the short run leads to high volatility of short-term interest and exchange rates which in turn causes economic instabilities.
- Keeping short-term interest rates fixed in times of changing macroeconomic conditions causes real effects of monetary policy – whether they are intended or not.

The preceding review of the inflation history since the 1970s underlines that inflation cannot be perfectly predicted and controlled.[32] Therefore the idea of a central bank trying to "fool" private market agents hardly captures the actual interaction of politics and markets. If we stick however to the game-theoretic framework we would have to model a dynamic sequence of discretionary decisions on interest rate variations under the condition of imperfect information. Because of control and information problems the market results cannot unambiguously be attributed to decisions and actions taken by one of the players involved. Private market agents, in particular, do not know exactly whether and when it is appropriate to modify the beliefs held about central bank's preferences.

Given these market conditions where shocks with unpredictable consequences occur and where monetary policy is plagued with unintentional control errors, the best, i.e. "rational" way of expectation formation on the part of private agents is to rely on an adaptive procedure. Decisive factors in the process of gradual learning then are not *methods,* but *results* of monetary policy where the long-run performance has a much higher weight than single appearances of positive or negative events. With reference to the distinction presented above we might conclude that monetary policy mainly has to act by using the *market channel* of transmission because the expectation channel does not work in a reliable manner. The growing credibility of the Fed and its president Volcker in the early 1980s "was probably based more on their demonstrated willingness to accept a painfully high level of (real) interest rates and a sharp downturn in output, rather than on the achievement of a particular monetary target".[33]

---

32 "There are two basic ways to obtain quantitative information about the economy: you can study econometric evidence, or you can ask your uncle" (Blinder 1997: 8, cf. Issing 1997).

33 Goodhart (1989: 304 - 5), cf. Cukierman (1992: 6, 139), Blinder (1997).

The key problem of market-channel control of the economy is that monetary policy for systematic reasons will hardly succeed in fine-tuning the macro dynamics around a stable path. A cursory inspection of figure 1 suggests that central banks in general orientate their interest rates at the course of inflation. The ex-post real rate of interest however provides only a rough *indicator* of the impact of monetary policy. This purely statistical variable does not seem to *cause* changes in macroeconomic development; in any case there is only a relatively weak correspondence with the cyclical movement of the economy. On the other hand, we observe a striking regularity between *nominal* short-term rates and the real growth rate: nearly every macroeconomic crisis follows with a lag (of one year in most cases) after a peak in interest rates (figure 2). The outstanding prediction property of nominal short-term interest rates is recognized in the literature since some years.[34] Besides the usual transmission processes working by altering exchange rates, long-term interest rates and the cost and liquidity aspects of interest payments this link between money rates and economic activity might be explained by the signalling effects which are triggered off by changes of the central bank's interest rates: it might indicate a "regime shift" in policy making which then will urge banks and investors to reassess investment projects. The *real* rate of interest, on the other hand, does not convey such an unbiased information to market agents.

The rate of interest, however, is but one of the factors which influence the decisions of private agents. Therefore, only a marked change or a continuing chain of slight interest rate changes will have a decisive effect on economic activity. In a cyclical upswing which is accompanied by rising prices and interest rates, e.g., entrepreneurs receive contradictory signals: on the one hand, the degree of capacity utilization, sales and the flow of profits might suggest to continue or even expand investment activities. On the other hand, entrepreneurs know that the central bank will not allow an unlimited increase of inflation; hence, the risks of at least some investment projects grow, particularly if their profitability depends on the reallocation of portfolios from financial to real assets (demand for real estate). In spite of these perceived risks investment activities may be continued for a while because of the existence of sunk costs. Finally, however, some minor event will modify the prevailing unstable balance between expansive and restrictive determinants and – comparable to the termination of a "hausse" at the stock exchange – will thus cause the ongoing boom to collapse. If the *expected* rate of interest starts to fall a rising number of firms will choose to "wait", i.e. switch to the temporary holding of financial assets. The cancellation or postponement of a critical volume of investment projects lowers cash flows and profits throughout the economy, leads to further investment decline and finally ends up in a recession.

With respect to the stabilization issue the "art" of central banking is to find a practical solution to a knife edge problem: moderate interest rates increases may

34 Cf. Bernanke / Blinder (1992), Filc (1992), Taylor (1995), Moersch (1996), Krupp / Cabos (1996).

leave the rise of prices and production unaffected whereas resolute steps produce an economic downturn.[35] Obviously, central banks will differ in their readiness to bear risks with regard to inflation and unemployment. Academic economists, too, reach different judgements on central banks' behaviour: some observers argue that they tend to postpone or soften necessary interest rate increases out of regard for employment issues.[36] Others find that by using decision-supporting devices as the production potential or the NAIRU policymakers would lean on over-cautious estimates so that the scope for expansive policy action shows a systematic downward bias; hence, monetary policy acts formally correct, but factually overly restrictive. Possibilities for higher growth and employment thus remain unused because the experience of a decreasing NAIRU only slowly leaves its mark in monetary policy decisions. "Some economists have been more eager to raise their estimate than to cut it. The NAIRU, like the wage rate, is downward sticky."[37]

Figure 3 exemplifies this issue with reference to Germany and the U.S. in the 1980s and 1990s. It is evident that the Bundesbank after 1988 tried hard by letting nominal and real interest rates increase to dampen the upswing which was accompanied by only a weak reduction of unemployment. This course was carried on when inflation accelerated in the aftermath of the German currency union. The final result was a deep recession which aggravated the huge problems of restructuring the economy in the new Eastern Länder and of financing this process. Given the assumption that the Bundesbank did not exert a substantial influence on the behaviour of wage and fiscal policies, there was hardly an alternative to the course of German interest rate policy. It surely makes no sense to claim in a retrospective view that the Bundesbank should have raised interest rates even faster already before 1990, just to convince the public that the bank was not pursuing a "fooling" strategy.

---

35 The non-mechanical link between monetary policy instruments and macroeconomic activity can be symbolized by the following formula where the path of inflation $\hat{p}_t$ during the cycle depends strongly on its own past history and – to a lesser extent – on previous interest-rate policies and shocks $\varepsilon_t$ which may exhibit serial correlation. The cyclical instability of the system may be expressed by the sudden change in the value of the parameters: some marginal decision in the field of monetary policies will cause $\varphi$ to shrink and $\mu$ to grow.

$$\hat{p}_t - \hat{p}_{t-1} = \varphi(\hat{p}_{t-1} - \hat{p}_{t-2}) - \mu(i_{t-1} - i_{t-2}) + \varepsilon_t$$

In contrast to this approach, in most cases only stochastic shocks enter into the Phillips curve equation in the Barro-Gordon literature. They are observed by the central bank after wage settlements have been fixed and thus allow a welfare-enhancing stabilization whereas inflation expectations of market agents are disappointed. This kind of disturbance complicates the game-theoretic setup of the analysis, but leaves the central bank's ability to control the economy unaffected, as a matter of principle, i.e., the stability of structural relationships of the macroeconomic system remains intact.

36 See, e.g., Goodhart (1994b). Blinder (1997) concedes that the Fed sometimes waits for a "convenient" constellation for its decisions on stiffening interest rates. For interesting accounts on disagreements between the Treasury and the Governor during the period before granting full instrument independence to the Bank of England in 1997 see Cobham (1997) and Frowen / Karakitsos (1997).

37 Galbraith (1997: 102).

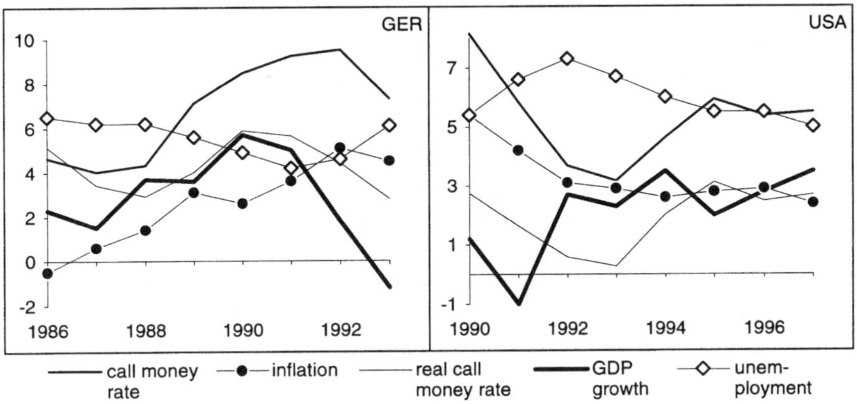


Figure 3: Inflation, interest rates, growth and unemployment in Germany and the US (data source: OECD)

The U.S. case is more interesting. After overcoming the 1991 crisis monetary policy rapidly turned to a restrictive course as unemployment approached the "natural" rate of 6%. The decreasing rate of inflation however stabilized around 3% and the Fed responded by keeping nominal and real interest rates constant. Then growth speeded up, unemployment came further down to 4,5% (March 1998), but so did the inflation rate! Facing these contradictory signals the Fed stuck to its "non-policy". This policy stance may be risky, but is nonetheless reasonable. There are good reasons to believe that measured "overemployment" is a statistical artefact. Actual price and productivity trends do not call for a preventive anti-inflation policy which would dampen growth dynamics without any other welfare gains.

If nevertheless inflation should revive in the near future conservative critics no doubt will see their fears confirmed. But even in that case the episode could hardly be interpreted as a Barro-Gordon game. There is an open discussion on whether to continue the current slightly expansive course of monetary policy or not, the Fed goes on to inform the public about its evaluation of the macroeconomic situation and the ensuing policy consequences. Thus it should be clear to everybody that the uncertainty of the macroeconomic development is not primarily due to some hidden preferences and targets of policymakers, but rather due to the difficulties of evaluating economic data and functional relationships:

- First, structural change and high-tech services make it more difficult to measure inflation accurately. Some argue that prices are already falling and are concerned about the destabilizing properties of deflation. The chairman of the Fed poses the – yet rhetorical – question whether monetary policy should rather aim at stabilizing the prices of financial assets instead of goods prices.[38]

38 Greenspan (1997).

- Second, the real economic variables which serve as points of reference for monetary-policy decisions do not seem to be neither constant nor even independent from the path of nominal demand. We turn to this problem in the following final section.

## VI. Real determinants of the nominal anchor or non-neutrality of monetary policy?

If monetary policy aims at preventing inflation reliable information on the state and path of resource endowments are needed to assess which course of nominal demand is compatible with the supply side. In Germany, for this purpose the Bundesbank uses an estimation of potential production which is derived from the stock of available capital and labour. In the U.S., the difference between actual employment and the NAIRU plays an important role; nearly each increase of employment seems to be accompanied by speculations about ensuing interest rate increases. If the stability of prices is the sole policy target the potential production seems to be the more appropriate criterion as it indicates a general outlook on the use of resources. Moreover, the rate of unemployment shows a non-uniform correspondence to the growth rate and therefore does not mirror the cyclical movement of the economy in some countries (figure 2). In Germany and the U.S., inflation seems to depend on the general degree of capacity utilization, on exchange rate movements and exogenous shocks, but not primarily on nominal wages. Gordon disapproves the fixation on wages and refers to Fisher who already in 1926 had discovered the Phillips curve as a direct link between unemployment and price inflation (ignoring the intermediate step of wage inflation).[39]

On the other hand, if the role of the NAIRU is downgraded as a point of reference for measuring the risk of inflation, the structure of the Barro-Gordon game is even more different from the actual market process. "If the natural rate hypothesis means anything at all, it must imply that inflation stems from pressure in the labor market and is therefore wage driven."[40] The German concept of orientating monetary policy at the potential production can be criticized for leaving open the question how the targeted low-inflation growth is compatible with full employment. The situation on the labour market has no role to play in the derivation of the money growth target; there is even no "extra" money supply provision for allowing an increase of the degree of capacity utilization when actual is below potential growth.[41] Unemployment in a regime of equilibrium growth is being regarded as a pure wage policy problem. Finally, the attempt of limiting nominal demand so that it can be served from *domestic* sources implies linking the goal of price stability to some implicit foreign balance target which is rarely being justified.

---

39 Gordon (1997: 17), cf. Franz / Gordon (1993).

40 Galbraith (1997: 99).

41 Cf. Bofinger et al. (1996: 253 - 6).

The decisive point, however, is the positive feedback mechanism between the *utilization* and the *stock* of marketable resources, i.e. productive and human capital. Investment activities to enlarge productive capacity in general responds to a surge of demand. A similar adjustment process is to be observed on the labour market. Whereas classical theory relied on Malthus' "law of population", modern labour market theory takes into account migration and, in particular, negative qualification effects which take place during the time of being unemployed. As a consequence, the hypothetical equilibrium growth rate and the NAIRU follow with a lag to the actual path of growth and employment. The more general conclusion is that the supply side of the economy cannot even be defined independently of the medium-term path of effective demand.

In the U.S., this is particularly obvious with respect to the NAIRU. Its estimated value was step by step revised upwards, in the first place, and then downwards since 1984. If the NAIRU follows a random walk by mirroring the movement the actual unemployment rate, it is devalued as a point of reference for macro policy decisions. What is needed is not only an agreement on the "right" estimated figure but also on the "correct" theory which explains the movement of the NAIRU. The control problem in monetary policy reveals a circular logic: the central bank produces and stabilizes that level employment which then turns out as the equilibrium target level. "High unemployment is even worse than we thought, because it raises the NAIRU, and lower unemployment is even better than we thought because it reduces the NAIRU."[42]

The treatment of this hysteresis problem in the game-theoretic literature is not yet convincing: a basic drawback again is the ignorance of the time lag between the application of policy instruments and the ensuing macroeconomic effects. From an intertemporal point of view, this leads to a downward-biased evaluation of an employment target because inflation – as the policy instrument in the *modelled* economy – rises at once whereas employment gains, enlarged by persistence effects, accrue later and thus have to be discounted. This sequence of events may be reversed in the real world however. The endogenous enlargement of supply-side forces which accompanies a demand expansion may dampen inflationary pressure; and it is questionable to make a definite prediction about inflation expectations. In a Barro-Gordon game, however, inflation expectations definitely rise if employment dynamics show at least some persistence as this increases the benefit of launching a surprise inflation on the part of policymakers.[43] For similar reasons, we should assume that inflation expectations will generally rise in times of high unemployment (if the probabilities of the appearance of "hard-nosed" and "wet" policymakers are constant); this is not what we observe. At best it could be argued that wage inflation is kept in check on account of *involuntary* unemployment – but this category is unknown in new classical economics. Finally it seems hardly con-

42 Stiglitz (1997: 8), cf. Galbraith (1997), Vogt (1995).

43 Cf. Svensson (1997).

vincing, in the case of true hysteresis, to define a "hard-nosed" policymaker as showing absolutely no interest in employment.[44] Perfect hysteresis implies the existence of multiple equilibria which in principle can be attained at stable prices. Under these conditions, lowering equilibrium unemployment can be a free lunch which should not be rejected.

In general, Barro-Gordon games tend to emphasize the long-run neutrality of money. This is acceptable if this approach aims only at the analysis of short-term aspects in the interactive process of decision making. But we should hesitate to give central bankers the advice to design the strategy of monetary policy according to the new classical approach. This warning may be unnecessary, but some ingredients of that approach often are taken for granted without further reasoning. Such a basic proposition is that monetary policy cannot solve the problem of "structural" unemployment. This statement, however, deserves some qualifications.

It is useful to state the opposite proposition: *there is no structural unemployment;* this category represents a confusion of macro and micro topics, employment and efficiency, respectively.[45] For methodological reasons unemployment is always and everywhere a macroeconomic variable, some quantity of unemployed persons, a subgroup of potential labour supply (which itself cannot be defined independently from macroeconomic conditions). The volume of employment is always and everywhere directly determined by goods demand and – linked through production technology – labour demand, although of course other macroeconomic variables like, e.g., even the nominal wage rate may exert an indirect influence on goods demand.

Workers whether employed or not in general will differ in their qualification and productivity. An efficient labour-turnover process will allocate workers according to these abilities on the available jobs so that person equipped with the lowest qualification remain unemployed. The empirical finding that unemployed workers have a low qualification, however, does not explain the extent of unemployment. From this it follows that it is impossible to define a definite amount of structural unemployment irrespective of the state of macro demand. This would be an arbitrary and misleading procedure as nearly every level of demand-determined unemployment, if maintained, tends to alter its shape so that it *appears* to be supply-side determined.

If effective demand falls firms respond by laying off workers thus combining a quantitative adjustment with an efficiency-enhancing strategy: firing workers with the lowest qualification implies that the average productivity of the employed workforce increases. Isolated policy strategies which enhance labour market flexibility thus will only support the realization of efficiency gains whereas the level of employment is bound to fall. On the other hand, it is always possible to expand

---

[44] Cf. Grüner (1996).

[45] Riese (1997).

total employment in the economy by way of an increased demand; it may lead however to a loss of efficiency on the micro level. A high level of employment thus will be associated with relatively low real income per head whereas a shrinking level of employment allows to solve efficiency problems within the firms and therefore to pay higher incomes to the employed persons. "Matching" problems which nowadays seem to explain a substantial part of contemporary structural unemployment surely were of equal importance in the 1960s; but they had to be tackled on the *firm level* as vigorous demand dynamics left no other choices to the employers.

Of course, firms have to be compensated for bearing efficiency losses if demand policies call for a higher level of employment and if a spiral of rising wages and prices is to be avoided. This may justify a complementary policy of wage moderation and wage differentiation. But an isolated policy of wage reduction will not be effective. The unions for decades were told by the German Council of Economic Advisers that nominal wage policies could not succeed in altering income distribution in favour of wage earners; now the same group of experts recommends that wage increases for several years should be kept below productivity growth in order to raise profits.[46] The most probable outcome – instead of promoting investment – would be a further reduction of inflation and an appreciation of the mark. Wage moderation supports demand relative to given money growth. In case of low inflation it is preferable, however, to increase money growth by keeping money wages constant as the opposite combination may trigger off a period of true deflation.[47] Particularly, if hysteresis effects prevail expansive monetary policy is the appropriate strategy. Therefore, the predominating approach of monetary policy acting in a "game against market agents" should be substituted by an attempt of evaluating the scope of economic policy cooperation.

## VII. Summary: Six propositions

- *The new institutionalism: Does inflation depend on the state of the economic policy system?* The perhaps unintended outcome of the new classical revolution in macro theory is that not market forces but rather policy institutions and their strategies and reputation are said to determine macroeconomic results. The Barro-Gordon model purports to give a solid microfoundation of an inflation bias which should be eliminated by way of economic policy reforms. However, evidence does not lend much support to that approach. Behaving in contradiction to the rules of the Barro-Gordon game does not seem to produce inflationary expectations and disinflation still is costly in terms of employment even and especially if central banks have high reputation.

46 Sachverständigenrat (1997: para. 368).

47 Cf. Keynes (1936: 266).

- *Looking at the wrong side of the Phillips curve.* The Barro-Gordon model argues that monetary policy aims at excess employment by means of a surprise inflation. Keynes and Friedman agree that going beyond full employment will start a dynamic inflationary process. Instead of opposing to Friedman's critique of the Phillips curve approach of policy making Postkeynesians should have insisted that the main task is to raise employment to the natural rate and not beyond it. The reasons given in the Barro-Gordon approach for the attributed overemployment target are dubious even in a political vote-getting strategy. As a surprise inflation lowers real wages of the majority of workers, a left-wing party in particular would lose popularity amongst its own followers while there is nothing to win amongst the owners of financial wealth anyway.

- *Central bankers cannot launch surprise inflation even if they would like to.* The scientific "discovery" of a time inconsistency problem follows from an inadequate modelling of central banks. It is ignored that these institutions typically behave with a Rogoff bias because being banks they have to preserve the confidence of their customers and they usually obtain their staff from the financial community. They could opt for a surprise inflation only in the unlikely case of a high time preference as the "game against the market" may have long-run consequences in terms of inflationary expectations. Moreover, the Barro-Gordon model ignores the time lags in the transmission process. The rate of inflation cannot be controlled directly. Any monetary expansion has to start by lowering short-term interest rates whereas employment and price effects follow with a lag. If interest rate policies can be observed by market agents expected and actual inflation would rise long before any additional employment could be gained. Thus even a one-period game makes no sense; there is no temptation to run a surprise inflation. Accordingly, the expectation-driven inflation bias of the Barro-Gordon literature disappears.

- *The history of inflation does not resemble a Barro-Gordon game.* In most countries the two waves of inflation in previous decades were driven from the supply side. Although monetary policy then differed in its vigour to fight inflation people hardly could derive the impression that "weak" central banks tried to fool the market. The issue obviously was "gradualism" versus "cold turkey" but not time inconsistency. In many cases monetary policy was restrictive although actual unemployment was above the estimated natural rate; the fact that these figures have been revised upwards in subsequent studies is irrelevant for an evaluation of the actual stance of policy decisions. The only two episodes of purely money-driven inflation happened in Germany and Switzerland where inflation was allowed to recover from zero to two percent, but was attacked hereafter.

- *The art of central banking: controlling a knife edge problem.* As monetary policy cannot even control its intermediate targets without noise or delay, market agents' rational choice is adaptive expectations. Single or short-run market results cannot be attributed to distinct decisions of any of the market players. Reputation has to be earned by long-run results of monetary policy irrespective of its methods. It is nearly impossible to keep demand on an equilibrium path where resources are fully employed but not in short supply. Because of the cumulative character of the business cycle occasional weak interest rate signals will not change the course of the economy while a series of interest rate increases sooner or later will cause an overreaction, i.e. recession and unemployment. The economy's supply capacity is difficult to predict and reacts endogenously to changes in demand. Therefore, a policy which acts overcautiously and gives away possible scope for growth and employment has no welfare advantage compared to a policy which might lead to rising prices. Again, it is a matter of risk, not of fooling.

– *The NAIRU is no independent barrier to demand policies.* In spite of cursory and unsatisfactory treatments of persistence and hysteresis effects the Barro-Gordon literature generally stresses the long-run neutrality of money. Given the feedback from the use of resources to investment in human and productive capital this traditional dogma is far from being true. In particular, the NAIRU cannot be defined without reference to overall labour demand. With heterogeneous labour any demand-determined pool of unemployment changes to "structural" unemployment in the labour turnover process. In former times of full employment the problem of low worker qualification appeared as low efficiency in production. Thus demand-driven employment increases are possible if firms are compensated for the accompanying rise in costs. On the other hand, lowering wages and enhancing labour market flexibility will revalue the currency, increase efficiency, but not employment.

## References

*Ball,* L. (1995): Disinflation with Imperfect Credibility. Journal of Monetary Economics, 35, 5 - 23. – *Barro,* R. J. / *Gordon,* D. B. (1983): A Positive Theory of Monetary Policy in a Natural Rate Model. Journal of Political Economy, 91, 589 - 610. – *Bernanke,* B. S. / *Blinder,* A. S. (1992): The Federal Funds Rate and the Channels of Monetary Transmission. American Economic Review, 82, 901 - 21. – *Blackburn,* K. / *Christensen,* M. (1989): Monetary Policy and Credibility – Theories and Evidence. Journal of Economic Literature, 27, 1 - 45. – *Blinder,* A. S. (1987): Keynes, Lucas, and Scientific Progress. American Economic Review, Papers and Proceedings, 77, 130 - 6. – *Blinder,* A. S. (1997): What Central Bankers Could Learn from Academics – and Vice Versa. Journal of Economic Perspectives, 11, 2, 3 - 19. – *Bofinger,* P. et al. (1996): Geldpolitik – Ziele, Institutionen, Strategien und Instrumente. München. – *Canzoneri,* M. B. (1985): Monetary Policy Games and the Role of Private Information. American Economic Review, 75, 1056 - 70. – *Cobham,* D. (1997): The Post-ERM Framework for Monetary Policy in the United Kingdom – Bounded Credibility. Economic Journal, 107, 1128 - 41. – *Cukierman,* A. (1992): Central Bank Strategy, Credibility and Independence – Theory and Evidence. Cambridge / London: MIT Press. – *Deutsche Bundesbank* (1992): Zum Zusammenhang zwischen Geldmengen- und Preisentwicklung in der Bundesrepublik

Deutschland. Monatsbericht Januar, 20 - 9. – *Filc,* W. (1992): Monetäre Fundierung einer angebotsorientierten Stabilitätspolitik. Konjunkturpolitik, 38, 316 - 39. – *Fischer,* S. (1985): The Problem of Disinflation. Zeitschrift für Wirtschafts- und Sozialwissenschaften, 105, 123 - 31. – *Fischer,* S. (1990): Rules versus Discretion in Monetary Policy. In: Friedman, B. M. / Hahn, F. H., eds.: Handbook of Monetary Economics. Bd. 2, 1155 - 84. – *Franz,* W. (1996): Theoretische Ansätze zur Erklärung der Arbeitslosigkeit. In: Gahlen, B. et al., eds.: Arbeitslosigkeit und Möglichkeiten ihrer Überwindung. Tübingen: Mohr, 3 - 45. – *Franz,* W. / *Gordon,* R. J. (1993): German and American Wage and Price Dynamics – Differences and Common Themes. European Economic Review, 37, 719 - 62. – *Friedman,* M. (1968): The Role of Monetary Policy. American Economic Review, 58, 1 - 17. – *Frowen,* S. F. / *Karakitsos,* E. (1997): An Evaluation of Inflation Targeting in Germany and the UK. Kredit und Kapital, 30, 501 - 532. – *Galbraith,* J. K. (1997): Time to Ditch the NAIRU. Journal of Economic Perspectives, 11, 1, 93 - 108. – *Goodhart,* C. A. E. (1989): The Conduct of Monetary Policy. Economic Journal, 99, 293 - 346. – *Goodhart,* C. A. E. (1994a): Game Theory for Central Bankers – A Report to the Governor of the Bank of England. Journal of Economic Literature, 32, 101 - 14. – *Goodhart,* C. A. E. (1994b): What Should Central Banks Do? What Should Be Their Macroeconomic Objectives and Operations? Economic Journal, 104, 1424 - 36. – *Gordon,* R. J. (1997): The Time-Varying NAIRU and its Implications for Economic Policy. Journal of Economic Perspectives, 11, 1, 11 - 32. – *Greenspan,* A. (1997): Remarks. In: Deutsche Bundesbank, ed.: Auszüge aus Presseartikeln, No. 60, 15. 10. 97, 16 - 9. – *Grüner,* H. P. (1996): Monetary Policy, Reputation and Hysteresis. Zeitschrift für Wirtschafts- und Sozialwissenschaften, 116, 15 - 29. – *Hahn,* F. H. (1982): Money and Inflation. Oxford: Basil Blackwell. – *Hargreaves* Heap, S. P. (1980): Choosing the Wrong 'Natural' Rate – Accelerating Inflation or Decelerating Employment and Growth. Economic Journal, 90, 611 - 20. – *Illing,* G. (1997): Theorie der Geldpolitik – Eine spieltheoretische Einführung. Berlin et al.: Springer. – *Issing,* O. (1997): Monetary Theory as a Basis for Monetary Policy – Reflections of a Central Banker. In: Deutsche Bundesbank, ed.: Auszüge aus Presseartikeln, No. 50, 8. 9. 97, 6 - 10. – *Jordan,* T. J. (1997): Disinflation Costs, Accelerating Inflation Gains, and Central Bank Independence. Weltwirtschaftliches Archiv, 133, 1 - 21. – *Keynes,* J. M. (1936): General Theory of Employment, Interest, and Money. London: MacMillan. – *Krupp,* H. J. / *Cabos,* K. (1996): Geldpolitik und Beschäftigung. In: Gahlen, B. et al., eds.: Arbeitslosigkeit und Möglichkeiten ihrer Überwindung. Tübingen, 363 - 87. – *Kydland,* F. E. / *Prescott,* E. C. (1977): Rules Rather than Discretion – The Inconsistency of Optimal Plans. Journal of Political Economy, 85, 473 - 91. – *Lucas,* R. E. (1972): Expectations and the Neutrality of Money. Journal of Economic Theory, 4, 103 - 24. – *McCallum,* B. T. (1995): Two Fallacies Concerning Central-Bank Independence. American Economic Review, Papers and Proceedings, 85, 207 - 11. – *McCallum,* B. T. (1997): Crucial Issues Concerning Central Bank Independence. Journal of Monetary Economics, 39, 99 - 112. – *Moersch,* M. (1996): Interest Rates or Spreads as Predictors of Real Economic Activity? Konjunkturpolitik, 42, 40 - 51. – *Phelps,* E. S. (1972): Inflation Policy and Unemployment Theory – The Cost- Benefit Approach to Monetary Planning. London: MacMillan. – *Pohl,* R. (1979): Akzeptierte Arbeitslosigkeit und dauerhafte Trade-Offs – Zur Dichotomie kurzfristiger Anpassungen und langfristiger Gleichgewichtszustände. Zeitschrift für die gesamte Staatswissenschaft, 135, 17 - 40. – *Rich,* G. (1997): Monetary Targets as a Policy Rule – Lessons from the Swiss Experience. Journal of Monetary Economics, 39, 113 - 41. – *Riese,* H. (1997): Unemployment – A German Subject. Contribution to the conference of the German Association for Political Economy: "Unemployment in Europe", Maastricht. – *Rogoff,* K. (1985): The Optimal Degree of Commitment to an Intermediate Monetary Target. Quarterly Journal of Economics, 100, 1169 - 89. –

*Rothschild,* K. W. (1971): The Phillips Curve and All That. Scottish Journal of Political Economy, 18, 245 - 80. – *Sachverständigenrat* (1997): Jahresgutachten 1997 / 98. Wachstum, Beschäftigung, Währungsunion – Orientierungen für die Zukunft. Bundestagsdrucksache 13 / 9090, Bonn. – *Samuelson,* P. A. / *Solow,* R. M. (1960): Analytical Aspects of Anti-Inflation Policy. American Economic Review, Papers and Proceedings, 50, 185 - 94. – *Scharpf,* F. W. (1988): Inflation und Arbeitslosigkeit in Westeuropa – Eine spieltheoretische Interpretation. Politische Vierteljahresschrift, 29, 6- 41. – *Sievert,* O. (1979): Die Steuerbarkeit der Konjunktur durch den Staat. In: Weizsäcker, C. C. von, ed.: Staat und Wirtschaft. Schriften des Vereins für Socialpolitik, 102, Berlin: Duncker & Humblot, 809- 46. – *Spahn,* H.-P. (1997a): Credibility, Reputation, and the Instability of the EMS. In: Cohen, A. J. et al., eds.: Money, Financial Institutions and Macroeconomics. Boston et al., 235 - 51. – *Spahn,* H.-P. (1997b): Disinflation und Arbeitslosigkeit – Über die Nichtneutralität der Geldpolitik. Diskussionsbeiträge aus dem Volkswirtschaftlichen Institut der Universität Hohenheim, No. 139, Stuttgart. – *Stiglitz,* J. (1997): Reflections on the Natural Rate Hypothesis. Journal of Economic Perspectives, 11, 1, 3 - 10. – *Svensson,* L. E. O. (1997): Optimal Inflation Targets, "Conservative" Central Banks, and Linear Inflation Contracts. American Economic Review, 87, 98 - 114. – *Taylor,* J. B. (1995): The Monetary Transmission Mechanism – An Empirical Framework. Journal of Economic Perspectives, 9, 4, 11 - 26. – *Tobin,* J. (1972): Inflation and Unemployment. American Economic Review, 62, 1 - 18. – *Vogt,* W. (1995): Makroökonomische Auswirkungen von beschränkter Marktmacht auf dem Güter- und Arbeitsmarkt. In: Flemmig, J., ed.: Moderne Makroökonomik – Eine kritische Bestandsaufnahme. Marburg: Metropolis, 167 - 208. – *Walsh,* C. E. (1995a): Is New Zealand's Reserve Bank Act of 1989 an Optimal Central Bank Contract? Journal of Money, Credit, and Banking, 27, 1179 - 91. – *Walsh,* C. E. (1995b): Optimal Contracts for Central Bankers. American Economic Review, 85, 150 - 67. – *Walsh,* C. E. (1995c): Central Bank Independence and the Short-Run Output- Inflation Trade-off in the European Community. In: Eichengreen, B. et al., eds.: Monetary and Fiscal Policy in an Integrated Europe. Berlin et al., 12 - 37.

# The Impact of Monetary Policy on Employment

By Hans-Jürgen Krupp and Karen Cabos, Hamburg

## I. The relationship between monetary policy and employment policy

The question of the impact of monetary policy on the employment situation touches upon an issue that does not occupy a central place in thinking about monetary policy. Indeed, there are some who may well look upon it as an act of heresy even to pose the question, given their belief that the sole purpose of monetary policy is to maintain price stability.

There is both a normative dimension to this issue and an empirical one – and to some extent the two are connected. First of all, we need to establish by empirical means whether monetary policy does indeed influence the employment situation. If the answer is "no", then we need not pursue the matter further. The normative question – *should* monetary policy also aim employment – could then be dismissed as an irrelevance, since we would already have established that it cannot do this anyway.

It is well understood, of course, that central banks in different countries take a different view of this question. In the United States the Federal Reserve Act states that the central bank shall pursue the twin aims of fostering economic growth and maintaining a stable currency,[1] while in Germany – and also in the coming European Monetary Union – the maintenance of stable prices takes absolute priority.[2] The pursuit of aims dictated by employment policy is only relevant in so far as the central bank is required to support the general economic policy of the government subject to its principal aim of maintaining price stability.

The statutory definition of aims does appear to leave room for the idea, therefore, that monetary policy should take account of the possible effects on employment.

---

1 "The Board of Governors of the Federal Reserve System and the Federal Open Market Committee shall maintain long run growth of the monetary and credit aggregates commensurate with the economy's long run potential to increase production, so as to promote effectively the goals of maximum employment, stable prices, and moderate long-term interest rates ". (Federal Reserve Act § 2)

2 "The principal aim of the European Central Bank is to guarantee price stability." (Article 105 of the Treaty establishing the European Community)

On the other hand this normative requirement, which rates different priorities under different national central banking systems, would effectively be meaningless if monetary policy had no impact on the employment situation. The discussion that follows will therefore concern itself not so much with the normative question of whether, and to what extent, monetary policy should take account of its effects on employment, but rather with the empirical question of whether monetary policy does, in fact, have an impact on the employment situation.

The orthodox monetarist position has always been clear: the theory demonstrates that monetary policy cannot have any real long-term effects on the economy, although the possibility of short-term effects cannot be excluded. Monetary measures affect the rate of inflation, but they do not affect what is actually happening in the economy. This view has increasingly come to be questioned. If, for example, central banks are able to shorten periods of recession and extend periods of recovery by the use of monetary measures, it is possible to look upon these initially as short-term effects. But it is not plausible to suppose that such transitory real effects will be entirely without long-term consequences.

More important has been the collapse of monetarist ideas about the links between monetary policy and inflation at the empirical level. The worldwide abandonment of monetary targeting has revived the debate about economic indicators, and with it the question of how changes in monetary policy impact on inflation. As a result, the monetary transmission mechanisms have attracted increasing attention again in recent years. Monetary policy in the US, moreover, which is directed towards employment as much as towards inflation, has helped to renew the debate about the magnitude and persistence of the real effects of monetary policy. If the strength of these effects – contrary to what has long been believed – is not such that they can be ignored, then we need to ask ourselves exactly how this transmission takes place.

The impact of monetary policy on employment is very closely related to the output effects of monetary policy. And not only the links between monetary policy and production are determined by a variety of different transmission channels, but so are the links between production and employment, i.e. the situation in the labour market.

In Germany the experience of the nineties has shown that positive growth in GDP does not necessarily go hand in hand with a rise in employment – and even less so with a fall in unemployment. Here again we need to distinguish between the short-term and the long-term effects. In the long term there are many indications that the so-called employment threshold – which is to say, the minimum rate of growth needed to stimulate a rise in employment – is gradually falling. The structural shift in favour of the services sector is associated with a decline in average overall labour productivity, which implies a connection between employment and growth.[3] In the short term, though, there are significant fluctuations, and sud-

3 International Labour Office (1996), Weeber (1997).

den spurts in productivity in certain areas of the economy may mean that the employment threshold is relatively high in a particular year. Another important factor is the sectoral structure of growth and employment: advances in productivity vary considerably from one branch of industry to another. But in general there can be no doubt that increased production leads to higher employment. So it seems reasonable to suppose that the principal way in which monetary policy affects employment is via the growth in production.

At the same time we cannot rule out the possibility that causality runs the other way round: the situation in the labour market may have a significant impact on prices, and hence on monetary policy. So it is not surprising that in the heyday of monetarism the link between inflation and unemployment played a key role, even after the simple and somewhat Keynesian Phillips curve models were superseded by the literature on the NAIRU (non-accelerating inflation rate of unemployment). In its original form the NAIRU model differs little from the natural rate hypothesis: pushing unemployment down below a certain (equilibrium) level leads to rising inflation, because the redistribution struggle sets off a wage-price spiral.

For a long time it was assumed that the NAIRU is time invariant. And for all practical purposes the concept only makes sense if this is the case. This would make it possible to gear monetary policy to the observable rate of unemployment. However, the empirical experiences of many countries have shown that over long periods of time trend-induced changes in the unemployment rate may be accompanied by more or less stationary rates of inflation. And it works both ways. While the more or less continuous decline in unemployment rates in the US since the early 1980s has been accompanied by consistently low inflation, Germany has experienced the opposite: since the mid-1980s unemployment has risen steadily, while inflation has remained more or less unchanged.

The search for the causes of this time-varying NAIRU has led to the advancement of the so-called hysteresis hypothesis, which states that the equilibrium unemployment rate depends on past unemployment rates. Or to put it another way: if unemployment remains above its equilibrium level for an extended period as a result of policy errors, then the NAIRU rises – and *vice-versa.* Estimates for Germany indicate that the NAIRU rose by some two percentage points in the 1980s, from just under 4% to just under 6%.[4] A similar study of the US economy shows that the NAIRU, having peaked at 6.5% at the start of the 1980s, has since fallen by more than one percentage point and is now approaching the 5% mark.[5]

What are the implications of this for monetary policy? Clearly the labour markets, which lag far behind in the transmission mechanism, form an important connecting link between monetary policy and price levels. For the US Stiglitz estimates that approximately 20% of the variation in inflation can be explained by un-

---

4 Cf. Franz (1991), p. 362.

5 Cf. Gordon (1997), p. 21.

employment alone.[6] This contrasts with the monetarist view that the real effects of monetary policy are only temporary and that their only long run effect is on price levels.

According to this, therefore, even temporary output effects of monetary policy could influence employment levels in the long run by helping to make unemployment deviate from its equilibrium "for long enough". All this focuses attention back on the magnitude and persistence of the real effects of monetary policy on the economy.

Against this background it is tempting to conduct the debate about the real impact of monetary policy not just at a theoretical level, but rather to begin by asking, with the aid of empirical studies, whether these real effects can legitimately be classified as merely "temporary". Or do they persist for long enough to admit of shifts in the NAIRU in the meantime?

We certainly need to go beyond empirical studies. Any analysis of the real effects of monetary policy must take account of the transmission mechanisms involved. Are conventional ideas about monetary policy transmission really adequate in the sense that they pay due regard to the essential channels through which monetary policy is transmitted?

## II. Empirical studies on the real effects of monetary policy

The debate about real effects of monetary policy has been very much influenced by the seminal work of Bernanke and Blinder (1992). In contrast to the hitherto prevailing view that the monetary transmission mechanism begins with changes in monetary growth,[7] they start from the view that in empirical studies the impact of monetary policy can best be measured by changes in the Federal Funds Rate.[8] This idea that monetary growth and the Funds Rate are not two distinct components of the monetary transmission mechanism, but are alternative measures of the monetary policy stance, is empirically supported by the fact that in forecasts of economic growth only one of these two variables is of significant explanatory value. To substantiate their claim Bernanke and Blinder argue that changes in the Funds Rate can be plausibly explained in terms of a monetary policy reaction function.

Bernanke and Blinder also turn their attention to the question of the monetary transmission mechanism that is set in motion by changes in very short-term interest rates. Using Granger causality tests and variance decompositions they demonstrate that the Funds Rate, when compared with different monetary aggregates and short- and long-term interest rates, is the best indicator of economic growth.[9]

6 Stiglitz (1997), p. 5.

7 Cf. Friedman / Schwartz (1963), Sims (1972) and (1980).

8 A similar line of argument is pursued by McCallum (1983).

From the fact that the Funds Rate is so much more useful as an indicator than the other traditional elements of the transmission mechanism, Bernanke and Blinder conclude that other transmission channels for monetary policy must also exist. It follows from this that monetary policy exercises stronger real effects than is implied by conventional thinking. Bernanke and Gertler (1995) reach to similar conclusions about the US, in which they argue primarily that the timing and the strength of the reactions of individual demand components appear to contradict conventional views of the transmission mechanism. The initial reaction to a monetary tightening in the US is a decline in some components of ultimate demand, namely residential investment and consumer demand, followed by a decline in output. The last component to respond is business fixed investment, which according to the neo-classical view ought to be first in line in the transmission mechanism.

These findings tend to indicate, then, that studies of the real effects of monetary policy which are based on traditional thinking systematically underestimate those effects because they fail to appreciate the full complexity of the transmission mechanism.

The second question that arises concerns the persistence of output effects. Orthodox monetarist thinking holds that the real effects of monetary policy are short-term at most – and given the existence of rational expectations, are limited to unanticipated policy actions. It follows that the attempt to exploit these effects as part of an activist policy only raises inflation in the long run.

Yet, a series of more recent studies based on VAR models have concluded that the real effects of a change in monetary policy stance last for a minimum of three to four years in the US.[10]

It would undoubtedly be an over-simplification to take these findings for the US and apply them wholesale to Germany or Europe. As in so many other cases, far fewer studies are available for Germany than for the US. A recent contribution that analyses the transmission channels of monetary policy in European countries is the work of Barran, Coudert and Mojon (1997). Their conclusion is that the contractive effect of an interest-rate jump in Germany only peaks after 12 quarters, and thereafter diminishes only very gradually. In a European comparison undertaken by the authors Germany ranks among the countries where the real effects of monetary policy are most pronounced. Comparing the G7 countries, Gerlach and Smets (1995) however conclude that the real effects of monetary policy shocks are much

9 In a comparison of the exlanatory power of the Funds Rate with an interest differential between publicly and privately issued bonds of the same maturity it has to be said that the Funds Rate does not perform conspicuously better. This finding accords with earlier results by Friedman / Kuttner (1992) and Kashyap / Stein / Wilcox (1993). Bernanke (1990) points out, however, that this spread is itself a measure of the monetary policy stance.

10 44 months according to Bernanke / Gertler (1995), 12 quarters according to the BIS (1994) and Romer / Romer (1994). The latter also make the point that the VAR methodology normally used in this type of analysis tends, if anything, to underestimate the actual persistence.

the same in all these countries, and that these effects last for a period of three to four years.[11] In terms of the magnitude and persistence of the real effects of monetary policy, these findings do point to substantial similarities between the US on the one hand and Germany and the other EMS states on the other, even though it has to be conceded that they all stem from VAR models, and may therefore all be subject to the same specification errors with regard to the identification of shocks.[12] And needless to say they tell us little about the underlying transmission mechanisms.

A recent study by Kirchgässner and Savioz (1997) offers some information concerning the monetary transmission mechanisms in Germany. They investigate the information content of various monetary indicators for real GDP growth. The indicators in question are the growth rates of the monetary aggregates M1, M2 and M3, plus the overnight rate, the three-month interest rate on the money market, the yield on bonds outstanding as a long-term rate, the corresponding spreads and the difference in interest rates on loans from private and public lenders. The analytical methods used by the authors include OLS estimates and out-of-sample forecasts as well as Granger causality tests. In terms of the choice of indicators, therefore, but also in terms of the econometric methods used, this study closely parallels parts of the study carried out by Bernanke and Blinder for the US.

The conclusion reached by Kirchgässner and Savioz is that the overnight rate and the growth of M1 are the best single indicators of economic growth, while the best compound indicators – combinations of M1 or M3 with various short-term interest rates – are M1 on the one hand and the yield on bonds outstanding followed by the overnight rate on the other hand. On balance the overnight rate dominates that of all other interest rates in Germany.

However, the authors are extremely cautious in their interpretation of their meticulously documented findings, confining themselves to a discussion of their indicator value. Citing the Lucas critique, they refuse – doubtless rightly – to be drawn further on the monetary implications, in particular eschewing any specific recommendations about interest-rate targets. Movements in the capital markets are too closely tied to the expectations of the market players. The problem with a monetary policy linked to interest-rate targets is that it would ultimately have to base itself to a very large degree on the expectations of market players about the direction of that policy. Woodford (1994) and Bernanke / Woodford (1997) have clearly demonstrated the instability that results from setting a direct inflation target linked solely to nominal interest rates.[13]

---

[11] The only exceptions are the United Kingdom and Japan, with a notably higher persistence.

[12] This point is also made by the European Commission (1997), p. 30 ff.

[13] This does not apply, however, where monetary policy is linked to real interest rate levels – see Woodford (1997).

But the thesis put forward by Bernanke / Blinder, Romer / Romer and others, namely that the findings published by Kirchgässner / Savioz can be interpreted in terms of economic causality, and can thus be seen as proof of the existence of direct real effects and as an indicator of the underlying transmission channels, falls far short of an interim statement of purpose. All that is claimed is that real effects of monetary policy are observable under the prevailing monetary regime, and that these effects are both more deep-seated, in terms of the existence of hitherto neglected transmission channels, and longer-lasting than has hitherto been supposed.

At the risk of being accused, with the aforementioned authors, of succumbing to the *post hoc, ergo propter hoc* fallacy,[14] we are bound to ask what can be learned from these findings about monetary transmission mechanisms in Germany.

First and foremost, the fact that the overnight rate is a better indicator of real economic activity than all other interest-rate indicators demonstrates that in Germany, too, we need to take account of transmission channels that go beyond traditional ideas about the linkage between prices and the capital markets. This conclusion corresponds with the findings of other authors about the US.

The most important difference between Kirchgässner / Savioz and the American findings lies in the predictive power of monetary aggregates. Whereas studies for the USA show that different measures of monetary growth and the Funds Rate provide identical information, this finding is borne out in Germany only in the case of M3. M1 contains information that goes beyond that of other indicators. One obvious interpretation of this difference is that in Germany the transmission channels that matter are not the same as those in the US, as indeed has been concluded by other authors.[15] This would then mean that the central role of money demand consistently maintained by the Bundesbank is crucial to the transmission mechanism. If we want a more elaborate explanation, we could do worse than cite the critique advanced by Lucas once more. In all probability this difference between the German and American findings is partly due to the different monetary regimes in the two countries. In Germany monetary aggregates play a part in the monetary transmission mechanism because the Bundesbank has placed them at the centre of its monetary policy. This appears all the more probable in view of the fact that most of the study by Kirchgässner and Savioz relates to the period prior to Germany's reunification.[16]

---

14 See for example Hoover / Perez (1994).

15 See for example Sauer / Scheide (1995).

16 The period since 1990 is examined in a separate section, but the authors point out that the data sample is too small for them to draw any reliable conclusions. Consequently the 1990s, when the focus has shifted increasingly to other monetary indicators, have relatively little significance for the results of the study.

## III. Theoretical attempts at an explanation

At the centre of attempts to arrive at a theoretical explanation of this empirical evidence gathered from a number of countries is a view of transmission channels that emphasizes the process of money supply. This may be summarized as the credit channel view. In its various forms this view assumes that credit rationing imposed by financial market creates a situation in which monetary policy changes impact more directly and immediately on the real economy.[17] In other words, such models emphasize quantity reactions rather than price reactions. The rationing is the product of asymmetric information between creditors and debtors, and can be derived from principal-agent models, for example. An asymmetric distribution of information or the cost incurred by creditors in obtaining information mean that the price of external borrowing for a company is higher than the opportunity costs of financing by internally raised funds. In other words, companies effectively pay a premium for financing their operations with externally raised funds. In these models the central hypothesis for transmission states that the external finance premium is directly influenced by monetary policy. It increases during phases of monetary tightening and falls during phases of high liquidity.

The theoretical approaches underlying the credit channel view of the transmission mechanism can be roughly divided into two groups: transmission via a balance-sheet channel, which starts from the credit-worthiness of companies as evidenced by the structure of their balance sheets, and the – more contentious – transmission via the rationing of credit supply by the commercial banking sector.[18]

To explain the balance-sheet channel we need to start from the hypothesis that monetary policy influences the balance-sheet positions of a company – and hence its options for incurring short-term debt – in a number of different ways. A raising of the general interest-rate level, for example, affects the asset position of a company by immediately altering its interest debt. The scale of the impact depends on the amount of credit advanced at variable interest rates. Meanwhile higher interest rates on the capital markets lead to a fall in the prices of asset titles. So a rise in interest rates produces a decline in the net asset position of a company and hence in its credit-worthiness. At the same time, however, the liquid assets available to the company are immediately reduced, possibly forcing it to increase its borrowing. These effects can also be magnified in the business sector by delays in settling accounts between companies at different stages of the production cycle.

One obvious implication of these models is that small and comparatively undercapitalized companies are likely to be especially hard hit by this transmission me-

---

17 Cf. Mishkin (1995), Bernanke / Gertler (1995).

18 Bernanke / Blinder (1988) have developed a theoretical model for the bank lending channel. This channel is not discussed further here because it starts out from the contentious premise that the commercial banking sector is rationed in terms of quantity. See also Bernanke / Gertler (1995), p. 40 ff.

chanism. The study by Gertler and Gilchrist (1994) supports this hypothesis for the US.

The effectiveness of this transmission channel is critically dependent on three factors: Corporate decision-making must think in terms of short-term borrowings, the interest rates on these loans must be closely tied to the overnight rate and the interest on the relevant borrowings must be charged at a variable rate.

At first glance it looks as though the US comes closer to meeting these requirements than Germany (and a number of other European countries). In 1994 the BIS set out to examine these requirements for the G7 countries. It emerged that the proportion of loans at fixed rates of interest in the whole of the private sector in Germany and France is far higher than it is in the Anglo-American countries – and far higher also than in Japan. On the other hand, the period for which credit is extended and the structuring of repayments is essentially similar in all countries, with long-term loans predominating.[19] The consequence is a certain built-in time-lag in the transmission mechanism: a change of direction in monetary policy has to be sustained for some time before it begins to take effect via the balance-sheet channel. Once it does make itself felt, however, the effects are long-lasting.

A further indicator of the effectiveness of the balance-sheet channel is the responsiveness of gross interest payments (or their share in GDP) to changes in short-term interest rates. The existence of a linkage as such between the two has been demonstrated for all countries, but they are more closely connected in the USA, the UK and Canada than they are, for example, in France, which is much closer to Germany in this respect, given the similarities in financial market structures between the two countries. It is hardly surprising, therefore, that the results of empirical studies concerning the existence of a credit channel in Germany are less conclusive than the results of similar studies for the US.[20]

There could be a completely different explanation for this, of course. The American economy is far less open than its European counterparts. To that extent the exchange rate dependency of the US is significantly less than that of the European countries, while it also has to be remembered that a significant proportion of international trade transactions are invoiced in dollars.

The situation in Europe is completely different. For example, the effect of dollar devaluation has generally been not only to push up the value of the D-Mark relative to the dollar, but also to increase the pressure for upward revaluation within the EMS – which in turn has made it difficult for individual countries to compete on even terms even within Europe. All this has taken place in a highly open economy environment.

Against this background one could picture a very different transmission mechanism at work in small, open economies, whereby the short-term interest rate leads to

---

19 See for example Borio (1995).

20 See for example Guender / Moersch (1997).

a change in the exchange rate, which in turn affects the overall level of demand in the country concerned via foreign trade movements.

In an open economy, then, there are at least three basic transmission channels of monetary policy: the traditional one operating via long-term interest rates and investment demand; the credit channel operating via short-term interest rates and liquidity in the non-banking sector; and finally the exchange-rate channel, which operates via the exchange rate and foreign trade movements.

There are a number of possible explanations for the fact that the literature contains far fewer empirical studies of the exchange-rate channel than of the other transmission channels listed. One obvious explanation is that the debate is influenced to a very large extent by American economists – and as we have seen, this transmission channel plays a very subordinate role in the US because the US economy is less open. Another possible explanation lies in the considerable methodological problems that arise with the empirical analysis. How far can we hope to distinguish, for example, between those real effects of monetary policy which are transmitted via the exchange-rate route and those that are attributable to the other two transmission channels? It would be extremely difficult to analyze an interest-rate-induced reaction in a specific demand component, such as investment in plant and equipment, in terms of how far each transmission channel has contributed to that reaction. And an empirical analysis of the exchange-rate channel would presuppose not least that we are able to distinguish between fluctuations in the exchange rate that are interest-rate induced and fluctuations that are due to other causes.[21] And finally, the time-paths of interest rate and exchange-rate movements are likely to be very largely interdependent, and mutually influenced by expectations.

To that extent, therefore, the attempt to demonstrate the existence and operation of an exchange-rate channel by empirical analysis encounters considerable difficulties. One clear pointer is the fact that direct real effects of short-term interest-rate fluctuations in Germany appear to be far stronger than can plausibly be explained in terms of the credit channel – via gross interest payments, for example. Beyond that one can break down the exchange-rate channel into its component parts by investigating the real effects of exchange-rate movements on the one hand and the interest-rate dependency of exchange rates on the other.

In a recent empirical study on the exchange-rate dependency of Germany's foreign trade the Bundesbank has established that the elasticities involved here are considerable. It was found that the elasticity of the external contribution (the sum of the elasticities of import and export demand) in response to a change in the exchange value of the D-Mark is just below one.[22] A more difficult question to answer is the extent to which movements in the exchange rate are in fact attributable

---

21 See for example Taylor (1995), McCallum (1994). Eichenbaum / Evans (1995) have analyzed interest-rate-induced fluctuations in exchange rates in the US.

22 The German Bundesbank, Monthly Reports 1 / 1998.

to changes in short-term interest rates. There can be no doubt that short-term interest rates are not the only determinants of exchange rates.

Persuasive evidence for the interest-rate dependency of exchange rates can be seen in the success of the exchange rate policies pursued by many European countries. It is quite clearly possible to stabilize the exchange rate by the appropriate use of monetary policy. If we consider both elements of the exchange-rate channel, taking the elasticity of foreign trade in response to the exchange rate together with our past experience of exchange-rate-oriented policies, we are again led to conclude that the exchange-rate channel can play a very important role in a small, open economy. Any differences in the quantitative significance of this channel in the individual countries of the European Monetary System probably reflect differences in the direction and emphasis of monetary policies in those countries.

Countries that pursue a monetary policy linked to the exchange rate of the D-Mark have abandoned the pursuit of an autonomous policy, i.e. a policy that pursues domestic economic goals. Their principal concern was to stabilize the exchange value of their currency relative to the D-Mark, which also meant that they sought as far as possible to eliminate any impact on the domestic economy caused by movements in the exchange rate, even if there were real effects associated with this. But they had to accept effects that arose from exchange rate movements between the D-Mark and third currencies, which more often than not meant the dollar or the yen. To that extent the problems experienced by these countries are not so very different from the problems here in Germany.

Germany found itself in a very different situation, however. The question here was how far an anchor currency country can pursue an exchange-rate-oriented monetary policy without jeopardizing its role as an anchor currency country. As a rule the Bundesbank has hesitated to take the exchange rate as a guide to policy. Or to put it another way, German monetary policy has not reacted to movements in the exchange rate, nor have its measures been designed to take account of the possible effects on the exchange rate in the future. Which is not to say that this transmission channel has not been effective in Germany. On the contrary, it has tended to amplify monetary signals beyond the degree that would be expected if one is looking purely at the domestic economy. Had the Bundesbank been guided by purely domestic economic considerations, as is claimed, this would have had a destabilizing effect.

Some might find this view less than wholly persuasive, and wonder if it might not have been possible even for an anchor currency country to take more account of exchange rates. If, for example, we had used monetary measures – and specifically an earlier lowering of short-term interest rates – to curtail the rise in the value of the D-Mark in 1994/95, this would have had very substantial positive real effects.

So the significance of the exchange-rate channel has varied widely from one European country to the next. The central banks of those countries whose currencies were pegged to the D-Mark looked primarily to the exchange rate for guidance. This the Bundesbank has conspicuously *not* done.

## IV. Monetary policy in the context of European Monetary Union

At this point it can be concluded that monetary policy does indeed have perceptible real effects in all countries and that these effects are not solely attributable to the traditional notion of a monetary transmission mechanism. Whereas in the Anglo-Saxon countries most of the direct output effects can be attributed to the credit channel, this is not the case in some European countries such as Germany and France. It can be assumed that the exchange-rate channel played a role in this context. Presumably the real effects of monetary policy are transmitted simultaneously via long-term interest rates, exchange rates and the credit supply.

The introduction of a single European currency will lead to significant changes. These will include the uniform monetary policies of the European Central Bank, uniform short-term interest rates, the end of internal exchange rates within the Monetary Union, as well as a single external exchange rate. Europe's exchange-rate dependence will decline perceptibly – and with it the significance of the exchange rate channel.

It may well be that the reduced importance of the exchange-rate channel will temper the real economic effects of monetary policy. At the same time there will no longer be the same need to cushion exchange rate shocks. Exchange rates will no longer depend to the former extent on short-term interest rates; instead they will belong to the potential disturbances inherent in the real economy.

The situation will change significantly with regard to the exchange-rate orientation of monetary policy. Once European Monetary Union has been established, this issue will no longer evoke differing strategies. Given the reduced degree of openness, there will no longer be the same necessity to pay attention to the exchange rate. Monetary policy can then be geared primarily to domestic economic requirements. However, the "domestic" economy will have increased in size.

In future, domestic economic factors will exert a greater potential influence on interest rate policies than the (erratic) fluctuations in exchange rates. If the goal is to achieve price stability and steady economic development, short-term interest rates must be adapted to the current economic situation. This applies both in the case of the classical transmission mechanism argument *and* in the case of the credit channel argument.

However, problems could arise during the transitional period. To the extent that the individual countries diverge in terms of their cyclical position there is a likelihood that a convergence of short-term interest rates will have differing effects in the various countries concerned. However, a recently published OECD study indicates that the potential EMU members will display a high degree of economic convergence from the outset.[23]

A further problem could be that uniform monetary impulses in the individual countries could induce differing real effects, due to the specific characteristics of the national financial markets and the transmission mechanisms that operate in these markets. The EU Commission (1997) adheres to this view, for example, even though convincing evidence has yet to be presented. This underscores the importance of analyzing monetary transmission mechanisms from a national standpoint.

This being said, it is likely that European Monetary Union will lead not only to economic convergence but also to a uniform transmission mechanism throughout the Union. All the signs are that the credit channel and the associated real economic effects will play a major role – as is the case in the US.

With regard to the employment situation in Europe all this provides grounds for optimism. On the one hand it is correct to say that monetary union will not solve unemployment problems, and that monetary policies are not a substitute for employment policies. However, there will be an improvement in the conditions under which employment policies can operate. Exchange rate disturbances – and the constraints these disturbances place on policy-making (albeit in different ways) – will become less important. Monetary policy will acquire greater freedom of action. It is important that this freedom is used effectively. In the light of the considerable real economic effects it is not sufficient just to secure price stability. At the same time it is essential to exploit the possibilities for real economic expansion, without thereby endangering price stability. In many respects Europe will become more comparable to the US. It would be good if this were also to apply to the field of monetary policy.

## References

*Barran,* Fernando / *Coudert,* Virginie and *Mojon,* Benoît: "The Transmission of Monetary Policy in the European Countries", in: Collignon, Stefan (ed.): European Monetary Policy, 1997, London, Washington:81 - 111. – *Bank for International Settlements:* 64. Annual Report, June 1994, Basle. – *Bernanke,* Ben: "On the Predictive Power of Interest Rates and Interest Rate Spreads", New England Economic Review (Federal Reserve Bank of Boston), November / December 1990: 51 - 68. – *Bernanke,* Ben and *Blinder,* Alan: "Credit, Money and Aggregate Demand", American Economic Review, May 1988, 78: 435 - 439. – *Bernanke,* Ben and *Blinder,* Alan: "The Federal Funds Rate and the Channels of Monetary Transmission", American Economic Review, September 1992, 82: 901 - 921. – *Bernanke,* Ben and *Gertler,* Mark: "Inside the Black Box: The Credit Channel of Monetary Policy Transmission", Journal of Economic Perspectives, Fall 1995, 9: 27 - 48. – *Bernanke,* Ben and *Woodford,* Michael: "Inflation Forecasts and Monetary Policy", NBER working paper no. 6157,

23 OECD, Economic Outlook 62, December 1997, p. 21.

September 1997. – *Borio,* Claudio: "The Structure of Credit to the Non-Government Sector and the Transmission Mechanism of Monetary Policy: A Cross-Country Comparison", BIS working paper no. 24, April 1995.– *Deutsche Bundesbank:* Monthly Report, January 1998: 49 - 59. – *Eichenbaum,* Martin and *Evans,* Charles: "Some Empirical Evidence on the Effects of Shocks to Monetary Policy on Exchange Rates", Quarterly Journal of Economics, November 1995, 110: 975 - 1009. – *European Commission:* Directorate General II, Economic Policy in EMU, Part B, Specific Topics, November 1997, no.125. – *Franz,* Wolfgang: Arbeitsmarktökonomik, Berlin et al., 1991. – *Friedman,* Benjamin and *Kuttner,* Kenneth: "Money, Income, Prices, and Interest Rates", American Economic Review, June 1992, 82: 472 - 492. – *Friedman,* Milton and *Schwartz,* Anna: A Monetary History of the United States, Princeton, 1963. – *Gerlach,* Stefan and *Smets,* Frank: "The Monetary Transmission Mechanism: Evidence from the G-7 Countries", BIS working paper no. 26, April 1995. – *Gertler,* Mark and *Gilchrist,* Simon: "Monetary Policy, Business Cycles and the Behaviour of Small Manufacturing Firms", Quarterly Journal of Economics, May 1994, 109: 309 - 340. – *Gordon,* Robert: "The Time-Varying NAIRU and its Implications for Economic Policy", Journal of Economic Perspectives, Winter 1997, 11: 11 - 32. – *Guender,* Alfred and *Moersch,* Mathias: "On the Existence of a Credit Channel of Monetary Policy in Germany", Kredit und Kapital, 2/1997, 30, 173 - 185. – *Hoover,* K. D. and *Perez,* S. J.: "Post-hoc-ergo-propter once more: An Evaluation of 'Does Monetary Policy Matter?' in the Spirit of James Tobin", Journal of Monetary Economics, 1994, 34: 47 - 73. – *International Labour Office:* World Employment 1996/1997, Geneva, 1996. – *Kashyap,* Anil/*Stein,* Jeremy and *Wilcox,* David: "Monetary Policy and Credit Conditions", American Economic Review, June 1993, 83: 78 - 98. – *Kirchgässner,* Gebhard and *Savioz,* Marcel: "Monetary Policy and Forecasts for Real GDP Growth: An Empirical Investigation for the Federal Republic of Germany", Universität St.Gallen, paper presented at the Annual Meeting of the Verein für Socialpolitik in Bern 1997. – *McCallum,* Bennet: "A Reconsideration of Sims' Evidence Concerning Monetarism", Economics Letters, 1983, 13: 167 - 171. – *McCallum,* Bennet: "A Reconsideration of the Uncovered Interest Rate Parity Relationship", Journal of Monetary Economics, Febuary 1994, 33: 105 - 132. – *Mishkin,* Frederic: "Symposium on the Monetary Transmission Mechanism", Journal of Economic Perspectives, Fall 1995, 9: 3 - 10. – *OECD:* Economic Outlook, December 1997, 62: 21. – *Romer,* Christina and *Romer,* David: "What Ends Recessions?", NBER Macroeconomics Annual 1994, 9: 121 - 170. – *Sauer,* Christine and *Scheide,* Joachim: "Money, Interest Rate Spreads, and Economic Activity", Weltwirtschaftliches Archiv, 1995, 131: 708 - 722. – *Sims,* Christopher: "Money, Income, and Causality", American Economic Review, September 1972, 62: 540 - 552. – *Sims,* Christopher: "Comparison of Interwar and Postwar Business Cycles": "Monetarism Reconsidered", American Economic Review, May 1980, 70: 250 - 257. – *Stiglitz,* Joseph: "Reflections on the Natural Rate Hypothesis", Journal of Economic Perspectives, Winter 1997, 11, 3 - 10. – *Taylor,* John: "The Monetary Transmission Mechanism: An Empirical Framework", Journal of Economic Perspectives, Fall 1995, 9: 11 - 26. – *Weeber,* Joachim: "Wann führt Wachstum zu mehr Beschäftigung?", Wirtschaftsdienst, March 1997, 77: 180 - 184. – *Woodford,* Michael: "Nonstandard Indicators for Monetary Policy: Can their Usefulness be Judged from Forecasting Regressions?", in: Mankiw, Gregory (ed.), Monetary Policy, Chicago, 1994. – *Woodford,* Michael: "Doing Without Money: Controlling Inflation in a Post-Monetary World", NBER working paper no. 6188, September 1997.

# Zur Koordination von Geld- und Lohnpolitik

## Eine empirische Analyse für die USA und Deutschland

Von Gustav A. Horn, Berlin

### I. Einleitung

Nach den Ölpreisschocks der siebziger Jahre, deren Wirkungen auch noch bis an den Anfang des vergangenen Jahrzehnt hineinreichten, schien die konjunkturelle Entwicklung in den westlichen Industrieländern stabil zu sein. Schließlich setzte in den achtziger Jahren ein Aufschwung ein, der zumeist weitaus länger als bislang üblich, anhielt. Allerdings mündete diese Entwicklung ab 1988 / 89 – in Deutschland aufgrund der Vereinigung verzögert – in vielen Ländern in eine Rezession. Auffallend ist, daß die Krise in den USA weniger tief und kürzer war als z. B. in Deutschland und anderen Ländern Europas. Dies geschah, obwohl die wirtschaftliche Entwicklung in den westlichen Industrieländern durch keinerlei „exogene" Schocks wie z. B. eine drastische Steigerung der Ölpreise beeinträchtigt wurde. Im Gegenteil, sinkende Ölpreise sorgten sogar für günstige Rahmenbedingungen. Negative Anstöße fehlten also. Will man diese Konjunkturkrisen somit erklären, muß sich der Blick folglich auf „endogene", in den Industrieländern selbst liegende, Ursachen für diese Entwicklung richten.

Im Zuge der mit den Ölpreiskrisen verbundenen Rezessionen hatte sich in den meisten Ländern Europas ein hoher Sockel an Arbeitslosigkeit gebildet, der auch durch die konjunkturelle Aufwärtsentwicklung der achtziger Jahre nicht abgebaut wurde. Dies lenkte den Blick auf die Rolle des Lohnbildungsmechanismus sowohl speziell bei der Verarbeitung der Ölpreisschocks als auch generell bei der Entstehung von Rezessionen.[1] Vielfach wird in ihm die Ursache der hohen Arbeitslosigkeit insbesondere in Deutschland und Europa gesehen, da die Löhne zu inflexibel auf die Gegebenheiten des Arbeitsmarktes reagiert hätten, als daß eine Markträumung erfolgen könnte.[2] Als positives Beispiel werden zumeist die USA genannt, wo seit der letzten Rezession 1991 die Beschäftigung spürbar ausgeweitet werden konnte, während die Arbeitslosigkeit ihren tiefsten Stand seit 1970 erreichte.[3]

1 Siehe vor allem Bruno / Sachs (1985).

2 Vgl. DIW (1997).

3 Vgl. Horn (1998).

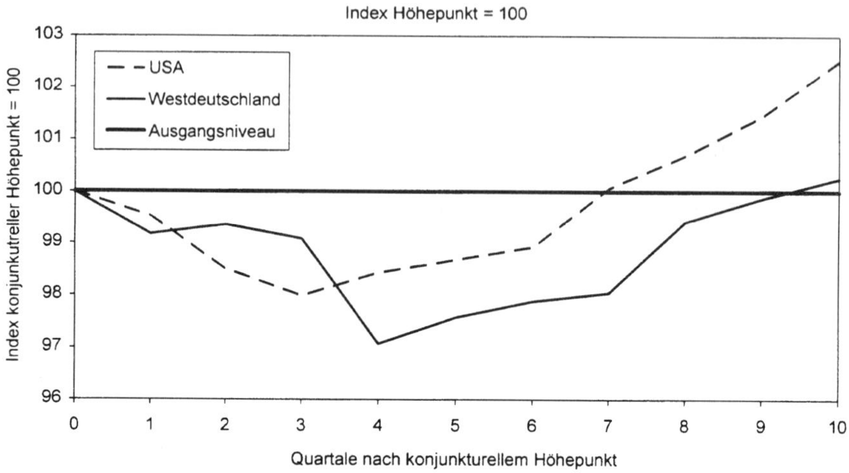


Abbildung 1: Entwicklung des Bruttoinlandsprodukts

Waren jedoch die Lohnzuwächse auch in Deutschland in den siebziger und auch zu Beginn der achtziger Jahre gemessen an der Produktivitätsentwicklung und der Inflationsrate sehr hoch, zeichneten sich die späten achtziger und auch die neunziger Jahre in fast allen großen Industrieländern freilich durch sehr moderate nominale Lohnerhöhungen aus.[4] Insofern stellt sich die Frage, ob im Vorfeld der jüngsten Rezessionen tatsächlich Gefährdungen der Inflationsziele von der Lohnentwicklung ausgingen. Dafür spricht, daß die Geldpolitik in diesem Zeitraum ihre Inflationsziele nach unten revidierte. In den europäischen Ländern außer Deutschland lag dies vor allem an den Bemühungen um eine Konvergenz der Inflationsraten auf das deutsche Niveau im Zuge der wachsenden Integration auf dem europäischen Binnenmarkt, und auch in den USA sowie in Kanada gewann die Bekämpfung der Inflation nach der massiven Geldentwertung zu Beginn der achtziger Jahre an Gewicht. Insofern stellt sich die Frage, ob nicht trotz der mäßigeren Lohnsteigerungen die strengeren Inflationsvorgaben einen Konflikt zwischen Lohn- und Geldpolitik auslösten, der zur Entstehung von Rezessionen beigetragen hat, weil die Lohnbildung nicht maßvoll genug war, um die engeren Ziele einhalten zu können. Hätte hingegen die Lohnbildung frühzeitig auf geldpolitische Signale reagiert, und wäre der Lohnanstieg rasch in mit den Inflationsvorstellungen kompatibler Form moderater ausgefallen, wäre der zusätzliche Druck auf die Löhne über die erhöhte Arbeitslosigkeit nicht erforderlich gewesen.

Diese Überlegungen führen zu der allgemeineren Frage inwieweit überhaupt eine Koordination oder zumindest eine Interaktion zwischen Lohnfindung und

---

4 Die europäische Entwicklung ist dargestellt in Horn / Scheremet / Zwiener (1997). Die nordamerikanische in Horn (1998).

Geldpolitik stattfindet, über die sich z. B. strengere Inflationsvorgaben vermitteln. Dieser Frage soll im folgenden mittels empirischer Methoden nachgegangen werden. Von der Antwort hängt ab, ob diese Interaktion bzw. ihr Fehlen überhaupt eine Erklärung für die jüngsten Rezessionen sein kann. Ein wesentliches Element in dieser Analyse ist die Geschwindigkeit, mit der auf veränderte Gegebenheiten reagiert wird. Nur bei einer raschen Wechselwirkung von Geldpolitik und Lohnfindung ergeben sich keine Folgen für die realwirtschaftliche Entwicklung.

Untersucht werden soll diese Interaktion anhand eines Vergleichs zwischen Deutschland und den USA. Die Lohn und geldpolitischen Variablen werden dabei in ein System interdependenter monetärer und Arbeitsmarktvariablen eingebettet. Dies geschieht mittels der ökonometrischen Schätzung eines Systems von Vektor Autoregressiven Gleichungen (VAR), durch die wechselseitige Reaktionen und auch die Geschwindigkeit der Reaktionen deutlich gemacht werden können. Insbesondere lassen sich die Reaktion der Geldpolitik auf Lohnentwicklungen sowie die Reaktion der Löhne auf geldpolitische Entscheidungen aufzeigen. Ökonometrische Zeitreihenschätzungen ermitteln den Informationsgehalt, den die Variablen wechselseitig für einander aufweisen.

Die Resultate weisen auf einen unterschiedlichen zeitlichen Horizont bei der Inflationsbekämpfung hin. In den USA findet sie vor allem im Vorfeld, durch Beachtung von Impulsen aus der Lohnentwicklung und der Inflationserwartungen auf den Kapitalmärkten, statt. In Deutschland agiert die Bundesbank offenbar erst, wenn eine Beschleunigung des Preisauftriebs beobachtbar wird. Die Lohnreaktionen sprechen dafür, daß die Lohnbildung in Deutschland erst in jüngster Zeit auf Signale der Geldpolitik reagiert. Für die achtziger Jahre läßt sich eine Kooperation mit der Geldpolitik nicht nachweisen. Die Geldpolitik berücksichtigt Lohnsignale bei ihren Entscheidungen in den achtzigern überhaupt nicht und in den neunzigern nur für eine kurze Zeitspanne.

Im folgenden Kapitel sollen die theoretischen Grundlagen einer Interaktion von Lohn- und Geldpolitik kurz skizziert werden. In Kapitel III steht die Konstruktion eines Systems Vektor Autoregressiver Schätzungen im Mittelpunkt. Kapitel IV enthält die empirischen Resultate und im letzten Abschnitt werden einige Schlußfolgerungen aus der Analyse gezogen.

## II. Zur Interaktion von Geld- und Lohnpolitik

In der theoretischen Literatur wird seit einiger Zeit der Interaktion wirtschaftspolitischer Institutionen, darunter werden im allgemeinen auch die Lohnfindung und die Geldpolitik subsumiert, verstärkte Aufmerksamkeit gewidmet.[5] Interaktion

5 Siehe Hamada (1976), Ghosh(1986), Rogoff (1985) und Kehoe (1989). Zur Methodik siehe Kydland / Prescott (1977) . Siehe auch Bryson / Jensen / Van Hoose (1993).

wird dabei in der Regel als Kooperation im spieltheoretischen Sinn gesehen.[6] Im Mittelpunkt steht allerdings fast immer internationale Kooperation, insbesondere der Geldpolitik.[7] Dabei hat sich eine zunehmend kritische Einschätzung der Effekte von wirtschaftspolitischer Kooperation durchgesetzt. Zeigten Hamada[8] und auch Oudiz und Sachs[9] noch die möglichen positiven Wirkungen von Kooperation für Wachstum und Beschäftigung auf, wurde dieses Resultat von Rogoff[10] in Frage gestellt. Zwar leitet er ab, daß bei internationaler geldpolitischer Kooperation sich ein höherer Output bei niedriger Inflation als ohne Kooperation erzielen läßt, weil es im Gegensatz zum Fall isolierter Geldpolitik nicht zu einer Abwertung kommt. Diese günstige Konstellation wird jedoch von der Lohnfindung (wage setters) konterkariert, in dem die Beschäftigten sich diese Kooperationsrente durch höhere Lohnsteigerungen aneignen und damit den Output-Inflation-Zusammenhang im Vergleich zu einer Situation ohne Kooperation letztlich unverändert lassen. Auf diese Weise zeigen sich dann jedoch keine positiven Effekte von Kooperation mehr.

Die Kritik an dem Ansatz von Rogoff konzentrierte sich im wesentlichen auf seine Modellierung der Zielfunktionen. Zum einen wurde bemerkt, daß er sich lediglich auf die Ziele von politischen Instanzen beschränke, nicht aber die der privaten Wirtschaftsteilnehmer einbeziehe.[11] Wäre dies der Fall, würden die von ihm hergeleiteten Lohnerhöhungen nicht erfolgen, weil die Gewerkschaften die Nachteile eines solchen Verhaltens in ihr Kalkül einbeziehen würden. Unter diesen Umständen wäre die Kooperation der Nicht Kooperation überlegen. Ein solches Argument rührt an ein entscheidendes Problem: Ob Kooperation erfolgreich ist oder nicht hängt wesentlich von den institutionellen Rahmenbedingungen ab.[12] Vorteile aus Kooperation ergeben sich nur dann, wenn die Lohnfindung anders gestaltet ist als im Modell von Rogoff, wenn sich nämlich die Löhne im vollständigen Wettbewerb zwischen Arbeitsanbietern ergeben.

Kehoe[13] zeigt die institutionelle Bedingtheit der Resultate deutlich auf, in dem er auf die unterschiedlichen Ergebnisse für verschiedene Zielfunktionen bei der Lohnfindung hinweist. Demnach hätte internationale Kooperation von Geldpolitik sehr wohl positive Effekte, wenn die Lohnfindung dezentral im Wettbewerb erfol-

---

6 Siehe Oudiz / Sachs (1984).

7 Siehe u. a. Kehoe (1989), Rothschild (1990), Neumann (1994). Siehe auch die empirische Analyse in Bryant et al. (1988) und Krupp / Cabos (1995).

8 Siehe Hamada (1976).

9 Siehe Oudiz / Sachs (1984).

10 Siehe Rogoff (1985). Siehe hierzu auch die kritischen Bemerkungen von Rothschild (1990).

11 Siehe Canzoneri / Henderson (1988). Ein ähnlich gelagerter Einwand ist, daß diese Lohnerhöhungen nur bei starken Gewerkschaften möglich sind; siehe hierzu Kehoe (1989).

12 Siehe Kehoe (1989).

13 Siehe Kehoe (1989).

gen würde, weil dann, ohne Gewerkschaften mit Monopolmacht über das Arbeitsangebot, die von Rogoff befürchteten Lohnsteigerungen nicht durchzusetzen wären. Falls aber die Lohnbildung doch wegen der Existenz von Gewerkschaften gleichsam zentralisiert würde, wäre hingegen die Nicht Kooperation von Regierungen vorteilhafter. In diesem Fall ließe internationale Steuerkonkurrenz nur niedrige Steuersätze zu. Folglich könnten die Regierungen nur eine zurückhaltende Fiskalpolitik durchführen und es bestünde aus dieser Richtung keine Inflationsgefahr.

Auch in der empirisch orientierten Literatur wird der Interaktion zwischen Lohn- und Geldpolitik kaum Aufmerksamkeit geschenkt. Calmfors und Drifill und, mit neueren Daten, die OECD untersuchen zwar den Zusammenhang zwischen Formen der Lohnbildung und gesamtwirtschaftlicher Entwicklung, aber ohne daß explizit auf die Interaktion von Politikbereichen eingegangen wird.[14] Zumeist konzentrieren sich die neueren empirischen Untersuchungen zudem auf die geldpolitischen Impulse [15]

Diese Überlegungen zeigen, daß bei diesen Ansätzen eine Lücke im Hinblick auf binnenwirtschaftliche Interaktionen von wirtschaftspolitischen Institutionen besteht. Insbesondere stellt sich angesichts der Bedeutung der Lohnreaktionen die Frage nach der Interaktion zwischen Lohnfindung und vor allem der Geldpolitik. Wie die theoretischen Analysen zeigen, ist dies zum Beispiel entscheidend für die Konsequenzen von internationaler wirtschaftspolitischer Kooperation. Vieles spricht aus der Sicht der theoretischen Ansätze dafür, daß die Art und Weise, in der die Lohnfindung mit den übrigen Politikfeldern interagiert, maßgeblich für deren Wirkung ist.

Besteht, wie in dem Ansatz von Rogoff, keinerlei binnenwirtschaftliche Kooperation zwischen Lohn- und Geldpolitik und existieren zugleich Gewerkschaften mit Monopolmacht sind negative Effekte von geldpolitischen Maßnahmen wahrscheinlich. In diesem extremen Fall lassen weder die Gewerkschaften geldpolitische Signale in ihre Entscheidungen einfließen, noch berücksichtigt die Zentralbank Lohnsignale. Unter diesen Umständen finden Stabilitätsvorstellungen der Zentralbank und die hieraus abgeleiteten Entscheidungen über die Geldmarktzinsen keinen Eingang in die Lohnfindung. Potentielle Stabilitätsverletzungen werden also bei Lohnabschlüssen nicht zur Kenntnis genommen. Gleichzeitig schreitet aber auch die Zentralbank bei Vorliegen solcher Verletzungen erst spät ein, nämlich dann wenn sie als beschleunigte Inflationsrate sichtbar werden. Unter diesen Voraussetzungen ist die Einhaltung der Stabilitätsziele in realwirtschaftlicher Sicht kostspielig, da sie nur über eine Stabilisierungsrezession erzwungen werden kann. Jede expansivere Ausrichtung von Geld- oder auch Fiskalpolitik übersetzt sich in

---

14 Siehe Calmfors / Driffil (1988) und OECD (1997).

15 Siehe Bernanke / Blinder (1992) und als Vorläufer Stock / Watson (1989). Diese Methodik wird weitergeführt in Bernanke / Mihov(1995), Shioji(1997) und Bagliano / Favero (1997).

diesem Modellrahmen auch durch Lohnsteigerungen rasch in höhere Inflation und läßt, wenn überhaupt, nur eine geringe reale Wirkung zu.

Ein anderer Extremfall ist, wenn bei der Lohnfindung mögliche negative Effekte einer Verletzung von Inflationszielen in die Entscheidungen einfließen, also auf geldpolitische Signale reagiert wird, um Stabilitätsvorgaben nicht zu gefährden. Wenn eine solche Verhaltensweise ihr Äquivalent in einer Zentralbank findet, die Lohnimpulse aufgreift, lassen sich Stabilitätsvorgaben realisieren, ohne daß dies negative realwirtschaftliche Konsequenzen haben müßte. Voraussetzung hierfür ist, daß beide Seiten diese Ausrichtung in glaubwürdiger Weise verfolgen, ansonsten würde die Beachtung der wechselseitigen Signale sinnlos sein.

Zwischen diesen beiden Extremfällen sind Zwischenformen von Interaktionen denkbar, bei denen nur eine Seite entsprechende Signale achtet. Reagiert z. B. nur die Lohnpolitik auf geldpolitische Signale, nicht aber die Geldpolitik auf die Lohnpolitik, ist die Einhaltung von Inflationszielen wahrscheinlich. Gleichwohl würden Verletzungen erst recht spät, möglicherweise unter hohen realen Kosten bekämpft. Beachtet umgekehrt die Lohnfindung die geldpolitischen Signale nicht, sind Stabilitätsverletzungen wahrscheinlicher. Agiert die Zentralbank aber früh, schon bei Auftreten entsprechender Lohnimpulse, sollten sich die realen Kosten der Inflationsbekämpfung in Grenzen halten.

Will man diese Zusammenhänge empirisch analysieren, ist eine interdependente Modellierung der Lohnfindung und der Geldpolitik unabdingbar. Soll auch die Geschwindigkeit der Reaktion und ihre Nachhaltigkeit deutlich gemacht werden, muß eine Untersuchung der Impulse und ihrer Verarbeitung erfolgen. All dies läßt sich mittels Schätzungen von Vektor Autoregressiven Systemen (VAR) bewerkstelligen, die Interdependenzen zulassen und gleichzeitig die Verarbeitung von Impulsen, die von den einzelnen Variablen ausgehen, erkennbar werden lassen.

## III. Ein System interdependenter Lohn- und monetärer Entwicklungen

### *1. Die Variablen*

Im folgenden soll daher ein VAR System begründet werden, mit dem sich die Interdependenzen zwischen Lohnentwicklung und Geldpolitik abbilden lassen. Die wesentlichen Größen sind die Kennzahlen für die Lohnentwicklung und die geldpolitischen Variablen. Für die USA werden die Effektivverdienste je Stunde der abhängig Beschäftigten im privaten Sektor, die vom Bureau of Labour Statistics erhoben werden, als Lohnvariable verwendet. An dieser Größe sollten Lohnimpulse deutlich werden. Da in Deutschland Signale seitens der Lohnpolitik vor allem von den Tarifvereinbarungen ausgehen, und Werte für Effektivverdienste nicht in der notwendigen Frequenz (Monate) verfügbar sind, wird hier der Tariflohnindex der Bundesbank als Lohnindikator eingesetzt.

Als geldpolitische Variable für die USA wird zum einen die Federal Funds Rate, der für die USA relevante geldpolitisch determinierte Zinssatz, in die Analyse einbezogen. Die ausschließliche Berücksichtigung des Geldmarktzinses blendet Kapitalmarkteffekte aus. Dies kann sinnvoll sein, wenn ohnehin ein Gleichlauf zwischen Geld- und Kapitalmarktzinsen bestünde, da auf diese Weise die Einbeziehung unnötiger Variablen vermieden wird. Als Alternative wurde die Zinsdifferenz zwischen kurz- und langfristigen Anlageformen verwendet. Diese Variante nimmt die Zinsdifferenz als Indikator für die geldpolitische Ausrichtung[16], die sich aus der Kombination von Zinssetzungen der Zentralbank und Kapitalmarktreaktionen ergibt. Um die Kapitalmarktreaktionen explizit zu berücksichtigen wurden in Alternativschätzungen explizit die Kapitalmarktzinsen, für private Anleihen mit 5 Jähriger Restlaufzeit, eingeführt. Hierdurch wird der Unterschied zwischen geldpolitischen Entscheidungen und Kapitalmarktentwicklungen explizit. Damit lassen sich möglicherweise divergierende Tendenzen, die z. B. aus plötzlichen von der Geldpolitik nicht vorhergesehen Inflationsbefürchtungen auf den Kapitalmärkten resultieren können, aufzeigen. Alle Zinsreihen entstammen der Datenbank des Federal Reserve Boards. Für Deutschland werden der Pensionszinssatz (Repo -Rate) als geldpolitischer Zins und der Zinssatz für Anleihen mit 10jähriger Restlaufzeit für die Kapitalmarktzinsen verwendet. Die Reihen basieren auf den Daten der Bundesbank.

Neben diesen Schlüsselgrößen sind noch die Inflationsrate und die Arbeitslosenquote Teil des VAR System. Beide Größen sollten sowohl für die Lohnfindung als auch für die geldpolitischen Entscheidungen von Bedeutung sein. Hier spielen im Hinblick auf die Lohnfindung Phillipskurvenüberlegungen eine Rolle, nach denen die Lohnzuwächse sowohl auf Inflation als auch auf die Überschußnachfrage am Arbeitsmarkt reagiert. Des weiteren wird die Geldpolitik sowohl Inflation als auch die konjunkturelle Entwicklung, die sich auch in der Arbeitslosenquote widerspiegelt in ihr Kalkül aufnehmen. Die Arbeitslosenquote für Deutschland bezieht sich lediglich auf Westdeutschland, um die Transformationsprobleme Ostdeutschlands auszublenden. Außerdem wurde die Standardisierte Reihe der OECD verwendet, um gleichartige Konzepte zur Messung von Arbeitslosigkeit zu haben. Die Zeitreihen entstammen sowohl für die USA als auch für Deutschland den Main Economic Indicators der OECD. Schließlich fließt auch noch der reale effektive Wechselkurs in die Analyse ein, um die außenwirtschaftliche Stabilität der Währung zu berücksichtigen. Hier bildet wiederum die entsprechende Reihe der OECD Main Economic Indicators für beide Länder die Grundlage.

### *2. Zur Reihung der Variablen*

Zur Konstruktion ein VAR Systems ist es erforderlich, durch grobe theoretische Vorüberlegungen eine Reihenfolge der Variablen zu bestimmen, die sich an der Re-

[16] Siehe hierzu z. B. Bernanke / Blinder (1992).

aktionsgeschwindigkeit auf Schocks der übrigen Variablen orientieren muß.[17] Mit Hilfe solcher Überlegungen lassen sich Restriktionen gewinnen, die für die Aufspaltung der Varianz einer Variable, und damit zur Identifizierung der einzelnen Impulse von Bedeutung sind. Wenn unterstellt wird, daß eine Variable z. B. nur sehr langsam auf Impulse von anderen Größen reagiert, dann wird im Rahmen einer VAR in der ersten Periode die gesamte Varianz aus eigenen Veränderungen erklärt. Erst in nachfolgenden Perioden schlagen sich Impulse von anderen Größen nieder. Anders bei einer nachgeordnet plazierten Variable. Hier wird gleich in der ersten Periode ein Einfluß von vorher eingeordneten Größen angenommen. Aus alldem folgt, daß die im Rahmen einer VAR gewonnenen Ergebnisse von der Reihenfolge der verwendeten Variablen abhängig sind; diese ist also zu begründen.

Unterstellt man eine Preisbildung unter monopolistischer Konkurrenz, überwälzen Unternehmen Lohnerhöhungen auf die Preise. Erst dann erfolgt über Inflationserwartungen eine Reaktion der Löhne auf die Preise. Ein Lohnschock hat demnach rasche Preiswirkungen, während die Rückwirkung mehr Zeit erfordert. Diese Annahmen implizieren, daß die Lohnvariable im VAR System vor der Preisvariable plaziert wird. Weiterhin sei unterstellt, daß die Arbeitslosigkeit auf Lohn- wie auch auf Preisschocks langsamer reagiert als Löhne und Preise auf Arbeitslosigkeit; mit anderen Worten Preise schneller reagieren als Mengen.[18] Dies bedeutet die Arbeitslosenquote ist die erste in der Reihe der Variablen.

Für die Geldpolitik wird eine höhere Reaktionsgeschwindigkeit als der Lohnfindung unterstellt und damit, daß sie Schocks der Lohn- und Inflationsvariablen schneller aufnimmt als umgekehrt. Aus diesem Grund belegt sie einen Rang nach diesen Größen im Rahmen der VAR Systems. Als noch flexibler wurden die Reaktionen auf den Kapitalmärkten angesehen, so daß die Kapitalmarktzinsen nach den Geldmarktzinsen plaziert werden. Die flexibelste Reaktion auf Schocks wird der Wechselkursvariable unterstellt, die somit auf den letzten Rang gesetzt wird.

### *3. Die Darstellung des VAR Systems*

Die obigen Überlegungen lassen sich in folgender Gleichung darstellen:

$$Y_t = A_0 Y_t + A_1 Y_{t-1} + B_0 X_t + u_t \quad \text{with} \quad t \leq T$$

Dabei ist $Y$ der Vektor der einzelnen Variablen mit $Y = (UR, \tilde{w}, \pi, i, il, exr)$. $UR$ ist die Arbeitslosenquote, $\tilde{w}, \pi$ sind die (prozentualen) Lohnänderungen bzw. die Inflationsrate. Die übrigen Bezeichnungen sind in der oben angegebenen Reihen-

17 Siehe Lütkepohl (1991) und als Beispiel Bernanke / Blinder (1992).

18 Diese Annahme impliziert nicht zwangsläufig, daß Löhne und Preise hinreichend flexibel wären, um eine fortwährend Markträumung zu erreichen. Es ist lediglich angenommen, daß sie sich im Vergleich zu den Mengen rascher anpassen.

folge, ein als geldpolitisches Instrument dienender Zinssatz, ein langfristige Zinssatz sowie die Wechselkurse. Die Matrizen $A_0$ und $A_1$ enthalten die gleichzeitigen bzw. die verzögerten wechselseitigen Einflüsse. Die Matrix $X$ besteht aus exogenen Variablen, hier nur das Absolutglied, und die Matrix $B$ gibt deren Einfluß an. Die Residuen sind mit $u_t$ bezeichnet, der Schätzzeitraum umfaßt $T$ Perioden.

Um dieses System identifizieren zu können, sind Restriktionen auf $A_0$ und $A_1$ erforderlich. In Übereinstimmung mit anderen Ansätzen[19] wird hier unterstellt, daß Restriktionen ausschließlich auf $A_0$ liegen. In Verbindung mit oben gemachten Überlegungen zur Geschwindigkleit bedeutet dies, daß $A_0$ eine untere Dreiecksstruktur aufweist, also rekursiv ist. Unter dieser Voraussetzung kann eine unrestringierte VAR angewendet werden. [20]

## *4. Zu den Schätzungen des VAR Systems*

Für die Schätzungen werden Monatsdaten verwendet. Diese Frequenz scheint angemessen, um den möglicherweise raschen Reaktionen vor allem der Geldpolitik sowie der Kapital- und Devisenmärkte Rechnung zu tragen. Der Schätzzeitraum reicht in einem ersten Ansatz für die USA von Januar 1972 bis Oktober 1997. In Deutschland mußte ein sehr viel kürzere Schätzzeitraum zugrunde gelegt werden, da die monatlichen Tariflohndaten erst ab 1985 verfügbar sind. Die Schätzung endet 1995 mit dem Ende der Verfügbarkeit für die westdeutschen standardisierten Arbeitslosenquoten seitens der OECD.

Eine generelles Problem bei der Anwendung von VAR Systemen besteht in der Erfassung von Strukturänderungen.[21] Sind Strukturveränderungen bekannt, wie zum Beispiel eine grundsätzliche Änderung der geldpolitischen Strategie, so sollte sich dies in einem entsprechend aufgespaltenen Schätzzeitraum niederschlagen. Für die USA hat ein solcher fundamentaler Wechsel in der Geldpolitik 1979/81 stattgefunden, als die Fed mehrfache Wechsel von Zins zu Mengenpolitik und zurück vollzog. Dem wird im folgenden Rechnung getragen, in dem für die USA ein verkürzter Schätzzeitraum ab 1982 gewählt wird. In Deutschland ist die Vereinigung eine offenkundiger Strukturbruch. Deshalb werden hier Schätzungen für die Zeiträume von 1985 bis 1990 und von 1991 bis 1995 durchgeführt. Durch diese Unterteilungen können Verhaltensänderungen, die bei der Gesamtschätzung „untergehen“, offenbar werden.

Zwischen den verschiedenen oben dargestellten Varianten soll anhand von Effizienzkriterien diskriminiert werden. Jene Schätzungen sollen also vorgezogen werden, die den höchsten Erklärungsgehalt mit dem geringsten Aufwand an Variablen

---

19 Siehe Bernanke / Blinder (1992) und Sims (1980).

20 Siehe Lütkepohl (1991).

21 Siehe Bernanke / Blinder (1992) und Shioji (1997).

erzielen. Zur Messung dieser Effizienz werden der Akaike und der Schwarz Test verwendet.[22] Diese Tests zeigen zum einen mittels Likelihood Test an, welchen Erklärungsgehalt das jeweilige Modell aufweist. Dieser wird gewichtet mit der Zahl der hierzu verwendeten Variablen. Dabei ist dieses Gewicht beim Schwarz Test etwas größer als beim Akaike Test.

Aus den VAR Schätzungen lassen sich sog. Impulsreaktionen ermitteln. Dies ist die Reaktion aller Variablen des Systems auf einen standardisierten Schock für eine Variable. Dabei ist zu beachten, daß Impulsreaktionen immer die Reaktion des gesamten Systems wiedergeben. Es handelt sich damit nicht nur um partielle und unmittelbare Zusammenhänge, die hier wirksam werden, sondern um vollständige Effekte, einschließlich der mittelbaren Folgewirkungen. Auf z. B. einen Preisschock reagieren nicht nur unmittelbar die Kapitalmarktzinsen und Wechselkurse, sondern mittelbar und vielleicht auch später und durchgreifender die Geldpolitik. Alle diese Reaktionen können den ursprünglichen Impuls abschwächen oder sogar letztlich ins Gegenteil verkehren. Aus diesem Grund werden theoretisch eindeutig determinierte partikuläre Zusammenhänge nicht notwendigerweise deutlich. Über einen längeren Zeitraum ist dies angesichts der dann möglicherweise einsetzenden „Gegenreaktionen“ immer weniger wahrscheinlich.

## IV. Die Resultate

### *1. VAR Systeme für die USA und Deutschland*

Für beide Länder wurden vier VAR Systeme über den aus Datengründen maximal möglichen Zeitraum geschätzt. Unterschiede zwischen den Systemen resultieren im wesentlichen aus einer variierenden Modellierung der Geldpolitik. Im allgemeinsten Fall wurden sowohl der Geldmarktzinssatz als auch der langfristige Zinssatz explizit in die Analyse einbezogen. Als eine Variante dient die Berücksichtigung der Zinsstruktur. Als letzte Alternative wurde nur der kurzfristige Zinssatz zur Abbildung der monetären Bedingungen verwendet. Dies mag auf den ersten Blick als eine für die Geldpolitik der Bundesbank, die ja ein Geldmengenkonzept verfolgt, nicht angemessene Modellierung erscheinen. Allerdings ist die Praxis der Bundesbank weitaus weniger von Geldmengenüberlegungen beeinflußt als durch zinspolitische Entscheidungen.[23] Schließlich wurde in einer Version noch der effektive Wechselkurs integriert, um der Bedeutung der außenwirtschaftlichen Verflechtungen für die Preisstabilität Rechnung zu tragen.

Die Beurteilung der Modelle erfolgt anhand der oben geschilderten Kriterien. Dabei kam ein zweistufiges Verfahren zur Anwendung. Auf einer erste Stufe wird für ein VAR System des jeweiligen Modellansatzes die Länge der zu verwenden-

---

22 Siehe Pindyck und Rubinfeld (1991).

23 Siehe Horn, Scheremet, Zwiener (1997).

den Lags ermittelt. Mit Hilfe des Akaike und des Schwarz Kriteriums läßt sich zeigen, bei welcher Zahl von Lags ein möglichst hoher Erklärungsgehalt sich mit möglichst wenigen Variablen erzielen läßt. Die Ergebnisse deuten daraufhin, daß lediglich Verzögerungen von zwei oder drei Monaten sinnvoll sind. Alle längeren Verzögerungen wurden anhand der beiden Kriterien eindeutig zurückgewiesen. Zwischen den Varianten zwei und drei Monate ließ sich keine eindeutige Entscheidung finden; nach dem Akaike Kriterium war die dreimonatige Verzögerung marginal überlegen, nach dem Schwarz Kriterium war es umgekehrt. Beide Möglichkeiten sind demnach gleichwertig. Im folgenden werden allerdings nur die Ergebnisse mit einem Lag von zwei Monaten präsentiert.

Vergleicht man nun die verschiedenen VAR Systeme mit gleicher Laglänge läßt sich bei Beachtung der Restriktion, daß der Schätzzeitraum für alle gleich sein muß, eine endgültige Auswahl treffen. Die Testergebnisse (Tabelle 1) legen nahe,

*Tabelle 1*

**VAR Teststatistik USA**
1972.01 - 1997.10

| Kriterium / Variable | Akaike | Schwarz | Lags |
|---|---|---|---|
| U,P,W,IS,IL,EXR | -9,85 | -8,90 | 2 |
| U,P,W,IS,IL | -10,74 | -10,07 | 2 |
| U,P,W,Yield | -8,72 | -8,29 | 2 |
| U,P,W,IS | -8,46 | -8,02 | 2 |

U - Arbeitslosenquote, P - Inflationsrate, W - Effektivlohnveränderungen in %, IS - Federal Funds Rate, IL - langfristiger Zinssatz (5 Jahre), Yield - langfristiger Zinssatz minus kurzfristigen, EXR - nominaler effektiver Wechselkurs des USD.

**VAR Teststatistik Deutschland**
1986.04 - 1995.07

| Kriterium / Variable | Akaike | Schwarz | Lags |
|---|---|---|---|
| U,P,W,IS,IL,EXR | -15,97 | -14,08 | 2 |
| U,P,W,IS,IL | -16,03 | -14,70 | 2 |
| U,P,W,Yield | -12,02 | -11,14 | 2 |
| U,P,W,IS | -12,77 | -11,90 | 2 |

U - Arbeitslosenquote, P - Inflationsrate, W - Tariflohnveränderungen in %, IS - Repo Rate, IL - langfristiger Zinssatz (5 Jahre), Yield - langfristiger Zinssatz minus kurzfristigen, EXR - nominaler effektiver Wechselkurs der DM.

den Ansatz zu verwenden, bei dem Geld- und Kapitalmarktzinsen explizit berücksichtigt werden. Sowohl das Akaike als auch das Schwarz Kriterium zeigen, daß dieser Ansatz effizienter ist als die beiden übrigen. Für die USA ergibt sich zudem, daß die Berücksichtigung der Wechselkursvariable die Effizienz der Schätzung verschlechtert. Anders in Deutschland. Hier erweist sich das Modell mit Wechselkursvariable dem Modell, in dem Kapital- und Geldmarktzinsen explizit berücksichtigt werden, als ebenbürtig. Folglich wurde für Deutschland das Modell mit Wechselkursvariablen den folgenden Untersuchungen zugrunde gelegt.

### *2. Die Ausrichtung der Geldpolitik*

Die Ausrichtung der Geldpolitik läßt sich anhand der Impulsreaktion der Geldpolitikvariable ermessen. Über den gesamten Zeitraum gesehen, zeigt sich für die USA, daß die Geldpolitik im wesentlichen auf Impulse seitens Arbeitslosigkeit und der langfristigen Zinsen reagiert.[24] Wählt man den verkürzten Zeitraum seit 1982 tritt allerdings noch die Lohnvariable als relevante Orientierungsgröße hinzu. Die Bedeutsamkeit einer Reaktionen läßt sich über ihren Anteil an der Gesamtvarianz für eine Prognose der abhängigen Variable ermitteln. Insgesamt kommt die Arbeitslosigkeit auf gut 40% (Gesamtzeitraum), bei einer zweijährigen Vorhersage. Für die Zeit seit 1982 ergibt sich freilich ein erheblich niedrigerer Wert von nur noch 15%.

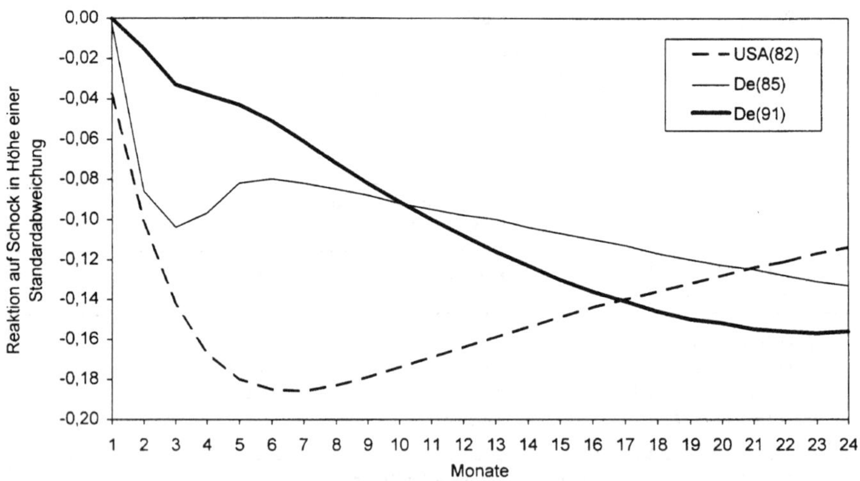


Abbildung 2: Impulsreaktion der Geldpolitik auf Arbeitslosigkeit

24 Daneben weist die Zinsvariable wie alle übrigen auch Autoregressitivät auf.

Dies läßt darauf schließen, daß die Arbeitslosigkeit mit der Neuorientierung der Geldpolitik in den USA an Bedeutung für geldpolitische Entscheidungen verloren hat. Gleichwohl zeigt sich, daß die Fed relativ rasch auf einen Anstieg der Arbeitslosigkeit reagiert. Die Impulsreaktion des Geldmarktzinses ist über ein Jahr nach einem Anstieg der Arbeitslosigkeit noch signifikant negativ. Erst nach etwa 16 Monaten verliert sich ihr Einfluß.

Seit der Umorientierung der amerikanischen Geldpolitik zu Beginn der achtziger Jahre findet die Lohnentwicklung eine stärkere Berücksichtigung und zudem scheint sich die Autoregressivität der Zinsentwicklung erhöht zu haben. Gerade in letzterem offenbart sich wahrscheinlich der geldpolitische Regimewechsel, der in einer ausgeprägteren Zinssteuerung besteht. Unter diesen Umständen dürfte die Geldpolitik eine größere Stetigkeit bei der Zinsentwicklung einhalten als bei einer Geldmengensteuerung mit frei floatendem Zinssatz. Die Inflationsrate hat demgegenüber nur einen geringen Erklärungsgehalt für die Entwicklung der Geldmarktzinsen. Die Reaktion auf Inflationsimpulse ist zu keinem Zeitpunkt signifikant. Sie spielt also für geldpolitische Maßnahmen der Fed wohl keine größere Rolle.

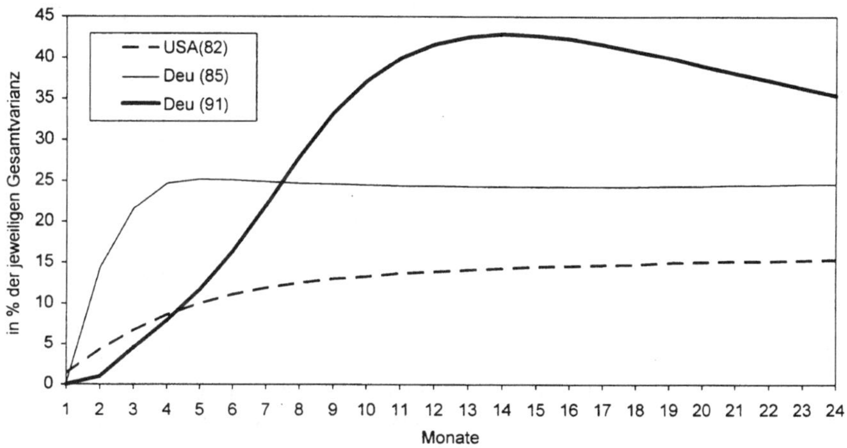


Abbildung 3: Varianzzerlegung – Geldpolitische Reaktion auf Arbeitslosigkeit

Andere Indikatoren sind wichtiger. Zum einen weisen die langfristigen Zinsen, in denen sich Inflationserwartungen der Kapitalmärkte widerspiegeln können, auf kurze Sicht einen erheblich größeren Einfluß auf als die aktuelle Inflationsrate. Bis knapp ein Jahr nach einem Anstieg der Kapitalmarktzinsen sind signifikant höhere Geldmarktzinsen festzustellen. Zum zweiten deuten die Ergebnisse daraufhin, daß Impulse aus der Lohnentwicklung, in denen gleichfalls zukünftige Inflationstendenzen erkennbar werden, maßgeblicher für die Entscheidungen der amerikanischen Zentralbank sind. Bereits nach zwei bis sechs Monaten erreichen diese ihren maximalen Wert, ihre Bedeutung für die Varianz der Vorhersage nimmt im Verlauf von zwei Jahren sogar noch zu auf zuletzt etwa 20%. Auch läßt sich für einen Zeitraum von knapp einem Jahr eine signifikante Reaktion feststellen. Offensichtlich reagiert die Fed rasch auf Lohnzuwächse und hält einen entsprechenden Kurs auch über einen längeren Zeitpunkt bei. Beschleunigen sich also die Lohnzuwächse plötzlich, erfolgt nach diesen Ergebnissen bereits wenige Monate später eine Zinsanhebung, die auch nach Abklingen des anfänglichen Impulses über längere Zeit beibehalten wird. Beides, die Reaktion auf Kapitalmarktzinsen und auch Lohnentwicklung, zeigen, daß die Fed auf eine frühzeitige Inflationsbekämpfung abzielt.

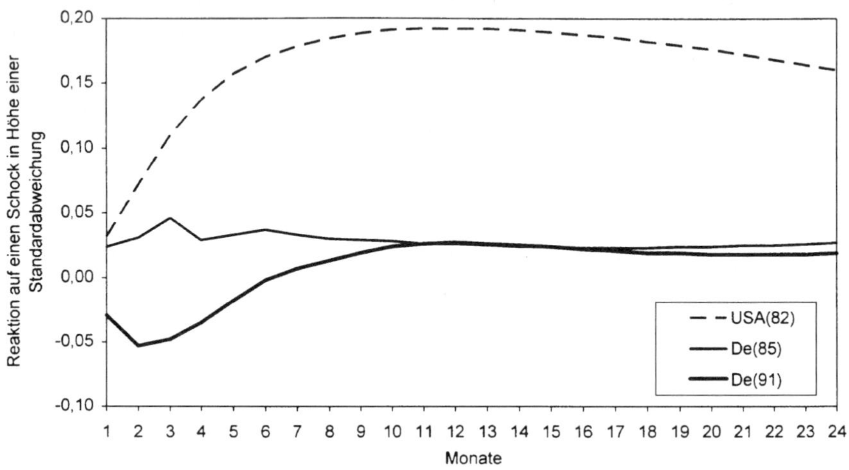


Abbildung 4: Impulsreaktion der Geldpolitik auf die Lohnentwicklung

Die Geldpolitik in Deutschland ähnelt der amerikanischen in der Hinsicht, daß die Variable Arbeitslosigkeit einen erheblichen Informationsgehalt für Aussagen über die geldpolitische Ausrichtung aufweist. Nach einem Anstieg der Arbeitslosigkeit erfolgt eine spürbare zinssenkende Reaktion und dieser Kurs wird auch über einen längeren Zeitraum beibehalten. Die Aussage gilt sowohl für die Schätzung des gesamten als auch für beide verkürzte Zeiträume. Die Größenordnung für die Varianz liegen mit 25% (85 - 90), 35% (91 - 95) und gut 45% (Gesamtzeitraum) sogar etwas höher als für die USA. Es fällt allerdings auf, daß für die Schätzung ab 1991 die Reaktion erst nach einigen Monaten signifikant wird. Dies läßt auf eine eher späte Antwort auf eine Veränderung der Arbeitsmarktlage schließen. Gleichwohl scheint für die Politik der Bundesbank die Bekämpfung von Arbeitslosigkeit eine etwa ebenso hohe Priorität zu besitzen wie für die Fed.

Es zeigen sich aber auch wesentliche Unterschiede. So hat die aktuelle Inflationsentwicklung für die deutsche Geldpolitik eine größere Bedeutung als für die amerikanische. Jede Inflationsbeschleunigung führt zu relativ raschen Zinserhöhungen. Es deutet sich allerdings eine Verhaltensänderung im Hinblick auf die Dauerhaftigkeit bei der Reaktion auf Inflationsimpulse zwischen den achtzigern und den neunziger Jahren an. Zuletzt scheint die Reaktion kurzfristigerer Natur zu sein. Zinssteigernde Impulse lassen sich signifikant nur noch für einen Zeitraum von knapp 10 Monaten nachweisen und auch der Anteil an der Gesamtvarianz bei der Vorhersage geht deutlich zurück. In den achtziger Jahren läßt sich eine signifikante Reaktion erst nach gut 10 Monaten nachweisen. Dies spricht dafür, daß neuerdings auf längere Sicht andere Faktoren als die aktuelle Inflationsrate Bedeutung für die deutsche Geldpolitik haben.

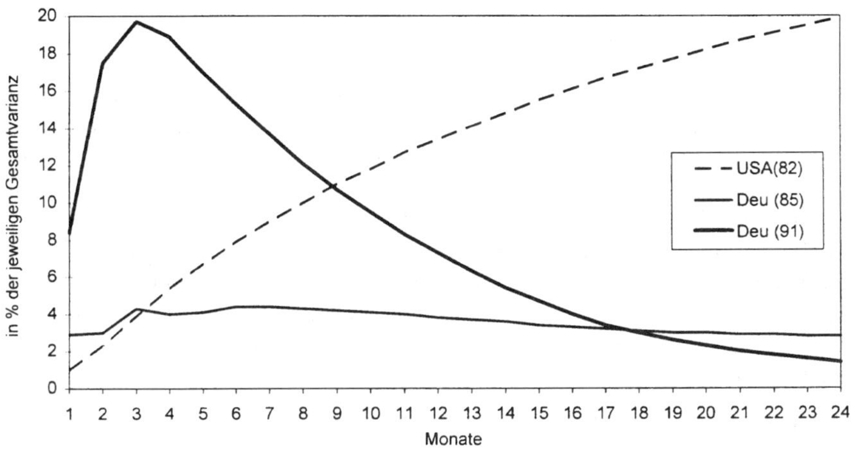


Abbildung 5: Varianzzerlegung – Reaktion der Geldpolitik auf Lohnzuwächse

Hier ist vor allem – und dies ist gleichfalls ein wesentlicher Unterschied zu den USA, wo dieses Modell zurückgewiesen wurde – die Wechselkursentwicklung zu nennen. Allerdings reagiert die Bundesbank anfänglich zwar signifikant, aber nicht sehr stark (85 - 91) oder gar nicht (91 - 95) auf Auf- oder Abwertungen. Für den Zeitraum seit 1991 erst nach etwa 6 -8 Monaten sind z. B. signifikante Zinssenkungen als Antwort auf Aufwertungen nachweisbar. Die Wechselkursvariable wirkt also weniger unmittelbar auf die Geldpolitik ein als indirekt über andere Größen des Modells. So dürften die als Antwort auf eine Aufwertung in den Ergebnissen aufscheinenden Zinssenkungen erst durch die hierdurch gedämpfte Inflationsentwicklung und die gestiegene Arbeitslosigkeit auf die Geldpolitik Einfluß ausüben.

Bemerkenswert ist, daß Reaktionen auf Lohnimpulse oder auf Änderungen der Kapitalmarktzinsen insgesamt nur eine untergeordnete Bedeutung für die deutsche Geldpolitik zu haben scheinen. Zu keinem Zeitpunkt läßt sich eine signifikante Reaktion nachweisen. Es spricht also wenig dafür, daß in Deutschland Lohnimpulse oder Kapitalmarktentwicklungen von der Bundesbank systematisch als Vorboten für Inflation aufgefaßt werden und zu entsprechenden Reaktionen führen.

Damit zeichnet sich die deutsche Geldpolitik im Vergleich zur amerikanischen durch eine eher reaktive Inflationsbekämpfung aus. Anstatt Inflationsindikatoren zu nutzen, um frühzeitig Signale insbesondere an die Lohnpolitik zu vermitteln, daß die Stabilität in Gefahr gesehen wird und eine Straffung des geldpolitischen Kurses droht, schreitet die Bundesbank offensichtlich erst mit dem Eintreten der Inflationseffekte ein. Gleichzeitig bekämpft sie allerdings die Arbeitslosigkeit, die möglicherweise erst als Folge von Stabilitätsverletzungen entstanden ist auch im Vergleich zur Fed energisch.

### *3. Die Ausrichtung der Lohnentwicklung*

Ob eine Interaktion von Geldpolitik und Lohnentwicklung stattfindet, hängt zur einen Hälfte auch an der Ausrichtung der Lohnentwicklung. Gefragt ist nach ihrer Reaktion auf Änderungen der Geldmarktzinssätze. Bei Erhöhungen der Geldmarktsätze, sollten sich bei kooperativem Verhalten relativ rasch mäßigere Lohnsteigerungen einstellen. Für die USA zeigt sich, daß die Geldmarktzinsen keine wesentliche Bedeutung für die Lohnentwicklung aufweisen, schon gar nicht in einem kooperativen Sinne. Die Impulsreaktion ist zu keinem Zeitpunkt signifikant. Hieraus folgt, daß von seiten der Lohnbildung in den USA keine unmittelbare Reaktion auf geldpolitischen Entscheidungen erfolgt, von einer Kooperation oder Interaktion die Rede nicht sein kann.

Vielmehr ist für die USA eine ausgeprägte Autoregressivität der Lohnentwicklung zu konstatieren, also Reaktionen auf Impulse von anderen als den vorangegangen Lohnsteigerungen eine nur untergeordnete Bedeutung haben. Selbst eine höhere Arbeitslosigkeit führt in den USA nicht zu signifikant reduzierten Lohnsteigerungen. Demgegenüber ist der Einfluß der Inflationsrate größer. Ein stärkerer Preisauftrieb erhöht kurzfristig die Lohnsteigerungen, jedoch ist dieser Effekt nur für wenige Monate von nennenswerter Bedeutung. Das bedeutet auch, daß amerikanischen Arbeitnehmer sich allenfalls rudimentär an erwarteten Reallohnentwicklungen orientieren.

Für Deutschland ergibt sich im Grunde ein ähnliches Bild wie für die USA. Eine dauerhafte signifikante Reaktion der Lohnentwicklung auf geldpolitische Entscheidungen ist nicht nachzuweisen. Während des Zeitraumes von 1985 bis 1990 dominieren konjunkturelle Effekte, die sogar kurzfristig eine prozyklische Lohnreaktion anzeigen.

Es fällt aber bei den deutschen Lohnreaktionen auf, daß monetäre Impulse auf andere Weise als über Geldmarktzinsen wirksam werden. So ist eine ausgeprägte Reaktion auf Wechselkursänderungen zu konstatieren. Bei einer Aufwertung fallen die Lohnabschlüsse nach kurzer Zeit signifikant moderater aus. Die Reaktionszeit

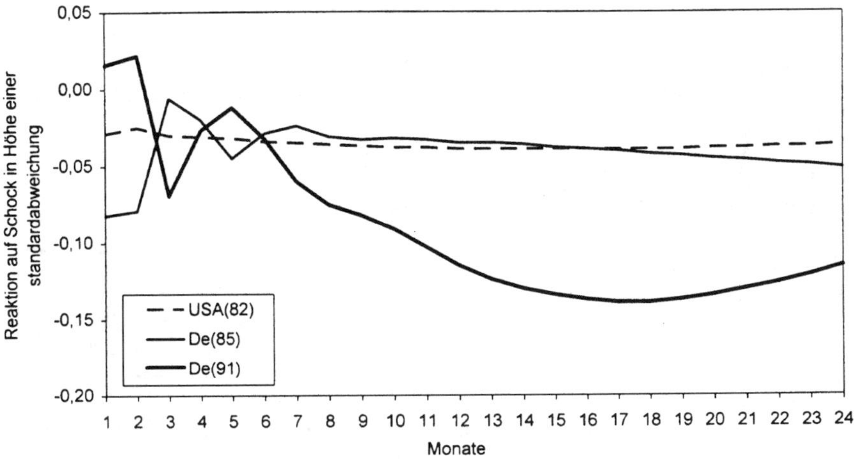


Abbildung 6: Impulsreaktion der Lohnentwicklung auf Arbeitslosigkeit

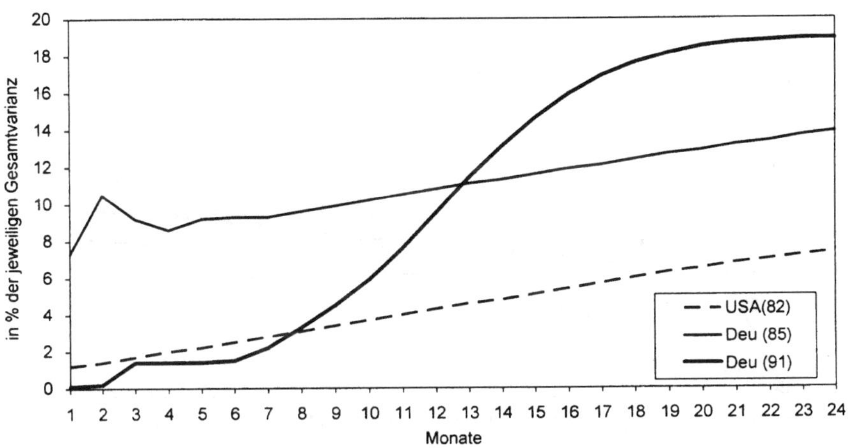


Abbildung 7: Varianzzerlegung – Reaktion der Lohnentwicklung auf Arbeitslosigkeit

war im ersten Schätzzeitraum sogar noch kürzer als im zweiten, wo eine signifikante Reaktion erst nach 5 Monaten feststellbar ist. Die Wechselkursimpulse besitzen auch einen hohen Informationsgehalt. Zwar sind sie auf kurze Sicht nur von geringer Bedeutung für die Variation der Lohnvariable. Aber etwa nach gut einem Jahr ist ihr Anteil an der Gesamtvarianz der Vorhersage beträchtlich. Dies entspricht der Zeitspanne, die offenbar erforderlich ist, daß z. B. Aufwertungen negative Konsequenzen für die wirtschaftliche Entwicklung haben und daher über

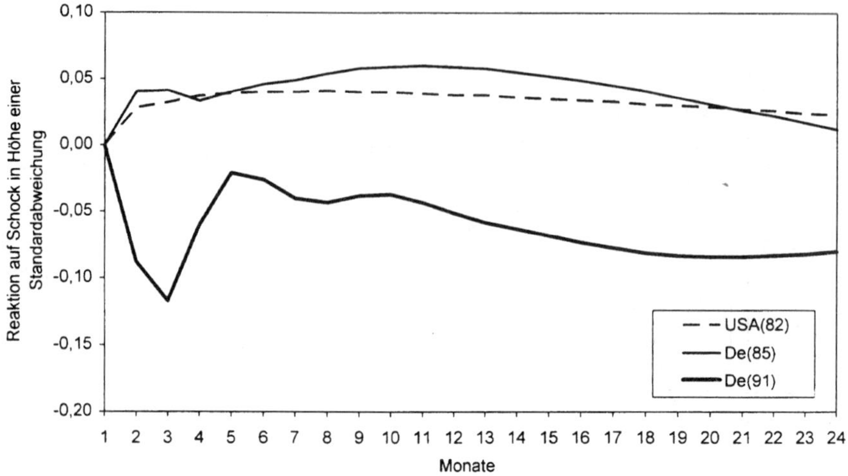


Abbildung 8: Impulsreaktion der Lohnentwicklung auf Geldmarktzinsen

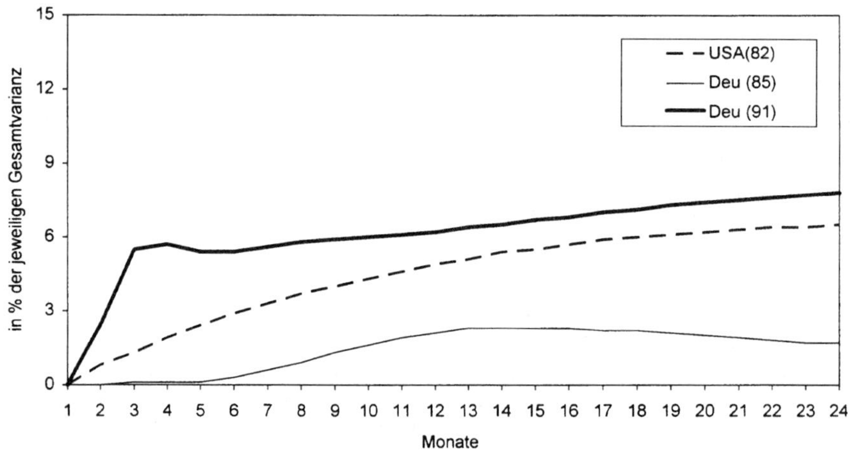


Abbildung 9: Varianzzerlegung – Reaktion der Lohnentwicklung auf Geldmarktzinsen

einen Anstieg der Arbeitslosenquote zu Lohnmäßigung führen. Dieser Effekt scheint für Deutschland, unabhängig vom Schätzzeitraum von Bedeutung zu sein.

Ein wichtiges Ergebnis ist, daß die Arbeitslosenquote für die Lohnbildung in Deutschland offenbar von größerer Relevanz ist als in den USA. Dies erklärt auch, warum die indirekte Effekte von Wechselkurseffekten relativ ausgeprägt sind. Sobald sie nämlich die Arbeitslosenquote tangieren, stellt sich eine merkliche Lohnreaktion ein. Dabei erfolgte die Reaktion in beiden Subperioden eher zögerlich. Im weiteren Verlauf ist der Effekt jedoch um so kräftiger. In jeder der beiden Subperioden ist die Lohnreaktion aber stärker ausgeprägt als in den USA. Dies deutet an, daß die Lohnfindung in Deutschland flexibler auf Änderungen der Überschußnachfrage am Arbeitsmarkt reagiert. Im Falle steigender Arbeitslosenquoten ist die Lohnzurückhaltung ausgeprägter. Umgekehrt steigen die Löhne offenbar auch rasch wieder an, wenn sich die Lage auf dem Arbeitsmarkt bessert.

Alles in allem läßt sich die Schlußfolgerung ziehen, daß die Lohnfindung sowohl in den USA als auch in Deutschland kaum auf monetäre Signale reagiert. Es fällt auf die Lohnpolitik in Deutschland insgesamt „offener“ auf Impulse reagiert während in den USA sich ein eher stetiger, unabhängig von äußeren Ereignissen, ablaufender Lohnpfad ergibt.

## V. Schlußfolgerungen für die Koordination von Geld- und Lohnpolitik

Die Ergebnisse zeigen, daß sowohl in den USA als auch in Deutschland eine Kooperation im Sinne einer wechselseitigen Berücksichtigung der jeweiligen Entscheidungen während der vergangenen beiden Jahrzehnte nicht stattgefunden hat. Dieser positive Extremfall, bei dem sich Stabilisierungsrezessionen wohl hätten vermeiden lassen, wird durch die empirische Analyse zurückgewiesen. Offensichtlich werden hier wechselseitig verfügbare Informationen nicht ausgenutzt. Es wäre allerdings falsch zu behaupten, daß überhaupt keine Form von Interaktion existieren würde. In den USA läßt die Geldpolitik Entwicklungen bei Frühindikatoren zur Erkennung von Inflationsgefahren, zu denen neben den Kapitalmarktzinsen die Lohnentwicklung gehört, in ihre Zinsentscheidungen einfließen. Damit reagiert sie frühzeitig auf Stabilitätsgefahren und kann die realen Kosten in Grenzen halten. Erschwert wird die Aufgabe der Fed allerdings dadurch, daß die Lohnfindung in den USA auf geldpolitische Signale nicht reagiert. Erst ein Anstieg der Arbeitslosigkeit, der im übrigen auch kräftiger als in Deutschland sein muß, um den gleichen Effekt zu zeigen, führt die Lohnentwicklung hier auf einen Stabilitätspfad zurück.

In Deutschland krankt die Kooperation sowohl an der Ausrichtung der Bundesbank als auch an der Lohnpolitik. Sie berücksichtigen beide kaum vorauslaufende Inflationsindikatoren. Insbesondere läßt sich bei der Bundesbank keine Tendenz zu einer frühzeitigen Inflationsbekämpfung erkennen. Lediglich im Hinblick auf die außenwirtschaftliche Stabilität nimmt sie stärker Rücksicht als die Fed, in dem sie Wechselkursänderungen in ihre Entscheidungen einfließen läßt.

Insgesamt bleibt damit festzuhalten, daß Koordinationsmängel damit durchaus einen Erklärungsbeitrag zu den jüngsten Rezessionen leisten. Die Konstellationen der Interaktionen geben auch Hinweise darauf, warum die Rezession in den USA nicht so tiefgreifend und von kürzerer Dauer war als in Deutschland. Das frühzeitige Bremsen und Lockern der Geldpolitik begrenzte die realwirtschaftlichen Kosten. In Deutschland hingegen bremste die Bundesbank später und länger mit entsprechenden Konsequenzen für die realwirtschaftliche Entwicklung.

Eine wesentliche Erweiterung der obigen Analyse könnte in der expliziteren Berücksichtigung von Erwartungen bestehen. Zum einen könnten die Erwartungen über geldpolitische Maßnahmen über die Zinsdifferenzen eingehen, die den Unterschied zwischen dem durch die Geldpolitik fixierten Zinssatz, also z. B. der Federal Funds Rate und dem Zinssatz für Anleihen mit einmonatiger Restlaufzeit, in dem die Erwartungen über die kurzfristige im wesentlichen geldpolitisch determinierte Zinsentwicklung aufscheinen sollten. Aus einer Differenz läßt sich dann der mögliche Überraschungseffekt geldpolitischer Entscheidungen ablesen. Auch für die Lohnfindung lassen sich zumindest für Deutschland Erwartungen einbeziehen, die auf Tarifabschlüssen beruhen, die ja in der Regel für die Zukunft gelten sollen und insofern der tatsächlichen Tariflohnentwicklung vorauseilen.

Die Ergebnisse für Deutschland leiden noch unter relativ kurzen Datenreihe. Diese Problem läßt sich bei weiteren Forschungsvorhaben mildern, wenn auf die Berücksichtigung der standardisierten Arbeitslosenquote verzichtet wird, und statt dessen die registrierte Arbeitslosenquote verwendet wird, für die weiterhin Daten für Westdeutschland vorliegen. Damit sind allerdings die Konzepte zur Messung der Arbeitslosigkeit zwischen beiden Länder nicht mehr unmittelbar vergleichbar. Zur Erweiterung der Datenbasis kann auch die Verwendung von Effektivlöhnen anstelle der Tariflöhne beitragen, wobei diese jedoch nur als Quartalsdaten vorliegen. Damit besteht die Gefahr, daß die Schnelligkeit von Reaktionen nicht sichtbar wird. Aber auch dies wäre durch weitere Analysen zu klären, deren Ziel es ist, ein noch klareres Bild über die Rolle von Koordinationsmängeln für das Entstehen von Rezessionen zu erhalten.

## Literaturverzeichnis

*Bagliano,* Fabio C. and *Favero,* C. A. (1997): Measuring Monetary Policy with VAR Models: An Evaluation, CEPR Discussion Papers no 1743. – *Bernanke,* Ben and *Blinder,* Alan (1992): The Federal Funds Rate and the Channels of Monetary Transmissions, in: AER vol 82 no 4, p 901 ff. – *Bernanke,* Ben and *Mihov,* I. (1995): What Does the Bundesbank Target? in : NBER working paper no 5764. – *Bruno,* Michael / *Sachs,* Jeffrey (1985): Economics of Worldwide Stagflation, Cambridge, MA., Harvard University Press. – *Bryant,* Ralph C. / *Henderson,* Dale / *Holtham,* Gerald / *Hooper,* Peter / *Symansky,* Steven (1988): Empirical Macroeconomics for Interdependent Economies, The Brookings Institution. – *Bryson,* Jay H. / *Jensen,* Hendrik / *Van Hoose,* David. D. (1993): Rules, Discretion and International Monetary and Fiscal Policy Coordination, in: Open economies review no 4, pp 117 - 132. – *Calmfors,* L. / *Driffill,* J. (1988): Bargaining Structure, Corporatism and Macroeconomic Performance, in: Economic Policy, vol 6, p 14 - 61. – *Canzoneri,* M. B. / *Dale,* Henderson (1988): Is Sovereign Policymaking Bad?, in: Brunner, K. / A. Meltzer (eds), Stabilization Policies and Labor

Market, Amsterdam (north-Holland), pp. 93 - 140. – *DIW* (1997): Die Lage der Weltwirtschaft und der deutschen Wirtschaft im Herbst 1997. Gemeinschaftsgutachten der wirtschaftswissenschaftlichen Forschungsinstitute, in: DIW-Wochenbericht Nr. 44/97. – *Gosh,* Atish (1986): International Policy Coordination in an Uncertain World, in: Economic Letters 21, pp 271 - 276. – *Hamada,* Koichi (1976): A Strategic Analysis of Monetary Interdependence, in: Journal of Political Economy vol 84 no 4, pp 667 - 700. – *Horn,* Gustav A. (1986): Preisstabilisierende Geldpolitik, in: Kredit und Kapital 19. J./1. – *Horn,* Gustav A. (1997): The Price of Monetary Convergence, An Empirical Analysis, Manuscript. – *Horn,* Gustav A. (1998): Beschäftigungswachstum in den USA – ein erklärbares Wunder. in: DIW-Wochenbericht Nr. 9/98. – *Horn,* Gustav A./*Scheremet,* Wolfgang/*Zwiener,* Rudolf (1997): Rahmenbedingungen für den Arbeitsmarkt in einer erfolgreichen Wirtschafts- und Währungsunion der EU-Mitgliedsstaaten, in: Gutachten im Auftrag des Bundesministers für Wirtschaft. – *Kehoe,* Patrick (1989): Policy Cooperation Among Benevolent Governments May be Undesirable, in: Review of Economics Studies vol 56, pp 289 -296. – *Krupp,* Hans-Jürgen/*Cabos,* Karen (1995): Geldpolitik und Beschäftigung, 25. Wirtschaftswissenschaftliches Seminar Ottobeuren. – *Kydland,* Finn/*Prescott,* Edward C. (1997): Rules Rather Than Discretion, in: Journal of Political Economy vol 85, pp 473- 491. – *Lütkepohl,* Helmut (1991): Introduction to Multiple Time Series Analysis, Springer Verlag, Berlin, Heidelberg, New York. – *Neumann,* Manfred J. M.: Koordination der Makropolitik in Europa, in: Gahlen, R./Hesse, H./Ramser, H. J.: Europäische Integrationsprobleme aus wirtschaftlicher Sicht, Mohr Tübingen. – *OECD* (1997): Employment Outlook, Paris. – *Oudiz,* Gilles/*Sachs,* Jeffrey: Macroeconomic Policy Coordination Among the Industrial Economies, in: Brookings Papers on Economic Activity no 1, pp 1 - 64 – *Pindyck,* Robert/*Rubinfeld,* Daniel L. (1991): Econometric Models and Economic Forecasts, Mc Graw – Hill 3 ed. – *Romer,* Christina/*Romer,* David H. (1994): What Ends Recessions, NBER- Working Paper no. 4765. – *Rogoff,* Kenneth (1985): Can International Monetary Coordination be Counterproductive, in: Journal of International Economics vol. 18, pp 199 - 217. – *Rothschild,* Kurt (1990): Internationale Koordination der Wirtschaftspolitik. Ein Fragezeichen, in: Konjunkurpolitik 36. Jg, Heft 2/3, S. 80 - 90. – *Shioji,* Etsuro (1997): Identifiying Monetary Policy Shocks in Japan, in: CEPR Discussion Papers no.1733. – *Sims,* Chr. (1980) :Macroeconomics and Reality, in: Econometrica no 48, pp 1- 48. – *Stieglitz,* Joseph S. (1986): Theories of Wage Rigidities, in : J. Butkiewicz et al (rds): Keynes Economic Legacy: Contemporary Economic Theories, New York, Praeger Publishers – *Stock,* James/*Watson,* Mark (1989): New Indexes of Coincident and Leading Indicators, in: O. Blanchard/S. Fischer (eds.) NBER Macroeconomics Annual, Cambridge, MA., MIT-Press, pp 351 - 93.

## Editors and Authors

Dr. *Karen Cabos,* Landeszentralbank in der Freien und Hansestadt Hamburg, in Mecklenburg-Vorpommern und Schleswig-Holstein, Hamburg

Prof. Dr. *Norman Cameron,* University of Manitoba, Winnipeg

Prof. Dr. *Paul Davidson,* University of Tennessee, Knoxville

Prof. Dr. *Wolfgang Filc,* Universität Trier und Institut für Empirische Wirtschaftsforschung

Prof. Dr. *Wolfgang Franz,* Zentrum für Europäische Wirtschaftsforschung und Universität Mannheim

*Michael Frömmel,* Dipl.-Kfm., Rheinisch-Westfälische Technische Hochschule Aachen

Dr. *Lothar Funk,* Universität Trier

Dr. *Loek Groot,* Universiteit Utrecht

Prof. Dr. *Hans-Joachim Heinemann,* Universität Hannover

Priv. Doz. Dr. *Arne Heise,* WSI, Düsseldorf

Dr. *Michael Heise,* DG Bank, Frankfurt a.M.

Prof. Dr. *Carl-Ludwig Holtfrerich,* Freie Universität Berlin

Dr. *Gustav A. Horn,* Deutsches Institut für Wirtschaftsforschung, Berlin

Prof. Dr. *Derek Hum,* University of Manitoba, Winnipeg

Dr. *Alexander Juchems,* ifo Institut für Wirtschaftsforschung, München

Dr. *Henning Klodt,* Institut für Weltwirtschaft, Kiel

Prof. Dr. Dr. h. c. *Claus Köhler,* Johann Wolfgang Goethe-Universität, Frankfurt a. M. und Institut für Empirische Wirtschaftsforschung

Prof. Dr. *Hans-Jürgen Krupp,* Landeszentralbank in der Freien und Hansestadt Hamburg, in Mecklenburg-Vorpommern und Schleswig-Holstein, Hamburg

Dr. *Willi Leibfritz,* ifo Institut für Wirtschaftsforschung, München

Prof. Dr. *Lukas Menkhoff,* Rheinisch-Westfälische Technische Hochschule Aachen

Dr. *Mathias Moersch,* DG Bank, Frankfurt a. M.

Prof. Dr. *Ewald Nowotny,* Wirtschaftsuniversität Wien

Prof. Dr. *Attiat F. Ott,* Clark University, Worcester

Prof. Dr. *Jan Priewe,* Fachhochschule für Technik und Wirtschaft Berlin

Prof. Dr. Dr. h. c. *Rudolf Richter,* Universität des Saarlandes, Saarbrücken

Prof. Dr. *Ronald Schettkat,* Universiteit Utrecht

Prof. Dr. *Wayne Simpson,* University of Manitoba, Winnipeg

Prof. Dr. *Heinz-Peter Spahn,* Universität Hohenheim

Dr. *Peter Winker,* Universität Mannheim